EU Treaties and Legislation

Second Edition

D1495144

EDITED BY **ROBERT SCHÜTZE**

Professor of European Law at Durham University and Visiting Professor at the College of Europe (Bruges) and LUISS – Guido Carli (Rome)

CAMBRIDGE UNIVERSITY PRESS

CAMBRIDGE
UNIVERSITY PRESS

University Printing House, Cambridge CB2 8BS, United Kingdom

One Liberty Plaza, 20th Floor, New York, NY 10006, USA

477 Williamstown Road, Port Melbourne, VIC 3207, Australia

314–321, 3rd Floor, Plot 3, Splendor Forum, Jasola District Centre, New Delhi – 110025, India

79 Anson Road, #06–04/06, Singapore 079906

Cambridge University Press is part of the University of Cambridge.

It furthers the University's mission by disseminating knowledge in the pursuit of education, learning, and research at the highest international levels of excellence.

www.cambridge.org
Information on this title: www.cambridge.org/9781108456593
DOI: 10.1017/9781108624374

First edition © Cambridge University Press 2015
Second edition © Robert Schütze 2018

This publication is in copyright. Subject to statutory exception and to the provisions of relevant collective licensing agreements, no reproduction of any part may take place without the written permission of Cambridge University Press.

First published 2015
Reprinted 2017
Second edition 2018

Printed and bound in Great Britain by Clays Ltd, Elcograf S.p.A.

A catalogue record for this publication is available from the British Library.

Library of Congress Cataloging-in-Publication Data
Names: Schutze, Robert, editor.
Title: EU treaties and legislation / edited by Robert Schutze, Professor of European Law at Durham University and Visiting Professor at the College of Europe (Bruges) and LUISS - Universita Guido Carli (Rome).
Description: Second edition. | New York, NY : Cambridge University Press, 2018. | Includes index.
Identifiers: LCCN 2018022362 | ISBN 9781108456593 (paperback)
Subjects: LCSH: Law – European Union countries. | European Union. | BISAC: LAW / International. | LCGFT: Treaties. | Statutes and codes
Classification: LCC KJE916 .E93 2018 | DDC 341.3/7094–dc23
LC record available at https://lccn.loc.gov/2018022362

ISBN 978-1-108-45659-3 Paperback

Cambridge University Press has no responsibility for the persistence or accuracy of URLs for external or third-party internet websites referred to in this publication and does not guarantee that any content on such websites is, or will remain, accurate or appropriate.

19 NOV 2019

Contents

Preface to the Second Edition

No one can keep track of all legal developments within the European Union, and any collection on the law of the Union will thus have to be highly selective. This student edition of *EU Treaties and Legislation* presents the most essential primary and secondary sources of Union law. Part I contains the Union's primary law in consolidated form (except for the Treaty establishing the European Atomic Energy Community). Part II then offers a selection of twenty-six pieces of Union legislation in five core areas, which are of importance to undergraduate students of European Union law. Each legislative act is presented in its "Lisbonised" form and in its most updated "consolidated" version. In contrast to the first edition, this second edition now also includes the "Brussels I Regulation" and the "Damages Directive" for breaches of competition law.

An appendix contains extracts of the central United Kingdom acts governing British membership in the European Union: the European Communities Act 1972 as well as the European Union Act 2011. Yet in light of the British decision to withdraw from the European Union, this second edition now also includes extracts from three additional Brexit-related statutes, namely: the European Union (Notification of Withdrawal) Act 2017, the Constitutional Reform and Governance Act 2010, as well as the European Union (Withdrawal) Bill (as originally introduced by HM Government).

Regarding this second edition, thankful acknowledgement is again made to the European Union for its kind permission to reproduce primary and secondary Union law from its EUR-Lex website. It (almost) goes without saying that this student text is not "authentic" and therefore produces no legal effects. With a similar disclaimer in mind, I am equally grateful to Her Majesty's Stationery Office for allowing me to reproduce extracts from its legislation.gov.uk website. I would like to thank Sinéad Moloney for her belief in the original project and Caitlin Lisle for her assistance with regard to this second edition. I continue to be particularly indebted to Eszter Belteki for her "Tables of Equivalences", which are – in my view – the most refined and accurate Tables that presently exist.

Table of EU Treaties and Secondary Law

Table of UK Legislation on EU Matters

A. European Communities Act 1972: 1972 Chapter 68
B. European Union Act 2011: 2011 Chapter 12
C. European Union (Notification of Withdrawal) Act 2017: 2017 Chapter 9
D. Constitutional Reform and Governance Act 2010: 2010 Chapter 25
E. European Union (Withdrawal) Bill: HC Bill 5

Table of Equivalences

The EU Treaties have been amended many times; and following extensive treaty amendments, the EU Treaties have been renumbered. This has happened twice in the history of the European Union. The first renumbering took place through the 1997 Treaty of Amsterdam, and the second renumbering was effected by the 2007 Lisbon Treaty – the most significant textual change in the life of the European Union.

Special Keys:
a: Substantial changes made to the provision;
b: Amended by the Nice Treaty;
c: Introduced by the Single European Act;
d: Repealed and replaced by the 1965 Merger Treaty;
e: Introduced by the 1975 Treaty Amending Certain Financial Provisions.

1 TREATY ON EUROPEAN UNION (TEU)

Maastricht	Amsterdam	Lisbon
Article A	Article 1	Article 1
Article A[1]	Article 1[1]	Article 1[1]
Article A[2]	Article 1[2]	Article 1[2]
Article A[3]	Article 1[3]	Repealed
		Article 1[3]
Article B	Article 2	Article 3
Article B[1] 1st indent	Article 2[1] 1st indent	Article 3(1) and (4)
Article B[1] 2nd indent	Article 2[1] 2nd indent	Article 3(5)
Article B[1] 3rd indent	Article 2[1] 3rd indent	Article 3(2) and (5) 1st sentence
Article B[1] 4th indent	Article 2[1] 4th indent[a]	Article 3(2)
Article B[1] 5th indent	Article 2[1] 5th indent	Repealed
		Article 3(3)

(cont.)

Maastricht	Amsterdam	Lisbon
Article B[2]	Article 2[2]	Article 3(6)
Article C	Article 3	Articles 13(1) and 21(3) TEU and Article 7 TFEU
Article C[1]	Article 3[1]	Article 13(1) and Article 7 TFEU
Article C[2]	Article 3[2]	Article 21(3) TEU
		Article 4(1)
		Article 4(3)
Article D	Article 4	Article 15[a]
Article D[1]	Article 4[1]	Article 15(1)
Article D[2]	Article 4[2]	Article 15(2), (3) 1st and 2nd sentences and (6)(d)
Article D[2] 1st sentence	Article 4[2] 1st sentence	Article 15(2) 1st sentence
		Article 15(2) 2nd sentence
Article D[2] 2nd sentence	Article 4[2] 2nd sentence	Article 15(3) 2nd sentence[a]
Article D[2] 3rd sentence	Article 4[2] 3rd sentence	Article 15(3) 1st sentence
		Article 15(3) 3rd sentence
		Article 15(4)
		Article 15(5)
		Article 15(6)(a) to (c)
Article D[3]	Article 4[3]	Article 15(6)(d)
		Article 15(6)[2] and [3]
Article 3b TEC	Article 5 TEC	Article 5 TEU
		Article 5(1) TEU
Article 3b[1] TEC	Article 5[1] TEC	Article 5(2) TEU
Article 3b[2] TEC	Article 5[2] TEC	Article 5(3) TEU
Article 3b[3] TEC	Article 5[3] TEC	Article 5(4) TEU
Article E	Article 5	Article 13(2)
		Article 6(1)
		Article 6(2)
Article F	Article 6	Articles 2, 4(2), 6(3) and 311[1] TFEU

(cont.)

Maastricht	Amsterdam	Lisbon
Article F(1)	Article 6(1) and (3)	Article 4(2) and 2
Article F(1) 1st part	Article 6(3)	Article 4(2)
Article F(1) 2nd part	Article 6(1)	Article 2
Article F(2)	Article 6(2)	Article 6(3)
Article F(3)	Article 6(4)	Article 311[1] TFEU
	Article F.1 inserted and renumbered to Article 7	Articles 7 and 354 TFEU
	Article 7(1)[b]	Article 7(1)
	Article 7(2)[b]	Article 7(2)
	Article 7(3)[b]	Article 7(4)
	Article 7(4)[b]	Article 7(4)
		Article 7(5)
	Article 7(5)[b]	Article 354 TFEU
	Article 7(5) 1st sentence[b]	Article 354[1] 1st sentence TFEU
	Article 7(5) 2nd sentence[b]	Article 354[1] 2nd sentence TFEU
	Article 7(5) 3rd sentence[b]	Article 354[2] TFEU
	Article 7(5)[2][b]	Article 354[3] TFEU[a]
	Article 7(6)[b]	Article 354[4] TFEU
Article G	Article 8	Repealed
Article H	Article 9	Repealed
Article I	Article 10	Repealed
		Article 8
		Article 9
		Article 10
		Article 11
		Article 12
		Article 13(1)[2]
		Article 13(3) and (4)
Article 137 and 140[1] TEC	Articles 189[1] and [2], 190(1) to (3), 192[1], 197[1] TEC	Article 14

(cont.)

Maastricht	Amsterdam	Lisbon
Article 137 TEC	Article 189[1] TEC	Article 14(1) and (2) 1st sentence TEU
	Article 192[1] TEC	Article 14(1) TEU
	Article 189[2] TEC	Article 14(2) 2nd sentence TEU
	Article 190(2) TEC	Article 14(2) 3rd sentence TEU
		Article 14(2)[2] TEU
	Article 190(1) TEC	Article 14(3) TEU
	Article 190(3) TEC	Article 14(3) TEU
Article 140[1] TEC	Article 197[1] TEC	Article 14(4) TEU
Article 145 2nd indent TEC	Article 202 2nd indent TEC	Article 16(1) TEU
Article 146 TEC	Article 203 TEC	Article 16(2) and (9) TEU
Article 148(1) TEC	Article 205(1) TEC	Article 16(3) and Article 238(1) TFEU
Article 148(2) TEC	Article 205(2) TEC	Article 16(4) and (5) TEU and Article 238(3) TFEU
		Article 16(6) to (8)
Article 155 TEC	Article 211 TEC	Article 17(1)
		Article 17(2)
Article 158(1)	Article 214(1)	Article 17(3)[1]
1st sentence 3rd part TEC	1st sentence 3rd part TEC	
Article 157(1) TEC	Article 213(1) TEC	Article 17(3)[2] and (5)
Article 157(1)[1] TEC	Article 213(1)[1] TEC	Article 17(3)[2] and (5)[1]
Article 157(2) TEC	Article 213(2) TEC	Article 17(3)[3] and Article 245 TFEU
Article 157(2)[1] TEC	Article 213(2)[1] TEC	Article 17(3)[3] 1st sentence
Article 157(2)[2] 1st sentence TEC	Article 213(2)[2] 1st sentence TEC	Article 17(3)[3] 2nd sentence
Article 157(2)[2] 2nd sentence TEC	Article 213(2)[2] 2nd sentence TEC	Article 17(3)[3] 3rd sentence and Article 245[1] 1st sentence TFEU

(cont.)

Maastricht	Amsterdam	Lisbon
		Article 17(4)
Article 157(1)[2] TEC	Article 213(1)[2] TEC	Article 17(5)[1] penultimate and last part
Article 157(1)[3] TEC	Article 213(1)[3] TEC	Article 17(5)[2] 1st part of the 1st sentence
Article 157(1)[4] TEC	Article 213(1)[4] TEC	Article 17(5)[2] 2nd part of the 1st sentence[a]
		Article 17(5)[2] 2nd sentence
	Article 219[1] TEC	Article 17(6)(a)
		Article 17(6)(b)
Article 161 TEC[a]	Article 217 TEC[b]	Article 17(6)(c)
		Article 17(6)[2]
Article 158(2)[1] and [2] TEC	Article 214(2)[1] and [2] TEC	Article 17(7)[1] and [2][a]
Article 158(2)[3] TEC	Article 214(2)[3] TEC	Article 17(7)[3][a]
		Article 17(8)
		Article 18
		Article 19(1) 1st sentence
Article 164 TEC	Article 220 TEC	Article 19(1) 2nd sentence
		Article 19(1)[2]
Article 165[1] TEC	Article 221[1] TEC	Article 19(2) 1st sentence
		Article 19(2)[2] and [3]
		Article 19(3)
	Articles 27a to 27e, 40 to 40bb and 43 to 45	Article 20
Article J	Repealed	
Article J.1 and Article 130u(1) and (2) TEC	Article 11 and Article 177(1) and (2) TEC	Article 21
		Article 21(1)
Article J.1	Article 11	Articles 21(2) and 24(3)
Article J.1(1) and (2)	Article 11(1)	Article 21(2)

(cont.)

Maastricht	Amsterdam	Lisbon
Article J.1(2) 1st indent	Article 11(1) 1st indent	Article 21(2)(a)
Article J.1(2) 2nd indent	Article 11(1) 2nd indent	Article 21(2)(c)
Article J.1(2) 3rd indent	Article 11(1) 3rd indent	Article 21(2)(c)
Article J.1(2) 4th indent	Article 11(1) 4th indent	Article 21(2)(h)
Article J.1(2) 5th indent	Article 11(1) 5th indent	Article 21(2)(b)
		Article 21(2)(f) and (g)
Article 130u(2) TEC	Article 177(2) TEC	Article 21(2)(b)
		Article 21(2)(f) and (g)
Article 130u(1) TEC	Article 177(1) TEC	Article 208(1)[1] TFEU and Article 21(2)(d) and (e)
Article J.1(3)	Repealed	
Article J.1(4)	Article 11(2)	Article 24(3)
		Article 22
		Article 23
		Article 24(1) and (2)
	Article 12	Article 25
	Article 12[1]	Article 25[1]
	Article 12 1st indent	Article 25(a)
	Article 12 2nd indent	Article 25(b)(iii)
	Article 12 3rd indent	Article 25(b)(i)
	Article 12 4th indent	Article 25(b)(ii)
	Article 12 5th indent	Article 25(c)
Article J.8(1) and (2)		Article 26(1) 1st sentence and (2)[1] and [2]
Article J.8(1)	Article 13(1)	Article 26(1) 1st sentence
		Article 26(1) 2nd sentence
		Article 26(1)[2]
	Article 13(2)	Repealed
Article J.8(2)	Article 13(3)	Article 26(2)
Article J.8(2) 1st sentence	Article 13(3)[1]	Article 26(2)[1]

(cont.)

Maastricht	Amsterdam	Lisbon
	Article 13(3)[2]	Article 26(2)[2]
Article J.8(2) 2nd sentence	Article 13(3)[3]	Repealed
		Article 26(3)
		Article 27
Article J.3(1) and (3) to (7)	Article 14	Article 28
Article J.3(1) 1st sentence	Article 14(1) 1st and 2nd sentences	Article 28(1) 1st sentence[a]
Article J.3(1) 2nd sentence	Article 14(1) 3rd sentence	Article 28(1) 2nd sentence
Article J.3(3)	Article 14(2)	Article 28(1)[2]
Article J.3(4)	Article 14(3)	Article 28(2)
	Article 14(4)	Repealed
Article J.3(5)	Article 14(5)	Article 28(3)
Article J.3(6)	Article 14(6)	Article 28(4)
Article J.3(7)	Article 14(7)	Article 28(5)
Article J.2(2)	Article 15	Article 29
Article J.2(1)	Article 16	Article 32[a]
	Article 17	Article 42(1) to (3)
Article J.4(1)	Article 17(1)[1]	Article 42(2)[1]
Article J.4(2)	Article 17(1)[2]	Article 42(2)[2]
Article J.4(3)	Repealed	
Article J.4(4)	Article 17(1)[3]	Article 42(3)[1]
	Article 17(1)[4]	Repealed
	Article 17(2)	Article 42(1) 3rd sentence
		Article 42(1) 1st, 2nd and 4th sentences
Article J.4(2)	Article 17(3)	Repealed
Article J.4(5)	Article 17(4)	Repealed
Article J.4(6)	Article 17(5)	Repealed
		Article 42(3)[2] to (7)
Article J.5	Article 18	Article 33[a]
Article J.5(1)	Article 18(1)	Repealed

(cont.)

Maastricht	Amsterdam	Lisbon
Article J.5(2)	Article 18(2)	Repealed
	Article 18(3)	Repealed
Article J.5(3)	Article 18(4)	Repealed
	Article 18(5)	Article 33
Articles J.2(3) and J.5(4)	Article 19	Article 34
		Article 34(1) 3rd sentence
Article J.2(3)[2]	Article 19(1)[2]	Article 34(1)[2]
Article J.5(4)[1]	Article 19(2)[1]	Article 34(2)[1]
Article J.5(4)[2]	Article 19(2)[2]	Article 34(2)[2]
		Article 34(2)[3]
Article J.6	Article 20	Article 35[1] and [2]
Article J.6[1]	Article 20[1]	Article 35[1]
Article J.6[2]	Article 20[2]	Article 35[2]
		Article 35[3]
Article J.7	Article 21	Article 36
Article J.8(3) and (4)	Article J.12 inserted and renumbered to Article 22	Article 30
Articles J.3(2) and J.8(2)[2]	Article J.13 inserted and renumbered to Article 23	Article 31
Article J.8(2)[2]	Article 23(1)	Article 31(1)
Article J.3(2)	Article 23(2)	Article 31(2) to (4)
Article J.3(2)[1]	Article 23(2) 1st indent	Article 31(2) 1st and 2nd indents
Article J.3(2)[1]	Article 23(2) 2nd indent	Article 31(2) 3rd indent
		Article 31(2) 4th indent
	Article 23(2)[2]	Article 31(2)[2]
Article J.3(2)[2]	Article 23(2)[3]	Repealed
		Article 31(3)
	Article 23(2)[4]	Article 31(4)
	Article 23(3)	Article 31(5)
	Article J.14 inserted and renumbered to Article 24	Article 37[a]

(cont.)

Maastricht	Amsterdam	Lisbon
Article J.8(5)	Article 25	Article 38
Article J.8(5)	Article 25[1][b]	Article 38[1]
	Article 25[2][b]	Article 38[21]
	Article 25[3][b]	Article 38[31]
		Article 39
	Article J.16 inserted and renumbered to Article 26	Repealed
Article J.9	Article 27	Repealed
Article J.10	Repealed	
Article J.11	Article 28	Article 41
Article J.11(1)	Article 28(1)	Repealed
Article J.11(2)[1]	Article 28(2)	Article 41(1)
Article J.11(2)[2] 1st indent	Article 28(3)	Article 41(2)
Article J.11(2)[2] 2nd indent	Article 28(4)	Repealed
		Article 41(3)
		Article 43
		Article 44
		Article 45
		Article 46
		Article 47
Article K	Repealed	
Article K.1	Article 29	Article 67(3) TFEU
	Article 30	Articles 87 and 88 TFEU[a]
	Article 31	Articles 82, 83 and 85 TFEU[a]
	Article 32	Article 89 TFEU
Article K.2(1)	Repealed	
Article K.2(2)	Article 33	Article 72 TFEU
Articles K.3 and K.4(3)	Article 34	Repealed
	Article 35	Repealed
Article K.4(1) and (2)	Article 36	Article 71 TFEU
Article K.5	Article 37	Repealed

(cont.)

Maastricht	Amsterdam	Lisbon
	Article 38	Repealed
Article K.6	Article 39	Repealed
Article K.7	Article 40[a]	Repealed
	Article 40a[b] and 40[b]	Article 20 and Articles 326 to 334 TFEU
Article K.8	Article 41	Repealed
Article K.9	Article 42	Repealed
	Article K.15 inserted and renumbered to Article 43	Articles 326 to 334 TFEU
	Article 43[a]	Articles 326 to 334 TFEU
	Article 43[b]	Articles 326 to 334 TFEU
	Article K.16 inserted and renumbered to Article 44	Articles 326 to 334 TFEU
	Article 44a[b]	Articles 326 to 334 TFEU
	Article K.17 inserted and renumbered to Article 45	Articles 326 to 334 TFEU
Article L	Article 46	Repealed
Article M	Article 47	Article 40[a]
Article N	Article 48	Article 48[a]
Article O	Article 49	Article 49
Article P	Article 50	Repealed
		Article 50
		Article 51
		Article 52
Article Q	Article 51	Article 53
Article Q	Article 52	Article 54
Article S	Article 53	Article 55
Article S	Article 53[1]	Article 55[1]
	Article 53[2]	Article 55[1]
		Article 55[2]

2 TREATY ON THE FUNCTIONING OF THE EUROPEAN UNION (TFEU)

Rome	Maastricht	Amsterdam	Lisbon
Article 1	Article 1	Article 1	Repealed
			Article 1
			Article 2
			Article 3
			Article 4
			Article 5
			Article 6
	Article C[1] TEU	Article 3[1] TEU	Article 7
Article 2	Article 2	Article 2	Article 3 TEU
Article 3	Article 3	Article 3	Article 3 TEU
		Article 3(2)	Article 8
			Article 9
			Article 10
	Article 3a	Article 4	Article 119
	Article 3b	Article 5	Article 5 TEU
	Article 3b[1]	Article 5[1]	Article 5(2) TEU
	Article 3b[2]	Article 5[2]	Article 5(3) TEU
	Article 3b[3]	Article 5[3]	Article 5(4) TEU
		Article 3c inserted and renumbered to Article 6	Article 11
			Article 13
Article 4	Article 4	Article 7	Article 13 TEU
Article 4(1)	Article 4(1)	Article 7(1)	Article 13(1) TEU
Article 4(1) 2nd sentence	Article 4(1) 2nd sentence	Article 7(1) 2nd sentence	Article 13(2) TEU
Article 4(2)	Article 4(2)	Article 7(2)	Article 13(4) TEU
	Article 4a	Article 8	Article 13(1) 5th indent TEU and Article 282 TFEU

(cont.)

Rome	Maastricht	Amsterdam	Lisbon
	Article 4b	Article 9	Repealed
Article 5	Article 5	Article 10	Article 4(3)[2] and[3] TEU
Article 5[1]	Article 5[1]	Article 10[1]	Article 4(3)[2] TEU
Article 5[2]	Article 5[2]	Article 10[2]	Article 4(3)[3] TEU
		Article 5a inserted and renumbered to Article 11	Articles 326 to 334
		Article 11a[b]	Articles 326 to 334
		Article 40 TEU	Articles 326 to 334
			Article 17
Article 6	Repealed		Article 5
Article 6(1)	Repealed		Article 5(1) 1st sentence
Article 6(2)	Repealed		
Article 7	Article 6	Article 12	Article 18
		Article 6a inserted and renumbered to Article 13	Article 19
Article 8	Article 7	Repealed	
	Article 7a	Article 14	Article 26
	Article 7b	Repealed	
	Article 7c	Article 15	Article 27
		Article 7d inserted and renumbered to Article 16	Article 14
	Article 8	Article 17	Article 20
	Article 8a	Article 18	Article 21
	Article 8b	Article 19	Article 22
	Article 8c	Article 20	Article 23[1]
			Article 23[2]
			Article 24[1]

(cont.)

Rome	Maastricht	Amsterdam	Lisbon
	Article 8d	Article 21	Article 24[2] to[4]
	Article 8e	Article 22	Article 25
Article 9	Article 9	Article 23	Article 28
Article 10	Article 10	Article 24	Article 29
Article 10(1)	Article 10(1)	Article 24	Article 29
Article 10(2)	Article 10(2)	Repealed	
Article 11	Article 11	Repealed	
Article 12	Article 12	Article 25	Article 30
Article 13	Article 13	Repealed	Article 30
Article 14	Article 14	Repealed	
Article 15	Article 15	Repealed	
Article 16	Article 16	Repealed	Article 30
Article 17	Article 17	Repealed	Article 30
Article 18	Article 18	Repealed	
Article 19	Article 19	Repealed	
Article 20	Article 20	Repealed	
Article 21	Article 21	Repealed	
Article 22	Article 22	Repealed	
Article 23	Article 23	Repealed	
Article 24	Article 24	Repealed	
Article 25	Article 25	Repealed	
Article 26	Article 26	Repealed	
Article 27	Article 27	Repealed	
Article 28	Article 28	Article 26	Article 31
Article 29	Article 29	Article 27	Article 32
Article 30	Article 30	Article 28	Article 34
Article 31	Article 31	Repealed	
Article 32	Article 32	Repealed	
Article 33	Article 33	Repealed	
Article 34	Article 34	Article 29	Article 35

(cont.)

Rome	Maastricht	Amsterdam	Lisbon
Article 35	Article 35	Repealed	
Article 36	Article 36	Article 30	Article 36
Article 37	Article 37	Article 31	Article 37
Article 37(1)	Article 37(1)	Article 31(1)	Article 37(1)
Article 37(2)	Article 37(2)	Article 31(2)	Article 37(2)
Article 37(3)	Article 37(3)	Repealed	
Article 37(4)	Article 37(4)	Article 31(3)	Article 37(3)
Article 38	Article 38	Article 32	Article 38
Article 39	Article 39	Article 33	Article 39
Article 40	Article 40	Article 34	Article 40
Article 40(1)	Article 40(1)	Repealed	
Article 40(2)	Article 40(2)	Article 34(1)	Article 40(1)
Article 40(2)(a)	Article 40(2)(a)	Article 34(1)(a)	Article 40(1)(a)
Article 40(2)(b)	Article 40(2)(b)	Article 34(1)(b)	Article 40(1)(b)
Article 40(2)(c)	Article 40(2)(c)	Article 34(1)(c)	Article 40(1)(c)
Article 40(3)	Article 40(3)	Article 34(2)	Article 40(2)
Article 40(3)[1]	Article 40(3)[1]	Article 34(2)[1]	Article 40(2)[1]
Article 40(3)[2]	Article 40(3)[2]	Article 34(2)[2]	Article 40(2)[2]
Article 40(3)[3]	Article 40(3)[3]	Article 34(2)[3]	Article 40(2)[3]
Article 40(4)	Article 40(4)	Article 34(3)	Article 40(3)
Article 41	Article 41	Article 35	Article 41
Article 42	Article 42	Article 36	Article 42
Article 43	Article 43	Article 37	Article 43
Article 43(1)	Article 43(1)	Article 37(1)	Repealed
			Article 43(1)
Article 43(2)	Article 43(2)	Article 37(2)	Article 43(2) and (3)
Article 43(3)	Article 43(3)	Article 37(3)	Article 43(4)
			Article 43(5)
Article 44	Article 44	Repealed	
Article 45	Article 45	Repealed	
Article 46	Article 46	Article 38	Article 44

(cont.)

Rome	Maastricht	Amsterdam	Lisbon
Article 47	Article 47	Repealed	
Article 48	Article 48	Article 39	Article 45
Article 49	Article 49	Article 40	Article 46
Article 50	Article 50	Article 41	Article 47
Article 51	Article 51	Article 42	Article 48
Article 52	Article 52	Article 43	Article 49
Article 53	Article 53	Repealed	
Article 54	Article 54	Article 44	Article 50
Article 54(1)	Article 54(1)	Repealed	
Article 54(2)	Article 54(2)	Article 44(1)	Article 50(1)
Article 54(3)	Article 54(3)	Article 44(2)	Article 50(2)
Article 54(3)(a)	Article 54(3)(a)	Article 44(2)(a)	Article 50(2)(a)
Article 54(3)(b)	Article 54(3)(b)	Article 44(2)(b)	Article 50(2)(b)
Article 54(3)(c)	Article 54(3)(c)	Article 44(2)(c)	Article 50(2)(c)
Article 54(3)(d)	Article 54(3)(d)	Article 44(2)(d)	Article 50(2)(d)
Article 54(3)(e)	Article 54(3)(e)	Article 44(2)(e)	Article 50(2)(e)
Article 54(3)(f)	Article 54(3)(f)	Article 44(2)(f)	Article 50(2)(f)
Article 54(3)(g)	Article 54(3)(g)	Article 44(2)(g)	Article 50(2)(g)
Article 54(3)(h)	Article 54(3)(h)	Article 44(2)(h)	Article 50(2)(h)
Article 55	Article 55	Article 45	Article 51
Article 56	Article 56	Article 46	Article 52
Article 57	Article 57	Article 47	Article 53
Article 57(1)	Article 57(1)	Article 47(1)	Article 53(1)
Article 57(2)	Article 57(2)	Article 47(2)	Article 53(1)
			Article 53(2)
Article 58	Article 58	Article 48	Article 54
Article 59	Article 59	Article 49	Article 56
Article 60	Article 60	Article 50	Article 57
Article 61	Article 61	Article 51	Article 58
Article 62	Article 62	Repealed	
Article 63	Article 63	Article 52	Article 59

(cont.)

Rome	Maastricht	Amsterdam	Lisbon
Article 63(1)	Article 63(1)	Repealed	
Article 63(2)	Article 63(2)	Article 52(1)	Article 59(1)
Article 63(3)	Article 63(3)	Article 52(2)	Article 59(2)
Article 64	Article 64	Article 53	Article 60
Article 65	Article 65	Article 54	Article 61
Article 66	Article 66	Article 55	Article 62
Article 67	Article 67	Repealed	
Article 68	Article 68	Repealed	
Article 69	Article 69	Repealed	
Article 70	Article 70	Repealed	
Article 71	Article 71	Repealed	
Article 72	Article 72	Repealed	
Article 73	Article 73	Repealed	
	Article 73a	Repealed	
	Article 73b	Article 56	Article 63
	Article 73b(1)	Article 56(1)	Article 63(1)
	Article 73b(2)	Article 56(2)	Article 63(2)
	Article 73c	Article 57	Article 64
	Article 73c(1)	Article 57(1)	Article 64(1)
	Article 73c(2)	Article 57(2)	Article 64(2) and (3)
	Article 73c(2) 1st sentence	Article 57(2) 1st sentence	Article 64(2)
	Article 73c(2) 2nd sentence	Article 57(2) 2nd sentence	Article 64(3)
	Article 73d	Article 58	Article 65
	Article 73d(1)	Article 58(1)	Article 65(1)
	Article 73d(1)(a)	Article 58(1)(a)	Article 65(1)(a)
	Article 73d(1)(b)	Article 58(1)(b)	Article 65(1)(b)
	Article 73d(2)	Article 58(2)	Article 65(2)
	Article 73d(3)	Article 58(3)	Article 65(3)

(cont.)

Rome	Maastricht	Amsterdam	Lisbon
			Article 65(4)
	Article 73e	Repealed	
	Article 73f	Article 59	Article 66
			Article 67(2)
		Article 29 TEU	Article 67(3)
			Article 68
			Article 69
			Article 70
		Article 36 TEU	Article 71
			Article 73
	Article 73g	Article 60	Article 75
	Article 73g(1)	Article 60(1)	Article 75[1]
	Article 73g(2)	Article 60(2)	Repealed
Article 106	Article 73h	Repealed	
		Article 73i inserted and renumbered to Article 61	Article 67(1)
		Article 73j inserted and renumbered to Article 62	Article 77
		Article 73k points (1) and (2) inserted and renumbered to Article 63 points (1) and (2)	Article 78
		Article 73k points (3) and (4) inserted and renumbered to Article 63 points (3) and (4)	Article 79
		Article 73l(1) inserted and renumbered to Article 64(1) and Article 33 TEU	Article 72

(cont.)

Rome	Maastricht	Amsterdam	Lisbon
		Article 73l(2) inserted and renumbered to Article 64(2)	Article 78(3)
		Article 73m inserted and renumbered to Article 65	Article 81
		Article 73n inserted and renumbered to Article 66	Article 74
		Article 73o inserted and renumbered to Article 67	Repealed
		Article 73p inserted and renumbered to Article 68	Repealed
		Article 73q inserted and renumbered to Article 69	Repealed
			Article 76
			Article 80
			Article 81
		Article 31 TEU	Article 82
		Article 31 TEU	Article 83
			Article 84
		Article 31 TEU	Article 85
			Article 86
		Article 30 TEU	Article 87
		Article 30 TEU	Article 88
		Article 32 TEU	Article 89
Article 74	Article 74	Article 70	Article 90
Article 75	Article 75	Article 71	Article 91
Article 75(1)	Article 75(1)	Article 71(1)	Article 91(1)

(cont.)

Rome	Maastricht	Amsterdam	Lisbon
Article 75(1)(a)	Article 75(1)(a)	Article 71(1)(a)	Article 91(1)(a)
Article 75(1)(b)	Article 75(1)(b)	Article 71(1)(b)	Article 91(1)(b)
	Article 75(1)(c)	Article 71(1)(c)	Article 91(1)(c)
Article 75(1)(c)	Article 75(1)(d)	Article 71(1)(d)	Article 91(1)(d)
Article 75(2)	Article 75(2)	Repealed	
Article 75(3)	Article 75(3)	Article 71(2)	Article 91(2)
Article 76	Article 76	Article 72	Article 92
Article 77	Article 77	Article 73	Article 93
Article 78	Article 78	Article 74	Article 94
Article 79	Article 79	Article 75	Article 95
Article 80	Article 80	Article 76	Article 96
Article 81	Article 81	Article 77	Article 97
Article 82	Article 82	Article 78	Article 98
Article 83	Article 83	Article 79	Article 99
Article 84	Article 84	Article 80	Article 100
Article 84(1)	Article 84(1)	Article 80(1)	Article 100(1)
Article 84(2)	Article 84(2)	Article 80(2)	Article 100(2)
	Article 84(2)[1]	Article 80(2)[1]	Article 100(2) 1st sentence
	Article 84(2)[2]	Article 80(2)[2]	Article 100(2) 2nd sentence
Article 85	Article 85	Article 81	Article 101
Article 86	Article 86	Article 82	Article 102
Article 87	Article 87	Article 83	Article 103
Article 88	Article 88	Article 84	Article 104
Article 89	Article 89	Article 85	Article 105
Article 90	Article 90	Article 86	Article 106
Article 91	Article 91	Repealed	
Article 92	Article 92	Article 87	Article 107
Article 93	Article 93	Article 88	Article 108
Article 94	Article 94	Article 89	Article 109

(cont.)

Rome	Maastricht	Amsterdam	Lisbon
Article 95	Article 95	Article 90	Article 110
Article 95[1]	Article 95[1]	Article 90[1]	Article 110[1]
Article 95[2]	Article 95[2]	Article 90[2]	Article 110[2]
Article 95[3]	Article 95[3]	Repealed	
Article 96	Article 96	Article 91	Article 111
Article 97	Article 97	Repealed	
Article 98	Article 98	Article 92	Article 112
Article 99	Article 99	Article 93	Article 113
Article 100	Article 100	Article 94	Article 115
	Article 100a	Article 95	Article 114
	Article 100a(1)	Article 95(1)	Article 114(1)
	Article 100a(2)	Article 95(2)	Article 114(2)
	Article 100a(3)	Article 95(3)	Article 114(3)
	Article 100a(4)	Article 95(4)	Article 114(4)
	Article 100a(4)[1]	Article 95(4)	Article 114(4)
		Article 95(5)	Article 114(5)
	Article 100a(4)[2]	Article 95(6)[1]	Article 114(6)[1]
		Article 95(6)[2]	Article 114(6)[2]
		Article 95(6)[3]	Article 114(6)[3]
		Article 95(7)	Article 114(7)
		Article 95(8)	Article 114(8)
	Article 100a(4)[3]	Article 95(9)	Article 114(9)
	Article 100a(5)	Article 95(10)	Article 114(10)
	Article 100b	Repealed	
	Article 100c	Repealed	
	Article 100d	Repealed	
Article 101	Article 101	Article 96	Article 116
Article 102	Article 102	Article 97	Article 117
			Article 118

(cont.)

Rome	Maastricht	Amsterdam	Lisbon
Article 105	Article 102a	Article 98	Article 120
	Article 102a 1st sentence	Article 98 1st sentence	Article 120 1st sentence
	Article 102a 2nd sentence	Article 98 2nd sentence	Article 120 2nd sentence
Article 103	Article 103	Article 99	Article 121
	Article 103a	Article 100	Article 122
Article 104	Repealed		
	Article 104	Article 101	Article 123
	Article 104a	Article 102	Article 124
	Article 104b	Article 103	Article 125
	Article 104c	Article 104	Article 126
	Article 105	Article 105	Article 127
	Article 105a	Article 106	Article 128
	Article 106	Article 107	Article 129
	Article 107	Article 108	Article 130
	Article 108	Article 109	Article 131
	Article 108a	Article 110	Article 132
			Article 133
	Article 109	Article 111	Articles 138 and 219
	Article 109[1] to [3] and [5]	Article 111[1] to [3] and [5]	Article 219
	Article 109[4]	Article 111[4]	Article 138
	Article 109a	Article 112	Article 283
	Article 109b	Article 113	Article 284
	Article 109c	Article 114	Article 134
	Article 109d	Article 115	Article 135
			Article 136
			Article 137
			Article 139

(cont.)

Rome	Maastricht	Amsterdam	Lisbon
	Article 109e	Article 116	Repealed
	Article 109f(1), (2) 6th indent and (3) to (9)	Article 117(1), (2) 6th indent and (3) to (9)	Repealed
	Article 109f(2) 1st five indents	Article 117(2) 1st five indents	Article 141(2)
	Article 109g	Article 118	Repealed
Article 108	Article 109h	Article 119	Article 143
	Article 109h(4)	Article 119(4)	Repealed
Article 109	Article 109i	Article 120	Article 144
	Article 109i(4)	Article 120(4)	Repealed
Article 109j(1)	Article 121(1)	Article 140(1)	
Article 109j(2) to (4)	Article 121(2) to (4)	Repealed	
Article 109k(1), (2) 1st sentence, (3) to (6)	Article 122(1), (2) 1st sentence, (3) to (6)	Repealed	
	Article 109k(2) 2nd sentence	Article 122(2) 2nd sentence	Article 140(2)[1]
	Article 109l(1), (2) and (4)	Article 123(1), (2) and (4)	Repealed
	Article 109l(3)	Article 123(3)	Article 141(1)
	Article 109l(5)	Article 123(5)	Article 140(3)
Article 107(1)	Article 109m(1)[a]	Article 124(1)	Article 142
Article 107(2)	Repealed		
	Article 109m(2)	Article 124(2)	Repealed
		Article 109n inserted and renumbered to Article 125	Article 145
		Article 109o inserted and renumbered to Article 126	Article 146
		Article 109p inserted and renumbered to Article 127	Article 147

(cont.)

Rome	Maastricht	Amsterdam	Lisbon
		Article 109q inserted and renumbered to Article 128	Article 148
		Article 109r inserted and renumbered to Article 129	Article 149
		Article 109s inserted and renumbered to Article 130	Article 150
Article 110	Article 110	Article 131	Article 206
Article 111	Repealed		
Article 112	Article 112	Article 132	Repealed
Article 113	Article 113	Article 133	Article 207
Article 113(1)	Article 113(1)	Article 133(1)	Article 207(1)
Article 113(2)	Article 113(2)	Article 133(2)	Article 207(2)
Article 113(3)	Article 113(3)	Article 133(3)	Article 207(3)
Article 113(3)[1]	Article 113(3)[1]	Article 133(3)[1]	Article 207(3)[2]
Article 113(3)[2]	Article 113(3)[2]	Article 133(3)[2]	Article 207(3)[3]
	Article 113(3)[3]	Article 133(3)[3]	Article 207(3)[1]
Article 113(4)	Article 113(4)	Article 133(4)	Article 207(4) 1st sentence
			Article 207(4) 2nd sentence to [3](b)
			Article 207(5) and (6)
Article 114	Repealed		
Article 115	Article 115	Article 134	Repealed
Article 116	Repealed		
		Article 116 inserted and renumbered to Article 135	Article 33
Article 117	Article 117	Article 136	Article 151
			Article 152
Article 118	Article 118	Article 140	Article 156

(cont.)

Rome	Maastricht	Amsterdam	Lisbon
	Article 118a	Article 137	Article 153
	Article 118a(1)	Article 137(1)	Articles 151[1] and 153(1)
			Article 153(2)(a)
	Article 118a(2)	Article 137(2)	Article 153(2)(b)
	Article 118a(2) 1st sentence	Article 137(2) 1st sentence	Article 153(2)(b) 1st sentence
	Article 118a(2) 2nd sentence	Article 137(2) 2nd sentence	Article 153(2)(b) 2nd sentence
			Article 153(2)[2] to [4]
			Article 153(3)
			Article 153(4)[1] and 1st indent
	Article 118a(3)	Article 137(5)	Article 153(4) 2nd indent
			Article 153(5)
	Article 118b	Article 138	Article 154
		Article 139	Article 155
Article 119	Article 119	Article 141	Article 157
Article 119[1]	Article 119[1]	Article 141(1)	Article 157(1)
Article 119[2]	Article 119[2]	Article 141(2)	Article 157(2)
Article 119[3]	Article 119[3]	Article 141(2)[2]	Article 157(2)[2]
		Article 141(3)	Article 157(3)
		Article 141(4)	Article 157(4)
Article 120	Article 120	Article 142	Article 158
		Article 143[1]	Article 159
		Article 143[2]	Repealed
Article 121	Article 121	Article 144	Article 160
Article 122	Article 122	Article 145	Article 161
Article 123	Article 123	Article 146	Article 162
Article 124	Article 124	Article 147	Article 163

(cont.)

Rome	Maastricht	Amsterdam	Lisbon
Article 125	Repealed		
Article 126	Repealed		
Article 127	Repealed		
Article 128	Repealed		
	Article 125	Article 148	Article 164
	Article 126	Article 149	Article 165
	Article 127	Article 150	Article 166
	Article 128	Article 151	Article 167
Article 129	Article 128d	Article 266	Article 308
Article 129	Article 152	Article 168	
	Article 129(1)	Article 152(1)	Article 168(1)
	Article 129(1)[1] and [3]	Article 152(1)[1]	Article 168(1)[1]
	Article 129(1)[2]	Article 152(1)[2]	Article 168(1)[2]
		Article 152(1)[3]	Article 168(1)[3]
	Article 129(2)	Article 152(2)[2]	Article 168(2)[2]
		Article 152(2)[1]	Article 168(2)[1]
	Article 129(3)	Article 152(3)	Article 168(3)
	Article 129(4)	Article 152(4)	Article 168(4)
		Article 152(4)(a)	Article 168(4)(a)
		Article 152(4)(b)	Article 168(4)(b)
			Article 168(4)(c)
	Article 129(4) 1st indent	Article 152(4)(c)	Article 168(5)
	Article 129(4) 2nd indent	Article 152(4) last paragraph	Article 168(6)
		Article 152(5)	Article 168(7)
	Article 129a	Article 153	Article 169 and Article 12
		Article 153(1)	Article 169(1)
		Article 153(2)	Article 12

(cont.)

Rome	Maastricht	Amsterdam	Lisbon
	Article 129a(1)	Article 153(3)	Article 169(2)
	Article 129a(1)(a)	Article 153(3)(a)	Article 169(2)(a)
	Article 129a(1)(b)	Article 153(3)(b)	Article 169(2)(b)
			Article 169(3) and (4)
	Article 129b	Article 154	Article 170
	Article 129c	Article 155	Article 171
	Article 129d	Article 156	Article 172
	Article 129d[3]	Repealed	
Article 130	Article 198e	Article 267	Article 309
Article 130[1]	Article 198e[1]	Article 267[1]	Article 309[1]
	Article 198e[2]	Article 267[2]	Article 309[2]
	Article 130	Article 157	Article 173
Article 130a[c]	Article 130a	Article 158	Article 174
Article 130b	Article 130b[1]	Article 159[1]	Article 175[1]
	Article 130b[2]	Article 159[2]	Article 175[2]
	Article 130b[3]	Article 159[3]	Article 175[3]
Article 130c[c]	Article 130c	Article 160	Article 176
Article 130d[c]	Repealed		
	Article 130d	Article 161	Article 177
Article 130e[c]	Article 130e	Article 162	Article 178
Article 130f[c]	Article 130f	Article 163	Article 179
Article 130g[c]	Article 130g	Article 164	Article 180
Article 130h[c]	Article 130h	Article 165	Article 181
Article 130h 1st sentence	Article 130h(1)	Article 165(1)	Article 181(1)
Article 130h 2nd sentence	Article 130h(2)	Article 165(2)	Article 181(2)
Article 130i[c]	Article 130i	Article 166	Article 182
Article 130i(1)	Article 130i(1)	Article 166(1)	Article 182(1)
Article 130i(2)	Article 130i(2)	Article 166(2)	Article 182(2)

(cont.)

Rome	Maastricht	Amsterdam	Lisbon
	Article 130i(3)	Article 166(3)	Article 182(3)
	Article 130i(4)	Article 166(4)	Article 182(4)
			Article 182(5)
Article 130k[c]	Article 130j	Article 167	Article 183
Article 130l	Article 130k	Article 168	Article 184
Article 130m	Article 130l	Article 169	Article 185
Article 130n	Article 130m	Article 170	Article 186
Article 130o	Article 130n	Article 171	Article 187
Article 130p	Repealed		
Article 130q	Article 130o	Article 172	Article 188
Article 130q(1)	Article 130o[1]	Article 172[1]	Article 188[1]
Article 130q(2)	Article 130o[2]	Article 172[2]	Article 188[2]
			Article 189
	Article 130p	Article 173	Article 190
	Article 130q inserted and repealed		
Article 130r[c]	Article 130r	Article 174	Article 191
Article 130r(1)	Article 130r(1)	Article 174(1)	Article 191(1)
Article 130r(2)	Article 130r(2)	Article 174(2)	Article 191(2)
Article 130r(3)	Article 130r(3)	Article 174(3)	Article 191(3)
Article 130r(4) 1st sentence	Repealed		
Article 130r(4) 2nd sentence	Article 130s(4)	Article 175(4)	Article 192(4)
Article 130r(5)	Article 130r(4)	Article 174(4)	Article 191(4)
Article 130s[c]	Article 130s	Article 175	Article 192
Article 130s[1]	Article 130s(1)	Article 175(1)	Article 192(1)
	Article 130s(2)	Article 175(2)	Article 192(2)
	Article 130s(2)[1]	Article 175(2)[1]	Article 192(2)[1]
	Article 130s(2)[1] 1st indent	Article 175(2)[1] 1st indent	Article 192(2)(a)

(cont.)

Rome	Maastricht	Amsterdam	Lisbon
	Article 130s(2)[1] 2nd indent	Article 175(2)[1] 2nd indent	Article 192(2)(b)
	Article 130s(2)[1] 3rd indent	Article 175(2)[1] 3rd indent	Article 192(2)(c)
Article 130s[2]	Article 130s(2)[2]	Article 175(2)[2]	Article 192(2)[2]
	Article 130s(3)	Article 175(3)	Article 192(3)
	Article 130s(5)	Article 175(5)	Article 192(5)
Article 130t[c]	Article 130t	Article 176	Article 193
			Article 194
			Article 195
			Article 196
			Article 197
	Article 130u	Article 177	Article 208 and Article 21(2)(b), (d) and (e) TEU
	Article 130u(1)	Article 177(1)	Article 208(1)[1] and Article 21(2)(d) and (e) TEU
	Article 130u(2)	Article 177(2)	Article 21(2)(b) TEU
	Article 130u(3)	Article 177(3)	Article 208(2)
			Article 208(1)[2] 1st sentence
	Article 130v	Article 178	Article 208(1)[2] 2nd sentence
	Article 130w	Article 179	Article 209
	Article 130w(1)	Article 179(1)	Article 209(1)
	Article 130w(2)	Article 179(2)	Article 209(3)
	Article 130w(3)	Article 179(3)	Repealed
	Article 130x	Article 180	Article 210
	Article 130x(1)	Article 180(1)	Article 210(1)
	Article 130x(2)	Article 180(2)	Article 210(2)
	Article 130y	Article 181	Article 209(2) and Article 211

(cont.)

Rome	Maastricht	Amsterdam	Lisbon
	Article 130y[1]	Article 181[1]	Article 209(2)[1] and Article 211
	Article 130y[1] 1st sentence	Article 181[1] 1st sentence	Article 211
	Article 130y[1] 2nd sentence	Article 181[1] 2nd sentence	Article 209(2)[1]
	Article 130y[2]	Article 181[2]	Article 209(2)[2]
		Article 181a[b]	Article 212
			Article 213
			Article 214
Article 131	Article 131	Article 182	Article 198
Article 132	Article 132	Article 183	Article 199
Article 133	Article 133	Article 184	Article 200
Article 134	Article 134	Article 185	Article 201
Article 135	Article 135	Article 186	Article 202
Article 136	Article 136	Article 187	Article 203
Article 136[1]	Article 136[1]	Repealed	
Article 136[2]	Article 136[2]	Article 187	Article 203
	Article 136a	Article 188	Article 204
Article 137	Article 137	Article 189[1]	Article 14(1) and (2) 1st sentence TEU
		Article 189[2]	Article 14(2) 2nd sentence TEU
			Article 205
Article 138	Article 138	Article 190	Article 223
Article 138(1)	Lapsed on 17 July 1979	Article 190(1)	Article 14(3) TEU
Article 138(2)	Lapsed on 17 July 1979	Article 190(2)	Article 14(2) 3rd sentence TEU
		Article 190(3)	Article 14(3) TEU
Article 138(3)	Article 138(3)	Article 190(4)	Article 223(1)
		Article 190(5)	Article 223(2)
	Article 138a	Article 191	Article 10(4) TEU

(cont.)

Rome	Maastricht	Amsterdam	Lisbon
	Article 138b	Article 192	Article 225 and Article 14(1) TEU
	Article 138b[1]	Article 192[1]	Article 14(1) TEU
	Article 138b[2]	Article 192[2]	Article 225
	Article 138c	Article 193	Article 226
	Article 138d	Article 194	Article 227
	Article 138e	Article 195	Article 228
Article 139	Article 139	Article 196	Article 229
Article 140	Article 140	Article 197	Article 230 and Article 14(4) TEU
Article 140[1]	Article 140[1]	Article 197[1]	Article 14(4) TEU
Article 140[2]	Article 140[2]	Article 197[2]	Article 230[1]
Article 140[3]	Article 140[3]	Article 197[3]	Article 230[2]
Article 140[4]	Article 140[4]	Article 197[4]	Article 230[3]
Article 141	Article 141	Article 198	Article 231
Article 142	Article 142	Article 199	Article 232
Article 143	Article 143	Article 200	Article 233
Article 144	Article 144	Article 201	Article 234
			Article 235
			Article 236
Article 145	Article 145	Article 202	Article 16(1) TEU and Articles 290 and 291 TFEU
Article 145 1st indent	Article 145 1st indent	Article 202 1st indent	Article 121
Article 145 2nd indent	Article 145 2nd indent	Article 202 2nd indent	Article 16(1) TEU
	Article 145 3rd indent	Article 202 3rd indent	Article 291(2)–(4)
Article 146	Article 146	Article 203	Article 16(2) and (9) TEU

(cont.)

Rome	Maastricht	Amsterdam	Lisbon
Article 147	Article 147	Article 204	Article 237
Article 148	Article 148	Article 205	Article 16(3) to (5) TEU and Article 238(1), (3) and (4) TFEU
Article 148(1)	Article 148(1)	Article 205(1)	Article 16(3) TEU and Article 238(1)
			Article 238(2)
Article 148(2)	Article 148(2)	Article 205(2)	Article 16(4) and (5) TEU and Article 238(3)
Article 148(3)	Article 148(3)	Article 205(3)	Article 238(4)
Article 149	Repealed		
Article 150	Article 150	Article 206	Article 239
Article 151	Article 151(3)	Article 207(3)[1]	Article 240(3)
	Article 151	Article 207	Article 240
Article 152	Article 152	Article 208	Article 241
Article 153	Article 153	Article 209	Article 242
Article 154	Article 154	Article 210	Article 243
			Article 244
Article 155	Article 155	Article 211	Article 17(1) TEU
Article 156[d]	Article 156	Article 212	Article 249(2)
Article 157[d]	Article 157	Article 213	Article 17(3) and (5) TEU and Article 245
Article 157(1)	Article 157(1)	Article 213(1)	Article 17(3)[2] and (5) TEU
Article 157(1)[1]	Article 157(1)[1]	Article 213(1)[1]	Article 17(3)[2] and (5)[1] TEU
Article 157(1)[2]	Article 157(1)[2]	Article 213(1)[2]	Article 17(5)[1] penultimate and last part TEU
Article 157(1)[3]	Article 157(1)[3]	Article 213(1)[3]	Article 17(5)[2] 1st part of the 1st sentence TEU

(cont.)

Rome	Maastricht	Amsterdam	Lisbon
Article 157(1)[4]	Article 157(1)[4]	Article 213(1)[4]	Article 17(5)[2] 2nd part of the 1st sentence TEU[a]
Article 157(2)	Article 157(2)	Article 213(2)	Article 17(3)[3] TEU and Article 245
Article 157(2)[1]	Article 157(2)[1]	Article 213(2)[1]	Article 17(3)[3] 1st sentence TEU
Article 157(2)[2]	Article 157(2)[2] 1st sentence	Article 213(2)[2] 1st sentence	Article 17(3)[3] 2nd sentence TEU
Article 157(2)[3]	Article 157(2)[2] 2nd sentence	Article 213(2)[2] 2nd sentence	Article 17(3)[3] 3rd sentence TEU and Article 245[1] 1st sentence
Article 157(2)[4]	Article 157(2)[2] 3rd sentence	Article 213(2)[2] 3rd sentence	Article 245[1] 2nd sentence
Article 157(2)[5]	Article 157(2)[3]	Article 213(2)[3]	Article 245[2]
Article 158[d]	Article 158	Article 214	Article 17(3)[1] and (7) TEU
Article 158[1]	Article 158(1)[1]	Article 214(1)[1]	Repealed
	Article 158(2)[1] and [2]	Article 214(2)[1] and [2]	Article 17(7)[1] and [2] TEU[a]
Article 158[2] 1st sentence	Article 158(1) 1st sentence 3rd part	Article 214(1) 1st sentence 3rd part	Article 17(3)[1] TEU
Article 158[2] 2nd sentence	Article 158(1)[2]	Article 214(1)[2]	Repealed
	Article 158(2)[3]	Article 214(2)[3]	Article 17(7)[3] TEU[a]
	Article 158(3)	Repealed	
Article 159[d]	Article 159	Article 215	Article 246
Article 159[1]	Article 159[1]	Article 215[1]	Article 246[1]
Article 159[2] 1st sentence	Article 159[2] 1st sentence	Article 215[2] 1st sentence	Article 246[2]
Article 159[2] 2nd sentence	Article 159[2] 2nd sentence	Article 215[2] 2nd sentence	Article 246[3]
	Article 159[3]	Article 215[3]	Article 246[4]

(cont.)

Rome	Maastricht	Amsterdam	Lisbon
			Article 246[5]
Article 159[3]	Article 159[4]	Article 215[4]	Article 246[6]
Article 160[d]	Article 160	Article 216	Article 247
Article 161	Article 161[a]	Article 217	Article 17(6)(c) TEU
Article 161[1]	Article 161[a]	Article 217	Article 17(6)(c) TEU
Article 161[2] to[4]	Repealed		
			Article 248
Article 162[d]	Article 162	Article 218	Articles 249(1) and 295
Article 162[1][d]	Article 162(1)	Article 218(1)	Article 295
Article 162[2][d]	Article 162(2)	Article 218(2)	Article 249(1)
Article 163	Article 163	Article 219	Article 250 and Article 17(6)(a) TEU
		Article 219[1]	Article 17(6)(a) TEU
Article 163[1]	Article 163[1]	Article 219[2]	Article 250[1]
Article 163[2]	Article 163[2]	Article 219[3]	Article 250[2]
Article 164	Article 164	Article 220	Article 19(1) 2nd sentence TEU
Article 165	Article 165	Article 221	Article 251 and Article 19(2) 1st sentence TEU
Article 165[1]	Article 165[1]	Article 221[1]	Article 19(2) 1st sentence TEU
Article 165[2] 1st sentence	Article 165[2] 1st sentence	Article 221[2] 1st sentence	Article 251[2]
Article 165[2] 2nd sentence	Article 165[2] 2nd sentence	Article 221[2] 2nd sentence	Article 251[1]
Article 165[3]	Article 165[3][a]	Article 221[3]	Article 251[2]
Article 165[4]	Article 165[4]	Article 221[4]	Repealed
Article 166	Article 166	Article 222	Article 252
Article 166[1]	Article 166[1]	Article 222[1]	Article 252 1st sentence
Article 166[2]	Article 166[2]	Article 222[2]	Article 252[2]

(cont.)

Rome	Maastricht	Amsterdam	Lisbon
Article 166[3]	Article 166[3]	Article 222[3]	Article 252 2nd sentence
Article 167	Article 167	Article 223	Article 253
Article 167[1]	Article 167[1]	Article 223[1]	Article 253[1]
Article 167[2]	Article 167[2]	Article 223[2]	Article 253[2]
Article 167[3]	Article 167[3]	Article 223[3]	Article 253[2]
Article 167[4]	Article 167[4]	Article 223[4]	Article 253[4]
Article 167[5]	Article 167[5]	Article 223[5]	Article 253[3]
Article 168	Article 168	Article 224	Article 253[5]
			Article 254[1], [3], [4] and [6]
	Article 168a	Article 225	Article 254[2] and [5] and (6) and Article 256(1)
	Article 168a(1)	Article 225(1)	Article 256(1) 1st and 3rd sentences
	Article 168a(2)	Article 225(2)	Article 254(6) and Article 256(1) 2nd sentence
	Article 168a(3)	Article 225(3)	Article 254[2]
	Article 168a(4)	Article 225(4)	Article 254[5]
			Article 256(1)[2]
			Article 256(2) and (3)
		Article 225a[b]	Article 257[a]
			Article 255
Article 169	Article 169	Article 226	Article 258
Article 170	Article 170	Article 227	Article 259
Article 171	Article 171(1)	Article 228(1)	Article 260(1)
	Article 171(2)	Article 228(2)	Article 260(2)
			Article 260(3)
Article 172	Article 172	Article 229	Article 261
		Article 229a[b]	Article 262

(cont.)

Rome	Maastricht	Amsterdam	Lisbon
Article 173	Article 173	Article 230	Article 263
Article 173[1]	Article 173[1]	Article 230[1]	Article 263[1]
Article 173[2]		Article 230[2]	Article 263[2]
	Article 173[3]	Article 230[3]	Article 263[3]
Article 173[2]	Article 173[4]	Article 230[4]	Article 263[4]
			Article 263[5]
Article 173[3]	Article 173[5]	Article 230[5]	Article 263[6]
Article 174	Article 174	Article 231	Article 264
Article 175	Article 175	Article 232	Article 265
Article 175[1]	Article 175[1]	Article 232[1]	Article 265[1]
Article 175[2]	Article 175[2]	Article 232[2]	Article 265[2]
Article 175[3]	Article 175[3]	Article 232[3]	Article 265[3]
	Article 175[4]	Article 232[4]	Repealed
Article 176	Article 176	Article 233	Article 266
Article 176[1]	Article 176[1]	Article 233[1]	Article 266[1]
Article 176[2]	Article 176[2]	Article 233[2]	Article 266[2]
	Article 176[3]	Article 233[3]	Repealed
Article 177	Article 177	Article 234	Article 267
Article 177[1](a)	Article 177[1](a)	Article 234[1](a)	Article 267[1](a)
Article 177[1](b)	Article 177[1](b)	Article 234[1](b)	Article 267[1](b)
Article 177[1](c)	Article 177[1](c)	Article 234[1](c)	Repealed
Article 177[2]	Article 177[2]	Article 234[2]	Article 267[2]
Article 177[3]	Article 177[3]	Article 234[3]	Article 267[3]
			Article 267[4]
Article 178	Article 178	Article 235	Article 268
			Article 269
Article 179	Article 179	Article 236	Article 270
Article 180	Article 180	Article 237	Article 271
Article 180(a)	Article 180(a)	Article 237(a)	Article 271(a)
Article 180(b)	Article 180(b)	Article 237(b)	Article 271(b)

(cont.)

Rome	Maastricht	Amsterdam	Lisbon
Article 180(c)	Article 180(c)	Article 237(c)	Article 271(c)
	Article 180(d)	Article 237(d)	Article 271(d)
Article 181	Article 181	Article 238	Article 272
Article 182	Article 182	Article 239	Article 273
Article 183	Article 183	Article 240	Article 274
			Article 275
			Article 276
Article 184	Article 184	Article 241	Article 277
Article 185	Article 185	Article 242	Article 278
Article 186	Article 186	Article 243	Article 279
Article 187	Article 187	Article 244	Article 280
Article 188	Article 188	Article 245	Article 281
Article 188[1]	Article 188[1]	Article 245[1]	Article 281[1]
Article 188[2]	Article 188[2]	Article 245[2]	Article 281[2]
Article 188[3]	Article 188[3]	Article 245[3]	Article 253[6]
	Article 188a	Article 246	Article 285[1]
	Article 188b	Article 247	Articles 285[2] and 286
	Article 188b(1) and (4)[1]	Article 247(1)	Article 285[2] 1st sentence
	Article 188b(2)	Article 247(2)	Article 286(1)
	Article 188b(3)[1]	Article 247(3)[1]	Article 286(2) 1st and 2nd sentences
	Article 188b(3)[2]	Repealed	
	Article 188b(3)[3]	Article 247(3)[2]	Article 286(2) 3rd sentence
	Article 188b(3)[4]	Article 247(3)[4]	Article 286(2)[2]
	Article 188b(4)[1]	Article 247(4)[1]	Article 285[2] 2nd sentence
	Article 188b(4)[2]	Article 247(4)[2]	Article 286(3)
	Article 188b(5)	Article 247(5)	Article 286(4)

(cont.)

Rome	Maastricht	Amsterdam	Lisbon
	Article 188b(6)	Article 247(6)	Article 286(5)
	Article 188b(7)	Article 247(7)	Article 286(6)
	Article 188b(8)	Article 247(8)	Article 286(7)
	Article 188b(9)	Article 247(9)	Article 286(8)
Article 206[e]	Article 188c	Article 248	Article 287
	Article 188c(1)	Article 248(1)	Article 287(1)
	Article 188c(2)	Article 248(2)	Article 287(2)
Article 206[2][e]	Article 188c(3)[1]	Article 248(3)[1]	Article 287(3)[1]
	Article 188c(3)[2]	Article 248(3)[2]	Article 287(3)[2]
		Article 248(3)[3]	Article 287(3)[3]
Article 206[2][e]	Article 188c(4)	Article 248(4)	Article 287(4)
	Article 188c(4)[1]	Article 248(4)[1]	Article 287(4)[1]
	Article 188c(4)[2]	Article 248(4)[2]	Article 287(4)[2]
	Article 188c(4)[3]	Article 248(4)[3]	Article 287(4)[3]
			Article 287(4)[4]
Article 189	Article 189	Article 249	Article 288
			Article 289
			Article 290
			Article 291
			Article 292
	Article 189a	Article 250	Article 293
	Article 189b	Article 251	Article 294
	Article 189b(1)	Article 251(1)	Article 294(1)
	Article 189b(2)	Article 251(2)	Article 294(2) to (7)
	Article 189b(2)[1]	Article 251(2)[1]	Article 294(2)
	Article 189b(2)[2]	Article 251(2) 1st part of the sentence and 3rd indent	Article 294(3), (5) and (6)
		Article 251(2) 1st and 2nd indents	Article 294(4)

(cont.)

Rome	Maastricht	Amsterdam	Lisbon
	Article 189b(2)[3]	Article 251(2)[3]	Article 294(7)
	Article 189b(3)	Article 251(3)	Article 294(8) and (9)
	Article 189b(4) 1st and 3rd sentences	Article 251(4) 1st and 3rd sentences	Article 294(10)
	Article 189b(4) 2nd sentence	Article 251(4) 2nd sentence	Article 294(11)
	Article 189b(5)	Article 251(5)	Article 294(13)
	Article 189b(6)	Article 251(6)	Article 294(12)
	Article 189b(7)	Article 251(7)	Article 294(14)
			Article 294(15)
	Article 189b(8)	Repealed	
	Article 189c	Article 252	Repealed
Article 190	Article 190	Article 253	Article 296
Article 191	Article 191	Article 254	Article 297(1) and (2)[2] and [3]
Article 191[1]	Article 191(1)	Article 254(1)	Article 297(1)
			Article 297(2)[1]
	Article 191(2)	Article 254(2)	Article 297(2)[2]
Article 191[2]	Article 191(3)	Article 254(3)	Article 297(2)[3]
			Article 298
			Article 15(1) and (2)
		Article 191a inserted and renumbered to Article 255	Article 15(3)[1] to [3]
		Article 255(1)	Article 15(3)[1]
		Article 255(2)	Article 15(3)[2]
		Article 255(3)	Article 15(3)[3]
			Article 15(3)[4] and [5]
Article 192	Article 192	Article 256	Article 299

(cont.)

Rome	Maastricht	Amsterdam	Lisbon
Article 193	Article 193	Article 257	Article 300(1) and (2)
Article 193[1]	Article 193[1]	Article 257[1]	Article 300(1)[a]
Article 193[2]	Article 193[2]	Article 257[2]	Article 300(2)
Article 194	Article 194	Article 258	Article 300(4), 301[1] and [3] and Article 302(1) 1st and 3rd sentences
Article 194[1]	Article 194[1]	Article 258[1]	Article 301[1]
Article 194[2]	Article 194[2]	Article 258[2]	Article 302(1) 1st and 3rd sentences
Article 194[3]	Article 194[3]a	Article 258[3]	Article 300(4)
	Article 194[4]	Article 258[4]	Article 301[3]
Article 195	Article 195	Article 259	Article 302(1) 2nd sentence and (2)
Article 195(1)[1]	Article 195(1)[1]	Article 259(1)[1]	Article 302(1) 2nd sentence
Article 195(1)[2]	Article 195(1)[2]	Article 259(1)[2]	Repealed
Article 195(2)	Article 195(2)	Article 259(2)	Article 302(2)
			Article 301[2]
Article 196	Article 196	Article 260	Article 303
Article 197	Article 197	Article 261	Repealed
Article 197[1]	Article 197[1]	Article 261[1]	Repealed
Article 197[2]	Article 197[2]	Repealed	
Article 197[3]	Article 197[3]	Article 261[2]	Repealed
Article 197[4]	Article 197[4]	Article 261[3]	Repealed
Article 197[5]	Article 197[5]	Article 261[4]	Repealed
Article 198	Article 198	Article 262	Article 304
Article 198[1]	Article 198[1]	Article 262[1]	Article 304[1]
Article 198[2]	Article 198[2]	Article 262[2]	Article 304[2]
Article 198[3]	Article 198[3]	Article 262[3]	Article 304[3]
		Article 262[4]	Article 304[1] 1st sentence

(cont.)

Rome	Maastricht	Amsterdam	Lisbon
	Article 198a	Article 263	Article 300(3) and (5) and Article 305[1] and [3]
	Article 198a[1]	Article 263[1]	Article 300(3)
	Article 198a[2]	Article 263[2]	Article 305[1]
			Article 305[2]
	Article 198a[3]	Article 263[3]	Article 305[3]
	Article 198a[4]	Article 263[4]	Article 300(4)
			Article 300(5)
	Article 198b	Article 264	Article 306
	Article 198c	Article 265	Article 307
	Article 198c[1]	Article 265[1]	Article 307[1]
	Article 198c[2]	Article 265[2]	Article 307[2]
	Article 198c[3]	Article 265[3]	Article 307[3]
		Article 265[4]	Article 307 1st sentence
	Article 198c[4]	Article 265[5]	Article 307[4]
	Article 198c[5]	Article 265[6]	Article 307[5]
Article 199	Article 199	Article 268	Article 310(1)[1] and [3]
Article 199[1]	Article 199[1]	Article 268[1]	Article 310(1)[1]
			Article 310(1)[2]
	Article 199[2]	Article 268[2]	Repealed
Article 199[2]	Article 199[3]	Article 268[3]	Article 310(1)[3]
Article 200	Repealed		
Article 201	Article 201	Article 269	Article 311
	Article F(3) TEU	Article 6(4) TEU	Article 311[1]
Article 201[1]	Article 201[1z][a]	Article 269[1]	Article 311[2]
Article 201[2]	Article 201 2nd sentence 1st part	Article 269 2nd sentence 1st part	Repealed

(cont.)

Rome	Maastricht	Amsterdam	Lisbon
Article 201[3]	Article 201[2]	Article 269[2]	Article 311[3]
			Article 311[4]
			Article 312
			Article 310(3), (5) and (6)
	Article 201a	Article 270	Article 310(4)
Article 202	Article 202	Article 271	Article 310(2) and 316
Article 202[1]	Article 202[1]	Article 271[1]	Article 310(2)
Article 202[2]	Article 202[2]	Article 271[2]	Article 316[1]
Article 202[3]	Article 202[3]	Article 271[3]	Article 316[2]
Article 202[4]	Article 202[4]	Article 271[4]	Article 316[3]
Article 203	Article 203	Article 272	Articles 313 and 314(1) to (4), (6), (7), (9) and (10)
Article 203(1)	Article 203(1)	Article 272(1)	Article 313
Article 203(2)	Article 203(2)	Article 272(2)	Article 314(1)
Article 203(3)	Article 203(3)	Article 272(3)	Article 314(2) and (3)[3] 1st sentence
Article 203(3)[1]	Article 203(3)[1]	Article 272(3)[1]	Article 314(2)[1]
Article 203(3)[2]	Article 203(3)[2]	Article 272(3)[2]	Article 314(2)[2]
Article 203(3)[3]	Article 203(3)[3]	Article 272(3)[3]	Article 314(3)[3] 1st sentence
Article 203(4)	Article 203(4)	Article 272(4)	Article 314(3) and (4)
			Article 314(5)
Article 203(5)	Article 203(5)	Article 272(5)	Article 314(6) and (7)
Article 203(6)	Article 203(6)	Article 272(6)	Article 314(7)
			Article 314(8)
Article 203(7)	Article 203(7)	Article 272(7)	Article 314(9)
	Article 203(8)	Article 272(8)	Article 314(7)(b) and (c)

(cont.)

Rome	Maastricht	Amsterdam	Lisbon
Article 203(8)	Article 203(9)	Article 272(9)	Repealed
Article 203(9)	Article 203(10)	Article 272(10)	Article 314(10)
Article 204	Article 204	Article 273	Article 315
Article 204[1]	Article 204[1]	Article 273[1]	Article 315[1]
Article 204[2]	Article 204[2]	Article 273[2]	Article 315[2]
	Article 204[3]	Article 273[3]	Repealed
	Article 204[4]	Article 273[4]	Article 315[3]
			Article 315[4]
Article 205	Article 205	Article 274	Article 317
Article 205a[e]	Article 205a	Article 275	Article 318[1]
			Article 318[2]
	Article 206	Article 276	Article 319
Article 207	Article 207	Article 277	Article 320
Article 207[1]	Article 207[1]	Article 277	Article 320
Article 207[2] to [5]	Article 207[2] to [5]	Repealed	
Article 208	Article 208	Article 278	Article 321
Article 209[e]	Article 209	Article 279	Article 322
Article 209(a)	Article 209(a)	Article 279(a)	Article 322(1)(a)
Article 209(b)	Article 209(b)	Article 279(b)	Article 322(2)
Article 209(c)	Article 209(c)	Article 279(c)	Article 322(1)(b)
			Article 323
			Article 324
	Article 209a	Article 280	Article 325
		Article 280(1)	Article 325(1)
	Article 209a[1]	Article 280(2)	Article 325(2)
	Article 209a[2]	Article 280(3)	Article 325(3)
		Article 280(4)	Article 325(4)
		Article 280(5)	Article 325(5)
Article 210	Article 210	Article 281	Article 47 TEU
Article 211	Article 211	Article 282	Article 335

(cont.)

Rome	Maastricht	Amsterdam	Lisbon
Article 212[d]	Article 212	Article 283	Article 336
Article 212(1)[1]	Article 212(1)[1]	Repealed	
Article 212(1)[2]	Article 212(1)[2]	Article 283	Article 336
Article 213	Article 213	Article 284	Article 337
		Article 213a inserted and renumbered Article 285	Article 338
			Article 16(1)
		Article 213b inserted and renumbered Article 286	Article 16(2)[1]
		Article 286(1)	Article 16(2)[1]
		Article 286(2)	Repealed
Article 214	Article 214	Article 287	Article 339
Article 215	Article 215	Article 288	Article 340
Article 215[1]	Article 215[1]	Article 288[1]	Article 340[1]
Article 215[2]	Article 215[2]	Article 288[2]	Article 340[2]
	Article 215[3]	Article 288[3]	Article 340[3]
Article 215[3]	Article 215[4]	Article 288[4]	Article 340[4]
Article 216	Article 216	Article 289	Article 341
Article 217	Article 217	Article 290	Article 342
Article 218[d]	Article 218	Article 291	Article 343
Article 219	Article 219	Article 292	Article 344
Article 220	Article 220	Article 293	Repealed
Article 221	Article 221	Article 294	Article 55
Article 222	Article 222	Article 295	Article 345
Article 223	Article 223	Article 296	Article 346
Article 223(1)	Article 223(1)	Article 296(1)	Article 346(1)
Article 223(1)(a)	Article 223(1)(a)	Article 296(1)(a)	Article 346(1)(a)
Article 223(1)(b)	Article 223(1)(b)	Article 296(1)(b)	Article 346(1)(b)
Article 223(2)	Article 223(2)	Repealed	
Article 223(3)	Article 223(3)	Article 296(2)	Article 346(2)

(cont.)

Rome	Maastricht	Amsterdam	Lisbon
Article 224	Article 224	Article 297	Article 347
Article 225	Article 225	Article 298	Article 348
Article 226	Article 226	Repealed	
Article 227	Article 227	Article 299	Articles 349 and 355 and Article 52(1) TEU
Article 227(1)	Article 227(1)	Article 299(1)	Article 52(1) TEU
Article 227(2)	Article 227(2)[1]	Article 299(2)[1]	Article 355(1)
	Article 227(2)[2]	Repealed	
	Article 227(2)[3]	Repealed	
		Article 299(2)[2]	Article 349[1]
		Article 299(2)[3]	Article 349[2]
		Article 299(2)[4]	Article 349[3]
Article 227(3)	Article 227(3)	Article 299(3)	Article 355(2)
Article 227(4)	Article 227(4)	Article 299(4)	Article 355(3)
		Article 299(5)	Article 355(4)
Article 227(5)	Article 227(5)	Article 299(6)	Article 355(5)
			Article 355(6)
Article 228	Article 228	Article 300	Articles 218(1) to (9), (11) and 216(2)
Article 228(1)	Article 228(1)	Article 300(1)	Article 218(1) to (8)
Article 228(1) 1st sentence	Article 228(1) 1st and 2nd sentences	Article 300(1) 1st and 2nd sentences	Article 218(1) to (7)
	Article 228(1)[2]	Article 300(1)[2]	Article 218(8)
Article 228(1) 2nd sentence	Article 228(2)	Article 300(2)	Article 218(8) 1st sentence
		Article 300(3)[2]	Article 218(9)
	Article 228(3)[1]	Article 300(3)[1]	Article 218(6)[2] indent (b)
	Article 228(3)[2]	Article 300(3)[2]	Article 218(6)[2] indent (a)

(cont.)

Rome	Maastricht	Amsterdam	Lisbon
	Article 228(3)[3]	Article 300(3)[3]	Article 218(6)[2] indent (a) last sentence
	Article 228(4)	Article 300(4)	Article 218(7)
	Article 228(5)	Article 300(5)	Repealed
			Article 218(10)
Article 228(1)[2]	Article 228(6)	Article 300(6)	Article 218(11)
Article 228(2)	Article 228(7)	Article 300(7)	Article 216(2)
	Article 228a	Article 301	Article 215
Article 229	Article 229	Article 302	Article 220(1)
Article 229[1]	Article 229[1]	Article 302[1]	Article 220(1)[1]
Article 229[2]	Article 229[2]	Article 302[2]	Article 220(1)[2]
Article 230	Article 230	Article 303	Article 220(1)[1]
Article 231	Article 231	Article 304	Article 220(1)[1]
			Article 221
			Article 222
			Article 224
Article 232	Article 232	Article 305	Repealed
Article 233	Article 233	Article 306	Article 350
Article 234	Article 234	Article 307	Article 351
Article 235	Article 235	Article 308	Article 352(1) 1st sentence
			Article 352(1) 2nd sentence and (2) to (4)
Article 236	Repealed		Article 48 TEU
Article 236[1]			Article 48(2) TEU
Article 236[2]			Article 48(3) and (4)[1] TEU
Article 236[3]			Article 48(4)[2] TEU
		Article 236 inserted and renumbered to Article 309	Article 354[a]

(cont.)

Rome	Maastricht	Amsterdam	Lisbon
Article 237	Repealed		Article 49 TEU
Article 238	Article 238	Article 310	Article 217
Article 239	Article 239	Article 311	Article 51 TEU
Article 240	Article 240	Article 312	Article 53 TEU and Article 356
Article 241	Article 241	Repealed	
Article 242	Article 242	Repealed	
Article 243	Article 243	Repealed	
Article 244	Article 244	Repealed	
Article 245	Article 245	Repealed	
Article 246	Article 246	Repealed	
Article 247	Article 247	Article 313	Article 357
Article 248	Article 248	Article 314	Article 358[2] and [3]
Article 248[1]	Article 248[1]	Article 314[1]	Repealed
Article 248[2]	Article 248[2]	Article 314[2]	Repealed
			Article 358[1]
Article 248[3]	Article 248[3]	Article 314[3]	Article 358[2]
Article 248[4]	Article 248[4]	Article 314[4]	Article 358[3]

PART I
Union Primary Law: Treaties and Charter

1

Treaty on European Union (TEU)

Contents

PREAMBLE

HIS MAJESTY THE KING OF THE BELGIANS, HER MAJESTY THE QUEEN OF DENMARK, THE PRESIDENT OF THE FEDERAL REPUBLIC OF GERMANY, THE PRESIDENT OF IRELAND, THE PRESIDENT OF THE HELLENIC REPUBLIC, HIS MAJESTY THE KING OF SPAIN, THE PRESIDENT OF THE FRENCH REPUBLIC, THE PRESIDENT OF THE ITALIAN REPUBLIC, HIS ROYAL HIGHNESS THE GRAND DUKE OF LUXEMBOURG, HER MAJESTY THE QUEEN OF THE NETHERLANDS, THE PRESIDENT OF THE PORTUGUESE REPUBLIC, HER MAJESTY THE QUEEN OF THE UNITED KINGDOM OF GREAT BRITAIN AND NORTHERN IRELAND,[1]

RESOLVED to mark a new stage in the process of European integration undertaken with the establishment of the European Communities,

---

[1] The Republic of Bulgaria, the Czech Republic, the Republic of Estonia, the Republic of Croatia, the Republic of Cyprus, the Republic of Latvia, the Republic of Lithuania, the Republic of Hungary, the Republic of Malta, the Republic of Austria, the Republic of Poland, Romania, the Republic of Slovenia, the Slovak Republic, the Republic of Finland and the Kingdom of Sweden have since become members of the European Union.

DRAWING INSPIRATION from the cultural, religious and humanist inheritance of Europe, from which have developed the universal values of the inviolable and inalienable rights of the human person, freedom, democracy, equality and the rule of law,

RECALLING the historic importance of the ending of the division of the European continent and the need to create firm bases for the construction of the future Europe,

CONFIRMING their attachment to the principles of liberty, democracy and respect for human rights and fundamental freedoms and of the rule of law,

CONFIRMING their attachment to fundamental social rights as defined in the European Social Charter signed at Turin on 18 October 1961 and in the 1989 Community Charter of the Fundamental Social Rights of Workers,

DESIRING to deepen the solidarity between their peoples while respecting their history, their culture and their traditions,

DESIRING to enhance further the democratic and efficient functioning of the institutions so as to enable them better to carry out, within a single institutional framework, the tasks entrusted to them,

RESOLVED to achieve the strengthening and the convergence of their economies and to establish an economic and monetary union including, in accordance with the provisions of this Treaty and of the Treaty on the Functioning of the European Union, a single and stable currency,

DETERMINED to promote economic and social progress for their peoples, taking into account the principle of sustainable development and within the context of the accomplishment of the internal market and of reinforced cohesion and environmental protection, and to implement policies ensuring that advances in economic integration are accompanied by parallel progress in other fields,

RESOLVED to establish a citizenship common to nationals of their countries,

RESOLVED to implement a common foreign and security policy including the progressive framing of a common defence policy, which might lead to a common defence in accordance with the provisions of Article 42, thereby reinforcing the European identity and its independence in order to promote peace, security and progress in Europe and in the world,

RESOLVED to facilitate the free movement of persons, while ensuring the safety and security of their peoples, by establishing an area of freedom, security and justice, in accordance with the provisions of this Treaty and of the Treaty on the Functioning of the European Union,

RESOLVED to continue the process of creating an ever closer union among the peoples of Europe, in which decisions are taken as closely as possible to the citizen in accordance with the principle of subsidiarity,

IN VIEW of further steps to be taken in order to advance European integration,

HAVE DECIDED to establish a European Union and to this end have designated as their Plenipotentiaries:

(List of plenipotentiaries not reproduced)

WHO, having exchanged their full powers, found in good and due form, have agreed as follows:

TITLE I COMMON PROVISIONS

Article 1

By this Treaty, the HIGH CONTRACTING PARTIES establish among themselves a EUROPEAN UNION, hereinafter called 'the Union', on which the Member States confer competences to attain objectives they have in common.

This Treaty marks a new stage in the process of creating an ever closer union among the peoples of Europe, in which decisions are taken as openly as possible and as closely as possible to the citizen.

The Union shall be founded on the present Treaty and on the Treaty on the Functioning of the European Union (hereinafter referred to as 'the Treaties'). Those two Treaties shall have the same legal value. The Union shall replace and succeed the European Community.

Article 2

The Union is founded on the values of respect for human dignity, freedom, democracy, equality, the rule of law and respect for human rights, including the rights of persons belonging to minorities. These values are common to the Member States in a society in which pluralism, non-discrimination, tolerance, justice, solidarity and equality between women and men prevail.

Article 3

1. The Union's aim is to promote peace, its values and the well-being of its peoples.
2. The Union shall offer its citizens an area of freedom, security and justice without internal frontiers, in which the free movement of persons is ensured in conjunction with appropriate measures with respect to external border controls, asylum, immigration and the prevention and combating of crime.
3. The Union shall establish an internal market. It shall work for the sustainable development of Europe based on balanced economic growth and price stability, a highly competitive social market economy, aiming at full employment and social progress, and a high level of protection and improvement of the quality of the environment. It shall promote scientific and technological advance.

   It shall combat social exclusion and discrimination, and shall promote social justice and protection, equality between women and men, solidarity between generations and protection of the rights of the child. It shall promote economic, social and territorial cohesion, and solidarity among Member States.

   It shall respect its rich cultural and linguistic diversity, and shall ensure that Europe's cultural heritage is safeguarded and enhanced.
4. The Union shall establish an economic and monetary union whose currency is the euro.
5. In its relations with the wider world, the Union shall uphold and promote its values and interests and contribute to the protection of its citizens. It shall contribute to peace, security, the sustainable development of the Earth, solidarity and mutual

respect among peoples, free and fair trade, eradication of poverty and the protection of human rights, in particular the rights of the child, as well as to the strict observance and the development of international law, including respect for the principles of the United Nations Charter.

6. The Union shall pursue its objectives by appropriate means commensurate with the competences which are conferred upon it in the Treaties.

Article 4

1. In accordance with Article 5, competences not conferred upon the Union in the Treaties remain with the Member States.

2. The Union shall respect the equality of Member States before the Treaties as well as their national identities, inherent in their fundamental structures, political and constitutional, inclusive of regional and local self-government. It shall respect their essential State functions, including ensuring the territorial integrity of the State, maintaining law and order and safeguarding national security. In particular, national security remains the sole responsibility of each Member State.

3. Pursuant to the principle of sincere cooperation, the Union and the Member States shall, in full mutual respect, assist each other in carrying out tasks which flow from the Treaties.

   The Member States shall take any appropriate measure, general or particular, to ensure fulfilment of the obligations arising out of the Treaties or resulting from the acts of the institutions of the Union.

   The Member States shall facilitate the achievement of the Union's tasks and refrain from any measure which could jeopardise the attainment of the Union's objectives.

Article 5

1. The limits of Union competences are governed by the principle of conferral. The use of Union competences is governed by the principles of subsidiarity and proportionality.

2. Under the principle of conferral, the Union shall act only within the limits of the competences conferred upon it by the Member States in the Treaties to attain the objectives set out therein. Competences not conferred upon the Union in the Treaties remain with the Member States.

3. Under the principle of subsidiarity, in areas which do not fall within its exclusive competence, the Union shall act only if and in so far as the objectives of the proposed action cannot be sufficiently achieved by the Member States, either at central level or at regional and local level, but can rather, by reason of the scale or effects of the proposed action, be better achieved at Union level.

   The institutions of the Union shall apply the principle of subsidiarity as laid down in the Protocol on the application of the principles of subsidiarity and proportionality. National Parliaments ensure compliance with the principle of subsidiarity in accordance with the procedure set out in that Protocol.

4. Under the principle of proportionality, the content and form of Union action shall not exceed what is necessary to achieve the objectives of the Treaties.

   The institutions of the Union shall apply the principle of proportionality as laid down in the Protocol on the application of the principles of subsidiarity and proportionality.

Article 6

1. The Union recognises the rights, freedoms and principles set out in the Charter of Fundamental Rights of the European Union of 7 December 2000, as adapted at Strasbourg, on 12 December 2007, which shall have the same legal value as the Treaties.

   The provisions of the Charter shall not extend in any way the competences of the Union as defined in the Treaties.

   The rights, freedoms and principles in the Charter shall be interpreted in accordance with the general provisions in Title VII of the Charter governing its interpretation and application and with due regard to the explanations referred to in the Charter, that set out the sources of those provisions.

2. The Union shall accede to the European Convention for the Protection of Human Rights and Fundamental Freedoms. Such accession shall not affect the Union's competences as defined in the Treaties.

3. Fundamental rights, as guaranteed by the European Convention for the Protection of Human Rights and Fundamental Freedoms and as they result from the constitutional traditions common to the Member States, shall constitute general principles of the Union's law.

Article 7

1. On a reasoned proposal by one third of the Member States, by the European Parliament or by the European Commission, the Council, acting by a majority of four fifths of its members after obtaining the consent of the European Parliament, may determine that there is a clear risk of a serious breach by a Member State of the values referred to in Article 2. Before making such a determination, the Council shall hear the Member State in question and may address recommendations to it, acting in accordance with the same procedure.

   The Council shall regularly verify that the grounds on which such a determination was made continue to apply.

2. The European Council, acting by unanimity on a proposal by one third of the Member States or by the Commission and after obtaining the consent of the European Parliament, may determine the existence of a serious and persistent breach by a Member State of the values referred to in Article 2, after inviting the Member State in question to submit its observations.

3. Where a determination under paragraph 2 has been made, the Council, acting by a qualified majority, may decide to suspend certain of the rights deriving from the application of the Treaties to the Member State in question, including the voting rights of the representative of the government of that Member State in the Council. In doing so, the Council shall take into account the possible consequences of such a suspension on the rights and obligations of natural and legal persons.

   The obligations of the Member State in question under the Treaties shall in any case continue to be binding on that State.

4. The Council, acting by a qualified majority, may decide subsequently to vary or revoke measures taken under paragraph 3 in response to changes in the situation which led to their being imposed.

5. The voting arrangements applying to the European Parliament, the European Council and the Council for the purposes of this Article are laid down in Article 354 of the Treaty on the Functioning of the European Union.

Article 8

1. The Union shall develop a special relationship with neighbouring countries, aiming to establish an area of prosperity and good neighbourliness, founded on the values of the Union and characterised by close and peaceful relations based on cooperation.
2. For the purposes of paragraph 1, the Union may conclude specific agreements with the countries concerned. These agreements may contain reciprocal rights and obligations as well as the possibility of undertaking activities jointly. Their implementation shall be the subject of periodic consultation.

TITLE II PROVISIONS ON DEMOCRATIC PRINCIPLES

Article 9

In all its activities, the Union shall observe the principle of the equality of its citizens, who shall receive equal attention from its institutions, bodies, offices and agencies. Every national of a Member State shall be a citizen of the Union. Citizenship of the Union shall be additional to and not replace national citizenship.

Article 10

1. The functioning of the Union shall be founded on representative democracy.
2. Citizens are directly represented at Union level in the European Parliament. Member States are represented in the European Council by their Heads of State or Government and in the Council by their governments, themselves democratically accountable either to their national Parliaments, or to their citizens.
3. Every citizen shall have the right to participate in the democratic life of the Union. Decisions shall be taken as openly and as closely as possible to the citizen.
4. Political parties at European level contribute to forming European political awareness and to expressing the will of citizens of the Union.

Article 11

1. The institutions shall, by appropriate means, give citizens and representative associations the opportunity to make known and publicly exchange their views in all areas of Union action.
2. The institutions shall maintain an open, transparent and regular dialogue with representative associations and civil society.
3. The European Commission shall carry out broad consultations with parties concerned in order to ensure that the Union's actions are coherent and transparent.
4. Not less than one million citizens who are nationals of a significant number of Member States may take the initiative of inviting the European Commission, within the framework of its powers, to submit any appropriate proposal on matters where citizens consider that a legal act of the Union is required for the purpose of implementing the Treaties.

The procedures and conditions required for such a citizens' initiative shall be determined in accordance with the first paragraph of Article 24 of the Treaty on the Functioning of the European Union.

Article 12

National Parliaments contribute actively to the good functioning of the Union:

(a) through being informed by the institutions of the Union and having draft legislative acts of the Union forwarded to them in accordance with the Protocol on the role of national Parliaments in the European Union;

(b) by seeing to it that the principle of subsidiarity is respected in accordance with the procedures provided for in the Protocol on the application of the principles of subsidiarity and proportionality;

(c) by taking part, within the framework of the area of freedom, security and justice, in the evaluation mechanisms for the implementation of the Union policies in that area, in accordance with Article 70 of the Treaty on the Functioning of the European Union, and through being involved in the political monitoring of Europol and the evaluation of Eurojust's activities in accordance with Articles 88 and 85 of that Treaty;

(d) by taking part in the revision procedures of the Treaties, in accordance with Article 48 of this Treaty;

(e) by being notified of applications for accession to the Union, in accordance with Article 49 of this Treaty;

(f) by taking part in the inter-parliamentary cooperation between national Parliaments and with the European Parliament, in accordance with the Protocol on the role of national Parliaments in the European Union.

TITLE III PROVISIONS ON THE INSTITUTIONS

Article 13

1. The Union shall have an institutional framework which shall aim to promote its values, advance its objectives, serve its interests, those of its citizens and those of the Member States, and ensure the consistency, effectiveness and continuity of its policies and actions.

    The Union's institutions shall be:
    — the European Parliament,
    — the European Council,
    — the Council,
    — the European Commission (hereinafter referred to as 'the Commission'),
    — the Court of Justice of the European Union,
    — the European Central Bank,
    — the Court of Auditors.

2. Each institution shall act within the limits of the powers conferred on it in the Treaties, and in conformity with the procedures, conditions and objectives set out in them. The institutions shall practice mutual sincere cooperation.

3. The provisions relating to the European Central Bank and the Court of Auditors and detailed provisions on the other institutions are set out in the Treaty on the Functioning of the European Union.

4. The European Parliament, the Council and the Commission shall be assisted by an Economic and Social Committee and a Committee of the Regions acting in an advisory capacity.

Article 14

1. The European Parliament shall, jointly with the Council, exercise legislative and budgetary functions. It shall exercise functions of political control and consultation as laid down in the Treaties. It shall elect the President of the Commission.
2. The European Parliament shall be composed of representatives of the Union's citizens. They shall not exceed seven hundred and fifty in number, plus the President. Representation of citizens shall be degressively proportional, with a minimum threshold of six members per Member State. No Member State shall be allocated more than ninety-six seats.

   The European Council shall adopt by unanimity, on the initiative of the European Parliament and with its consent, a decision establishing the composition of the European Parliament, respecting the principles referred to in the first subparagraph.
3. The members of the European Parliament shall be elected for a term of five years by direct universal suffrage in a free and secret ballot.
4. The European Parliament shall elect its President and its officers from among its members.

Article 15

1. The European Council shall provide the Union with the necessary impetus for its development and shall define the general political directions and priorities thereof. It shall not exercise legislative functions.
2. The European Council shall consist of the Heads of State or Government of the Member States, together with its President and the President of the Commission. The High Representative of the Union for Foreign Affairs and Security Policy shall take part in its work.
3. The European Council shall meet twice every six months, convened by its President. When the agenda so requires, the members of the European Council may decide each to be assisted by a minister and, in the case of the President of the Commission, by a member of the Commission. When the situation so requires, the President shall convene a special meeting of the European Council.
4. Except where the Treaties provide otherwise, decisions of the European Council shall be taken by consensus.
5. The European Council shall elect its President, by a qualified majority, for a term of two and a half years, renewable once. In the event of an impediment or serious misconduct, the European Council can end the President's term of office in accordance with the same procedure.
6. The President of the European Council:
   (a) shall chair it and drive forward its work;
   (b) shall ensure the preparation and continuity of the work of the European Council in cooperation with the President of the Commission, and on the basis of the work of the General Affairs Council;
   (c) shall endeavour to facilitate cohesion and consensus within the European Council;

(d) shall present a report to the European Parliament after each of the meetings of the European Council.

The President of the European Council shall, at his level and in that capacity, ensure the external representation of the Union on issues concerning its common foreign and security policy, without prejudice to the powers of the High Representative of the Union for Foreign Affairs and Security Policy.

The President of the European Council shall not hold a national office.

Article 16

1. The Council shall, jointly with the European Parliament, exercise legislative and budgetary functions. It shall carry out policy-making and coordinating functions as laid down in the Treaties.
2. The Council shall consist of a representative of each Member State at ministerial level, who may commit the government of the Member State in question and cast its vote.
3. The Council shall act by a qualified majority except where the Treaties provide otherwise.
4. As from 1 November 2014, a qualified majority shall be defined as at least 55% of the members of the Council, comprising at least fifteen of them and representing Member States comprising at least 65% of the population of the Union.

   A blocking minority must include at least four Council members, failing which the qualified majority shall be deemed attained.

   The other arrangements governing the qualified majority are laid down in Article 238(2) of the Treaty on the Functioning of the European Union.
5. The transitional provisions relating to the definition of the qualified majority which shall be applicable until 31 October 2014 and those which shall be applicable from 1 November 2014 to 31 March 2017 are laid down in the Protocol on transitional provisions.
6. The Council shall meet in different configurations, the list of which shall be adopted in accordance with Article 236 of the Treaty on the Functioning of the European Union.

   The General Affairs Council shall ensure consistency in the work of the different Council configurations. It shall prepare and ensure the follow-up to meetings of the European Council, in liaison with the President of the European Council and the Commission.

   The Foreign Affairs Council shall elaborate the Union's external action on the basis of strategic guidelines laid down by the European Council and ensure that the Union's action is consistent.
7. A Committee of Permanent Representatives of the Governments of the Member States shall be responsible for preparing the work of the Council.
8. The Council shall meet in public when it deliberates and votes on a draft legislative act. To this end, each Council meeting shall be divided into two parts, dealing respectively with deliberations on Union legislative acts and non-legislative activities.
9. The Presidency of Council configurations, other than that of Foreign Affairs, shall be held by Member State representatives in the Council on the basis of equal rotation, in accordance with the conditions established in accordance with Article 236 of the Treaty on the Functioning of the European Union.

Article 17

1. The Commission shall promote the general interest of the Union and take appropriate initiatives to that end. It shall ensure the application of the Treaties, and of measures adopted by the institutions pursuant to them. It shall oversee the application of Union law under the control of the Court of Justice of the European Union. It shall execute the budget and manage programmes. It shall exercise coordinating, executive and management functions, as laid down in the Treaties. With the exception of the common foreign and security policy, and other cases provided for in the Treaties, it shall ensure the Union's external representation. It shall initiate the Union's annual and multiannual programming with a view to achieving interinstitutional agreements.

2. Union legislative acts may only be adopted on the basis of a Commission proposal, except where the Treaties provide otherwise. Other acts shall be adopted on the basis of a Commission proposal where the Treaties so provide.

3. The Commission's term of office shall be five years.

   The members of the Commission shall be chosen on the ground of their general competence and European commitment from persons whose independence is beyond doubt.

   In carrying out its responsibilities, the Commission shall be completely independent. Without prejudice to Article 18(2), the members of the Commission shall neither seek nor take instructions from any Government or other institution, body, office or entity. They shall refrain from any action incompatible with their duties or the performance of their tasks.

4. The Commission appointed between the date of entry into force of the Treaty of Lisbon and 31 October 2014, shall consist of one national of each Member State, including its President and the High Representative of the Union for Foreign Affairs and Security Policy who shall be one of its Vice-Presidents.

5. As from 1 November 2014, the Commission shall consist of a number of members, including its President and the High Representative of the Union for Foreign Affairs and Security Policy, corresponding to two thirds of the number of Member States, unless the European Council, acting unanimously, decides to alter this number.

   The members of the Commission shall be chosen from among the nationals of the Member States on the basis of a system of strictly equal rotation between the Member States, reflecting the demographic and geographical range of all the Member States. This system shall be established unanimously by the European Council in accordance with Article 244 of the Treaty on the Functioning of the European Union.

6. The President of the Commission shall:

   (a) lay down guidelines within which the Commission is to work;

   (b) decide on the internal organisation of the Commission, ensuring that it acts consistently, efficiently and as a collegiate body;

   (c) appoint Vice-Presidents, other than the High Representative of the Union for Foreign Affairs and Security Policy, from among the members of the Commission.

   A member of the Commission shall resign if the President so requests. The High Representative of the Union for Foreign Affairs and Security Policy shall resign, in accordance with the procedure set out in Article 18(1), if the President so requests.

7. Taking into account the elections to the European Parliament and after having held the appropriate consultations, the European Council, acting by a qualified majority, shall propose to the European Parliament a candidate for President of the Commission. This candidate shall be elected by the European Parliament by a majority of its component members. If he does not obtain the required majority, the European Council, acting by a qualified majority, shall within one month propose a new candidate who shall be elected by the European Parliament following the same procedure.

The Council, by common accord with the President-elect, shall adopt the list of the other persons whom it proposes for appointment as members of the Commission. They shall be selected, on the basis of the suggestions made by Member States, in accordance with the criteria set out in paragraph 3, second subparagraph, and paragraph 5, second subparagraph.

The President, the High Representative of the Union for Foreign Affairs and Security Policy and the other members of the Commission shall be subject as a body to a vote of consent by the European Parliament. On the basis of this consent the Commission shall be appointed by the European Council, acting by a qualified majority.

8. The Commission, as a body, shall be responsible to the European Parliament. In accordance with Article 234 of the Treaty on the Functioning of the European Union, the European Parliament may vote on a motion of censure of the Commission. If such a motion is carried, the members of the Commission shall resign as a body and the High Representative of the Union for Foreign Affairs and Security Policy shall resign from the duties that he carries out in the Commission.

Article 18

1. The European Council, acting by a qualified majority, with the agreement of the President of the Commission, shall appoint the High Representative of the Union for Foreign Affairs and Security Policy. The European Council may end his term of office by the same procedure.

2. The High Representative shall conduct the Union's common foreign and security policy. He shall contribute by his proposals to the development of that policy, which he shall carry out as mandated by the Council. The same shall apply to the common security and defence policy.

3. The High Representative shall preside over the Foreign Affairs Council.

4. The High Representative shall be one of the Vice-Presidents of the Commission. He shall ensure the consistency of the Union's external action. He shall be responsible within the Commission for responsibilities incumbent on it in external relations and for coordinating other aspects of the Union's external action. In exercising these responsibilities within the Commission, and only for these responsibilities, the High Representative shall be bound by Commission procedures to the extent that this is consistent with paragraphs 2 and 3.

Article 19

1. The Court of Justice of the European Union shall include the Court of Justice, the General Court and specialised courts. It shall ensure that in the interpretation and application of the Treaties the law is observed.

Member States shall provide remedies sufficient to ensure effective legal protection in the fields covered by Union law.

2. The Court of Justice shall consist of one judge from each Member State. It shall be assisted by Advocates-General.

The General Court shall include at least one judge per Member State.

The Judges and the Advocates-General of the Court of Justice and the Judges of the General Court shall be chosen from persons whose independence is beyond doubt and who satisfy the conditions set out in Articles 253 and 254 of the Treaty on the Functioning of the European Union. They shall be appointed by common accord of the governments of the Member States for six years. Retiring Judges and Advocates-General may be reappointed.

3. The Court of Justice of the European Union shall, in accordance with the Treaties:
   (a) rule on actions brought by a Member State, an institution or a natural or legal person;
   (b) give preliminary rulings, at the request of courts or tribunals of the Member States, on the interpretation of Union law or the validity of acts adopted by the institutions;
   (c) rule in other cases provided for in the Treaties.

TITLE IV PROVISIONS ON ENHANCED COOPERATION

Article 20

1. Member States which wish to establish enhanced cooperation between themselves within the framework of the Union's non-exclusive competences may make use of its institutions and exercise those competences by applying the relevant provisions of the Treaties, subject to the limits and in accordance with the detailed arrangements laid down in this Article and in Articles 326 to 334 of the Treaty on the Functioning of the European Union.

   Enhanced cooperation shall aim to further the objectives of the Union, protect its interests and reinforce its integration process. Such cooperation shall be open at any time to all Member States, in accordance with Article 328 of the Treaty on the Functioning of the European Union.

2. The decision authorising enhanced cooperation shall be adopted by the Council as a last resort, when it has established that the objectives of such cooperation cannot be attained within a reasonable period by the Union as a whole, and provided that at least nine Member States participate in it. The Council shall act in accordance with the procedure laid down in Article 329 of the Treaty on the Functioning of the European Union.

3. All members of the Council may participate in its deliberations, but only members of the Council representing the Member States participating in enhanced cooperation shall take part in the vote. The voting rules are set out in Article 330 of the Treaty on the Functioning of the European Union.

4. Acts adopted in the framework of enhanced cooperation shall bind only participating Member States. They shall not be regarded as part of the acquis which has to be accepted by candidate States for accession to the Union.

TITLE V GENERAL PROVISIONS ON THE UNION'S EXTERNAL ACTION AND SPECIFIC PROVISIONS ON THE COMMON FOREIGN AND SECURITY POLICY

Chapter 1 General Provisions on the Union's External Action

Article 21

1. The Union's action on the international scene shall be guided by the principles which have inspired its own creation, development and enlargement, and which it seeks to advance in the wider world: democracy, the rule of law, the universality and indivisibility of human rights and fundamental freedoms, respect for human dignity, the principles of equality and solidarity, and respect for the principles of the United Nations Charter and international law.

   The Union shall seek to develop relations and build partnerships with third countries, and international, regional or global organisations which share the principles referred to in the first subparagraph. It shall promote multilateral solutions to common problems, in particular in the framework of the United Nations.

2. The Union shall define and pursue common policies and actions, and shall work for a high degree of cooperation in all fields of international relations, in order to:
   (a) safeguard its values, fundamental interests, security, independence and integrity;
   (b) consolidate and support democracy, the rule of law, human rights and the principles of international law;
   (c) preserve peace, prevent conflicts and strengthen international security, in accordance with the purposes and principles of the United Nations Charter, with the principles of the Helsinki Final Act and with the aims of the Charter of Paris, including those relating to external borders;
   (d) foster the sustainable economic, social and environmental development of developing countries, with the primary aim of eradicating poverty;
   (e) encourage the integration of all countries into the world economy, including through the progressive abolition of restrictions on international trade;
   (f) help develop international measures to preserve and improve the quality of the environment and the sustainable management of global natural resources, in order to ensure sustainable development;
   (g) assist populations, countries and regions confronting natural or man-made disasters; and
   (h) promote an international system based on stronger multilateral cooperation and good global governance.

3. The Union shall respect the principles and pursue the objectives set out in paragraphs 1 and 2 in the development and implementation of the different areas of the Union's external action covered by this Title and by Part Five of the Treaty on the Functioning of the European Union, and of the external aspects of its other policies.

   The Union shall ensure consistency between the different areas of its external action and between these and its other policies. The Council and the Commission, assisted by the High Representative of the Union for Foreign Affairs and Security Policy, shall ensure that consistency and shall cooperate to that effect.

Article 22

1. On the basis of the principles and objectives set out in Article 21, the European Council shall identify the strategic interests and objectives of the Union.

   Decisions of the European Council on the strategic interests and objectives of the Union shall relate to the common foreign and security policy and to other areas of the external action of the Union. Such decisions may concern the relations of the Union with a specific country or region or may be thematic in approach. They shall define their duration, and the means to be made available by the Union and the Member States.

   The European Council shall act unanimously on a recommendation from the Council, adopted by the latter under the arrangements laid down for each area. Decisions of the European Council shall be implemented in accordance with the procedures provided for in the Treaties.

2. The High Representative of the Union for Foreign Affairs and Security Policy, for the area of common foreign and security policy, and the Commission, for other areas of external action, may submit joint proposals to the Council.

Chapter 2 Specific Provisions on the Common Foreign and Security Policy

SECTION 1 COMMON PROVISIONS

Article 23

The Union's action on the international scene, pursuant to this Chapter, shall be guided by the principles, shall pursue the objectives of, and be conducted in accordance with, the general provisions laid down in Chapter 1.

Article 24

1. The Union's competence in matters of common foreign and security policy shall cover all areas of foreign policy and all questions relating to the Union's security, including the progressive framing of a common defence policy that might lead to a common defence.

   The common foreign and security policy is subject to specific rules and procedures. It shall be defined and implemented by the European Council and the Council acting unanimously, except where the Treaties provide otherwise. The adoption of legislative acts shall be excluded. The common foreign and security policy shall be put into effect by the High Representative of the Union for Foreign Affairs and Security Policy and by Member States, in accordance with the Treaties. The specific role of the European Parliament and of the Commission in this area is defined by the Treaties. The Court of Justice of the European Union shall not have jurisdiction with respect to these provisions, with the exception of its jurisdiction to monitor compliance with Article 40 of this Treaty and to review the legality of certain decisions as provided for by the second paragraph of Article 275 of the Treaty on the Functioning of the European Union.

2. Within the framework of the principles and objectives of its external action, the Union shall conduct, define and implement a common foreign and security policy, based on the development of mutual political solidarity among Member States, the identification

of questions of general interest and the achievement of an ever-increasing degree of convergence of Member States' actions.

3. The Member States shall support the Union's external and security policy actively and unreservedly in a spirit of loyalty and mutual solidarity and shall comply with the Union's action in this area.

   The Member States shall work together to enhance and develop their mutual political solidarity. They shall refrain from any action which is contrary to the interests of the Union or likely to impair its effectiveness as a cohesive force in international relations.

   The Council and the High Representative shall ensure compliance with these principles.

Article 25

The Union shall conduct the common foreign and security policy by:
   (a) defining the general guidelines;
   (b) adopting decisions defining:
       (i) actions to be undertaken by the Union;
       (ii) positions to be taken by the Union;
       (iii) arrangements for the implementation of the decisions referred to in points (i) and (ii); and by
   (c) strengthening systematic cooperation between Member States in the conduct of policy.

Article 26

1. The European Council shall identify the Union's strategic interests, determine the objectives of and define general guidelines for the common foreign and security policy, including for matters with defence implications. It shall adopt the necessary decisions.

   If international developments so require, the President of the European Council shall convene an extraordinary meeting of the European Council in order to define the strategic lines of the Union's policy in the face of such developments.

2. The Council shall frame the common foreign and security policy and take the decisions necessary for defining and implementing it on the basis of the general guidelines and strategic lines defined by the European Council.

   The Council and the High Representative of the Union for Foreign Affairs and Security Policy shall ensure the unity, consistency and effectiveness of action by the Union.

3. The common foreign and security policy shall be put into effect by the High Representative and by the Member States, using national and Union resources.

Article 27

1. The High Representative of the Union for Foreign Affairs and Security Policy, who shall chair the Foreign Affairs Council, shall contribute through his proposals to the development of the common foreign and security policy and shall ensure implementation of the decisions adopted by the European Council and the Council.

2. The High Representative shall represent the Union for matters relating to the common foreign and security policy. He shall conduct political dialogue with third parties on the Union's behalf and shall express the Union's position in international organisations and at international conferences.

3. In fulfilling his mandate, the High Representative shall be assisted by a European External Action Service. This service shall work in cooperation with the diplomatic services of the Member States and shall comprise officials from relevant departments of the General Secretariat of the Council and of the Commission as well as staff seconded from national diplomatic services of the Member States. The organisation and functioning of the European External Action Service shall be established by a decision of the Council. The Council shall act on a proposal from the High Representative after consulting the European Parliament and after obtaining the consent of the Commission.

Article 28

1. Where the international situation requires operational action by the Union, the Council shall adopt the necessary decisions. They shall lay down their objectives, scope, the means to be made available to the Union, if necessary their duration, and the conditions for their implementation.
   If there is a change in circumstances having a substantial effect on a question subject to such a decision, the Council shall review the principles and objectives of that decision and take the necessary decisions.
2. Decisions referred to in paragraph 1 shall commit the Member States in the positions they adopt and in the conduct of their activity.
3. Whenever there is any plan to adopt a national position or take national action pursuant to a decision as referred to in paragraph 1, information shall be provided by the Member State concerned in time to allow, if necessary, for prior consultations within the Council. The obligation to provide prior information shall not apply to measures which are merely a national transposition of Council decisions.
4. In cases of imperative need arising from changes in the situation and failing a review of the Council decision as referred to in paragraph 1, Member States may take the necessary measures as a matter of urgency having regard to the general objectives of that decision. The Member State concerned shall inform the Council immediately of any such measures.
5. Should there be any major difficulties in implementing a decision as referred to in this Article, a Member State shall refer them to the Council which shall discuss them and seek appropriate solutions. Such solutions shall not run counter to the objectives of the decision referred to in paragraph 1 or impair its effectiveness.

Article 29

The Council shall adopt decisions which shall define the approach of the Union to a particular matter of a geographical or thematic nature. Member States shall ensure that their national policies conform to the Union positions.

Article 30

1. Any Member State, the High Representative of the Union for Foreign Affairs and Security Policy, or the High Representative with the Commission's support, may refer any question relating to the common foreign and security policy to the Council and may submit to it, respectively, initiatives or proposals.

2. In cases requiring a rapid decision, the High Representative, of his own motion, or at the request of a Member State, shall convene an extraordinary Council meeting within 48 hours or, in an emergency, within a shorter period.

Article 31

1. Decisions under this Chapter shall be taken by the European Council and the Council acting unanimously, except where this Chapter provides otherwise. The adoption of legislative acts shall be excluded.

   When abstaining in a vote, any member of the Council may qualify its abstention by making a formal declaration under the present subparagraph. In that case, it shall not be obliged to apply the decision, but shall accept that the decision commits the Union. In a spirit of mutual solidarity, the Member State concerned shall refrain from any action likely to conflict with or impede Union action based on that decision and the other Member States shall respect its position. If the members of the Council qualifying their abstention in this way represent at least one third of the Member States comprising at least one third of the population of the Union, the decision shall not be adopted.

2. By derogation from the provisions of paragraph 1, the Council shall act by qualified majority:
   — when adopting a decision defining a Union action or position on the basis of a decision of the European Council relating to the Union's strategic interests and objectives, as referred to in Article 22(1),
   — when adopting a decision defining a Union action or position, on a proposal which the High Representative of the Union for Foreign Affairs and Security Policy has presented following a specific request from the European Council, made on its own initiative or that of the High Representative,
   — when adopting any decision implementing a decision defining a Union action or position,
   — when appointing a special representative in accordance with Article 33.
   If a member of the Council declares that, for vital and stated reasons of national policy, it intends to oppose the adoption of a decision to be taken by qualified majority, a vote shall not be taken. The High Representative will, in close consultation with the Member State involved, search for a solution acceptable to it. If he does not succeed, the Council may, acting by a qualified majority, request that the matter be referred to the European Council for a decision by unanimity.

3. The European Council may unanimously adopt a decision stipulating that the Council shall act by a qualified majority in cases other than those referred to in paragraph 2.

4. Paragraphs 2 and 3 shall not apply to decisions having military or defence implications.

5. For procedural questions, the Council shall act by a majority of its members.

Article 32

Member States shall consult one another within the European Council and the Council on any matter of foreign and security policy of general interest in order to determine a common approach. Before undertaking any action on the international scene or entering into any commitment which could affect the Union's interests, each Member State shall consult the others within the European Council or the Council. Member States shall ensure, through the convergence of their actions, that the Union is able to assert its interests and values on the international scene. Member States shall show mutual solidarity.

When the European Council or the Council has defined a common approach of the Union within the meaning of the first paragraph, the High Representative of the Union for Foreign Affairs and Security Policy and the Ministers for Foreign Affairs of the Member States shall coordinate their activities within the Council.

The diplomatic missions of the Member States and the Union delegations in third countries and at international organisations shall cooperate and shall contribute to formulating and implementing the common approach.

Article 33

The Council may, on a proposal from the High Representative of the Union for Foreign Affairs and Security Policy, appoint a special representative with a mandate in relation to particular policy issues. The special representative shall carry out his mandate under the authority of the High Representative.

Article 34

1. Member States shall coordinate their action in international organisations and at international conferences. They shall uphold the Union's positions in such forums. The High Representative of the Union for Foreign Affairs and Security Policy shall organise this coordination. In international organisations and at international conferences where not all the Member States participate, those which do take part shall uphold the Union's positions.
2. In accordance with Article 24(3), Member States represented in international organisations or international conferences where not all the Member States participate shall keep the other Member States and the High Representative informed of any matter of common interest. Member States which are also members of the United Nations Security Council will concert and keep the other Member States and the High Representative fully informed. Member States which are members of the Security Council will, in the execution of their functions, defend the positions and the interests of the Union, without prejudice to their responsibilities under the provisions of the United Nations Charter. When the Union has defined a position on a subject which is on the United Nations Security Council agenda, those Member States which sit on the Security Council shall request that the High Representative be invited to present the Union's position.

Article 35

The diplomatic and consular missions of the Member States and the Union delegations in third countries and international conferences, and their representations to international organisations, shall cooperate in ensuring that decisions defining Union positions and actions adopted pursuant to this Chapter are complied with and implemented.

They shall step up cooperation by exchanging information and carrying out joint assessments.

They shall contribute to the implementation of the right of citizens of the Union to protection in the territory of third countries as referred to in Article 20(2)(c) of the Treaty on the Functioning of the European Union and of the measures adopted pursuant to Article 23 of that Treaty.

Article 36

The High Representative of the Union for Foreign Affairs and Security Policy shall regularly consult the European Parliament on the main aspects and the basic choices of the common foreign and security policy and the common security and defence policy and inform it of how those policies evolve. He shall ensure that the views of the European Parliament are duly taken into consideration. Special representatives may be involved in briefing the European Parliament.

The European Parliament may address questions or make recommendations to the Council or the High Representative. Twice a year it shall hold a debate on progress in implementing the common foreign and security policy, including the common security and defence policy.

Article 37

The Union may conclude agreements with one or more States or international organisations in areas covered by this Chapter.

Article 38

Without prejudice to Article 240 of the Treaty on the Functioning of the European Union, a Political and Security Committee shall monitor the international situation in the areas covered by the common foreign and security policy and contribute to the definition of policies by delivering opinions to the Council at the request of the Council or of the High Representative of the Union for Foreign Affairs and Security Policy or on its own initiative. It shall also monitor the implementation of agreed policies, without prejudice to the powers of the High Representative.

Within the scope of this Chapter, the Political and Security Committee shall exercise, under the responsibility of the Council and of the High Representative, the political control and strategic direction of the crisis management operations referred to in Article 43.

The Council may authorise the Committee, for the purpose and for the duration of a crisis management operation, as determined by the Council, to take the relevant decisions concerning the political control and strategic direction of the operation.

Article 39

In accordance with Article 16 of the Treaty on the Functioning of the European Union and by way of derogation from paragraph 2 thereof, the Council shall adopt a decision laying down the rules relating to the protection of individuals with regard to the processing of personal data by the Member States when carrying out activities which fall within the scope of this Chapter, and the rules relating to the free movement of such data. Compliance with these rules shall be subject to the control of independent authorities.

Article 40

The implementation of the common foreign and security policy shall not affect the application of the procedures and the extent of the powers of the institutions laid down by the Treaties for the exercise of the Union competences referred to in Articles 3 to 6 of the Treaty on the Functioning of the European Union.

Similarly, the implementation of the policies listed in those Articles shall not affect the application of the procedures and the extent of the powers of the institutions laid down by the Treaties for the exercise of the Union competences under this Chapter.

Article 41

1. Administrative expenditure to which the implementation of this Chapter gives rise for the institutions shall be charged to the Union budget.
2. Operating expenditure to which the implementation of this Chapter gives rise shall also be charged to the Union budget, except for such expenditure arising from operations having military or defence implications and cases where the Council acting unanimously decides otherwise.

    In cases where expenditure is not charged to the Union budget, it shall be charged to the Member States in accordance with the gross national product scale, unless the Council acting unanimously decides otherwise. As for expenditure arising from operations having military or defence implications, Member States whose representatives in the Council have made a formal declaration under Article 31(1), second subparagraph, shall not be obliged to contribute to the financing thereof.
3. The Council shall adopt a decision establishing the specific procedures for guaranteeing rapid access to appropriations in the Union budget for urgent financing of initiatives in the framework of the common foreign and security policy, and in particular for preparatory activities for the tasks referred to in Article 42(1) and Article 43. It shall act after consulting the European Parliament.

    Preparatory activities for the tasks referred to in Article 42(1) and Article 43 which are not charged to the Union budget shall be financed by a start-up fund made up of Member States' contributions.

    The Council shall adopt by a qualified majority, on a proposal from the High Representative of the Union for Foreign Affairs and Security Policy, decisions establishing:
    (a) the procedures for setting up and financing the start-up fund, in particular the amounts allocated to the fund;
    (b) the procedures for administering the start-up fund;
    (c) the financial control procedures.

    When the task planned in accordance with Article 42(1) and Article 43 cannot be charged to the Union budget, the Council shall authorise the High Representative to use the fund. The High Representative shall report to the Council on the implementation of this remit.

SECTION 2 PROVISIONS ON THE COMMON SECURITY AND DEFENCE POLICY

Article 42

1. The common security and defence policy shall be an integral part of the common foreign and security policy. It shall provide the Union with an operational capacity drawing on civilian and military assets. The Union may use them on missions outside the Union for peace-keeping, conflict prevention and strengthening international security in accordance with the principles of the United Nations Charter. The performance of these tasks shall be undertaken using capabilities provided by the Member States.

2. The common security and defence policy shall include the progressive framing of a common Union defence policy. This will lead to a common defence, when the European Council, acting unanimously, so decides. It shall in that case recommend to the Member States the adoption of such a decision in accordance with their respective constitutional requirements.

   The policy of the Union in accordance with this Section shall not prejudice the specific character of the security and defence policy of certain Member States and shall respect the obligations of certain Member States, which see their common defence realised in the North Atlantic Treaty Organisation (NATO), under the North Atlantic Treaty and be compatible with the common security and defence policy established within that framework.

3. Member States shall make civilian and military capabilities available to the Union for the implementation of the common security and defence policy, to contribute to the objectives defined by the Council. Those Member States which together establish multinational forces may also make them available to the common security and defence policy.

   Member States shall undertake progressively to improve their military capabilities. The Agency in the field of defence capabilities development, research, acquisition and armaments (hereinafter referred to as 'the European Defence Agency') shall identify operational requirements, shall promote measures to satisfy those requirements, shall contribute to identifying and, where appropriate, implementing any measure needed to strengthen the industrial and technological base of the defence sector, shall participate in defining a European capabilities and armaments policy, and shall assist the Council in evaluating the improvement of military capabilities.

4. Decisions relating to the common security and defence policy, including those initiating a mission as referred to in this Article, shall be adopted by the Council acting unanimously on a proposal from the High Representative of the Union for Foreign Affairs and Security Policy or an initiative from a Member State. The High Representative may propose the use of both national resources and Union instruments, together with the Commission where appropriate.

5. The Council may entrust the execution of a task, within the Union framework, to a group of Member States in order to protect the Union's values and serve its interests. The execution of such a task shall be governed by Article 44.

6. Those Member States whose military capabilities fulfil higher criteria and which have made more binding commitments to one another in this area with a view to the most demanding missions shall establish permanent structured cooperation within the Union framework. Such cooperation shall be governed by Article 46. It shall not affect the provisions of Article 43.

7. If a Member State is the victim of armed aggression on its territory, the other Member States shall have towards it an obligation of aid and assistance by all the means in their power, in accordance with Article 51 of the United Nations Charter. This shall not prejudice the specific character of the security and defence policy of certain Member States.

   Commitments and cooperation in this area shall be consistent with commitments under the North Atlantic Treaty Organisation, which, for those States which are members of it, remains the foundation of their collective defence and the forum for its implementation.

Article 43

1. The tasks referred to in Article 42(1), in the course of which the Union may use civilian and military means, shall include joint disarmament operations, humanitarian and rescue tasks, military advice and assistance tasks, conflict prevention and peace-keeping tasks, tasks of combat forces in crisis management, including peace-making and post-conflict stabilisation. All these tasks may contribute to the fight against terrorism, including by supporting third countries in combating terrorism in their territories.

2. The Council shall adopt decisions relating to the tasks referred to in paragraph 1, defining their objectives and scope and the general conditions for their implementation. The High Representative of the Union for Foreign Affairs and Security Policy, acting under the authority of the Council and in close and constant contact with the Political and Security Committee, shall ensure coordination of the civilian and military aspects of such tasks.

Article 44

1. Within the framework of the decisions adopted in accordance with Article 43, the Council may entrust the implementation of a task to a group of Member States which are willing and have the necessary capability for such a task. Those Member States, in association with the High Representative of the Union for Foreign Affairs and Security Policy, shall agree among themselves on the management of the task.

2. Member States participating in the task shall keep the Council regularly informed of its progress on their own initiative or at the request of another Member State. Those States shall inform the Council immediately should the completion of the task entail major consequences or require amendment of the objective, scope and conditions determined for the task in the decisions referred to in paragraph 1. In such cases, the Council shall adopt the necessary decisions.

Article 45

1. The European Defence Agency referred to in Article 42(3), subject to the authority of the Council, shall have as its task to:
   (a) contribute to identifying the Member States' military capability objectives and evaluating observance of the capability commitments given by the Member States;
   (b) promote harmonisation of operational needs and adoption of effective, compatible procurement methods;
   (c) propose multilateral projects to fulfil the objectives in terms of military capabilities, ensure coordination of the programmes implemented by the Member States and management of specific cooperation programmes;
   (d) support defence technology research, and coordinate and plan joint research activities and the study of technical solutions meeting future operational needs;
   (e) contribute to identifying and, if necessary, implementing any useful measure for strengthening the industrial and technological base of the defence sector and for improving the effectiveness of military expenditure.

2. The European Defence Agency shall be open to all Member States wishing to be part of it. The Council, acting by a qualified majority, shall adopt a decision defining the Agency's statute, seat and operational rules. That decision should take account of the level of effective participation in the Agency's activities. Specific groups shall be set

up within the Agency bringing together Member States engaged in joint projects. The Agency shall carry out its tasks in liaison with the Commission where necessary.

Article 46

1. Those Member States which wish to participate in the permanent structured cooperation referred to in Article 42(6), which fulfil the criteria and have made the commitments on military capabilities set out in the Protocol on permanent structured cooperation, shall notify their intention to the Council and to the High Representative of the Union for Foreign Affairs and Security Policy.

2. Within three months following the notification referred to in paragraph 1 the Council shall adopt a decision establishing permanent structured cooperation and determining the list of participating Member States. The Council shall act by a qualified majority after consulting the High Representative.

3. Any Member State which, at a later stage, wishes to participate in the permanent structured cooperation shall notify its intention to the Council and to the High Representative.

   The Council shall adopt a decision confirming the participation of the Member State concerned which fulfils the criteria and makes the commitments referred to in Articles 1 and 2 of the Protocol on permanent structured cooperation. The Council shall act by a qualified majority after consulting the High Representative. Only members of the Council representing the participating Member States shall take part in the vote.

   A qualified majority shall be defined in accordance with Article 238(3)(a) of the Treaty on the Functioning of the European Union.

4. If a participating Member State no longer fulfils the criteria or is no longer able to meet the commitments referred to in Articles 1 and 2 of the Protocol on permanent structured cooperation, the Council may adopt a decision suspending the participation of the Member State concerned.

   The Council shall act by a qualified majority. Only members of the Council representing the participating Member States, with the exception of the Member State in question, shall take part in the vote.

   A qualified majority shall be defined in accordance with Article 238(3)(a) of the Treaty on the Functioning of the European Union.

5. Any participating Member State which wishes to withdraw from permanent structured cooperation shall notify its intention to the Council, which shall take note that the Member State in question has ceased to participate.

6. The decisions and recommendations of the Council within the framework of permanent structured cooperation, other than those provided for in paragraphs 2 to 5, shall be adopted by unanimity. For the purposes of this paragraph, unanimity shall be constituted by the votes of the representatives of the participating Member States only.

TITLE VI FINAL PROVISIONS

Article 47

The Union shall have legal personality.

Article 48

1. The Treaties may be amended in accordance with an ordinary revision procedure. They may also be amended in accordance with simplified revision procedures.

Ordinary revision procedure

2. The Government of any Member State, the European Parliament or the Commission may submit to the Council proposals for the amendment of the Treaties. These proposals may, inter alia, serve either to increase or to reduce the competences conferred on the Union in the Treaties. These proposals shall be submitted to the European Council by the Council and the national Parliaments shall be notified.

3. If the European Council, after consulting the European Parliament and the Commission, adopts by a simple majority a decision in favour of examining the proposed amendments, the President of the European Council shall convene a Convention composed of representatives of the national Parliaments, of the Heads of State or Government of the Member States, of the European Parliament and of the Commission. The European Central Bank shall also be consulted in the case of institutional changes in the monetary area. The Convention shall examine the proposals for amendments and shall adopt by consensus a recommendation to a conference of representatives of the governments of the Member States as provided for in paragraph 4.

    The European Council may decide by a simple majority, after obtaining the consent of the European Parliament, not to convene a Convention should this not be justified by the extent of the proposed amendments. In the latter case, the European Council shall define the terms of reference for a conference of representatives of the governments of the Member States.

4. A conference of representatives of the governments of the Member States shall be convened by the President of the Council for the purpose of determining by common accord the amendments to be made to the Treaties.

    The amendments shall enter into force after being ratified by all the Member States in accordance with their respective constitutional requirements.

5. If, two years after the signature of a treaty amending the Treaties, four fifths of the Member States have ratified it and one or more Member States have encountered difficulties in proceeding with ratification, the matter shall be referred to the European Council.

Simplified revision procedures

6. The Government of any Member State, the European Parliament or the Commission may submit to the European Council proposals for revising all or part of the provisions of Part Three of the Treaty on the Functioning of the European Union relating to the internal policies and action of the Union.

    The European Council may adopt a decision amending all or part of the provisions of Part Three of the Treaty on the Functioning of the European Union. The European Council shall act by unanimity after consulting the European Parliament and the Commission, and the European Central Bank in the case of institutional changes in the monetary area. That decision shall not enter into force until it is approved by the Member States in accordance with their respective constitutional requirements.

    The decision referred to in the second subparagraph shall not increase the competences conferred on the Union in the Treaties.

7. Where the Treaty on the Functioning of the European Union or Title V of this Treaty provides for the Council to act by unanimity in a given area or case, the European Council may adopt a decision authorising the Council to act by a qualified majority in that area or in that case. This subparagraph shall not apply to decisions with military implications or those in the area of defence.

Where the Treaty on the Functioning of the European Union provides for legislative acts to be adopted by the Council in accordance with a special legislative procedure, the European Council may adopt a decision allowing for the adoption of such acts in accordance with the ordinary legislative procedure.

Any initiative taken by the European Council on the basis of the first or the second subparagraph shall be notified to the national Parliaments. If a national Parliament makes known its opposition within six months of the date of such notification, the decision referred to in the first or the second subparagraph shall not be adopted. In the absence of opposition, the European Council may adopt the decision.

For the adoption of the decisions referred to in the first and second subparagraphs, the European Council shall act by unanimity after obtaining the consent of the European Parliament, which shall be given by a majority of its component members.

Article 49

Any European State which respects the values referred to in Article 2 and is committed to promoting them may apply to become a member of the Union. The European Parliament and national Parliaments shall be notified of this application. The applicant State shall address its application to the Council, which shall act unanimously after consulting the Commission and after receiving the consent of the European Parliament, which shall act by a majority of its component members. The conditions of eligibility agreed upon by the European Council shall be taken into account.

The conditions of admission and the adjustments to the Treaties on which the Union is founded, which such admission entails, shall be the subject of an agreement between the Member States and the applicant State. This agreement shall be submitted for ratification by all the contracting States in accordance with their respective constitutional requirements.

Article 50

1. Any Member State may decide to withdraw from the Union in accordance with its own constitutional requirements.
2. A Member State which decides to withdraw shall notify the European Council of its intention. In the light of the guidelines provided by the European Council, the Union shall negotiate and conclude an agreement with that State, setting out the arrangements for its withdrawal, taking account of the framework for its future relationship with the Union. That agreement shall be negotiated in accordance with Article 218(3) of the Treaty on the Functioning of the European Union. It shall be concluded on behalf of the Union by the Council, acting by a qualified majority, after obtaining the consent of the European Parliament.
3. The Treaties shall cease to apply to the State in question from the date of entry into force of the withdrawal agreement or, failing that, two years after the notification referred to in paragraph 2, unless the European Council, in agreement with the Member State concerned, unanimously decides to extend this period.
4. For the purposes of paragraphs 2 and 3, the member of the European Council or of the Council representing the withdrawing Member State shall not participate in the discussions of the European Council or Council or in decisions concerning it.

A qualified majority shall be defined in accordance with Article 238(3)(b) of the Treaty on the Functioning of the European Union.

5. If a State which has withdrawn from the Union asks to rejoin, its request shall be subject to the procedure referred to in Article 49.

Article 51
The Protocols and Annexes to the Treaties shall form an integral part thereof.

Article 52
1. The Treaties shall apply to the Kingdom of Belgium, the Republic of Bulgaria, the Czech Republic, the Kingdom of Denmark, the Federal Republic of Germany, the Republic of Estonia, Ireland, the Hellenic Republic, the Kingdom of Spain, the French Republic, the Republic of Croatia, the Italian Republic, the Republic of Cyprus, the Republic of Latvia, the Republic of Lithuania, the Grand Duchy of Luxembourg, the Republic of Hungary, the Republic of Malta, the Kingdom of the Netherlands, the Republic of Austria, the Republic of Poland, the Portuguese Republic, Romania, the Republic of Slovenia, the Slovak Republic, the Republic of Finland, the Kingdom of Sweden and the United Kingdom of Great Britain and Northern Ireland.
2. The territorial scope of the Treaties is specified in Article 355 of the Treaty on the Functioning of the European Union.

Article 53
This Treaty is concluded for an unlimited period.

Article 54
1. This Treaty shall be ratified by the High Contracting Parties in accordance with their respective constitutional requirements. The instruments of ratification shall be deposited with the Government of the Italian Republic.
2. This Treaty shall enter into force on 1 January 1993, provided that all the Instruments of ratification have been deposited, or, failing that, on the first day of the month following the deposit of the Instrument of ratification by the last signatory State to take this step.

Article 55
1. This Treaty, drawn up in a single original in the Bulgarian, Croatian, Czech, Danish, Dutch, English, Estonian, Finnish, French, German, Greek, Hungarian, Irish, Italian, Latvian, Lithuanian, Maltese, Polish, Portuguese, Romanian, Slovak, Slovenian, Spanish and Swedish languages, the texts in each of these languages being equally authentic, shall be deposited in the archives of the Government of the Italian Republic, which will transmit a certified copy to each of the governments of the other signatory States.
2. This Treaty may also be translated into any other languages as determined by Member States among those which, in accordance with their constitutional order, enjoy official status in all or part of their territory. A certified copy of such translations shall be provided by the Member States concerned to be deposited in the archives of the Council.

IN WITNESS WHEREOF the undersigned Plenipotentiaries have signed this Treaty.

Done at Maastricht on the seventh day of February in the year one thousand nine hundred and ninety-two.

(List of signatories not reproduced.)

1

2

Treaty on the Functioning of the European Union (TFEU)

Contents

2

2

PREAMBLE

HIS MAJESTY THE KING OF THE BELGIANS, THE PRESIDENT OF THE FEDERAL REPUBLIC OF GERMANY, THE PRESIDENT OF THE FRENCH REPUBLIC, THE PRESIDENT OF THE ITALIAN REPUBLIC, HER ROYAL HIGHNESS THE GRAND DUCHESS OF LUXEMBOURG, HER MAJESTY THE QUEEN OF THE NETHERLANDS,[1]

DETERMINED to lay the foundations of an ever closer union among the peoples of Europe,

RESOLVED to ensure the economic and social progress of their States by common action to eliminate the barriers which divide Europe,

AFFIRMING as the essential objective of their efforts the constant improvements of the living and working conditions of their peoples,

---

[1] The Republic of Bulgaria, the Czech Republic, the Kingdom of Denmark, the Republic of Estonia, Ireland, the Hellenic Republic, the Kingdom of Spain, the Republic of Cyprus, the Republic of Latvia, the Republic of Lithuania, the Republic of Hungary, the Republic of Malta, the Republic of Austria, the Republic of Poland, the Portuguese Republic, Romania, the Republic of Slovenia, the Slovak Republic, the Republic of Finland, the Kingdom of Sweden and the United Kingdom of Great Britain and Northern Ireland have since become members of the European Union.

RECOGNISING that the removal of existing obstacles calls for concerted action in order to guarantee steady expansion, balanced trade and fair competition,

ANXIOUS to strengthen the unity of their economies and to ensure their harmonious development by reducing the differences existing between the various regions and the backwardness of the less favoured regions,

DESIRING to contribute, by means of a common commercial policy, to the progressive abolition of restrictions on international trade,

INTENDING to confirm the solidarity which binds Europe and the overseas countries and desiring to ensure the development of their prosperity, in accordance with the principles of the Charter of the United Nations,

RESOLVED by thus pooling their resources to preserve and strengthen peace and liberty, and calling upon the other peoples of Europe who share their ideal to join in their efforts,

DETERMINED to promote the development of the highest possible level of knowledge for their peoples through a wide access to education and through its continuous updating, and to this end HAVE DESIGNATED as their Plenipotentiaries:

(List of plenipotentiaries not reproduced)

WHO, having exchanged their full powers, found in good and due form, have agreed as follows.

PART ONE PRINCIPLES

Article 1
1. This Treaty organises the functioning of the Union and determines the areas of, delimitation of, and arrangements for exercising its competences.
2. This Treaty and the Treaty on European Union constitute the Treaties on which the Union is founded. These two Treaties, which have the same legal value, shall be referred to as 'the Treaties'.

TITLE I CATEGORIES AND AREAS OF UNION COMPETENCE

Article 2
1. When the Treaties confer on the Union exclusive competence in a specific area, only the Union may legislate and adopt legally binding acts, the Member States being able to do so themselves only if so empowered by the Union or for the implementation of Union acts.
2. When the Treaties confer on the Union a competence shared with the Member States in a specific area, the Union and the Member States may legislate and adopt legally binding acts in that area. The Member States shall exercise their competence to the extent that the Union has not exercised its competence. The Member States shall again exercise their competence to the extent that the Union has decided to cease exercising its competence.
3. The Member States shall coordinate their economic and employment policies within arrangements as determined by this Treaty, which the Union shall have competence to provide.

4. The Union shall have competence, in accordance with the provisions of the Treaty on European Union, to define and implement a common foreign and security policy, including the progressive framing of a common defence policy.

5. In certain areas and under the conditions laid down in the Treaties, the Union shall have competence to carry out actions to support, coordinate or supplement the actions of the Member States, without thereby superseding their competence in these areas.

   Legally binding acts of the Union adopted on the basis of the provisions of the Treaties relating to these areas shall not entail harmonisation of Member States' laws or regulations.

6. The scope of and arrangements for exercising the Union's competences shall be determined by the provisions of the Treaties relating to each area.

Article 3

1. The Union shall have exclusive competence in the following areas:
   (a) customs union;
   (b) the establishing of the competition rules necessary for the functioning of the internal market;
   (c) monetary policy for the Member States whose currency is the euro;
   (d) the conservation of marine biological resources under the common fisheries policy;
   (e) common commercial policy.

2. The Union shall also have exclusive competence for the conclusion of an international agreement when its conclusion is provided for in a legislative act of the Union or is necessary to enable the Union to exercise its internal competence, or in so far as its conclusion may affect common rules or alter their scope.

Article 4

1. The Union shall share competence with the Member States where the Treaties confer on it a competence which does not relate to the areas referred to in Articles 3 and 6.

2. Shared competence between the Union and the Member States applies in the following principal areas:
   (a) internal market;
   (b) social policy, for the aspects defined in this Treaty;
   (c) economic, social and territorial cohesion;
   (d) agriculture and fisheries, excluding the conservation of marine biological resources;
   (e) environment;
   (f) consumer protection;
   (g) transport;
   (h) trans-European networks;
   (i) energy;
   (j) area of freedom, security and justice;
   (k) common safety concerns in public health matters, for the aspects defined in this Treaty.

3. In the areas of research, technological development and space, the Union shall have competence to carry out activities, in particular to define and implement programmes; however, the exercise of that competence shall not result in Member States being prevented from exercising theirs.

4. In the areas of development cooperation and humanitarian aid, the Union shall have competence to carry out activities and conduct a common policy; however, the exercise of that competence shall not result in Member States being prevented from exercising theirs.

Article 5

1. The Member States shall coordinate their economic policies within the Union. To this end, the Council shall adopt measures, in particular broad guidelines for these policies.

    Specific provisions shall apply to those Member States whose currency is the euro.
2. The Union shall take measures to ensure coordination of the employment policies of the Member States, in particular by defining guidelines for these policies.
3. The Union may take initiatives to ensure coordination of Member States' social policies.

Article 6

The Union shall have competence to carry out actions to support, coordinate or supplement the actions of the Member States. The areas of such action shall, at European level, be:

(a) protection and improvement of human health;
(b) industry;
(c) culture;
(d) tourism;
(e) education, vocational training, youth and sport;
(f) civil protection;
(g) administrative cooperation.

TITLE II PROVISIONS HAVING GENERAL APPLICATION

Article 7

The Union shall ensure consistency between its policies and activities, taking all of its objectives into account and in accordance with the principle of conferral of powers.

Article 8

In all its activities, the Union shall aim to eliminate inequalities, and to promote equality, between men and women.

Article 9

In defining and implementing its policies and activities, the Union shall take into account requirements linked to the promotion of a high level of employment, the guarantee of adequate social protection, the fight against social exclusion, and a high level of education, training and protection of human health.

Article 10

In defining and implementing its policies and activities, the Union shall aim to combat discrimination based on sex, racial or ethnic origin, religion or belief, disability, age or sexual orientation.

Article 11

Environmental protection requirements must be integrated into the definition and implementation of the Union's policies and activities, in particular with a view to promoting sustainable development.

Article 12

Consumer protection requirements shall be taken into account in defining and implementing other Union policies and activities.

Article 13

In formulating and implementing the Union's agriculture, fisheries, transport, internal market, research and technological development and space policies, the Union and the Member States shall, since animals are sentient beings, pay full regard to the welfare requirements of animals, while respecting the legislative or administrative provisions and customs of the Member States relating in particular to religious rites, cultural traditions and regional heritage.

Article 14

Without prejudice to Article 4 of the Treaty on European Union or to Articles 93, 106 and 107 of this Treaty, and given the place occupied by services of general economic interest in the shared values of the Union as well as their role in promoting social and territorial cohesion, the Union and the Member States, each within their respective powers and within the scope of application of the Treaties, shall take care that such services operate on the basis of principles and conditions, particularly economic and financial conditions, which enable them to fulfil their missions. The European Parliament and the Council, acting by means of regulations in accordance with the ordinary legislative procedure, shall establish these principles and set these conditions without prejudice to the competence of Member States, in compliance with the Treaties, to provide, to commission and to fund such services.

Article 15

1. In order to promote good governance and ensure the participation of civil society, the Union's institutions, bodies, offices and agencies shall conduct their work as openly as possible.
2. The European Parliament shall meet in public, as shall the Council when considering and voting on a draft legislative act.
3. Any citizen of the Union, and any natural or legal person residing or having its registered office in a Member State, shall have a right of access to documents of the Union's institutions, bodies, offices and agencies, whatever their medium, subject to the principles and the conditions to be defined in accordance with this paragraph.

    General principles and limits on grounds of public or private interest governing this right of access to documents shall be determined by the European Parliament and the Council, by means of regulations, acting in accordance with the ordinary legislative procedure.

    Each institution, body, office or agency shall ensure that its proceedings are transparent and shall elaborate in its own Rules of Procedure specific provisions regarding access to its documents, in accordance with the regulations referred to in the second subparagraph.

The Court of Justice of the European Union, the European Central Bank and the European Investment Bank shall be subject to this paragraph only when exercising their administrative tasks.

The European Parliament and the Council shall ensure publication of the documents relating to the legislative procedures under the terms laid down by the regulations referred to in the second subparagraph.

Article 16

1. Everyone has the right to the protection of personal data concerning them.
2. The European Parliament and the Council, acting in accordance with the ordinary legislative procedure, shall lay down the rules relating to the protection of individuals with regard to the processing of personal data by Union institutions, bodies, offices and agencies, and by the Member States when carrying out activities which fall within the scope of Union law, and the rules relating to the free movement of such data. Compliance with these rules shall be subject to the control of independent authorities.

   The rules adopted on the basis of this Article shall be without prejudice to the specific rules laid down in Article 39 of the Treaty on European Union.

Article 17

1. The Union respects and does not prejudice the status under national law of churches and religious associations or communities in the Member States.
2. The Union equally respects the status under national law of philosophical and non confessional organisations.
3. Recognising their identity and their specific contribution, the Union shall maintain an open, transparent and regular dialogue with these churches and organisations.

PART TWO NON-DISCRIMINATION AND CITIZENSHIP OF THE UNION

Article 18

Within the scope of application of the Treaties, and without prejudice to any special provisions contained therein, any discrimination on grounds of nationality shall be prohibited.

The European Parliament and the Council, acting in accordance with the ordinary legislative procedure, may adopt rules designed to prohibit such discrimination.

Article 19

1. Without prejudice to the other provisions of the Treaties and within the limits of the powers conferred by them upon the Union, the Council, acting unanimously in accordance with a special legislative procedure and after obtaining the consent of the European Parliament, may take appropriate action to combat discrimination based on sex, racial or ethnic origin, religion or belief, disability, age or sexual orientation.
2. By way of derogation from paragraph 1, the European Parliament and the Council, acting in accordance with the ordinary legislative procedure, may adopt the basic

principles of Union incentive measures, excluding any harmonisation of the laws and regulations of the Member States, to support action taken by the Member States in order to contribute to the achievement of the objectives referred to in paragraph 1.

Article 20

1. Citizenship of the Union is hereby established. Every person holding the nationality of a Member State shall be a citizen of the Union. Citizenship of the Union shall be additional to and not replace national citizenship.
2. Citizens of the Union shall enjoy the rights and be subject to the duties provided for in the Treaties. They shall have, inter alia:
   (a) the right to move and reside freely within the territory of the Member States;
   (b) the right to vote and to stand as candidates in elections to the European Parliament and in municipal elections in their Member State of residence, under the same conditions as nationals of that State;
   (c) the right to enjoy, in the territory of a third country in which the Member State of which they are nationals is not represented, the protection of the diplomatic and consular authorities of any Member State on the same conditions as the nationals of that State;
   (d) the right to petition the European Parliament, to apply to the European Ombudsman, and to address the institutions and advisory bodies of the Union in any of the Treaty languages and to obtain a reply in the same language.
   These rights shall be exercised in accordance with the conditions and limits defined by the Treaties and by the measures adopted thereunder.

Article 21

1. Every citizen of the Union shall have the right to move and reside freely within the territory of the Member States, subject to the limitations and conditions laid down in the Treaties and by the measures adopted to give them effect.
2. If action by the Union should prove necessary to attain this objective and the Treaties have not provided the necessary powers, the European Parliament and the Council, acting in accordance with the ordinary legislative procedure, may adopt provisions with a view to facilitating the exercise of the rights referred to in paragraph 1.
3. For the same purposes as those referred to in paragraph 1 and if the Treaties have not provided the necessary powers, the Council, acting in accordance with a special legislative procedure, may adopt measures concerning social security or social protection. The Council shall act unanimously after consulting the European Parliament.

Article 22

1. Every citizen of the Union residing in a Member State of which he is not a national shall have the right to vote and to stand as a candidate at municipal elections in the Member State in which he resides, under the same conditions as nationals of that State. This right shall be exercised subject to detailed arrangements adopted by the Council, acting unanimously in accordance with a special legislative procedure and after consulting the European Parliament; these arrangements may provide for derogations where warranted by problems specific to a Member State.

2. Without prejudice to Article 223(1) and to the provisions adopted for its implementation, every citizen of the Union residing in a Member State of which he is not a national shall have the right to vote and to stand as a candidate in elections to the European Parliament in the Member State in which he resides, under the same conditions as nationals of that State. This right shall be exercised subject to detailed arrangements adopted by the Council, acting unanimously in accordance with a special legislative procedure and after consulting the European Parliament; these arrangements may provide for derogations where warranted by problems specific to a Member State.

Article 23

Every citizen of the Union shall, in the territory of a third country in which the Member State of which he is a national is not represented, be entitled to protection by the diplomatic or consular authorities of any Member State, on the same conditions as the nationals of that State. Member States shall adopt the necessary provisions and start the international negotiations required to secure this protection.

The Council, acting in accordance with a special legislative procedure and after consulting the European Parliament, may adopt directives establishing the coordination and cooperation measures necessary to facilitate such protection.

Article 24

The European Parliament and the Council, acting by means of regulations in accordance with the ordinary legislative procedure, shall adopt the provisions for the procedures and conditions required for a citizens' initiative within the meaning of Article 11 of the Treaty on European Union, including the minimum number of Member States from which such citizens must come.

Every citizen of the Union shall have the right to petition the European Parliament in accordance with Article 227.

Every citizen of the Union may apply to the Ombudsman established in accordance with Article 228.

Every citizen of the Union may write to any of the institutions or bodies referred to in this Article or in Article 13 of the Treaty on European Union in one of the languages mentioned in Article 55(1) of the Treaty on European Union and have an answer in the same language.

Article 25

The Commission shall report to the European Parliament, to the Council and to the Economic and Social Committee every three years on the application of the provisions of this Part. This report shall take account of the development of the Union.

On this basis, and without prejudice to the other provisions of the Treaties, the Council, acting unanimously in accordance with a special legislative procedure and after obtaining the consent of the European Parliament, may adopt provisions to strengthen or to add to the rights listed in Article 20(2). These provisions shall enter into force after their approval by the Member States in accordance with their respective constitutional requirements.

PART THREE UNION POLICIES AND INTERNAL ACTIONS

TITLE I THE INTERNAL MARKET

Article 26

1. The Union shall adopt measures with the aim of establishing or ensuring the functioning of the internal market, in accordance with the relevant provisions of the Treaties.
2. The internal market shall comprise an area without internal frontiers in which the free movement of goods, persons, services and capital is ensured in accordance with the provisions of the Treaties.
3. The Council, on a proposal from the Commission, shall determine the guidelines and conditions necessary to ensure balanced progress in all the sectors concerned.

Article 27

When drawing up its proposals with a view to achieving the objectives set out in Article 26, the Commission shall take into account the extent of the effort that certain economies showing differences in development will have to sustain for the establishment of the internal market and it may propose appropriate provisions.

If these provisions take the form of derogations, they must be of a temporary nature and must cause the least possible disturbance to the functioning of the internal market.

TITLE II FREE MOVEMENT OF GOODS

Article 28

1. The Union shall comprise a customs union which shall cover all trade in goods and which shall involve the prohibition between Member States of customs duties on imports and exports and of all charges having equivalent effect, and the adoption of a common customs tariff in their relations with third countries.
2. The provisions of Article 30 and of Chapter 3 of this Title shall apply to products originating in Member States and to products coming from third countries which are in free circulation in Member States.

Article 29

Products coming from a third country shall be considered to be in free circulation in a Member State if the import formalities have been complied with and any customs duties or charges having equivalent effect which are payable have been levied in that Member State, and if they have not benefited from a total or partial drawback of such duties or charges.

Chapter 1 The Customs Union

Article 30

Customs duties on imports and exports and charges having equivalent effect shall be prohibited between Member States. This prohibition shall also apply to customs duties of a fiscal nature.

Article 31
Common Customs Tariff duties shall be fixed by the Council on a proposal from the Commission.

Article 32
In carrying out the tasks entrusted to it under this Chapter the Commission shall be guided by:
- (a) the need to promote trade between Member States and third countries;
- (b) developments in conditions of competition within the Union in so far as they lead to an improvement in the competitive capacity of undertakings;
- (c) the requirements of the Union as regards the supply of raw materials and semi-finished goods; in this connection the Commission shall take care to avoid distorting conditions of competition between Member States in respect of finished goods;
- (d) the need to avoid serious disturbances in the economies of Member States and to ensure rational development of production and an expansion of consumption within the Union.

Chapter 2 Customs Cooperation

Article 33
Within the scope of application of the Treaties, the European Parliament and the Council, acting in accordance with the ordinary legislative procedure, shall take measures in order to strengthen customs cooperation between Member States and between the latter and the Commission.

Chapter 3 Prohibition of Quantitative Restrictions between Member States

Article 34
Quantitative restrictions on imports and all measures having equivalent effect shall be prohibited between Member States.

Article 35
Quantitative restrictions on exports, and all measures having equivalent effect, shall be prohibited between Member States.

Article 36
The provisions of Articles 34 and 35 shall not preclude prohibitions or restrictions on imports, exports or goods in transit justified on grounds of public morality, public policy or public security; the protection of health and life of humans, animals or plants; the protection of national treasures possessing artistic, historic or archaeological value; or the protection of industrial and commercial property. Such prohibitions or restrictions shall not, however, constitute a means of arbitrary discrimination or a disguised restriction on trade between Member States.

Article 37
1. Member States shall adjust any State monopolies of a commercial character so as to ensure that no discrimination regarding the conditions under which goods are procured and marketed exists between nationals of Member States.

The provisions of this Article shall apply to any body through which a Member State, in law or in fact, either directly or indirectly supervises, determines or appreciably influences imports or exports between Member States. These provisions shall likewise apply to monopolies delegated by the State to others.

2. Member States shall refrain from introducing any new measure which is contrary to the principles laid down in paragraph 1 or which restricts the scope of the articles dealing with the prohibition of customs duties and quantitative restrictions between Member States.

3. If a State monopoly of a commercial character has rules which are designed to make it easier to dispose of agricultural products or obtain for them the best return, steps should be taken in applying the rules contained in this Article to ensure equivalent safeguards for the employment and standard of living of the producers concerned.

TITLE III AGRICULTURE AND FISHERIES

Article 38

1. The Union shall define and implement a common agriculture and fisheries policy.

   The internal market shall extend to agriculture, fisheries and trade in agricultural products. 'Agricultural products' means the products of the soil, of stock farming and of fisheries and products of first-stage processing directly related to these products. References to the common agricultural policy or to agriculture, and the use of the term 'agricultural', shall be understood as also referring to fisheries, having regard to the specific characteristics of this sector.

2. Save as otherwise provided in Articles 39 to 44, the rules laid down for the establishment and functioning of the internal market shall apply to agricultural products.

3. The products subject to the provisions of Articles 39 to 44 are listed in Annex I.

4. The operation and development of the internal market for agricultural products must be accompanied by the establishment of a common agricultural policy.

Article 39

1. The objectives of the common agricultural policy shall be:
   (a) to increase agricultural productivity by promoting technical progress and by ensuring the rational development of agricultural production and the optimum utilisation of the factors of production, in particular labour;
   (b) thus to ensure a fair standard of living for the agricultural community, in particular by increasing the individual earnings of persons engaged in agriculture;
   (c) to stabilise markets;
   (d) to assure the availability of supplies;
   (e) to ensure that supplies reach consumers at reasonable prices.

2. In working out the common agricultural policy and the special methods for its application, account shall be taken of:
   (a) the particular nature of agricultural activity, which results from the social structure of agriculture and from structural and natural disparities between the various agricultural regions;
   (b) the need to effect the appropriate adjustments by degrees;
   (c) the fact that in the Member States agriculture constitutes a sector closely linked with the economy as a whole.

Article 40

1. In order to attain the objectives set out in Article 39, a common organisation of agricultural markets shall be established.

   This organisation shall take one of the following forms, depending on the product concerned:

   (a) common rules on competition;

   (b) compulsory coordination of the various national market organisations;

   (c) a European market organisation.

2. The common organisation established in accordance with paragraph 1 may include all measures required to attain the objectives set out in Article 39, in particular regulation of prices, aids for the production and marketing of the various products, storage and carryover arrangements and common machinery for stabilising imports or exports.

   The common organisation shall be limited to pursuit of the objectives set out in Article 39 and shall exclude any discrimination between producers or consumers within the Union.

   Any common price policy shall be based on common criteria and uniform methods of calculation.

3. In order to enable the common organisation referred to in paragraph 1 to attain its objectives, one or more agricultural guidance and guarantee funds may be set up.

Article 41

To enable the objectives set out in Article 39 to be attained, provision may be made within the framework of the common agricultural policy for measures such as:

   (a) an effective coordination of efforts in the spheres of vocational training, of research and of the dissemination of agricultural knowledge; this may include joint financing of projects or institutions;

   (b) joint measures to promote consumption of certain products.

Article 42

The provisions of the Chapter relating to rules on competition shall apply to production of and trade in agricultural products only to the extent determined by the European Parliament and the Council within the framework of Article 43(2) and in accordance with the procedure laid down therein, account being taken of the objectives set out in Article 39.

   The Council, on a proposal from the Commission, may authorise the granting of aid:

   (a) for the protection of enterprises handicapped by structural or natural conditions;

   (b) within the framework of economic development programmes.

Article 43

1. The Commission shall submit proposals for working out and implementing the common agricultural policy, including the replacement of the national organisations by one of the forms of common organisation provided for in Article 40(1), and for implementing the measures specified in this Title.

   These proposals shall take account of the interdependence of the agricultural matters mentioned in this Title.

2. The European Parliament and the Council, acting in accordance with the ordinary legislative procedure and after consulting the Economic and Social Committee, shall

establish the common organisation of agricultural markets provided for in Article 40(1) and the other provisions necessary for the pursuit of the objectives of the common agricultural policy and the common fisheries policy.

3. The Council, on a proposal from the Commission, shall adopt measures on fixing prices, levies, aid and quantitative limitations and on the fixing and allocation of fishing opportunities.

4. In accordance with paragraph 2, the national market organisations may be replaced by the common organisation provided for in Article 40(1) if:

   (a) the common organisation offers Member States which are opposed to this measure and which have an organisation of their own for the production in question equivalent safeguards for the employment and standard of living of the producers concerned, account being taken of the adjustments that will be possible and the specialisation that will be needed with the passage of time;

   (b) such an organisation ensures conditions for trade within the Union similar to those existing in a national market.

5. If a common organisation for certain raw materials is established before a common organisation exists for the corresponding processed products, such raw materials as are used for processed products intended for export to third countries may be imported from outside the Union.

Article 44

Where in a Member State a product is subject to a national market organisation or to internal rules having equivalent effect which affect the competitive position of similar production in another Member State, a countervailing charge shall be applied by Member States to imports of this product coming from the Member State where such organisation or rules exist, unless that State applies a countervailing charge on export.

The Commission shall fix the amount of these charges at the level required to redress the balance; it may also authorise other measures, the conditions and details of which it shall determine.

TITLE IV FREE MOVEMENT OF PERSONS, SERVICES AND CAPITAL

Chapter 1 Workers

Article 45

1. Freedom of movement for workers shall be secured within the Union.

2. Such freedom of movement shall entail the abolition of any discrimination based on nationality between workers of the Member States as regards employment, remuneration and other conditions of work and employment.

3. It shall entail the right, subject to limitations justified on grounds of public policy, public security or public health:

   (a) to accept offers of employment actually made;

   (b) to move freely within the territory of Member States for this purpose;

   (c) to stay in a Member State for the purpose of employment in accordance with the provisions governing the employment of nationals of that State laid down by law, regulation or administrative action;

(d) to remain in the territory of a Member State after having been employed in that State, subject to conditions which shall be embodied in regulations to be drawn up by the Commission.

4. The provisions of this Article shall not apply to employment in the public service.

Article 46

The European Parliament and the Council shall, acting in accordance with the ordinary legislative procedure and after consulting the Economic and Social Committee, issue directives or make regulations setting out the measures required to bring about freedom of movement for workers, as defined in Article 45, in particular:

(a) by ensuring close cooperation between national employment services;

(b) by abolishing those administrative procedures and practices and those qualifying periods in respect of eligibility for available employment, whether resulting from national legislation or from agreements previously concluded between Member States, the maintenance of which would form an obstacle to liberalisation of the movement of workers;

(c) by abolishing all such qualifying periods and other restrictions provided for either under national legislation or under agreements previously concluded between Member States as imposed on workers of other Member States conditions regarding the free choice of employment other than those imposed on workers of the State concerned;

(d) by setting up appropriate machinery to bring offers of employment into touch with applications for employment and to facilitate the achievement of a balance between supply and demand in the employment market in such a way as to avoid serious threats to the standard of living and level of employment in the various regions and industries.

Article 47

Member States shall, within the framework of a joint programme, encourage the exchange of young workers.

Article 48

The European Parliament and the Council shall, acting in accordance with the ordinary legislative procedure, adopt such measures in the field of social security as are necessary to provide freedom of movement for workers; to this end, they shall make arrangements to secure for employed and self-employed migrant workers and their dependants:

(a) aggregation, for the purpose of acquiring and retaining the right to benefit and of calculating the amount of benefit, of all periods taken into account under the laws of the several countries;

(b) payment of benefits to persons resident in the territories of Member States.

Where a member of the Council declares that a draft legislative act referred to in the first subparagraph would affect important aspects of its social security system, including its scope, cost or financial structure, or would affect the financial balance of that system, it may request that the matter be referred to the European Council. In that case, the ordinary legislative procedure shall be suspended. After discussion, the European Council shall, within four months of this suspension, either:

(a) refer the draft back to the Council, which shall terminate the suspension of the ordinary legislative procedure; or

(b) take no action or request the Commission to submit a new proposal; in that case, the act originally proposed shall be deemed not to have been adopted.

Chapter 2 Right of Establishment

Article 49

Within the framework of the provisions set out below, restrictions on the freedom of establishment of nationals of a Member State in the territory of another Member State shall be prohibited. Such prohibition shall also apply to restrictions on the setting-up of agencies, branches or subsidiaries by nationals of any Member State established in the territory of any Member State.

Freedom of establishment shall include the right to take up and pursue activities as self-employed persons and to set up and manage undertakings, in particular companies or firms within the meaning of the second paragraph of Article 54, under the conditions laid down for its own nationals by the law of the country where such establishment is effected, subject to the provisions of the Chapter relating to capital.

Article 50

1. In order to attain freedom of establishment as regards a particular activity, the European Parliament and the Council, acting in accordance with the ordinary legislative procedure and after consulting the Economic and Social Committee, shall act by means of directives.

2. The European Parliament, the Council and the Commission shall carry out the duties devolving upon them under the preceding provisions, in particular:

(a) by according, as a general rule, priority treatment to activities where freedom of establishment makes a particularly valuable contribution to the development of production and trade;

(b) by ensuring close cooperation between the competent authorities in the Member States in order to ascertain the particular situation within the Union of the various activities concerned;

(c) by abolishing those administrative procedures and practices, whether resulting from national legislation or from agreements previously concluded between Member States, the maintenance of which would form an obstacle to freedom of establishment;

(d) by ensuring that workers of one Member State employed in the territory of another Member State may remain in that territory for the purpose of taking up activities therein as self-employed persons, where they satisfy the conditions which they would be required to satisfy if they were entering that State at the time when they intended to take up such activities;

(e) by enabling a national of one Member State to acquire and use land and buildings situated in the territory of another Member State, in so far as this does not conflict with the principles laid down in Article 39(2);

(f) by effecting the progressive abolition of restrictions on freedom of establishment in every branch of activity under consideration, both as regards the conditions for setting up agencies, branches or subsidiaries in the territory of a Member State and as regards the subsidiaries in the territory of a Member State and as regards the conditions governing the entry of personnel belonging to the main establishment into managerial or supervisory posts in such agencies, branches or subsidiaries;

(g) by coordinating to the necessary extent the safeguards which, for the protection of the interests of members and others, are required by Member States of companies or firms within the meaning of the second paragraph of Article 54 with a view to making such safeguards equivalent throughout the Union;

(h) by satisfying themselves that the conditions of establishment are not distorted by aids granted by Member States.

Article 51

The provisions of this Chapter shall not apply, so far as any given Member State is concerned, to activities which in that State are connected, even occasionally, with the exercise of official authority.

The European Parliament and the Council, acting in accordance with the ordinary legislative procedure, may rule that the provisions of this Chapter shall not apply to certain activities.

Article 52

1. The provisions of this Chapter and measures taken in pursuance thereof shall not prejudice the applicability of provisions laid down by law, regulation or administrative action providing for special treatment for foreign nationals on grounds of public policy, public security or public health.

2. The European Parliament and the Council shall, acting in accordance with the ordinary legislative procedure, issue directives for the coordination of the abovementioned provisions.

Article 53

1. In order to make it easier for persons to take up and pursue activities as self-employed persons, the European Parliament and the Council shall, acting in accordance with the ordinary legislative procedure, issue directives for the mutual recognition of diplomas, certificates and other evidence of formal qualifications and for the coordination of the provisions laid down by law, regulation or administrative action in Member States concerning the taking-up and pursuit of activities as self-employed persons.

2. In the case of the medical and allied and pharmaceutical professions, the progressive abolition of restrictions shall be dependent upon coordination of the conditions for their exercise in the various Member States.

Article 54

Companies or firms formed in accordance with the law of a Member State and having their registered office, central administration or principal place of business within the Union shall, for the purposes of this Chapter, be treated in the same way as natural persons who are nationals of Member States.

'Companies or firms' means companies or firms constituted under civil or commercial law, including cooperative societies, and other legal persons governed by public or private law, save for those which are non-profit-making.

Article 55

Member States shall accord nationals of the other Member States the same treatment as their own nationals as regards participation in the capital of companies or firms within the meaning of Article 54, without prejudice to the application of the other provisions of the Treaties.

Chapter 3 Services

Article 56

Within the framework of the provisions set out below, restrictions on freedom to provide services within the Union shall be prohibited in respect of nationals of Member States who are established in a Member State other than that of the person for whom the services are intended.

The European Parliament and the Council, acting in accordance with the ordinary legislative procedure, may extend the provisions of the Chapter to nationals of a third country who provide services and who are established within the Union.

Article 57

Services shall be considered to be 'services' within the meaning of the Treaties where they are normally provided for remuneration, in so far as they are not governed by the provisions relating to freedom of movement for goods, capital and persons.

'Services' shall in particular include:

(a) activities of an industrial character;
(b) activities of a commercial character;
(c) activities of craftsmen;
(d) activities of the professions.

Without prejudice to the provisions of the Chapter relating to the right of establishment, the person providing a service may, in order to do so, temporarily pursue his activity in the Member State where the service is provided, under the same conditions as are imposed by that State on its own nationals.

Article 58

1. Freedom to provide services in the field of transport shall be governed by the provisions of the Title relating to transport.
2. The liberalisation of banking and insurance services connected with movements of capital shall be effected in step with the liberalisation of movement of capital.

Article 59

1. In order to achieve the liberalisation of a specific service, the European Parliament and the Council, acting in accordance with the ordinary legislative procedure and after consulting the Economic and Social Committee, shall issue directives.
2. As regards the directives referred to in paragraph 1, priority shall as a general rule be given to those services which directly affect production costs or the liberalisation of which helps to promote trade in goods.

Article 60

The Member States shall endeavour to undertake the liberalisation of services beyond the extent required by the directives issued pursuant to Article 59(1), if their general economic situation and the situation of the economic sector concerned so permit.

To this end, the Commission shall make recommendations to the Member States concerned.

Article 61

As long as restrictions on freedom to provide services have not been abolished, each Member State shall apply such restrictions without distinction on grounds of nationality or residence to all persons providing services within the meaning of the first paragraph of Article 56.

Article 62

The provisions of Articles 51 to 54 shall apply to the matters covered by this Chapter.

Chapter 4 Capital and Payments

Article 63

1. Within the framework of the provisions set out in this Chapter, all restrictions on the movement of capital between Member States and between Member States and third countries shall be prohibited.
2. Within the framework of the provisions set out in this Chapter, all restrictions on payments between Member States and between Member States and third countries shall be prohibited.

Article 64

1. The provisions of Article 63 shall be without prejudice to the application to third countries of any restrictions which exist on 31 December 1993 under national or Union law adopted in respect of the movement of capital to or from third countries involving direct investment – including in real estate – establishment, the provision of financial services or the admission of securities to capital markets. In respect of restrictions existing under national law in Bulgaria, Estonia and Hungary, the relevant date shall be 31 December 1999. In respect of restrictions existing under national law in Croatia, the relevant date shall be 31 December 2002.
2. Whilst endeavouring to achieve the objective of free movement of capital between Member States and third countries to the greatest extent possible and without prejudice to the other Chapters of the Treaties, the European Parliament and the Council, acting in accordance with the ordinary legislative procedure, shall adopt the measures on the movement of capital to or from third countries involving direct investment – including investment in real estate – establishment, the provision of financial services or the admission of securities to capital markets.
3. Notwithstanding paragraph 2, only the Council, acting in accordance with a special legislative procedure, may unanimously, and after consulting the European Parliament, adopt measures which constitute a step backwards in Union law as regards the liberalisation of the movement of capital to or from third countries.

Article 65

1. The provisions of Article 63 shall be without prejudice to the right of Member States:
   (a) to apply the relevant provisions of their tax law which distinguish between taxpayers who are not in the same situation with regard to their place of residence or with regard to the place where their capital is invested;
   (b) to take all requisite measures to prevent infringements of national law and regulations, in particular in the field of taxation and the prudential supervision of financial institutions, or to lay down procedures for the declaration of capital movements for purposes of administrative or statistical information, or to take measures which are justified on grounds of public policy or public security.
2. The provisions of this Chapter shall be without prejudice to the applicability of restrictions on the right of establishment which are compatible with the Treaties.
3. The measures and procedures referred to in paragraphs 1 and 2 shall not constitute a means of arbitrary discrimination or a disguised restriction on the free movement of capital and payments as defined in Article 63.
4. In the absence of measures pursuant to Article 64(3), the Commission or, in the absence of a Commission decision within three months from the request of the Member State concerned, the Council, may adopt a decision stating that restrictive tax measures adopted by a Member State concerning one or more third countries are to be considered compatible with the Treaties in so far as they are justified by one of the objectives of the Union and compatible with the proper functioning of the internal market. The Council shall act unanimously on application by a Member State.

Article 66

Where, in exceptional circumstances, movements of capital to or from third countries cause, or threaten to cause, serious difficulties for the operation of economic and monetary union, the Council, on a proposal from the Commission and after consulting the European Central Bank, may take safeguard measures with regard to third countries for a period not exceeding six months if such measures are strictly necessary.

TITLE V AREA OF FREEDOM, SECURITY AND JUSTICE

Chapter 1 General Provisions

Article 67

1. The Union shall constitute an area of freedom, security and justice with respect for fundamental rights and the different legal systems and traditions of the Member States.
2. It shall ensure the absence of internal border controls for persons and shall frame a common policy on asylum, immigration and external border control, based on solidarity between Member States, which is fair towards third-country nationals. For the purpose of this Title, stateless persons shall be treated as third-country nationals.
3. The Union shall endeavour to ensure a high level of security through measures to prevent and combat crime, racism and xenophobia, and through measures for coordination and cooperation between police and judicial authorities and other competent authorities, as well as through the mutual recognition of judgments in criminal matters and, if necessary, through the approximation of criminal laws.

4. The Union shall facilitate access to justice, in particular through the principle of mutual recognition of judicial and extrajudicial decisions in civil matters.

Article 68

The European Council shall define the strategic guidelines for legislative and operational planning within the area of freedom, security and justice.

Article 69

National Parliaments ensure that the proposals and legislative initiatives submitted under Chapters 4 and 5 comply with the principle of subsidiarity, in accordance with the arrangements laid down by the Protocol on the application of the principles of subsidiarity and proportionality.

Article 70

Without prejudice to Articles 258, 259 and 260, the Council may, on a proposal from the Commission, adopt measures laying down the arrangements whereby Member States, in collaboration with the Commission, conduct objective and impartial evaluation of the implementation of the Union policies referred to in this Title by Member States' authorities, in particular in order to facilitate full application of the principle of mutual recognition. The European Parliament and national Parliaments shall be informed of the content and results of the evaluation.

Article 71

A standing committee shall be set up within the Council in order to ensure that operational cooperation on internal security is promoted and strengthened within the Union. Without prejudice to Article 240, it shall facilitate coordination of the action of Member States' competent authorities. Representatives of the Union bodies, offices and agencies concerned may be involved in the proceedings of this committee. The European Parliament and national Parliaments shall be kept informed of the proceedings.

Article 72

This Title shall not affect the exercise of the responsibilities incumbent upon Member States with regard to the maintenance of law and order and the safeguarding of internal security.

Article 73

It shall be open to Member States to organise between themselves and under their responsibility such forms of cooperation and coordination as they deem appropriate between the competent departments of their administrations responsible for safeguarding national security.

Article 74

The Council shall adopt measures to ensure administrative cooperation between the relevant departments of the Member States in the areas covered by this Title, as well as between those departments and the Commission. It shall act on a Commission proposal, subject to Article 76, and after consulting the European Parliament.

Article 75

Where necessary to achieve the objectives set out in Article 67, as regards preventing and combating terrorism and related activities, the European Parliament and the Council, acting by means of regulations in accordance with the ordinary legislative procedure, shall define a framework for administrative measures with regard to capital movements and payments, such as the freezing of funds, financial assets or economic gains belonging to, or owned or held by, natural or legal persons, groups or non-State entities.

The Council, on a proposal from the Commission, shall adopt measures to implement the framework referred to in the first paragraph.

The acts referred to in this Article shall include necessary provisions on legal safeguards.

Article 76

The acts referred to in Chapters 4 and 5, together with the measures referred to in Article 74 which ensure administrative cooperation in the areas covered by these Chapters, shall be adopted:

(a) on a proposal from the Commission, or

(b) on the initiative of a quarter of the Member States.

Chapter 2 Policies on Border Checks, Asylum and Immigration

2

Article 77

1. The Union shall develop a policy with a view to:

    (a) ensuring the absence of any controls on persons, whatever their nationality, when crossing internal borders;

    (b) carrying out checks on persons and efficient monitoring of the crossing of external borders;

    (c) the gradual introduction of an integrated management system for external borders.

2. For the purposes of paragraph 1, the European Parliament and the Council, acting in accordance with the ordinary legislative procedure, shall adopt measures concerning:

    (a) the common policy on visas and other short-stay residence permits;

    (b) the checks to which persons crossing external borders are subject;

    (c) the conditions under which nationals of third countries shall have the freedom to travel within the Union for a short period;

    (d) any measure necessary for the gradual establishment of an integrated management system for external borders;

    (e) the absence of any controls on persons, whatever their nationality, when crossing internal borders.

3. If action by the Union should prove necessary to facilitate the exercise of the right referred to in Article 20(2)(a), and if the Treaties have not provided the necessary powers, the Council, acting in accordance with a special legislative procedure, may adopt provisions concerning passports, identity cards, residence permits or any other such document. The Council shall act unanimously after consulting the European Parliament.

4. This Article shall not affect the competence of the Member States concerning the geographical demarcation of their borders, in accordance with international law.

Article 78

1. The Union shall develop a common policy on asylum, subsidiary protection and temporary protection with a view to offering appropriate status to any third-country national requiring international protection and ensuring compliance with the principle of non-refoulement. This policy must be in accordance with the Geneva Convention of 28 July 1951 and the Protocol of 31 January 1967 relating to the status of refugees, and other relevant treaties.

2. For the purposes of paragraph 1, the European Parliament and the Council, acting in accordance with the ordinary legislative procedure, shall adopt measures for a common European asylum system comprising:

   (a) a uniform status of asylum for nationals of third countries, valid throughout the Union;

   (b) a uniform status of subsidiary protection for nationals of third countries who, without obtaining European asylum, are in need of international protection;

   (c) a common system of temporary protection for displaced persons in the event of a massive inflow;

   (d) common procedures for the granting and withdrawing of uniform asylum or subsidiary protection status;

   (e) criteria and mechanisms for determining which Member State is responsible for considering an application for asylum or subsidiary protection;

   (f) standards concerning the conditions for the reception of applicants for asylum or subsidiary protection;

   (g) partnership and cooperation with third countries for the purpose of managing inflows of people applying for asylum or subsidiary or temporary protection.

3. In the event of one or more Member States being confronted by an emergency situation characterised by a sudden inflow of nationals of third countries, the Council, on a proposal from the Commission, may adopt provisional measures for the benefit of the Member State(s) concerned. It shall act after consulting the European Parliament.

Article 79

1. The Union shall develop a common immigration policy aimed at ensuring, at all stages, the efficient management of migration flows, fair treatment of third-country nationals residing legally in Member States, and the prevention of, and enhanced measures to combat, illegal immigration and trafficking in human beings.

2. For the purposes of paragraph 1, the European Parliament and the Council, acting in accordance with the ordinary legislative procedure, shall adopt measures in the following areas:

   (a) the conditions of entry and residence, and standards on the issue by Member States of long-term visas and residence permits, including those for the purpose of family reunification;

   (b) the definition of the rights of third-country nationals residing legally in a Member State, including the conditions governing freedom of movement and of residence in other Member States;

   (c) illegal immigration and unauthorised residence, including removal and repatriation of persons residing without authorisation;

   (d) combating trafficking in persons, in particular women and children.

3. The Union may conclude agreements with third countries for the readmission to their countries of origin or provenance of third-country nationals who do not or who no longer fulfil the conditions for entry, presence or residence in the territory of one of the Member States.

4. The European Parliament and the Council, acting in accordance with the ordinary legislative procedure, may establish measures to provide incentives and support for the action of Member States with a view to promoting the integration of third-country nationals residing legally in their territories, excluding any harmonisation of the laws and regulations of the Member States.

5. This Article shall not affect the right of Member States to determine volumes of admission of third-country nationals coming from third countries to their territory in order to seek work, whether employed or self-employed.

Article 80

The policies of the Union set out in this Chapter and their implementation shall be governed by the principle of solidarity and fair sharing of responsibility, including its financial implications, between the Member States. Whenever necessary, the Union acts adopted pursuant to this Chapter shall contain appropriate measures to give effect to this principle.

Chapter 3 Judicial Cooperation in Civil Matters

Article 81

1. The Union shall develop judicial cooperation in civil matters having cross-border implications, based on the principle of mutual recognition of judgments and of decisions in extrajudicial cases. Such cooperation may include the adoption of measures for the approximation of the laws and regulations of the Member States.

2. For the purposes of paragraph 1, the European Parliament and the Council, acting in accordance with the ordinary legislative procedure, shall adopt measures, particularly when necessary for the proper functioning of the internal market, aimed at ensuring:
   (a) the mutual recognition and enforcement between Member States of judgments and of decisions in extrajudicial cases;
   (b) the cross-border service of judicial and extrajudicial documents;
   (c) the compatibility of the rules applicable in the Member States concerning conflict of laws and of jurisdiction;
   (d) cooperation in the taking of evidence;
   (e) effective access to justice;
   (f) the elimination of obstacles to the proper functioning of civil proceedings, if necessary by promoting the compatibility of the rules on civil procedure applicable in the Member States;
   (g) the development of alternative methods of dispute settlement;
   (h) support for the training of the judiciary and judicial staff.

3. Notwithstanding paragraph 2, measures concerning family law with cross-border implications shall be established by the Council, acting in accordance with a special legislative procedure. The Council shall act unanimously after consulting the European Parliament.

The Council, on a proposal from the Commission, may adopt a decision determining those aspects of family law with cross-border implications which may be the subject of acts adopted by the ordinary legislative procedure. The Council shall act unanimously after consulting the European Parliament.

The proposal referred to in the second subparagraph shall be notified to the national Parliaments. If a national Parliament makes known its opposition within six months of the date of such notification, the decision shall not be adopted. In the absence of opposition, the Council may adopt the decision.

Chapter 4 Judicial Cooperation in Criminal Matters

Article 82

1. Judicial cooperation in criminal matters in the Union shall be based on the principle of mutual recognition of judgments and judicial decisions and shall include the approximation of the laws and regulations of the Member States in the areas referred to in paragraph 2 and in Article 83.

    The European Parliament and the Council, acting in accordance with the ordinary legislative procedure, shall adopt measures to:
    (a) lay down rules and procedures for ensuring recognition throughout the Union of all forms of judgments and judicial decisions;
    (b) prevent and settle conflicts of jurisdiction between Member States;
    (c) support the training of the judiciary and judicial staff;
    (d) facilitate cooperation between judicial or equivalent authorities of the Member States in relation to proceedings in criminal matters and the enforcement of decisions.

2. To the extent necessary to facilitate mutual recognition of judgments and judicial decisions and police and judicial cooperation in criminal matters having a cross-border dimension, the European Parliament and the Council may, by means of directives adopted in accordance with the ordinary legislative procedure, establish minimum rules. Such rules shall take into account the differences between the legal traditions and systems of the Member States.

    They shall concern:
    (a) mutual admissibility of evidence between Member States;
    (b) the rights of individuals in criminal procedure;
    (c) the rights of victims of crime;
    (d) any other specific aspects of criminal procedure which the Council has identified in advance by a decision; for the adoption of such a decision, the Council shall act unanimously after obtaining the consent of the European Parliament.

    Adoption of the minimum rules referred to in this paragraph shall not prevent Member States from maintaining or introducing a higher level of protection for individuals.

3. Where a member of the Council considers that a draft directive as referred to in paragraph 2 would affect fundamental aspects of its criminal justice system, it may request that the draft directive be referred to the European Council. In that case, the ordinary legislative procedure shall be suspended. After discussion, and in case of a consensus, the European Council shall, within four months of this suspension, refer the draft back to the Council, which shall terminate the suspension of the ordinary legislative procedure.

Within the same timeframe, in case of disagreement, and if at least nine Member States wish to establish enhanced cooperation on the basis of the draft directive concerned, they shall notify the European Parliament, the Council and the Commission accordingly. In such a case, the authorisation to proceed with enhanced cooperation referred to in Article 20(2) of the Treaty on European Union and Article 329(1) of this Treaty shall be deemed to be granted and the provisions on enhanced cooperation shall apply.

Article 83

1. The European Parliament and the Council may, by means of directives adopted in accordance with the ordinary legislative procedure, establish minimum rules concerning the definition of criminal offences and sanctions in the areas of particularly serious crime with a cross-border dimension resulting from the nature or impact of such offences or from a special need to combat them on a common basis.

   These areas of crime are the following: terrorism, trafficking in human beings and sexual exploitation of women and children, illicit drug trafficking, illicit arms trafficking, money laundering, corruption, counterfeiting of means of payment, computer crime and organised crime.

   On the basis of developments in crime, the Council may adopt a decision identifying other areas of crime that meet the criteria specified in this paragraph. It shall act unanimously after obtaining the consent of the European Parliament.

2. If the approximation of criminal laws and regulations of the Member States proves essential to ensure the effective implementation of a Union policy in an area which has been subject to harmonisation measures, directives may establish minimum rules with regard to the definition of criminal offences and sanctions in the area concerned. Such directives shall be adopted by the same ordinary or special legislative procedure as was followed for the adoption of the harmonisation measures in question, without prejudice to Article 76.

3. Where a member of the Council considers that a draft directive as referred to in paragraph 1 or 2 would affect fundamental aspects of its criminal justice system, it may request that the draft directive be referred to the European Council. In that case, the ordinary legislative procedure shall be suspended. After discussion, and in case of a consensus, the European Council shall, within four months of this suspension, refer the draft back to the Council, which shall terminate the suspension of the ordinary legislative procedure.

   Within the same timeframe, in case of disagreement, and if at least nine Member States wish to establish enhanced cooperation on the basis of the draft directive concerned, they shall notify the European Parliament, the Council and the Commission accordingly. In such a case, the authorisation to proceed with enhanced cooperation referred to in Article 20(2) of the Treaty on European Union and Article 329(1) of this Treaty shall be deemed to be granted and the provisions on enhanced cooperation shall apply.

Article 84

The European Parliament and the Council, acting in accordance with the ordinary legislative procedure, may establish measures to promote and support the action of Member States in the field of crime prevention, excluding any harmonisation of the laws and regulations of the Member States.

Article 85

1. Eurojust's mission shall be to support and strengthen coordination and cooperation between national investigating and prosecuting authorities in relation to serious crime affecting two or more Member States or requiring a prosecution on common bases, on the basis of operations conducted and information supplied by the Member States' authorities and by Europol.

   In this context, the European Parliament and the Council, by means of regulations adopted in accordance with the ordinary legislative procedure, shall determine Eurojust's structure, operation, field of action and tasks. These tasks may include:

   (a) the initiation of criminal investigations, as well as proposing the initiation of prosecutions conducted by competent national authorities, particularly those relating to offences against the financial interests of the Union;

   (b) the coordination of investigations and prosecutions referred to in point (a);

   (c) the strengthening of judicial cooperation, including by resolution of conflicts of jurisdiction and by close cooperation with the European Judicial Network.

   These regulations shall also determine arrangements for involving the European Parliament and national Parliaments in the evaluation of Eurojust's activities.

2. In the prosecutions referred to in paragraph 1, and without prejudice to Article 86, formal acts of judicial procedure shall be carried out by the competent national officials.

Article 86

1. In order to combat crimes affecting the financial interests of the Union, the Council, by means of regulations adopted in accordance with a special legislative procedure, may establish a European Public Prosecutor's Office from Eurojust. The Council shall act unanimously after obtaining the consent of the European Parliament.

   In the absence of unanimity in the Council, a group of at least nine Member States may request that the draft regulation be referred to the European Council. In that case, the procedure in the Council shall be suspended. After discussion, and in case of a consensus, the European Council shall, within four months of this suspension, refer the draft back to the Council for adoption.

   Within the same timeframe, in case of disagreement, and if at least nine Member States wish to establish enhanced cooperation on the basis of the draft regulation concerned, they shall notify the European Parliament, the Council and the Commission accordingly. In such a case, the authorisation to proceed with enhanced cooperation referred to in Article 20(2) of the Treaty on European Union and Article 329(1) of this Treaty shall be deemed to be granted and the provisions on enhanced cooperation shall apply.

2. The European Public Prosecutor's Office shall be responsible for investigating, prosecuting and bringing to judgment, where appropriate in liaison with Europol, the perpetrators of, and accomplices in, offences against the Union's financial interests, as determined by the regulation provided for in paragraph 1. It shall exercise the functions of prosecutor in the competent courts of the Member States in relation to such offences.

3. The regulations referred to in paragraph 1 shall determine the general rules applicable to the European Public Prosecutor's Office, the conditions governing the performance of its functions, the rules of procedure applicable to its activities, as well as those governing

the admissibility of evidence, and the rules applicable to the judicial review of procedural measures taken by it in the performance of its functions.

4. The European Council may, at the same time or subsequently, adopt a decision amending paragraph 1 in order to extend the powers of the European Public Prosecutor's Office to include serious crime having a cross-border dimension and amending accordingly paragraph 2 as regards the perpetrators of, and accomplices in, serious crimes affecting more than one Member State. The European Council shall act unanimously after obtaining the consent of the European Parliament and after consulting the Commission.

Chapter 5 Police Cooperation

Article 87

1. The Union shall establish police cooperation involving all the Member States' competent authorities, including police, customs and other specialised law enforcement services in relation to the prevention, detection and investigation of criminal offences.

2. For the purposes of paragraph 1, the European Parliament and the Council, acting in accordance with the ordinary legislative procedure, may establish measures concerning:
   (a) the collection, storage, processing, analysis and exchange of relevant information;
   (b) support for the training of staff, and cooperation on the exchange of staff, on equipment and on research into crime-detection;
   (c) common investigative techniques in relation to the detection of serious forms of organised crime.

3. The Council, acting in accordance with a special legislative procedure, may establish measures concerning operational cooperation between the authorities referred to in this Article. The Council shall act unanimously after consulting the European Parliament.

   In case of the absence of unanimity in the Council, a group of at least nine Member States may request that the draft measures be referred to the European Council. In that case, the procedure in the Council shall be suspended. After discussion, and in case of a consensus, the European Council shall, within four months of this suspension, refer the draft back to the Council for adoption.

   Within the same timeframe, in case of disagreement, and if at least nine Member States wish to establish enhanced cooperation on the basis of the draft measures concerned, they shall notify the European Parliament, the Council and the Commission accordingly. In such a case, the authorisation to proceed with enhanced cooperation referred to in Article 20(2) of the Treaty on European Union and Article 329(1) of this Treaty shall be deemed to be granted and the provisions on enhanced cooperation shall apply.

   The specific procedure provided for in the second and third subparagraphs shall not apply to acts which constitute a development of the Schengen acquis.

Article 88

1. Europol's mission shall be to support and strengthen action by the Member States' police authorities and other law enforcement services and their mutual cooperation in preventing and combating serious crime affecting two or more Member States, terrorism and forms of crime which affect a common interest covered by a Union policy.

2. The European Parliament and the Council, by means of regulations adopted in accordance with the ordinary legislative procedure, shall determine Europol's structure, operation, field of action and tasks. These tasks may include:

   (a) the collection, storage, processing, analysis and exchange of information, in particular that forwarded by the authorities of the Member States or third countries or bodies;

   (b) the coordination, organisation and implementation of investigative and operational action carried out jointly with the Member States' competent authorities or in the context of joint investigative teams, where appropriate in liaison with Eurojust. These regulations shall also lay down the procedures for scrutiny of Europol's activities by the European Parliament, together with national Parliaments.

3. Any operational action by Europol must be carried out in liaison and in agreement with the authorities of the Member State or States whose territory is concerned. The application of coercive measures shall be the exclusive responsibility of the competent national authorities.

Article 89

The Council, acting in accordance with a special legislative procedure, shall lay down the conditions and limitations under which the competent authorities of the Member States referred to in Articles 82 and 87 may operate in the territory of another Member State in liaison and in agreement with the authorities of that State. The Council shall act unanimously after consulting the European Parliament.

TITLE VI TRANSPORT

Article 90

The objectives of the Treaties shall, in matters governed by this Title, be pursued within the framework of a common transport policy.

Article 91

1. For the purpose of implementing Article 90, and taking into account the distinctive features of transport, the European Parliament and the Council shall, acting in accordance with the ordinary legislative procedure and after consulting the Economic and Social Committee and the Committee of the Regions, lay down:

   (a) common rules applicable to international transport to or from the territory of a Member State or passing across the territory of one or more Member States;

   (b) the conditions under which non-resident carriers may operate transport services within a Member State;

   (c) measures to improve transport safety;

   (d) any other appropriate provisions.

2. When the measures referred to in paragraph 1 are adopted, account shall be taken of cases where their application might seriously affect the standard of living and level of employment in certain regions, and the operation of transport facilities.

Article 92

Until the provisions referred to in Article 91(1) have been laid down, no Member State may, unless the Council has unanimously adopted a measure granting a derogation, make the various provisions governing the subject on 1 January 1958 or, for acceding States, the date of their accession less favourable in their direct or indirect effect on carriers of other Member States as compared with carriers who are nationals of that State.

Article 93

Aids shall be compatible with the Treaties if they meet the needs of coordination of transport or if they represent reimbursement for the discharge of certain obligations inherent in the concept of a public service.

Article 94

Any measures taken within the framework of the Treaties in respect of transport rates and conditions shall take account of the economic circumstances of carriers.

Article 95

1. In the case of transport within the Union, discrimination which takes the form of carriers charging different rates and imposing different conditions for the carriage of the same goods over the same transport links on grounds of the country of origin or of destination of the goods in question shall be prohibited.
2. Paragraph 1 shall not prevent the European Parliament and the Council from adopting other measures pursuant to Article 91(1).
3. The Council shall, on a proposal from the Commission and after consulting the European Parliament and the Economic and Social Committee, lay down rules for implementing the provisions of paragraph 1.

    The Council may in particular lay down the provisions needed to enable the institutions of the Union to secure compliance with the rule laid down in paragraph 1 and to ensure that users benefit from it to the full.
4. The Commission shall, acting on its own initiative or on application by a Member State, investigate any cases of discrimination falling within paragraph 1 and, after consulting any Member State concerned, shall take the necessary decisions within the framework of the rules laid down in accordance with the provisions of paragraph 3.

Article 96

1. The imposition by a Member State, in respect of transport operations carried out within the Union, of rates and conditions involving any element of support or protection in the interest of one or more particular undertakings or industries shall be prohibited, unless authorised by the Commission.
2. The Commission shall, acting on its own initiative or on application by a Member State, examine the rates and conditions referred to in paragraph 1, taking account in particular of the requirements of an appropriate regional economic policy, the needs of underdeveloped areas and the problems of areas seriously affected by political circumstances on the one hand, and of the effects of such rates and conditions on competition between the different modes of transport on the other.

    After consulting each Member State concerned, the Commission shall take the necessary decisions.
3. The prohibition provided for in paragraph 1 shall not apply to tariffs fixed to meet competition.

Article 97

Charges or dues in respect of the crossing of frontiers which are charged by a carrier in addition to the transport rates shall not exceed a reasonable level after taking the costs actually incurred thereby into account.

Member States shall endeavour to reduce these costs progressively. The Commission may make recommendations to Member States for the application of this Article.

Article 98

The provisions of this Title shall not form an obstacle to the application of measures taken in the Federal Republic of Germany to the extent that such measures are required in order to compensate for the economic disadvantages caused by the division of Germany to the economy of certain areas of the Federal Republic affected by that division. Five years after the entry into force of the Treaty of Lisbon, the Council, acting on a proposal from the Commission, may adopt a decision repealing this Article.

Article 99

An Advisory Committee consisting of experts designated by the governments of Member States shall be attached to the Commission. The Commission, whenever it considers it desirable, shall consult the Committee on transport matters.

Article 100

1. The provisions of this Title shall apply to transport by rail, road and inland waterway.
2. The European Parliament and the Council, acting in accordance with the ordinary legislative procedure, may lay down appropriate provisions for sea and air transport. They shall act after consulting the Economic and Social Committee and the Committee of the Regions.

TITLE VII COMMON RULES ON COMPETITION, TAXATION AND APPROXIMATION OF LAWS

Chapter 1 Rules on Competition

SECTION 1 RULES APPLYING TO UNDERTAKINGS

Article 101

1. The following shall be prohibited as incompatible with the internal market: all agreements between undertakings, decisions by associations of undertakings and concerted practices which may affect trade between Member States and which have as their object or effect the prevention, restriction or distortion of competition within the internal market, and in particular those which:
   (a) directly or indirectly fix purchase or selling prices or any other trading conditions;
   (b) limit or control production, markets, technical development, or investment;
   (c) share markets or sources of supply;
   (d) apply dissimilar conditions to equivalent transactions with other trading parties, thereby placing them at a competitive disadvantage;

(e) make the conclusion of contracts subject to acceptance by the other parties of supplementary obligations which, by their nature or according to commercial usage, have no connection with the subject of such contracts.

2. Any agreements or decisions prohibited pursuant to this Article shall be automatically void.

3. The provisions of paragraph 1 may, however, be declared inapplicable in the case of:
   — any agreement or category of agreements between undertakings,
   — any decision or category of decisions by associations of undertakings,
   — any concerted practice or category of concerted practices,

   which contributes to improving the production or distribution of goods or to promoting technical or economic progress, while allowing consumers a fair share of the resulting benefit, and which does not:
   (a) impose on the undertakings concerned restrictions which are not indispensable to the attainment of these objectives;
   (b) afford such undertakings the possibility of eliminating competition in respect of a substantial part of the products in question.

Article 102

Any abuse by one or more undertakings of a dominant position within the internal market or in a substantial part of it shall be prohibited as incompatible with the internal market in so far as it may affect trade between Member States.

Such abuse may, in particular, consist in:
   (a) directly or indirectly imposing unfair purchase or selling prices or other unfair trading conditions;
   (b) limiting production, markets or technical development to the prejudice of consumers;
   (c) applying dissimilar conditions to equivalent transactions with other trading parties, thereby placing them at a competitive disadvantage;
   (d) making the conclusion of contracts subject to acceptance by the other parties of supplementary obligations which, by their nature or according to commercial usage, have no connection with the subject of such contracts.

Article 103

1. The appropriate regulations or directives to give effect to the principles set out in Articles 101 and 102 shall be laid down by the Council, on a proposal from the Commission and after consulting the European Parliament.

2. The regulations or directives referred to in paragraph 1 shall be designed in particular:
   (a) to ensure compliance with the prohibitions laid down in Article 101(1) and in Article 102 by making provision for fines and periodic penalty payments;
   (b) to lay down detailed rules for the application of Article 101(3), taking into account the need to ensure effective supervision on the one hand, and to simplify administration to the greatest possible extent on the other;
   (c) to define, if need be, in the various branches of the economy, the scope of the provisions of Articles 101 and 102;

(d) to define the respective functions of the Commission and of the Court of Justice of the European Union in applying the provisions laid down in this paragraph;

(e) to determine the relationship between national laws and the provisions contained in this Section or adopted pursuant to this Article.

Article 104

Until the entry into force of the provisions adopted in pursuance of Article 103, the authorities in Member States shall rule on the admissibility of agreements, decisions and concerted practices and on abuse of a dominant position in the internal market in accordance with the law of their country and with the provisions of Article 101, in particular paragraph 3, and of Article 102.

Article 105

1. Without prejudice to Article 104, the Commission shall ensure the application of the principles laid down in Articles 101 and 102. On application by a Member State or on its own initiative, and in cooperation with the competent authorities in the Member States, which shall give it their assistance, the Commission shall investigate cases of suspected infringement of these principles. If it finds that there has been an infringement, it shall propose appropriate measures to bring it to an end.

2. If the infringement is not brought to an end, the Commission shall record such infringement of the principles in a reasoned decision. The Commission may publish its decision and authorise Member States to take the measures, the conditions and details of which it shall determine, needed to remedy the situation.

3. The Commission may adopt regulations relating to the categories of agreement in respect of which the Council has adopted a regulation or a directive pursuant to Article 103(2)(b).

Article 106

1. In the case of public undertakings and undertakings to which Member States grant special or exclusive rights, Member States shall neither enact nor maintain in force any measure contrary to the rules contained in the Treaties, in particular to those rules provided for in Article 18 and Articles 101 to 109.

2. Undertakings entrusted with the operation of services of general economic interest or having the character of a revenue-producing monopoly shall be subject to the rules contained in the Treaties, in particular to the rules on competition, in so far as the application of such rules does not obstruct the performance, in law or in fact, of the particular tasks assigned to them. The development of trade must not be affected to such an extent as would be contrary to the interests of the Union.

3. The Commission shall ensure the application of the provisions of this Article and shall, where necessary, address appropriate directives or decisions to Member States.

SECTION 2 AIDS GRANTED BY STATES

Article 107

1. Save as otherwise provided in the Treaties, any aid granted by a Member State or through State resources in any form whatsoever which distorts or threatens to distort

competition by favouring certain undertakings or the production of certain goods shall, in so far as it affects trade between Member States, be incompatible with the internal market.

2. The following shall be compatible with the internal market:
   (a) aid having a social character, granted to individual consumers, provided that such aid is granted without discrimination related to the origin of the products concerned;
   (b) aid to make good the damage caused by natural disasters or exceptional occurrences;
   (c) aid granted to the economy of certain areas of the Federal Republic of Germany affected by the division of Germany, in so far as such aid is required in order to compensate for the economic disadvantages caused by that division. Five years after the entry into force of the Treaty of Lisbon, the Council, acting on a proposal from the Commission, may adopt a decision repealing this point.

3. The following may be considered to be compatible with the internal market:
   (a) aid to promote the economic development of areas where the standard of living is abnormally low or where there is serious underemployment, and of the regions referred to in Article 349, in view of their structural, economic and social situation;
   (b) aid to promote the execution of an important project of common European interest or to remedy a serious disturbance in the economy of a Member State;
   (c) aid to facilitate the development of certain economic activities or of certain economic areas, where such aid does not adversely affect trading conditions to an extent contrary to the common interest;
   (d) aid to promote culture and heritage conservation where such aid does not affect trading conditions and competition in the Union to an extent that is contrary to the common interest;
   (e) such other categories of aid as may be specified by decision of the Council on a proposal from the Commission.

Article 108

1. The Commission shall, in cooperation with Member States, keep under constant review all systems of aid existing in those States. It shall propose to the latter any appropriate measures required by the progressive development or by the functioning of the internal market.

2. If, after giving notice to the parties concerned to submit their comments, the Commission finds that aid granted by a State or through State resources is not compatible with the internal market having regard to Article 107, or that such aid is being misused, it shall decide that the State concerned shall abolish or alter such aid within a period of time to be determined by the Commission.

   If the State concerned does not comply with this decision within the prescribed time, the Commission or any other interested State may, in derogation from the provisions of Articles 258 and 259, refer the matter to the Court of Justice of the European Union direct.

   On application by a Member State, the Council may, acting unanimously, decide that aid which that State is granting or intends to grant shall be considered to be compatible with the internal market, in derogation from the provisions of Article 107 or from the regulations provided for in Article 109, if such a decision is justified by exceptional circumstances. If, as regards the aid in question, the Commission has already initiated the procedure provided for in the first subparagraph of this paragraph, the fact that the State concerned has made its application to the Council shall have the effect of suspending that procedure until the Council has made its attitude known.

If, however, the Council has not made its attitude known within three months of the said application being made, the Commission shall give its decision on the case.

3. The Commission shall be informed, in sufficient time to enable it to submit its comments, of any plans to grant or alter aid. If it considers that any such plan is not compatible with the internal market having regard to Article 107, it shall without delay initiate the procedure provided for in paragraph 2. The Member State concerned shall not put its proposed measures into effect until this procedure has resulted in a final decision.

4. The Commission may adopt regulations relating to the categories of State aid that the Council has, pursuant to Article 109, determined may be exempted from the procedure provided for by paragraph 3 of this Article.

Article 109

The Council, on a proposal from the Commission and after consulting the European Parliament, may make any appropriate regulations for the application of Articles 107 and 108 and may in particular determine the conditions in which Article 108(3) shall apply and the categories of aid exempted from this procedure.

Chapter 2 Tax Provisions

Article 110

No Member State shall impose, directly or indirectly, on the products of other Member States any internal taxation of any kind in excess of that imposed directly or indirectly on similar domestic products.

Furthermore, no Member State shall impose on the products of other Member States any internal taxation of such a nature as to afford indirect protection to other products.

Article 111

Where products are exported to the territory of any Member State, any repayment of internal taxation shall not exceed the internal taxation imposed on them whether directly or indirectly.

Article 112

In the case of charges other than turnover taxes, excise duties and other forms of indirect taxation, remissions and repayments in respect of exports to other Member States may not be granted and countervailing charges in respect of imports from Member States may not be imposed unless the measures contemplated have been previously approved for a limited period by the Council on a proposal from the Commission.

Article 113

The Council shall, acting unanimously in accordance with a special legislative procedure and after consulting the European Parliament and the Economic and Social Committee, adopt provisions for the harmonisation of legislation concerning turnover taxes, excise duties and other forms of indirect taxation to the extent that such harmonisation is necessary to ensure the establishment and the functioning of the internal market and to avoid distortion of competition.

Chapter 3 Approximation of Laws

Article 114

1. Save where otherwise provided in the Treaties, the following provisions shall apply for the achievement of the objectives set out in Article 26. The European Parliament and the Council shall, acting in accordance with the ordinary legislative procedure and after consulting the Economic and Social Committee, adopt the measures for the approximation of the provisions laid down by law, regulation or administrative action in Member States which have as their object the establishment and functioning of the internal market.

2. Paragraph 1 shall not apply to fiscal provisions, to those relating to the free movement of persons nor to those relating to the rights and interests of employed persons.

3. The Commission, in its proposals envisaged in paragraph 1 concerning health, safety, environmental protection and consumer protection, will take as a base a high level of protection, taking account in particular of any new development based on scientific facts. Within their respective powers, the European Parliament and the Council will also seek to achieve this objective.

4. If, after the adoption of a harmonisation measure by the European Parliament and the Council, by the Council or by the Commission, a Member State deems it necessary to maintain national provisions on grounds of major needs referred to in Article 36, or relating to the protection of the environment or the working environment, it shall notify the Commission of these provisions as well as the grounds for maintaining them.

5. Moreover, without prejudice to paragraph 4, if, after the adoption of a harmonisation measure by the European Parliament and the Council, by the Council or by the Commission, a Member State deems it necessary to introduce national provisions based on new scientific evidence relating to the protection of the environment or the working environment on grounds of a problem specific to that Member State arising after the adoption of the harmonisation measure, it shall notify the Commission of the envisaged provisions as well as the grounds for introducing them.

6. The Commission shall, within six months of the notifications as referred to in paragraphs 4 and 5, approve or reject the national provisions involved after having verified whether or not they are a means of arbitrary discrimination or a disguised restriction on trade between Member States and whether or not they shall constitute an obstacle to the functioning of the internal market.

   In the absence of a decision by the Commission within this period the national provisions referred to in paragraphs 4 and 5 shall be deemed to have been approved.

   When justified by the complexity of the matter and in the absence of danger for human health, the Commission may notify the Member State concerned that the period referred to in this paragraph may be extended for a further period of up to six months.

7. When, pursuant to paragraph 6, a Member State is authorised to maintain or introduce national provisions derogating from a harmonisation measure, the Commission shall immediately examine whether to propose an adaptation to that measure.

8. When a Member State raises a specific problem on public health in a field which has been the subject of prior harmonisation measures, it shall bring it to the attention of the Commission which shall immediately examine whether to propose appropriate measures to the Council.

9. By way of derogation from the procedure laid down in Articles 258 and 259, the Commission and any Member State may bring the matter directly before the Court of Justice of the European Union if it considers that another Member State is making improper use of the powers provided for in this Article.

10. The harmonisation measures referred to above shall, in appropriate cases, include a safeguard clause authorising the Member States to take, for one or more of the non-economic reasons referred to in Article 36, provisional measures subject to a Union control procedure.

Article 115

Without prejudice to Article 114, the Council shall, acting unanimously in accordance with a special legislative procedure and after consulting the European Parliament and the Economic and Social Committee, issue directives for the approximation of such laws, regulations or administrative provisions of the Member States as directly affect the establishment or functioning of the internal market.

Article 116

Where the Commission finds that a difference between the provisions laid down by law, regulation or administrative action in Member States is distorting the conditions of competition in the internal market and that the resultant distortion needs to be eliminated, it shall consult the Member States concerned.

If such consultation does not result in an agreement eliminating the distortion in question, the European Parliament and the Council, acting in accordance with the ordinary legislative procedure, shall issue the necessary directives. Any other appropriate measures provided for in the Treaties may be adopted.

Article 117

1. Where there is a reason to fear that the adoption or amendment of a provision laid down by law, regulation or administrative action may cause distortion within the meaning of Article 116, a Member State desiring to proceed therewith shall consult the Commission. After consulting the Member States, the Commission shall recommend to the States concerned such measures as may be appropriate to avoid the distortion in question.

2. If a State desiring to introduce or amend its own provisions does not comply with the recommendation addressed to it by the Commission, other Member States shall not be required, pursuant to Article 116, to amend their own provisions in order to eliminate such distortion. If the Member State which has ignored the recommendation of the Commission causes distortion detrimental only to itself, the provisions of Article 116 shall not apply.

Article 118

In the context of the establishment and functioning of the internal market, the European Parliament and the Council, acting in accordance with the ordinary legislative procedure, shall establish measures for the creation of European intellectual property rights to provide uniform protection of intellectual property rights throughout the Union and for the setting up of centralised Union-wide authorisation, coordination and supervision arrangements.

The Council, acting in accordance with a special legislative procedure, shall by means of regulations establish language arrangements for the European intellectual property rights. The Council shall act unanimously after consulting the European Parliament.

TITLE VIII ECONOMIC AND MONETARY POLICY

Article 119

1. For the purposes set out in Article 3 of the Treaty on European Union, the activities of the Member States and the Union shall include, as provided in the Treaties, the adoption of an economic policy which is based on the close coordination of Member States' economic policies, on the internal market and on the definition of common objectives, and conducted in accordance with the principle of an open market economy with free competition.
2. Concurrently with the foregoing, and as provided in the Treaties and in accordance with the procedures set out therein, these activities shall include a single currency, the euro, and the definition and conduct of a single monetary policy and exchange-rate policy the primary objective of both of which shall be to maintain price stability and, without prejudice to this objective, to support the general economic policies in the Union, in accordance with the principle of an open market economy with free competition.
3. These activities of the Member States and the Union shall entail compliance with the following guiding principles: stable prices, sound public finances and monetary conditions and a sustainable balance of payments.

Chapter 1 Economic Policy

Article 120

Member States shall conduct their economic policies with a view to contributing to the achievement of the objectives of the Union, as defined in Article 3 of the Treaty on European Union, and in the context of the broad guidelines referred to in Article 121(2). The Member States and the Union shall act in accordance with the principle of an open market economy with free competition, favouring an efficient allocation of resources, and in compliance with the principles set out in Article 119.

Article 121

1. Member States shall regard their economic policies as a matter of common concern and shall coordinate them within the Council, in accordance with the provisions of Article 120.
2. The Council shall, on a recommendation from the Commission, formulate a draft for the broad guidelines of the economic policies of the Member States and of the Union, and shall report its findings to the European Council.

    The European Council shall, acting on the basis of the report from the Council, discuss a conclusion on the broad guidelines of the economic policies of the Member States and of the Union.

On the basis of this conclusion, the Council shall adopt a recommendation setting out these broad guidelines. The Council shall inform the European Parliament of its recommendation.

3. In order to ensure closer coordination of economic policies and sustained convergence of the economic performances of the Member States, the Council shall, on the basis of reports submitted by the Commission, monitor economic developments in each of the Member States and in the Union as well as the consistency of economic policies with the broad guidelines referred to in paragraph 2, and regularly carry out an overall assessment.

   For the purpose of this multilateral surveillance, Member States shall forward information to the Commission about important measures taken by them in the field of their economic policy and such other information as they deem necessary.

4. Where it is established, under the procedure referred to in paragraph 3, that the economic policies of a Member State are not consistent with the broad guidelines referred to in paragraph 2 or that they risk jeopardising the proper functioning of economic and monetary union, the Commission may address a warning to the Member State concerned. The Council, on a recommendation from the Commission, may address the necessary recommendations to the Member State concerned. The Council may, on a proposal from the Commission, decide to make its recommendations public.

   Within the scope of this paragraph, the Council shall act without taking into account the vote of the member of the Council representing the Member State concerned.

   A qualified majority of the other members of the Council shall be defined in accordance with Article 238(3)(a).

5. The President of the Council and the Commission shall report to the European Parliament on the results of multilateral surveillance. The President of the Council may be invited to appear before the competent committee of the European Parliament if the Council has made its recommendations public.

6. The European Parliament and the Council, acting by means of regulations in accordance with the ordinary legislative procedure, may adopt detailed rules for the multilateral surveillance procedure referred to in paragraphs 3 and 4.

Article 122

1. Without prejudice to any other procedures provided for in the Treaties, the Council, on a proposal from the Commission, may decide, in a spirit of solidarity between Member States, upon the measures appropriate to the economic situation, in particular if severe difficulties arise in the supply of certain products, notably in the area of energy.

2. Where a Member State is in difficulties or is seriously threatened with severe difficulties caused by natural disasters or exceptional occurrences beyond its control, the Council, on a proposal from the Commission, may grant, under certain conditions, Union financial assistance to the Member State concerned. The President of the Council shall inform the European Parliament of the decision taken.

Article 123

1. Overdraft facilities or any other type of credit facility with the European Central Bank or with the central banks of the Member States (hereinafter referred to as 'national central banks') in favour of Union institutions, bodies, offices or agencies, central governments,

regional, local or other public authorities, other bodies governed by public law, or public undertakings of Member States shall be prohibited, as shall the purchase directly from them by the European Central Bank or national central banks of debt instruments.

2. Paragraph 1 shall not apply to publicly owned credit institutions which, in the context of the supply of reserves by central banks, shall be given the same treatment by national central banks and the European Central Bank as private credit institutions.

Article 124

Any measure, not based on prudential considerations, establishing privileged access by Union institutions, bodies, offices or agencies, central governments, regional, local or other public authorities, other bodies governed by public law, or public undertakings of Member States to financial institutions, shall be prohibited.

Article 125

1. The Union shall not be liable for or assume the commitments of central governments, regional, local or other public authorities, other bodies governed by public law, or public undertakings of any Member State, without prejudice to mutual financial guarantees for the joint execution of a specific project. A Member State shall not be liable for or assume the commitments of central governments, regional, local or other public authorities, other bodies governed by public law, or public undertakings of another Member State, without prejudice to mutual financial guarantees for the joint execution of a specific project.

2. The Council, on a proposal from the Commission and after consulting the European Parliament, may, as required, specify definitions for the application of the prohibitions referred to in Articles 123 and 124 and in this Article.

Article 126

1. Member States shall avoid excessive government deficits.

2. The Commission shall monitor the development of the budgetary situation and of the stock of government debt in the Member States with a view to identifying gross errors. In particular it shall examine compliance with budgetary discipline on the basis of the following two criteria:

   (a) whether the ratio of the planned or actual government deficit to gross domestic product exceeds a reference value, unless:

   — either the ratio has declined substantially and continuously and reached a level that comes close to the reference value,

   — or, alternatively, the excess over the reference value is only exceptional and temporary and the ratio remains close to the reference value;

   (b) whether the ratio of government debt to gross domestic product exceeds a reference value, unless the ratio is sufficiently diminishing and approaching the reference value at a satisfactory pace.

   The reference values are specified in the Protocol on the excessive deficit procedure annexed to the Treaties.

3. If a Member State does not fulfil the requirements under one or both of these criteria, the Commission shall prepare a report. The report of the Commission shall also take into account whether the government deficit exceeds government investment expenditure

and take into account all other relevant factors, including the medium-term economic and budgetary position of the Member State.

The Commission may also prepare a report if, notwithstanding the fulfilment of the requirements under the criteria, it is of the opinion that there is a risk of an excessive deficit in a Member State.

4. The Economic and Financial Committee shall formulate an opinion on the report of the Commission.

5. If the Commission considers that an excessive deficit in a Member State exists or may occur, it shall address an opinion to the Member State concerned and shall inform the Council accordingly.

6. The Council shall, on a proposal from the Commission, and having considered any observations which the Member State concerned may wish to make, decide after an overall assessment whether an excessive deficit exists.

7. Where the Council decides, in accordance with paragraph 6, that an excessive deficit exists, it shall adopt, without undue delay, on a recommendation from the Commission, recommendations addressed to the Member State concerned with a view to bringing that situation to an end within a given period. Subject to the provisions of paragraph 8, these recommendations shall not be made public.

8. Where it establishes that there has been no effective action in response to its recommendations within the period laid down, the Council may make its recommendations public.

9. If a Member State persists in failing to put into practice the recommendations of the Council, the Council may decide to give notice to the Member State to take, within a specified time limit, measures for the deficit reduction which is judged necessary by the Council in order to remedy the situation.

In such a case, the Council may request the Member State concerned to submit reports in accordance with a specific timetable in order to examine the adjustment efforts of that Member State.

10. The rights to bring actions provided for in Articles 258 and 259 may not be exercised within the framework of paragraphs 1 to 9 of this Article.

11. As long as a Member State fails to comply with a decision taken in accordance with paragraph 9, the Council may decide to apply or, as the case may be, intensify one or more of the following measures:

— to require the Member State concerned to publish additional information, to be specified by the Council, before issuing bonds and securities,

— to invite the European Investment Bank to reconsider its lending policy towards the Member State concerned,

— to require the Member State concerned to make a non-interest-bearing deposit of an appropriate size with the Union until the excessive deficit has, in the view of the Council, been corrected,

— to impose fines of an appropriate size. The President of the Council shall inform the European Parliament of the decisions taken.

12. The Council shall abrogate some or all of its decisions or recommendations referred to in paragraphs 6 to 9 and 11 to the extent that the excessive deficit in the Member State concerned has, in the view of the Council, been corrected. If the Council has previously made public recommendations, it shall, as soon as the decision under

paragraph 8 has been abrogated, make a public statement that an excessive deficit in the Member State concerned no longer exists.

13. When taking the decisions or recommendations referred to in paragraphs 8, 9, 11 and 12, the Council shall act on a recommendation from the Commission.

When the Council adopts the measures referred to in paragraphs 6 to 9, 11 and 12, it shall act without taking into account the vote of the member of the Council representing the Member State concerned.

A qualified majority of the other members of the Council shall be defined in accordance with Article 238(3)(a).

14. Further provisions relating to the implementation of the procedure described in this Article are set out in the Protocol on the excessive deficit procedure annexed to the Treaties.

The Council shall, acting unanimously in accordance with a special legislative procedure and after consulting the European Parliament and the European Central Bank, adopt the appropriate provisions which shall then replace the said Protocol.

Subject to the other provisions of this paragraph, the Council shall, on a proposal from the Commission and after consulting the European Parliament, lay down detailed rules and definitions for the application of the provisions of the said Protocol.

Chapter 2 Monetary Policy

Article 127

1. The primary objective of the European System of Central Banks (hereinafter referred to as 'the ESCB') shall be to maintain price stability. Without prejudice to the objective of price stability, the ESCB shall support the general economic policies in the Union with a view to contributing to the achievement of the objectives of the Union as laid down in Article 3 of the Treaty on European Union. The ESCB shall act in accordance with the principle of an open market economy with free competition, favouring an efficient allocation of resources, and in compliance with the principles set out in Article 119.

2. The basic tasks to be carried out through the ESCB shall be:
   — to define and implement the monetary policy of the Union,
   — to conduct foreign-exchange operations consistent with the provisions of Article 219,
   — to hold and manage the official foreign reserves of the Member States,
   — to promote the smooth operation of payment systems.

3. The third indent of paragraph 2 shall be without prejudice to the holding and management by the governments of Member States of foreign-exchange working balances.

4. The European Central Bank shall be consulted:
   — on any proposed Union act in its fields of competence,
   — by national authorities regarding any draft legislative provision in its fields of competence, but within the limits and under the conditions set out by the Council in accordance with the procedure laid down in Article 129(4).

The European Central Bank may submit opinions to the appropriate Union institutions, bodies, offices or agencies or to national authorities on matters in its fields of competence.

5. The ESCB shall contribute to the smooth conduct of policies pursued by the competent authorities relating to the prudential supervision of credit institutions and the stability of the financial system.

6. The Council, acting by means of regulations in accordance with a special legislative procedure, may unanimously, and after consulting the European Parliament and the European Central Bank, confer specific tasks upon the European Central Bank concerning policies relating to the prudential supervision of credit institutions and other financial institutions with the exception of insurance undertakings.

Article 128

1. The European Central Bank shall have the exclusive right to authorise the issue of euro banknotes within the Union. The European Central Bank and the national central banks may issue such notes. The banknotes issued by the European Central Bank and the national central banks shall be the only such notes to have the status of legal tender within the Union.

2. Member States may issue euro coins subject to approval by the European Central Bank of the volume of the issue. The Council, on a proposal from the Commission and after consulting the European Parliament and the European Central Bank, may adopt measures to harmonise the denominations and technical specifications of all coins intended for circulation to the extent necessary to permit their smooth circulation within the Union.

Article 129

1. The ESCB shall be governed by the decision-making bodies of the European Central Bank which shall be the Governing Council and the Executive Board.

2. The Statute of the European System of Central Banks and of the European Central Bank (hereinafter referred to as 'the Statute of the ESCB and of the ECB') is laid down in a Protocol annexed to the Treaties.

3. Articles 5.1, 5.2, 5.3, 17, 18, 19.1, 22, 23, 24, 26, 32.2, 32.3, 32.4, 32.6, 33.1(a) and 36 of the Statute of the ESCB and of the ECB may be amended by the European Parliament and the Council, acting in accordance with the ordinary legislative procedure. They shall act either on a recommendation from the European Central Bank and after consulting the Commission or on a proposal from the Commission and after consulting the European Central Bank.

4. The Council, either on a proposal from the Commission and after consulting the European Parliament and the European Central Bank or on a recommendation from the European Central Bank and after consulting the European Parliament and the Commission, shall adopt the provisions referred to in Articles 4, 5.4, 19.2, 20, 28.1, 29.2, 30.4 and 34.3 of the Statute of the ESCB and of the ECB.

Article 130

When exercising the powers and carrying out the tasks and duties conferred upon them by the Treaties and the Statute of the ESCB and of the ECB, neither the European Central Bank, nor a national central bank, nor any member of their decision-making bodies shall seek or take instructions from Union institutions, bodies, offices or agencies, from any government of a Member State or from any other body. The Union institutions, bodies, offices or agencies and the governments of the Member States undertake to respect this principle and not to seek to influence the members of the decision-making bodies of the European Central Bank or of the national central banks in the performance of their tasks.

Article 131

Each Member State shall ensure that its national legislation including the statutes of its national central bank is compatible with the Treaties and the Statute of the ESCB and of the ECB.

Article 132

1. In order to carry out the tasks entrusted to the ESCB, the European Central Bank shall, in accordance with the provisions of the Treaties and under the conditions laid down in the Statute of the ESCB and of the ECB:
   — make regulations to the extent necessary to implement the tasks defined in Article 3.1, first indent, Articles 19.1, 22 and 25.2 of the Statute of the ESCB and of the ECB in cases which shall be laid down in the acts of the Council referred to in Article 129(4),
   — take decisions necessary for carrying out the tasks entrusted to the ESCB under the Treaties and the Statute of the ESCB and of the ECB,
   — make recommendations and deliver opinions.
2. The European Central Bank may decide to publish its decisions, recommendations and opinions.
3. Within the limits and under the conditions adopted by the Council under the procedure laid down in Article 129(4), the European Central Bank shall be entitled to impose fines or periodic penalty payments on undertakings for failure to comply with obligations under its regulations and decisions.

Article 133

Without prejudice to the powers of the European Central Bank, the European Parliament and the Council, acting in accordance with the ordinary legislative procedure, shall lay down the measures necessary for the use of the euro as the single currency. Such measures shall be adopted after consultation of the European Central Bank.

Chapter 3 Institutional Provisions

Article 134

1. In order to promote coordination of the policies of Member States to the full extent needed for the functioning of the internal market, an Economic and Financial Committee is hereby set up.
2. The Economic and Financial Committee shall have the following tasks:
   — to deliver opinions at the request of the Council or of the Commission, or on its own initiative for submission to those institutions,
   — to keep under review the economic and financial situation of the Member States and of the Union and to report regularly thereon to the Council and to the Commission, in particular on financial relations with third countries and international institutions,

— without prejudice to Article 240, to contribute to the preparation of the work of the Council referred to in Articles 66, 75, 121(2), (3), (4) and (6), 122, 124, 125, 126, 127(6), 128(2), 129(3) and (4), 138, 140(2) and (3), 143, 144(2) and (3), and in Article 219, and to carry out other advisory and preparatory tasks assigned to it by the Council,

— to examine, at least once a year, the situation regarding the movement of capital and the freedom of payments, as they result from the application of the Treaties and of measures adopted by the Council; the examination shall cover all measures relating to capital movements and payments; the Committee shall report to the Commission and to the Council on the outcome of this examination.

The Member States, the Commission and the European Central Bank shall each appoint no more than two members of the Committee.

3. The Council shall, on a proposal from the Commission and after consulting the European Central Bank and the Committee referred to in this Article, lay down detailed provisions concerning the composition of the Economic and Financial Committee. The President of the Council shall inform the European Parliament of such a decision.

4. In addition to the tasks set out in paragraph 2, if and as long as there are Member States with a derogation as referred to in Article 139, the Committee shall keep under review the monetary and financial situation and the general payments system of those Member States and report regularly thereon to the Council and to the Commission.

Article 135

For matters within the scope of Articles 121(4), 126 with the exception of paragraph 14, 138, 140(1), 140(2), first subparagraph, 140(3) and 219, the Council or a Member State may request the Commission to make a recommendation or a proposal, as appropriate. The Commission shall examine this request and submit its conclusions to the Council without delay.

Chapter 4 Provisions Specific to Member States Whose Currency is the Euro

Article 136

1. In order to ensure the proper functioning of economic and monetary union, and in accordance with the relevant provisions of the Treaties, the Council shall, in accordance with the relevant procedure from among those referred to in Articles 121 and 126, with the exception of the procedure set out in Article 126(14), adopt measures specific to those Member States whose currency is the euro:
   (a) to strengthen the coordination and surveillance of their budgetary discipline;
   (b) to set out economic policy guidelines for them, while ensuring that they are compatible with those adopted for the whole of the Union and are kept under surveillance.

2. For those measures set out in paragraph 1, only members of the Council representing Member States whose currency is the euro shall take part in the vote.

   A qualified majority of the said members shall be defined in accordance with Article 238(3)(a).

3. The Member States whose currency is the euro may establish a stability mechanism to be activated if indispensable to safeguard the stability of the euro area as a whole. The granting of any required financial assistance under the mechanism will be made subject to strict conditionality.

Article 137

Arrangements for meetings between ministers of those Member States whose currency is the euro are laid down by the Protocol on the Euro Group.

Article 138

1. In order to secure the euro's place in the international monetary system, the Council, on a proposal from the Commission, shall adopt a decision establishing common positions on matters of particular interest for economic and monetary union within the competent international financial institutions and conferences. The Council shall act after consulting the European Central Bank.
2. The Council, on a proposal from the Commission, may adopt appropriate measures to ensure unified representation within the international financial institutions and conferences. The Council shall act after consulting the European Central Bank.
3. For the measures referred to in paragraphs 1 and 2, only members of the Council representing Member States whose currency is the euro shall take part in the vote.

    A qualified majority of the said members shall be defined in accordance with Article 238(3)(a).

Chapter 5 Transitional Provisions

Article 139

1. Member States in respect of which the Council has not decided that they fulfil the necessary conditions for the adoption of the euro shall hereinafter be referred to as "Member States with a derogation".
2. The following provisions of the Treaties shall not apply to Member States with a derogation:
    (a) adoption of the parts of the broad economic policy guidelines which concern the euro area generally (Article 121(2));
    (b) coercive means of remedying excessive deficits (Article 126(9) and (11));
    (c) the objectives and tasks of the ESCB (Article 127(1) to (3) and (5));
    (d) issue of the euro (Article 128);
    (e) acts of the European Central Bank (Article 132);
    (f) measures governing the use of the euro (Article 133);
    (g) monetary agreements and other measures relating to exchange-rate policy (Article 219);
    (h) appointment of members of the Executive Board of the European Central Bank (Article 283(2));
    (i) decisions establishing common positions on issues of particular relevance for economic and monetary union within the competent international financial institutions and conferences (Article 138(1));
    (j) measures to ensure unified representation within the international financial institutions and conferences (Article 138(2)).

    In the Articles referred to in points (a) to (j), "Member States" shall therefore mean Member States whose currency is the euro.
3. Under Chapter IX of the Statute of the ESCB and of the ECB, Member States with a derogation and their national central banks are excluded from rights and obligations within the ESCB.

4. The voting rights of members of the Council representing Member States with a derogation shall be suspended for the adoption by the Council of the measures referred to in the Articles listed in paragraph 2, and in the following instances:

   (a) recommendations made to those Member States whose currency is the euro in the framework of multilateral surveillance, including on stability programmes and warnings (Article 121(4));

   (b) measures relating to excessive deficits concerning those Member States whose currency is the euro (Article 126(6), (7), (8), (12) and (13)).

A qualified majority of the other members of the Council shall be defined in accordance with Article 238(3)(a).

Article 140

1. At least once every two years, or at the request of a Member State with a derogation, the Commission and the European Central Bank shall report to the Council on the progress made by the Member States with a derogation in fulfilling their obligations regarding the achievement of economic and monetary union. These reports shall include an examination of the compatibility between the national legislation of each of these Member States, including the statutes of its national central bank, and Articles 130 and 131 and the Statute of the ESCB and of the ECB. The reports shall also examine the achievement of a high degree of sustainable convergence by reference to the fulfilment by each Member State of the following criteria:

— the achievement of a high degree of price stability; this will be apparent from a rate of inflation which is close to that of, at most, the three best performing Member States in terms of price stability,

— the sustainability of the government financial position; this will be apparent from having achieved a government budgetary position without a deficit that is excessive as determined in accordance with Article 126(6),

— the observance of the normal fluctuation margins provided for by the exchange-rate mechanism of the European Monetary System, for at least two years, without devaluing against the euro,

— the durability of convergence achieved by the Member State with a derogation and of its participation in the exchange-rate mechanism being reflected in the long-term interest-rate levels.

The four criteria mentioned in this paragraph and the relevant periods over which they are to be respected are developed further in a Protocol annexed to the Treaties. The reports of the Commission and the European Central Bank shall also take account of the results of the integration of markets, the situation and development of the balances of payments on current account and an examination of the development of unit labour costs and other price indices.

2. After consulting the European Parliament and after discussion in the European Council, the Council shall, on a proposal from the Commission, decide which Member States with a derogation fulfil the necessary conditions on the basis of the criteria set out in paragraph 1, and abrogate the derogations of the Member States concerned.

The Council shall act having received a recommendation of a qualified majority of those among its members representing Member States whose currency is the euro. These members shall act within six months of the Council receiving the Commission's proposal.

The qualified majority of the said members, as referred to in the second subparagraph, shall be defined in accordance with Article 238(3)(a).

3. If it is decided, in accordance with the procedure set out in paragraph 2, to abrogate a derogation, the Council shall, acting with the unanimity of the Member States whose currency is the euro and the Member State concerned, on a proposal from the Commission and after consulting the European Central Bank, irrevocably fix the rate at which the euro shall be substituted for the currency of the Member State concerned, and take the other measures necessary for the introduction of the euro as the single currency in the Member State concerned.

Article 141

1. If and as long as there are Member States with a derogation, and without prejudice to Article 129(1), the General Council of the European Central Bank referred to in Article 44 of the Statute of the ESCB and of the ECB shall be constituted as a third decision-making body of the European Central Bank.

2. If and as long as there are Member States with a derogation, the European Central Bank shall, as regards those Member States:
   — strengthen cooperation between the national central banks,
   — strengthen the coordination of the monetary policies of the Member States, with the aim of ensuring price stability,
   — monitor the functioning of the exchange-rate mechanism,
   — hold consultations concerning issues falling within the competence of the national central banks and affecting the stability of financial institutions and markets,
   — carry out the former tasks of the European Monetary Cooperation Fund which had subsequently been taken over by the European Monetary Institute.

Article 142

Each Member State with a derogation shall treat its exchange-rate policy as a matter of common interest. In so doing, Member States shall take account of the experience acquired in cooperation within the framework of the exchange-rate mechanism.

Article 143

1. Where a Member State with a derogation is in difficulties or is seriously threatened with difficulties as regards its balance of payments either as a result of an overall disequilibrium in its balance of payments, or as a result of the type of currency at its disposal, and where such difficulties are liable in particular to jeopardise the functioning of the internal market or the implementation of the common commercial policy, the Commission shall immediately investigate the position of the State in question and the action which, making use of all the means at its disposal, that State has taken or may take in accordance with the provisions of the Treaties. The Commission shall state what measures it recommends the State concerned to take.

   If the action taken by a Member State with a derogation and the measures suggested by the Commission do not prove sufficient to overcome the difficulties which have arisen or which threaten, the Commission shall, after consulting the Economic and Financial Committee, recommend to the Council the granting of mutual assistance and appropriate methods therefor.

The Commission shall keep the Council regularly informed of the situation and of how it is developing.

2. The Council shall grant such mutual assistance; it shall adopt directives or decisions laying down the conditions and details of such assistance, which may take such forms as:

(a) a concerted approach to or within any other international organisations to which Member States with a derogation may have recourse;

(b) measures needed to avoid deflection of trade where the Member State with a derogation which is in difficulties maintains or reintroduces quantitative restrictions against third countries;

(c) the granting of limited credits by other Member States, subject to their agreement.

3. If the mutual assistance recommended by the Commission is not granted by the Council or if the mutual assistance granted and the measures taken are insufficient, the Commission shall authorise the Member State with a derogation which is in difficulties to take protective measures, the conditions and details of which the Commission shall determine.

Such authorisation may be revoked and such conditions and details may be changed by the Council.

Article 144

1. Where a sudden crisis in the balance of payments occurs and a decision within the meaning of Article 143(2) is not immediately taken, a Member State with a derogation may, as a precaution, take the necessary protective measures. Such measures must cause the least possible disturbance in the functioning of the internal market and must not be wider in scope than is strictly necessary to remedy the sudden difficulties which have arisen.

2. The Commission and the other Member States shall be informed of such protective measures not later than when they enter into force. The Commission may recommend to the Council the granting of mutual assistance under Article 143.

3. After the Commission has delivered a recommendation and the Economic and Financial Committee has been consulted, the Council may decide that the Member State concerned shall amend, suspend or abolish the protective measures referred to above.

TITLE IX EMPLOYMENT

Article 145

Member States and the Union shall, in accordance with this Title, work towards developing a coordinated strategy for employment and particularly for promoting a skilled, trained and adaptable workforce and labour markets responsive to economic change with a view to achieving the objectives defined in Article 3 of the Treaty on European Union.

Article 146

1. Member States, through their employment policies, shall contribute to the achievement of the objectives referred to in Article 145 in a way consistent with the broad guidelines of the economic policies of the Member States and of the Union adopted pursuant to Article 121(2).

2. Member States, having regard to national practices related to the responsibilities of management and labour, shall regard promoting employment as a matter of common concern and shall coordinate their action in this respect within the Council, in accordance with the provisions of Article 148.

Article 147

1. The Union shall contribute to a high level of employment by encouraging cooperation between Member States and by supporting and, if necessary, complementing their action. In doing so, the competences of the Member States shall be respected.
2. The objective of a high level of employment shall be taken into consideration in the formulation and implementation of Union policies and activities.

Article 148

1. The European Council shall each year consider the employment situation in the Union and adopt conclusions thereon, on the basis of a joint annual report by the Council and the Commission.
2. On the basis of the conclusions of the European Council, the Council, on a proposal from the Commission and after consulting the European Parliament, the Economic and Social Committee, the Committee of the Regions and the Employment Committee referred to in Article 150, shall each year draw up guidelines which the Member States shall take into account in their employment policies. These guidelines shall be consistent with the broad guidelines adopted pursuant to Article 121(2).
3. Each Member State shall provide the Council and the Commission with an annual report on the principal measures taken to implement its employment policy in the light of the guidelines for employment as referred to in paragraph 2.
4. The Council, on the basis of the reports referred to in paragraph 3 and having received the views of the Employment Committee, shall each year carry out an examination of the implementation of the employment policies of the Member States in the light of the guidelines for employment. The Council, on a recommendation from the Commission, may, if it considers it appropriate in the light of that examination, make recommendations to Member States.
5. On the basis of the results of that examination, the Council and the Commission shall make a joint annual report to the European Council on the employment situation in the Union and on the implementation of the guidelines for employment.

Article 149

The European Parliament and the Council, acting in accordance with the ordinary legislative procedure and after consulting the Economic and Social Committee and the Committee of the Regions, may adopt incentive measures designed to encourage cooperation between Member States and to support their action in the field of employment through initiatives aimed at developing exchanges of information and best practices, providing comparative analysis and advice as well as promoting innovative approaches and evaluating experiences, in particular by recourse to pilot projects.

Those measures shall not include harmonisation of the laws and regulations of the Member States.

Article 150

The Council, acting by a simple majority after consulting the European Parliament, shall establish an Employment Committee with advisory status to promote coordination between Member States on employment and labour market policies. The tasks of the Committee shall be:

— to monitor the employment situation and employment policies in the Member States and the Union,

— without prejudice to Article 240, to formulate opinions at the request of either the Council or the Commission or on its own initiative, and to contribute to the preparation of the Council proceedings referred to in Article 148.

In fulfilling its mandate, the Committee shall consult management and labour.

Each Member State and the Commission shall appoint two members of the Committee.

TITLE X SOCIAL POLICY

Article 151

The Union and the Member States, having in mind fundamental social rights such as those set out in the European Social Charter signed at Turin on 18 October 1961 and in the 1989 Community Charter of the Fundamental Social Rights of Workers, shall have as their objectives the promotion of employment, improved living and working conditions, so as to make possible their harmonisation while the improvement is being maintained, proper social protection, dialogue between management and labour, the development of human resources with a view to lasting high employment and the combating of exclusion.

To this end the Union and the Member States shall implement measures which take account of the diverse forms of national practices, in particular in the field of contractual relations, and the need to maintain the competitiveness of the Union economy.

They believe that such a development will ensue not only from the functioning of the internal market, which will favour the harmonisation of social systems, but also from the procedures provided for in the Treaties and from the approximation of provisions laid down by law, regulation or administrative action.

Article 152

The Union recognises and promotes the role of the social partners at its level, taking into account the diversity of national systems. It shall facilitate dialogue between the social partners, respecting their autonomy.

The Tripartite Social Summit for Growth and Employment shall contribute to social dialogue.

Article 153

1. With a view to achieving the objectives of Article 151, the Union shall support and complement the activities of the Member States in the following fields:

   (a) improvement in particular of the working environment to protect workers' health and safety;

   (b) working conditions;

   (c) social security and social protection of workers;

   (d) protection of workers where their employment contract is terminated;

(e) the information and consultation of workers;

(f) representation and collective defence of the interests of workers and employers, including co-determination, subject to paragraph 5;

(g) conditions of employment for third-country nationals legally residing in Union territory;

(h) the integration of persons excluded from the labour market, without prejudice to Article 166;

(i) equality between men and women with regard to labour market opportunities and treatment at work;

(j) the combating of social exclusion;

(k) the modernisation of social protection systems without prejudice to point (c).

2. To this end, the European Parliament and the Council:

(a) may adopt measures designed to encourage cooperation between Member States through initiatives aimed at improving knowledge, developing exchanges of information and best practices, promoting innovative approaches and evaluating experiences, excluding any harmonisation of the laws and regulations of the Member States;

(b) may adopt, in the fields referred to in paragraph 1(a) to (i), by means of directives, minimum requirements for gradual implementation, having regard to the conditions and technical rules obtaining in each of the Member States. Such directives shall avoid imposing administrative, financial and legal constraints in a way which would hold back the creation and development of small and medium-sized undertakings.

The European Parliament and the Council shall act in accordance with the ordinary legislative procedure after consulting the Economic and Social Committee and the Committee of the Regions.

In the fields referred to in paragraph 1(c), (d), (f) and (g), the Council shall act unanimously, in accordance with a special legislative procedure, after consulting the European Parliament and the said Committees.

The Council, acting unanimously on a proposal from the Commission, after consulting the European Parliament, may decide to render the ordinary legislative procedure applicable to paragraph 1(d), (f) and (g).

3. A Member State may entrust management and labour, at their joint request, with the implementation of directives adopted pursuant to paragraph 2, or, where appropriate, with the implementation of a Council decision adopted in accordance with Article 155.

In this case, it shall ensure that, no later than the date on which a directive or a decision must be transposed or implemented, management and labour have introduced the necessary measures by agreement, the Member State concerned being required to take any necessary measure enabling it at any time to be in a position to guarantee the results imposed by that directive or that decision.

4. The provisions adopted pursuant to this Article:

— shall not affect the right of Member States to define the fundamental principles of their social security systems and must not significantly affect the financial equilibrium thereof,

— shall not prevent any Member State from maintaining or introducing more stringent protective measures compatible with the Treaties.

5. The provisions of this Article shall not apply to pay, the right of association, the right to strike or the right to impose lock-outs.

Article 154

1. The Commission shall have the task of promoting the consultation of management and labour at Union level and shall take any relevant measure to facilitate their dialogue by ensuring balanced support for the parties.
2. To this end, before submitting proposals in the social policy field, the Commission shall consult management and labour on the possible direction of Union action.
3. If, after such consultation, the Commission considers Union action advisable, it shall consult management and labour on the content of the envisaged proposal. Management and labour shall forward to the Commission an opinion or, where appropriate, a recommendation.
4. On the occasion of the consultation referred to in paragraphs 2 and 3, management and labour may inform the Commission of their wish to initiate the process provided for in Article 155. The duration of this process shall not exceed nine months, unless the management and labour concerned and the Commission decide jointly to extend it.

Article 155

1. Should management and labour so desire, the dialogue between them at Union level may lead to contractual relations, including agreements.
2. Agreements concluded at Union level shall be implemented either in accordance with the procedures and practices specific to management and labour and the Member States or, in matters covered by Article 153, at the joint request of the signatory parties, by a Council decision on a proposal from the Commission. The European Parliament shall be informed.

    The Council shall act unanimously where the agreement in question contains one or more provisions relating to one of the areas for which unanimity is required pursuant to Article 153(2).

Article 156

With a view to achieving the objectives of Article 151 and without prejudice to the other provisions of the Treaties, the Commission shall encourage cooperation between the Member States and facilitate the coordination of their action in all social policy fields under this Chapter, particularly in matters relating to:

— employment,
— labour law and working conditions,
— basic and advanced vocational training,
— social security,
— prevention of occupational accidents and diseases,
— occupational hygiene,
— the right of association and collective bargaining between employers and workers.

To this end, the Commission shall act in close contact with Member States by making studies, delivering opinions and arranging consultations both on problems arising at national level and on those of concern to international organisations, in particular initiatives aiming at the establishment of guidelines and indicators, the organisation of exchange of best practice, and the preparation of the necessary elements for periodic monitoring and evaluation. The European Parliament shall be kept fully informed.

Before delivering the opinions provided for in this Article, the Commission shall consult the Economic and Social Committee.

Article 157

1. Each Member State shall ensure that the principle of equal pay for male and female workers for equal work or work of equal value is applied.
2. For the purpose of this Article, "pay" means the ordinary basic or minimum wage or salary and any other consideration, whether in cash or in kind, which the worker receives directly or indirectly, in respect of his employment, from his employer.

    Equal pay without discrimination based on sex means:
    (a) that pay for the same work at piece rates shall be calculated on the basis of the same unit of measurement;
    (b) that pay for work at time rates shall be the same for the same job.
3. The European Parliament and the Council, acting in accordance with the ordinary legislative procedure, and after consulting the Economic and Social Committee, shall adopt measures to ensure the application of the principle of equal opportunities and equal treatment of men and women in matters of employment and occupation, including the principle of equal pay for equal work or work of equal value.
4. With a view to ensuring full equality in practice between men and women in working life, the principle of equal treatment shall not prevent any Member State from maintaining or adopting measures providing for specific advantages in order to make it easier for the underrepresented sex to pursue a vocational activity or to prevent or compensate for disadvantages in professional careers.

Article 158

Member States shall endeavour to maintain the existing equivalence between paid holiday schemes.

Article 159

The Commission shall draw up a report each year on progress in achieving the objectives of Article 151, including the demographic situation in the Union. It shall forward the report to the European Parliament, the Council and the Economic and Social Committee.

Article 160

The Council, acting by a simple majority after consulting the European Parliament, shall establish a Social Protection Committee with advisory status to promote cooperation on social protection policies between Member States and with the Commission. The tasks of the Committee shall be:

— to monitor the social situation and the development of social protection policies in the Member States and the Union,

— to promote exchanges of information, experience and good practice between Member States and with the Commission,

— without prejudice to Article 240, to prepare reports, formulate opinions or undertake other work within its fields of competence, at the request of either the Council or the Commission or on its own initiative.

In fulfilling its mandate, the Committee shall establish appropriate contacts with management and labour.

Each Member State and the Commission shall appoint two members of the Committee.

Article 161

The Commission shall include a separate chapter on social developments within the Union in its annual report to the European Parliament.

The European Parliament may invite the Commission to draw up reports on any particular problems concerning social conditions.

TITLE XI THE EUROPEAN SOCIAL FUND

Article 162

In order to improve employment opportunities for workers in the internal market and to contribute thereby to raising the standard of living, a European Social Fund is hereby established in accordance with the provisions set out below; it shall aim to render the employment of workers easier and to increase their geographical and occupational mobility within the Union, and to facilitate their adaptation to industrial changes and to changes in production systems, in particular through vocational training and retraining.

Article 163

The Fund shall be administered by the Commission.

The Commission shall be assisted in this task by a Committee presided over by a Member of the Commission and composed of representatives of governments, trade unions and employers' organisations.

Article 164

The European Parliament and the Council, acting in accordance with the ordinary legislative procedure and after consulting the Economic and Social Committee and the Committee of the Regions, shall adopt implementing regulations relating to the European Social Fund.

TITLE XII EDUCATION, VOCATIONAL TRAINING, YOUTH AND SPORT

Article 165

1. The Union shall contribute to the development of quality education by encouraging cooperation between Member States and, if necessary, by supporting and supplementing their action, while fully respecting the responsibility of the Member States for the content of teaching and the organisation of education systems and their cultural and linguistic diversity.

   The Union shall contribute to the promotion of European sporting issues, while taking account of the specific nature of sport, its structures based on voluntary activity and its social and educational function.

2. Union action shall be aimed at:
   — developing the European dimension in education, particularly through the teaching and dissemination of the languages of the Member States,
   — encouraging mobility of students and teachers, by encouraging inter alia, the academic recognition of diplomas and periods of study,

— promoting cooperation between educational establishments,

— developing exchanges of information and experience on issues common to the education systems of the Member States,

— encouraging the development of youth exchanges and of exchanges of socio-educational instructors, and encouraging the participation of young people in democratic life in Europe,

— encouraging the development of distance education,

— developing the European dimension in sport, by promoting fairness and openness in sporting competitions and cooperation between bodies responsible for sports, and by protecting the physical and moral integrity of sportsmen and sportswomen, especially the youngest sportsmen and sportswomen.

3. The Union and the Member States shall foster cooperation with third countries and the competent international organisations in the field of education and sport, in particular the Council of Europe.

4. In order to contribute to the achievement of the objectives referred to in this Article:

— the European Parliament and the Council, acting in accordance with the ordinary legislative procedure, after consulting the Economic and Social Committee and the Committee of the Regions, shall adopt incentive measures, excluding any harmonisation of the laws and regulations of the Member States,

— the Council, on a proposal from the Commission, shall adopt recommendations.

Article 166

1. The Union shall implement a vocational training policy which shall support and supplement the action of the Member States, while fully respecting the responsibility of the Member States for the content and organisation of vocational training.

2. Union action shall aim to:

— facilitate adaptation to industrial changes, in particular through vocational training and retraining,

— improve initial and continuing vocational training in order to facilitate vocational integration and reintegration into the labour market,

— facilitate access to vocational training and encourage mobility of instructors and trainees and particularly young people,

— stimulate cooperation on training between educational or training establishments and firms,

— develop exchanges of information and experience on issues common to the training systems of the Member States.

3. The Union and the Member States shall foster cooperation with third countries and the competent international organisations in the sphere of vocational training.

4. The European Parliament and the Council, acting in accordance with the ordinary legislative procedure and after consulting the Economic and Social Committee and the Committee of the Regions, shall adopt measures to contribute to the achievement of the objectives referred to in this Article, excluding any harmonisation of the laws and regulations of the Member States, and the Council, on a proposal from the Commission, shall adopt recommendations.

TITLE XIII CULTURE

Article 167

1. The Union shall contribute to the flowering of the cultures of the Member States, while respecting their national and regional diversity and at the same time bringing the common cultural heritage to the fore.

2. Action by the Union shall be aimed at encouraging cooperation between Member States and, if necessary, supporting and supplementing their action in the following areas:
   — improvement of the knowledge and dissemination of the culture and history of the European peoples,
   — conservation and safeguarding of cultural heritage of European significance,
   — non-commercial cultural exchanges,
   — artistic and literary creation, including in the audiovisual sector.

3. The Union and the Member States shall foster cooperation with third countries and the competent international organisations in the sphere of culture, in particular the Council of Europe.

4. The Union shall take cultural aspects into account in its action under other provisions of the Treaties, in particular in order to respect and to promote the diversity of its cultures.

5. In order to contribute to the achievement of the objectives referred to in this Article:
   — the European Parliament and the Council acting in accordance with the ordinary legislative procedure and after consulting the Committee of the Regions, shall adopt incentive measures, excluding any harmonisation of the laws and regulations of the Member States,
   — the Council, on a proposal from the Commission, shall adopt recommendations.

TITLE XIV PUBLIC HEALTH

Article 168

1. A high level of human health protection shall be ensured in the definition and implementation of all Union policies and activities.

   Union action, which shall complement national policies, shall be directed towards improving public health, preventing physical and mental illness and diseases, and obviating sources of danger to physical and mental health. Such action shall cover the fight against the major health scourges, by promoting research into their causes, their transmission and their prevention, as well as health information and education, and monitoring, early warning of and combating serious cross-border threats to health.

   The Union shall complement the Member States' action in reducing drugs-related health damage, including information and prevention.

2. The Union shall encourage cooperation between the Member States in the areas referred to in this Article and, if necessary, lend support to their action. It shall in particular encourage cooperation between the Member States to improve the complementarity of their health services in cross-border areas.

Member States shall, in liaison with the Commission, coordinate among themselves their policies and programmes in the areas referred to in paragraph 1. The Commission may, in close contact with the Member States, take any useful initiative to promote such coordination, in particular initiatives aiming at the establishment of guidelines and indicators, the organisation of exchange of best practice, and the preparation of the necessary elements for periodic monitoring and evaluation. The European Parliament shall be kept fully informed.

3. The Union and the Member States shall foster cooperation with third countries and the competent international organisations in the sphere of public health.

4. By way of derogation from Article 2(5) and Article 6(a) and in accordance with Article 4(2)(k) the European Parliament and the Council, acting in accordance with the ordinary legislative procedure and after consulting the Economic and Social Committee and the Committee of the Regions, shall contribute to the achievement of the objectives referred to in this Article through adopting in order to meet common safety concerns:

  (a) measures setting high standards of quality and safety of organs and substances of human origin, blood and blood derivatives; these measures shall not prevent any Member State from maintaining or introducing more stringent protective measures;

  (b) measures in the veterinary and phytosanitary fields which have as their direct objective the protection of public health;

  (c) measures setting high standards of quality and safety for medicinal products and devices for medical use.

5. The European Parliament and the Council, acting in accordance with the ordinary legislative procedure and after consulting the Economic and Social Committee and the Committee of the Regions, may also adopt incentive measures designed to protect and improve human health and in particular to combat the major cross-border health scourges, measures concerning monitoring, early warning of and combating serious cross-border threats to health, and measures which have as their direct objective the protection of public health regarding tobacco and the abuse of alcohol, excluding any harmonisation of the laws and regulations of the Member States.

6. The Council, on a proposal from the Commission, may also adopt recommendations for the purposes set out in this Article.

7. Union action shall respect the responsibilities of the Member States for the definition of their health policy and for the organisation and delivery of health services and medical care. The responsibilities of the Member States shall include the management of health services and medical care and the allocation of the resources assigned to them. The measures referred to in paragraph 4(a) shall not affect national provisions on the donation or medical use of organs and blood.

TITLE XV CONSUMER PROTECTION

Article 169

1. In order to promote the interests of consumers and to ensure a high level of consumer protection, the Union shall contribute to protecting the health, safety and economic interests of consumers, as well as to promoting their right to information, education and to organise themselves in order to safeguard their interests.

2. The Union shall contribute to the attainment of the objectives referred to in paragraph 1 through:
   (a) measures adopted pursuant to Article 114 in the context of the completion of the internal market;
   (b) measures which support, supplement and monitor the policy pursued by the Member States.
3. The European Parliament and the Council, acting in accordance with the ordinary legislative procedure and after consulting the Economic and Social Committee, shall adopt the measures referred to in paragraph 2(b).
4. Measures adopted pursuant to paragraph 3 shall not prevent any Member State from maintaining or introducing more stringent protective measures. Such measures must be compatible with the Treaties. The Commission shall be notified of them.

TITLE XVI TRANS-EUROPEAN NETWORKS

Article 170
1. To help achieve the objectives referred to in Articles 26 and 174 and to enable citizens of the Union, economic operators and regional and local communities to derive full benefit from the setting-up of an area without internal frontiers, the Union shall contribute to the establishment and development of trans-European networks in the areas of transport, telecommunications and energy infrastructures.
2. Within the framework of a system of open and competitive markets, action by the Union shall aim at promoting the interconnection and interoperability of national networks as well as access to such networks. It shall take account in particular of the need to link island, landlocked and peripheral regions with the central regions of the Union.

Article 171
1. In order to achieve the objectives referred to in Article 170, the Union:
   — shall establish a series of guidelines covering the objectives, priorities and broad lines of measures envisaged in the sphere of trans-European networks; these guidelines shall identify projects of common interest,
   — shall implement any measures that may prove necessary to ensure the interoperability of the networks, in particular in the field of technical standardisation,
   — may support projects of common interest supported by Member States, which are identified in the framework of the guidelines referred to in the first indent, particularly through feasibility studies, loan guarantees or interest-rate subsidies; the Union may also contribute, through the Cohesion Fund set up pursuant to Article 177, to the financing of specific projects in Member States in the area of transport infrastructure.
   The Union's activities shall take into account the potential economic viability of the projects.
2. Member States shall, in liaison with the Commission, coordinate among themselves the policies pursued at national level which may have a significant impact on the achievement of the objectives referred to in Article 170. The Commission may, in close cooperation with the Member State, take any useful initiative to promote such coordination.
3. The Union may decide to cooperate with third countries to promote projects of mutual interest and to ensure the interoperability of networks.

Article 172

The guidelines and other measures referred to in Article 171(1) shall be adopted by the European Parliament and the Council, acting in accordance with the ordinary legislative procedure and after consulting the Economic and Social Committee and the Committee of the Regions.

Guidelines and projects of common interest which relate to the territory of a Member State shall require the approval of the Member State concerned.

TITLE XVII INDUSTRY

Article 173

1. The Union and the Member States shall ensure that the conditions necessary for the competitiveness of the Union's industry exist.

   For that purpose, in accordance with a system of open and competitive markets, their action shall be aimed at:
   — speeding up the adjustment of industry to structural changes,
   — encouraging an environment favourable to initiative and to the development of undertakings throughout the Union, particularly small and medium-sized undertakings,
   — encouraging an environment favourable to cooperation between undertakings,
   — fostering better exploitation of the industrial potential of policies of innovation, research and technological development.

2. The Member States shall consult each other in liaison with the Commission and, where necessary, shall coordinate their action. The Commission may take any useful initiative to promote such coordination, in particular initiatives aiming at the establishment of guidelines and indicators, the organisation of exchange of best practice, and the preparation of the necessary elements for periodic monitoring and evaluation. The European Parliament shall be kept fully informed.

3. The Union shall contribute to the achievement of the objectives set out in paragraph 1 through the policies and activities it pursues under other provisions of the Treaties. The European Parliament and the Council, acting in accordance with the ordinary legislative procedure and after consulting the Economic and Social Committee, may decide on specific measures in support of action taken in the Member States to achieve the objectives set out in paragraph 1, excluding any harmonisation of the laws and regulations of the Member States.

   This Title shall not provide a basis for the introduction by the Union of any measure which could lead to a distortion of competition or contains tax provisions or provisions relating to the rights and interests of employed persons.

TITLE XVIII ECONOMIC, SOCIAL AND TERRITORIAL COHESION

Article 174

In order to promote its overall harmonious development, the Union shall develop and pursue its actions leading to the strengthening of its economic, social and territorial cohesion.

In particular, the Union shall aim at reducing disparities between the levels of development of the various regions and the backwardness of the least favoured regions.

Among the regions concerned, particular attention shall be paid to rural areas, areas affected by industrial transition, and regions which suffer from severe and permanent natural or demographic handicaps such as the northernmost regions with very low population density and island, cross-border and mountain regions.

Article 175

Member States shall conduct their economic policies and shall coordinate them in such a way as, in addition, to attain the objectives set out in Article 174. The formulation and implementation of the Union's policies and actions and the implementation of the internal market shall take into account the objectives set out in Article 174 and shall contribute to their achievement. The Union shall also support the achievement of these objectives by the action it takes through the Structural Funds (European Agricultural Guidance and Guarantee Fund, Guidance Section; European Social Fund; European Regional Development Fund), the European Investment Bank and the other existing Financial Instruments.

The Commission shall submit a report to the European Parliament, the Council, the Economic and Social Committee and the Committee of the Regions every three years on the progress made towards achieving economic, social and territorial cohesion and on the manner in which the various means provided for in this Article have contributed to it. This report shall, if necessary, be accompanied by appropriate proposals.

If specific actions prove necessary outside the Funds and without prejudice to the measures decided upon within the framework of the other Union policies, such actions may be adopted by the European Parliament and the Council acting in accordance with the ordinary legislative procedure and after consulting the Economic and Social Committee and the Committee of the Regions.

Article 176

The European Regional Development Fund is intended to help to redress the main regional imbalances in the Union through participation in the development and structural adjustment of regions whose development is lagging behind and in the conversion of declining industrial regions.

Article 177

Without prejudice to Article 178, the European Parliament and the Council, acting by means of regulations in accordance with the ordinary legislative procedure and consulting the Economic and Social Committee and the Committee of the Regions, shall define the tasks, priority objectives and the organisation of the Structural Funds, which may involve grouping the Funds. The general rules applicable to them and the provisions necessary to ensure their effectiveness and the coordination of the Funds with one another and with the other existing Financial Instruments shall also be defined by the same procedure.

A Cohesion Fund set up in accordance with the same procedure shall provide a financial contribution to projects in the fields of environment and trans-European networks in the area of transport infrastructure.

Article 178

Implementing regulations relating to the European Regional Development Fund shall be taken by the European Parliament and the Council, acting in accordance with the ordinary legislative procedure and after consulting the Economic and Social Committee and the Committee of the Regions.

With regard to the European Agricultural Guidance and Guarantee Fund, Guidance Section, and the European Social Fund, Articles 43 and 164 respectively shall continue to apply.

TITLE XIX RESEARCH AND TECHNOLOGICAL DEVELOPMENT AND SPACE

Article 179

1. The Union shall have the objective of strengthening its scientific and technological bases by achieving a European research area in which researchers, scientific knowledge and technology circulate freely, and encouraging it to become more competitive, including in its industry, while promoting all the research activities deemed necessary by virtue of other Chapters of the Treaties.

2. For this purpose the Union shall, throughout the Union, encourage undertakings, including small and medium-sized undertakings, research centres and universities in their research and technological development activities of high quality; it shall support their efforts to cooperate with one another, aiming, notably, at permitting researchers to cooperate freely across borders and at enabling undertakings to exploit the internal market potential to the full, in particular through the opening-up of national public contracts, the definition of common standards and the removal of legal and fiscal obstacles to that cooperation.

3. All Union activities under the Treaties in the area of research and technological development, including demonstration projects, shall be decided on and implemented in accordance with the provisions of this Title.

Article 180

In pursuing these objectives, the Union shall carry out the following activities, complementing the activities carried out in the Member States:

(a) implementation of research, technological development and demonstration programmes, by promoting cooperation with and between undertakings, research centres and universities;

(b) promotion of cooperation in the field of Union research, technological development and demonstration with third countries and international organisations;

(c) dissemination and optimisation of the results of activities in Union research, technological development and demonstration;

(d) stimulation of the training and mobility of researchers in the Union.

Article 181

1. The Union and the Member States shall coordinate their research and technological development activities so as to ensure that national policies and Union policy are mutually consistent.

2. In close cooperation with the Member State, the Commission may take any useful initiative to promote the coordination referred to in paragraph 1, in particular initiatives aiming at the establishment of guidelines and indicators, the organisation of exchange of best practice, and the preparation of the necessary elements for periodic monitoring and evaluation. The European Parliament shall be kept fully informed.

Article 182

1. A multiannual framework programme, setting out all the activities of the Union, shall be adopted by the European Parliament and the Council, acting in accordance with the ordinary legislative procedure after consulting the Economic and Social Committee.

   The framework programme shall:
   — establish the scientific and technological objectives to be achieved by the activities provided for in Article 180 and fix the relevant priorities,
   — indicate the broad lines of such activities,
   — fix the maximum overall amount and the detailed rules for Union financial participation in the framework programme and the respective shares in each of the activities provided for.

2. The framework programme shall be adapted or supplemented as the situation changes.

3. The framework programme shall be implemented through specific programmes developed within each activity. Each specific programme shall define the detailed rules for implementing it, fix its duration and provide for the means deemed necessary. The sum of the amounts deemed necessary, fixed in the specific programmes, may not exceed the overall maximum amount fixed for the framework programme and each activity.

4. The Council, acting in accordance with a special legislative procedure and after consulting the European Parliament and the Economic and Social Committee, shall adopt the specific programmes.

5. As a complement to the activities planned in the multiannual framework programme, the European Parliament and the Council, acting in accordance with the ordinary legislative procedure and after consulting the Economic and Social Committee, shall establish the measures necessary for the implementation of the European research area.

Article 183

For the implementation of the multiannual framework programme the Union shall:
— determine the rules for the participation of undertakings, research centres and universities,
— lay down the rules governing the dissemination of research results.

Article 184

In implementing the multiannual framework programme, supplementary programmes may be decided on involving the participation of certain Member States only, which shall finance them subject to possible Union participation.

The Union shall adopt the rules applicable to supplementary programmes, particularly as regards the dissemination of knowledge and access by other Member States.

Article 185

In implementing the multiannual framework programme, the Union may make provision, in agreement with the Member States concerned, for participation in research and development programmes undertaken by several Member States, including participation in the structures created for the execution of those programmes.

Article 186

In implementing the multiannual framework programme the Union may make provision for cooperation in Union research, technological development and demonstration with third countries or international organisations.

The detailed arrangements for such cooperation may be the subject of agreements between the Union and the third parties concerned.

Article 187

The Union may set up joint undertakings or any other structure necessary for the efficient execution of Union research, technological development and demonstration programmes.

Article 188

The Council, on a proposal from the Commission and after consulting the European Parliament and the Economic and Social Committee, shall adopt the provisions referred to in Article 187.

The European Parliament and the Council, acting in accordance with the ordinary legislative procedure and after consulting the Economic and Social Committee, shall adopt the provisions referred to in Articles 183, 184 and 185. Adoption of the supplementary programmes shall require the agreement of the Member States concerned.

Article 189

1. To promote scientific and technical progress, industrial competitiveness and the implementation of its policies, the Union shall draw up a European space policy. To this end, it may promote joint initiatives, support research and technological development and coordinate the efforts needed for the exploration and exploitation of space.
2. To contribute to attaining the objectives referred to in paragraph 1, the European Parliament and the Council, acting in accordance with the ordinary legislative procedure, shall establish the necessary measures, which may take the form of a European space programme, excluding any harmonisation of the laws and regulations of the Member States.
3. The Union shall establish any appropriate relations with the European Space Agency.
4. This Article shall be without prejudice to the other provisions of this Title.

Article 190

At the beginning of each year the Commission shall send a report to the European Parliament and to the Council. The report shall include information on research and technological development activities and the dissemination of results during the previous year, and the work programme for the current year.

TITLE XX ENVIRONMENT

Article 191

1. Union policy on the environment shall contribute to pursuit of the following objectives:
   — preserving, protecting and improving the quality of the environment,
   — protecting human health,

— prudent and rational utilisation of natural resources,
— promoting measures at international level to deal with regional or worldwide environmental problems, and in particular combating climate change.

2. Union policy on the environment shall aim at a high level of protection taking into account the diversity of situations in the various regions of the Union. It shall be based on the precautionary principle and on the principles that preventive action should be taken, that environmental damage should as a priority be rectified at source and that the polluter should pay.

In this context, harmonisation measures answering environmental protection requirements shall include, where appropriate, a safeguard clause allowing Member States to take provisional measures, for non-economic environmental reasons, subject to a procedure of inspection by the Union.

3. In preparing its policy on the environment, the Union shall take account of:
— available scientific and technical data,
— environmental conditions in the various regions of the Union,
— the potential benefits and costs of action or lack of action,
— the economic and social development of the Union as a whole and the balanced development of its regions.

4. Within their respective spheres of competence, the Union and the Member States shall cooperate with third countries and with the competent international organisations. The arrangements for Union cooperation may be the subject of agreements between the Union and the third parties concerned.

The previous subparagraph shall be without prejudice to Member States' competence to negotiate in international bodies and to conclude international agreements.

Article 192

1. The European Parliament and the Council, acting in accordance with the ordinary legislative procedure and after consulting the Economic and Social Committee and the Committee of the Regions, shall decide what action is to be taken by the Union in order to achieve the objectives referred to in Article 191.

2. By way of derogation from the decision-making procedure provided for in paragraph 1 and without prejudice to Article 114, the Council acting unanimously in accordance with a special legislative procedure and after consulting the European Parliament, the Economic and Social Committee and the Committee of the Regions, shall adopt:
   (a) provisions primarily of a fiscal nature;
   (b) measures affecting:
      — town and country planning,
      — quantitative management of water resources or affecting, directly or indirectly, the availability of those resources,
      — land use, with the exception of waste management;
   (c) measures significantly affecting a Member State's choice between different energy sources and the general structure of its energy supply.

The Council, acting unanimously on a proposal from the Commission and after consulting the European Parliament, the Economic and Social Committee and the

Committee of the Regions, may make the ordinary legislative procedure applicable to the matters referred to in the first subparagraph.

3. General action programmes setting out priority objectives to be attained shall be adopted by the European Parliament and the Council, acting in accordance with the ordinary legislative procedure and after consulting the Economic and Social Committee and the Committee of the Regions.

   The measures necessary for the implementation of these programmes shall be adopted under the terms of paragraph 1 or 2, as the case may be.

4. Without prejudice to certain measures adopted by the Union, the Member States shall finance and implement the environment policy.

5. Without prejudice to the principle that the polluter should pay, if a measure based on the provisions of paragraph 1 involves costs deemed disproportionate for the public authorities of a Member State, such measure shall lay down appropriate provisions in the form of:
   — temporary derogations, and/or
   — financial support from the Cohesion Fund set up pursuant to Article 177.

Article 193

The protective measures adopted pursuant to Article 192 shall not prevent any Member State from maintaining or introducing more stringent protective measures. Such measures must be compatible with the Treaties. They shall be notified to the Commission.

TITLE XXI ENERGY

Article 194

1. In the context of the establishment and functioning of the internal market and with regard for the need to preserve and improve the environment, Union policy on energy shall aim, in a spirit of solidarity between Member States, to:
   (a) ensure the functioning of the energy market;
   (b) ensure security of energy supply in the Union;
   (c) promote energy efficiency and energy saving and the development of new and renewable forms of energy; and
   (d) promote the interconnection of energy networks.

2. Without prejudice to the application of other provisions of the Treaties, the European Parliament and the Council, acting in accordance with the ordinary legislative procedure, shall establish the measures necessary to achieve the objectives in paragraph 1. Such measures shall be adopted after consultation of the Economic and Social Committee and the Committee of the Regions.

   Such measures shall not affect a Member State's right to determine the conditions for exploiting its energy resources, its choice between different energy sources and the general structure of its energy supply, without prejudice to Article 192(2)(c).

3. By way of derogation from paragraph 2, the Council, acting in accordance with a special legislative procedure, shall unanimously and after consulting the European Parliament, establish the measures referred to therein when they are primarily of a fiscal nature.

TITLE XXII TOURISM

Article 195

1. The Union shall complement the action of the Member States in the tourism sector, in particular by promoting the competitiveness of Union undertakings in that sector.

   To that end, Union action shall be aimed at:

   (a) encouraging the creation of a favourable environment for the development of undertakings in this sector;

   (b) promoting cooperation between the Member States, particularly by the exchange of good practice.

2. The European Parliament and the Council, acting in accordance with the ordinary legislative procedure, shall establish specific measures to complement actions within the Member States to achieve the objectives referred to in this Article, excluding any harmonisation of the laws and regulations of the Member States.

TITLE XXIII CIVIL PROTECTION

Article 196

1. The Union shall encourage cooperation between Member States in order to improve the effectiveness of systems for preventing and protecting against natural or man-made disasters. Union action shall aim to:

   (a) support and complement Member States' action at national, regional and local level in risk prevention, in preparing their civil-protection personnel and in responding to natural or man-made disasters within the Union;

   (b) promote swift, effective operational cooperation within the Union between national civil-protection services;

   (c) promote consistency in international civil-protection work.

2. The European Parliament and the Council, acting in accordance with the ordinary legislative procedure shall establish the measures necessary to help achieve the objectives referred to in paragraph 1, excluding any harmonisation of the laws and regulations of the Member States.

TITLE XXIV ADMINISTRATIVE COOPERATION

Article 197

1. Effective implementation of Union law by the Member States, which is essential for the proper functioning of the Union, shall be regarded as a matter of common interest.

2. The Union may support the efforts of Member States to improve their administrative capacity to implement Union law. Such action may include facilitating the exchange of information and of civil servants as well as supporting training schemes. No Member State shall be obliged to avail itself of such support. The European Parliament and the Council, acting by means of regulations in accordance with the ordinary legislative procedure, shall establish the necessary measures to this end, excluding any harmonisation of the laws and regulations of the Member States.

3. This Article shall be without prejudice to the obligations of the Member States to implement Union law or to the prerogatives and duties of the Commission. It shall also be without prejudice to other provisions of the Treaties providing for administrative cooperation among the Member States and between them and the Union.

PART FOUR ASSOCIATION OF THE OVERSEAS COUNTRIES AND TERRITORIES

Article 198

The Member States agree to associate with the Union the non-European countries and territories which have special relations with Denmark, France, the Netherlands and the United Kingdom. These countries and territories (hereinafter called the 'countries and territories') are listed in Annex II.

The purpose of association shall be to promote the economic and social development of the countries and territories and to establish close economic relations between them and the Union as a whole.

In accordance with the principles set out in the preamble to this Treaty, association shall serve primarily to further the interests and prosperity of the inhabitants of these countries and territories in order to lead them to the economic, social and cultural development to which they aspire.

Article 199

Association shall have the following objectives.

1. Member States shall apply to their trade with the countries and territories the same treatment as they accord each other pursuant to the Treaties.
2. Each country or territory shall apply to its trade with Member States and with the other countries and territories the same treatment as that which it applies to the European State with which is has special relations.
3. The Member States shall contribute to the investments required for the progressive development of these countries and territories.
4. For investments financed by the Union, participation in tenders and supplies shall be open on equal terms to all natural and legal persons who are nationals of a Member State or of one of the countries and territories.
5. In relations between Member States and the countries and territories the right of establishment of nationals and companies or firms shall be regulated in accordance with the provisions and procedures laid down in the Chapter relating to the right of establishment and on a non-discriminatory basis, subject to any special provisions laid down pursuant to Article 203.

Article 200

1. Customs duties on imports into the Member States of goods originating in the countries and territories shall be prohibited in conformity with the prohibition of customs duties between Member States in accordance with the provisions of the Treaties.
2. Customs duties on imports into each country or territory from Member States or from the other countries or territories shall be prohibited in accordance with the provisions of Article 30.

3. The countries and territories may, however, levy customs duties which meet the needs of their development and industrialisation or produce revenue for their budgets.

The duties referred to in the preceding subparagraph may not exceed the level of those imposed on imports of products from the Member State with which each country or territory has special relations.

4. Paragraph 2 shall not apply to countries and territories which, by reason of the particular international obligations by which they are bound, already apply a non-discriminatory customs tariff.

5. The introduction of or any change in customs duties imposed on goods imported into the countries and territories shall not, either in law or in fact, give rise to any direct or indirect discrimination between imports from the various Member States.

Article 201

If the level of the duties applicable to goods from a third country on entry into a country or territory is liable, when the provisions of Article 200(1) have been applied, to cause deflections of trade to the detriment of any Member State, the latter may request the Commission to propose to the other Member States the measures needed to remedy the situation.

Article 202

Subject to the provisions relating to public health, public security or public policy, freedom of movement within Member States for workers from the countries and territories, and within the countries and territories for workers from Member States, shall be regulated by acts adopted in accordance with Article 203.

Article 203

The Council, acting unanimously on a proposal from the Commission, shall, on the basis of the experience acquired under the association of the countries and territories with the Union and of the principles set out in the Treaties, lay down provisions as regards the detailed rules and the procedure for the association of the countries and territories with the Union. Where the provisions in question are adopted by the Council in accordance with a special legislative procedure, it shall act unanimously on a proposal from the Commission and after consulting the European Parliament.

Article 204

The provisions of Articles 198 to 203 shall apply to Greenland, subject to the specific provisions for Greenland set out in the Protocol on special arrangements for Greenland, annexed to the Treaties.

PART FIVE THE UNION'S EXTERNAL ACTION

TITLE I GENERAL PROVISIONS ON THE UNION'S EXTERNAL ACTION

Article 205

The Union's action on the international scene, pursuant to this Part, shall be guided by the principles, pursue the objectives and be conducted in accordance with the general provisions laid down in Chapter 1 of Title V of the Treaty on European Union.

TITLE II COMMON COMMERCIAL POLICY

Article 206

By establishing a customs union in accordance with Articles 28 to 32, the Union shall contribute, in the common interest, to the harmonious development of world trade, the progressive abolition of restrictions on international trade and on foreign direct investment, and the lowering of customs and other barriers.

Article 207

1. The common commercial policy shall be based on uniform principles, particularly with regard to changes in tariff rates, the conclusion of tariff and trade agreements relating to trade in goods and services, and the commercial aspects of intellectual property, foreign direct investment, the achievement of uniformity in measures of liberalisation, export policy and measures to protect trade such as those to be taken in the event of dumping or subsidies. The common commercial policy shall be conducted in the context of the principles and objectives of the Union's external action.

2. The European Parliament and the Council, acting by means of regulations in accordance with the ordinary legislative procedure, shall adopt the measures defining the framework for implementing the common commercial policy.

3. Where agreements with one or more third countries or international organisations need to be negotiated and concluded, Article 218 shall apply, subject to the special provisions of this Article.

   The Commission shall make recommendations to the Council, which shall authorise it to open the necessary negotiations. The Council and the Commission shall be responsible for ensuring that the agreements negotiated are compatible with internal Union policies and rules.

   The Commission shall conduct these negotiations in consultation with a special committee appointed by the Council to assist the Commission in this task and within the framework of such directives as the Council may issue to it. The Commission shall report regularly to the special committee and to the European Parliament on the progress of negotiations.

4. For the negotiation and conclusion of the agreements referred to in paragraph 3, the Council shall act by a qualified majority.

   For the negotiation and conclusion of agreements in the fields of trade in services and the commercial aspects of intellectual property, as well as foreign direct investment, the Council shall act unanimously where such agreements include provisions for which unanimity is required for the adoption of internal rules.

   The Council shall also act unanimously for the negotiation and conclusion of agreements:

   (a) in the field of trade in cultural and audiovisual services, where these agreements risk prejudicing the Union's cultural and linguistic diversity;

   (b) in the field of trade in social, education and health services, where these agreements risk seriously disturbing the national organisation of such services and prejudicing the responsibility of Member States to deliver them.

5. The negotiation and conclusion of international agreements in the field of transport shall be subject to Title VI of Part Three and to Article 218.

6. The exercise of the competences conferred by this Article in the field of the common commercial policy shall not affect the delimitation of competences between the Union and the Member States, and shall not lead to harmonisation of legislative or regulatory provisions of the Member States in so far as the Treaties exclude such harmonisation.

TITLE III COOPERATION WITH THIRD COUNTRIES AND HUMANITARIAN AID

Chapter 1 Development Cooperation

Article 208

1. Union policy in the field of development cooperation shall be conducted within the framework of the principles and objectives of the Union's external action. The Union's development cooperation policy and that of the Member States complement and reinforce each other.

   Union development cooperation policy shall have as its primary objective the reduction and, in the long term, the eradication of poverty. The Union shall take account of the objectives of development cooperation in the policies that it implements which are likely to affect developing countries.
2. The Union and the Member States shall comply with the commitments and take account of the objectives they have approved in the context of the United Nations and other competent international organisations.

Article 209

1. The European Parliament and the Council, acting in accordance with the ordinary legislative procedure, shall adopt the measures necessary for the implementation of development cooperation policy, which may relate to multiannual cooperation programmes with developing countries or programmes with a thematic approach.
2. The Union may conclude with third countries and competent international organisations any agreement helping to achieve the objectives referred to in Article 21 of the Treaty on European Union and in Article 208 of this Treaty.

   The first subparagraph shall be without prejudice to Member States' competence to negotiate in international bodies and to conclude agreements.
3. The European Investment Bank shall contribute, under the terms laid down in its Statute, to the implementation of the measures referred to in paragraph 1.

Article 210

1. In order to promote the complementarity and efficiency of their action, the Union and the Member States shall coordinate their policies on development cooperation and shall consult each other on their aid programmes, including in international organisations and during international conferences. They may undertake joint action. Member States shall contribute if necessary to the implementation of Union aid programmes.
2. The Commission may take any useful initiative to promote the coordination referred to in paragraph 1.

Article 211

Within their respective spheres of competence, the Union and the Member States shall cooperate with third countries and with the competent international organisations.

Chapter 2 Economic, Financial and Technical Cooperation with Third Countries

Article 212

1. Without prejudice to the other provisions of the Treaties, and in particular Articles 208 to 211, the Union shall carry out economic, financial and technical cooperation measures, including assistance, in particular financial assistance, with third countries other than developing countries. Such measures shall be consistent with the development policy of the Union and shall be carried out within the framework of the principles and objectives of its external action. The Union's operations and those of the Member States shall complement and reinforce each other.

2. The European Parliament and the Council, acting in accordance with the ordinary legislative procedure, shall adopt the measures necessary for the implementation of paragraph 1.

3. Within their respective spheres of competence, the Union and the Member States shall cooperate with third countries and the competent international organisations. The arrangements for Union cooperation may be the subject of agreements between the Union and the third parties concerned.

    The first subparagraph shall be without prejudice to the Member States' competence to negotiate in international bodies and to conclude international agreements.

Article 213

When the situation in a third country requires urgent financial assistance from the Union, the Council shall adopt the necessary decisions on a proposal from the Commission.

Chapter 3 Humanitarian Aid

Article 214

1. The Union's operations in the field of humanitarian aid shall be conducted within the framework of the principles and objectives of the external action of the Union. Such operations shall be intended to provide ad hoc assistance and relief and protection for people in third countries who are victims of natural or man-made disasters, in order to meet the humanitarian needs resulting from these different situations. The Union's measures and those of the Member States shall complement and reinforce each other.

2. Humanitarian aid operations shall be conducted in compliance with the principles of international law and with the principles of impartiality, neutrality and non-discrimination.

3. The European Parliament and the Council, acting in accordance with the ordinary legislative procedure, shall establish the measures defining the framework within which the Union's humanitarian aid operations shall be implemented.

4. The Union may conclude with third countries and competent international organisations any agreement helping to achieve the objectives referred to in paragraph 1 and in Article 21 of the Treaty on European Union.

   The first subparagraph shall be without prejudice to Member States' competence to negotiate in international bodies and to conclude agreements.

5. In order to establish a framework for joint contributions from young Europeans to the humanitarian aid operations of the Union, a European Voluntary Humanitarian Aid Corps shall be set up. The European Parliament and the Council, acting by means of regulations in accordance with the ordinary legislative procedure, shall determine the rules and procedures for the operation of the Corps.

6. The Commission may take any useful initiative to promote coordination between actions of the Union and those of the Member States, in order to enhance the efficiency and complementarity of Union and national humanitarian aid measures.

7. The Union shall ensure that its humanitarian aid operations are coordinated and consistent with those of international organisations and bodies, in particular those forming part of the United Nations system.

TITLE IV RESTRICTIVE MEASURES

Article 215

1. Where a decision, adopted in accordance with Chapter 2 of Title V of the Treaty on European Union, provides for the interruption or reduction, in part or completely, of economic and financial relations with one or more third countries, the Council, acting by a qualified majority on a joint proposal from the High Representative of the Union for Foreign Affairs and Security Policy and the Commission, shall adopt the necessary measures. It shall inform the European Parliament thereof.

2. Where a decision adopted in accordance with Chapter 2 of Title V of the Treaty on European Union so provides, the Council may adopt restrictive measures under the procedure referred to in paragraph 1 against natural or legal persons and groups or non-State entities.

3. The acts referred to in this Article shall include necessary provisions on legal safeguards.

TITLE V INTERNATIONAL AGREEMENTS

Article 216

1. The Union may conclude an agreement with one or more third countries or international organisations where the Treaties so provide or where the conclusion of an agreement is necessary in order to achieve, within the framework of the Union's policies, one of the objectives referred to in the Treaties, or is provided for in a legally binding Union act or is likely to affect common rules or alter their scope.

2. Agreements concluded by the Union are binding upon the institutions of the Union and on its Member States.

Article 217

The Union may conclude with one or more third countries or international organisations agreements establishing an association involving reciprocal rights and obligations, common action and special procedure.

Article 218

1. Without prejudice to the specific provisions laid down in Article 207, agreements between the Union and third countries or international organisations shall be negotiated and concluded in accordance with the following procedure.
2. The Council shall authorise the opening of negotiations, adopt negotiating directives, authorise the signing of agreements and conclude them.
3. The Commission, or the High Representative of the Union for Foreign Affairs and Security Policy where the agreement envisaged relates exclusively or principally to the common foreign and security policy, shall submit recommendations to the Council, which shall adopt a decision authorising the opening of negotiations and, depending on the subject of the agreement envisaged, nominating the Union negotiator or the head of the Union's negotiating team.
4. The Council may address directives to the negotiator and designate a special committee in consultation with which the negotiations must be conducted.
5. The Council, on a proposal by the negotiator, shall adopt a decision authorising the signing of the agreement and, if necessary, its provisional application before entry into force.
6. The Council, on a proposal by the negotiator, shall adopt a decision concluding the agreement.

　　Except where agreements relate exclusively to the common foreign and security policy, the Council shall adopt the decision concluding the agreement:

(a) after obtaining the consent of the European Parliament in the following cases:
   (i) association agreements;
   (ii) agreement on Union accession to the European Convention for the Protection of Human Rights and Fundamental Freedoms;
   (iii) agreements establishing a specific institutional framework by organising cooperation procedures;
   (iv) agreements with important budgetary implications for the Union;
   (v) agreements covering fields to which either the ordinary legislative procedure applies, or the special legislative procedure where consent by the European Parliament is required.

　　The European Parliament and the Council may, in an urgent situation, agree upon a time-limit for consent.

(b) after consulting the European Parliament in other cases. The European Parliament shall deliver its opinion within a time-limit which the Council may set depending on the urgency of the matter. In the absence of an opinion within that time-limit, the Council may act.

7. When concluding an agreement, the Council may, by way of derogation from paragraphs 5, 6 and 9, authorise the negotiator to approve on the Union's behalf modifications to the agreement where it provides for them to be adopted by a simplified procedure or by a body set up by the agreement. The Council may attach specific conditions to such authorisation.

2

8. The Council shall act by a qualified majority throughout the procedure.

    However, it shall act unanimously when the agreement covers a field for which unanimity is required for the adoption of a Union act as well as for association agreements and the agreements referred to in Article 212 with the States which are candidates for accession. The Council shall also act unanimously for the agreement on accession of the Union to the European Convention for the Protection of Human Rights and Fundamental Freedoms; the decision concluding this agreement shall enter into force after it has been approved by the Member States in accordance with their respective constitutional requirements.

9. The Council, on a proposal from the Commission or the High Representative of the Union for Foreign Affairs and Security Policy, shall adopt a decision suspending application of an agreement and establishing the positions to be adopted on the Union's behalf in a body set up by an agreement, when that body is called upon to adopt acts having legal effects, with the exception of acts supplementing or amending the institutional framework of the agreement.

10. The European Parliament shall be immediately and fully informed at all stages of the procedure.

11. A Member State, the European Parliament, the Council or the Commission may obtain the opinion of the Court of Justice as to whether an agreement envisaged is compatible with the Treaties. Where the opinion of the Court is adverse, the agreement envisaged may not enter into force unless it is amended or the Treaties are revised.

Article 219

1. By way of derogation from Article 218, the Council, either on a recommendation from the European Central Bank or on a recommendation from the Commission and after consulting the European Central Bank, in an endeavour to reach a consensus consistent with the objective of price stability, may conclude formal agreements on an exchange-rate system for the euro in relation to the currencies of third States. The Council shall act unanimously after consulting the European Parliament and in accordance with the procedure provided for in paragraph 3.

    The Council may, either on a recommendation from the European Central Bank or on a recommendation from the Commission, and after consulting the European Central Bank, in an endeavour to reach a consensus consistent with the objective of price stability, adopt, adjust or abandon the central rates of the euro within the exchange-rate system. The President of the Council shall inform the European Parliament of the adoption, adjustment or abandonment of the euro central rates.

2. In the absence of an exchange-rate system in relation to one or more currencies of third States as referred to in paragraph 1, the Council, either on a recommendation from the Commission and after consulting the European Central Bank or on a recommendation from the European Central Bank, may formulate general orientations for exchange-rate policy in relation to these currencies. These general orientations shall be without prejudice to the primary objective of the ESCB to maintain price stability.

3. By way of derogation from Article 218, where agreements concerning monetary or foreign exchange regime matters need to be negotiated by the Union with one or more third States or international organisations, the Council, on a recommendation from the Commission and after consulting the European Central Bank, shall decide the

arrangements for the negotiation and for the conclusion of such agreements. These arrangements shall ensure that the Union expresses a single position. The Commission shall be fully associated with the negotiations.

4. Without prejudice to Union competence and Union agreements as regards economic and monetary union, Member States may negotiate in international bodies and conclude international agreements.

TITLE VI THE UNION'S RELATIONS WITH INTERNATIONAL ORGANISATIONS AND THIRD COUNTRIES AND UNION DELEGATIONS

Article 220

1. The Union shall establish all appropriate forms of cooperation with the organs of the United Nations and its specialised agencies, the Council of Europe, the Organisation for Security and Cooperation in Europe and the Organisation for Economic Cooperation and Development.

   The Union shall also maintain such relations as are appropriate with other international organisations.

2. The High Representative of the Union for Foreign Affairs and Security Policy and the Commission shall implement this Article.

Article 221

1. Union delegations in third countries and at international organisations shall represent the Union.

2. Union delegations shall be placed under the authority of the High Representative of the Union for Foreign Affairs and Security Policy. They shall act in close cooperation with Member States' diplomatic and consular missions.

TITLE VII SOLIDARITY CLAUSE

Article 222

1. The Union and its Member States shall act jointly in a spirit of solidarity if a Member State is the object of a terrorist attack or the victim of a natural or man-made disaster. The Union shall mobilise all the instruments at its disposal, including the military resources made available by the Member States, to:

   (a) — prevent the terrorist threat in the territory of the Member States;
   — protect democratic institutions and the civilian population from any terrorist attack;
   — assist a Member State in its territory, at the request of its political authorities, in the event of a terrorist attack;

   (b) assist a Member State in its territory, at the request of its political authorities, in the event of a natural or man-made disaster.

2. Should a Member State be the object of a terrorist attack or the victim of a natural or man-made disaster, the other Member States shall assist it at the request of its political authorities. To that end, the Member States shall coordinate between themselves in the Council.

3. The arrangements for the implementation by the Union of the solidarity clause shall be defined by a decision adopted by the Council acting on a joint proposal by

the Commission and the High Representative of the Union for Foreign Affairs and Security Policy. The Council shall act in accordance with Article 31(1) of the Treaty on European Union where this decision has defence implications. The European Parliament shall be informed.

For the purposes of this paragraph and without prejudice to Article 240, the Council shall be assisted by the Political and Security Committee with the support of the structures developed in the context of the common security and defence policy and by the Committee referred to in Article 71; the two committees shall, if necessary, submit joint opinions.

4. The European Council shall regularly assess the threats facing the Union in order to enable the Union and its Member States to take effective action.

PART SIX INSTITUTIONAL AND FINANCIAL PROVISIONS

TITLE I INSTITUTIONAL PROVISIONS

Chapter 1 The Institutions

SECTION 1 THE EUROPEAN PARLIAMENT

Article 223

1. The European Parliament shall draw up a proposal to lay down the provisions necessary for the election of its Members by direct universal suffrage in accordance with a uniform procedure in all Member States or in accordance with principles common to all Member States.

The Council, acting unanimously in accordance with a special legislative procedure and after obtaining the consent of the European Parliament, which shall act by a majority of its component Members, shall lay down the necessary provisions. These provisions shall enter into force following their approval by the Member States in accordance with their respective constitutional requirements.

2. The European Parliament, acting by means of regulations on its own initiative in accordance with a special legislative procedure after seeking an opinion from the Commission and with the consent of the Council, shall lay down the regulations and general conditions governing the performance of the duties of its Members. All rules or conditions relating to the taxation of Members or former Members shall require unanimity within the Council.

Article 224

The European Parliament and the Council, acting in accordance with the ordinary legislative procedure, by means of regulations, shall lay down the regulations governing political parties at European level referred to in Article 10(4) of the Treaty on European Union and in particular the rules regarding their funding.

Article 225

The European Parliament may, acting by a majority of its component Members, request the Commission to submit any appropriate proposal on matters on which it considers that a Union act is required for the purpose of implementing the Treaties. If the Commission does not submit a proposal, it shall inform the European Parliament of the reasons.

Article 226

In the course of its duties, the European Parliament may, at the request of a quarter of its component Members, set up a temporary Committee of Inquiry to investigate, without prejudice to the powers conferred by the Treaties on other institutions or bodies, alleged contraventions or maladministration in the implementation of Union law, except where the alleged facts are being examined before a court and while the case is still subject to legal proceedings.

The temporary Committee of Inquiry shall cease to exist on the submission of its report.

The detailed provisions governing the exercise of the right of inquiry shall be determined by the European Parliament, acting by means of regulations on its own initiative in accordance with a special legislative procedure, after obtaining the consent of the Council and the Commission.

Article 227

Any citizen of the Union, and any natural or legal person residing or having its registered office in a Member State, shall have the right to address, individually or in association with other citizens or persons, a petition to the European Parliament on a matter which comes within the Union's fields of activity and which affects him, her or it directly.

Article 228

1. A European Ombudsman, elected by the European Parliament, shall be empowered to receive complaints from any citizen of the Union or any natural or legal person residing or having its registered office in a Member State concerning instances of maladministration in the activities of the Union institutions, bodies, offices or agencies, with the exception of the Court of Justice of the European Union acting in its judicial role. He or she shall examine such complaints and report on them.

   In accordance with his duties, the Ombudsman shall conduct inquiries for which he finds grounds, either on his own initiative or on the basis of complaints submitted to him direct or through a Member of the European Parliament, except where the alleged facts are or have been the subject of legal proceedings. Where the Ombudsman establishes an instance of maladministration, he shall refer the matter to the institution, body, office or agency concerned, which shall have a period of three months in which to inform him of its views. The Ombudsman shall then forward a report to the European Parliament and the institution, body, office or agency concerned. The person lodging the complaint shall be informed of the outcome of such inquiries.

   The Ombudsman shall submit an annual report to the European Parliament on the outcome of his inquiries.

2. The Ombudsman shall be elected after each election of the European Parliament for the duration of its term of office. The Ombudsman shall be eligible for reappointment.

   The Ombudsman may be dismissed by the Court of Justice at the request of the European Parliament if he no longer fulfils the conditions required for the performance of his duties or if he is guilty of serious misconduct.

3. The Ombudsman shall be completely independent in the performance of his duties. In the performance of those duties he shall neither seek nor take instructions from any Government, institution, body, office or entity. The Ombudsman may not, during his term of office, engage in any other occupation, whether gainful or not.

4. The European Parliament acting by means of regulations on its own initiative in accordance with a special legislative procedure shall, after seeking an opinion from the Commission and with the consent of the Council, lay down the regulations and general conditions governing the performance of the Ombudsman's duties.

Article 229

The European Parliament shall hold an annual session. It shall meet, without requiring to be convened, on the second Tuesday in March.

The European Parliament may meet in extraordinary part-session at the request of a majority of its component Members or at the request of the Council or of the Commission.

Article 230

The Commission may attend all the meetings and shall, at its request, be heard.

The Commission shall reply orally or in writing to questions put to it by the European Parliament or by its Members.

The European Council and the Council shall be heard by the European Parliament in accordance with the conditions laid down in the Rules of Procedure of the European Council and those of the Council.

Article 231

Save as otherwise provided in the Treaties, the European Parliament shall act by a majority of the votes cast.

The Rules of Procedure shall determine the quorum.

Article 232

The European Parliament shall adopt its Rules of Procedure, acting by a majority of its Members.

The proceedings of the European Parliament shall be published in the manner laid down in the Treaties and in its Rules of Procedure.

Article 233

The European Parliament shall discuss in open session the annual general report submitted to it by the Commission.

Article 234

If a motion of censure on the activities of the Commission is tabled before it, the European Parliament shall not vote thereon until at least three days after the motion has been tabled and only by open vote.

If the motion of censure is carried by a two-thirds majority of the votes cast, representing a majority of the component Members of the European Parliament, the members of the Commission shall resign as a body and the High Representative of the Union for Foreign Affairs and Security Policy shall resign from duties that he or she carries out in the Commission. They shall remain in office and continue to deal with current business until they are replaced in accordance with Article 17 of the Treaty on European Union. In this case, the term of office of the members of the Commission appointed to replace them shall expire on the date on which the term of office of the members of the Commission obliged to resign as a body would have expired.

SECTION 2 THE EUROPEAN COUNCIL

Article 235

1. Where a vote is taken, any member of the European Council may also act on behalf of not more than one other member.

   Article 16(4) of the Treaty on European Union and Article 238(2) of this Treaty shall apply to the European Council when it is acting by a qualified majority. Where the European Council decides by vote, its President and the President of the Commission shall not take part in the vote.

   Abstentions by members present in person or represented shall not prevent the adoption by the European Council of acts which require unanimity.

2. The President of the European Parliament may be invited to be heard by the European Council.

3. The European Council shall act by a simple majority for procedural questions and for the adoption of its Rules of Procedure.

4. The European Council shall be assisted by the General Secretariat of the Council.

Article 236

The European Council shall adopt by a qualified majority:

   (a) a decision establishing the list of Council configurations, other than those of the General Affairs Council and of the Foreign Affairs Council, in accordance with Article 16(6) of the Treaty on European Union;

   (b) a decision on the Presidency of Council configurations, other than that of Foreign Affairs, in accordance with Article 16(9) of the Treaty on European Union.

SECTION 3 THE COUNCIL

Article 237

The Council shall meet when convened by its President on his own initiative or at the request of one of its Members or of the Commission.

Article 238

1. Where it is required to act by a simple majority, the Council shall act by a majority of its component members.

2. By way of derogation from Article 16(4) of the Treaty on European Union, as from 1 November 2014 and subject to the provisions laid down in the Protocol

on transitional provisions, where the Council does not act on a proposal from the Commission or from the High Representative of the Union for Foreign Affairs and Security Policy, the qualified majority shall be defined as at least 72% of the members of the Council, representing Member States comprising at least 65% of the population of the Union.

3. As from 1 November 2014 and subject to the provisions laid down in the Protocol on transitional provisions, in cases where, under the Treaties, not all the members of the Council participate in voting, a qualified majority shall be defined as follows:

   (a) A qualified majority shall be defined as at least 55% of the members of the Council representing the participating Member States, comprising at least 65% of the population of these States.

   A blocking minority must include at least the minimum number of Council members representing more than 35% of the population of the participating Member States, plus one member, failing which the qualified majority shall be deemed attained;

   (b) By way of derogation from point (a), where the Council does not act on a proposal from the Commission or from the High Representative of the Union for Foreign Affairs and Security Policy, the qualified majority shall be defined as at least 72% of the members of the Council representing the participating Member States, comprising at least 65% of the population of these States.

4. Abstentions by Members present in person or represented shall not prevent the adoption by the Council of acts which require unanimity.

Article 239

Where a vote is taken, any Member of the Council may also act on behalf of not more than one other member.

Article 240

1. A committee consisting of the Permanent Representatives of the Governments of the Member States shall be responsible for preparing the work of the Council and for carrying out the tasks assigned to it by the latter. The Committee may adopt procedural decisions in cases provided for in the Council's Rules of Procedure.

2. The Council shall be assisted by a General Secretariat, under the responsibility of a Secretary-General appointed by the Council.

   The Council shall decide on the organisation of the General Secretariat by a simple majority.

3. The Council shall act by a simple majority regarding procedural matters and for the adoption of its Rules of Procedure.

Article 241

The Council, acting by a simple majority, may request the Commission to undertake any studies the Council considers desirable for the attainment of the common objectives, and to submit to it any appropriate proposals. If the Commission does not submit a proposal, it shall inform the Council of the reasons.

Article 242

The Council, acting by a simple majority shall, after consulting the Commission, determine the rules governing the committees provided for in the Treaties.

Article 243

The Council shall determine the salaries, allowances and pensions of the President of the European Council, the President of the Commission, the High Representative of the Union for Foreign Affairs and Security Policy, the Members of the Commission, the Presidents, Members and Registrars of the Court of Justice of the European Union, and the Secretary-General of the Council. It shall also determine any payment to be made instead of remuneration.

SECTION 4 THE COMMISSION

Article 244

In accordance with Article 17(5) of the Treaty on European Union, the Members of the Commission shall be chosen on the basis of a system of rotation established unanimously by the European Council and on the basis of the following principles:

(a) Member States shall be treated on a strictly equal footing as regards determination of the sequence of, and the time spent by, their nationals as members of the Commission; consequently, the difference between the total number of terms of office held by nationals of any given pair of Member States may never be more than one;

(b) subject to point (a), each successive Commission shall be so composed as to reflect satisfactorily the demographic and geographical range of all the Member States.

Article 245

The Members of the Commission shall refrain from any action incompatible with their duties. Member States shall respect their independence and shall not seek to influence them in the performance of their tasks.

The Members of the Commission may not, during their term of office, engage in any other occupation, whether gainful or not. When entering upon their duties they shall give a solemn undertaking that, both during and after their term of office, they will respect the obligations arising therefrom and in particular their duty to behave with integrity and discretion as regards the acceptance, after they have ceased to hold office, of certain appointments or benefits. In the event of any breach of these obligations, the Court of Justice may, on application by the Council acting by a simple majority or the Commission, rule that the Member concerned be, according to the circumstances, either compulsorily retired in accordance with Article 247 or deprived of his right to a pension or other benefits in its stead.

Article 246

Apart from normal replacement, or death, the duties of a Member of the Commission shall end when he resigns or is compulsorily retired.

A vacancy caused by resignation, compulsory retirement or death shall be filled for the remainder of the Member's term of office by a new Member of the same nationality appointed by the Council, by common accord with the President of the Commission, after consulting the European Parliament and in accordance with the criteria set out in the second subparagraph of Article 17(3) of the Treaty on European Union.

The Council may, acting unanimously on a proposal from the President of the Commission, decide that such a vacancy need not be filled, in particular when the remainder of the Member's term of office is short.

In the event of resignation, compulsory retirement or death, the President shall be replaced for the remainder of his term of office. The procedure laid down in the first subparagraph of Article 17(7) of the Treaty on European Union shall be applicable for the replacement of the President.

In the event of resignation, compulsory retirement or death, the High Representative of the Union for Foreign Affairs and Security Policy shall be replaced, for the remainder of his or her term of office, in accordance with Article 18(1) of the Treaty on European Union.

In the case of the resignation of all the Members of the Commission, they shall remain in office and continue to deal with current business until they have been replaced, for the remainder of their term of office, in accordance with Article 17 of the Treaty on European Union.

Article 247

If any Member of the Commission no longer fulfils the conditions required for the performance of his duties or if he has been guilty of serious misconduct, the Court of Justice may, on application by the Council acting by a simple majority or the Commission, compulsorily retire him.

Article 248

Without prejudice to Article 18(4) of the Treaty on European Union, the responsibilities incumbent upon the Commission shall be structured and allocated among its members by its President, in accordance with Article 17(6) of that Treaty. The President may reshuffle the allocation of those responsibilities during the Commission's term of office. The Members of the Commission shall carry out the duties devolved upon them by the President under his authority.

Article 249

1. The Commission shall adopt its Rules of Procedure so as to ensure that both it and its departments operate. It shall ensure that these Rules are published.
2. The Commission shall publish annually, not later than one month before the opening of the session of the European Parliament, a general report on the activities of the Union.

Article 250

The Commission shall act by a majority of its Members.

Its Rules of Procedure shall determine the quorum.

SECTION 5 THE COURT OF JUSTICE OF THE EUROPEAN UNION

Article 251

The Court of Justice shall sit in chambers or in a Grand Chamber, in accordance with the rules laid down for that purpose in the Statute of the Court of Justice of the European Union.

When provided for in the Statute, the Court of Justice may also sit as a full Court.

Article 252

The Court of Justice shall be assisted by eight Advocates-General. Should the Court of Justice so request, the Council, acting unanimously, may increase the number of Advocates-General.*

It shall be the duty of the Advocate-General, acting with complete impartiality and independence, to make, in open court, reasoned submissions on cases which, in accordance with the Statute of the Court of Justice of the European Union, require his involvement.

Article 253

The Judges and Advocates-General of the Court of Justice shall be chosen from persons whose independence is beyond doubt and who possess the qualifications required for appointment to the highest judicial offices in their respective countries or who are juris consults of recognised competence; they shall be appointed by common accord of the governments of the Member States for a term of six years, after consultation of the panel provided for in Article 255.

Every three years there shall be a partial replacement of the Judges and Advocates-General, in accordance with the conditions laid down in the Statute of the Court of Justice of the European Union.

The Judges shall elect the President of the Court of Justice from among their number for a term of three years. He may be re-elected.

Retiring Judges and Advocates-General may be reappointed. The Court of Justice shall appoint its Registrar and lay down the rules governing his service.

The Court of Justice shall establish its Rules of Procedure. Those Rules shall require the approval of the Council.

Article 254

The number of Judges of the General Court shall be determined by the Statute of the Court of Justice of the European Union. The Statute may provide for the General Court to be assisted by Advocates-General.

The members of the General Court shall be chosen from persons whose independence is beyond doubt and who possess the ability required for appointment to high judicial office. They shall be appointed by common accord of the governments of the Member States for a term of six years, after consultation of the panel provided for in Article 255. The membership shall be partially renewed every three years. Retiring members shall be eligible for reappointment.

---

* The present number of Advocates-General is set at 11, see (Council) Decision 2013/336 increasing the number of Advocates-General of the Court of Justice of the European Union [2013] OJ L179/92.

The Judges shall elect the President of the General Court from among their number for a term of three years. He may be re-elected.

The General Court shall appoint its Registrar and lay down the rules governing his service.

The General Court shall establish its Rules of Procedure in agreement with the Court of Justice. Those Rules shall require the approval of the Council.

Unless the Statute of the Court of Justice of the European Union provides otherwise, the provisions of the Treaties relating to the Court of Justice shall apply to the General Court.

Article 255

A panel shall be set up in order to give an opinion on candidates' suitability to perform the duties of Judge and Advocate-General of the Court of Justice and the General Court before the governments of the Member States make the appointments referred to in Articles 253 and 254.

The panel shall comprise seven persons chosen from among former members of the Court of Justice and the General Court, members of national supreme courts and lawyers of recognised competence, one of whom shall be proposed by the European Parliament. The Council shall adopt a decision establishing the panel's operating rules and a decision appointing its members. It shall act on the initiative of the President of the Court of Justice.

Article 256

1. The General Court shall have jurisdiction to hear and determine at first instance actions or proceedings referred to in Articles 263, 265, 268, 270 and 272, with the exception of those assigned to a specialised court set up under Article 257 and those reserved in the Statute for the Court of Justice. The Statute may provide for the General Court to have jurisdiction for other classes of action or proceeding.

   Decisions given by the General Court under this paragraph may be subject to a right of appeal to the Court of Justice on points of law only, under the conditions and within the limits laid down by the Statute.

2. The General Court shall have jurisdiction to hear and determine actions or proceedings brought against decisions of the specialised courts.

   Decisions given by the General Court under this paragraph may exceptionally be subject to review by the Court of Justice, under the conditions and within the limits laid down by the Statute, where there is a serious risk of the unity or consistency of Union law being affected.

3. The General Court shall have jurisdiction to hear and determine questions referred for a preliminary ruling under Article 267, in specific areas laid down by the Statute.

   Where the General Court considers that the case requires a decision of principle likely to affect the unity or consistency of Union law, it may refer the case to the Court of Justice for a ruling.

   Decisions given by the General Court on questions referred for a preliminary ruling may exceptionally be subject to review by the Court of Justice, under the conditions and within the limits laid down by the Statute, where there is a serious risk of the unity or consistency of Union law being affected.

Article 257

The European Parliament and the Council, acting in accordance with the ordinary legislative procedure, may establish specialised courts attached to the General

Court to hear and determine at first instance certain classes of action or proceeding brought in specific areas. The European Parliament and the Council shall act by means of regulations either on a proposal from the Commission after consultation of the Court of Justice or at the request of the Court of Justice after consultation of the Commission.

The regulation establishing a specialised court shall lay down the rules on the organisation of the court and the extent of the jurisdiction conferred upon it.

Decisions given by specialised courts may be subject to a right of appeal on points of law only or, when provided for in the regulation establishing the specialised court, a right of appeal also on matters of fact, before the General Court.

The members of the specialised courts shall be chosen from persons whose independence is beyond doubt and who possess the ability required for appointment to judicial office. They shall be appointed by the Council, acting unanimously.

The specialised courts shall establish their Rules of Procedure in agreement with the Court of Justice. Those Rules shall require the approval of the Council.

Unless the regulation establishing the specialised court provides otherwise, the provisions of the Treaties relating to the Court of Justice of the European Union and the provisions of the Statute of the Court of Justice of the European Union shall apply to the specialised courts. Title I of the Statute and Article 64 thereof shall in any case apply to the specialised courts.

Article 258

If the Commission considers that a Member State has failed to fulfil an obligation under the Treaties, it shall deliver a reasoned opinion on the matter after giving the State concerned the opportunity to submit its observations.

If the State concerned does not comply with the opinion within the period laid down by the Commission, the latter may bring the matter before the Court of Justice of the European Union.

Article 259

A Member State which considers that another Member State has failed to fulfil an obligation under the Treaties may bring the matter before the Court of Justice of the European Union.

Before a Member State brings an action against another Member State for an alleged infringement of an obligation under the Treaties, it shall bring the matter before the Commission.

The Commission shall deliver a reasoned opinion after each of the States concerned has been given the opportunity to submit its own case and its observations on the other party's case both orally and in writing.

If the Commission has not delivered an opinion within three months of the date on which the matter was brought before it, the absence of such opinion shall not prevent the matter from being brought before the Court.

Article 260

1. If the Court of Justice of the European Union finds that a Member State has failed to fulfil an obligation under the Treaties, the State shall be required to take the necessary measures to comply with the judgment of the Court.

2. If the Commission considers that the Member State concerned has not taken the necessary measures to comply with the judgment of the Court, it may bring the case before the Court after giving that State the opportunity to submit its observations. It shall specify the amount of the lump sum or penalty payment to be paid by the Member State concerned which it considers appropriate in the circumstances.

If the Court finds that the Member State concerned has not complied with its judgment it may impose a lump sum or penalty payment on it.

This procedure shall be without prejudice to Article 259.

3. When the Commission brings a case before the Court pursuant to Article 258 on the grounds that the Member State concerned has failed to fulfil its obligation to notify measures transposing a directive adopted under a legislative procedure, it may, when it deems appropriate, specify the amount of the lump sum or penalty payment to be paid by the Member State concerned which it considers appropriate in the circumstances. If the Court finds that there is an infringement it may impose a lump sum or penalty payment on the Member State concerned not exceeding the amount specified by the Commission. The payment obligation shall take effect on the date set by the Court in its judgment.

Article 261

Regulations adopted jointly by the European Parliament and the Council, and by the Council, pursuant to the provisions of the Treaties, may give the Court of Justice of the European Union unlimited jurisdiction with regard to the penalties provided for in such regulations.

Article 262

Without prejudice to the other provisions of the Treaties, the Council, acting unanimously in accordance with a special legislative procedure and after consulting the European Parliament, may adopt provisions to confer jurisdiction, to the extent that it shall determine, on the Court of Justice of the European Union in disputes relating to the application of acts adopted on the basis of the Treaties which create European intellectual property rights. These provisions shall enter into force after their approval by the Member States in accordance with their respective constitutional requirements.

Article 263

The Court of Justice of the European Union shall review the legality of legislative acts, of acts of the Council, of the Commission and of the European Central Bank, other than recommendations and opinions, and of acts of the European Parliament and of the European Council intended to produce legal effects vis-à-vis third parties. It shall also review the legality of acts of bodies, offices or agencies of the Union intended to produce legal effects vis-à-vis third parties.

It shall for this purpose have jurisdiction in actions brought by a Member State, the European Parliament, the Council or the Commission on grounds of lack of competence, infringement of an essential procedural requirement, infringement of the Treaties or of any rule of law relating to their application, or misuse of powers.

The Court shall have jurisdiction under the same conditions in actions brought by the Court of Auditors, by the European Central Bank and by the Committee of the Regions for the purpose of protecting their prerogatives.

Any natural or legal person may, under the conditions laid down in the first and second paragraphs, institute proceedings against an act addressed to that person or which is of direct and individual concern to them, and against a regulatory act which is of direct concern to them and does not entail implementing measures.

Acts setting up bodies, offices and agencies of the Union may lay down specific conditions and arrangements concerning actions brought by natural or legal persons against acts of these bodies, offices or agencies intended to produce legal effects in relation to them.

The proceedings provided for in this Article shall be instituted within two months of the publication of the measure, or of its notification to the plaintiff, or, in the absence thereof, of the day on which it came to the knowledge of the latter, as the case may be.

Article 264

If the action is well founded, the Court of Justice of the European Union shall declare the act concerned to be void.

However, the Court shall, if it considers this necessary, state which of the effects of the act which it has declared void shall be considered as definitive.

Article 265

Should the European Parliament, the European Council, the Council, the Commission or the European Central Bank, in infringement of the Treaties, fail to act, the Member States and the other institutions of the Union may bring an action before the Court of Justice of the European Union to have the infringement established. This Article shall apply, under the same conditions, to bodies, offices and agencies of the Union which fail to act.

The action shall be admissible only if the institution, body, office or agency concerned has first been called upon to act. If, within two months of being so called upon, the institution, body, office or agency concerned has not defined its position, the action may be brought within a further period of two months.

Any natural or legal person may, under the conditions laid down in the preceding paragraphs, complain to the Court that an institution, body, office or agency of the Union has failed to address to that person any act other than a recommendation or an opinion.

Article 266

The institution whose act has been declared void or whose failure to act has been declared contrary to the Treaties shall be required to take the necessary measures to comply with the judgment of the Court of Justice of the European Union.

This obligation shall not affect any obligation which may result from the application of the second paragraph of Article 340.

Article 267

The Court of Justice of the European Union shall have jurisdiction to give preliminary rulings concerning:
(a) the interpretation of the Treaties;
(b) the validity and interpretation of acts of the institutions, bodies, offices or agencies of the Union[.]

Where such a question is raised before any court or tribunal of a Member State, that court or tribunal may, if it considers that a decision on the question is necessary to enable it to give judgment, request the Court to give a ruling thereon.

Where any such question is raised in a case pending before a court or tribunal of a Member State against whose decisions there is no judicial remedy under national law, that court or tribunal shall bring the matter before the Court.

If such a question is raised in a case pending before a court or tribunal of a Member State with regard to a person in custody, the Court of Justice of the European Union shall act with the minimum of delay.

Article 268
The Court of Justice of the European Union shall have jurisdiction in disputes relating to compensation for damage provided for in the second and third paragraphs of Article 340.

Article 269
The Court of Justice shall have jurisdiction to decide on the legality of an act adopted by the European Council or by the Council pursuant to Article 7 of the Treaty on European Union solely at the request of the Member State concerned by a determination of the European Council or of the Council and in respect solely of the procedural stipulations contained in that Article.

Such a request must be made within one month from the date of such determination. The Court shall rule within one month from the date of the request.

Article 270
The Court of Justice of the European Union shall have jurisdiction in any dispute between the Union and its servants within the limits and under the conditions laid down in the Staff Regulations of Officials and the Conditions of Employment of other servants of the Union.

Article 271
The Court of Justice of the European Union shall, within the limits hereinafter laid down, have jurisdiction in disputes concerning:
  (a) the fulfilment by Member States of obligations under the Statute of the European Investment Bank. In this connection, the Board of Directors of the Bank shall enjoy the powers conferred upon the Commission by Article 258;
  (b) measures adopted by the Board of Governors of the European Investment Bank. In this connection, any Member State, the Commission or the Board of Directors of the Bank may institute proceedings under the conditions laid down in Article 263;
  (c) measures adopted by the Board of Directors of the European Investment Bank. Proceedings against such measures may be instituted only by Member States or by the Commission, under the conditions laid down in Article 263, and solely on the grounds of non-compliance with the procedure provided for in Article 19(2), (5), (6) and (7) of the Statute of the Bank;
  (d) the fulfilment by national central banks of obligations under the Treaties and the Statute of the ESCB and of the ECB. In this connection the powers of the

Governing Council of the European Central Bank in respect of national central banks shall be the same as those conferred upon the Commission in respect of Member States by Article 258. If the Court finds that a national central bank has failed to fulfil an obligation under the Treaties, that bank shall be required to take the necessary measures to comply with the judgment of the Court.

Article 272

The Court of Justice of the European Union shall have jurisdiction to give judgment pursuant to any arbitration clause contained in a contract concluded by or on behalf of the Union, whether that contract be governed by public or private law.

Article 273

The Court of Justice shall have jurisdiction in any dispute between Member States which relates to the subject matter of the Treaties if the dispute is submitted to it under a special agreement between the parties.

Article 274

Save where jurisdiction is conferred on the Court of Justice of the European Union by the Treaties, disputes to which the Union is a party shall not on that ground be excluded from the jurisdiction of the courts or tribunals of the Member States.

Article 275

The Court of Justice of the European Union shall not have jurisdiction with respect to the provisions relating to the common foreign and security policy nor with respect to acts adopted on the basis of those provisions.

However, the Court shall have jurisdiction to monitor compliance with Article 40 of the Treaty on European Union and to rule on proceedings, brought in accordance with the conditions laid down in the fourth paragraph of Article 263 of this Treaty, reviewing the legality of decisions providing for restrictive measures against natural or legal persons adopted by the Council on the basis of Chapter 2 of Title V of the Treaty on European Union.

Article 276

In exercising its powers regarding the provisions of Chapters 4 and 5 of Title V of Part Three relating to the area of freedom, security and justice, the Court of Justice of the European Union shall have no jurisdiction to review the validity or proportionality of operations carried out by the police or other law-enforcement services of a Member State or the exercise of the responsibilities incumbent upon Member States with regard to the maintenance of law and order and the safeguarding of internal security.

Article 277

Notwithstanding the expiry of the period laid down in Article 263, sixth paragraph, any party may, in proceedings in which an act of general application adopted by an institution, body, office or agency of the Union is at issue, plead the grounds specified in Article 263, second paragraph, in order to invoke before the Court of Justice of the European Union the inapplicability of that act.

Article 278

Actions brought before the Court of Justice of the European Union shall not have suspensory effect. The Court may, however, if it considers that circumstances so require, order that application of the contested act be suspended.

Article 279

The Court of Justice of the European Union may in any cases before it prescribe any necessary interim measures.

Article 280

The judgments of the Court of Justice of the European Union shall be enforceable under the conditions laid down in Article 299.

Article 281

The Statute of the Court of Justice of the European Union shall be laid down in a separate Protocol.

The European Parliament and the Council, acting in accordance with the ordinary legislative procedure, may amend the provisions of the Statute, with the exception of Title I and Article 64. The European Parliament and the Council shall act either at the request of the Court of Justice and after consultation of the Commission, or on a proposal from the Commission and after consultation of the Court of Justice.

SECTION 6 THE EUROPEAN CENTRAL BANK

Article 282

1. The European Central Bank, together with the national central banks, shall constitute the European System of Central Banks (ESCB). The European Central Bank, together with the national central banks of the Member States whose currency is the euro, which constitute the Eurosystem, shall conduct the monetary policy of the Union.
2. The ESCB shall be governed by the decision-making bodies of the European Central Bank. The primary objective of the ESCB shall be to maintain price stability. Without prejudice to that objective, it shall support the general economic policies in the Union in order to contribute to the achievement of the latter's objectives.
3. The European Central Bank shall have legal personality. It alone may authorise the issue of the euro. It shall be independent in the exercise of its powers and in the management of its finances. Union institutions, bodies, offices and agencies and the governments of the Member States shall respect that independence.
4. The European Central Bank shall adopt such measures as are necessary to carry out its tasks in accordance with Articles 127 to 133, with Article 138, and with the conditions laid down in the Statute of the ESCB and of the ECB. In accordance with these same Articles, those Member States whose currency is not the euro, and their central banks, shall retain their powers in monetary matters.
5. Within the areas falling within its responsibilities, the European Central Bank shall be consulted on all proposed Union acts, and all proposals for regulation at national level, and may give an opinion.

Article 283

1. The Governing Council of the European Central Bank shall comprise the members of the Executive Board of the European Central Bank and the Governors of the national central banks of the Member States whose currency is the euro.

2. The Executive Board shall comprise the President, the Vice-President and four other members.

   The President, the Vice-President and the other members of the Executive Board shall be appointed by the European Council, acting by a qualified majority, from among persons of recognised standing and professional experience in monetary or banking matters, on a recommendation from the Council, after it has consulted the European Parliament and the Governing Council of the European Central Bank.

   Their term of office shall be eight years and shall not be renewable. Only nationals of Member States may be members of the Executive Board.

Article 284

1. The President of the Council and a Member of the Commission may participate, without having the right to vote, in meetings of the Governing Council of the European Central Bank.

   The President of the Council may submit a motion for deliberation to the Governing Council of the European Central Bank.

2. The President of the European Central Bank shall be invited to participate in Council meetings when the Council is discussing matters relating to the objectives and tasks of the ESCB.

3. The European Central Bank shall address an annual report on the activities of the ESCB and on the monetary policy of both the previous and current year to the European Parliament, the Council and the Commission, and also to the European Council. The President of the European Central Bank shall present this report to the Council and to the European Parliament, which may hold a general debate on that basis.

   The President of the European Central Bank and the other members of the Executive Board may, at the request of the European Parliament or on their own initiative, be heard by the competent committees of the European Parliament.

SECTION 7 THE COURT OF AUDITORS

Article 285

The Court of Auditors shall carry out the Union's audit.

It shall consist of one national of each Member State. Its Members shall be completely independent in the performance of their duties, in the Union's general interest.

Article 286

1. The Members of the Court of Auditors shall be chosen from among persons who belong or have belonged in their respective States to external audit bodies or who are especially qualified for this office. Their independence must be beyond doubt.

2. The Members of the Court of Auditors shall be appointed for a term of six years. The Council, after consulting the European Parliament, shall adopt the list of Members

drawn up in accordance with the proposals made by each Member State. The term of office of the Members of the Court of Auditors shall be renewable.

They shall elect the President of the Court of Auditors from among their number for a term of three years. The President may be re-elected.

3. In the performance of these duties, the Members of the Court of Auditors shall neither seek nor take instructions from any government or from any other body. The Members of the Court of Auditors shall refrain from any action incompatible with their duties.

4. The Members of the Court of Auditors may not, during their term of office, engage in any other occupation, whether gainful or not. When entering upon their duties they shall give a solemn undertaking that, both during and after their term of office, they will respect the obligations arising therefrom and in particular their duty to behave with integrity and discretion as regards the acceptance, after they have ceased to hold office, of certain appointments or benefits.

5. Apart from normal replacement, or death, the duties of a Member of the Court of Auditors shall end when he resigns, or is compulsorily retired by a ruling of the Court of Justice pursuant to paragraph 6.

The vacancy thus caused shall be filled for the remainder of the Member's term of office.

Save in the case of compulsory retirement, Members of the Court of Auditors shall remain in office until they have been replaced.

6. A Member of the Court of Auditors may be deprived of his office or of his right to a pension or other benefits in its stead only if the Court of Justice, at the request of the Court of Auditors, finds that he no longer fulfils the requisite conditions or meets the obligations arising from his office.

7. The Council shall determine the conditions of employment of the President and the Members of the Court of Auditors and in particular their salaries, allowances and pensions. It shall also determine any payment to be made instead of remuneration.

8. The provisions of the Protocol on the privileges and immunities of the European Union applicable to the Judges of the Court of Justice of the European Union shall also apply to the Members of the Court of Auditors.

Article 287

1. The Court of Auditors shall examine the accounts of all revenue and expenditure of the Union. It shall also examine the accounts of all revenue and expenditure of all bodies, offices or agencies set up by the Union in so far as the relevant constituent instrument does not preclude such examination.

The Court of Auditors shall provide the European Parliament and the Council with a statement of assurance as to the reliability of the accounts and the legality and regularity of the underlying transactions which shall be published in the Official Journal of the European Union. This statement may be supplemented by specific assessments for each major area of Union activity.

2. The Court of Auditors shall examine whether all revenue has been received and all expenditure incurred in a lawful and regular manner and whether the financial management has been sound. In doing so, it shall report in particular on any cases of irregularity.

The audit of revenue shall be carried out on the basis both of the amounts established as due and the amounts actually paid to the Union.

The audit of expenditure shall be carried out on the basis both of commitments undertaken and payments made.

These audits may be carried out before the closure of accounts for the financial year in question.

3. The audit shall be based on records and, if necessary, performed on the spot in the other institutions of the Union, on the premises of any body, office or agency which manages revenue or expenditure on behalf of the Union and in the Member States, including on the premises of any natural or legal person in receipt of payments from the budget. In the Member States the audit shall be carried out in liaison with national audit bodies or, if these do not have the necessary powers, with the competent national departments. The Court of Auditors and the national audit bodies of the Member States shall cooperate in a spirit of trust while maintaining their independence. These bodies or departments shall inform the Court of Auditors whether they intend to take part in the audit.

The other institutions of the Union, any bodies, offices or agencies managing revenue or expenditure on behalf of the Union, any natural or legal person in receipt of payments from the budget, and the national audit bodies or, if these do not have the necessary powers, the competent national departments, shall forward to the Court of Auditors, at its request, any document or information necessary to carry out its task.

In respect of the European Investment Bank's activity in managing Union expenditure and revenue, the Court's rights of access to information held by the Bank shall be governed by an agreement between the Court, the Bank and the Commission. In the absence of an agreement, the Court shall nevertheless have access to information necessary for the audit of Union expenditure and revenue managed by the Bank.

4. The Court of Auditors shall draw up an annual report after the close of each financial year. It shall be forwarded to the other institutions of the Union and shall be published, together with the replies of these institutions to the observations of the Court of Auditors, in the *Official Journal of the European Union*.

The Court of Auditors may also, at any time, submit observations, particularly in the form of special reports, on specific questions and deliver opinions at the request of one of the other institutions of the Union.

It shall adopt its annual reports, special reports or opinions by a majority of its Members. However, it may establish internal chambers in order to adopt certain categories of reports or opinions under the conditions laid down by its Rules of Procedure.

It shall assist the European Parliament and the Council in exercising their powers of control over the implementation of the budget.

The Court of Auditors shall draw up its Rules of Procedure. Those rules shall require the approval of the Council.

Chapter 2 Legal Acts of the Union, Adoption Procedures and Other Provisions

SECTION 1 THE LEGAL ACTS OF THE UNION

Article 288

To exercise the Union's competences, the institutions shall adopt regulations, directives, decisions, recommendations and opinions.

A regulation shall have general application. It shall be binding in its entirety and directly applicable in all Member States.

A directive shall be binding, as to the result to be achieved, upon each Member State to which it is addressed, but shall leave to the national authorities the choice of form and methods.

A decision shall be binding in its entirety. A decision which specifies those to whom it is addressed shall be binding only on them.

Recommendations and opinions shall have no binding force.

Article 289

1. The ordinary legislative procedure shall consist in the joint adoption by the European Parliament and the Council of a regulation, directive or decision on a proposal from the Commission. This procedure is defined in Article 294.
2. In the specific cases provided for by the Treaties, the adoption of a regulation, directive or decision by the European Parliament with the participation of the Council, or by the latter with the participation of the European Parliament, shall constitute a special legislative procedure.
3. Legal acts adopted by legislative procedure shall constitute legislative acts.
4. In the specific cases provided for by the Treaties, legislative acts may be adopted on the initiative of a group of Member States or of the European Parliament, on a recommendation from the European Central Bank or at the request of the Court of Justice or the European Investment Bank.

Article 290

1. A legislative act may delegate to the Commission the power to adopt non-legislative acts of general application to supplement or amend certain non-essential elements of the legislative act.

   The objectives, content, scope and duration of the delegation of power shall be explicitly defined in the legislative acts. The essential elements of an area shall be reserved for the legislative act and accordingly shall not be the subject of a delegation of power.
2. Legislative acts shall explicitly lay down the conditions to which the delegation is subject; these conditions may be as follows:
   (a) the European Parliament or the Council may decide to revoke the delegation;
   (b) the delegated act may enter into force only if no objection has been expressed by the European Parliament or the Council within a period set by the legislative act.

   For the purposes of (a) and (b), the European Parliament shall act by a majority of its component members, and the Council by a qualified majority.
3. The adjective 'delegated' shall be inserted in the title of delegated acts.

Article 291

1. Member States shall adopt all measures of national law necessary to implement legally binding Union acts.
2. Where uniform conditions for implementing legally binding Union acts are needed, those acts shall confer implementing powers on the Commission, or, in duly justified specific cases and in the cases provided for in Articles 24 and 26 of the Treaty on European Union, on the Council.
3. For the purposes of paragraph 2, the European Parliament and the Council, acting by means of regulations in accordance with the ordinary legislative procedure, shall lay

down in advance the rules and general principles concerning mechanisms for control by Member States of the Commission's exercise of implementing powers.

4. The word 'implementing' shall be inserted in the title of implementing acts.

Article 292

The Council shall adopt recommendations. It shall act on a proposal from the Commission in all cases where the Treaties provide that it shall adopt acts on a proposal from the Commission. It shall act unanimously in those areas in which unanimity is required for the adoption of a Union act. The Commission, and the European Central Bank in the specific cases provided for in the Treaties, shall adopt recommendations.

SECTION 2 PROCEDURES FOR THE ADOPTION OF ACTS AND OTHER PROVISIONS

Article 293

1. Where, pursuant to the Treaties, the Council acts on a proposal from the Commission, it may amend that proposal only by acting unanimously, except in the cases referred to in paragraphs 10 and 13 of Article 294, in Articles 310, 312 and 314 and in the second paragraph of Article 315.
2. As long as the Council has not acted, the Commission may alter its proposal at any time during the procedures leading to the adoption of a Union act.

Article 294

1. Where reference is made in the Treaties to the ordinary legislative procedure for the adoption of an act, the following procedure shall apply.
2. The Commission shall submit a proposal to the European Parliament and the Council.

First reading

3. The European Parliament shall adopt its position at first reading and communicate it to the Council.
4. If the Council approves the European Parliament's position, the act concerned shall be adopted in the wording which corresponds to the position of the European Parliament.
5. If the Council does not approve the European Parliament's position, it shall adopt its position at first reading and communicate it to the European Parliament.
6. The Council shall inform the European Parliament fully of the reasons which led it to adopt its position at first reading. The Commission shall inform the European Parliament fully of its position.

Second reading

7. If, within three months of such communication, the European Parliament:
   (a) approves the Council's position at first reading or has not taken a decision, the act concerned shall be deemed to have been adopted in the wording which corresponds to the position of the Council;
   (b) rejects, by a majority of its component members, the Council's position at first reading, the proposed act shall be deemed not to have been adopted;

(c) proposes, by a majority of its component members, amendments to the Council's position at first reading, the text thus amended shall be forwarded to the Council and to the Commission, which shall deliver an opinion on those amendments.

8. If, within three months of receiving the European Parliament's amendments, the Council, acting by a qualified majority:

(a) approves all those amendments, the act in question shall be deemed to have been adopted;

(b) does not approve all the amendments, the President of the Council, in agreement with the President of the European Parliament, shall within six weeks convene a meeting of the Conciliation Committee.

9. The Council shall act unanimously on the amendments on which the Commission has delivered a negative opinion.

Conciliation

10. The Conciliation Committee, which shall be composed of the members of the Council or their representatives and an equal number of members representing the European Parliament, shall have the task of reaching agreement on a joint text, by a qualified majority of the members of the Council or their representatives and by a majority of the members representing the European Parliament within six weeks of its being convened, on the basis of the positions of the European Parliament and the Council at second reading.

11. The Commission shall take part in the Conciliation Committee's proceedings and shall take all necessary initiatives with a view to reconciling the positions of the European Parliament and the Council.

12. If, within six weeks of its being convened, the Conciliation Committee does not approve the joint text, the proposed act shall be deemed not to have been adopted.

Third reading

13. If, within that period, the Conciliation Committee approves a joint text, the European Parliament, acting by a majority of the votes cast, and the Council, acting by a qualified majority, shall each have a period of six weeks from that approval in which to adopt the act in question in accordance with the joint text. If they fail to do so, the proposed act shall be deemed not to have been adopted.

14. The periods of three months and six weeks referred to in this Article shall be extended by a maximum of one month and two weeks respectively at the initiative of the European Parliament or the Council.

Special provisions

15. Where, in the cases provided for in the Treaties, a legislative act is submitted to the ordinary legislative procedure on the initiative of a group of Member States, on a recommendation by the European Central Bank, or at the request of the Court of Justice, paragraph 2, the second sentence of paragraph 6, and paragraph 9 shall not apply.

In such cases, the European Parliament and the Council shall communicate the proposed act to the Commission with their positions at first and second readings. The European Parliament or the Council may request the opinion of the Commission throughout the procedure, which the Commission may also deliver on its own initiative. It may also, if it deems it necessary, take part in the Conciliation Committee in accordance with paragraph 11.

Article 295

The European Parliament, the Council and the Commission shall consult each other and by common agreement make arrangements for their cooperation. To that end, they may, in compliance with the Treaties, conclude interinstitutional agreements which may be of a binding nature.

Article 296

Where the Treaties do not specify the type of act to be adopted, the institutions shall select it on a case-by-case basis, in compliance with the applicable procedures and with the principle of proportionality.

Legal acts shall state the reasons on which they are based and shall refer to any proposals, initiatives, recommendations, requests or opinions required by the Treaties.

When considering draft legislative acts, the European Parliament and the Council shall refrain from adopting acts not provided for by the relevant legislative procedure in the area in question.

Article 297

1. Legislative acts adopted under the ordinary legislative procedure shall be signed by the President of the European Parliament and by the President of the Council.

   Legislative acts adopted under a special legislative procedure shall be signed by the President of the institution which adopted them.

   Legislative acts shall be published in the Official Journal of the European Union. They shall enter into force on the date specified in them or, in the absence thereof, on the twentieth day following that of their publication.

2. Non-legislative acts adopted in the form of regulations, directives or decisions, when the latter do not specify to whom they are addressed, shall be signed by the President of the institution which adopted them.

   Regulations and directives which are addressed to all Member States, as well as decisions which do not specify to whom they are addressed, shall be published in the *Official Journal of the European Union*. They shall enter into force on the date specified in them or, in the absence thereof, on the twentieth day following that of their publication.

   Other directives, and decisions which specify to whom they are addressed, shall be notified to those to whom they are addressed and shall take effect upon such notification.

Article 298

1. In carrying out their missions, the institutions, bodies, offices and agencies of the Union shall have the support of an open, efficient and independent European administration.
2. In compliance with the Staff Regulations and the Conditions of Employment adopted on the basis of Article 336, the European Parliament and the Council, acting by means of regulations in accordance with the ordinary legislative procedure, shall establish provisions to that end.

Article 299

Acts of the Council, the Commission or the European Central Bank which impose a pecuniary obligation on persons other than States, shall be enforceable.

Enforcement shall be governed by the rules of civil procedure in force in the State in the territory of which it is carried out. The order for its enforcement shall be appended to the decision, without other formality than verification of the authenticity of the decision, by the national authority which the government of each Member State shall designate for this purpose and shall make known to the Commission and to the Court of Justice of the European Union.

When these formalities have been completed on application by the party concerned, the latter may proceed to enforcement in accordance with the national law, by bringing the matter directly before the competent authority.

Enforcement may be suspended only by a decision of the Court. However, the courts of the country concerned shall have jurisdiction over complaints that enforcement is being carried out in an irregular manner.

Chapter 3 The Union's Advisory Bodies

Article 300

1. The European Parliament, the Council and the Commission shall be assisted by an Economic and Social Committee and a Committee of the Regions, exercising advisory functions.
2. The Economic and Social Committee shall consist of representatives of organisations of employers, of the employed, and of other parties representative of civil society, notably in socio-economic, civic, professional and cultural areas.
3. The Committee of the Regions shall consist of representatives of regional and local bodies who either hold a regional or local authority electoral mandate or are politically accountable to an elected assembly.
4. The members of the Economic and Social Committee and of the Committee of the Regions shall not be bound by any mandatory instructions. They shall be completely independent in the performance of their duties, in the Union's general interest.
5. The rules referred to in paragraphs 2 and 3 governing the nature of the composition of the Committees shall be reviewed at regular intervals by the Council to take account of economic, social and demographic developments within the Union. The Council, on a proposal from the Commission, shall adopt decisions to that end.

SECTION 1 THE ECONOMIC AND SOCIAL COMMITTEE

Article 301

The number of members of the Economic and Social Committee shall not exceed 350.

The Council, acting unanimously on a proposal from the Commission, shall adopt a decision determining the Committee's composition.

The Council shall determine the allowances of members of the Committee.

Article 302

1. The members of the Committee shall be appointed for five years The Council shall adopt the list of members drawn up in accordance with the proposals made by each Member State. The term of office of the members of the Committee shall be renewable.

2. The Council shall act after consulting the Commission. It may obtain the opinion of European bodies which are representative of the various economic and social sectors and of civil society to which the Union's activities are of concern.

Article 303

The Committee shall elect its chairman and officers from among its members for a term of two and a half years.

It shall adopt its Rules of Procedure.

The Committee shall be convened by its chairman at the request of the European Parliament, the Council or of the Commission. It may also meet on its own initiative.

Article 304

The Committee shall be consulted by the European Parliament, by the Council or by the Commission where the Treaties so provide. The Committee may be consulted by these institutions in all cases in which they consider it appropriate. It may issue an opinion on its own initiative in cases in which it considers such action appropriate.

The European Parliament, the Council or the Commission shall, if it considers it necessary, set the Committee, for the submission of its opinion, a time limit which may not be less than one month from the date on which the chairman receives notification to this effect. Upon expiry of the time limit, the absence of an opinion shall not prevent further action.

The opinion of the Committee, together with a record of the proceedings, shall be forwarded to the European Parliament, to the Council and to the Commission.

SECTION 2 THE COMMITTEE OF THE REGIONS

Article 305

The number of members of the Committee of the Regions shall not exceed 350.

The Council, acting unanimously on a proposal from the Commission, shall adopt a decision determining the Committee's composition.

The members of the Committee and an equal number of alternate members shall be appointed for five years. Their term of office shall be renewable. The Council shall adopt the list of members and alternate members drawn up in accordance with the proposals made by each Member State. When the mandate referred to in Article 300(3) on the basis of which they were proposed comes to an end, the term of office of members of the Committee shall terminate automatically and they shall then be replaced for the remainder of the said term of office in accordance with the same procedure. No member of the Committee shall at the same time be a Member of the European Parliament.

Article 306

The Committee of the Regions shall elect its chairman and officers from among its members for a term of two and a half years.

It shall adopt its Rules of Procedure. The Committee shall be convened by its chairman at the request of the European Parliament, the Council or of the Commission. It may also meet on its own initiative.

Article 307

The Committee of the Regions shall be consulted by the European Parliament, by the Council or by the Commission where the Treaties so provide and in all other cases, in particular those which concern cross-border cooperation, in which one of these institutions considers it appropriate.

The European Parliament, the Council or the Commission shall, if it considers it necessary, set the Committee, for the submission of its opinion, a time limit which may not be less than one month from the date on which the chairman receives notification to this effect. Upon expiry of the time limit, the absence of an opinion shall not prevent further action.

Where the Economic and Social Committee is consulted pursuant to Article 304, the Committee of the Regions shall be informed by the European Parliament, the Council or the Commission of the request for an opinion. Where it considers that specific regional interests are involved, the Committee of the Regions may issue an opinion on the matter.

It may issue an opinion on its own initiative in cases in which it considers such action appropriate.

The opinion of the Committee, together with a record of the proceedings, shall be forwarded to the European Parliament, to the Council and to the Commission.

Chapter 4 The European Investment Bank

Article 308

The European Investment Bank shall have legal personality.

The members of the European Investment Bank shall be the Member States. The Statute of the European Investment Bank is laid down in a Protocol annexed to the Treaties. The Council acting unanimously in accordance with a special legislative procedure, at the request of the European Investment Bank and after consulting the European Parliament and the Commission, or on a proposal from the Commission and after consulting the European Parliament and the European Investment Bank, may amend the Statute of the Bank.

Article 309

The task of the European Investment Bank shall be to contribute, by having recourse to the capital market and utilising its own resources, to the balanced and steady development of the internal market in the interest of the Union. For this purpose the Bank shall, operating on a non-profit-making basis, grant loans and give guarantees which facilitate the financing of the following projects in all sectors of the economy:

(a) projects for developing less-developed regions;

(b) projects for modernising or converting undertakings or for developing fresh activities called for by the establishment or functioning of the internal market, where these projects are of such a size or nature that they cannot be entirely financed by the various means available in the individual Member States;

(c) projects of common interest to several Member States which are of such a size or nature that they cannot be entirely financed by the various means available in the individual Member States.

In carrying out its task, the Bank shall facilitate the financing of investment programmes in conjunction with assistance from the Structural Funds and other Union Financial Instruments.

TITLE II FINANCIAL PROVISIONS

Article 310
1. All items of revenue and expenditure of the Union shall be included in estimates to be drawn up for each financial year and shall be shown in the budget.

    The Union's annual budget shall be established by the European Parliament and the Council in accordance with Article 314.

    The revenue and expenditure shown in the budget shall be in balance.
2. The expenditure shown in the budget shall be authorised for the annual budgetary period in accordance with the regulation referred to in Article 322.
3. The implementation of expenditure shown in the budget shall require the prior adoption of a legally binding Union act providing a legal basis for its action and for the implementation of the corresponding expenditure in accordance with the regulation referred to in Article 322, except in cases for which that law provides.
4. With a view to maintaining budgetary discipline, the Union shall not adopt any act which is likely to have appreciable implications for the budget without providing an assurance that the expenditure arising from such an act is capable of being financed within the limit of the Union's own resources and in compliance with the multiannual financial framework referred to in Article 312.
5. The budget shall be implemented in accordance with the principle of sound financial management. Member States shall cooperate with the Union to ensure that the appropriations entered in the budget are used in accordance with this principle.
6. The Union and the Member States, in accordance with Article 325, shall counter fraud and any other illegal activities affecting the financial interests of the Union.

Chapter 1 The Union's Own Resources

Article 311
The Union shall provide itself with the means necessary to attain its objectives and carry through its policies.

Without prejudice to other revenue, the budget shall be financed wholly from own resources.

The Council, acting in accordance with a special legislative procedure, shall unanimously and after consulting the European Parliament adopt a decision laying down the provisions relating to the system of own resources of the Union. In this context it may establish new categories of own resources or abolish an existing category. That decision shall not enter into force until it is approved by the Member States in accordance with their respective constitutional requirements.

The Council, acting by means of regulations in accordance with a special legislative procedure, shall lay down implementing measures for the Union's own resources system in so far as this is provided for in the decision adopted on the basis of the third paragraph. The Council shall act after obtaining the consent of the European Parliament.

2

Chapter 2 The Multiannual Financial Framework

Article 312

1. The multiannual financial framework shall ensure that Union expenditure develops in an orderly manner and within the limits of its own resources.

   It shall be established for a period of at least five years.

   The annual budget of the Union shall comply with the multiannual financial framework.

2. The Council, acting in accordance with a special legislative procedure, shall adopt a regulation laying down the multiannual financial framework. The Council shall act unanimously after obtaining the consent of the European Parliament, which shall be given by a majority of its component members.

   The European Council may, unanimously, adopt a decision authorising the Council to act by a qualified majority when adopting the regulation referred to in the first subparagraph.

3. The financial framework shall determine the amounts of the annual ceilings on commitment appropriations by category of expenditure and of the annual ceiling on payment appropriations. The categories of expenditure, limited in number, shall correspond to the Union's major sectors of activity.

   The financial framework shall lay down any other provisions required for the annual budgetary procedure to run smoothly.

4. Where no Council regulation determining a new financial framework has been adopted by the end of the previous financial framework, the ceilings and other provisions corresponding to the last year of that framework shall be extended until such time as that act is adopted.

5. Throughout the procedure leading to the adoption of the financial framework, the European Parliament, the Council and the Commission shall take any measure necessary to facilitate its adoption.

Chapter 3 The Union's Annual Budget

Article 313

The financial year shall run from 1 January to 31 December.

Article 314

The European Parliament and the Council, acting in accordance with a special legislative procedure, shall establish the Union's annual budget in accordance with the following provisions.

1. With the exception of the European Central Bank, each institution shall, before 1 July, draw up estimates of its expenditure for the following financial year. The Commission shall consolidate these estimates in a draft budget, which may contain different estimates.

   The draft budget shall contain an estimate of revenue and an estimate of expenditure.

2. The Commission shall submit a proposal containing the draft budget to the European Parliament and to the Council not later than 1 September of the year preceding that in which the budget is to be implemented.

   The Commission may amend the draft budget during the procedure until such time as the Conciliation Committee, referred to in paragraph 5, is convened.

3. The Council shall adopt its position on the draft budget and forward it to the European Parliament not later than 1 October of the year preceding that in which the budget is to be implemented. The Council shall inform the European Parliament in full of the reasons which led it to adopt its position.

4. If, within forty-two days of such communication, the European Parliament:
   (a) approves the position of the Council, the budget shall be adopted;
   (b) has not taken a decision, the budget shall be deemed to have been adopted;
   (c) adopts amendments by a majority of its component members, the amended draft shall be forwarded to the Council and to the Commission. The President of the European Parliament, in agreement with the President of the Council, shall immediately convene a meeting of the Conciliation Committee. However, if within ten days of the draft being forwarded the Council informs the European Parliament that it has approved all its amendments, the Conciliation Committee shall not meet.

5. The Conciliation Committee, which shall be composed of the members of the Council or their representatives and an equal number of members representing the European Parliament, shall have the task of reaching agreement on a joint text, by a qualified majority of the members of the Council or their representatives and by a majority of the representatives of the European Parliament within twenty-one days of its being convened, on the basis of the positions of the European Parliament and the Council.

   The Commission shall take part in the Conciliation Committee's proceedings and shall take all the necessary initiatives with a view to reconciling the positions of the European Parliament and the Council.

6. If, within the twenty-one days referred to in paragraph 5, the Conciliation Committee agrees on a joint text, the European Parliament and the Council shall each have a period of fourteen days from the date of that agreement in which to approve the joint text.

7. If, within the period of fourteen days referred to in paragraph 6:
   (a) the European Parliament and the Council both approve the joint text or fail to take a decision, or if one of these institutions approves the joint text while the other one fails to take a decision, the budget shall be deemed to be definitively adopted in accordance with the joint text; or
   (b) the European Parliament, acting by a majority of its component members, and the Council both reject the joint text, or if one of these institutions rejects the joint text while the other one fails to take a decision, a new draft budget shall be submitted by the Commission; or
   (c) the European Parliament, acting by a majority of its component members, rejects the joint text while the Council approves it, a new draft budget shall be submitted by the Commission; or
   (d) the European Parliament approves the joint text whilst the Council rejects it, the European Parliament may, within fourteen days from the date of the rejection by the Council and acting by a majority of its component members and three-fifths of the votes cast, decide to confirm all or some of the amendments referred to in paragraph 4(c). Where a European Parliament amendment is not confirmed, the position agreed in the Conciliation Committee on the budget heading which is the subject of the amendment shall be retained. The budget shall be deemed to be definitively adopted on this basis.

8. If, within the twenty-one days referred to in paragraph 5, the Conciliation Committee does not agree on a joint text, a new draft budget shall be submitted by the Commission.

9. When the procedure provided for in this Article has been completed, the President of the European Parliament shall declare that the budget has been definitively adopted.

10. Each institution shall exercise the powers conferred upon it under this Article in compliance with the Treaties and the acts adopted thereunder, with particular regard to the Union's own resources and the balance between revenue and expenditure.

Article 315

If, at the beginning of a financial year, the budget has not yet been definitively adopted, a sum equivalent to not more than one twelfth of the budget appropriations for the preceding financial year may be spent each month in respect of any chapter of the budget in accordance with the provisions of the Regulations made pursuant to Article 322; that sum shall not, however, exceed one twelfth of the appropriations provided for in the same chapter of the draft budget.

The Council on a proposal by the Commission, may, provided that the other conditions laid down in the first paragraph are observed, authorise expenditure in excess of one twelfth in accordance with the regulations made pursuant to Article 322. The Council shall forward the decision immediately to the European Parliament.

The decision referred to in the second paragraph shall lay down the necessary measures relating to resources to ensure application of this Article, in accordance with the acts referred to in Article 311.

It shall enter into force thirty days following its adoption if the European Parliament, acting by a majority of its component Members, has not decided to reduce this expenditure within that time-limit.

Article 316

In accordance with conditions to be laid down pursuant to Article 322, any appropriations, other than those relating to staff expenditure, that are unexpended at the end of the financial year may be carried forward to the next financial year only.

Appropriations shall be classified under different chapters grouping items of expenditure according to their nature or purpose and subdivided in accordance with the regulations made pursuant to Article 322.

The expenditure of the European Parliament, the European Council and the Council, the Commission and the Court of Justice of the European Union shall be set out in separate parts of the budget, without prejudice to special arrangements for certain common items of expenditure.

Chapter 4 Implementation of the Budget and Discharge

Article 317

The Commission shall implement the budget in cooperation with the Member States, in accordance with the provisions of the regulations made pursuant to Article 322, on its own responsibility and within the limits of the appropriations, having regard to the principles of sound financial management. Member States shall cooperate with the Commission to ensure that the appropriations are used in accordance with the principles of sound financial management.

The regulations shall lay down the control and audit obligations of the Member States in the implementation of the budget and the resulting responsibilities. They shall also lay down the responsibilities and detailed rules for each institution concerning its part in effecting its own expenditure.

Within the budget, the Commission may, subject to the limits and conditions laid down in the regulations made pursuant to Article 322, transfer appropriations from one chapter to another or from one subdivision to another.

Article 318

The Commission shall submit annually to the European Parliament and to the Council the accounts of the preceding financial year relating to the implementation of the budget. The Commission shall also forward to them a financial statement of the assets and liabilities of the Union.

The Commission shall also submit to the European Parliament and to the Council an evaluation report on the Union's finances based on the results achieved, in particular in relation to the indications given by the European Parliament and the Council pursuant to Article 319.

Article 319

1. The European Parliament, acting on a recommendation from the Council, shall give a discharge to the Commission in respect of the implementation of the budget. To this end, the Council and the European Parliament in turn shall examine the accounts, the financial statement and the evaluation report referred to in Article 318, the annual report by the Court of Auditors together with the replies of the institutions under audit to the observations of the Court of Auditors, the statement of assurance referred to in Article 287(1), second subparagraph and any relevant special reports by the Court of Auditors.
2. Before giving a discharge to the Commission, or for any other purpose in connection with the exercise of its powers over the implementation of the budget, the European Parliament may ask to hear the Commission give evidence with regard to the execution of expenditure or the operation of financial control systems. The Commission shall submit any necessary information to the European Parliament at the latter's request.
3. The Commission shall take all appropriate steps to act on the observations in the decisions giving discharge and on other observations by the European Parliament relating to the execution of expenditure, as well as on comments accompanying the recommendations on discharge adopted by the Council.

    At the request of the European Parliament or the Council, the Commission shall report on the measures taken in the light of these observations and comments and in particular on the instructions given to the departments which are responsible for the implementation of the budget. These reports shall also be forwarded to the Court of Auditors.

Chapter 5 Common Provisions

Article 320
The multiannual financial framework and the annual budget shall be drawn up in euro.

Article 321
The Commission may, provided it notifies the competent authorities of the Member States concerned, transfer into the currency of one of the Member States its holdings in the currency of another Member State, to the extent necessary to enable them to be used for purposes which come within the scope of the Treaties. The Commission shall as far as possible avoid making such transfers if it possesses cash or liquid assets in the currencies which it needs.

The Commission shall deal with each Member State through the authority designated by the State concerned. In carrying out financial operations the Commission shall employ the services of the bank of issue of the Member State concerned or of any other financial institution approved by that State.

Article 322
1. The European Parliament and the Council, acting in accordance with the ordinary legislative procedure, and after consulting the Court of Auditors, shall adopt by means of regulations:
   (a) the financial rules which determine in particular the procedure to be adopted for establishing and implementing the budget and for presenting and auditing accounts;
   (b) rules providing for checks on the responsibility of financial actors, in particular authorising officers and accounting officers.
2. The Council, acting on a proposal from the Commission and after consulting the European Parliament and the Court of Auditors, shall determine the methods and procedure whereby the budget revenue provided under the arrangements relating to the Union's own resources shall be made available to the Commission, and determine the measures to be applied, if need be, to meet cash requirements.

Article 323
The European Parliament, the Council and the Commission shall ensure that the financial means are made available to allow the Union to fulfil its legal obligations in respect of third parties.

Article 324
Regular meetings between the Presidents of the European Parliament, the Council and the Commission shall be convened, on the initiative of the Commission, under the budgetary procedures referred to in this Title. The Presidents shall take all the necessary steps to promote consultation and the reconciliation of the positions of the institutions over which they preside in order to facilitate the implementation of this Title.

Chapter 6 Combatting Fraud

Article 325

1. The Union and the Member States shall counter fraud and any other illegal activities affecting the financial interests of the Union through measures to be taken in accordance with this Article, which shall act as a deterrent and be such as to afford effective protection in the Member States, and in all the Union's institutions, bodies, offices and agencies.

2. Member States shall take the same measures to counter fraud affecting the financial interests of the Union as they take to counter fraud affecting their own financial interests.

3. Without prejudice to other provisions of the Treaties, the Member States shall coordinate their action aimed at protecting the financial interests of the Union against fraud. To this end they shall organise, together with the Commission, close and regular cooperation between the competent authorities.

4. The European Parliament and the Council, acting in accordance with the ordinary legislative procedure, after consulting the Court of Auditors, shall adopt the necessary measures in the fields of the prevention of and fight against fraud affecting the financial interests of the Union with a view to affording effective and equivalent protection in the Member States and in all the Union's institutions, bodies, offices and agencies.

5. The Commission, in cooperation with Member States, shall each year submit to the European Parliament and to the Council a report on the measures taken for the implementation of this Article.

TITLE III ENHANCED COOPERATION

Article 326

Any enhanced cooperation shall comply with the Treaties and Union law.

Such cooperation shall not undermine the internal market or economic, social and territorial cohesion. It shall not constitute a barrier to or discrimination in trade between Member States, nor shall it distort competition between them.

Article 327

Any enhanced cooperation shall respect the competences, rights and obligations of those Member States which do not participate in it. Those Member States shall not impede its implementation by the participating Member States.

Article 328

1. When enhanced cooperation is being established, it shall be open to all Member States, subject to compliance with any conditions of participation laid down by the authorising decision. It shall also be open to them at any other time, subject to compliance with the acts already adopted within that framework, in addition to those conditions.

The Commission and the Member States participating in enhanced cooperation shall ensure that they promote participation by as many Member States as possible.

2. The Commission and, where appropriate, the High Representative of the Union for Foreign Affairs and Security Policy shall keep the European Parliament and the Council regularly informed regarding developments in enhanced cooperation.

Article 329

1. Member States which wish to establish enhanced cooperation between themselves in one of the areas covered by the Treaties, with the exception of fields of exclusive competence and the common foreign and security policy, shall address a request to the Commission, specifying the scope and objectives of the enhanced cooperation proposed. The Commission may submit a proposal to the Council to that effect. In the event of the Commission not submitting a proposal, it shall inform the Member States concerned of the reasons for not doing so.

   Authorisation to proceed with the enhanced cooperation referred to in the first subparagraph shall be granted by the Council, on a proposal from the Commission and after obtaining the consent of the European Parliament.

2. The request of the Member States which wish to establish enhanced cooperation between themselves within the framework of the common foreign and security policy shall be addressed to the Council. It shall be forwarded to the High Representative of the Union for Foreign Affairs and Security Policy, who shall give an opinion on whether the enhanced cooperation proposed is consistent with the Union's common foreign and security policy, and to the Commission, which shall give its opinion in particular on whether the enhanced cooperation proposed is consistent with other Union policies. It shall also be forwarded to the European Parliament for information.

   Authorisation to proceed with enhanced cooperation shall be granted by a decision of the Council acting unanimously.

Article 330

All members of the Council may participate in its deliberations, but only members of the Council representing the Member States participating in enhanced cooperation shall take part in the vote.

Unanimity shall be constituted by the votes of the representatives of the participating Member States only.

A qualified majority shall be defined in accordance with Article 238(3).

Article 331

1. Any Member State which wishes to participate in enhanced cooperation in progress in one of the areas referred to in Article 329(1) shall notify its intention to the Council and the Commission.

   The Commission shall, within four months of the date of receipt of the notification, confirm the participation of the Member State concerned. It shall note where necessary that the conditions of participation have been fulfilled and shall adopt any transitional measures necessary with regard to the application of the acts already adopted within the framework of enhanced cooperation.

However, if the Commission considers that the conditions of participation have not been fulfilled, it shall indicate the arrangements to be adopted to fulfil those conditions and shall set a deadline for re-examining the request. On the expiry of that deadline, it shall re-examine the request, in accordance with the procedure set out in the second subparagraph. If the Commission considers that the conditions of participation have still not been met, the Member State concerned may refer the matter to the Council, which shall decide on the request. The Council shall act in accordance with Article 330. It may also adopt the transitional measures referred to in the second subpara-graph on a proposal from the Commission.

2. Any Member State which wishes to participate in enhanced cooperation in progress in the framework of the common foreign and security policy shall notify its intention to the Council, the High Representative of the Union for Foreign Affairs and Security Policy and the Commission.

The Council shall confirm the participation of the Member State concerned, after consulting the High Representative of the Union for Foreign Affairs and Security Policy and after noting, where necessary, that the conditions of participation have been fulfilled. The Council, on a proposal from the High Representative, may also adopt any transitional measures necessary with regard to the application of the acts already adopted within the framework of enhanced cooperation. However, if the Council considers that the conditions of participation have not been fulfilled, it shall indicate the arrangements to be adopted to fulfil those conditions and shall set a deadline for re-examining the request for participation.

For the purposes of this paragraph, the Council shall act unanimously and in accordance with Article 330.

Article 332

Expenditure resulting from implementation of enhanced cooperation, other than administrative costs entailed for the institutions, shall be borne by the participating Member States, unless all members of the Council, acting unanimously after consulting the European Parliament, decide otherwise.

Article 333

1. Where a provision of the Treaties which may be applied in the context of enhanced cooperation stipulates that the Council shall act unanimously, the Council, acting unanimously in accordance with the arrangements laid down in Article 330, may adopt a decision stipulating that it will act by a qualified majority.

2. Where a provision of the Treaties which may be applied in the context of enhanced cooperation stipulates that the Council shall adopt acts under a special legislative procedure, the Council, acting unanimously in accordance with the arrangements laid down in Article 330, may adopt a decision stipulating that it will act under the ordinary legislative procedure. The Council shall act after consulting the European Parliament.

3. Paragraphs 1 and 2 shall not apply to decisions having military or defence implications.

Article 334

The Council and the Commission shall ensure the consistency of activities undertaken in the context of enhanced cooperation and the consistency of such activities with the policies of the Union, and shall cooperate to that end.

PART SEVEN GENERAL AND FINAL PROVISIONS

Article 335

In each of the Member States, the Union shall enjoy the most extensive legal capacity accorded to legal persons under their laws; it may, in particular, acquire or dispose of movable and immovable property and may be a party to legal proceedings. To this end, the Union shall be represented by the Commission. However, the Union shall be represented by each of the institutions, by virtue of their administrative autonomy, in matters relating to their respective operation.

Article 336

The European Parliament and the Council shall, acting by means of regulations in accordance with the ordinary legislative procedure and after consulting the other institutions concerned, lay down the Staff Regulations of Officials of the European Union and the Conditions of Employment of other servants of the Union.

Article 337

The Commission may, within the limits and under conditions laid down by the Council acting by a simple majority in accordance with the provisions of the Treaties, collect any information and carry out any checks required for the performance of the tasks entrusted to it.

Article 338

1. Without prejudice to Article 5 of the Protocol on the Statute of the European System of Central Banks and of the European Central Bank, the European Parliament and the Council, acting in accordance with the ordinary legislative procedure, shall adopt measures for the production of statistics where necessary for the performance of the activities of the Union.
2. The production of Union statistics shall conform to impartiality, reliability, objectivity, scientific independence, cost-effectiveness and statistical confidentiality; it shall not entail excessive burdens on economic operators.

Article 339

The members of the institutions of the Union, the members of committees, and the officials and other servants of the Union shall be required, even after their duties have ceased, not to disclose information of the kind covered by the obligation of professional secrecy, in particular information about undertakings, their business relations or their cost components.

Article 340

The contractual liability of the Union shall be governed by the law applicable to the contract in question.

In the case of non-contractual liability, the Union shall, in accordance with the general principles common to the laws of the Member States, make good any damage caused by its institutions or by its servants in the performance of their duties.

Notwithstanding the second paragraph, the European Central Bank shall, in accordance with the general principles common to the laws of the Member States, make good any damage caused by it or by its servants in the performance of their duties.

The personal liability of its servants towards the Union shall be governed by the provisions laid down in their Staff Regulations or in the Conditions of Employment applicable to them.

Article 341

The seat of the institutions of the Union shall be determined by common accord of the governments of the Member States.

Article 342

The rules governing the languages of the institutions of the Union shall, without prejudice to the provisions contained in the Statute of the Court of Justice of the European Union, be determined by the Council, acting unanimously by means of regulations.

Article 343

The Union shall enjoy in the territories of the Member States such privileges and immunities as are necessary for the performance of its tasks, under the conditions laid down in the Protocol of 8 April 1965 on the privileges and immunities of the European Union. The same shall apply to the European Central Bank and the European Investment Bank.

Article 344

Member States undertake not to submit a dispute concerning the interpretation or application of the Treaties to any method of settlement other than those provided for therein.

Article 345

The Treaties shall in no way prejudice the rules in Member States governing the system of property ownership.

Article 346

1. The provisions of the Treaties shall not preclude the application of the following rules:
   (a) no Member State shall be obliged to supply information the disclosure of which it considers contrary to the essential interests of its security;
   (b) any Member State may take such measures as it considers necessary for the protection of the essential interests of its security which are connected with the production of or trade in arms, munitions and war material; such measures shall not adversely affect the conditions of competition in the internal market regarding products which are not intended for specifically military purposes.
2. The Council may, acting unanimously on a proposal from the Commission, make changes to the list, which it drew up on 15 April 1958, of the products to which the provisions of paragraph 1(b) apply.

Article 347

Member States shall consult each other with a view to taking together the steps needed to prevent the functioning of the internal market being affected by measures which a Member State may be called upon to take in the event of serious internal disturbances affecting the maintenance of law and order, in the event of war, serious international tension constituting a threat of war, or in order to carry out obligations it has accepted for the purpose of maintaining peace and international security.

Article 348

If measures taken in the circumstances referred to in Articles 346 and 347 have the effect of distorting the conditions of competition in the internal market, the Commission shall, together with the State concerned, examine how these measures can be adjusted to the rules laid down in the Treaties.

By way of derogation from the procedure laid down in Articles 258 and 259, the Commission or any Member State may bring the matter directly before the Court of Justice if it considers that another Member State is making improper use of the powers provided for in Articles 346 and 347. The Court of Justice shall give its ruling in camera.

Article 349

Taking account of the structural social and economic situation of Guadeloupe, French Guiana, Martinique, Réunion, Saint-Barthélemy, Saint-Martin, the Azores, Madeira and the Canary Islands, which is compounded by their remoteness, insularity, small size, difficult topography and climate, economic dependence on a few products, the permanence and combination of which severely restrain their development, the Council, on a proposal from the Commission and after consulting the European Parliament, shall adopt specific measures aimed, in particular, at laying down the conditions of application of the Treaties to those regions, including common policies. Where the specific measures in question are adopted by the Council in accordance with a special legislative procedure, it shall also act on a proposal from the Commission and after consulting the European Parliament.

The measures referred to in the first paragraph concern in particular areas such as customs and trade policies, fiscal policy, free zones, agriculture and fisheries policies, conditions for supply of raw materials and essential consumer goods, State aids and conditions of access to structural funds and to horizontal Union programmes.

The Council shall adopt the measures referred to in the first paragraph taking into account the special characteristics and constraints of the outermost regions without undermining the integrity and the coherence of the Union legal order, including the internal market and common policies.

Article 350

The provisions of the Treaties shall not preclude the existence or completion of regional unions between Belgium and Luxembourg, or between Belgium, Luxembourg and the Netherlands, to the extent that the objectives of these regional unions are not attained by application of the Treaties.

Article 351

The rights and obligations arising from agreements concluded before 1 January 1958 or, for acceding States, before the date of their accession, between one or more Member States on the one hand, and one or more third countries on the other, shall not be affected by the provisions of the Treaties.

To the extent that such agreements are not compatible with the Treaties, the Member State or States concerned shall take all appropriate steps to eliminate the incompatibilities established. Member States shall, where necessary, assist each other to this end and shall, where appropriate, adopt a common attitude.

In applying the agreements referred to in the first paragraph, Member States shall take into account the fact that the advantages accorded under the Treaties by each Member State form an integral part of the establishment of the Union and are thereby inseparably linked with the creation of common institutions, the conferring of powers upon them and the granting of the same advantages by all the other Member States.

Article 352

1. If action by the Union should prove necessary, within the framework of the policies defined in the Treaties, to attain one of the objectives set out in the Treaties, and the Treaties have not provided the necessary powers, the Council, acting unanimously on a proposal from the Commission and after obtaining the consent of the European Parliament, shall adopt the appropriate measures. Where the measures in question are adopted by the Council in accordance with a special legislative procedure, it shall also act unanimously on a proposal from the Commission and after obtaining the consent of the European Parliament.

2. Using the procedure for monitoring the subsidiarity principle referred to in Article 5(3) of the Treaty on European Union, the Commission shall draw national Parliaments' attention to proposals based on this Article.

3. Measures based on this Article shall not entail harmonisation of Member States' laws or regulations in cases where the Treaties exclude such harmonisation.

4. This Article cannot serve as a basis for attaining objectives pertaining to the common foreign and security policy and any acts adopted pursuant to this Article shall respect the limits set out in Article 40, second paragraph, of the Treaty on European Union.

Article 353

Article 48(7) of the Treaty on European Union shall not apply to the following Articles:
— Article 311, third and fourth paragraphs,
— Article 312(2), first subparagraph,
— Article 352, and
— Article 354.

Article 354

For the purposes of Article 7 of the Treaty on European Union on the suspension of certain rights resulting from Union membership, the member of the European Council or of the Council representing the Member State in question shall not take part in the vote and the Member State in question shall not be counted in the calculation of the one third or four fifths of Member States referred to in paragraphs 1 and 2 of that Article.

Abstentions by members present in person or represented shall not prevent the adoption of decisions referred to in paragraph 2 of that Article.

For the adoption of the decisions referred to in paragraphs 3 and 4 of Article 7 of the Treaty on European Union, a qualified majority shall be defined in accordance with Article 238(3)(b) of this Treaty.

Where, following a decision to suspend voting rights adopted pursuant to paragraph 3 of Article 7 of the Treaty on European Union, the Council acts by a qualified majority on the basis of a provision of the Treaties, that qualified majority shall be defined in accordance with Article 238(3)(b) of this Treaty, or, where the Council acts on a proposal from the Commission or from the High Representative of the Union for Foreign Affairs and Security Policy, in accordance with Article 238(3)(a).

For the purposes of Article 7 of the Treaty on European Union, the European Parliament shall act by a two-thirds majority of the votes cast, representing the majority of its component Members.

Article 355

In addition to the provisions of Article 52 of the Treaty on European Union relating to the territorial scope of the Treaties, the following provisions shall apply:

1. The provisions of the Treaties shall apply to Guadeloupe, French Guiana, Martinique, Réunion, Saint-Barthélemy, Saint-Martin, the Azores, Madeira and the Canary Islands in accordance with Article 349.
2. The special arrangements for association set out in Part Four shall apply to the overseas countries and territories listed in Annex II.

   The Treaties shall not apply to those overseas countries and territories having special relations with the United Kingdom of Great Britain and Northern Ireland which are not included in the aforementioned list.
3. The provisions of the Treaties shall apply to the European territories for whose external relations a Member State is responsible.
4. The provisions of the Treaties shall apply to the Åland Islands in accordance with the provisions set out in Protocol 2 to the Act concerning the conditions of accession of the Republic of Austria, the Republic of Finland and the Kingdom of Sweden.
5. Notwithstanding Article 52 of the Treaty on European Union and paragraphs 1 to 4 of this Article:
   (a) the Treaties shall not apply to the Faeroe Islands;
   (b) the Treaties shall not apply to the United Kingdom Sovereign Base Areas of Akrotiri and Dhekelia in Cyprus except to the extent necessary to ensure the implementation of the arrangements set out in the Protocol on the Sovereign Base Areas of the United Kingdom of Great Britain and Northern Ireland in Cyprus annexed to the Act concerning the conditions of accession of the Czech Republic, the Republic of Estonia, the Republic of Cyprus, the Republic of Latvia, the Republic of Lithuania, the Republic of Hungary, the Republic of Malta, the Republic of Poland, the Republic of Slovenia and the Slovak Republic to the European Union and in accordance with the terms of that Protocol;

(c) the Treaties shall apply to the Channel Islands and the Isle of Man only to the extent necessary to ensure the implementation of the arrangements for those islands set out in the Treaty concerning the accession of new Member States to the European Economic Community and to the European Atomic Energy Community signed on 22 January 1972.

6. The European Council may, on the initiative of the Member State concerned, adopt a decision amending the status, with regard to the Union, of a Danish, French or Netherlands country or territory referred to in paragraphs 1 and 2. The European Council shall act unanimously after consulting the Commission.

Article 356
This Treaty is concluded for an unlimited period.

Article 357
This Treaty shall be ratified by the High Contracting Parties in accordance with their respective constitutional requirements. The Instruments of ratification shall be deposited with the Government of the Italian Republic.

This Treaty shall enter into force on the first day of the month following the deposit of the Instrument of ratification by the last signatory State to take this step. If, however, such deposit is made less than 15 days before the beginning of the following month, this Treaty shall not enter into force until the first day of the second month after the date of such deposit.

Article 358
The provisions of Article 55 of the Treaty on European Union shall apply to this Treaty.

IN WITNESS WHEREOF, the undersigned Plenipotentiaries have signed this Treaty. Done at Rome this twenty-fifth day of March in the year one thousand nine hundred and fifty-seven.

(List of signatories not reproduced.)

2

3

Protocols and Annexes to the Treaties (Selection)

Contents

PROTOCOL (NO 1) ON THE ROLE OF NATIONAL PARLIAMENTS IN THE EUROPEAN UNION

THE HIGH CONTRACTING PARTIES,

RECALLING that the way in which national Parliaments scrutinise their governments in relation to the activities of the Union is a matter for the particular constitutional organisation and practice of each Member State,

DESIRING to encourage greater involvement of national Parliaments in the activities of the European Union and to enhance their ability to express their views on draft legislative acts of the Union as well as on other matters which may be of particular interest to them,

HAVE AGREED UPON the following provisions, which shall be annexed to the Treaty on European Union, to the Treaty on the Functioning of the European Union and to the Treaty establishing the European Atomic Energy Community:

TITLE I INFORMATION FOR NATIONAL PARLIAMENTS

Article 1

Commission consultation documents (green and white papers and communications) shall be forwarded directly by the Commission to national Parliaments upon publication. The Commission shall also forward the annual legislative programme as well as any other instrument of legislative planning or policy to national Parliaments, at the same time as to the European Parliament and the Council.

Article 2

Draft legislative acts sent to the European Parliament and to the Council shall be forwarded to national Parliaments.

For the purposes of this Protocol, "draft legislative acts" shall mean proposals from the Commission, initiatives from a group of Member States, initiatives from the European Parliament, requests from the Court of Justice, recommendations from the European Central Bank and requests from the European Investment Bank, for the adoption of a legislative act.

Draft legislative acts originating from the Commission shall be forwarded to national Parliaments directly by the Commission, at the same time as to the European Parliament and the Council.

Draft legislative acts originating from the European Parliament shall be forwarded to national Parliaments directly by the European Parliament.

Draft legislative acts originating from a group of Member States, the Court of Justice, the European Central Bank or the European Investment Bank shall be forwarded to national Parliaments by the Council.

Article 3

National Parliaments may send to the Presidents of the European Parliament, the Council and the Commission a reasoned opinion on whether a draft legislative act complies with the principle of subsidiarity, in accordance with the procedure laid down in the Protocol on the application of the principles of subsidiarity and proportionality.

If the draft legislative act originates from a group of Member States, the President of the Council shall forward the reasoned opinion or opinions to the governments of those Member States.

If the draft legislative act originates from the Court of Justice, the European Central Bank or the European Investment Bank, the President of the Council shall forward the reasoned opinion or opinions to the institution or body concerned.

Article 4

An eight-week period shall elapse between a draft legislative act being made available to national Parliaments in the official languages of the Union and the date when it is placed on a provisional agenda for the Council for its adoption or for adoption of a position under a legislative procedure. Exceptions shall be possible in cases of urgency, the reasons for which shall be stated in the act or position of the Council. Save in urgent cases for which due reasons have been given, no agreement may be reached on a draft legislative act during those eight weeks. Save in urgent cases for which due reasons have been given, a ten-day period shall elapse between the placing of a draft legislative act on the provisional agenda for the Council and the adoption of a position.

Article 5

The agendas for and the outcome of meetings of the Council, including the minutes of meetings where the Council is deliberating on draft legislative acts, shall be forwarded directly to national Parliaments, at the same time as to Member States' governments.

Article 6

When the European Council intends to make use of the first or second subparagraphs of Article 48(7) of the Treaty on European Union, national Parliaments shall be informed of the initiative of the European Council at least six months before any decision is adopted.

Article 7

The Court of Auditors shall forward its annual report to national Parliaments, for information, at the same time as to the European Parliament and to the Council.

Article 8

Where the national Parliamentary system is not unicameral, Articles 1 to 7 shall apply to the component chambers.

TITLE II INTERPARLIAMENTARY COOPERATION

Article 9

The European Parliament and national Parliaments shall together determine the organisation and promotion of effective and regular inter parliamentary cooperation within the Union.

Article 10

A conference of Parliamentary Committees for Union Affairs may submit any contribution it deems appropriate for the attention of the European Parliament, the Council and the Commission. That conference shall in addition promote the exchange of information and best practice between national Parliaments and the European Parliament, including their special committees. It may also organise inter parliamentary conferences on specific topics, in particular to debate matters of common foreign and security policy, including common security and defence policy. Contributions from the conference shall not bind national Parliaments and shall not prejudge their positions.

PROTOCOL (NO 2) ON THE APPLICATION OF THE PRINCIPLES OF SUBSIDIARITY AND PROPORTIONALITY

THE HIGH CONTRACTING PARTIES,

WISHING to ensure that decisions are taken as closely as possible to the citizens of the Union,

RESOLVED to establish the conditions for the application of the principles of subsidiarity and proportionality, as laid down in Article 5 of the Treaty on European Union, and to establish a system for monitoring the application of those principles,

HAVE AGREED UPON the following provisions, which shall be annexed to the Treaty on European Union and to the Treaty on the Functioning of the European Union:

Article 1
Each institution shall ensure constant respect for the principles of subsidiarity and proportionality, as laid down in Article 5 of the Treaty on European Union.

Article 2
Before proposing legislative acts, the Commission shall consult widely. Such consultations shall, where appropriate, take into account the regional and local dimension of the action envisaged. In cases of exceptional urgency, the Commission shall not conduct such consultations. It shall give reasons for its decision in its proposal.

Article 3
For the purposes of this Protocol, "draft legislative acts" shall mean proposals from the Commission, initiatives from a group of Member States, initiatives from the European Parliament, requests from the Court of Justice, recommendations from the European Central Bank and requests from the European Investment Bank, for the adoption of a legislative act.

Article 4
The Commission shall forward its draft legislative acts and its amended drafts to national Parliaments at the same time as to the Union legislator.

The European Parliament shall forward its draft legislative acts and its amended drafts to national Parliaments.

The Council shall forward draft legislative acts originating from a group of Member States, the Court of Justice, the European Central Bank or the European Investment Bank and amended drafts to national Parliaments.

Upon adoption, legislative resolutions of the European Parliament and positions of the Council shall be forwarded by them to national Parliaments.

Article 5

Draft legislative acts shall be justified with regard to the principles of subsidiarity and proportionality. Any draft legislative act should contain a detailed statement making it possible to appraise compliance with the principles of subsidiarity and proportionality. This statement should contain some assessment of the proposal's financial impact and, in the case of a directive, of its implications for the rules to be put in place by Member States, including, where necessary, the regional legislation. The reasons for concluding that a Union objective can be better achieved at Union level shall be substantiated by qualitative and, wherever possible, quantitative indicators. Draft legislative acts shall take account of the need for any burden, whether financial or administrative, falling upon the Union, national governments, regional or local authorities, economic operators and citizens, to be minimised and commensurate with the objective to be achieved.

Article 6

Any national Parliament or any chamber of a national Parliament may, within eight weeks from the date of transmission of a draft legislative act, in the official languages of the Union, send to the Presidents of the European Parliament, the Council and the Commission a reasoned opinion stating why it considers that the draft in question does not comply with the principle of subsidiarity. It will be for each national Parliament or each chamber of a national Parliament to consult, where appropriate, regional parliaments with legislative powers.

If the draft legislative act originates from a group of Member States, the President of the Council shall forward the opinion to the governments of those Member States.

If the draft legislative act originates from the Court of Justice, the European Central Bank or the European Investment Bank, the President of the Council shall forward the opinion to the institution or body concerned.

Article 7

1. The European Parliament, the Council and the Commission, and, where appropriate, the group of Member States, the Court of Justice, the European Central Bank or the European Investment Bank, if the draft legislative act originates from them, shall take account of the reasoned opinions issued by national Parliaments or by a chamber of a national Parliament.

   Each national Parliament shall have two votes, shared out on the basis of the national Parliamentary system. In the case of a bicameral Parliamentary system, each of the two chambers shall have one vote.

2. Where reasoned opinions on a draft legislative act's non-compliance with the principle of subsidiarity represent at least one third of all the votes allocated to the national Parliaments in accordance with the second subparagraph of paragraph 1, the draft must be reviewed. This threshold shall be a quarter in the case of a draft legislative act submitted on the basis of Article 76 of the Treaty on the Functioning of the European Union on the area of freedom, security and justice.

   After such review, the Commission or, where appropriate, the group of Member States, the European Parliament, the Court of Justice, the European Central Bank or the European Investment Bank, if the draft legislative act originates from them, may decide to maintain, amend or withdraw the draft. Reasons must be given for this decision.

3. Furthermore, under the ordinary legislative procedure, where reasoned opinions on the non-compliance of a proposal for a legislative act with the principle of subsidiarity represent at least a simple majority of the votes allocated to the national Parliaments in accordance with the second subparagraph of paragraph 1, the proposal must be reviewed. After such review, the Commission may decide to maintain, amend or withdraw the proposal.

If it chooses to maintain the proposal, the Commission will have, in a reasoned opinion, to justify why it considers that the proposal complies with the principle of subsidiarity. This reasoned opinion, as well as the reasoned opinions of the national Parliaments, will have to be submitted to the Union legislator, for consideration in the procedure:

(a) before concluding the first reading, the legislator (the European Parliament and the Council) shall consider whether the legislative proposal is compatible with the principle of subsidiarity, taking particular account of the reasons expressed and shared by the majority of national Parliaments as well as the reasoned opinion of the Commission;

(b) if, by a majority of 55% of the members of the Council or a majority of the votes cast in the European Parliament, the legislator is of the opinion that the proposal is not compatible with the principle of subsidiarity, the legislative proposal shall not be given further consideration.

Article 8

The Court of Justice of the European Union shall have jurisdiction in actions on grounds of infringement of the principle of subsidiarity by a legislative act, brought in accordance with the rules laid down in Article 263 of the Treaty on the Functioning of the European Union by Member States, or notified by them in accordance with their legal order on behalf of their national Parliament or a chamber thereof.

In accordance with the rules laid down in the said Article, the Committee of the Regions may also bring such actions against legislative acts for the adoption of which the Treaty on the Functioning of the European Union provides that it be consulted.

Article 9

The Commission shall submit each year to the European Council, the European Parliament, the Council and national Parliaments a report on the application of Article 5 of the Treaty on European Union. This annual report shall also be forwarded to the Economic and Social Committee and the Committee of the Regions.

PROTOCOL (NO 3) ON THE STATUTE OF THE COURT OF JUSTICE OF THE EUROPEAN UNION

THE HIGH CONTRACTING PARTIES,

DESIRING to lay down the Statute of the Court of Justice of the European Union provided for in Article 281 of the Treaty on the Functioning of the European Union,

HAVE AGREED UPON the following provisions, which shall be annexed to the Treaty on European Union, the Treaty on the Functioning of the European Union and the Treaty establishing the European Atomic Energy Community:

Article 1

The Court of Justice of the European Union shall be constituted and shall function in accordance with the provisions of the Treaties, of the Treaty establishing the European Atomic Energy Community (the EAEC Treaty) and of this Statute.

TITLE I JUDGES AND ADVOCATES-GENERAL

Article 2

Before taking up his duties each Judge shall, before the Court of Justice sitting in open court, take an oath to perform his duties impartially and conscientiously and to preserve the secrecy of the deliberations of the Court.

Article 3

The Judges shall be immune from legal proceedings. After they have ceased to hold office, they shall continue to enjoy immunity in respect of acts performed by them in their official capacity, including words spoken or written.

The Court of Justice, sitting as a full Court, may waive the immunity. If the decision concerns a member of the General Court or of a specialised court, the Court shall decide after consulting the court concerned.

Where immunity has been waived and criminal proceedings are instituted against a Judge, he shall be tried, in any of the Member States, only by the court competent to judge the members of the highest national judiciary.

Articles 11 to 14 and Article 17 of the Protocol on the privileges and immunities of the European Union shall apply to the Judges, Advocates-General, Registrar and Assistant Rapporteurs of the Court of Justice of the European Union, without prejudice to the provisions relating to immunity from legal proceedings of Judges which are set out in the preceding paragraphs.

Article 4

The Judges may not hold any political or administrative office.

They may not engage in any occupation, whether gainful or not, unless exemption is exceptionally granted by the Council, acting by a simple majority.

When taking up their duties, they shall give a solemn undertaking that, both during and after their term of office, they will respect the obligations arising therefrom, in particular the duty to behave with integrity and discretion as regards the acceptance, after they have ceased to hold office, of certain appointments or benefits.

Any doubt on this point shall be settled by decision of the Court of Justice. If the decision concerns a member of the General Court or of a specialised court, the Court shall decide after consulting the court concerned.

Article 5

Apart from normal replacement, or death, the duties of a Judge shall end when he resigns.

Where a Judge resigns, his letter of resignation shall be addressed to the President of the Court of Justice for transmission to the President of the Council. Upon this notification a vacancy shall arise on the bench.

Save where Article 6 applies, a Judge shall continue to hold office until his successor takes up his duties.

Article 6

A Judge may be deprived of his office or of his right to a pension or other benefits in its stead only if, in the unanimous opinion of the Judges and Advocates-General of the Court of Justice, he no longer fulfils the requisite conditions or meets the obligations arising from his office. The Judge concerned shall not take part in any such deliberations. If the person concerned is a member of the General Court or of a specialised court, the Court shall decide after consulting the court concerned.

The Registrar of the Court shall communicate the decision of the Court to the President of the European Parliament and to the President of the Commission and shall notify it to the President of the Council.

In the case of a decision depriving a Judge of his office, a vacancy shall arise on the bench upon this latter notification.

Article 7

A Judge who is to replace a member of the Court whose term of office has not expired shall be appointed for the remainder of his predecessor's term.

Article 8

The provisions of Articles 2 to 7 shall apply to the Advocates-General.

TITLE II ORGANISATION OF THE COURT OF JUSTICE

Article 9

When, every three years, the Judges are partially replaced, one half of the number of Judges shall be replaced. If the number of Judges is an uneven number, the number of Judges who shall be replaced shall alternately be the number which is the next above one half of the number of Judges and the number which is next below one half.

The first paragraph shall also apply when the Advocates General are partially replaced, every three years.

Article 9a

The Judges shall elect the President and the Vice-President of the Court of Justice from among their number for a term of three years. They may be re-elected.

The Vice-President shall assist the President in accordance with the conditions laid down in the Rules of Procedure. He shall take the President's place when the latter is prevented from attending or when the office of President is vacant.

Article 10

The Registrar shall take an oath before the Court of Justice to perform his duties impartially and conscientiously and to preserve the secrecy of the deliberations of the Court of Justice.

Article 11

The Court of Justice shall arrange for replacement of the Registrar on occasions when he is prevented from attending the Court of Justice.

Article 12

Officials and other servants shall be attached to the Court of Justice to enable it to function. They shall be responsible to the Registrar under the authority of the President.

Article 13

At the request of the Court of Justice, the European Parliament and the Council may, acting in accordance with the ordinary legislative procedure, provide for the appointment of Assistant Rapporteurs and lay down the rules governing their service. The Assistant Rapporteurs may be required, under conditions laid down in the Rules of Procedure, to participate in preparatory inquiries in cases pending before the Court and to cooperate with the Judge who acts as Rapporteur.

The Assistant Rapporteurs shall be chosen from persons whose independence is beyond doubt and who possess the necessary legal qualifications; they shall be appointed by the Council, acting by a simple majority. They shall take an oath before the Court to perform their duties impartially and conscientiously and to preserve the secrecy of the deliberations of the Court.

Article 14

The Judges, the Advocates-General and the Registrar shall be required to reside at the place where the Court of Justice has its seat.

Article 15

The Court of Justice shall remain permanently in session. The duration of the judicial vacations shall be determined by the Court with due regard to the needs of its business.

Article 16

The Court of Justice shall form chambers consisting of three and five Judges. The Judges shall elect the Presidents of the chambers from among their number. The Presidents of the chambers of five Judges shall be elected for three years. They may be re-elected once.

The Grand Chamber shall consist of 15 Judges. It shall be presided over by the President of the Court. The Vice- President of the Court and, in accordance with the conditions laid down in the Rules of Procedure, three of the Presidents of the chambers of five Judges and other Judges shall also form part of the Grand Chamber.

The Court shall sit in a Grand Chamber when a Member State or an institution of the Union that is party to the proceedings so requests.

The Court shall sit as a full Court where cases are brought before it pursuant to Article 228(2), Article 245(2), Article 247 or Article 286(6) of the Treaty on the Functioning of the European Union.

Moreover, where it considers that a case before it is of exceptional importance, the Court may decide, after hearing the Advocate-General, to refer the case to the full Court.

Article 17

Decisions of the Court of Justice shall be valid only when an uneven number of its members is sitting in the deliberations.

Decisions of the chambers consisting of either three or five Judges shall be valid only if they are taken by three Judges.

Decisions of the Grand Chamber shall be valid only if 11 Judges are sitting.

Decisions of the full Court shall be valid only if 17 Judges are sitting.

In the event of one of the Judges of a chamber being prevented from attending, a Judge of another chamber may be called upon to sit in accordance with conditions laid down in the Rules of Procedure.

Article 18

No Judge or Advocate-General may take part in the disposal of any case in which he has previously taken part as agent or adviser or has acted for one of the parties, or in which he has been called upon to pronounce as a member of a court or tribunal, of a commission of inquiry or in any other capacity.

If, for some special reason, any Judge or Advocate-General considers that he should not take part in the judgment or examination of a particular case, he shall so inform the President. If, for some special reason, the President considers that any Judge or Advocate-General should not sit or make submissions in a particular case, he shall notify him accordingly.

Any difficulty arising as to the application of this Article shall be settled by decision of the Court of Justice.

A party may not apply for a change in the composition of the Court or of one of its chambers on the grounds of either the nationality of a Judge or the absence from the Court or from the chamber of a Judge of the nationality of that party.

TITLE III PROCEDURE BEFORE THE COURT OF JUSTICE

Article 19

The Member States and the institutions of the Union shall be represented before the Court of Justice by an agent appointed for each case; the agent may be assisted by an adviser or by a lawyer.

The States, other than the Member States, which are parties to the Agreement on the European Economic Area and also the EFTA Surveillance Authority referred to in that Agreement shall be represented in same manner.

Other parties must be represented by a lawyer.

Only a lawyer authorised to practise before a court of a Member State or of another State which is a party to the Agreement on the European Economic Area may represent or assist a party before the Court.

Such agents, advisers and lawyers shall, when they appear before the Court, enjoy the rights and immunities necessary to the independent exercise of their duties, under conditions laid down in the Rules of Procedure.

As regards such advisers and lawyers who appear before it, the Court shall have the powers normally accorded to courts of law, under conditions laid down in the Rules of Procedure.

University teachers being nationals of a Member State whose law accords them a right of audience shall have the same rights before the Court as are accorded by this Article to lawyers.

Article 20

The procedure before the Court of Justice shall consist of two parts: written and oral.

The written procedure shall consist of the communication to the parties and to the institutions of the Union whose decisions are in dispute, of applications, statements of case, defences and observations, and of replies, if any, as well as of all papers and documents in support or of certified copies of them.

Communications shall be made by the Registrar in the order and within the time laid down in the Rules of Procedure.

The oral procedure shall consist of the hearing by the Court of agents, advisers and lawyers and of the submissions of the Advocate-General, as well as the hearing, if any, of witnesses and experts.

Where it considers that the case raises no new point of law, the Court may decide, after hearing the Advocate-General, that the case shall be determined without a submission from the Advocate-General.

Article 21

A case shall be brought before the Court of Justice by a written application addressed to the Registrar. The application shall contain the applicant's name and permanent address and the description of the signatory, the name of the party or names of the parties against whom the application is made, the subject-matter of the dispute, the form of order sought and a brief statement of the pleas in law on which the application is based.

The application shall be accompanied, where appropriate, by the measure the annulment of which is sought or, in the circumstances referred to in Article 265 of the Treaty on the Functioning of the European Union, by documentary evidence of the date on which an institution was, in accordance with those Articles, requested to act. If the documents are not submitted with the application, the Registrar shall ask the party concerned to produce them within a reasonable period, but in that event the rights of the party shall not lapse even if such documents are produced after the time limit for bringing proceedings.

Article 22

A case governed by Article 18 of the EAEC Treaty shall be brought before the Court of Justice by an appeal addressed to the Registrar. The appeal shall contain the name and permanent address of the applicant and the description of the signatory, a reference to the decision against which the appeal is brought, the names of the respondents, the subject-matter of the dispute, the submissions and a brief statement of the grounds on which the appeal is based.

The appeal shall be accompanied by a certified copy of the decision of the Arbitration Committee which is contested.

If the Court rejects the appeal, the decision of the Arbitration Committee shall become final.

If the Court annuls the decision of the Arbitration Committee, the matter may be re-opened, where appropriate, on the initiative of one of the parties in the case, before the Arbitration Committee. The latter shall conform to any decisions on points of law given by the Court.

Article 23

In the cases governed by Article 267 of the Treaty on the Functioning of the European Union, the decision of the court or tribunal of a Member State which suspends its proceedings and refers a case to the Court of Justice shall be notified to the Court by the court or tribunal concerned. The decision shall then be notified by the Registrar of the Court to the parties, to the Member States and to the Commission, and to the institution, body, office or agency of the Union which adopted the act the validity or interpretation of which is in dispute.

Within two months of this notification, the parties, the Member States, the Commission and, where appropriate, the institution, body, office or agency which adopted the act the validity or interpretation of which is in dispute, shall be entitled to submit statements of case or written observations to the Court.

In the cases governed by Article 267 of the Treaty on the Functioning of the European Union, the decision of the national court or tribunal shall, moreover, be notified by the Registrar of the Court to the States, other than the Member States, which are parties to the Agreement on the European Economic Area and also to the EFTA Surveillance Authority referred to in that Agreement which may, within two months of notification, where one of the fields of application of that Agreement is concerned, submit statements of case or written observations to the Court.

Where an agreement relating to a specific subject matter, concluded by the Council and one or more non-member States, provides that those States are to be entitled to submit statements of case or written observations where a court or tribunal of a Member State refers to the Court of Justice for a preliminary ruling a question falling within the scope of the agreement, the decision of the national court or tribunal containing that question shall also be notified to the non-member States concerned. Within two months from such notification, those States may lodge at the Court statements of case or written observations.

Article 23a(*)

The Rules of Procedure may provide for an expedited or accelerated procedure and, for references for a preliminary ruling relating to the area of freedom, security and justice, an urgent procedure.

Those procedures may provide, in respect of the submission of statements of case or written observations, for a shorter period than that provided for by Article 23, and, in derogation from the fourth paragraph of Article 20, for the case to be determined without a submission from the Advocate-General.

In addition, the urgent procedure may provide for restriction of the parties and other interested persons mentioned in Article 23, authorised to submit statements of case or written observations and, in cases of extreme urgency, for the written stage of the procedure to be omitted.

Article 24

The Court of Justice may require the parties to produce all documents and to supply all information which the Court considers desirable. Formal note shall be taken of any refusal.

---

* Article inserted by Decision 2008/79/EC, Euratom [2008] OJ L24/42, 29 January 2008.

The Court may also require the Member States and institutions, bodies, offices and agencies not being parties to the case to supply all information which the Court considers necessary for the proceedings.

Article 25
The Court of Justice may at any time entrust any individual, body, authority, committee or other organisation it chooses with the task of giving an expert opinion.

Article 26
Witnesses may be heard under conditions laid down in the Rules of Procedure.

Article 27
With respect to defaulting witnesses the Court of Justice shall have the powers generally granted to courts and tribunals and may impose pecuniary penalties under conditions laid down in the Rules of Procedure.

Article 28
Witnesses and experts may be heard on oath taken in the form laid down in the Rules of Procedure or in the manner laid down by the law of the country of the witness or expert.

Article 29
The Court of Justice may order that a witness or expert be heard by the judicial authority of his place of permanent residence.

The order shall be sent for implementation to the competent judicial authority under conditions laid down in the Rules of Procedure. The documents drawn up in compliance with the letters rogatory shall be returned to the Court under the same conditions.

The Court shall defray the expenses, without prejudice to the right to charge them, where appropriate, to the parties.

Article 30
A Member State shall treat any violation of an oath by a witness or expert in the same manner as if the offence had been committed before one of its courts with jurisdiction in civil proceedings. At the instance of the Court of Justice, the Member State concerned shall prosecute the offender before its competent court.

Article 31
The hearing in court shall be public, unless the Court of Justice, of its own motion or on application by the parties, decides otherwise for serious reasons.

Article 32
During the hearings the Court of Justice may examine the experts, the witnesses and the parties themselves. The latter, however, may address the Court of Justice only through their representatives.

Article 33
Minutes shall be made of each hearing and signed by the President and the Registrar.

Article 34

The case list shall be established by the President.

Article 35

The deliberations of the Court of Justice shall be and shall remain secret.

Article 36

Judgments shall state the reasons on which they are based. They shall contain the names of the Judges who took part in the deliberations.

Article 37

Judgments shall be signed by the President and the Registrar. They shall be read in open court.

Article 38

The Court of Justice shall adjudicate upon costs.

Article 39

The President of the Court of Justice may, by way of summary procedure, which may, in so far as necessary, differ from some of the rules contained in this Statute and which shall be laid down in the Rules of Procedure, adjudicate upon applications to suspend execution, as provided for in Article 278 of the Treaty on the Functioning of the European Union and Article 157 of the EAEC Treaty, or to prescribe interim measures pursuant to Article 279 of the Treaty on the Functioning of the European Union, or to suspend enforcement in accordance with the fourth paragraph of Article 299 of the Treaty on the Functioning of the European Union or the third paragraph of Article 164 of the EAEC Treaty.

The powers referred to in the first paragraph may, under the conditions laid down in the Rules of Procedure, be exercised by the Vice-President of the Court of Justice.

Should the President and the Vice-President be prevented from attending, another Judge shall take their place under the conditions laid down in the Rules of Procedure.

The ruling of the President or of the Judge replacing him shall be provisional and shall in no way prejudice the decision of the Court on the substance of the case.

Article 40

Member States and institutions of the Union may intervene in cases before the Court of Justice.

The same right shall be open to the bodies, offices and agencies of the Union and to any other person which can establish an interest in the result of a case submitted to the Court. Natural or legal persons shall not intervene in cases between Member States, between institutions of the Union or between Member States and institutions of the Union.

Without prejudice to the second paragraph, the States, other than the Member States, which are parties to the Agreement on the European Economic Area, and also the EFTA Surveillance Authority referred to in that Agreement, may intervene in cases before the Court where one of the fields of application of that Agreement is concerned.

An application to intervene shall be limited to supporting the form of order sought by one of the parties.

Article 41

Where the defending party, after having been duly summoned, fails to file written submissions in defence, judgment shall be given against that party by default. An objection may be lodged against the judgment within one month of it being notified. The objection shall not have the effect of staying enforcement of the judgment by default unless the Court of Justice decides otherwise.

Article 42

Member States, institutions, bodies, offices and agencies of the Union and any other natural or legal persons may, in cases and under conditions to be determined by the Rules of Procedure, institute third-party proceedings to contest a judgment rendered without their being heard, where the judgment is prejudicial to their rights.

Article 43

If the meaning or scope of a judgment is in doubt, the Court of Justice shall construe it on application by any party or any institution of the Union establishing an interest therein.

Article 44

An application for revision of a judgment may be made to the Court of Justice only on discovery of a fact which is of such a nature as to be a decisive factor, and which, when the judgment was given, was unknown to the Court and to the party claiming the revision.

The revision shall be opened by a judgment of the Court expressly recording the existence of a new fact, recognising that it is of such a character as to lay the case open to revision and declaring the application admissible on this ground.

No application for revision may be made after the lapse of 10 years from the date of the judgment.

Article 45

Periods of grace based on considerations of distance shall be determined by the Rules of Procedure.

No right shall be prejudiced in consequence of the expiry of a time limit if the party concerned proves the existence of unforeseeable circumstances or of force majeure.

Article 46

Proceedings against the Union in matters arising from non-contractual liability shall be barred after a period of five years from the occurrence of the event giving rise thereto. The period of limitation shall be interrupted if proceedings are instituted before the Court of Justice or if prior to such proceedings an application is made by the aggrieved party to the relevant institution of the Union. In the latter event the proceedings must be instituted within the period of two months provided for in Article 263 of the Treaty on the Functioning of the European Union; the provisions of the second paragraph of Article 265 of the Treaty on the Functioning of the European Union shall apply where appropriate.

This Article shall also apply to proceedings against the European Central Bank regarding non-contractual liability.

TITLE IV GENERAL COURT

Article 47
The first paragraph of Article 9, Article 9a, Articles 14 and 15, the first, second, fourth and fifth paragraphs of Article 17 and Article 18 shall apply to the General Court and its members.

The fourth paragraph of Article 3 and Articles 10, 11 and 14 shall apply to the Registrar of the General Court *mutatis mutandis*.

Article 48
The General Court shall consist of:
(a) 40 Judges as from 25 December 2015;
(b) 47 Judges as from 1 September 2016;
(c) two Judges per Member State as from 1 September 2019.

Article 49
The Members of the General Court may be called upon to perform the task of an Advocate-General.

It shall be the duty of the Advocate-General, acting with complete impartiality and independence, to make, in open court, reasoned submissions on certain cases brought before the General Court in order to assist the General Court in the performance of its task.

The criteria for selecting such cases, as well as the procedures for designating the Advocates-General, shall be laid down in the Rules of Procedure of the General Court.

A Member called upon to perform the task of Advocate-General in a case may not take part in the judgment of the case.

Article 50
The General Court shall sit in chambers of three or five Judges. The Judges shall elect the Presidents of the chambers from among their number. The Presidents of the chambers of five Judges shall be elected for three years. They may be re-elected once.

The composition of the chambers and the assignment of cases to them shall be governed by the Rules of Procedure. In certain cases governed by the Rules of Procedure, the General Court may sit as a full court or be constituted by a single Judge.

The Rules of Procedure may also provide that the General Court may sit in a Grand Chamber in cases and under the conditions specified therein.

Article 50a
1. The General Court shall exercise at first instance jurisdiction in disputes between the Union and its servants as referred to in Article 270 of the Treaty on the Functioning of the European Union, including disputes between all institutions, bodies, offices or agencies, on the one hand, and their servants, on the other, in respect of which jurisdiction is conferred on the Court of Justice of the European Union.
2. At all stages of the procedure, including the time when the application is filed, the General Court may examine the possibilities of an amicable settlement of the dispute and may try to facilitate such settlement.

Article 51

By way of derogation from the rule laid down in Article 256(1) of the Treaty on the Functioning of the European Union, jurisdiction shall be reserved to the Court of Justice in the actions referred to in Articles 263 and 265 of the Treaty on the Functioning of the European Union when they are brought by a Member State against:

(a) an act of or failure to act by the European Parliament or the Council, or by those institutions acting jointly, except for:
 — decisions taken by the Council under the third subparagraph of Article 108(2) of the Treaty on the Functioning of the European Union;
 — acts of the Council adopted pursuant to a Council regulation concerning measures to protect trade within the meaning of Article 207 of the Treaty on the Functioning of the European Union;
 — acts of the Council by which the Council exercises implementing powers in accordance with the second paragraph of Article 291 of the Treaty on the Functioning of the European Union;

(b) against an act of or failure to act by the Commission under the first paragraph of Article 331 of the Treaty on the Functioning of the European Union.

Jurisdiction shall also be reserved to the Court of Justice in the actions referred to in the same Articles when they are brought by an institution of the Union against an act of or failure to act by the European Parliament, the Council, both those institutions acting jointly, or the Commission, or brought by an institution of the Union against an act of or failure to act by the European Central Bank.

Article 52

The President of the Court of Justice and the President of the General Court shall determine, by common accord, the conditions under which officials and other servants attached to the Court of Justice shall render their services to the General Court to enable it to function. Certain officials or other servants shall be responsible to the Registrar of the General Court under the authority of the President of the General Court.

Article 53

The procedure before the General Court shall be governed by Title III.

Such further and more detailed provisions as may be necessary shall be laid down in its Rules of Procedure. The Rules of Procedure may derogate from the fourth paragraph of Article 40 and from Article 41 in order to take account of the specific features of litigation in the field of intellectual property.

Notwithstanding the fourth paragraph of Article 20, the Advocate-General may make his reasoned submissions in writing.

Article 54

Where an application or other procedural document addressed to the General Court is lodged by mistake with the Registrar of the Court of Justice, it shall be transmitted immediately by that Registrar to the Registrar of the General Court; likewise, where an application or other procedural document addressed to the Court of Justice is lodged by mistake with the Registrar of the General Court, it shall be transmitted immediately by that Registrar to the Registrar of the Court of Justice.

Where the General Court finds that it does not have jurisdiction to hear and determine an action in respect of which the Court of Justice has jurisdiction, it shall refer that action to the Court of Justice; likewise, where the Court of Justice finds that an action falls within the jurisdiction of the General Court, it shall refer that action to the General Court, whereupon that Court may not decline jurisdiction.

Where the Court of Justice and the General Court are seised of cases in which the same relief is sought, the same issue of interpretation is raised or the validity of the same act is called in question, the General Court may, after hearing the parties, stay the proceedings before it until such time as the Court of Justice has delivered judgment or, where the action is one brought pursuant to Article 263 of the Treaty on the Functioning of the European Union, may decline jurisdiction so as to allow the Court of Justice to rule on such actions. In the same circumstances, the Court of Justice may also decide to stay the proceedings before it; in that event, the proceedings before the General Court shall continue.

Where a Member State and an institution of the Union are challenging the same act, the General Court shall decline jurisdiction so that the Court of Justice may rule on those applications.

Article 55

Final decisions of the General Court, decisions disposing of the substantive issues in part only or disposing of a procedural issue concerning a plea of lack of competence or inadmissibility, shall be notified by the Registrar of the General Court to all parties as well as all Member States and the institutions of the Union even if they did not intervene in the case before the General Court.

Article 56

An appeal may be brought before the Court of Justice, within two months of the notification of the decision appealed against, against final decisions of the General Court and decisions of that Court disposing of the substantive issues in part only or disposing of a procedural issue concerning a plea of lack of competence or inadmissibility.

Such an appeal may be brought by any party which has been unsuccessful, in whole or in part, in its submissions. However, interveners other than the Member States and the institutions of the Union may bring such an appeal only where the decision of the General Court directly affects them.

With the exception of cases relating to disputes between the Union and its servants, an appeal may also be brought by Member States and institutions of the Union which did not intervene in the proceedings before the General Court. Such Member States and institutions shall be in the same position as Member States or institutions which intervened at first instance.

Article 57

Any person whose application to intervene has been dismissed by the General Court may appeal to the Court of Justice within two weeks from the notification of the decision dismissing the application.

The parties to the proceedings may appeal to the Court of Justice against any decision of the General Court made pursuant to Article 278 or Article 279 or the fourth paragraph of Article 299 of the Treaty on the Functioning of the European Union or Article 157 or the third paragraph of Article 164 of the EAEC Treaty within two months from their notification.

The appeal referred to in the first two paragraphs of this Article shall be heard and determined under the procedure referred to in Article 39.

Article 58

An appeal to the Court of Justice shall be limited to points of law. It shall lie on the grounds of lack of competence of the General Court, a breach of procedure before it which adversely affects the interests of the appellant as well as the infringement of Union law by the General Court.

No appeal shall lie regarding only the amount of the costs or the party ordered to pay them.

Article 59

Where an appeal is brought against a decision of the General Court, the procedure before the Court of Justice shall consist of a written part and an oral part. In accordance with conditions laid down in the Rules of Procedure, the Court of Justice, having heard the Advocate-General and the parties, may dispense with the oral procedure.

Article 60

Without prejudice to Articles 278 and 279 of the Treaty on the Functioning of the European Union or Article 157 of the EAEC Treaty, an appeal shall not have suspensory effect.

By way of derogation from Article 280 of the Treaty on the Functioning of the European Union, decisions of the General Court declaring a regulation to be void shall take effect only as from the date of expiry of the period referred to in the first paragraph of Article 56 of this Statute or, if an appeal shall have been brought within that period, as from the date of dismissal of the appeal, without prejudice, however, to the right of a party to apply to the Court of Justice, pursuant to Articles 278 and 279 of the Treaty on the Functioning of the European Union or Article 157 of the EAEC Treaty, for the suspension of the effects of the regulation which has been declared void or for the prescription of any other interim measure.

Article 61

If the appeal is well founded, the Court of Justice shall quash the decision of the General Court. It may itself give final judgment in the matter, where the state of the proceedings so permits, or refer the case back to the General Court for judgment.

Where a case is referred back to the General Court, that Court shall be bound by the decision of the Court of Justice on points of law.

When an appeal brought by a Member State or an institution of the Union, which did not intervene in the proceedings before the General Court, is well founded, the Court of Justice may, if it considers this necessary, state which of the effects of the decision of the General Court which has been quashed shall be considered as definitive in respect of the parties to the litigation.

Article 62

In the cases provided for in Article 256(2) and (3) of the Treaty on the Functioning of the European Union, where the First Advocate-General considers that there is a serious risk of the unity or consistency of Union law being affected, he may propose that the Court of Justice review the decision of the General Court.

The proposal must be made within one month of delivery of the decision by the General Court. Within one month of receiving the proposal made by the First Advocate-General, the Court of Justice shall decide whether or not the decision should be reviewed.

Article 62a

The Court of Justice shall give a ruling on the questions which are subject to review by means of an urgent procedure on the basis of the file forwarded to it by the General Court.

Those referred to in Article 23 of this Statute and, in the cases provided for in Article 256(2) of the [Treaty on the Functioning of the European Union], the parties to the proceedings before the General Court shall be entitled to lodge statements or written observations with the Court of Justice relating to questions which are subject to review within a period prescribed for that purpose.

The Court of Justice may decide to open the oral procedure before giving a ruling.

Article 62b

In the cases provided for in Article 256(2) of the Treaty on the Functioning of the European Union, without prejudice to Articles 278 and 279 of the Treaty on the Functioning of the European Union, proposals for review and decisions to open the review procedure shall not have suspensory effect. If the Court of Justice finds that the decision of the General Court affects the unity or consistency of Union law, it shall refer the case back to the General Court which shall be bound by the points of law decided by the Court of Justice; the Court of Justice may state which of the effects of the decision of the General Court are to be considered as definitive in respect of the parties to the litigation. If, however, having regard to the result of the review, the outcome of the proceedings flows from the findings of fact on which the decision of the General Court was based, the Court of Justice shall give final judgment.

In the cases provided for in Article 256(3) of the Treaty on the Functioning of the European Union, in the absence of proposals for review or decisions to open the review procedure, the answer(s) given by the General Court to the questions submitted to it shall take effect upon expiry of the periods prescribed for that purpose in the second paragraph of Article 62. Should a review procedure be opened, the answer(s) subject to review shall take effect following that procedure, unless the Court of Justice decides otherwise. If the Court of Justice finds that the decision of the General Court affects the unity or consistency of Union law, the answer given by the Court of Justice to the questions subject to review shall be substituted for that given by the General Court.

TITLE IVa SPECIALISED COURTS

Article 62c

The provisions relating to the jurisdiction, composition, organisation and procedure of any specialised court established under Article 257 of the Treaty on the Functioning of the European Union shall be contained in an Annex to this Statute.

TITLE V FINAL PROVISIONS

Article 63

The Rules of Procedure of the Court of Justice and of the General Court shall contain any provisions necessary for applying and, where required, supplementing this Statute.

Article 64

The rules governing the language arrangements applicable at the Court of Justice of the European Union shall be laid down by a regulation of the Council acting unanimously. This regulation shall be adopted either at the request of the Court of Justice and after consultation of the Commission and the European Parliament, or on a proposal from the Commission and after consultation of the Court of Justice and of the European Parliament.

Until those rules have been adopted, the provisions of the Rules of Procedure of the Court of Justice and of the Rules of Procedure of the General Court governing language arrangements shall continue to apply. By way of derogation from Articles 253 and 254 of the Treaty on the Functioning of the European Union, those provisions may only be amended or repealed with the unanimous consent of the Council.

ANNEX THE EUROPEAN UNION CIVIL SERVICE TRIBUNAL (repealed)*

Article 1

The European Union Civil Service Tribunal (hereafter 'the Civil Service Tribunal') shall exercise at first instance jurisdiction in disputes between the Union and its servants referred to in Article 270 of the Treaty on the Functioning of the European Union, including disputes between all bodies or agencies and their servants in respect of which jurisdiction is conferred on the Court of Justice of the European Union.

Article 2

1. The Civil Service Tribunal shall consist of seven judges. Should the Court of Justice so request, the Council, acting by a qualified majority, may increase the number of judges.

   The judges shall be appointed for a period of six years. Retiring judges may be reappointed.

   Any vacancy shall be filled by the appointment of a new judge for a period of six years.
2. Temporary Judges shall be appointed, in addition to the Judges referred to in the first subparagraph of paragraph 1, in order to cover the absence of Judges who, while not suffering from disablement deemed to be total, are prevented from participating in the disposal of cases for a lengthy period of time.

---

* The Annex was deleted, together with the Civil Service Tribunal, by Regulation 2016/1192 on the transfer to the General Court of jurisdiction at first instance in disputes between the European Union and its servants [2016] OJ L200/137. According to art. 4 of the Regulation, however, certain provisions continue to apply: "Articles 9 to 12 of Annex I to Protocol No. 3 shall continue to apply to the appeals against decisions of the Civil Service Tribunal of which the General Court is seised as at 31 August 2016 or which are brought after that date. If the General Court sets aside a decision of the Civil Service Tribunal but considers that the state of the proceedings does not permit a decision, it shall refer the case to a chamber other than that which rules on the appeal".

Article 3

1. The judges shall be appointed by the Council, acting in accordance with the fourth paragraph of Article 257 of the Treaty on the Functioning of the European Union, after consulting the committee provided for by this Article. When appointing judges, the Council shall ensure a balanced composition of the Civil Service Tribunal on as broad a geographical basis as possible from among nationals of the Member States and with respect to the national legal systems represented.

2. Any person who is a Union citizen and fulfils the conditions laid down in the fourth paragraph of Article 257 of the Treaty on the Functioning of the European Union may submit an application. The Council, acting on a recommendation from the Court of Justice, shall determine the conditions and the arrangements governing the submission and processing of such applications.

3. A committee shall be set up comprising seven persons chosen from among former members of the Court of Justice and the General Court and lawyers of recognised competence. The committee's membership and operating rules shall be determined by the Council, acting on a recommendation by the President of the Court of Justice.

4. The committee shall give an opinion on candidates' suitability to perform the duties of judge at the Civil Service Tribunal. The committee shall append to its opinion a list of candidates having the most suitable high-level experience. Such list shall contain the names of at least twice as many candidates as there are judges to be appointed by the Council.

Article 4

1. The judges shall elect the President of the Civil Service Tribunal from among their number for a term of three years. He may be re-elected.

2. The Civil Service Tribunal shall sit in chambers of three judges. It may, in certain cases determined by its rules of procedure, sit in full court or in a chamber of five judges or of a single judge.

3. The President of the Civil Service Tribunal shall preside over the full court and the chamber of five judges. The Presidents of the chambers of three judges shall be designated as provided in paragraph 1. If the President of the Civil Service Tribunal is assigned to a chamber of three judges, he shall preside over that chamber.

4. The jurisdiction of and quorum for the full court as well as the composition of the chambers and the assignment of cases to them shall be governed by the Rules of Procedure.

Article 5

Articles 2 to 6, 14, 15, the first, second and fifth paragraphs of Article 17, and Article 18 of the Statute of the Court of Justice of the European Union shall apply to the Civil Service Tribunal and its members.

The oath referred to in Article 2 of the Statute shall be taken before the Court of Justice, and the decisions referred to in Articles 3, 4 and 6 thereof shall be adopted by the Court of Justice after consulting the Civil Service Tribunal.

Article 6

1. The Civil Service Tribunal shall be supported by the departments of the Court of Justice and of the General Court. The President of the Court of Justice or, in appropriate cases, the President of the General Court, shall determine by common accord with the President of the Civil Service Tribunal the conditions under which officials and other servants attached to the Court of Justice or the General Court shall render their services to the Civil Service Tribunal to enable it to function. Certain officials or other servants shall be responsible to the Registrar of the Civil Service Tribunal under the authority of the President of that Tribunal.

2. The Civil Service Tribunal shall appoint its Registrar and lay down the rules governing his service. The fourth paragraph of Article 3 and Articles 10, 11 and 14 of the Statute of the Court of Justice of the European Union shall apply to the Registrar of the Tribunal.

Article 7

1. The procedure before the Civil Service Tribunal shall be governed by Title III of the Statute of the Court of Justice of the European Union, with the exception of Articles 22 and 23. Such further and more detailed provisions as may be necessary shall be laid down in the Rules of Procedure.

2. The provisions concerning the General Court's language arrangements shall apply to the Civil Service Tribunal.

3. The written stage of the procedure shall comprise the presentation of the application and of the statement of defence, unless the Civil Service Tribunal decides that a second exchange of written pleadings is necessary. Where there is such second exchange, the Civil Service Tribunal may, with the agreement of the parties, decide to proceed to judgment without an oral procedure.

4. At all stages of the procedure, including the time when the application is filed, the Civil Service Tribunal may examine the possibilities of an amicable settlement of the dispute and may try to facilitate such settlement.

5. The Civil Service Tribunal shall rule on the costs of a case. Subject to the specific provisions of the Rules of Procedure, the unsuccessful party shall be ordered to pay the costs should the court so decide.

Article 8

1. Where an application or other procedural document addressed to the Civil Service Tribunal is lodged by mistake with the Registrar of the Court of Justice or General Court, it shall be transmitted immediately by that Registrar to the Registrar of the Civil Service Tribunal. Likewise, where an application or other procedural document addressed to the Court of Justice or to the General Court is lodged by mistake with the Registrar of the Civil Service Tribunal, it shall be transmitted immediately by that Registrar to the Registrar of the Court of Justice or General Court.

2. Where the Civil Service Tribunal finds that it does not have jurisdiction to hear and determine an action in respect of which the Court of Justice or the General Court has jurisdiction, it shall refer that action to the Court of Justice or to the General Court. Likewise, where the Court of Justice or the General Court finds that an action falls within the jurisdiction of the Civil Service Tribunal, the Court seised shall refer

that action to the Civil Service Tribunal, whereupon that Tribunal may not decline jurisdiction.

3. Where the Civil Service Tribunal and the General Court are seised of cases in which the same issue of interpretation is raised or the validity of the same act is called in question, the Civil Service Tribunal, after hearing the parties, may stay the proceedings until the judgment of the General Court has been delivered.

   Where the Civil Service Tribunal and the General Court are seised of cases in which the same relief is sought, the Civil Service Tribunal shall decline jurisdiction so that the General Court may act on those cases.

Article 9

An appeal may be brought before the General Court, within two months of notification of the decision appealed against, against final decisions of the Civil Service Tribunal and decisions of that Tribunal disposing of the substantive issues in part only or disposing of a procedural issue concerning a plea of lack of jurisdiction or inadmissibility.

Such an appeal may be brought by any party which has been unsuccessful, in whole or in part, in its submissions. However, interveners other than the Member States and the institutions of the Union may bring such an appeal only where the decision of the Civil Service Tribunal directly affects them.

Article 10

1. Any person whose application to intervene has been dismissed by the Civil Service Tribunal may appeal to the General Court within two weeks of notification of the decision dismissing the application.

2. The parties to the proceedings may appeal to the General Court against any decision of the Civil Service Tribunal made pursuant to Article 278 or Article 279 or the fourth paragraph of Article 299 of the Treaty on the Functioning of the European Union or Article 157 or the third paragraph of Article 164 of the EAEC Treaty within two months of its notification.

3. The President of the General Court may, by way of summary procedure, which may, in so far as necessary, differ from some of the rules contained in this Annex and which shall be laid down in the rules of procedure of the General Court, adjudicate upon appeals brought in accordance with paragraphs 1 and 2.

Article 11

1. An appeal to the General Court shall be limited to points of law. It shall lie on the grounds of lack of jurisdiction of the Civil Service Tribunal, a breach of procedure before it which adversely affects the interests of the appellant, as well as the infringement of Union law by the Tribunal.

2. No appeal shall lie regarding only the amount of the costs or the party ordered to pay them.

Article 12

1. Without prejudice to Articles 278 and 279 of the Treaty on the Functioning of the European Union or Article 157 of the EAEC Treaty, an appeal before the General Court shall not have suspensory effect.

2. Where an appeal is brought against a decision of the Civil Service Tribunal, the procedure before the General Court shall consist of a written part and an oral part. In accordance with conditions laid down in the rules of procedure, the General Court, having heard the parties, may dispense with the oral procedure.

Article 13

1. If the appeal is well founded, the General Court shall quash the decision of the Civil Service Tribunal and itself give judgment in the matter. It shall refer the case back to the Civil Service Tribunal for judgment where the state of the proceedings does not permit a decision by the Court.
2. Where a case is referred back to the Civil Service Tribunal, the Tribunal shall be bound by the decision of the General Court on points of law.

PROTOCOL (NO 4) ON THE STATUTE OF THE EUROPEAN SYSTEM OF CENTRAL BANKS AND OF THE EUROPEAN CENTRAL BANK

THE HIGH CONTRACTING PARTIES,

DESIRING to lay down the Statute of the European System of Central Banks and of the European Central Bank provided for in the second paragraph of Article 129 of the Treaty on the Functioning of the European Union,

HAVE AGREED upon the following provisions, which shall be annexed to the Treaty on European Union and to the Treaty on the Functioning of the European Union:

Chapter I The European System of Central Banks

Article 1

The European System of Central Banks

In accordance with Article 282(1) of the Treaty on the Functioning of the European Union, the European Central Bank (ECB) and the national central banks shall constitute the European System of Central Banks (ESCB). The ECB and the national central banks of those Member States whose currency is the euro shall constitute the Eurosystem.

The ESCB and the ECB shall perform their tasks and carry on their activities in accordance with the provisions of the Treaties and of this Statute.

Chapter II Objectives and Tasks of the ESCB

Article 2

Objectives

In accordance with Article 127(1) and Article 282(2) of the Treaty on the Functioning of the European Union, the primary objective of the ESCB shall be to maintain price stability. Without prejudice to the objective of price stability, it shall support the general economic policies in the Union with a view to contributing to the achievement of the objectives of the Union as laid down in Article 3 of the Treaty on European Union. The ESCB shall act in accordance with the principle of an open market economy with free competition, favouring an efficient allocation of resources, and in compliance with the principles set out in Article 119 of the Treaty on the Functioning of the European Union.

Article 3
Tasks

3.1. In accordance with Article 127(2) of the Treaty on the Functioning of the European Union, the basic tasks to be carried out through the ESCB shall be:
— to define and implement the monetary policy of the Union;
— to conduct foreign-exchange operations consistent with the provisions of Article 219 of that Treaty;
— to hold and manage the official foreign reserves of the Member States;
— to promote the smooth operation of payment systems.

3.2. In accordance with Article 127(3) of the Treaty on the Functioning of the European Union, the third indent of Article 3.1 shall be without prejudice to the holding and management by the governments of Member States of foreign-exchange working balances.

3.3. In accordance with Article 127(5) of the Treaty on the Functioning of the European Union, the ESCB shall contribute to the smooth conduct of policies pursued by the competent authorities relating to the prudential supervision of credit institutions and the stability of the financial system.

Article 4
Advisory functions

In accordance with Article 127(4) of the Treaty on the Functioning of the European Union:
(a) the ECB shall be consulted:
— on any proposed Union act in its fields of competence;
— by national authorities regarding any draft legislative provision in its fields of competence, but within the limits and under the conditions set out by the Council in accordance with the procedure laid down in Article 41;
(b) the ECB may submit opinions to the Union institutions, bodies, offices or agencies or to national authorities on matters in its fields of competence.

Article 5
Collection of statistical information

5.1. In order to undertake the tasks of the ESCB, the ECB, assisted by the national central banks, shall collect the necessary statistical information either from the competent national authorities or directly from economic agents. For these purposes it shall cooperate with the Union institutions, bodies, offices or agencies and with the competent authorities of the Member States or third countries and with international organisations.

5.2. The national central banks shall carry out, to the extent possible, the tasks described in Article 5.1.

5.3. The ECB shall contribute to the harmonisation, where necessary, of the rules and practices governing the collection, compilation and distribution of statistics in the areas within its fields of competence.

5.4. The Council, in accordance with the procedure laid down in Article 41, shall define the natural and legal persons subject to reporting requirements, the confidentiality regime and the appropriate provisions for enforcement.

Article 6
International cooperation

6.1. In the field of international cooperation involving the tasks entrusted to the ESCB, the ECB shall decide how the ESCB shall be represented.

6.2. The ECB and, subject to its approval, the national central banks may participate in international monetary institutions.

6.3. Articles 6.1 and 6.2 shall be without prejudice to Article 138 of the Treaty on the Functioning of the European Union.

Chapter III Organisation of the ESCB

Article 7
Independence

In accordance with Article 130 of the Treaty on the Functioning of the European Union, when exercising the powers and carrying out the tasks and duties conferred upon them by the Treaties and this Statute, neither the ECB, nor a national central bank, nor any member of their decision-making bodies shall seek or take instructions from Union institutions, bodies, offices or agencies, from any government of a Member State or from any other body. The Union institutions, bodies, offices or agencies and the governments of the Member States undertake to respect this principle and not to seek to influence the members of the decision-making bodies of the ECB or of the national central banks in the performance of their tasks.

Article 8
General principle

The ESCB shall be governed by the decision-making bodies of the ECB.

Article 9
The European Central Bank

9.1. The ECB which, in accordance with Article 282(3) of the Treaty on the Functioning of the European Union, shall have legal personality, shall enjoy in each of the Member States the most extensive legal capacity accorded to legal persons under its law; it may, in particular, acquire or dispose of movable and immovable property and may be a party to legal proceedings.

9.2. The ECB shall ensure that the tasks conferred upon the ESCB under Article 127(2),(3) and (5) of the Treaty on the Functioning of the European Union are implemented either by its own activities pursuant to this Statute or through the national central banks pursuant to Articles 12.1 and 14.

9.3. In accordance with Article 129(1) of the Treaty on the Functioning of the European Union, the decision making bodies of the ECB shall be the Governing Council and the Executive Board.

Article 10
The Governing Council

10.1. In accordance with Article 283(1) of the Treaty on the Functioning of the European Union, the Governing Council shall comprise the members of the Executive Board of the ECB and the governors of the national central banks of the Member States whose currency is the euro.

10.2. Each member of the Governing Council shall have one vote. As from the date on which the number of members of the Governing Council exceeds 21, each member of the Executive Board shall have one vote and the number of governors with a voting right shall be 15. The latter voting rights shall be assigned and shall rotate as follows:

— as from the date on which the number of governors exceeds 15, until it reaches 22, the governors shall be allocated to two groups, according to a ranking of the size of the share of their national central bank's Member State in the aggregate gross domestic product at market prices and in the total aggregated balance sheet of the monetary financial institutions of the Member States whose currency is the euro. The shares in the aggregate gross domestic product at market prices and in the total aggregated balance sheet of the monetary financial institutions shall be assigned weights of 5/6 and 1/6, respectively. The first group shall be composed of five governors and the second group of the remaining governors. The frequency of voting rights of the governors allocated to the first group shall not be lower than the frequency of voting rights of those of the second group. Subject to the previous sentence, the first group shall be assigned four voting rights and the second group eleven voting rights,

— as from the date on which the number of governors reaches 22, the governors shall be allocated to three groups according to a ranking based on the above criteria. The first group shall be composed of five governors and shall be assigned four voting rights. The second group shall be composed of half of the total number of governors, with any fraction rounded up to the nearest integer, and shall be assigned eight voting rights. The third group shall be composed of the remaining governors and shall be assigned three voting rights,

— within each group, the governors shall have their voting rights for equal amounts of time,

— for the calculation of the shares in the aggregate gross domestic product at market prices Article 29.2 shall apply. The total aggregated balance sheet of the monetary financial institutions shall be calculated in accordance with the statistical framework applying in the Union at the time of the calculation,

— whenever the aggregate gross domestic product at market prices is adjusted in accordance with Article 29.3, or whenever the number of governors increases, the size and/or composition of the groups shall be adjusted in accordance with the above principles,

— the Governing Council, acting by a two-thirds majority of all its members, with and without a voting right, shall take all measures necessary for the implementation of the above principles and may decide to postpone the start of the rotation system until the date on which the number of governors exceeds 18.

The right to vote shall be exercised in person. By way of derogation from this rule, the Rules of Procedure referred to in Article 12.3 may lay down that members of the Governing Council may cast their vote by means of teleconferencing. These rules shall also provide that a member of the Governing Council who is prevented from attending meetings of the Governing Council for a prolonged period may appoint an alternate as a member of the Governing Council.

The provisions of the previous paragraphs are without prejudice to the voting rights of all members of the Governing Council, with and without a voting right, under Articles 10.3, 40.2 and 40.3.

Save as otherwise provided for in this Statute, the Governing Council shall act by a simple majority of the members having a voting right. In the event of a tie, the President shall have the casting vote.

In order for the Governing Council to vote, there shall be a quorum of two-thirds of the members having a voting right. If the quorum is not met, the President may convene an extraordinary meeting at which decisions may be taken without regard to the quorum.

10.3. For any decisions to be taken under Articles 28, 29, 30, 32 and 33, the votes in the Governing Council shall be weighted according to the national central banks' shares in the subscribed capital of the ECB. The weights of the votes of the members of the Executive Board shall be zero. A decision requiring a qualified majority shall be adopted if the votes cast in favour represent at least two thirds of the subscribed capital of the ECB and represent at least half of the shareholders. If a Governor is unable to be present, he may nominate an alternate to cast his weighted vote.

10.4. The proceedings of the meetings shall be confidential. The Governing Council may decide to make the outcome of its deliberations public.

10.5. The Governing Council shall meet at least 10 times a year.

Article 11

The Executive Board

11.1. In accordance with the first subparagraph of Article 283(2) of the Treaty on the Functioning of the European Union, the Executive Board shall comprise the President, the Vice-President and four other members.

The members shall perform their duties on a full-time basis. No member shall engage in any occupation, whether gainful or not, unless exemption is exceptionally granted by the Governing Council.

11.2. In accordance with the second subparagraph of Article 283(2) of the Treaty on the Functioning of the European Union, the President, the Vice-President and the other members of the Executive Board shall be appointed by the European Council, acting by a qualified majority, from among persons of recognised standing and professional experience in monetary or banking matters, on a recommendation from the Council after it has consulted the European Parliament and the Governing Council. Their term of office shall be eight years and shall not be renewable.

Only nationals of Member States may be members of the Executive Board.

11.3. The terms and conditions of employment of the members of the Executive Board, in particular their salaries, pensions and other social security benefits shall be the subject of contracts with the ECB and shall be fixed by the Governing Council on a proposal from a Committee comprising three members appointed by the

Governing Council and three members appointed by the Council. The members of the Executive Board shall not have the right to vote on matters referred to in this paragraph.

11.4. If a member of the Executive Board no longer fulfils the conditions required for the performance of his duties or if he has been guilty of serious misconduct, the Court of Justice may, on application by the Governing Council or the Executive Board, compulsorily retire him.

11.5. Each member of the Executive Board present in person shall have the right to vote and shall have, for that purpose, one vote. Save as otherwise provided, the Executive Board shall act by a simple majority of the votes cast. In the event of a tie, the President shall have the casting vote. The voting arrangements shall be specified in the Rules of Procedure referred to in Article 12.3.

11.6. The Executive Board shall be responsible for the current business of the ECB.

11.7. Any vacancy on the Executive Board shall be filled by the appointment of a new member in accordance with Article 11.2.

Article 12
Responsibilities of the decision-making bodies

12.1. The Governing Council shall adopt the guidelines and take the decisions necessary to ensure the performance of the tasks entrusted to the ESCB under these Treaties and this Statute. The Governing Council shall formulate the monetary policy of the Union including, as appropriate, decisions relating to intermediate monetary objectives, key interest rates and the supply of reserves in the ESCB, and shall establish the necessary guidelines for their implementation.

The Executive Board shall implement monetary policy in accordance with the guidelines and decisions laid down by the Governing Council. In doing so the Executive Board shall give the necessary instructions to national central banks. In addition the Executive Board may have certain powers delegated to it where the Governing Council so decides.

To the extent deemed possible and appropriate and without prejudice to the provisions of this Article, the ECB shall have recourse to the national central banks to carry out operations which form part of the tasks of the ESCB.

12.2. The Executive Board shall have responsibility for the preparation of meetings of the Governing Council.

12.3. The Governing Council shall adopt Rules of Procedure which determine the internal organisation of the ECB and its decision-making bodies.

12.4. The Governing Council shall exercise the advisory functions referred to in Article 4.

12.5. The Governing Council shall take the decisions referred to in Article 6.

Article 13
The President

13.1. The President or, in his absence, the Vice-President shall chair the Governing Council and the Executive Board of the ECB.

13.2. Without prejudice to Article 38, the President or his nominee shall represent the ECB externally.

Article 14

National central banks

14.1. In accordance with Article 131 of the Treaty on the Functioning of the European Union, each Member State shall ensure that its national legislation, including the statutes of its national central bank, is compatible with these Treaties and this Statute.

14.2. The statutes of the national central banks shall, in particular, provide that the term of office of a Governor of a national central bank shall be no less than five years.

A Governor may be relieved from office only if he no longer fulfils the conditions required for the performance of his duties or if he has been guilty of serious misconduct. A decision to this effect may be referred to the Court of Justice by the Governor concerned or the Governing Council on grounds of infringement of these Treaties or of any rule of law relating to their application. Such proceedings shall be instituted within two months of the publication of the decision or of its notification to the plaintiff or, in the absence thereof, of the day on which it came to the knowledge of the latter, as the case may be.

14.3. The national central banks are an integral part of the ESCB and shall act in accordance with the guidelines and instructions of the ECB. The Governing Council shall take the necessary steps to ensure compliance with the guidelines and instructions of the ECB, and shall require that any necessary information be given to it.

14.4. National central banks may perform functions other than those specified in this Statute unless the Governing Council finds, by a majority of two thirds of the votes cast, that these interfere with the objectives and tasks of the ESCB. Such functions shall be performed on the responsibility and liability of national central banks and shall not be regarded as being part of the functions of the ESCB.

Article 15

Reporting commitments

15.1. The ECB shall draw up and publish reports on the activities of the ESCB at least quarterly.

15.2. A consolidated financial statement of the ESCB shall be published each week.

15.3. In accordance with Article 284(3) of the Treaty on the Functioning of the European Union, the ECB shall address an annual report on the activities of the ESCB and on the monetary policy of both the previous and the current year to the European Parliament, the Council and the Commission, and also to the European Council.

15.4. The reports and statements referred to in this Article shall be made available to interested parties free of charge.

Article 16

Banknotes

In accordance with Article 128(1) of the Treaty on the Functioning of the European Union, the Governing Council shall have the exclusive right to authorise the issue of euro banknotes within the Union. The ECB and the national central banks may issue such notes. The banknotes issued by the ECB and the national central banks shall be the only such notes to have the status of legal tender within the Union.

The ECB shall respect as far as possible existing practices regarding the issue and design of banknotes.

Chapter IV Monetary Functions and Operations of the ESCB

Article 17
Accounts with the ECB and the national central banks
In order to conduct their operations, the ECB and the national central banks may open accounts for credit institutions, public entities and other market participants and accept assets, including book entry securities, as collateral.

Article 18
Open market and credit operations
18.1. In order to achieve the objectives of the ESCB and to carry out its tasks, the ECB and the national central banks may:
  — operate in the financial markets by buying and selling outright (spot and forward) or under repurchase agreement and by lending or borrowing claims and marketable instruments, whether in euro or other currencies, as well as precious metals;
  — conduct credit operations with credit institutions and other market participants, with lending being based on adequate collateral.
18.2. The ECB shall establish general principles for open market and credit operations carried out by itself or the national central banks, including for the announcement of conditions under which they stand ready to enter into such transactions.

Article 19
Minimum reserves
19.1. Subject to Article 2, the ECB may require credit institutions established in Member States to hold minimum reserve on accounts with the ECB and national central banks in pursuance of monetary policy objectives. Regulations concerning the calculation and determination of the required minimum reserves may be established by the Governing Council. In cases of non-compliance the ECB shall be entitled to levy penalty interest and to impose other sanctions with comparable effect.
19.2. For the application of this Article, the Council shall, in accordance with the procedure laid down in Article 41, define the basis for minimum reserves and the maximum permissible ratios between those reserves and their basis, as well as the appropriate sanctions in cases of non-compliance.

Article 20
Other instruments of monetary control
The Governing Council may, by a majority of two thirds of the votes cast, decide upon the use of such other operational methods of monetary control as it sees fit, respecting Article 2.

The Council shall, in accordance with the procedure laid down in Article 41, define the scope of such methods if they impose obligations on third parties.

Article 21
Operations with public entities
21.1. In accordance with Article 123 of the Treaty on the Functioning of the European Union, overdrafts or any other type of credit facility with the ECB or with the national

central banks in favour of Union institutions, bodies, offices or agencies, central governments, regional, local or other public authorities, other bodies governed by public law, or public undertakings of Member States shall be prohibited, as shall the purchase directly from them by the ECB or national central banks of debt instruments.

21.2. The ECB and national central banks may act as fiscal agents for the entities referred to in Article 21.1.

21.3. The provisions of this Article shall not apply to publicly owned credit institutions which, in the context of the supply of reserves by central banks, shall be given the same treatment by national central banks and the ECB as private credit institutions.

Article 22
Clearing and payment systems
The ECB and national central banks may provide facilities, and the ECB may make regulations, to ensure efficient and sound clearing and payment systems within the Union and with other countries.

Article 23
External operations
The ECB and national central banks may:
— establish relations with central banks and financial institutions in other countries and, where appropriate, with international organisations;
— acquire and sell spot and forward all types of foreign exchange assets and precious metals; the term "foreign exchange asset" shall include securities and all other assets in the currency of any country or units of account and in whatever form held;
— hold and manage the assets referred to in this Article;
— conduct all types of banking transactions in relations with third countries and international organisations, including borrowing and lending operations.

Article 24
Other operations
In addition to operations arising from their tasks, the ECB and national central banks may enter into operations for their administrative purposes or for their staff.

Chapter V Prudential Supervision

Article 25
Prudential supervision
25.1. The ECB may offer advice to and be consulted by the Council, the Commission and the competent authorities of the Member States on the scope and implementation of Union legislation relating to the prudential supervision of credit institutions and to the stability of the financial system.

25.2. In accordance with any regulation of the Council under Article 127(6) of the Treaty on the Functioning of the European Union, the ECB may perform specific tasks concerning policies relating to the prudential supervision of credit institutions and other financial institutions with the exception of insurance undertakings.

Chapter VI Financial Provisions of the ESCB

Article 26
Financial accounts

26.1. The financial year of the ECB and national central banks shall begin on the first day of January and end on the last day of December.

26.2. The annual accounts of the ECB shall be drawn up by the Executive Board, in accordance with the principles established by the Governing Council. The accounts shall be approved by the Governing Council and shall thereafter be published.

26.3. For analytical and operational purposes, the Executive Board shall draw up a consolidated balance sheet of the ESCB, comprising those assets and liabilities of the national central banks that fall within the ESCB.

26.4. For the application of this Article, the Governing Council shall establish the necessary rules for standardising the accounting and reporting of operations undertaken by the national central banks.

Article 27
Auditing

27.1. The accounts of the ECB and national central banks shall be audited by independent external auditors recommended by the Governing Council and approved by the Council. The auditors shall have full power to examine all books and accounts of the ECB and national central banks and obtain full information about their transactions.

27.2. The provisions of Article 287 of the Treaty on the Functioning of the European Union shall only apply to an examination of the operational efficiency of the management of the ECB.

Article 28
Capital of the ECB

28.1. The capital of the ECB shall be euro 5 000 million. The capital may be increased by such amounts as may be decided by the Governing Council acting by the qualified majority provided for in Article 10.3, within the limits and under the conditions set by the Council under the procedure laid down in Article 41.

28.2. The national central banks shall be the sole subscribers to and holders of the capital of the ECB. The subscription of capital shall be according to the key established in accordance with Article 29.

28.3. The Governing Council, acting by the qualified majority provided for in Article 10.3, shall determine the extent to which and the form in which the capital shall be paid up.

28.4. Subject to Article 28.5, the shares of the national central banks in the subscribed capital of the ECB may not be transferred, pledged or attached.

28.5. If the key referred to in Article 29 is adjusted, the national central banks shall transfer among themselves capital shares to the extent necessary to ensure that the distribution of capital shares corresponds to the adjusted key. The Governing Council shall determine the terms and conditions of such transfers.

Article 29
Key for capital subscription

29.1. The key for subscription of the ECB's capital, fixed for the first time in 1998 when the ESCB was established, shall be determined by assigning to each national central bank a weighting in this key equal to the sum of:

— 50% of the share of its respective Member State in the population of the Union in the penultimate year preceding the establishment of the ESCB;

— 50% of the share of its respective Member State in the gross domestic product at market prices of the Union as recorded in the last five years preceding the penultimate year before the establishment of the ESCB. The percentages shall be rounded up or down to the nearest multiple of 0,0001 percentage points.

29.2. The statistical data to be used for the application of this Article shall be provided by the Commission in accordance with the rules adopted by the Council under the procedure provided for in Article 41.

29.3. The weightings assigned to the national central banks shall be adjusted every five years after the establishment of the ESCB by analogy with the provisions laid down in Article 29.1. The adjusted key shall apply with effect from the first day of the following year.

29.4. The Governing Council shall take all other measures necessary for the application of this Article.

Article 30
Transfer of foreign reserve assets to the ECB

30.1. Without prejudice to Article 28, the ECB shall be provided by the national central banks with foreign reserve assets, other than Member States' currencies, euro, IMF reserve positions and SDRs, up to an amount equivalent to euro 50 000 million. The Governing Council shall decide upon the proportion to be called up by the ECB following its establishment and the amounts called up at later dates. The ECB shall have the full right to hold and manage the foreign reserves that are transferred to it and to use them for the purposes set out in this Statute.

30.2. The contributions of each national central bank shall be fixed in proportion to its share in the subscribed capital of the ECB.

30.3. Each national central bank shall be credited by the ECB with a claim equivalent to its contribution. The Governing Council shall determine the denomination and remuneration of such claims.

30.4. Further calls of foreign reserve assets beyond the limit set in Article 30.1 may be effected by the ECB, in accordance with Article 30.2, within the limits and under the conditions set by the Council in accordance with the procedure laid down in Article 41.

30.5. The ECB may hold and manage IMF reserve positions and SDRs and provide for the pooling of such assets.

30.6. The Governing Council shall take all other measures necessary for the application of this Article.

Article 31
Foreign reserve assets held by national central banks

31.1. The national central banks shall be allowed to perform transactions in fulfilment of their obligations towards international organisations in accordance with Article 23.

31.2. All other operations in foreign reserve assets remaining with the national central banks after the transfers referred to in Article 30, and Member States' transactions with their foreign exchange working balances shall, above a certain limit to be established within the framework of Article 31.3, be subject to approval by the ECB in order to ensure consistency with the exchange rate and monetary policies of the Union.

31.3. The Governing Council shall issue guidelines with a view to facilitating such operations.

Article 32
Allocation of monetary income of national central banks

32.1. The income accruing to the national central banks in the performance of the ESCB's monetary policy function (hereinafter referred to as "monetary income") shall be allocated at the end of each financial year in accordance with the provisions of this Article.

32.2. The amount of each national central bank's monetary income shall be equal to its annual income derived from its assets held against notes in circulation and deposit liabilities to credit institutions. These assets shall be earmarked by national central banks in accordance with guidelines to be established by the Governing Council.

32.3. If, after the introduction of the euro, the balance sheet structures of the national central banks do not, in the judgment of the Governing Council, permit the application of Article 32.2, the Governing Council, acting by a qualified majority, may decide that, by way of derogation from Article 32.2, monetary income shall be measured according to an alternative method for a period of not more than five years.

32.4. The amount of each national central bank's monetary income shall be reduced by an amount equivalent to any interest paid by that central bank on its deposit liabilities to credit institutions in accordance with Article 19.

The Governing Council may decide that national central banks shall be indemnified against costs incurred in connection with the issue of banknotes or in exceptional circumstances for specific losses arising from monetary policy operations undertaken for the ESCB. Indemnification shall be in a form deemed appropriate in the judgment of the Governing Council; these amounts may be offset against the national central banks' monetary income.

32.5. The sum of the national central banks' monetary income shall be allocated to the national central banks in proportion to their paid up shares in the capital of the ECB, subject to any decision taken by the Governing Council pursuant to Article 33.2.

32.6. The clearing and settlement of the balances arising from the allocation of monetary income shall be carried out by the ECB in accordance with guidelines established by the Governing Council.

32.7. The Governing Council shall take all other measures necessary for the application of this Article.

Article 33
Allocation of net profits and losses of the ECB

33.1. The net profit of the ECB shall be transferred in the following order:
   (a) an amount to be determined by the Governing Council, which may not exceed 20% of the net profit, shall be transferred to the general reserve fund subject to a limit equal to 100% of the capital;

(b) the remaining net profit shall be distributed to the shareholders of the ECB in proportion to their paid-up shares.

33.2. In the event of a loss incurred by the ECB, the shortfall may be offset against the general reserve fund of the ECB and, if necessary, following a decision by the Governing Council, against the monetary income of the relevant financial year in proportion and up to the amounts allocated to the national central banks in accordance with Article 32.5.

Chapter VII General Provisions

Article 34
Legal acts

34.1. In accordance with Article 132 of the Treaty on the Functioning of the European Union, the ECB shall:
— make regulations to the extent necessary to implement the tasks defined in Article 3.1, first indent, Articles 19.1, 22 or 25.2 and in cases which shall be laid down in the acts of the Council referred to in Article 41;
— take decisions necessary for carrying out the tasks entrusted to the ESCB under these Treaties and this Statute;
— make recommendations and deliver opinions.

34.2. The ECB may decide to publish its decisions, recommendations and opinions.

34.3. Within the limits and under the conditions adopted by the Council under the procedure laid down in Article 41, the ECB shall be entitled to impose fines or periodic penalty payments on undertakings for failure to comply with obligations under its regulations and decisions.

Article 35
Judicial control and related matters

35.1. The acts or omissions of the ECB shall be open to review or interpretation by the Court of Justice of the European Union in the cases and under the conditions laid down in the Treaty on the Functioning of the European Union. The ECB may institute proceedings in the cases and under the conditions laid down in the Treaties.

35.2. Disputes between the ECB, on the one hand, and its creditors, debtors or any other person, on the other, shall be decided by the competent national courts, save where jurisdiction has been conferred upon the Court of Justice of the European Union.

35.3. The ECB shall be subject to the liability regime provided for in Article 340 of the Treaty on the Functioning of the European Union. The national central banks shall be liable according to their respective national laws.

35.4. The Court of Justice of the European Union shall have jurisdiction to give judgment pursuant to any arbitration clause contained in a contract concluded by or on behalf of the ECB, whether that contract be governed by public or private law.

35.5. A decision of the ECB to bring an action before the Court of Justice of the European Union shall be taken by the Governing Council.

35.6. The Court of Justice of the European Union shall have jurisdiction in disputes concerning the fulfilment by a national central bank of obligations under the Treaties and this Statute. If the ECB considers that a national central bank has failed to fulfil an obligation under the Treaties and this Statute, it shall deliver a reasoned opinion on the matter after giving the national central bank concerned the opportunity to submit its observations. If the national central bank concerned does not comply with the opinion within the period laid down by the ECB, the latter may bring the matter before the Court of Justice of the European Union.

Article 36
Staff
36.1. The Governing Council, on a proposal from the Executive Board, shall lay down the conditions of employment of the staff of the ECB.

36.2. The Court of Justice of the European Union shall have jurisdiction in any dispute between the ECB and its servants within the limits and under the conditions laid down in the conditions of employment.

Article 37
Professional secrecy
37.1. Members of the governing bodies and the staff of the ECB and the national central banks shall be required, even after their duties have ceased, not to disclose information of the kind covered by the obligation of professional secrecy.

37.2. Persons having access to data covered by Union legislation imposing an obligation of secrecy shall be subject to such legislation.

Article 38
Signatories
The ECB shall be legally committed to third parties by the President or by two members of the Executive Board or by the signatures of two members of the staff of the ECB who have been duly authorised by the President to sign on behalf of the ECB.

Article 39
Privileges and immunities
The ECB shall enjoy in the territories of the Member States such privileges and immunities as are necessary for the performance of its tasks, under the conditions laid down in the Protocol on the privileges and immunities of the European Union.

Chapter VIII Amendment of the Statute and Complementary Legislation

Article 40
Simplified amendment procedure
40.1. In accordance with Article 129(3) of the Treaty on the Functioning of the European Union, Articles 5.1, 5.2, 5.3, 17, 18, 19.1, 22, 23, 24, 26, 32.2, 32.3, 32.4, 32.6, 33.1(a) and 36 of this Statute may be amended by the European Parliament and the Council, acting in accordance with the ordinary legislative procedure either on a recommendation from the ECB and after consulting the Commission, or on a proposal from the Commission and after consulting the ECB.

40.2. Article 10.2 may be amended by a decision of the European Council, acting unanimously, either on a recommendation from the European Central Bank and after consulting the European Parliament and the Commission, or on a recommendation from the Commission and after consulting the European Parliament and the European Central Bank. These amendments shall not enter into force until they are approved by the Member States in accordance with their respective constitutional requirements.

40.3. A recommendation made by the ECB under this Article shall require a unanimous decision by the Governing Council.

Article 41
Complementary legislation

In accordance with Article 129(4) of the Treaty on the Functioning of the European Union, the Council, either on a proposal from the Commission and after consulting the European Parliament and the ECB or on a recommendation from the ECB and after consulting the European Parliament and the Commission, shall adopt the provisions referred to in Articles 4, 5.4, 19.2, 20, 28.1, 29.2, 30.4 and 34.3 of this Statute.

Chapter IX Transitional and Other Provisions for the ESCB

Article 42
General provisions

42.1. A derogation as referred to in Article 139 of the Treaty on the Functioning of the European Union shall entail that the following Articles of this Statute shall not confer any rights or impose any obligations on the Member State concerned: 3, 6, 9.2, 12.1, 14.3, 16, 18, 19, 20, 22, 23, 26.2, 27, 30, 31, 32, 33, 34, and 49.

42.2. The central banks of Member States with a derogation as specified in Article 139(1) of the Treaty on the Functioning of the European Union shall retain their powers in the field of monetary policy according to national law.

42.3. In accordance with Article 139 of the Treaty on the Functioning of the European Union, "Member States" shall be read as "Member States whose currency is the euro" in the following Articles of this Statute: 3, 11.2 and 19.

42.4. "National central banks" shall be read as "central banks of Member States whose currency is the euro" in the following Articles of this Statute: 9.2, 10.2, 10.3, 12.1, 16, 17, 18, 22, 23, 27, 30, 31, 32, 33.2 and 49.

42.5. "Shareholders" shall be read as "central banks of Member States whose currency is the euro" in Articles 10.3 and 33.1.

42.6. "Subscribed capital of the ECB" shall be read as "capital of the ECB subscribed by the central banks of Member States whose currency is the euro" in Articles 10.3 and 30.2.

Article 43
Transitional tasks of the ECB

The ECB shall take over the former tasks of the EMI referred to in Article 141(2) of the Treaty on the Functioning of the European Union which, because of the derogations of one or more Member States, still have to be performed after the introduction of the euro.

The ECB shall give advice in the preparations for the abrogation of the derogations specified in Article 140 of the Treaty on the Functioning of the European Union.

Article 44
The General Council of the ECB

44.1. Without prejudice to Article 129(1) of the Treaty on the Functioning of the European Union, the General Council shall be constituted as a third decision-making body of the ECB.

44.2. The General Council shall comprise the President and Vice-President of the ECB and the Governors of the national central banks. The other members of the Executive Board may participate, without having the right to vote, in meetings of the General Council.

44.3. The responsibilities of the General Council are listed in full in Article 46 of this Statute.

Article 45
Rules of Procedure of the General Council

45.1. The President or, in his absence, the Vice-President of the ECB shall chair the General Council of the ECB.

45.2. The President of the Council and a Member of the Commission may participate, without having the right to vote, in meetings of the General Council.

45.3. The President shall prepare the meetings of the General Council.

45.4. By way of derogation from Article 12.3, the General Council shall adopt its Rules of Procedure.

45.5. The Secretariat of the General Council shall be provided by the ECB.

Article 46
Responsibilities of the General Council

46.1. The General Council shall:
   — perform the tasks referred to in Article 43;
   — contribute to the advisory functions referred to in Articles 4 and 25.1.

46.2. The General Council shall contribute to:
   — the collection of statistical information as referred to in Article 5;
   — the reporting activities of the ECB as referred to in Article 15;
   — the establishment of the necessary rules for the application of Article 26 as referred to in Article 26.4;
   — the taking of all other measures necessary for the application of Article 29 as referred to in Article 29.4;
   — the laying down of the conditions of employment of the staff of the ECB as referred to in Article 36.

46.3. The General Council shall contribute to the necessary preparations for irrevocably fixing the exchange rates of the currencies of Member States with a derogation against the euro as referred to in Article 140(3) of the Treaty on the Functioning of the European Union.

46.4. The General Council shall be informed by the President of the ECB of decisions of the Governing Council.

Article 47
Transitional provisions for the capital of the ECB
In accordance with Article 29.1, each national central bank shall be assigned a weighting in the key for subscription of the ECB's capital. By way of derogation from Article 28.3, central banks of Member States with a derogation shall not pay up their subscribed capital unless the General Council, acting by a majority representing at least two thirds of the subscribed capital of the ECB and at least half of the shareholders, decides that a minimal percentage has to be paid up as a contribution to the operational costs of the ECB.

Article 48
Deferred payment of capital, reserves and provisions of the ECB
48.1. The central bank of a Member State whose derogation has been abrogated shall pay up its subscribed share of the capital of the ECB to the same extent as the central banks of other Member States whose currency is the euro, and shall transfer to the ECB foreign reserve assets in accordance with Article 30.1. The sum to be transferred shall be determined by multiplying the euro value at current exchange rates of the foreign reserve assets which have already been transferred to the ECB in accordance with Article 30.1, by the ratio between the number of shares subscribed by the national central bank concerned and the number of shares already paid up by the other national central banks.

48.2. In addition to the payment to be made in accordance with Article 48.1, the central bank concerned shall contribute to the reserves of the ECB, to those provisions equivalent to reserves, and to the amount still to be appropriated to the reserves and provisions corresponding to the balance of the profit and loss account as at 31 December of the year prior to the abrogation of the derogation. The sum to be contributed shall be determined by multiplying the amount of the reserves, as defined above and as stated in the approved balance sheet of the ECB, by the ratio between the number of shares subscribed by the central bank concerned and the number of shares already paid up by the other central banks.

48.3. Upon one or more countries becoming Member States and their respective national central banks becoming part of the ESCB, the subscribed capital of the ECB and the limit on the amount of foreign reserve assets that may be transferred to the ECB shall be automatically increased. The increase shall be determined by multiplying the respective amounts then prevailing by the ratio, within the expanded capital key, between the weighting of the entering national central banks concerned and the weighting of the national central banks already members of the ESCB. Each national central bank's weighting in the capital key shall be calculated by analogy with Article 29.1 and in compliance with Article 29.2. The reference periods to be used for the statistical data shall be identical to those applied for the latest quinquennial adjustment of the weightings under Article 29.3.

Article 49
Exchange of banknotes in the currencies of the Member States
Following the irrevocable fixing of exchange rates in accordance with Article 140 of the Treaty on the Functioning of the European Union, the Governing Council shall take the

necessary measures to ensure that banknotes denominated in currencies with irrevocably fixed exchange rates are exchanged by the national central banks at their respective par values.

Article 50
Applicability of the transitional provisions
If and as long as there are Member States with a derogation, Articles 42 to 47 shall be applicable.

PROTOCOL (NO 10) ON PERMANENT STRUCTURED COOPERATION ESTABLISHED BY ARTICLE 42 OF THE TREATY ON EUROPEAN UNION

THE HIGH CONTRACTING PARTIES,

HAVING REGARD TO Article 42(6) and Article 46 of the Treaty on European Union,

RECALLING that the Union is pursuing a common foreign and security policy based on the achievement of growing convergence of action by Member States,

RECALLING that the common security and defence policy is an integral part of the common foreign and security policy; that it provides the Union with operational capacity drawing on civil and military assets; that the Union may use such assets in the tasks referred to in Article 43 of the Treaty on European Union outside the Union for peace-keeping, conflict prevention and strengthening international security in accordance with the principles of the United Nations Charter; that the performance of these tasks is to be undertaken using capabilities provided by the Member States in accordance with the principle of a single set of forces,

RECALLING that the common security and defence policy of the Union does not prejudice the specific character of the security and defence policy of certain Member States,

RECALLING that the common security and defence policy of the Union respects the obligations under the North Atlantic Treaty of those Member States which see their common defence realised in the North Atlantic Treaty Organisation, which remains the foundation of the collective defence of its members, and is compatible with the common security and defence policy established within that framework,

CONVINCED that a more assertive Union role in security and defence matters will contribute to the vitality of a renewed Atlantic Alliance, in accordance with the Berlin Plus arrangements,

DETERMINED to ensure that the Union is capable of fully assuming its responsibilities within the international community,

RECOGNISING that the United Nations Organisation may request the Union's assistance for the urgent implementation of missions undertaken under Chapters VI and VII of the United Nations Charter,

RECOGNISING that the strengthening of the security and defence policy will require efforts by Member States in the area of capabilities,

CONSCIOUS that embarking on a new stage in the development of the European security and defence policy involves a determined effort by the Member States concerned,

RECALLING the importance of the High Representative of the Union for Foreign Affairs and Security Policy being fully involved in proceedings relating to permanent structured cooperation,

HAVE AGREED UPON the following provisions, which shall be annexed to the Treaty on European Union and to the Treaty on the Functioning of the European Union:

Article 1

The permanent structured cooperation referred to in Article 42(6) of the Treaty on European Union shall be open to any Member State which undertakes, from the date of entry into force of the Treaty of Lisbon, to:

(a) proceed more intensively to develop its defence capacities through the development of its national contributions and participation, where appropriate, in multinational forces, in the main European equipment programmes, and in the activity of the Agency in the field of defence capabilities development, research, acquisition and armaments (European Defence Agency)[;] and

(b) have the capacity to supply by 2010 at the latest, either at national level or as a component of multinational force groups, targeted combat units for the missions planned, structured at a tactical level as a battle group, with support elements including transport and logistics, capable of carrying out the tasks referred to in Article 43 of the Treaty on European Union, within a period of five to 30 days, in particular in response to requests from the United Nations Organisation, and which can be sustained for an initial period of 30 days and be extended up to at least 120 days.

Article 2

To achieve the objectives laid down in Article 1, Member States participating in permanent structured cooperation shall undertake to:

(a) cooperate, as from the entry into force of the Treaty of Lisbon, with a view to achieving approved objectives concerning the level of investment expenditure on defence equipment, and regularly review these objectives, in the light of the security environment and of the Union's international responsibilities;

(b) bring their defence apparatus into line with each other as far as possible, particularly by harmonising the identification of their military needs, by pooling and, where appropriate, specialising their defence means and capabilities, and by encouraging cooperation in the fields of training and logistics;

(c) take concrete measures to enhance the availability, interoperability, flexibility and deployability of their forces, in particular by identifying common objectives regarding the commitment of forces, including possibly reviewing their national decision-making procedures;

(d) work together to ensure that they take the necessary measures to make good, including through multinational approaches, and without prejudice to undertakings in this regard within the North Atlantic Treaty Organisation, the shortfalls perceived in the framework of the "Capability Development Mechanism";

(e) take part, where appropriate, in the development of major joint or European equipment programmes in the framework of the European Defence Agency.

Article 3

The European Defence Agency shall contribute to the regular assessment of participating Member States' contributions with regard to capabilities, in particular contributions made in accordance with the criteria to be established, inter alia, on the basis of Article 2, and shall report thereon at least once a year. The assessment may serve as a basis for Council recommendations and decisions adopted in accordance with Article 46 of the Treaty on European Union.

PROTOCOL (NO 12) ON THE EXCESSIVE DEFICIT PROCEDURE

THE HIGH CONTRACTING PARTIES,

DESIRING TO lay down the details of the excessive deficit procedure referred to in Article 126 of the Treaty on the Functioning of the European Union,

HAVE AGREED upon the following provisions, which shall be annexed to the Treaty on European Union and to the Treaty on the Functioning of the European Union:

Article 1

The reference values referred to in Article 126(2) of the Treaty on the Functioning of the European Union are:
— 3% for the ratio of the planned or actual government deficit to gross domestic product at market prices;
— 60% for the ratio of government debt to gross domestic product at market prices.

Article 2

In Article 126 of the said Treaty and in this Protocol:
— "government" means general government, that is central government, regional or local government and social security funds, to the exclusion of commercial operations, as defined in the European System of Integrated Economic Accounts;
— "deficit" means net borrowing as defined in the European System of Integrated Economic Accounts;
— "investment" means gross fixed capital formation as defined in the European System of Integrated Economic Accounts;
— "debt" means total gross debt at nominal value outstanding at the end of the year and consolidated between and within the sectors of general government as defined in the first indent.

Article 3

In order to ensure the effectiveness of the excessive deficit procedure, the governments of the Member States shall be responsible under this procedure for the deficits of general government as defined in the first indent of Article 2. The Member States shall ensure that national procedures in the budgetary area enable them to meet their obligations in this area deriving from these Treaties. The Member States shall report their planned and actual deficits and the levels of their debt promptly and regularly to the Commission.

Article 4
The statistical data to be used for the application of this Protocol shall be provided by the Commission.

PROTOCOL (NO 13) ON THE CONVERGENCE CRITERIA

THE HIGH CONTRACTING PARTIES,

DESIRING to lay down the details of the convergence criteria which shall guide the Union in taking decisions to end the derogations of those Member States with a derogation, referred to in Article 140 of the Treaty on the Functioning of the European Union,

HAVE AGREED upon the following provisions, which shall be annexed to the Treaty on European Union and to the Treaty on the Functioning of the European Union:

Article 1
The criterion on price stability referred to in the first indent of Article 140(1) of the Treaty on the Functioning of the European Union shall mean that a Member State has a price performance that is sustainable and an average rate of inflation, observed over a period of one year before the examination, that does not exceed by more than 1½ percentage points that of, at most, the three best performing Member States in terms of price stability. Inflation shall be measured by means of the consumer price index on a comparable basis taking into account differences in national definitions.

Article 2
The criterion on the government budgetary position referred to in the second indent of Article 140(1) of the said Treaty shall mean that at the time of the examination the Member State is not the subject of a Council decision under Article 126(6) of the said Treaty that an excessive deficit exists.

Article 3
The criterion on participation in the Exchange Rate mechanism of the European Monetary System referred to in the third indent of Article 140(1) of the said Treaty shall mean that a Member State has respected the normal fluctuation margins provided for by the exchange-rate mechanism on the European Monetary System without severe tensions for at least the last two years before the examination. In particular, the Member State shall not have devalued its currency's bilateral central rate against the euro on its own initiative for the same period.

Article 4
The criterion on the convergence of interest rates referred to in the fourth indent of Article 140(1) of the said Treaty shall mean that, observed over a period of one year before the examination, a Member State has had an average nominal long-term interest rate that does not exceed by more than two percentage points that of, at most, the three best performing Member States in terms of price stability. Interest rates shall be measured on the basis of long-term government bonds or comparable securities, taking into account differences in national definitions.

Article 5

The statistical data to be used for the application of this Protocol shall be provided by the Commission.

Article 6

The Council shall, acting unanimously on a proposal from the Commission and after consulting the European Parliament, the ECB and the Economic and Financial Committee, adopt appropriate provisions to lay down the details of the convergence criteria referred to in Article 140(1) of the said Treaty, which shall then replace this Protocol.

PROTOCOL (NO 14) ON THE EURO GROUP

THE HIGH CONTRACTING PARTIES,

DESIRING to promote conditions for stronger economic growth in the European Union and, to that end, to develop ever-closer coordination of economic policies within the euro area,

CONSCIOUS of the need to lay down special provisions for enhanced dialogue between the Member States whose currency is the euro, pending the euro becoming the currency of all Member States of the Union,

HAVE AGREED UPON the following provisions, which shall be annexed to the Treaty on European Union and to the Treaty on the Functioning of the European Union:

3

Article 1

The Ministers of the Member States whose currency is the euro shall meet informally. Such meetings shall take place, when necessary, to discuss questions related to the specific responsibilities they share with regard to the single currency. The Commission shall take part in the meetings. The European Central Bank shall be invited to take part in such meetings, which shall be prepared by the representatives of the Ministers with responsibility for finance of the Member States whose currency is the euro and of the Commission.

Article 2

The Ministers of the Member States whose currency is the euro shall elect a president for two and a half years, by a majority of those Member States.

PROTOCOL (NO 15) ON CERTAIN PROVISIONS RELATING TO THE UNITED KINGDOM OF GREAT BRITAIN AND NORTHERN IRELAND

THE HIGH CONTRACTING PARTIES,

RECOGNISING that the United Kingdom shall not be obliged or committed to adopt the euro without a separate decision to do so by its government and parliament,

GIVEN that on 16 October 1996 and 30 October 1997 the United Kingdom government notified the Council of its intention not to participate in the third stage of economic and monetary union,

NOTING the practice of the government of the United Kingdom to fund its borrowing requirement by the sale of debt to the private sector,

HAVE AGREED upon the following provisions, which shall be annexed to the Treaty on European Union and to the Treaty on the Functioning of the European Union:

1. Unless the United Kingdom notifies the Council that it intends to adopt the euro, it shall be under no obligation to do so.
2. In view of the notice given to the Council by the United Kingdom government on 16 October 1996 and 30 October 1997, paragraphs 3 to 8 and 10 shall apply to the United Kingdom.
3. The United Kingdom shall retain its powers in the field of monetary policy according to national law.
4. Articles 119, second paragraph, 126(1), (9) and (11), 127(1) to (5), 128, 130, 131, 132, 133, 138, 140(3), 219, 282(2), with the exception of the first and last sentences thereof, 282(5), and 283 of the Treaty on the Functioning of the European Union shall not apply to the United Kingdom. The same applies to Article 121(2) of this Treaty as regards the adoption of the parts of the broad economic policy guidelines which concern the euro area generally. In these provisions references to the Union or the Member States shall not include the United Kingdom and references to national central banks shall not include the Bank of England.
5. The United Kingdom shall endeavour to avoid an excessive government deficit. Articles 143 and 144 of the Treaty on the Functioning of the European Union shall continue to apply to the United Kingdom. Articles 134(4) and 142 shall apply to the United Kingdom as if it had a derogation.
6. The voting rights of the United Kingdom shall be suspended in respect of acts of the Council referred to in the Articles listed in paragraph 4 and in the instances referred to in the first subparagraph of Article 139(4) of the Treaty on the Functioning of the European Union. For this purpose the second subparagraph of Article 139(4) of the Treaty shall apply.

    The United Kingdom shall also have no right to participate in the appointment of the President, the Vice-President and the other members of the Executive Board of the ECB under the second subparagraph of Article 283(2) of the said Treaty.
7. Articles 3, 4, 6, 7, 9.2, 10.1, 10.3, 11.2, 12.1, 14, 16, 18 to 20, 22, 23, 26, 27, 30 to 34 and 49 of the Protocol on the Statute of the European System of Central Banks and of the European Central Bank ("the Statute") shall not apply to the United Kingdom.

    In those Articles, references to the Union or the Member States shall not include the United Kingdom and references to national central banks or shareholders shall not include the Bank of England.

    References in Articles 10.3 and 30.2 of the Statute to "subscribed capital of the ECB" shall not include capital subscribed by the Bank of England.
8. Article 141(1) of the Treaty on the Functioning of the European Union and Articles 43 to 47 of the Statute shall have effect, whether or not there is any Member State with a derogation, subject to the following amendments:
    (a) References in Article 43 to the tasks of the ECB and the EMI shall include those tasks that still need to be performed in the third stage owing to any decision of the United Kingdom not to adopt the euro.

(b) In addition to the tasks referred to in Article 46, the ECB shall also give advice in relation to and contribute to the preparation of any decision of the Council with regard to the United Kingdom taken in accordance with paragraphs 9(a) and 9(c).

(c) The Bank of England shall pay up its subscription to the capital of the ECB as a contribution to its operational costs on the same basis as national central banks of Member States with a derogation.

9. The United Kingdom may notify the Council at any time of its intention to adopt the euro. In that event:

(a) The United Kingdom shall have the right to adopt the euro provided only that it satisfies the necessary conditions. The Council, acting at the request of the United Kingdom and under the conditions and in accordance with the procedure laid down in Article 140(1) and (2) of the Treaty on the Functioning of the European Union, shall decide whether it fulfils the necessary conditions.

(b) The Bank of England shall pay up its subscribed capital, transfer to the ECB foreign reserve assets and contribute to its reserves on the same basis as the national central bank of a Member State whose derogation has been abrogated.

(c) The Council, acting under the conditions and in accordance with the procedure laid down in Article 140(3) of the said Treaty, shall take all other necessary decisions to enable the United Kingdom to adopt the euro.

If the United Kingdom adopts the euro pursuant to the provisions of this Protocol, paragraphs 3 to 8 shall cease to have effect.

10. Notwithstanding Article 123 of the Treaty on the Functioning of the European Union and Article 21.1 of the Statute, the Government of the United Kingdom may maintain its "ways and means" facility with the Bank of England if and so long as the United Kingdom does not adopt the euro.

PROTOCOL (NO 20) ON THE APPLICATION OF CERTAIN ASPECTS OF ARTICLE 26 OF THE TREATY ON THE FUNCTIONING OF THE EUROPEAN UNION TO THE UNITED KINGDOM AND TO IRELAND

THE HIGH CONTRACTING PARTIES,

DESIRING to settle certain questions relating to the United Kingdom and Ireland,

HAVING REGARD to the existence for many years of special travel arrangements between the United Kingdom and Ireland,

HAVE AGREED UPON the following provisions, which shall be annexed to the Treaty on European Union and the Treaty on the Functioning of the European Union:

Article 1

The United Kingdom shall be entitled, notwithstanding Articles 26 and 77 of the Treaty on the Functioning of the European Union, any other provision of that Treaty or of the Treaty on European Union, any measure adopted under those Treaties, or any international agreement concluded by the Union or by the Union and its Member States with one or more third States, to exercise at its frontiers with other Member States such controls on persons seeking to enter the United Kingdom as it may consider necessary for the purpose:

(a) of verifying the right to enter the United Kingdom of citizens of Member States and of their dependants exercising rights conferred by Union law, as well as citizens of other States on whom such rights have been conferred by an agreement by which the United Kingdom is bound; and

(b) of determining whether or not to grant other persons permission to enter the United Kingdom.

Nothing in Articles 26 and 77 of the Treaty on the Functioning of the European Union or in any other provision of that Treaty or of the Treaty on European Union or in any measure adopted under them shall prejudice the right of the United Kingdom to adopt or exercise any such controls. References to the United Kingdom in this Article shall include territories for whose external relations the United Kingdom is responsible.

Article 2

The United Kingdom and Ireland may continue to make arrangements between themselves relating to the movement of persons between their territories ("the Common Travel Area"), while fully respecting the rights of persons referred to in Article 1, first paragraph, point (a) of this Protocol. Accordingly, as long as they maintain such arrangements, the provisions of Article 1 of this Protocol shall apply to Ireland under the same terms and conditions as for the United Kingdom. Nothing in Articles 26 and 77 of the Treaty on the Functioning of the European Union, in any other provision of that Treaty or of the Treaty on European Union or in any measure adopted under them, shall affect any such arrangements.

Article 3

The other Member States shall be entitled to exercise at their frontiers or at any point of entry into their territory such controls on persons seeking to enter their territory from the United Kingdom or any territories whose external relations are under its responsibility for the same purposes stated in Article 1 of this Protocol, or from Ireland as long as the provisions of Article 1 of this Protocol apply to Ireland.

Nothing in Articles 26 and 77 of the Treaty on the Functioning of the European Union or in any other provision of that Treaty or of the Treaty on European Union or in any measure adopted under them shall prejudice the right of the other Member States to adopt or exercise any such controls.

PROTOCOL (NO 21) ON THE POSITION OF THE UNITED KINGDOM AND IRELAND IN RESPECT OF THE AREA OF FREEDOM, SECURITY AND JUSTICE

THE HIGH CONTRACTING PARTIES,

DESIRING to settle certain questions relating to the United Kingdom and Ireland,

HAVING REGARD to the Protocol on the application of certain aspects of Article 26 of the Treaty on the Functioning of the European Union to the United Kingdom and to Ireland,

HAVE AGREED UPON the following provisions, which shall be annexed to the Treaty on European Union and the Treaty on the Functioning of the European Union:

Article 1

Subject to Article 3, the United Kingdom and Ireland shall not take part in the adoption by the Council of proposed measures pursuant to Title V of Part Three of the Treaty on the Functioning of the European Union. The unanimity of the members of the Council, with the exception of the representatives of the governments of the United Kingdom and Ireland, shall be necessary for decisions of the Council which must be adopted unanimously.

For the purposes of this Article, a qualified majority shall be defined in accordance with Article 238(3) of the Treaty on the Functioning of the European Union.

Article 2

In consequence of Article 1 and subject to Articles 3, 4 and 6, none of the provisions of Title V of Part Three of the Treaty on the Functioning of the European Union, no measure adopted pursuant to that Title, no provision of any international agreement concluded by the Union pursuant to that Title, and no decision of the Court of Justice interpreting any such provision or measure shall be binding upon or applicable in the United Kingdom or Ireland; and no such provision, measure or decision shall in any way affect the competences, rights and obligations of those States; and no such provision, measure or decision shall in any way affect the Community or Union *acquis* nor form part of Union law as they apply to the United Kingdom or Ireland.

Article 3

1. The United Kingdom or Ireland may notify the President of the Council in writing, within three months after a proposal or initiative has been presented to the Council pursuant to Title V of Part Three of the Treaty on the Functioning of the European Union, that it wishes to take part in the adoption and application of any such proposed measure, whereupon that State shall be entitled to do so.

   The unanimity of the members of the Council, with the exception of a member which has not made such a notification, shall be necessary for decisions of the Council which must be adopted unanimously. A measure adopted under this paragraph shall be binding upon all Member States which took part in its adoption.

   Measures adopted pursuant to Article 70 of the Treaty on the Functioning of the European Union shall lay down the conditions for the participation of the United Kingdom and Ireland in the evaluations concerning the areas covered by Title V of Part Three of that Treaty.

   For the purposes of this Article, a qualified majority shall be defined in accordance with Article 238(3) of the Treaty on the Functioning of the European Union.

2. If after a reasonable period of time a measure referred to in paragraph 1 cannot be adopted with the United Kingdom or Ireland taking part, the Council may adopt such measure in accordance with Article 1 without the participation of the United Kingdom or Ireland. In that case Article 2 applies.

Article 4

The United Kingdom or Ireland may at any time after the adoption of a measure by the Council pursuant to Title V of Part Three of the Treaty on the Functioning of the European Union notify its intention to the Council and to the Commission that it wishes to accept that measure. In that case, the procedure provided for in Article 331(1) of the Treaty on the Functioning of the European Union shall apply mutatis mutandis.

Article 4a

1. The provisions of this Protocol apply for the United Kingdom and Ireland also to measures proposed or adopted pursuant to Title V of Part Three of the Treaty on the Functioning of the European Union amending an existing measure by which they are bound.

2. However, in cases where the Council, acting on a proposal from the Commission, determines that the non-participation of the United Kingdom or Ireland in the amended version of an existing measure makes the application of that measure inoperable for other Member States or the Union, it may urge them to make a notification under Article 3 or 4. For the purposes of Article 3, a further period of two months starts to run as from the date of such determination by the Council.

   If at the expiry of that period of two months from the Council's determination the United Kingdom or Ireland has not made a notification under Article 3 or Article 4, the existing measure shall no longer be binding upon or applicable to it, unless the Member State concerned has made a notification under Article 4 before the entry into force of the amending measure. This shall take effect from the date of entry into force of the amending measure or of expiry of the period of two months, whichever is the later.

   For the purpose of this paragraph, the Council shall, after a full discussion of the matter, act by a qualified majority of its members representing the Member States participating or having participated in the adoption of the amending measure. A qualified majority of the Council shall be defined in accordance with Article 238(3)(a) of the Treaty on the Functioning of the European Union.

3. The Council, acting by a qualified majority on a proposal from the Commission, may determine that the United Kingdom or Ireland shall bear the direct financial consequences, if any, necessarily and unavoidably incurred as a result of the cessation of its participation in the existing measure.

4. This Article shall be without prejudice to Article 4.

Article 5

A Member State which is not bound by a measure adopted pursuant to Title V of Part Three of the Treaty on the Functioning of the European Union shall bear no financial consequences of that measure other than administrative costs entailed for the institutions, unless all members of the Council, acting unanimously after consulting the European Parliament, decide otherwise.

Article 6

Where, in cases referred to in this Protocol, the United Kingdom or Ireland is bound by a measure adopted by the Council pursuant to Title V of Part Three of the Treaty on the Functioning of the European Union, the relevant provisions of the Treaties shall apply to that State in relation to that measure.

Article 6a

The United Kingdom and Ireland shall not be bound by the rules laid down on the basis of Article 16 of the Treaty on the Functioning of the European Union which relate to the processing of personal data by the Member States when carrying out activities which fall within the scope of Chapter 4 or Chapter 5 of Title V of Part Three of that Treaty where the United Kingdom and Ireland are not bound by the rules governing the forms of judicial cooperation in criminal matters or police cooperation which require compliance with the provisions laid down on the basis of Article 16.

Article 7

Articles 3, 4 and 4a shall be without prejudice to the Protocol on the Schengen acquis integrated into the framework of the European Union.

Article 8

Ireland may notify the Council in writing that it no longer wishes to be covered by the terms of this Protocol. In that case, the normal treaty provisions will apply to Ireland.

Article 9

With regard to Ireland, this Protocol shall not apply to Article 75 of the Treaty on the Functioning of the European Union.

3

PROTOCOL (NO 26) ON SERVICES OF GENERAL INTEREST

THE HIGH CONTRACTING PARTIES,

WISHING to emphasise the importance of services of general interest,

HAVE AGREED UPON the following interpretative provisions, which shall be annexed to the Treaty on European Union and to the Treaty on the Functioning of the European Union:

Article 1

The shared values of the Union in respect of services of general economic interest within the meaning of Article 14 of the Treaty on the Functioning of the European Union include in particular:
— the essential role and the wide discretion of national, regional and local authorities in providing, commissioning and organising services of general economic interest as closely as possible to the needs of the users;
— the diversity between various services of general economic interest and the differences in the needs and preferences of users that may result from different geographical, social or cultural situations;
— a high level of quality, safety and affordability, equal treatment and the promotion of universal access and of user rights.

Article 2

The provisions of the Treaties do not affect in any way the competence of Member States to provide, commission and organise non-economic services of general interest.

PROTOCOL (NO 28) ON ECONOMIC, SOCIAL AND TERRITORIAL COHESION

THE HIGH CONTRACTING PARTIES,

RECALLING that Article 3 of the Treaty on European Union includes the objective of promoting economic, social and territorial cohesion and solidarity between Member States and that the said cohesion figures among the areas of shared competence of the Union listed in Article 4(2)(c) of the Treaty on the Functioning of the European Union,

RECALLING that the provisions of Part Three, Title XVIII, on economic, social and territorial cohesion as a whole provide the legal basis for consolidating and further developing the Union's action in the field of economic, social and territorial cohesion, including the creation of a new fund,

RECALLING that the provisions of Article 177 of the Treaty on the Functioning of the European Union envisage setting up a Cohesion Fund,

NOTING that the European Investment Bank is lending large and increasing amounts for the benefit of the poorer regions,

NOTING the desire for greater flexibility in the arrangements for allocations from the Structural Funds,

NOTING the desire for modulation of the levels of Union participation in programmes and projects in certain countries,

NOTING the proposal to take greater account of the relative prosperity of Member States in the system of own resources,

REAFFIRM that the promotion of economic, social and territorial cohesion is vital to the full development and enduring success of the Union,

REAFFIRM their conviction that the Structural Funds should continue to play a considerable part in the achievement of Union objectives in the field of cohesion,

REAFFIRM their conviction that the European Investment Bank should continue to devote the majority of its resources to the promotion of economic, social and territorial cohesion, and declare their willingness to review the capital needs of the European Investment Bank as soon as this is necessary for that purpose,

AGREE that the Cohesion Fund will provide Union financial contributions to projects in the fields of environment and trans-European networks in Member States with a per capita GNP of less than 90% of the Union average which have a programme leading to the fulfilment of the conditions of economic convergence as set out in Article 126,

DECLARE their intention of allowing a greater margin of flexibility in allocating financing from the Structural Funds to specific needs not covered under the present Structural Funds regulations,

DECLARE their willingness to modulate the levels of Union participation in the context of programmes and projects of the Structural Funds, with a view to avoiding excessive increases in budgetary expenditure in the less prosperous Member States,

RECOGNISE the need to monitor regularly the progress made towards achieving economic, social and territorial cohesion and state their willingness to study all necessary measures in this respect,

DECLARE their intention of taking greater account of the contributive capacity of individual Member States in the system of own resources, and of examining means of correcting, for the less prosperous Member States, regressive elements existing in the present own resources system,

AGREE to annex this Protocol to the Treaty on European Union and the Treaty on the Functioning of the European Union.

PROTOCOL (NO 30) ON THE APPLICATION OF THE CHARTER OF FUNDAMENTAL RIGHTS OF THE EUROPEAN UNION TO POLAND AND TO THE UNITED KINGDOM

THE HIGH CONTRACTING PARTIES,

WHEREAS in Article 6 of the Treaty on European Union, the Union recognises the rights, freedoms and principles set out in the Charter of Fundamental Rights of the European Union,

WHEREAS the Charter is to be applied in strict accordance with the provisions of the aforementioned Article 6 and Title VII of the Charter itself,

WHEREAS the aforementioned Article 6 requires the Charter to be applied and interpreted by the courts of Poland and of the United Kingdom strictly in accordance with the explanations referred to in that Article,

WHEREAS the Charter contains both rights and principles,

WHEREAS the Charter contains both provisions which are civil and political in character and those which are economic and social in character,

WHEREAS the Charter reaffirms the rights, freedoms and principles recognised in the Union and makes those rights more visible, but does not create new rights or principles,

RECALLING the obligations devolving upon Poland and the United Kingdom under the Treaty on European Union, the Treaty on the Functioning of the European Union, and Union law generally,

NOTING the wish of Poland and the United Kingdom to clarify certain aspects of the application of the Charter,

DESIROUS therefore of clarifying the application of the Charter in relation to the laws and administrative action of Poland and of the United Kingdom and of its justiciability within Poland and within the United Kingdom,

REAFFIRMING that references in this Protocol to the operation of specific provisions of the Charter are strictly without prejudice to the operation of other provisions of the Charter,

REAFFIRMING that this Protocol is without prejudice to the application of the Charter to other Member States,

REAFFIRMING that this Protocol is without prejudice to other obligations devolving upon Poland and the United Kingdom under the Treaty on European Union, the Treaty on the Functioning of the European Union, and Union law generally,

HAVE AGREED UPON the following provisions, which shall be annexed to the Treaty on European Union and to the Treaty on the Functioning of the European Union:

Article 1

1. The Charter does not extend the ability of the Court of Justice of the European Union, or any court or tribunal of Poland or of the United Kingdom, to find that the laws, regulations or administrative provisions, practices or action of Poland or of the United Kingdom are inconsistent with the fundamental rights, freedoms and principles that it reaffirms.
2. In particular, and for the avoidance of doubt, nothing in Title IV of the Charter creates justiciable rights applicable to Poland or the United Kingdom except in so far as Poland or the United Kingdom has provided for such rights in its national law.

Article 2

To the extent that a provision of the Charter refers to national laws and practices, it shall only apply to Poland or the United Kingdom to the extent that the rights or principles that it contains are recognised in the law or practices of Poland or of the United Kingdom.

PROTOCOL (NO 35) ON ARTICLE 40.3.3 OF THE CONSTITUTION OF IRELAND

THE HIGH CONTRACTING PARTIES,

HAVE AGREED upon the following provision, which shall be annexed to the Treaty on European Union and to the Treaty on the Functioning of the European Union and to the Treaty establishing the European Atomic Energy Community: Nothing in the Treaties, or in the Treaty establishing the European Atomic Energy Community, or in the Treaties or Acts modifying or supplementing those Treaties, shall affect the application in Ireland of Article 40.3.3 of the Constitution of Ireland.

PROTOCOL (NO 36) ON TRANSITIONAL PROVISIONS

THE HIGH CONTRACTING PARTIES,

WHEREAS, in order to organise the transition from the institutional provisions of the Treaties applicable prior to the entry into force of the Treaty of Lisbon to the provisions contained in that Treaty, it is necessary to lay down transitional provisions,

HAVE AGREED UPON the following provisions, which shall be annexed to the Treaty on European Union, to the Treaty on the Functioning of the European Union and to the Treaty establishing the European Atomic Energy Community:

Article 1

In this Protocol, the words 'the Treaties' shall mean the Treaty on European Union, the Treaty on the Functioning of the European Union and the Treaty establishing the European Atomic Energy Community.

TITLE I PROVISIONS CONCERNING THE EUROPEAN PARLIAMENT

Article 2

1. For the period of the 2009–2014 parliamentary term remaining at the date of entry into force of this Article, and by way of derogation from Articles 189, second paragraph, and 190(2) of the Treaty establishing the European Community and Articles 107, second paragraph, and 108(2) of the Treaty establishing the European Atomic Energy Community, which were in force at the time of the European Parliament elections in June 2009, and by way of derogation from the number of seats provided for in the first subparagraph of Article 14(2) of the Treaty on European Union, the following 18 seats shall be added to the existing 736 seats, thus provisionally bringing the total number of members of the European Parliament to 754 until the end of the 2009–2014 parliamentary term:

Bulgaria	1	Netherlands	1
Spain	4	Austria	2
France	2	Poland	1
Italy	1	Slovenia	1
Latvia	1	Sweden	2
Malta	1	United Kingdom	1

2. By way of derogation from Article 14(3) of the Treaty on European Union, the Member States concerned shall designate the persons who will fill the additional seats referred to in paragraph 1, in accordance with the legislation of the Member States concerned and provided that the persons in question have been elected by direct universal suffrage:
   (a) in ad hoc elections by direct universal suffrage in the Member State concerned, in accordance with the provisions applicable for elections to the European Parliament;
   (b) by reference to the results of the European Parliament elections from 4 to 7 June 2009; or
   (c) by designation, by the national parliament of the Member State concerned from among its members, of the requisite number of members, according to the procedure determined by each of those Member States.

3. In accordance with the second subparagraph of Article 14(2) of the Treaty on European Union, the European Council shall adopt a decision determining the composition of the European Parliament in good time before the 2014 European Parliament elections.

TITLE II PROVISIONS CONCERNING THE QUALIFIED MAJORITY

Article 3

1. In accordance with Article 16(4) of the Treaty on European Union, the provisions of that paragraph and of Article 238(2) of the Treaty on the Functioning of the European Union relating to the definition of the qualified majority in the European Council and the Council shall take effect on 1 November 2014.

2. Between 1 November 2014 and 31 March 2017, when an act is to be adopted by qualified majority, a member of the Council may request that it be adopted in accordance with the qualified majority as defined in paragraph 3. In that case, paragraphs 3 and 4 shall apply.

3. Until 31 October 2014, the following provisions shall remain in force, without prejudice to the second subparagraph of Article 235(1) of the Treaty on the Functioning of the European Union.

   For acts of the European Council and of the Council requiring a qualified majority, members' votes shall be weighted as follows:

Belgium	12	Lithuania	7
Bulgaria	10	Luxembourg	4
Czech Republic	12	Hungary	12
Denmark	7	Malta	3
Germany	29	Netherlands	13
Estonia	4	Austria	10
Ireland	7	Poland	27
Greece	12	Portugal	12
Spain	27	Romania	14
France	29	Slovenia	4
Croatia	7	Slovakia	7
Italy	29	Finland	7
Cyprus	4	Sweden	10
Latvia	4	United Kingdom	29

   Acts shall be adopted if there are at least 260 votes in favour representing a majority of the members where, under the Treaties, they must be adopted on a proposal from the Commission. In other cases decisions shall be adopted if there are at least 260 votes in favour representing at least two thirds of the members.

   A member of the European Council or the Council may request that, where an act is adopted by the European Council or the Council by a qualified majority, a check is made to ensure that the Member States comprising the qualified majority represent at least 62% of the total population of the Union. If that proves not to be the case, the act shall not be adopted.

4. Until 31 October 2014, the qualified majority shall, in cases where, under the Treaties, not all the members of the Council participate in voting, namely in the cases where

reference is made to the qualified majority as defined in Article 238(3) of the Treaty on the Functioning of the European Union, be defined as the same proportion of the weighted votes and the same proportion of the number of the Council members and, if appropriate, the same percentage of the population of the Member States concerned as laid down in paragraph 3 of this Article.

TITLE III PROVISIONS CONCERNING THE CONFIGURATIONS OF THE COUNCIL

Article 4
Until the entry into force of the decision referred to in the first subparagraph of Article 16(6) of the Treaty on European Union, the Council may meet in the configurations laid down in the second and third subparagraphs of that paragraph and in the other configurations on the list established by a decision of the General Affairs Council, acting by a simple majority.

TITLE IV PROVISIONS CONCERNING THE COMMISSION, INCLUDING THE HIGH REPRESENTATIVE OF THE UNION FOR FOREIGN AFFAIRS AND SECURITY POLICY

Article 5
The members of the Commission in office on the date of entry into force of the Treaty of Lisbon shall remain in office until the end of their term of office. However, on the day of the appointment of the High Representative of the Union for Foreign Affairs and Security Policy, the term of office of the member having the same nationality as the High Representative shall end.

TITLE V PROVISIONS CONCERNING THE SECRETARY-GENERAL OF THE COUNCIL, HIGH REPRESENTATIVE FOR THE COMMON FOREIGN AND SECURITY POLICY, AND THE DEPUTY SECRETARY-GENERAL OF THE COUNCIL

Article 6
The terms of office of the Secretary-General of the Council, High Representative for the common foreign and security policy, and the Deputy Secretary-General of the Council shall end on the date of entry into force of the Treaty of Lisbon. The Council shall appoint a Secretary-General in conformity with Article 240(2) of the Treaty on the Functioning of the European Union.

TITLE VI PROVISIONS CONCERNING ADVISORY BODIES

Article 7
Until the entry into force of the decision referred to in Article 301 of the Treaty on the Functioning of the European Union, the allocation of members of the Economic and Social Committee shall be as follows:

Belgium	12	Lithuania	9
Bulgaria	12	Luxembourg	6
Czech Republic	12	Hungary	12
Denmark	9	Malta	5
Germany	24	Netherlands	12
Estonia	7	Austria	12
Ireland	9	Poland	21
Greece	12	Portugal	12
Spain	21	Romania	15
France	24	Slovenia	7
Croatia	9	Slovakia	9
Italy	24	Finland	9
Cyprus	6	Sweden	12
Latvia	7	United Kingdom	24

Article 8

Until the entry into force of the decision referred to in Article 305 of the Treaty on the Functioning of the European Union, the allocation of members of the Committee of the Regions shall be as follows:

Belgium	12	Lithuania	9
Bulgaria	12	Luxembourg	6
Czech Republic	12	Hungary	12
Denmark	9	Malta	5
Germany	24	Netherlands	12
Estonia	7	Austria	12
Ireland	9	Poland	21
Greece	12	Portugal	12
Spain	21	Romania	15
France	24	Slovenia	7
Croatia	9	Slovakia	9
Italy	24	Finland	9
Cyprus	6	Sweden	12
Latvia	7	United Kingdom	24

TITLE VII TRANSITIONAL PROVISIONS CONCERNING ACTS ADOPTED ON THE BASIS OF TITLES V AND VI OF THE TREATY ON EUROPEAN UNION PRIOR TO THE ENTRY INTO FORCE OF THE TREATY OF LISBON

Article 9

The legal effects of the acts of the institutions, bodies, offices and agencies of the Union adopted on the basis of the Treaty on European Union prior to the entry into force of the

Treaty of Lisbon shall be preserved until those acts are repealed, annulled or amended in implementation of the Treaties. The same shall apply to agreements concluded between Member States on the basis of the Treaty on European Union.

Article 10

1. As a transitional measure, and with respect to acts of the Union in the field of police cooperation and judicial cooperation in criminal matters which have been adopted before the entry into force of the Treaty of Lisbon, the powers of the institutions shall be the following at the date of entry into force of that Treaty: the powers of the Commission under Article 258 of the Treaty on the Functioning of the European Union shall not be applicable and the powers of the Court of Justice of the European Union under Title VI of the Treaty on European Union, in the version in force before the entry into force of the Treaty of Lisbon, shall remain the same, including where they have been accepted under Article 35(2) of the said Treaty on European Union.

2. The amendment of an act referred to in paragraph 1 shall entail the applicability of the powers of the institutions referred to in that paragraph as set out in the Treaties with respect to the amended act for those Member States to which that amended act shall apply.

3. In any case, the transitional measure mentioned in paragraph 1 shall cease to have effect five years after the date of entry into force of the Treaty of Lisbon.

4. At the latest six months before the expiry of the transitional period referred to in paragraph 3, the United Kingdom may notify to the Council that it does not accept, with respect to the acts referred to in paragraph 1, the powers of the institutions referred to in paragraph 1 as set out in the Treaties. In case the United Kingdom has made that notification, all acts referred to in paragraph 1 shall cease to apply to it as from the date of expiry of the transitional period referred to in paragraph 3. This subparagraph shall not apply with respect to the amended acts which are applicable to the United Kingdom as referred to in paragraph 2.

   The Council, acting by a qualified majority on a proposal from the Commission, shall determine the necessary consequential and transitional arrangements. The United Kingdom shall not participate in the adoption of this decision. A qualified majority of the Council shall be defined in accordance with Article 238(3)(a) of the Treaty on the Functioning of the European Union.

   The Council, acting by a qualified majority on a proposal from the Commission, may also adopt a decision determining that the United Kingdom shall bear the direct financial consequences, if any, necessarily and unavoidably incurred as a result of the cessation of its participation in those acts.

5. The United Kingdom may, at any time afterwards, notify the Council of its wish to participate in acts which have ceased to apply to it pursuant to paragraph 4, first subparagraph. In that case, the relevant provisions of the Protocol on the Schengen acquis integrated into the framework of the European Union or of the Protocol on the position of the United Kingdom and Ireland in respect of the area of freedom, security and justice, as the case may be, shall apply. The powers of the institutions with regard to those acts shall be those set out in the Treaties. When acting under the relevant Protocols, the Union institutions and the United Kingdom shall seek to reestablish the widest possible measure of participation of the United Kingdom in the acquis of

the Union in the area of freedom, security and justice without seriously affecting the practical operability of the various parts thereof, while respecting their coherence.

ANNEX II OVERSEAS COUNTRIES AND TERRITORIES TO WHICH THE PROVISIONS OF PART IV OF THE TREATY ON THE FUNCTIONING OF THE EUROPEAN UNION APPLY

— Greenland,
— New Caledonia and Dependencies,
— French Polynesia,
— French Southern and Antarctic Territories,
— Wallis and Futuna Islands,
— Mayotte,
— Saint Pierre and Miquelon,
— Aruba,
— Netherlands Antilles:
— Bonaire,
— Curaçao,
— Saba,
— Sint Eustatius,
— Sint Maarten,
— Anguilla,
— Cayman Islands,
— Falkland Islands,
— South Georgia and the South Sandwich Islands,
— Montserrat,
— Pitcairn,
— Saint Helena and Dependencies,
— British Antarctic Territory,
— British Indian Ocean Territory,
— Turks and Caicos Islands,
— British Virgin Islands,
— Bermuda.

4

Charter of Fundamental Rights of the European Union (with explanations)

Contents

PREAMBLE

The peoples of Europe, in creating an ever closer union among them, are resolved to share a peaceful future based on common values.

Conscious of its spiritual and moral heritage, the Union is founded on the indivisible, universal values of human dignity, freedom, equality and solidarity; it is based on the principles of democracy and the rule of law. It places the individual at the heart of its activities, by establishing the citizenship of the Union and by creating an area of freedom, security and justice.

The Union contributes to the preservation and to the development of these common values while respecting the diversity of the cultures and traditions of the peoples of Europe as well as the national identities of the Member States and the organisation of their public authorities at national, regional and local levels; it seeks to promote balanced and sustainable development and ensures free movement of persons, services, goods and capital, and the freedom of establishment.

To this end, it is necessary to strengthen the protection of fundamental rights in the light of changes in society, social progress and scientific and technological developments by making those rights more visible in a Charter.

This Charter reaffirms, with due regard for the powers and tasks of the Union and for the principle of subsidiarity, the rights as they result, in particular, from the constitutional traditions and international obligations common to the Member States,

4

the European Convention for the Protection of Human Rights and Fundamental Freedoms, the Social Charters adopted by the Union and by the Council of Europe and the case-law of the Court of Justice of the European Union and of the European Court of Human Rights. In this context the Charter will be interpreted by the courts of the Union and the Member States with due regard to the explanations prepared under the authority of the Praesidium of the Convention which drafted the Charter and updated under the responsibility of the Praesidium of the European Convention.

Enjoyment of these rights entails responsibilities and duties with regard to other persons, to the human community and to future generations.

The Union therefore recognises the rights, freedoms and principles set out hereafter.

TITLE I DIGNITY

Article 1
Human dignity
Human dignity is inviolable. It must be respected and protected.

Article 2
Right to life
1. Everyone has the right to life.
2. No one shall be condemned to the death penalty, or executed.

Article 3
Right to the integrity of the person
1. Everyone has the right to respect for his or her physical and mental integrity.
2. In the fields of medicine and biology, the following must be respected in particular:
    (a) the free and informed consent of the person concerned, according to the procedures laid down by law;
    (b) the prohibition of eugenic practices, in particular those aiming at the selection of persons;
    (c) the prohibition on making the human body and its parts as such a source of financial gain;
    (d) the prohibition of the reproductive cloning of human beings.

Article 4
Prohibition of torture and inhuman or degrading treatment or punishment
No one shall be subjected to torture or to inhuman or degrading treatment or punishment.

Article 5
Prohibition of slavery and forced labour
1. No one shall be held in slavery or servitude.
2. No one shall be required to perform forced or compulsory labour.
3. Trafficking in human beings is prohibited.

TITLE II FREEDOMS

Article 6
Right to liberty and security
Everyone has the right to liberty and security of person.

Article 7
Respect for private and family life
Everyone has the right to respect for his or her private and family life, home and communications.

Article 8
Protection of personal data
1. Everyone has the right to the protection of personal data concerning him or her.
2. Such data must be processed fairly for specified purposes and on the basis of the consent of the person concerned or some other legitimate basis laid down by law. Everyone has the right of access to data which has been collected concerning him or her, and the right to have it rectified.
3. Compliance with these rules shall be subject to control by an independent authority.

Article 9
Right to marry and right to found a family
The right to marry and the right to found a family shall be guaranteed in accordance with the national laws governing the exercise of these rights.

Article 10
Freedom of thought, conscience and religion
1. Everyone has the right to freedom of thought, conscience and religion. This right includes freedom to change religion or belief and freedom, either alone or in community with others and in public or in private, to manifest religion or belief, in worship, teaching, practice and observance.
2. The right to conscientious objection is recognised, in accordance with the national laws governing the exercise of this right.

Article 11
Freedom of expression and information
1. Everyone has the right to freedom of expression. This right shall include freedom to hold opinions and to receive and impart information and ideas without interference by public authority and regardless of frontiers.
2. The freedom and pluralism of the media shall be respected.

Article 12
Freedom of assembly and of association
1. Everyone has the right to freedom of peaceful assembly and to freedom of association at all levels, in particular in political, trade union and civic matters, which implies the

right of everyone to form and to join trade unions for the protection of his or her interests.

2. Political parties at Union level contribute to expressing the political will of the citizens of the Union.

Article 13
Freedom of the arts and sciences
The arts and scientific research shall be free of constraint. Academic freedom shall be respected.

Article 14
Right to education
1. Everyone has the right to education and to have access to vocational and continuing training.
2. This right includes the possibility to receive free compulsory education.
3. The freedom to found educational establishments with due respect for democratic principles and the right of parents to ensure the education and teaching of their children in conformity with their religious, philosophical and pedagogical convictions shall be respected, in accordance with the national laws governing the exercise of such freedom and right.

Article 15
Freedom to choose an occupation and right to engage in work
1. Everyone has the right to engage in work and to pursue a freely chosen or accepted occupation.
2. Every citizen of the Union has the freedom to seek employment, to work, to exercise the right of establishment and to provide services in any Member State.
3. Nationals of third countries who are authorised to work in the territories of the Member States are entitled to working conditions equivalent to those of citizens of the Union.

Article 16
Freedom to conduct a business
The freedom to conduct a business in accordance with Union law and national laws and practices is recognised.

Article 17
Right to property
1. Everyone has the right to own, use, dispose of and bequeath his or her lawfully acquired possessions. No one may be deprived of his or her possessions, except in the public interest and in the cases and under the conditions provided for by law, subject to fair compensation being paid in good time for their loss. The use of property may be regulated by law in so far as is necessary for the general interest.
2. Intellectual property shall be protected.

Article 18
Right to asylum

The right to asylum shall be guaranteed with due respect for the rules of the Geneva Convention of 28 July 1951 and the Protocol of 31 January 1967 relating to the status of refugees and in accordance with the Treaty on European Union and the Treaty on the Functioning of the European Union (hereinafter referred to as 'the Treaties').

Article 19
Protection in the event of removal, expulsion or extradition

1. Collective expulsions are prohibited.
2. No one may be removed, expelled or extradited to a State where there is a serious risk that he or she would be subjected to the death penalty, torture or other inhuman or degrading treatment or punishment.

TITLE III EQUALITY

Article 20
Equality before the law

Everyone is equal before the law.

Article 21
Non-discrimination

1. Any discrimination based on any ground such as sex, race, colour, ethnic or social origin, genetic features, language, religion or belief, political or any other opinion, membership of a national minority, property, birth, disability, age or sexual orientation shall be prohibited.
2. Within the scope of application of the Treaties and without prejudice to any of their specific provisions, any discrimination on grounds of nationality shall be prohibited.

Article 22
Cultural, religious and linguistic diversity

The Union shall respect cultural, religious and linguistic diversity.

Article 23
Equality between women and men

Equality between women and men must be ensured in all areas, including employment, work and pay.

The principle of equality shall not prevent the maintenance or adoption of measures providing for specific advantages in favour of the under-represented sex.

Article 24
The rights of the child

1. Children shall have the right to such protection and care as is necessary for their well-being. They may express their views freely. Such views shall be taken into consideration on matters which concern them in accordance with their age and maturity.

4

2. In all actions relating to children, whether taken by public authorities or private institutions, the child's best interests must be a primary consideration.
3. Every child shall have the right to maintain on a regular basis a personal relationship and direct contact with both his or her parents, unless that is contrary to his or her interests.

Article 25
The rights of the elderly
The Union recognises and respects the rights of the elderly to lead a life of dignity and independence and to participate in social and cultural life.

Article 26
Integration of persons with disabilities
The Union recognises and respects the right of persons with disabilities to benefit from measures designed to ensure their independence, social and occupational integration and participation in the life of the community.

TITLE IV SOLIDARITY

Article 27
Workers' right to information and consultation within the undertaking
Workers or their representatives must, at the appropriate levels, be guaranteed information and consultation in good time in the cases and under the conditions provided for by Union law and national laws and practices.

Article 28
Right of collective bargaining and action
Workers and employers, or their respective organisations, have, in accordance with Union law and national laws and practices, the right to negotiate and conclude collective agreements at the appropriate levels and, in cases of conflicts of interest, to take collective action to defend their interests, including strike action.

Article 29
Right of access to placement services
Everyone has the right of access to a free placement service.

Article 30
Protection in the event of unjustified dismissal
Every worker has the right to protection against unjustified dismissal, in accordance with Union law and national laws and practices.

Article 31
Fair and just working conditions
1. Every worker has the right to working conditions which respect his or her health, safety and dignity.
2. Every worker has the right to limitation of maximum working hours, to daily and weekly rest periods and to an annual period of paid leave.

Article 32

Prohibition of child labour and protection of young people at work

The employment of children is prohibited. The minimum age of admission to employment may not be lower than the minimum school-leaving age, without prejudice to such rules as may be more favourable to young people and except for limited derogations.

Young people admitted to work must have working conditions appropriate to their age and be protected against economic exploitation and any work likely to harm their safety, health or physical, mental, moral or social development or to interfere with their education.

Article 33

Family and professional life

1. The family shall enjoy legal, economic and social protection.
2. To reconcile family and professional life, everyone shall have the right to protection from dismissal for a reason connected with maternity and the right to paid maternity leave and to parental leave following the birth or adoption of a child.

Article 34

Social security and social assistance

1. The Union recognises and respects the entitlement to social security benefits and social services providing protection in cases such as maternity, illness, industrial accidents, dependency or old age, and in the case of loss of employment, in accordance with the rules laid down by Union law and national laws and practices.
2. Everyone residing and moving legally within the European Union is entitled to social security benefits and social advantages in accordance with Union law and national laws and practices.
3. In order to combat social exclusion and poverty, the Union recognises and respects the right to social and housing assistance so as to ensure a decent existence for all those who lack sufficient resources, in accordance with the rules laid down by Union law and national laws and practices.

Article 35

Health care

Everyone has the right of access to preventive health care and the right to benefit from medical treatment under the conditions established by national laws and practices. A high level of human health protection shall be ensured in the definition and implementation of all the Union's policies and activities.

Article 36

Access to services of general economic interest

The Union recognises and respects access to services of general economic interest as provided for in national laws and practices, in accordance with the Treaties, in order to promote the social and territorial cohesion of the Union.

Article 37
Environmental protection
A high level of environmental protection and the improvement of the quality of the environment must be integrated into the policies of the Union and ensured in accordance with the principle of sustainable development.

Article 38
Consumer protection
Union policies shall ensure a high level of consumer protection.

TITLE V CITIZENS' RIGHTS

Article 39
Right to vote and to stand as a candidate at elections to the European Parliament
1. Every citizen of the Union has the right to vote and to stand as a candidate at elections to the European Parliament in the Member State in which he or she resides, under the same conditions as nationals of that State.
2. Members of the European Parliament shall be elected by direct universal suffrage in a free and secret ballot.

Article 40
Right to vote and to stand as a candidate at municipal elections
Every citizen of the Union has the right to vote and to stand as a candidate at municipal elections in the Member State in which he or she resides under the same conditions as nationals of that State.

Article 41
Right to good administration
1. Every person has the right to have his or her affairs handled impartially, fairly and within a reasonable time by the institutions, bodies, offices and agencies of the Union.
2. This right includes:
    (a) the right of every person to be heard, before any individual measure which would affect him or her adversely is taken;
    (b) the right of every person to have access to his or her file, while respecting the legitimate interests of confidentiality and of professional and business secrecy;
    (c) the obligation of the administration to give reasons for its decisions.
3. Every person has the right to have the Union make good any damage caused by its institutions or by its servants in the performance of their duties, in accordance with the general principles common to the laws of the Member States.
4. Every person may write to the institutions of the Union in one of the languages of the Treaties and must have an answer in the same language.

Article 42
Right of access to documents
Any citizen of the Union, and any natural or legal person residing or having its registered office in a Member State, has a right of access to documents of the institutions, bodies, offices and agencies of the Union, whatever their medium.

Article 43

European Ombudsman

Any citizen of the Union and any natural or legal person residing or having its registered office in a Member State has the right to refer to the European Ombudsman cases of maladministration in the activities of the institutions, bodies, offices or agencies of the Union, with the exception of the Court of Justice of the European Union acting in its judicial role.

Article 44

Right to petition

Any citizen of the Union and any natural or legal person residing or having its registered office in a Member State has the right to petition the European Parliament.

Article 45

Freedom of movement and of residence

1. Every citizen of the Union has the right to move and reside freely within the territory of the Member States.
2. Freedom of movement and residence may be granted, in accordance with the Treaties, to nationals of third countries legally resident in the territory of a Member State.

Article 46

Diplomatic and consular protection

Every citizen of the Union shall, in the territory of a third country in which the Member State of which he or she is a national is not represented, be entitled to protection by the diplomatic or consular authorities of any Member State, on the same conditions as the nationals of that Member State.

TITLE VI JUSTICE

Article 47

Right to an effective remedy and to a fair trial

Everyone whose rights and freedoms guaranteed by the law of the Union are violated has the right to an effective remedy before a tribunal in compliance with the conditions laid down in this Article.

Everyone is entitled to a fair and public hearing within a reasonable time by an independent and impartial tribunal previously established by law. Everyone shall have the possibility of being advised, defended and represented.

Legal aid shall be made available to those who lack sufficient resources in so far as such aid is necessary to ensure effective access to justice.

Article 48

Presumption of innocence and right of defence

1. Everyone who has been charged shall be presumed innocent until proved guilty according to law.
2. Respect for the rights of the defence of anyone who has been charged shall be guaranteed.

Article 49
Principles of legality and proportionality of criminal offences and penalties

1. No one shall be held guilty of any criminal offence on account of any act or omission which did not constitute a criminal offence under national law or international law at the time when it was committed. Nor shall a heavier penalty be imposed than the one that was applicable at the time the criminal offence was committed. If, subsequent to the commission of a criminal offence, the law provides for a lighter penalty, that penalty shall be applicable.
2. This Article shall not prejudice the trial and punishment of any person for any act or omission which, at the time when it was committed, was criminal according to the general principles recognised by the community of nations.
3. The severity of penalties must not be disproportionate to the criminal offence.

Article 50
Right not to be tried or punished twice in criminal proceedings for the same criminal offence

No one shall be liable to be tried or punished again in criminal proceedings for an offence for which he or she has already been finally acquitted or convicted within the Union in accordance with the law.

TITLE VII GENERAL PROVISIONS GOVERNING THE INTERPRETATION AND APPLICATION OF THE CHARTER

Article 51
Field of application

1. The provisions of this Charter are addressed to the institutions, bodies, offices and agencies of the Union with due regard for the principle of subsidiarity and to the Member States only when they are implementing Union law. They shall therefore respect the rights, observe the principles and promote the application thereof in accordance with their respective powers and respecting the limits of the powers of the Union as conferred on it in the Treaties.
2. The Charter does not extend the field of application of Union law beyond the powers of the Union or establish any new power or task for the Union, or modify powers and tasks as defined in the Treaties.

Article 52
Scope and interpretation of rights and principles

1. Any limitation on the exercise of the rights and freedoms recognised by this Charter must be provided for by law and respect the essence of those rights and freedoms. Subject to the principle of proportionality, limitations may be made only if they are necessary and genuinely meet objectives of general interest recognised by the Union or the need to protect the rights and freedoms of others.
2. Rights recognised by this Charter for which provision is made in the Treaties shall be exercised under the conditions and within the limits defined by those Treaties.
3. In so far as this Charter contains rights which correspond to rights guaranteed by the Convention for the Protection of Human Rights and Fundamental Freedoms, the

meaning and scope of those rights shall be the same as those laid down by the said Convention. This provision shall not prevent Union law providing more extensive protection.

4. In so far as this Charter recognises fundamental rights as they result from the constitutional traditions common to the Member States, those rights shall be interpreted in harmony with those traditions.

5. The provisions of this Charter which contain principles may be implemented by legislative and executive acts taken by institutions, bodies, offices and agencies of the Union, and by acts of Member States when they are implementing Union law, in the exercise of their respective powers. They shall be judicially cognisable only in the interpretation of such acts and in the ruling on their legality.

6. Full account shall be taken of national laws and practices as specified in this Charter.

7. The explanations drawn up as a way of providing guidance in the interpretation of this Charter shall be given due regard by the courts of the Union and of the Member States.

Article 53

Level of protection

Nothing in this Charter shall be interpreted as restricting or adversely affecting human rights and fundamental freedoms as recognised, in their respective fields of application, by Union law and international law and by international agreements to which the Union or all the Member States are party, including the European Convention for the Protection of Human Rights and Fundamental Freedoms, and by the Member States' constitutions.

Article 54

Prohibition of abuse of rights

Nothing in this Charter shall be interpreted as implying any right to engage in any activity or to perform any act aimed at the destruction of any of the rights and freedoms recognised in this Charter or at their limitation to a greater extent than is provided for herein.

4

EXPLANATIONS RELATING TO THE CHARTER OF FUNDAMENTAL RIGHTS

These explanations were originally prepared under the authority of the Praesidium of the Convention which drafted the Charter of Fundamental Rights of the European Union. They have been updated under the responsibility of the Praesidium of the European Convention, in the light of the drafting adjustments made to the text of the Charter by that Convention (notably to Articles 51 and 52) and of further developments of Union law. Although they do not as such have the status of law, they are a valuable tool of interpretation intended to clarify the provisions of the Charter.

TITLE I DIGNITY

Explanation on Article 1 – Human dignity

The dignity of the human person is not only a fundamental right in itself but constitutes the real basis of fundamental rights. The 1948 Universal Declaration of Human Rights enshrined human dignity in its preamble: 'Whereas recognition of the inherent dignity and of the equal and inalienable rights of all members of the human family is the foundation of freedom, justice and peace in the world.' In its judgment of 9 October 2001 in Case C-377/98 *Netherlands v European Parliament and Council* [2001] ECR I-7079, at grounds 70–77, the Court of Justice confirmed that a fundamental right to human dignity is part of Union law.

It results that none of the rights laid down in this Charter may be used to harm the dignity of another person, and that the dignity of the human person is part of the substance of the rights laid down in this Charter. It must therefore be respected, even where a right is restricted.

Explanation on Article 2 – Right to life

1. Paragraph 1 of this Article is based on the first sentence of Article 2(1) of the ECHR, which reads as follows:
   '1.   Everyone's right to life shall be protected by law …'.
2. The second sentence of the provision, which referred to the death penalty, was superseded by the entry into force of Article 1 of Protocol No 6 to the ECHR, which reads as follows:
   'The death penalty shall be abolished. No-one shall be condemned to such penalty or executed.'
   Article 2(2) of the Charter is based on that provision.
3. The provisions of Article 2ofthe Charter correspond to those of the above Articles of the ECHR and its Protocol. They have the same meaning and the same scope, in accordance with Article 52(3) of the Charter. Therefore, the 'negative' definitions appearing in the ECHR must be regarded as also forming part of the Charter:
   (a) Article 2(2) of the ECHR:
      'Deprivation of life shall not be regarded as inflicted in contravention of this article when it results from the use of force which is no more than absolutely necessary:
      (a) in defence of any person from unlawful violence;
      (b) in order to effect a lawful arrest or to prevent the escape of a person lawfully detained;
      (c) in action lawfully taken for the purpose of quelling a riot or insurrection.'
   (b) Article 2 of Protocol No 6 to the ECHR:
      'A State may make provision in its law for the death penalty in respect of acts committed in time of war or of imminent threat of war; such penalty shall be applied only in the instances laid down in the law and in accordance with its provisions …'.

Explanation on Article 3 – Right to the integrity of the person

1. In its judgment of 9 October 2001 in Case C-377/98 *Netherlands v European Parliament and Council* [2001] ECR-I 7079, at grounds 70, 78 to 80, the Court of Justice confirmed that a fundamental right to human integrity is part of Union law and encompasses, in the context of medicine and biology, the free and informed consent of the donor and recipient.
2. The principles of Article 3 of the Charter are already included in the Convention on Human Rights and Biomedicine, adopted by the Council of Europe (ETS 164 and additional protocol ETS 168). The Charter does not set out to depart from those principles, and therefore prohibits only reproductive cloning. It neither authorises nor

prohibits other forms of cloning. Thus it does not in any way prevent the legislature from prohibiting other forms of cloning.

3. The reference to eugenic practices, in particular those aiming at the selection of persons, relates to possible situations in which selection programmes are organised and implemented, involving campaigns for sterilisation, forced pregnancy, compulsory ethnic marriage among others, all acts deemed to be international crimes in the Statute of the International Criminal Court adopted in Rome on 17 July 1998 (see its Article 7(1)(g)).

Explanation on Article 4 – Prohibition of torture and inhuman or degrading treatment or punishment

The right in Article 4 is the right guaranteed by Article 3 of the ECHR, which has the same wording: 'No one shall be subjected to torture or to inhuman or degrading treatment or punishment'. By virtue of Article 52(3) of the Charter, it therefore has the same meaning and the same scope as the ECHR Article.

Explanation on Article 5 – Prohibition of slavery and forced labour

1. The right in Article 5(1) and (2) corresponds to Article 4(1) and (2) of the ECHR, which has the same wording. It therefore has the same meaning and scope as the ECHR Article, by virtue of Article 52(3) of the Charter. Consequently:
   — no limitation may legitimately affect the right provided for in paragraph 1,
   — in paragraph 2, 'forced or compulsory labour' must be understood in the light of the 'negative' definitions contained in Article 4(3) of the ECHR:
   'For the purpose of this article the term "forced or compulsory labour" shall not include:
   (a) any work required to be done in the ordinary course of detention imposed according to the provisions of Article 5 of this Convention or during conditional release from such detention;
   (b) any service of a military character or, in case of conscientious objectors in countries where they are recognised, service exacted instead of compulsory military service;
   (c) any service exacted in case of an emergency or calamity threatening the life or well-being of the community;
   (d) any work or service which forms part of normal civic obligations.'

2. Paragraph 3 stems directly from human dignity and takes account of recent developments in organised crime, such as the organisation of lucrative illegal immigration or sexual exploitation networks. The Annex to the Europol Convention contains the following definition which refers to trafficking for the purpose of sexual exploitation: 'traffic in human beings: means subjection of a person to the real and illegal sway of other persons by using violence or menaces or by abuse of authority or intrigue with a view to the exploitation of prostitution, forms of sexual exploitation and assault of minors or trade in abandoned children'. Chapter VI of the Convention implementing the Schengen Agreement, which has been integrated into the Union's acquis, in which the United Kingdom and Ireland participate, contains the following wording in Article 27(1) which refers to illegal immigration networks: 'The Contracting Parties undertake to impose appropriate penalties on any person who, for financial gain, assists or tries to assist an alien to enter or reside within the territory of one of the Contracting

Parties in breach of that Contracting Party's laws on the entry and residence of aliens.' On 19 July 2002, the Council adopted a framework decision on combating trafficking in human beings (OJ L 203, 1.8.2002, p. 1) whose Article 1 defines in detail the offences concerning trafficking in human beings for the purposes of labour exploitation or sexual exploitation, which the Member States must make punishable by virtue of that framework decision.

TITLE II FREEDOMS

Explanation on Article 6 – Right to liberty and security

The rights in Article 6 are the rights guaranteed by Article 5 of the ECHR, and in accordance with Article 52(3) of the Charter, they have the same meaning and scope. Consequently, the limitations which may legitimately be imposed on them may not exceed those permitted by the ECHR, in the wording of Article 5:

1. 'Everyone has the right to liberty and security of person. No one shall be deprived of his liberty save in the following cases and in accordance with a procedure prescribed by law:
   (a) the lawful detention of a person after conviction by a competent court;
   (b) the lawful arrest or detention of a person for non-compliance with the lawful order of a court or in order to secure the fulfilment of any obligation prescribed by law;
   (c) the lawful arrest or detention of a person effected for the purpose of bringing him before the competent legal authority on reasonable suspicion of having committed an offence or when it is reasonably considered necessary to prevent his committing an offence or fleeing after having done so;
   (d) the detention of a minor by lawful order for the purpose of educational supervision or his lawful detention for the purpose of bringing him before the competent legal authority;
   (e) the lawful detention of persons for the prevention of the spreading of infectious diseases, of persons of unsound mind, alcoholics or drug addicts or vagrants;
   (f) the lawful arrest or detention of a person to prevent his effecting an unauthorised entry into the country or of a person against whom action is being taken with a view to deportation or extradition.
2. Everyone who is arrested shall be informed promptly, in a language which he understands, of the reasons for his arrest and of any charge against him.
3. Everyone arrested or detained in accordance with the provisions of paragraph 1.c of this Article shall be brought promptly before a judge or other officer authorised by law to exercise judicial power and shall be entitled to trial within a reasonable time or to release pending trial. Release may be conditioned by guarantees to appear for trial.
4. Everyone who is deprived of his liberty by arrest or detention shall be entitled to take proceedings by which the lawfulness of his detention shall be decided speedily by a court and his release ordered if the detention is not lawful.
5. Everyone who has been the victim of arrest or detention in contravention of the provisions of this Article shall have an enforceable right to compensation.'

The rights enshrined in Article 6 must be respected particularly when the European Parliament and the Council adopt legislative acts in the area of judicial cooperation in criminal matters, on the basis of Articles 82, 83 and 85 of the Treaty on the Functioning of the European Union, notably to define common minimum provisions as regards the categorisation of offences and punishments and certain aspects of procedural law.

Explanation on Article 7 – Respect for private and family life

The rights guaranteed in Article 7 correspond to those guaranteed by Article 8 of the ECHR. To take account of developments in technology the word 'correspondence' has been replaced by 'communications'.

In accordance with Article 52(3), the meaning and scope of this right are the same as those of the corresponding article of the ECHR. Consequently, the limitations which may legitimately be imposed on this right are the same as those allowed by Article 8 of the ECHR:

'1. Everyone has the right to respect for his private and family life, his home and his correspondence.

2. There shall be no interference by a public authority with the exercise of this right except such as is in accordance with the law and is necessary in a democratic society in the interests of national security, public safety or the economic well-being of the country, for the prevention of disorder or crime, for the protection of health or morals, or for the protection of the rights and freedoms of others.'

Explanation on Article 8 – Protection of personal data

This Article has been based on Article 286 of the Treaty establishing the European Community [Article 16 of the Treaty on the Functioning of the European Union] and Directive 95/46/EC of the European Parliament and of the Council on the protection of individuals with regard to the processing of personal data and on the free movement of such data (OJ L 281, 23.11.1995, p. 31) as well as on Article 8 of the ECHR and on the Council of Europe Convention of 28 January 1981 for the Protection of Individuals with regard to Automatic Processing of Personal Data, which has been ratified by all the Member States. Article 286 of the EC Treaty is now replaced by Article 16 of the Treaty on the Functioning of the European Union and Article 39 of the Treaty on European Union. Reference is also made to Regulation (EC) No. 45/2001 of the European Parliament and of the Council on the protection of individuals with regard to the processing of personal data by the [Union] institutions and bodies and on the free movement of such data (OJ L 8, 12.1.2001, p. 1). The above-mentioned Directive and Regulation contain conditions and limitations for the exercise of the right to the protection of personal data.

Explanation on Article 9 – Right to marry and right to found a family

This Article is based on Article 12 of the ECHR, which reads as follows: 'Men and women of marriageable age have the right to marry and to found a family according to the national laws governing the exercising of this right.' The wording of the Article has been modernised to cover cases in which national legislation recognises arrangements other than marriage for founding a family. This Article neither prohibits nor imposes the granting of the status of marriage to unions between people of the same sex. This right is thus similar to that afforded by the ECHR, but its scope may be wider when national legislation so provides.

Explanation on Article 10 – Freedom of thought, conscience and religion

The right guaranteed in paragraph 1 corresponds to the right guaranteed in Article 9 of the ECHR and, in accordance with Article 52(3) of the Charter, has the same meaning and scope. Limitations must therefore respect Article 9(2) of the Convention, which reads as follows: 'Freedom to manifest one's religion or beliefs shall be subject only to such limitations as are prescribed by law and are necessary in a democratic society in the interests of public safety, for the protection of public order, health or morals, or for the protection of the rights and freedoms of others.'

The right guaranteed in paragraph 2 corresponds to national constitutional traditions and to the development of national legislation on this issue.

Explanation on Article 11 – Freedom of expression and information

1. Article 11 corresponds to Article 10 of the European Convention on Human Rights, which reads as follows:

   '1. Everyone has the right to freedom of expression. This right shall include freedom to hold opinions and to receive and impart information and ideas without interference by public authority and regardless of frontiers. This Article shall not prevent States from requiring the licensing of broadcasting, television or cinema enterprises.

   2. The exercise of these freedoms, since it carries with it duties and responsibilities, may be subject to such formalities, conditions, restrictions or penalties as are prescribed by law and are necessary in a democratic society, in the interests of national security, territorial integrity or public safety, for the prevention of disorder or crime, for the protection of health or morals, for the protection of the reputation or rights of others, for preventing the disclosure of information received in confidence, or for maintaining the authority and impartiality of the judiciary.' Pursuant to Article 52(3) of the Charter, the meaning and scope of this right are the same as those guaranteed by the ECHR. The limitations which may be imposed on it may therefore not exceed those provided for in Article 10(2) of the Convention, without prejudice to any restrictions which the competition law of the Union may impose on Member States' right to introduce the licensing arrangements referred to in the third sentence of Article 10(1) of the ECHR.

2. Paragraph 2 of this Article spells out the consequences of paragraph 1 regarding freedom of the media. It is based in particular on Court of Justice case-law regarding television, particularly in Case C-288/89 (judgment of 25 July 1991, *Stichting Collectieve Antennevoorziening Gouda and others* [1991] ECR I-4007), and on the Protocol on the system of public broadcasting in the Member States annexed to the EC Treaty and now to the Treaties, and on Council Directive 89/552/EC (particularly its seventeenth recital).

Explanation on Article 12 – Freedom of assembly and of association

1. Paragraph 1 of this Article corresponds to Article 11 of the ECHR, which reads as follows:

   '1. Everyone has the right to freedom of peaceful assembly and to freedom of association with others, including the right to form and to join trade unions for the protection of his interests.

2. No restrictions shall be placed on the exercise of these rights other than such as are prescribed by law and are necessary in a democratic society in the interests of national security or public safety, for the prevention of disorder or crime, for the protection of health or morals or for the protection of the rights and freedoms of others. This article shall not prevent the imposition of lawful restrictions on the exercise of these rights by members of the armed forces, of the police or of the administration of the State.'

The meaning of the provisions of paragraph 1 of this Article 12 is the same as that of the ECHR, but their scope is wider since they apply at all levels including European level. In accordance with Article 52(3) of the Charter, limitations on that right may not exceed those considered legitimate by virtue of Article 11(2) of the ECHR.

2. This right is also based on Article 11 of the [Union] Charter of the Fundamental Social Rights of Workers.

3. Paragraph 2 of this Article corresponds to Article 10(4) of the Treaty on European Union.

Explanation on Article 13 – Freedom of the arts and sciences
This right is deduced primarily from the right to freedom of thought and expression. It is to be exercised having regard to Article 1 and may be subject to the limitations authorised by Article 10 of the ECHR.

Explanation on Article 14 – Right to education
1. This Article is based on the common constitutional traditions of Member States and on Article 2 of the Protocol to the ECHR, which reads as follows:
    'No person shall be denied the right to education. In the exercise of any functions which it assumes in relation to education and to teaching, the State shall respect the right of parents to ensure such education and teaching in conformity with their own religious and philosophical convictions.'

    It was considered useful to extend this Article to access to vocational and continuing training (see point 15 of the [Union] Charter of the Fundamental Social Rights of Workers and Article 10 of the Social Charter) and to add the principle of free compulsory education. As it is worded, the latter principle merely implies that as regards compulsory education, each child has the possibility of attending an establishment which offers free education. It does not require all establishments which provide education or vocational and continuing training, in particular private ones, to be free of charge. Nor does it exclude certain specific forms of education having to be paid for, if the State takes measures to grant financial compensation. In so far as the Charter applies to the Union, this means that in its training policies the Union must respect free compulsory education, but this does not, of course, create new powers. Regarding the right of parents, it must be interpreted in conjunction with the provisions of Article 24.

2. Freedom to found public or private educational establishments is guaranteed as one of the aspects of freedom to conduct a business but it is limited by respect for democratic principles and is exercised in accordance with the arrangements defined by national legislation.

Explanation on Article 15 – Freedom to choose an occupation and right to engage in work

Freedom to choose an occupation, as enshrined in Article 15(1), is recognised in Court of Justice case-law (see inter alia judgment of 14 May 1974, Case 4/73 *Nold* [1974] ECR 491, paragraphs 12 to 14 of the grounds; judgment of 13 December 1979, Case 44/79 *Hauer* [1979] ECR 3727; judgment of 8 October 1986, Case 234/85 *Keller* [1986] ECR 2897, paragraph 8 of the grounds).

This paragraph also draws upon Article 1(2) of the European Social Charter, which was signed on 18 October 1961 and has been ratified by all the Member States, and on point 4 of the [Union] Charter of the Fundamental Social Rights of Workers of 9 December 1989. The expression 'working conditions' is to be understood in the sense of Article 156 of the Treaty on the Functioning of the European Union.

Paragraph 2 deals with the three freedoms guaranteed by Articles 26, 45, 49 and 56 of the Treaty on the Functioning of the European Union, namely freedom of movement for workers, freedom of establishment and freedom to provide services.

Paragraph 3 has been based on Article 153(1)(g) of the Treaty on the Functioning of the European Union, and on Article 19(4) of the European Social Charter signed on 18 October 1961 and ratified by all the Member States. Article 52(2) of the Charter is therefore applicable. The question of recruitment of seamen having the nationality of third States for the crews of vessels flying the flag of a Member State of the Union is governed by Union law and national legislation and practice.

Explanation on Article 16 – Freedom to conduct a business

This Article is based on Court of Justice case-law which has recognised freedom to exercise an economic or commercial activity (see judgments of 14 May 1974, Case 4/73 *Nold* [1974] ECR 491, paragraph 14 of the grounds, and of 27 September 1979, Case 230–78 *SpA Eridiana and others* [1979] ECR 2749, paragraphs 20 and 31 of the grounds) and freedom of contract (see inter alia *Sukkerfabriken Nykøbing* judgment, Case 151/78 [1979] ECR 1, paragraph 19 of the grounds, and judgment of 5 October 1999, C-240/97 *Spain v Commission* [1999] ECR I-6571, paragraph 99 of the grounds) and Article 119(1) and (3) of the Treaty on the Functioning of the European Union, which recognises free competition. Of course, this right is to be exercised with respect for Union law and national legislation. It may be subject to the limitations provided for in Article 52(1) of the Charter.

Explanation on Article 17 – Right to property

This Article is based on Article 1 of the Protocol to the ECHR:

'Every natural or legal person is entitled to the peaceful enjoyment of his possessions. No one shall be deprived of his possessions except in the public interest and subject to the conditions provided for by law and by the general principles of international law.

The preceding provisions shall not, however, in any way impair the right of a State to enforce such laws as it deems necessary to control the use of property in accordance with the general interest or to secure the payment of taxes or other contributions or penalties.'

This is a fundamental right common to all national constitutions. It has been recognised on numerous occasions by the case-law of the Court of Justice, initially in the *Hauer* judgment (13 December 1979, [1979] ECR 3727). The wording has been updated but, in accordance with Article 52(3), the meaning and scope of the right are the same as those of the right guaranteed by the ECHR and the limitations may not exceed those provided for there.

   Protection of intellectual property, one aspect of the right of property, is explicitly mentioned in paragraph 2 because of its growing importance and [Union] secondary legislation. Intellectual property covers not only literary and artistic property but also *inter alia* patent and trademark rights and associated rights. The guarantees laid down in paragraph 1 shall apply as appropriate to intellectual property.

Explanation on Article 18 – Right to asylum

The text of the Article has been based on TEC Article 63, now replaced by Article 78 of the Treaty on the Functioning of the European Union, which requires the Union to respect the Geneva Convention on refugees. Reference should be made to the Protocols relating to the United Kingdom and Ireland, annexed to the Treaties, and to Denmark, to determine the extent to which those Member States implement Union law in this area and the extent to which this Article is applicable to them. This Article is in line with the Protocol on Asylum annexed to the Treaties.

Explanation on Article 19 – Protection in the event of removal, expulsion or extradition

Paragraph 1 of this Article has the same meaning and scope as Article 4 of Protocol No 4 to the ECHR concerning collective expulsion. Its purpose is to guarantee that every decision is based on a specific examination and that no single measure can be taken to expel all persons having the nationality of a particular State (see also Article 13 of the Covenant on Civil and Political Rights).

   Paragraph 2 incorporates the relevant case-law from the European Court of Human Rights regarding Article 3 of the ECHR (see *Ahmed v Austria*, judgment of 17 December 1996, 1996-VI, p. 2206, and *Soering*, judgment of 7 July 1989).

TITLE III EQUALITY

Explanation on Article 20 – Equality before the law

This Article corresponds to a general principle of law which is included in all European constitutions and has also been recognised by the Court of Justice as a basic principle of [Union] law (judgment of 13 November 1984, Case 283/83 *Racke* [1984] ECR 3791, judgment of 17 April 1997, Case C-15/95 *EARL* [1997] ECR I–1961, and judgment of 13 April 2000, Case C-292/97 *Karlsson* [2000] ECR 2737).

Explanation on Article 21 – Non-discrimination

Paragraph 1 draws on Article 13 of the EC Treaty, now replaced by Article 19 of the Treaty on the Functioning of the European Union, Article 14 of the ECHR and Article 11 of the Convention on Human Rights and Biomedicine as regards genetic heritage. In so far as this corresponds to Article 14 of the ECHR, it applies in compliance with it.

   There is no contradiction or incompatibility between paragraph 1 and Article 19 of the Treaty on the Functioning of the European Union which has a different scope and purpose: Article 19 confers power on the Union to adopt legislative acts, including harmonisation of the Member States' laws and regulations, to combat certain forms of discrimination, listed exhaustively in that Article. Such legislation may cover action of Member State authorities (as well as relations between private individuals) in any area within the limits of the Union's powers. In contrast, the provision in Article 21(1) does not create any power to enact anti-discrimination laws in these areas of Member State or private action, nor does it lay down a sweeping ban of discrimination in such wide-ranging areas. Instead, it only addresses discriminations by the institutions and bodies of the Union themselves, when exercising powers conferred under the Treaties, and by Member States only when they are implementing Union law. Paragraph 1 therefore does not alter the extent of powers granted under Article 19 nor the interpretation given to that Article.

Paragraph 2 corresponds to the first paragraph of Article 18 of the Treaty on the Functioning of the European Union and must be applied in compliance with that Article.

Explanation on Article 22 – Cultural, religious and linguistic diversity

This Article has been based on Article 6 of the Treaty on European Union and on Article 151(1) and (4) of the EC Treaty, now replaced by Article 167(1) and (4) of the Treaty on the Functioning of the European Union, concerning culture. Respect for cultural and linguistic diversity is now also laid down in Article 3(3) of the Treaty on European Union. The Article is also inspired by Declaration No 11 to the Final Act of the Amsterdam Treaty on the status of churches and non-confessional organisations, now taken over in Article 17 of the Treaty on the Functioning of the European Union.

Explanation on Article 23 – Equality between women and men

The first paragraph has been based on Articles 2 and 3(2) of the EC Treaty, now replaced by Article 3 of the Treaty on European Union and Article 8 of the Treaty on the Functioning of the European Union which impose the objective of promoting equality between men and women on the Union, and on Article 157(1) of the Treaty on the Functioning of the European Union. It draws on Article 20 of the revised European Social Charter of 3 May 1996 and on point 16 of the [Union] Charter on the rights of workers.

It is also based on Article 157(3) of the Treaty on the Functioning of the European Union and Article 2(4) of Council Directive 76/207/EEC on the implementation of the principle of equal treatment for men and women as regards access to employment, vocational training and promotion, and working conditions.

The second paragraph takes over in shorter form Article 157(4) of the Treaty on the Functioning of the European Union which provides that the principle of equal treatment does not prevent the maintenance or adoption of measures providing for specific advantages in order to make it easier for the under-represented sex to pursue a vocational activity or to prevent or compensate for disadvantages in professional careers. In accordance with Article 52(2), the present paragraph does not amend Article 157(4).

Explanation on Article 24 – The rights of the child

This Article is based on the New York Convention on the Rights of the Child signed on 20 November 1989 and ratified by all the Member States, particularly Articles 3, 9, 12 and 13 thereof.

Paragraph 3 takes account of the fact that, as part of the establishment of an area of freedom, security and justice, the legislation of the Union on civil matters having cross-border implications, for which Article 81 of the Treaty on the Functioning of the European

Union confers power, may include notably visiting rights ensuring that children can maintain on a regular basis a personal and direct contact with both of their parents.

Explanation on Article 25 – The rights of the elderly
This Article draws on Article 23 of the revised European Social Charter and Articles 24 and 25 of the [Union] Charter of the Fundamental Social Rights of Workers. Of course, participation in social and cultural life also covers participation in political life.

Explanation on Article 26 – Integration of persons with disabilities
The principle set out in this Article is based on Article 15 of the European Social Charter and also draws on point 26 of the [Union] Charter of the Fundamental Social Rights of Workers.

TITLE IV SOLIDARITY

Explanation on Article 27 – Workers' right to information and consultation within the undertaking
This Article appears in the revised European Social Charter (Article 21) and in the [Union] Charter on the rights of workers (points 17 and 18). It applies under the conditions laid down by Union law and by national laws. The reference to appropriate levels refers to the levels laid down by Union law or by national laws and practices, which might include the European level when Union legislation so provides. There is a considerable Union acquis in this field: Articles 154 and 155 of the Treaty on the Functioning of the European Union, and Directives 2002/14/EC (general framework for informing and consulting employees in the European [Union]), 98/59/EC (collective redundancies), 2001/23/EC (transfers of undertakings) and 94/45/EC (European works councils).

Explanation on Article 28 – Right of collective bargaining and action
This Article is based on Article 6 of the European Social Charter and on the [Union] Charter of the Fundamental Social Rights of Workers (points 12 to 14). The right of collective action was recognised by the European Court of Human Rights as one of the elements of trade union rights laid down by Article 11 of the ECHR. As regards the appropriate levels at which collective negotiation might take place, see the explanation given for the above Article. The modalities and limits for the exercise of collective action, including strike action, come under national laws and practices, including the question of whether it may be carried out in parallel in several Member States.

Explanation on Article 29 – Right of access to placement services
This Article is based on Article 1(3) of the European Social Charter and point 13 of the [Union] Charter of the Fundamental Social Rights of Workers.

Explanation on Article 30 – Protection in the event of unjustified dismissal
This Article draws on Article 24 of the revised Social Charter. See also Directive 2001/23/EC on the safeguarding of employees' rights in the event of transfers of undertakings, and Directive 80/987/EEC on the protection of employees in the event of the insolvency of their employer, as amended by Directive 2002/74/EC.

4

Explanation on Article 31 – Fair and just working conditions

1. Paragraph 1 of this Article is based on Directive 89/391/EEC on the introduction of measures to encourage improvements in the safety and health of workers at work. It also draws on Article 3 of the Social Charter and point 19 of the [Union] Charter on the rights of workers, and, as regards dignity at work, on Article 26 of the revised Social Charter. The expression 'working conditions' is to be understood in the sense of Article 156 of the Treaty on the Functioning of the European Union.

2. Paragraph 2 is based on Directive 93/104/EC concerning certain aspects of the organisation of working time, Article 2 of the European Social Charter and point 8 of the [Union] Charter on the rights of workers.

Explanation on Article 32 – Prohibition of child labour and protection of young people at work

This Article is based on Directive 94/33/EC on the protection of young people at work, Article 7 of the European Social Charter and points 20 to 23 of the [Union] Charter of the Fundamental Social Rights of Workers.

Explanation on Article 33 – Family and professional life

Article 33(1) is based on Article 16 of the European Social Charter.

Paragraph 2 draws on Council Directive 92/85/EEC on the introduction of measures to encourage improvements in the safety and health at work of pregnant workers and workers who have recently given birth or are breastfeeding and Directive 96/34/EC on the framework agreement on parental leave concluded by UNICE, CEEP and the ETUC. It is also based on Article 8 (protection of maternity) of the European Social Charter and draws on Article 27 (right of workers with family responsibilities to equal opportunities and equal treatment) of the revised Social Charter. 'Maternity' covers the period from conception to weaning.

Explanation on Article 34 – Social security and social assistance

The principle set out in Article 34(1) is based on Articles 153 and 156 of the Treaty on the Functioning of the European Union, Article 12 of the European Social Charter and point 10 of the [Union] Charter on the rights of workers. The Union must respect it when exercising the powers conferred on it by Articles 153 and 156 of the Treaty on the Functioning of the European Union. The reference to social services relates to cases in which such services have been introduced to provide certain advantages but does not imply that such services must be created where they do not exist. 'Maternity' must be understood in the same sense as in the preceding Article.

Paragraph 2 is based on Articles 12(4) and 13(4) of the European Social Charter and point 2 of the [Union] Charter of the Fundamental Social Rights of Workers and reflects the rules arising from Regulation (EEC) No 1408/71 and Regulation (EEC) No 1612/68.

Paragraph 3 draws on Article 13 of the European Social Charter and Articles 30 and 31 of the revised Social Charter and point 10 of the [Union] Charter. The Union must respect it in the context of policies based on Article 153 of the Treaty on the Functioning of the European Union.

Explanation on Article 35 – Health care
The principles set out in this Article are based on Article 152 of the EC Treaty, now replaced by Article 168 of the Treaty on the Functioning of the European Union, and on Articles 11 and 13 of the European Social Charter. The second sentence of the Article takes over Article 168(1).

Explanation on Article 36 – Access to services of general economic interest
This Article is fully in line with Article 14 of the Treaty on the Functioning of the European Union and does not create any new right. It merely sets out the principle of respect by the Union for the access to services of general economic interest as provided for by national provisions, when those provisions are compatible with Union law.

Explanation on Article 37 – Environmental protection
The principles set out in this Article have been based on Articles 2, 6 and 174 of the EC Treaty, which have now been replaced by Article 3(3) of the Treaty on European Union and Articles 11 and 191 of the Treaty on the Functioning of the European Union.
It also draws on the provisions of some national constitutions.

Explanation on Article 38 – Consumer protection
The principles set out in this Article have been based on Article 169 of the Treaty on the Functioning of the European Union.

TITLE V CITIZENS' RIGHTS

Explanation on Article 39 – Right to vote and to stand as a candidate at elections to the European Parliament
Article 39 applies under the conditions laid down in the Treaties, in accordance with Article 52(2) of the Charter. Article 39(1) corresponds to the right guaranteed in Article 20(2) of the Treaty on the Functioning of the European Union (cf. also the legal base in Article 22 of the Treaty on the Functioning of the European Union for the adoption of detailed arrangements for the exercise of that right) and Article 39(2) corresponds to Article 14(3) of the Treaty on European Union. Article 39(2) takes over the basic principles of the electoral system in a democratic State.

Explanation on Article 40 – Right to vote and to stand as a candidate at municipal elections
This Article corresponds to the right guaranteed by Article 20(2) of the Treaty on the Functioning of the European Union (cf. also the legal base in Article 22 of the Treaty on the Functioning of the European Union for the adoption of detailed arrangements for the exercise of that right). In accordance with Article 52(2) of the Charter, it applies under the conditions defined in these Articles in the Treaties.

Explanation on Article 41 – Right to good administration
Article 41 is based on the existence of the Union as subject to the rule of law whose characteristics were developed in the case-law which enshrined inter alia good administration

as a general principle of law (see inter alia Court of Justice judgment of 31 March 1992 in Case C-255/90 P *Burban* [1992] ECR I-2253, and Court of First Instance judgments of 18 September 1995 in Case T-167/94 *Nölle* [1995] ECR II-2589, and 9 July 1999 in Case T-231/97 *New Europe Consulting and others* [1999] ECR II-2403). The wording for that right in the first two paragraphs results from the case-law (Court of Justice judgment of 15 October 1987 in Case 222/86 *Heylens* [1987] ECR 4097, paragraph 15 of the grounds, judgment of 18 October 1989 in Case 374/87 *Orkem* [1989] ECR 3283, judgment of 21 November 1991 in Case C-269/90 *TU München* [1991] ECR I-5469, and Court of First Instance judgments of 6 December 1994 in Case T-450/93 *Lisrestal* [1994] ECR II-1177, 18 September 1995 in Case T-167/94 *Nölle* [1995] ECR II-2589) and the wording regarding the obligation to give reasons comes from Article 296 of the Treaty on the Functioning of the European Union (cf. also the legal base in Article 298 of the Treaty on the Functioning of the European Union for the adoption of legislation in the interest of an open, efficient and independent European administration).

Paragraph 3 reproduces the right now guaranteed by Article 340 of the Treaty on the Functioning of the European Union. Paragraph 4 reproduces the right now guaranteed by Article 20(2)(d) and Article 25 of the Treaty on the Functioning of the European Union. In accordance with Article 52(2) of the Charter, those rights are to be applied under the conditions and within the limits defined by the Treaties.

The right to an effective remedy, which is an important aspect of this question, is guaranteed in Article 47 of this Charter.

Explanation on Article 42 – Right of access to documents

The right guaranteed in this Article has been taken over from Article 255 of the EC Treaty [now Article 15(3) TFEU], on the basis of which Regulation (EC) No. 1049/2001 has subsequently been adopted. The European Convention has extended this right to documents of institutions, bodies and agencies generally, regardless of their form (see Article 15(3) of the Treaty on the Functioning of the European Union). In accordance with Article 52(2) of the Charter, the right of access to documents is exercised under the conditions and within the limits for which provision is made in Article 15(3) of the Treaty on the Functioning of the European Union.

Explanation on Article 43 – European Ombudsman

The right guaranteed in this Article is the right guaranteed by Articles 20 and 228 of the Treaty on the Functioning of the European Union. In accordance with Article 52(2) of the Charter, it applies under the conditions defined in these two Articles.

Explanation on Article 44 – Right to petition

The right guaranteed in this Article is the right guaranteed by Articles 20 and 227 of the Treaty on the Functioning of the European Union. In accordance with Article 52(2) of the Charter, it applies under the conditions defined in these two Articles.

Explanation on Article 45 – Freedom of movement and of residence

The right guaranteed by paragraph 1 is the right guaranteed by Article 20(2)(a) of the Treaty on the Functioning of the European Union (cf. also the legal base in Article 21; and the judgment of the Court of Justice of 17 September 2002, Case C-413/99 *Baumbast*

[2002] ECR I-7091). In accordance with Article 52(2) of the Charter, those rights are to be applied under the conditions and within the limits defined by the Treaties.

Paragraph 2 refers to the power granted to the Union by Articles 77, 78 and 79 of the Treaty on the Functioning of the European Union. Consequently, the granting of this right depends on the institutions exercising that power.

Explanation on Article 46 – Diplomatic and consular protection
The right guaranteed in this Article is the right guaranteed by Article 20 of the Treaty on the Functioning of the European Union (cf. also the legal base in Article 23). In accordance with Article 52(2) of the Charter, it applies under the conditions defined in these two Articles.

TITLE VI JUSTICE

Explanation on Article 47 – Right to an effective remedy and to a fair trial
The first paragraph is based on Article 13 of the ECHR:
'Everyone whose rights and freedoms as set forth in this Convention are violated shall have an effective remedy before a national authority notwithstanding that the violation has been committed by persons acting in an official capacity.'
However, in Union law the protection is more extensive since it guarantees the right to an effective remedy before a court. The Court of Justice enshrined that right in its judgment of 15 May 1986 as a general principle of Union law (Case 222/84 *Johnston* [1986] ECR 1651; see also judgment of 15 October 1987, Case 222/86 *Heylens* [1987] ECR 4097 and judgment of 3 December 1992, Case C-97/91 *Borelli* [1992] ECR I-6313). According to the Court, that general principle of Union law also applies to the

Member States when they are implementing Union law. The inclusion of this precedent in the Charter has not been intended to change the system of judicial review laid down by the Treaties, and particularly the rules relating to admissibility for direct actions before the Court of Justice of the European Union. The European Convention has considered the Union's system of judicial review including the rules on admissibility, and confirmed them while amending them as to certain aspects, as reflected in Articles 251 to 281 of the Treaty on the Functioning of the European Union, and in particular in the fourth paragraph of Article 263. Article 47 applies to the institutions of the Union and of Member States when they are implementing Union law and does so for all rights guaranteed by Union law.

The second paragraph corresponds to Article 6(1) of the ECHR which reads as follows:
'In the determination of his civil rights and obligations or of any criminal charge against him, everyone is entitled to a fair and public hearing within a reasonable time by an independent and impartial tribunal established by law. Judgment shall be pronounced publicly but the press and public may be excluded from all or part of the trial in the interests of morals, public order or national security in a democratic society, where the interests of juveniles or the protection of the private life of the parties so require, or to the extent strictly necessary in the opinion of the court in special circumstances where publicity would prejudice the interests of justice.'
In Union law, the right to a fair hearing is not confined to disputes relating to civil law rights and obligations. That is one of the consequences of the fact that the Union is a

community based on the rule of law as stated by the Court in Case 294/83, 'Les Verts' v European Parliament (judgment of 23 April 1986, [1986] ECR 1339). Nevertheless, in all respects other than their scope, the guarantees afforded by the ECHR apply in a similar way to the Union.

With regard to the third paragraph, it should be noted that in accordance with the case-law of the European Court of Human Rights, provision should be made for legal aid where the absence of such aid would make it impossible to ensure an effective remedy (ECHR judgment of 9 October 1979, Airey, Series A, Volume 32, p. 11). There is also a system of legal assistance for cases before the Court of Justice of the European Union.

Explanation on Article 48 – Presumption of innocence and right of defence
Article 48 is the same as Article 6(2) and (3) of the ECHR, which reads as follows:

'2. Everyone charged with a criminal offence shall be presumed innocent until proved guilty according to law.

3. Everyone charged with a criminal offence has the following minimum rights:
    (a) to be informed promptly, in a language which he understands and in detail, of the nature and cause of the accusation against him;
    (b) to have adequate time and facilities for the preparation of his defence;
    (c) to defend himself in person or through legal assistance of his own choosing or, if he has not sufficient means to pay for legal assistance, to be given it free when the interests of justice so require;
    (d) to examine or have examined witnesses against him and to obtain the attendance and examination of witnesses on his behalf under the same conditions as witnesses against him;
    (e) to have the free assistance of an interpreter if he cannot understand or speak the language used in court.'

In accordance with Article 52(3), this right has the same meaning and scope as the right guaranteed by the ECHR.

Explanation on Article 49 – Principles of legality and proportionality of criminal offences and penalties
This Article follows the traditional rule of the non-retroactivity of laws and criminal sanctions. There has been added the rule of the retroactivity of a more lenient penal law, which exists in a number of Member States and which features in Article 15 of the Covenant on Civil and Political Rights.

Article 7 of the ECHR is worded as follows:

'1. No one shall be held guilty of any criminal offence on account of any act or omission which did not constitute a criminal offence under national or international law at the time when it was committed. Nor shall a heavier penalty be imposed than the one that was applicable at the time the criminal offence was committed.

2. This Article shall not prejudice the trial and punishment of any person for any act or omission which, at the time when it was committed, was criminal according to the general principles of law recognised by civilised nations.'

In paragraph 2, the reference to 'civilised' nations has been deleted; this does not change the meaning of this paragraph, which refers to crimes against humanity in particular.

In accordance with Article 52(3), the right guaranteed here therefore has the same meaning and scope as the right guaranteed by the ECHR.

Paragraph 3 states the general principle of proportionality between penalties and criminal offences which is enshrined in the common constitutional traditions of the Member States and in the case-law of the Court of Justice of the [European Union].

Explanation on Article 50 – Right not to be tried or punished twice in criminal proceedings for the same criminal offence

Article 4 of Protocol No 7 to the ECHR reads as follows:

'1. No one shall be liable to be tried or punished again in criminal proceedings under the jurisdiction of the same State for an offence for which he has already been finally acquitted or convicted in accordance with the law and penal procedure of that State.

2. The provisions of the preceding paragraph shall not prevent the reopening of the case in accordance with the law and the penal procedure of the State concerned, if there is evidence of new or newly discovered facts, or if there has been a fundamental defect in the previous proceedings, which could affect the outcome of the case.

3. No derogation from this Article shall be made under Article 15 of the Convention.'

The '*non bis in idem*' rule applies in Union law (see, among the many precedents, the judgment of 5 May 1966, Joined Cases 18/65 and 35/65 *Gutmann v Commission* [1966] ECR 149 and a recent case, the decision of the Court of First Instance of 20 April 1999, Joined Cases T-305/94 and others *Limburgse Vinyl Maatschappij NV v Commission* [1999] ECR II-931). The rule prohibiting cumulation refers to cumulation of two penalties of the same kind, that is to say criminal-law penalties.

In accordance with Article 50, the '*non bis in idem*' rule applies not only within the jurisdiction of one State but also between the jurisdictions of several Member States. That corresponds to the *acquis* in Union law; see Articles 54 to 58 of the Schengen Convention and the judgment of the Court of Justice of 11 February 2003, C-187/01 *Gözütok* [2003] ECR I-1345, Article 7 of the Convention on the Protection of the European [Union's] Financial Interests and Article 10 of the Convention on the fight against corruption. The very limited exceptions in those Conventions permitting the Member States to derogate from the '*non bis in idem*' rule are covered by the horizontal clause in Article 52(1) of the Charter concerning limitations. As regards the situations referred to by Article 4 of Protocol No 7, namely the application of the principle within the same Member State, the guaranteed right has the same meaning and the same scope as the corresponding right in the ECHR.

TITLE VII GENERAL PROVISIONS GOVERNING THE INTERPRETATION AND APPLICATION OF THE CHARTER

Explanation on Article 51 – Field of application

The aim of Article 51 is to determine the scope of the Charter. It seeks to establish clearly that the Charter applies primarily to the institutions and bodies of the Union, in compliance with the principle of subsidiarity. This provision was drafted in keeping with Article 6(2) of the Treaty on European Union, which required the Union to respect fundamental rights, and with the mandate issued by the Cologne European Council. The term 'institutions' is enshrined in the Treaties. The expression 'bodies, offices and agencies' is commonly used in the Treaties to refer to all the authorities set up by the Treaties or by secondary legislation (see, e.g., Articles 15 or 16 of the Treaty on the Functioning of the European Union).

As regards the Member States, it follows unambiguously from the case-law of the Court of Justice that the requirement to respect fundamental rights defined in the context of the Union is only binding on the Member States when they act in the scope of Union law (judgment of 13 July 1989, Case 5/88 *Wachauf* [1989] ECR 2609; judgment of 18 June 1991, Case C-260/89 *ERT* [1991] ECR I-2925; judgment of 18 December 1997, Case C-309/96 *Annibaldi* [1997] ECR I-7493). The Court of Justice confirmed this case-law in the following terms: 'In addition, it should be remembered that the requirements flowing from the protection of fundamental rights in the [Union] legal order are also binding on Member States when they implement [Union] rules ... ' (judgment of 13 April 2000, Case C-292/97 [2000] ECR I-2737, paragraph 37 of the grounds). Of course this rule, as enshrined in this Charter, applies to the central authorities as well as to regional or local bodies, and to public organisations, when they are implementing Union law.

Paragraph 2, together with the second sentence of paragraph 1, confirms that the Charter may not have the effect of extending the competences and tasks which the Treaties confer on the Union. Explicit mention is made here of the logical consequences of the principle of subsidiarity and of the fact that the Union only has those powers which have been conferred upon it. The fundamental rights as guaranteed in the Union do not have any effect other than in the context of the powers determined by the Treaties. Consequently, an obligation, pursuant to the second sentence of paragraph 1, for the Union's institutions to promote principles laid down in the Charter may arise only within the limits of these same powers.

Paragraph 2 also confirms that the Charter may not have the effect of extending the field of application of Union law beyond the powers of the Union as established in the Treaties. The Court of Justice has already established this rule with respect to the fundamental rights recognised as part of Union law (judgment of 17 February 1998, C-249/96 *Grant* [1998] ECR I-621, paragraph 45 of the grounds). In accordance with this rule, it goes without saying that the reference to the Charter in Article 6 of the Treaty on European Union cannot be understood as extending by itself the range of Member State action considered to be 'implementation of Union law' (within the meaning of paragraph 1 and the above-mentioned case-law).

Explanation on Article 52 – Scope and interpretation of rights and principles

The purpose of Article 52 is to set the scope of the rights and principles of the Charter, and to lay down rules for their interpretation. Paragraph 1 deals with the arrangements for the limitation of rights. The wording is based on the case-law of the Court of Justice: ' ... it is well established in the case-law of the Court that restrictions may be imposed on the exercise of fundamental rights, in particular in the context of a common organisation of the market, provided that those restrictions in fact correspond to objectives of general interest pursued by the [Union] and do not constitute, with regard to the aim pursued, disproportionate and unreasonable interference undermining the very substance of those rights' (judgment of 13 April 2000, Case C-292/97, paragraph 45 of the grounds). The reference to general interests recognised by the Union covers both the objectives mentioned in Article 3 of the Treaty on European Union and other interests protected by specific provisions of the Treaties such as Article 4(1) of the Treaty on European Union and Articles 35(3), 36 and 346 of the Treaty on the Functioning of the European Union.

Paragraph 2 refers to rights which were already expressly guaranteed in the Treaty establishing the European Community and have been recognised in the Charter, and which are now found in the Treaties (notably the rights derived from Union citizenship). It clarifies that such rights remain subject to the conditions and limits applicable to the Union law on which they are based, and for which provision is made in the Treaties. The Charter does not alter the system of rights conferred by the EC Treaty and taken over by the Treaties.

Paragraph 3 is intended to ensure the necessary consistency between the Charter and the ECHR by establishing the rule that, in so far as the rights in the present Charter also correspond to rights guaranteed by the ECHR, the meaning and scope of those rights, including authorised limitations, are the same as those laid down by the ECHR. This means in particular that the legislator, in laying down limitations to those rights, must comply with the same standards as are fixed by the detailed limitation arrangements laid down in the ECHR, which are thus made applicable for the rights covered by this paragraph, without thereby adversely affecting the autonomy of Union law and of that of the Court of Justice of the European Union.

The reference to the ECHR covers both the Convention and the Protocols to it. The meaning and the scope of the guaranteed rights are determined not only by the text of those instruments, but also by the case-law of the European Court of Human Rights and by the Court of Justice of the European Union. The last sentence of the paragraph is designed to allow the Union to guarantee more extensive protection. In any event, the level of protection afforded by the Charter may never be lower than that guaranteed by the ECHR.

The Charter does not affect the possibilities of Member States to avail themselves of Article 15 ECHR, allowing derogations from ECHR rights in the event of war or of other public dangers threatening the life of the nation, when they take action in the areas of national defence in the event of war and of the maintenance of law and order, in accordance with their responsibilities recognised in Article 4(1) of the Treaty on European Union and in Articles 72 and 347 of the Treaty on the Functioning of the European Union.

The list of rights which may at the present stage, without precluding developments in the law, legislation and the Treaties, be regarded as corresponding to rights in the ECHR within the meaning of the present paragraph is given hereafter. It does not include rights additional to those in the ECHR.

1. Articles of the Charter where both the meaning and the scope are the same as the corresponding Articles of the ECHR:
   — Article 2 corresponds to Article 2 of the ECHR,
   — Article 4 corresponds to Article 3 of the ECHR,
   — Article 5(1) and (2) corresponds to Article 4 of the ECHR,
   — Article 6 corresponds to Article 5 of the ECHR,
   — Article 7 corresponds to Article 8 of the ECHR,
   — Article 10(1) corresponds to Article 9 of the ECHR,
   — Article 11 corresponds to Article 10 of the ECHR without prejudice to any restrictions which Union law may impose on Member States' right to introduce the licensing arrangements referred to in the third sentence of Article 10(1) of the ECHR,

— Article 17 corresponds to Article 1 of the Protocol to the ECHR,
— Article 19(1) corresponds to Article 4 of Protocol No 4,
— Article 19(2) corresponds to Article 3 of the ECHR as interpreted by the European Court of Human Rights,
— Article 48 corresponds to Article 6(2) and(3) of the ECHR,
— Article 49(1) (with the exception of the last sentence) and (2) correspond to Article 7 of the ECHR.

2. Articles where the meaning is the same as the corresponding Articles of the ECHR, but where the scope is wider:
— Article 9 covers the same field as Article 12 of the ECHR, but its scope may be extended to other forms of marriage if these are established by national legislation,
— Article 12(1) corresponds to Article 11 of the ECHR, but its scope is extended to European Union level,
— Article 14(1) corresponds to Article 2 of the Protocol to the ECHR, but its scope is extended to cover access to vocational and continuing training,
— Article 14(3) corresponds to Article 2 of the Protocol to the ECHR as regards the rights of parents,
— Article 47(2) and (3) corresponds to Article 6(1) of the ECHR, but the limitation to the determination of civil rights and obligations or criminal charges does not apply as regards Union law and its implementation,
— Article 50 corresponds to Article 4 of Protocol No 7 to the ECHR, but its scope is extended to European Union level between the Courts of the Member States,
— Finally, citizens of the European Union may not be considered as aliens in the scope of the application of Union law, because of the prohibition of any discrimination on grounds of nationality. The limitations provided for by Article 16 of the ECHR as regards the rights of aliens therefore do not apply to them in this context.

The rule of interpretation contained in paragraph 4 has been based on the wording of Article 6(3) of the Treaty on European Union and takes due account of the approach to common constitutional traditions followed by the Court of Justice (e.g., judgment of 13 December 1979, Case 44/79 *Hauer* [1979] ECR 3727; judgment of 18 May 1982, Case 155/79 *AM&S* [1982] ECR 1575). Under that rule, rather than following a rigid approach of 'a lowest common denominator', the Charter rights concerned should be interpreted in a way offering a high standard of protection which is adequate for the law of the Union and in harmony with the common constitutional traditions.

Paragraph 5 clarifies the distinction between 'rights' and 'principles' set out in the Charter. According to that distinction, subjective rights shall be respected, whereas principles shall be observed (Article 51(1)). Principles may be implemented through legislative or executive acts (adopted by the Union in accordance with its powers, and by the Member States only when they implement Union law); accordingly, they become significant for the Courts only when such acts are interpreted or reviewed. They do not however give rise to direct claims for positive action by the Union's institutions or Member States' authorities. This is consistent both with case-law of the Court of Justice (cf. notably case-law on the 'precautionary principle' in Article 191(2) of the Treaty on the Functioning of the European Union: judgment of the CFI of 11 September 2002, Case T-13/99 *Pfizer v Council*, with numerous references to earlier case-law; and a series of judgments on Article 33 (ex-39) on the principles of agricultural law, e.g. judgment of the Court of Justice in Case 265/85 *Van den Berg* [1987] ECR 1155: scrutiny of the principle of market stabilisation and of reasonable expectations) and with the approach of the Member States' constitutional systems to 'principles', particularly in the field of social law. For illustration, examples for principles, recognised in the Charter include e.g. Articles 25, 26 and 37. In some cases, an Article of the Charter may contain both elements of a right and of a principle, e.g. Articles 23, 33 and 34.

Paragraph 6 refers to the various Articles in the Charter which, in the spirit of subsidiarity, make reference to national laws and practices.

Explanation on Article 53 – Level of protection

This provision is intended to maintain the level of protection currently afforded within their respective scope by Union law, national law and international law. Owing to its importance, mention is made of the ECHR.

Explanation on Article 54 – Prohibition of abuse of rights

This Article corresponds to Article 17 of the ECHR:

'Nothing in this Convention may be interpreted as implying for any State, group or person any right to engage in any activity or perform any act aimed at the destruction of any of the rights and freedoms set forth herein or at their limitation to a greater extent than is provided for in the Convention.'

4

PART II
Union Secondary Law: Legislation and Other Acts

5

1976 Act Concerning the Election of the Members of the European Parliament by Direct Universal Suffrage

Article 1

1. In each Member State, members of the European Parliament shall be elected on the basis of proportional representation, using the list system or the single transferable vote.
2. Member States may authorise voting based on a preferential list system in accordance with the procedure they adopt.
3. Elections shall be by direct universal suffrage and shall be free and secret.

Article 2

In accordance with its specific national situation, each Member State may establish constituencies for elections to the European Parliament or subdivide its electoral area in a different manner, without generally affecting the proportional nature of the voting system.

Article 3

Member States may set a minimum threshold for the allocation of seats. At national level this threshold may not exceed 5 per cent of votes cast.

Article 4

Each Member State may set a ceiling for candidates' campaign expenses.

Article 5

1. The five-year term for which members of the European Parliament are elected shall begin at the opening of the first session following each election.
   It may be extended or curtailed pursuant to the second subparagraph of Article 10(2).
2. The term of office of each member shall begin and end at the same time as the period referred to in paragraph 1.

Article 6

1. Members of the European Parliament shall vote on an individual and personal basis. They shall not be bound by any instructions and shall not receive a binding mandate.
2. Members of the European Parliament shall enjoy the privileges and immunities applicable to them by virtue of the Protocol of 8 April 1965 on the privileges and immunities of the European [Union].

Article 7

1. The office of member of the European Parliament shall be incompatible with that of:
   — member of the government of a Member State,

— member of the Commission of the European [Union],
— Judge, Advocate-General or Registrar of the Court of Justice of the European [Union] or of the Court of First Instance,
— member of the Board of Directors of the European Central Bank,
— member of the Court of Auditors of the European [Union],
— Ombudsman of the European [Union],
— member of the Economic and Social Committee of the European [Union] and of the European Atomic Energy Community,
— member of the Committee of the Regions,
— member of committees or other bodies set up pursuant to the Treaties [on the Functioning of the European Union] and the European Atomic Energy Community for the purposes of managing the [Union's] funds or carrying out a permanent direct administrative task,
— member of the Board of Directors, Management Committee or staff of the European Investment Bank,
— active official or servant of the institutions of the European [Union] or of the specialised bodies attached to them or of the European Central Bank.

2. From the European Parliament elections in 2004, the office of member of the European Parliament shall be incompatible with that of member of a national parliament.

By way of derogation from that rule and without prejudice to paragraph 3:
— members of the Irish National Parliament who are elected to the European Parliament at a subsequent poll may have a dual mandate until the next election to the Irish National Parliament, at which juncture the first subparagraph of this paragraph shall apply;
— members of the United Kingdom Parliament who are also members of the European Parliament during the five-year term preceding election to the European Parliament in 2004 may have a dual mandate until the 2009 European Parliament elections, when the first subparagraph of this paragraph shall apply.

3. In addition, each Member State may, in the circumstances provided for in Article 8, extend rules at national level relating to incompatibility.

4. Members of the European Parliament to whom paragraphs 1, 2 and 3 become applicable in the course of the five-year period referred to in Article 5 shall be replaced in accordance with Article 13.

Article 8

Subject to the provisions of this Act, the electoral procedure shall be governed in each Member State by its national provisions.

These national provisions, which may if appropriate take account of the specific situation in the Member States, shall not affect the essentially proportional nature of the voting system.

Article 9

No one may vote more than once in any election of members of the European Parliament.

Article 10

1. Elections to the European Parliament shall be held on the date and at the times fixed by each Member State; for all Member States this date shall fall within the same period starting on a Thursday morning and ending on the following Sunday.

2. Member States may not officially make public the results of their count until after the close of polling in the Member State whose electors are the last to vote within the period referred to in paragraph 1.

Article 11

1. The Council, acting unanimously after consulting the European Parliament, shall determine the electoral period for the first elections.
2. Subsequent elections shall take place in the corresponding period in the last year of the five-year period referred to in Article 5.

   Should it prove impossible to hold the elections in the [Union] during that period, the Council acting unanimously shall, after consulting the European Parliament, determine, at least one year before the end of the five-year term referred to in Article 5, another electoral period which shall not be more than two months before or one month after the period fixed pursuant to the preceding subparagraph.
3. Without prejudice to Article [229 of the Treaty on the Functioning of the European Union] and Article 109 of the Treaty establishing the European Atomic Energy Community, the European Parliament shall meet, without requiring to be convened, on the first Tuesday after expiry of an interval of one month from the end of the electoral period.
4. The powers of the European Parliament shall cease upon the opening of the first sitting of the new European Parliament.

Article 12

The European Parliament shall verify the credentials of members of the European Parliament. For this purpose it shall take note of the results declared officially by the Member States and shall rule on any disputes which may arise out of the provisions of this Act other than those arising out of the national provisions to which the Act refers.

Article 13

1. A seat shall fall vacant when the mandate of a member of the European Parliament ends as a result of resignation, death or withdrawal of the mandate.
2. Subject to the other provisions of this Act, each Member State shall lay down appropriate procedures for filling any seat which falls vacant during the five-year term of office referred to in Article 5 for the remainder of that period.
3. Where the law of a Member State makes explicit provision for the withdrawal of the mandate of a member of the European Parliament, that mandate shall end pursuant to those legal provisions. The competent national authorities shall inform the European Parliament thereof.
4. Where a seat falls vacant as a result of resignation or death, the President of the European Parliament shall immediately inform the competent authorities of the Member State concerned thereof.

Article 14

Should it appear necessary to adopt measures to implement this Act, the Council, acting unanimously on a proposal from the European Parliament after consulting the Commission, shall adopt such measures after endeavouring to reach agreement with the

European Parliament in a conciliation committee consisting of the Council and representatives of the European Parliament.

Article 15

This Act is drawn up in the Danish, Dutch, English, Finnish, French, German, Greek, Irish, Italian, Portuguese, Spanish and Swedish languages, all the texts being equally authentic.

Annexes I and II shall form an integral part of this Act.

Article 16

The provisions of this Act shall enter into force on the first day of the month following that during which the last of the notifications referred to in the Decision is received.

ANNEX I

The United Kingdom will apply the provisions of this Act only in respect of the United Kingdom.

ANNEX II DECLARATION ON ARTICLE 14

As regards the procedure to be followed by the Conciliation Committee, it is agreed to have recourse to the provisions of paragraphs 5, 6 and 7 of the procedure laid down in the joint declaration of the European Parliament, the Council and the Commission of 4 March 1975.

5

6

Regulation 1141/2014 on the Statute and Funding of European Political Parties and European Political Foundations

Contents

THE EUROPEAN PARLIAMENT AND THE COUNCIL OF THE EUROPEAN UNION,

Having regard to the Treaty on the Functioning of the European Union, and in particular Article 224 thereof …

Acting in accordance with the ordinary legislative procedure …

HAVE ADOPTED THIS REGULATION:

Chapter I General Provisions

Article 1
Subject matter

This Regulation lays down the conditions governing the statute and funding of political parties at European level ('European political parties') and political foundations at European level ('European political foundations').

Article 2
Definitions

For the purposes of this Regulation:

(1) 'political party' means an association of citizens:
   — which pursues political objectives, and
   — which is either recognised by, or established in accordance with, the legal order of at least one Member State;

(2) 'political alliance' means structured cooperation between political parties and/or citizens;

(3) 'European political party' means a political alliance which pursues political objectives and is registered with the Authority for European political parties and foundations established in Article 6, in accordance with the conditions and procedures laid down in this Regulation;

(4) 'European political foundation' means an entity which is formally affiliated with a European political party, which is registered with the Authority in accordance with the conditions and procedures laid down in this Regulation, and which through its activities, within the aims and fundamental values pursued by the Union, underpins and complements the objectives of the European political party by performing one or more of the following tasks:

 (a) observing, analysing and contributing to the debate on European public policy issues and on the process of European integration;

 (b) developing activities linked to European public policy issues, such as organising and supporting seminars, training, conferences and studies on such issues between relevant stakeholders, including youth organisations and other representatives of civil society;

 (c) developing cooperation in order to promote democracy, including in third countries;

 (d) serving as a framework for national political foundations, academics, and other relevant actors to work together at European level;

(5) 'regional parliament' or 'regional assembly' means a body whose members either hold a regional electoral mandate or are politically accountable to an elected assembly;

(6) 'funding from the general budget of the European Union' means a grant awarded in accordance with Title VI of Part One or a contribution awarded in accordance with Title VIII of Part Two of Regulation (EU, Euratom) No. 966/2012 of the European Parliament and of the Council ('the Financial Regulation');

(7) 'donation' means any cash offering, any offering in kind, the provision below market value of any goods, services (including loans) or works, and/or any other transaction which constitutes an economic advantage for the European political party or the European political foundation concerned, with the exception of contributions from members and of usual political activities carried out on a voluntary basis by individuals;

(8) 'contribution from members' means any payment in cash, including membership fees, or any contribution in kind, or the provision below market value of any goods, services (including loans) or works, and/or any other transaction which constitutes an economic advantage for the European political party or the European political foundation concerned, when provided to that European political party or to that European political foundation by one of its members, with the exception of usual political activities carried out on a voluntary basis by individual members;

(9) 'annual budget' for the purposes of Articles 20 and 27 means the total amount of expenditure in a given year as reported in the annual financial statements of the European political party or of the European political foundation concerned;

(10) 'National Contact Point' means one of the liaison points designated for issues related to the central exclusion database referred to in Article 108 of the Financial Regulation and in Article 144 of Commission Delegated Regulation (EU) No.

1268/2012, or any other person or persons specifically designated by the relevant authorities in the Member States for the purpose of exchanging information in the application of this Regulation;

(11) 'seat' means the location where the European political party or the European political foundation has its central administration;

(12) 'concurrent infringements' means two or more infringements committed as part of the same unlawful act;

(13) 'repeated infringement' means an infringement committed within five years of a sanction having been imposed on its perpetrator for the same type of infringement.

Chapter II Statute for European Political Parties and European Political Foundations

Article 3
Conditions for registration

1. A political alliance shall be entitled to apply to register as a European political party subject to the following conditions:

   (a) it must have its seat in a Member State as indicated in its statutes;

   (b) it or its members must be, or be represented by, in at least one quarter of the Member States, members of the European Parliament, of national parliaments, of regional parliaments or of regional assemblies, or
   it or its member parties must have received, in at least one quarter of the Member States, at least three per cent of the votes cast in each of those Member States at the most recent elections to the European Parliament;

   (c) it must observe, in particular in its programme and in its activities, the values on which the Union is founded, as expressed in Article 2 TEU, namely respect for human dignity, freedom, democracy, equality, the rule of law and respect for human rights, including the rights of persons belonging to minorities;

   (d) it or its members must have participated in elections to the European Parliament, or have expressed publicly the intention to participate in the next elections to the European Parliament; and

   (e) it must not pursue profit goals.

2. An applicant shall be entitled to apply to register as a European political foundation subject to the following conditions:

   (a) it must be affiliated with a European political party registered in accordance with the conditions and procedures laid down in this Regulation;

   (b) it must have its seat in a Member State as indicated in its statutes;

   (c) it must observe, in particular in its programme and in its activities, the values on which the Union is founded, as expressed in Article 2 TEU, namely respect for human dignity, freedom, democracy, equality, the rule of law and respect for human rights, including the rights of persons belonging to minorities;

   (d) its objectives must complement the objectives of the European political party with which it is formally affiliated;

   (e) its governing body must be composed of members from at least one quarter of the Member States; and

   (f) it must not pursue profit goals.

3. A European political party can have only one formally affiliated European political foundation. Each European political party and the affiliated European political foundation shall ensure a separation between their respective day-to-day management, governing structures and financial accounts.

Article 4
Governance of European political parties

1. The statutes of a European political party shall comply with the applicable law of the Member State in which it has its seat and shall include provisions covering at least the following:

   (a) its name and logo, which must be clearly distinguishable from those of any existing European political party or European political foundation;

   (b) the address of its seat;

   (c) a political programme setting out its purpose and objectives;

   (d) a statement, in conformity with point (e) of Article 3(1), that it does not pursue profit goals;

   (e) where relevant, the name of its affiliated political foundation and a description of the formal relationship between them;

   (f) its administrative and financial organisation and procedures, specifying in particular the bodies and offices holding the powers of administrative, financial and legal representation and the rules on the establishment, approval and verification of annual accounts; and

   (g) the internal procedure to be followed in the event of its voluntary dissolution as a European political party.

2. The statutes of a European political party shall include provisions on internal party organisation covering at least the following:

   (a) the modalities for the admission, resignation and exclusion of its members, the list of its member parties being annexed to the statutes;

   (b) the rights and duties associated with all types of membership and the relevant voting rights;

   (c) the powers, responsibilities and composition of its governing bodies, specifying for each the criteria for the selection of candidates and the modalities for their appointment and dismissal;

   (d) its internal decision-making processes, in particular the voting procedures and quorum requirements;

   (e) its approach to transparency, in particular in relation to bookkeeping, accounts and donations, privacy and the protection of personal data; and

   (f) the internal procedure for amending its statutes.

3. The Member State of the seat may impose additional requirements for the statutes, provided those additional requirements are not inconsistent with this Regulation.

Article 5
Governance of European political foundations

1. The statutes of a European political foundation shall comply with the applicable law of the Member State in which it has its seat and shall include provisions covering at least the following:

(a) its name and logo, which must be clearly distinguishable from those of any existing European political party or European political foundation;

(b) the address of its seat;

(c) a description of its purpose and objectives, which must be compatible with the tasks listed in point (4) of Article 2;

(d) a statement, in conformity with point (f) of Article 3(2), that it does not pursue profit goals;

(e) the name of the European political party with which it is directly affiliated, and a description of the formal relationship between them;

(f) a list of its bodies, specifying for each its powers, responsibilities and composition, and including the modalities for the appointment and dismissal of the members and managers of such bodies;

(g) its administrative and financial organisation and procedures, specifying in particular the bodies and offices holding the powers of administrative, financial and legal representation and the rules on the establishment, approval and verification of annual accounts;

(h) the internal procedure for amending its statutes; and

(i) the internal procedure to be followed in the event of its voluntary dissolution as a European political foundation.

2. The Member State of the seat may impose additional requirements for the statutes, provided those additional requirements are not inconsistent with this Regulation.

Article 6
Authority for European political parties and European political foundations

1. An Authority for European political parties and European political foundations (the 'Authority') is hereby established for the purpose of registering, controlling and imposing sanctions on European political parties and European political foundations in accordance with this Regulation.

2. The Authority shall have legal personality. It shall be independent and shall exercise its functions in full compliance with this Regulation.

   The Authority shall decide on the registration and de-registration of European political parties and European political foundations in accordance with the procedures and conditions laid down in this Regulation. In addition, the Authority shall regularly verify that the registration conditions laid down in Article 3 and the governance provisions set out in accordance with points (a), (b) and (d) to (f) of Article 4(1) and in points (a) to (e) and (g) of Article 5(1) continue to be complied with by the registered European political parties and European political foundations.

   In its decisions, the Authority shall give full consideration to the fundamental right of freedom of association and to the need to ensure pluralism of political parties in Europe. The Authority shall be represented by its Director who shall take all decisions of the Authority on its behalf.

3. The Director of the Authority shall be appointed for a five-year non-renewable term by the European Parliament, the Council and the Commission (jointly referred to as the 'appointing authority') by common accord, on the basis of proposals made by a selection committee composed of the Secretaries-General of those institutions following an open call for candidates.

The Director of the Authority shall be selected on the basis of his or her personal and professional qualities. He or she shall not be a member of the European Parliament, hold any electoral mandate or be a current or former employee of a European political party or a European political foundation. The Director selected shall not have a conflict of interests between his or her duty as Director of the Authority and any other official duties, in particular in relation to the application of the provisions of this Regulation.

A vacancy caused by resignation, retirement, dismissal or death shall be filled in accordance with the same procedure.

In the event of a normal replacement or voluntary resignation the Director shall continue his or her functions until a replacement has taken up his or her duties.

If the Director of the Authority no longer fulfils the conditions required for the performance of his or her duties, he or she may be dismissed by common accord by at least two of the three institutions referred to in the first subparagraph and on the basis of a report drawn up by the selection committee referred to in the first subparagraph on its own initiative or following a request from any of the three institutions.

The Director of the Authority shall be independent in the performance of his or her duties. When acting on behalf of the Authority, the Director shall neither seek nor take instructions from any institution or government or from any other body, office or agency. The Director of the Authority shall refrain from any act which is incompatible with the nature of his or her duties.

The European Parliament, the Council and the Commission shall exercise jointly, with regard to the Director, the powers conferred on the appointing authority by the Staff Regulations of Officials (and the Conditions of Employment of Other Servants of the Union) laid down in Council Regulation (EEC, Euratom, ECSC) No. 259/68. Without prejudice to decisions on appointment and dismissal, the three institutions may agree to entrust the exercise of some or all of the remaining powers conferred on the appointing authority to any one of them.

The appointing authority may assign the Director to other tasks provided that such tasks are not incompatible with the workload resulting from his or her duties as Director of the Authority and are not liable to create any conflict of interests or to jeopardise the full independence of the Director.

4. The Authority shall be physically located in the European Parliament, which shall provide the Authority with the necessary offices and administrative support facilities.

5. The Director of the Authority shall be assisted by staff from one or more institutions of the Union. When working for the Authority, such staff shall act under the sole authority of the Director of the Authority.

The selection of the staff shall not be liable to result in a conflict of interests between their duties at the Authority and any other official duties, and they shall refrain from any act which is incompatible with the nature of their duties.

6. The Authority shall conclude agreements with the European Parliament and, if appropriate, with other institutions on any administrative arrangements necessary to enable it to carry out its tasks, in particular agreements regarding the staff, services and support provided pursuant to paragraphs 4, 5 and 8.

7. The appropriations for the expenditure of the Authority shall be provided under a separate Title in the Section for the European Parliament in the general budget of the European Union. The appropriations shall be sufficient to ensure the full and independent operation of the Authority. A draft budgetary plan for the Authority shall be submitted to the European Parliament by the Director, and shall be made public. The European Parliament shall delegate the duties of Authorising Officer with respect to those appropriations to the Director of the Authority.

8. Council Regulation No. 1 shall apply to the Authority.

   The translation services required for the functioning of the Authority and the Register shall be provided by the Translation Centre for the Bodies of the European Union.

9. The Authority and the Authorising Officer of the European Parliament shall share all information necessary for the execution of their respective responsibilities under this Regulation.

10. The Director shall submit annually a report to the European Parliament, the Council and the Commission on the activities of the Authority.

11. The Court of Justice of the European Union shall review the legality of the decisions of the Authority in accordance with Article 263 TFEU and shall have jurisdiction in disputes relating to compensation for damage caused by the Authority in accordance with Articles 268 and 340 TFEU. Should the Authority fail to take a decision where it is required to do so by this Regulation, proceedings for failure to act may be brought before the Court of Justice of the European Union in accordance with Article 265 TFEU.

Article 7
Register of European political parties and foundations

1. The Authority shall establish and manage a Register of European political parties and European political foundations. Information from the Register shall be available online in accordance with Article 32.

2. In order to ensure the proper functioning of the Register, the Commission shall be empowered to adopt delegated acts in accordance with Article 36 and within the scope of the relevant provisions of this Regulation concerning:

   (a) the information and supporting documents held by the Authority for which the Register is to be the competent repository, which shall include the statutes of a European political party or European political foundation, any other documents submitted as part of an application for registration in accordance with Article 8(2), any documents received from the Member State of the seat as referred to in Article 15(2), and information on the identity of the persons who are members of bodies or hold offices that are vested with powers of administrative, financial and legal representation, as referred to in point (f) of Article 4(1) and point (g) of Article 5(1);

   (b) materials from the Register as referred to in point (a) of this paragraph for which the Register is to be competent to certify legality as established by the Authority pursuant to its competences under this Regulation. The Authority shall not be competent to verify compliance by a European political party or European political foundation with any obligation or requirement imposed on the party or foundation in question by the Member State of the seat pursuant to Articles 4, 5 and Article 14(2) which is additional to the obligations and requirements laid down by this Regulation.

3. The Commission shall by implementing acts specify the details of the registration number system to be applied for the Register and standard extracts from the Register to be made available to third parties upon request, including the content of letters and documents. Such extracts shall not include personal data other than the identity of the persons who are members of bodies or hold offices that are vested with powers of administrative, financial and legal representation, as referred to in point (f) of Article 4(1) and point (g) of Article 5(1). Those implementing acts shall be adopted in accordance with the examination procedure referred to in Article 37.

Article 8
Application for registration

1. An application for registration shall be filed with the Authority. An application for registration as a European political foundation shall be filed only through the European political party with which the applicant is formally affiliated.
2. The application shall be accompanied by:
   (a) documents proving that the applicant satisfies the conditions laid down in Article 3, including a standard formal declaration in the form set out in the Annex;
   (b) the statutes of the party or foundation, containing the provisions required by Articles 4 and 5, including the relevant annexes and, where applicable, the statement of the Member State of the seat referred to in Article 15(2).
3. The Commission shall be empowered to adopt delegated acts in accordance with Article 36 and within the scope of the relevant provisions of this Regulation:
   (a) to identify any supplementary information or supporting document in relation to paragraph 2 necessary to allow the Authority to fully discharge its responsibilities under this Regulation in relation to the operation of the Register;
   (b) to amend the standard formal declaration in the Annex in respect of the particulars to be filled in by the applicant where necessary, in order to ensure that sufficient information is being held in relation to the signatory, his or her mandate and the European political party or European political foundation which he or she is mandated to represent for the purposes of the declaration.
4. Documentation submitted to the Authority as part of the application shall be published immediately on the website referred to in Article 32.

Article 9
Examination of the application and decision of the Authority

1. The application shall be examined by the Authority in order to determine whether the applicant satisfies the conditions for registration laid down in Article 3 and whether the statutes contain the provisions required by Articles 4 and 5.
2. The Authority shall adopt a decision to register the applicant, unless it establishes that the applicant does not satisfy the conditions for registration laid down in Article 3 or that the statutes do not contain the provisions required by Articles 4 and 5.

   The Authority shall publish its decision to register the applicant within one month following receipt of the application for registration or, where the procedures set out in Article 15(4) are applicable, within four months following receipt of the application for registration.

Where an application is incomplete, the Authority shall ask the applicant without delay to submit any additional information required. For the purposes of the deadline laid down in the second subparagraph, time shall only start to run from the date of receipt by the Authority of a complete application.

3. The standard formal declaration referred to in point (a) of Article 8(2) shall be considered sufficient for the Authority to ascertain that the applicant complies with the conditions specified in point (c) of Article 3(1) or point (c) of Article 3(2), whichever is applicable.

4. A decision of the Authority to register an applicant shall be published in the *Official Journal of the European Union*, together with the statutes of the party or foundation concerned. A decision not to register an applicant shall be published in the *Official Journal of the European Union*, together with the detailed grounds for rejection.

5. Any amendments to the documents or statutes submitted as part of the application for registration in accordance with Article 8(2) shall be notified to the Authority, which shall update the registration in accordance with the procedures set out in Article 15(2) and (4), mutatis mutandis.

6. The updated list of member parties of a European political party, annexed to the party statutes in accordance with Article 4(2), shall be sent to the Authority each year. Any changes following which the European political party might no longer satisfy the condition laid down in point (b) of Article 3(1) shall be communicated to the Authority within four weeks of any such change.

Article 10
Verification of compliance with registration conditions and requirements

1. Without prejudice to the procedure laid down in paragraph 3, the Authority shall regularly verify that the conditions for registration laid down in Article 3, and the governance provisions set out in points (a), (b) and (d) to (f) of Article 4(1) and points (a) to (e) and (g) of Article 5(1), continue to be complied with by registered European political parties and European political foundations.

2. If the Authority finds that any of the conditions for registration or governance provisions referred to in paragraph 1, with the exception of the conditions in point (c) of Article 3(1) and point (c) of Article 3(2), are no longer complied with, it shall notify the European political party or foundation concerned.

3. The European Parliament, the Council or the Commission may lodge with the Authority a request for verification of compliance by a specific European political party or European political foundation with the conditions laid down in point (c) of Article 3(1) and point (c) of Article 3(2). In such cases, and in the cases referred to in point (a) of Article 16(3), the Authority shall ask the committee of independent eminent persons established by Article 11 for an opinion on the subject. The committee shall give its opinion within two months.

Where the Authority becomes aware of facts which may give rise to doubts concerning compliance by a specific European political party or European political foundation with the conditions laid down in point (c) of Article 3(1) and point (c) of Article 3(2), it shall inform the European Parliament, the Council and the Commission with a view to allowing any of them to lodge a request for verification as referred to in the first subparagraph. Without prejudice to the first subparagraph, the European Parliament, the Council and the Commission shall indicate their intention within two months of receiving that information.

The procedures laid down in the first and second subparagraphs shall not be initiated within a period of two months prior to elections to the European Parliament.

Having regard to the committee's opinion, the Authority shall decide whether to de-register the European political party or European political foundation concerned. The decision of the Authority shall be duly reasoned.

A decision of the Authority to de-register on grounds of non-compliance with the conditions set out in point (c) of Article 3(1) or point (c) of Article 3(2) may only be adopted in the event of manifest and serious breach of those conditions. It shall be subject to the procedure set out in paragraph 4.

4. A decision of the Authority to de-register a European political party or foundation on the ground of a manifest and serious breach as regards compliance with the conditions set out in point (c) of Article 3(1) or point (c) of Article 3(2) shall be communicated to the European Parliament and the Council. The decision shall enter into force only if no objection is expressed by the European Parliament and the Council within a period of three months of the communication of the decision to the European Parliament and the Council or if, before the expiry of that period, the European Parliament and the Council have both informed the Authority that they will not object. In the event of an objection by the European Parliament and by the Council, the European political party or foundation shall remain registered.

The European Parliament and the Council may object to the decision only on grounds related to the assessment of compliance with the conditions for registration set out in point (c) of Article 3(1) and point (c) of Article 3(2).

The European political party or European political foundation concerned shall be informed that objections have been raised to the decision of the Authority to de-register it.

The European Parliament and the Council shall adopt a position in accordance with their respective decision-making rules as established in conformity with the Treaties. Any objection shall be duly reasoned and shall be made public.

5. A decision of the Authority to de-register a European political party or a European political foundation, to which no objections have been raised under the procedure laid down in paragraph 4, shall be published in the *Official Journal of the European Union*, together with the detailed grounds for de-registration, and shall enter into force three months following the date of such publication.

6. A European political foundation shall automatically forfeit its status as such if the European political party with which it is affiliated is removed from the Register.

Article 11
Committee of independent eminent persons

1. A committee of independent eminent persons is hereby established. It shall consist of six members, with the European Parliament, the Council and the Commission each appointing two members. The members of the committee shall be selected on the basis of their personal and professional qualities. They shall neither be members of the European Parliament, the Council or the Commission, nor hold any electoral mandate, be officials or other servants of the European Union or be

current or former employees of a European political party or a European political foundation.

Members of the committee shall be independent in the performance of their duties. They shall neither seek nor take instructions from any institution or government or from any other body, office or agency, and shall refrain from any act which is incompatible with the nature of their duties.

The committee shall be renewed within six months after the end of the first session of the European Parliament following each election to the European Parliament. The mandate of the members shall not be renewable.

2. The committee shall adopt its own rules of procedure. The chair of the committee shall be elected by its members from amongst their number in accordance with those rules. The secretariat and funding of the committee shall be provided by the European Parliament. The secretariat of the committee shall act under the sole authority of the committee.

3. When requested by the Authority, the committee shall give an opinion on any possible manifest and serious breach of the values on which the Union is founded, as referred to in point (c) of Article 3(1) and point (c) of Article 3(2), by a European political party or a European political foundation. To that end, the committee may request any relevant document and evidence from the Authority, the European Parliament, the European political party or European political foundation concerned, other political parties, political foundations or other stakeholders, and it may request to hear their representatives.

In its opinions, the committee shall give full consideration to the fundamental right of freedom of association and to the need to ensure pluralism of political parties in Europe.

The opinions of the committee shall be made public without delay.

Chapter III Legal Status of European Political Parties and European Political Foundations

Article 12
Legal personality
European political parties and European political foundations shall have European legal personality.

Article 13
Legal recognition and capacity
European political parties and European political foundations shall enjoy legal recognition and capacity in all Member States.

Article 14
Applicable law
1. European political parties and European political foundations shall be governed by this Regulation.
2. For matters not regulated by this Regulation or, where matters are only partly regulated by it, for those aspects which are not covered by it, European political parties

and European political foundations shall be governed by the applicable provisions of national law in the Member State in which they have their respective seats.

Activities carried out by European political parties and European political foundations in other Member States shall be governed by the relevant national laws of those Member States.

3. For matters not regulated by this Regulation or by the applicable provisions pursuant to paragraph 2 or, where matters are only partly regulated by them, for those aspects which are not covered by them, European political parties and European political foundations shall be governed by the provisions of their respective statutes.

Article 15
Acquisition of European legal personality

1. A European political party or a European political foundation shall acquire European legal personality on the date of publication in the *Official Journal of the European Union* of the decision of the Authority to register it, pursuant to Article 9.
2. If the Member State in which an applicant for registration as a European political party or a European political foundation has its seat so requires, the application submitted pursuant to Article 8 shall be accompanied by a statement issued by that Member State, certifying that the applicant has complied with all relevant national requirements for application, and that its statutes are in conformity with the applicable law referred to in the first subparagraph of Article 14(2).
3. Where the applicant enjoys legal personality under the law of a Member State, the acquisition of European legal personality shall be regarded by that Member State as a conversion of the national legal personality into a successor European legal personality. The latter shall fully maintain any pre-existing rights and obligations of the former national legal entity, which shall cease to exist as such. The Member States concerned shall not apply prohibitive conditions in the context of such conversion. The applicant shall maintain its seat in the Member State concerned until a decision in accordance with Article 9 has been published.
4. If the Member State in which the applicant has its seat so requires, the Authority shall fix the date of the publication referred to in paragraph 1 only after consultation with that Member State.

Article 16
Termination of European legal personality

1. A European political party or a European political foundation shall lose its European legal personality upon the entry into force of a decision of the Authority to remove it from the Register as published in the *Official Journal of the European Union*. The decision shall enter into force three months after such publication unless the European political party or the European political foundation concerned requests a shorter period.
2. A European political party or a European political foundation shall be removed from the Register by a decision of the Authority:
   (a) as a consequence of a decision adopted pursuant to Article 10(2) to (5);
   (b) in the circumstances provided for in Article 10(6);

(c) at the request of the European political party or European political foundation concerned; or

(d) in the cases referred to in point (b) of the first subparagraph of paragraph 3 of this Article.

3. If a European political party or a European political foundation has seriously failed to fulfil relevant obligations under national law applicable by virtue of the first subparagraph of Article 14(2), the Member State of the seat may address to the Authority a duly reasoned request for de-registration which must identify precisely and exhaustively the illegal actions and the specific national requirements that have not been complied with. In such cases, the Authority shall:

(a) for matters relating exclusively or predominantly to elements affecting respect for the values on which the Union is founded, as expressed in Article 2 TEU, initiate a verification procedure in accordance with Article 10(3). Article 10(4), (5) and (6) shall also apply;

(b) for any other matter, and when the reasoned request of the Member State concerned confirms that all national remedies have been exhausted, decide to remove the European political party or European political foundation concerned from the Register.

If a European political party or a European political foundation has seriously failed to fulfil relevant obligations under national law applicable by virtue of the second subparagraph of Article 14(2), and if the matter relates exclusively or predominantly to elements affecting respect of the values on which the Union is founded, as expressed in Article 2 TEU, the Member State concerned may address a request to the Authority in accordance with the provisions of the first subparagraph of this paragraph. The Authority shall proceed in accordance with point (a) of the first subparagraph of this paragraph.

In all cases, the Authority shall act without undue delay. The Authority shall inform the Member State concerned and the European political party or European political foundation concerned of the follow-up given to the reasoned request for de-registration.

4. The Authority shall fix the date of the publication referred to in paragraph 1 after consultation with the Member State in which the European political party or European political foundation has its seat.

5. If the European political party or European political foundation concerned acquires legal personality under the law of the Member State of its seat, such acquisition shall be regarded by that Member State as a conversion of the European legal personality into a national legal personality that fully maintains the pre-existing rights and obligations of the former European legal entity. The Member State in question shall not apply prohibitive conditions in the context of such conversion.

6. If the European political party or European political foundation does not acquire legal personality under the law of the Member State of its seat, it shall be wound up in accordance with the applicable law of that Member State. The Member State concerned may require that such winding-up be preceded by the acquisition by the party or foundation concerned of national legal personality in accordance with paragraph 5.

7. In all situations referred to in paragraphs 5 and 6, the Member State concerned shall ensure that the not-for-profit condition laid down in Article 3 is fully respected. The

Authority and the Authorising Officer of the European Parliament may agree with the Member State concerned the modalities for termination of the European legal personality, in particular in order to ensure the recovery of any funds received from the general budget of the European Union and the payment of any financial sanctions imposed in accordance with Article 27.

Chapter IV Funding Provisions

Article 17
Funding conditions

1. A European political party which is registered in accordance with the conditions and procedures laid down in this Regulation, which is represented in the European Parliament by at least one of its members, and which is not in one of the situations of exclusion referred to in Article 106(1) of the Financial Regulation may apply for funding from the general budget of the European Union, in accordance with the terms and conditions published by the Authorising Officer of the European Parliament in a call for contributions.

2. A European political foundation which is affiliated with a European political party eligible to apply for funding under paragraph 1, which is registered in accordance with the conditions and procedures laid down in this Regulation, and which is not in one of the situations of exclusion referred to in Article 106(1) of the Financial Regulation may apply for funding from the general budget of the European Union, in accordance with the terms and conditions published by the Authorising Officer of the European Parliament in a call for proposals.

3. For the purposes of determining eligibility for funding from the general budget of the European Union in accordance with paragraph 1 of this Article and point (b) of Article 3(1), and for the application of Article 19(1), a member of the European Parliament shall be considered as a member of only one European political party, which shall, where relevant, be the one to which his or her national or regional political party is affiliated on the final date for the submission of applications for funding.

4. Financial contributions or grants from the general budget of the European Union shall not exceed 85 % of the annual reimbursable expenditure indicated in the budget of a European political party and 85 % of the eligible costs incurred by a European political foundation. European political parties may use any unused part of the Union contribution awarded to cover reimbursable expenditure within the financial year following its award. Amounts still unused after that financial year shall be recovered in accordance with the Financial Regulation.

5. Within the limits set out in Articles 21 and 22, the expenditure reimbursable through a financial contribution shall include administrative expenditure and expenditure linked to technical assistance, meetings, research, cross-border events, studies, information and publications, as well as expenditure linked to campaigns.

Article 18
Application for funding

1. In order to receive funding from the general budget of the European Union, a European political party or European political foundation which satisfies the conditions of

Article 17(1) or (2) shall file an application with the European Parliament following a call for contributions or proposals.

2. The European political party and the European political foundation must, at the time of its application, comply with the obligations listed in Article 23, and, from the date of its application until the end of the financial year or of the action covered by the contribution or grant, remain registered in the Register and may not be the subject of any of the sanctions provided for in Article 27(1) and in points (a)(v) and (vi) of Article 27(2).

3. A European political foundation shall include in its application its annual work programme or action plan.

4. The Authorising Officer of the European Parliament shall adopt a decision within three months after closure of the call for contributions or call for proposals, and shall authorise and manage the corresponding appropriations in accordance with the Financial Regulation.

5. A European political foundation may apply for funding from the general budget of the European Union only through the European political party with which it is affiliated.

Article 19

Award criteria and distribution of funding

1. The respective appropriations available to those European political parties and European political foundations which have been awarded contributions or grants in accordance with Article 18 shall be distributed annually on the basis of the following distribution key:
   - 15 % shall be distributed in equal shares among the beneficiary European political parties,
   - 85 % shall be distributed in proportion to their share of elected members of the European Parliament among the beneficiary European political parties.

   The same distribution key shall be used to award funding to European political foundations, on the basis of their affiliation with a European political party.

2. The distribution referred to in paragraph 1 shall be based on the number of elected members of the European Parliament who are members of the applicant European political party on the final date for the submission of applications for funding, taking into account Article 17(3).

   After that date, any changes to the number shall not affect the respective share of funding between European political parties or European political foundations. This is without prejudice to the requirement in Article 17(1) for a European political party to be represented in the European Parliament by at least one of its members.

Article 20

Donations and contributions

1. European political parties and European political foundations may accept donations from natural or legal persons of up to a value of EUR 18 000 per year and per donor.

2. European political parties and European political foundations shall, at the time of the submission of their annual financial statements in accordance with Article 23, also transmit a list of all donors with their corresponding donations, indicating both the nature and the value of the individual donations. This paragraph shall also apply to

contributions made by member parties of European political parties and member organisations of European political foundations.

For donations from natural persons the value of which exceeds EUR 1 500 and is below or equal to EUR 3 000, the European political party or European political foundation concerned shall indicate whether the corresponding donors have given their prior written consent to publication in accordance with point (e) of Article 32(1).

3. Donations received by European political parties and European political foundations within six months prior to elections to the European Parliament shall be reported on a weekly basis to the Authority in writing and in accordance with paragraph 2.

4. Single donations the value of which exceeds EUR 12 000 that have been accepted by European political parties and European political foundations shall be immediately reported to the Authority in writing and in accordance with paragraph 2.

5. European political parties and European political foundations shall not accept any of the following:

   (a) anonymous donations or contributions;

   (b) donations from the budgets of political groups in the European Parliament;

   (c) donations from any public authority from a Member State or a third country, or from any undertaking over which such a public authority may exercise, directly or indirectly, a dominant influence by virtue of its ownership of it, its financial participation therein, or the rules which govern it; or

   (d) donations from any private entities based in a third country or from individuals from a third country who are not entitled to vote in elections to the European Parliament.

6. Any donation that is not permitted under this Regulation shall within 30 days following the date of its receipt by a European political party or a European political foundation:

   (a) be returned to the donor or to any person acting on the donor's behalf; or

   (b) where it is not possible to return it, be reported to the Authority and the European Parliament. The Authorising Officer of the European Parliament shall establish the amount receivable and authorise the recovery in accordance with the provisions laid down in Articles 78 and 79 of the Financial Regulation. The funds shall be entered as general revenue in the European Parliament section of the general budget of the European Union.

7. Contributions to a European political party from its members shall be permitted. The value of such contributions shall not exceed 40 % of the annual budget of that European political party.

8. Contributions to a European political foundation from its members, and from the European political party with which it is affiliated, shall be permitted. The value of such contributions shall not exceed 40 % of the annual budget of that European political foundation and may not derive from funds received by a European political party pursuant to this Regulation from the general budget of the European Union.

The burden of proof shall rest with the European political party concerned, which shall clearly indicate in its accounts the origin of funds used to finance its affiliated European political foundation.

9. Without prejudice to paragraphs 7 and 8, European political parties and European political foundations may accept from citizens who are their members contributions

up to a value of EUR 18 000 per year and per member, where such contributions are made by the member concerned on his or her own behalf.

The ceiling laid down in the first subparagraph shall not apply where the member concerned is also an elected member of the European Parliament, of a national parliament or of a regional parliament or regional assembly.

10. Any contribution that is not permitted under this Regulation shall be returned in accordance with paragraph 6.

Article 21
Financing of campaigns in the context of elections to the European Parliament

1. Subject to the second subparagraph, the funding of European political parties from the general budget of the European Union or from any other source may be used to finance campaigns conducted by the European political parties in the context of elections to the European Parliament in which they or their members participate as required by point (d) of Article 3(1).

   In accordance with Article 8 of the Act concerning the election of the members of the European Parliament by direct universal suffrage, the funding and possible limitation of election expenses for all political parties, candidates and third parties in, in addition to their participation in, elections to the European Parliament is governed in each Member State by national provisions.

2. Expenditure linked to the campaigns referred to in paragraph 1 shall be clearly identified as such by the European political parties in their annual financial statements.

Article 22
Prohibition of funding

1. Notwithstanding Article 21(1), the funding of European political parties from the general budget of the European Union or from any other source shall not be used for the direct or indirect funding of other political parties, and in particular national parties or candidates. Those national political parties and candidates shall continue to be governed by national rules.

2. The funding of European political foundations from the general budget of the European Union or from any other source shall not be used for any other purpose than for financing their tasks as listed in point (4) of Article 2 and to meet expenditure directly linked to the objectives set out in their statutes in accordance with Article 5. It shall in particular not be used for the direct or indirect funding of elections, political parties, or candidates or other foundations.

3. The funding of European political parties and European political foundations from the general budget of the European Union or from any other source shall not be used to finance referendum campaigns.

Chapter V Control and Sanctions

Article 23
Accounts, reporting and audit obligations

1. At the latest within six months following the end of the financial year, European political parties and European political foundations shall submit to the Authority, with

a copy to the Authorising Officer of the European Parliament and to the competent National Contact Point of the Member State of their seat:

(a) their annual financial statements and accompanying notes, covering their revenue and expenditure, assets and liabilities at the beginning and at the end of the financial year, in accordance with the law applicable in the Member State in which they have their seat and their annual financial statements on the basis of the international accounting standards defined in Article 2 of Regulation (EC) No. 1606/2002 of the European Parliament and of the Council;

(b) an external audit report on the annual financial statements, covering both the reliability of those financial statements and the legality and regularity of their revenue and expenditure, carried out by an independent body or expert; and

(c) the list of donors and contributors and their corresponding donations or contributions reported in accordance with Article 20(2), (3) and (4).

2. Where expenditure is implemented by European political parties jointly with national political parties or by European political foundations jointly with national political foundations, or with other organisations, evidence of the expenditure incurred by the European political parties or by the European political foundations directly or through those third parties shall be included in the annual financial statements referred to in paragraph 1.

3. The independent external bodies or experts referred to in point (b) of paragraph 1 shall be selected, mandated and paid by the European Parliament. They shall be duly authorised to audit accounts under the law applicable in the Member State in which they have their seat or establishment.

4. European political parties and European political foundations shall provide any information requested by the independent bodies or experts for the purpose of their audit.

5. The independent bodies or experts shall inform the Authority and the Authorising Officer of the European Parliament of any suspected illegal activity, fraud or corruption which may harm the financial interests of the Union. The Authority and the Authorising Officer of the European Parliament shall inform the National Contact Points concerned thereof.

Article 24
General rules on control

1. Control of compliance by European political parties and European political foundations with their obligations under this Regulation shall be exercised, in cooperation, by the Authority, by the Authorising Officer of the European Parliament and by the competent Member States.

2. The Authority shall control compliance by European political parties and European political foundations with their obligations under this Regulation, in particular in relation to Article 3, points (a), (b), and (d) to (f) of Article 4(1), points (a) to (e) and (g) of Article 5(1), Article 9(5) and (6), and Articles 20, 21 and 22.

The Authorising Officer of the European Parliament shall control compliance by European political parties and European political foundations with the obligations relating to Union funding under this Regulation in accordance with the Financial Regulation. In carrying out such controls, the European Parliament shall take the necessary measures in the fields of the prevention of and the fight against fraud affecting the financial interests of the Union.

3. The control by the Authority and by the Authorising Officer of the European Parliament referred to in paragraph 2 shall not extend to compliance by European political parties and European political foundations with their obligations under applicable national law as referred to in Article 14.

4. European political parties and European political foundations shall provide any information requested by the Authority, the Authorising Officer of the European Parliament, the Court of Auditors, the European Anti-Fraud Office (OLAF) or Member States which is necessary for the purpose of carrying out the controls for which they are responsible under this Regulation.

    Upon request and for the purpose of controlling compliance with Article 20, European political parties and European political foundations shall provide the Authority with information concerning contributions made by individual members and the identity of such members. Moreover, where appropriate, the Authority may require European political parties to provide signed confirmatory statements from members holding elected mandates for the purpose of controlling compliance with the condition laid down in the first subparagraph of point (b) of Article 3(1).

Article 25
Implementation and control in respect of Union funding

1. Appropriations for the funding of European political parties and European political foundations shall be determined under the annual budgetary procedure and shall be implemented in accordance with this Regulation and the Financial Regulation.

    The terms and conditions for contributions and grants shall be laid down by the Authorising Officer of the European Parliament in the call for contributions and the call for proposals.

2. Control of funding received from the general budget of the European Union and its use shall be exercised in accordance with the Financial Regulation.

    Control shall also be exercised on the basis of annual certification by an external and independent audit, as provided for in Article 23(1).

3. The Court of Auditors shall exercise its audit powers in accordance with Article 287 TFEU.

4. Any document or information required by the Court of Auditors in order to enable it to carry out its task shall be supplied to it at its request by the European political parties and the European political foundations that receive funding in accordance with this Regulation.

5. The contribution and grant decision or agreement shall expressly provide for auditing by the European Parliament and the Court of Auditors, on the basis of records and on the spot, of the European political party which has received a contribution or the European political foundation which has received a grant from the general budget of the European Union.

6. The Court of Auditors and the Authorising Officer of the European Parliament, or any other external body authorised by the Authorising Officer of the European Parliament, may carry out the necessary checks and verifications on the spot in order to verify the legality of expenditure and the proper implementation of the provisions of the

contribution and grant decision or agreement, and, in the case of European political foundations, the proper implementation of the work programme or action. The European political party or European political foundation in question shall supply any document or information needed to carry out this task.

7. OLAF may carry out investigations, including on-the-spot checks and inspections, in accordance with the provisions and procedures laid down in Regulation (EU, Euratom) No. 883/2013 of the European Parliament and of the Council and Council Regulation (Euratom, EC) No. 2185/96, with a view to establishing whether there has been fraud, corruption or any other illegal activity affecting the financial interests of the Union in connection with contributions or grants under this Regulation. If appropriate, its findings may give rise to recovery decisions by the Authorising Officer of the European Parliament.

Article 26

Technical support

All technical support provided by the European Parliament to European political parties shall be based on the principle of equal treatment. It shall be granted on conditions no less favourable than those granted to other external organisations and associations that may be accorded similar facilities and shall be supplied against invoice and payment.

Article 27

Sanctions

1. In accordance with Article 16, the Authority shall decide to remove a European political party or a European political foundation from the Register by way of sanction in any of the following situations:
   (a) where the party or foundation in question has been found by a judgment having the force of res judicata to have engaged in illegal activities detrimental to the financial interests of the Union as defined in Article 106(1) of the Financial Regulation;
   (b) where it is established, in accordance with the procedures set out in Article 10(2) to (5), that it no longer fulfils one or more of the conditions set out in points (a), (c) and (e) of Article 3(1) or in Article 3(2); or
   (c) where a request by a Member State for de-registration on grounds of serious failure to fulfil obligations under national law meets the requirements set out in point (b) of Article 16(3).

2. The Authority shall impose financial sanctions in the following situations:
   (a) non-quantifiable infringements:
      (i) in the event of non-compliance with the requirements of Article 9(5) or (6);
      (ii) in the event of non-compliance with the commitments entered into and the information provided by a European political party or European political foundation in accordance with points (a), (b) and (d) to (f) of Article 4(1) and with points (a), (b), (d) and (e) of Article 5(1);
      (iii) in the event of failure to transmit the list of donors and their corresponding donations in accordance with Article 20(2) or to report donations in accordance with Article 20(3) and (4);
      (iv) where a European political party or a European political foundation has infringed the obligations laid down in Article 23(1) or Article 24(4);

(v) where a European political party or a European political foundation has been found by a judgment having the force of res judicata to have engaged in illegal activities detrimental to the financial interests of the Union as defined in Article 106(1) of the Financial Regulation;

(vi) where the European political party or the European political foundation concerned has at any time intentionally omitted to provide information or has intentionally provided incorrect or misleading information, or where the bodies authorised by this Regulation to audit or conduct checks on the beneficiaries of funding from the general budget of the European Union detect inaccuracies in the annual financial statements which are regarded as constituting material omissions or misstatements of items in accordance with the international accounting standards defined in Article 2 of Regulation (EC) No. 1606/2002;

(b) quantifiable infringements:

(i) where a European political party or a European political foundation has accepted donations and contributions that are not permitted under Article 20(1) or (5), unless the conditions laid down in Article 20(6) are met;

(ii) in the event of non-compliance with the requirements laid down in Articles 21 and 22.

3. The Authorising Officer of the European Parliament may exclude a European political party or a European political foundation from future Union funding for up to five years, or up to 10 years in cases of an infringement repeated within a five-year period, when it has been found guilty of any of the infringements listed in points (v) and (vi) of point (a) of paragraph 2. This is without prejudice to the powers of the Authorising Officer of the European Parliament as set out in Article 204n of the Financial Regulation.

4. For the purposes of paragraphs 2 and 3, the following financial sanctions shall be imposed on a European political party or a European political foundation:

(a) in cases of non-quantifiable infringements, a fixed percentage of the annual budget of the European political party or European political foundation concerned:

— 5 %, or

— 7,5 % if there are concurrent infringements, or

— 20 % if the infringement in question is a repeated infringement, or

— a third of the percentages set out above if the European political party or European political foundation concerned has voluntarily declared the infringement before the Authority has officially opened an investigation, even in the case of a concurrent infringement or a repeated infringement, and the party or foundation concerned has taken the appropriate corrective measures,

— 50 % of the annual budget of the European political party or European political foundation concerned for the preceding year, when it has been found by a judgment having the force of res judicata to have engaged in illegal activities detrimental to the financial interests of the Union as defined in Article 106(1) of the Financial Regulation;

(b) in cases of quantifiable infringements, a fixed percentage of the amount of the irregular sums received or not reported in accordance with the following scale, up to a maximum of 10 % of the annual budget of the European political party or European political foundation concerned:

— 100 % of the irregular sums received or not reported where those sums do not exceed EUR 50 000, or

— 150 % of the irregular sums received or not reported where those sums exceed EUR 50 000 but do not exceed EUR 100 000, or

— 200 % of the irregular sums received or not reported where those sums exceed EUR 100 000 but do not exceed EUR 150 000, or

— 250 % of the irregular sums received or not reported where those sums exceed EUR 150 000 but do not exceed EUR 200 000, or

— 300 % of the irregular sums received or not reported where those sums exceed EUR 200 000, or

— one third of the percentages indicated above if the European political party or European political foundation concerned has voluntarily declared the infringement before the Authority and/or the Authorising Officer of the European Parliament has officially opened an investigation and the party or foundation concerned has taken the appropriate corrective measures.

For the application of the percentages indicated above, each donation or contribution shall be considered separately.

5. Whenever a European political party or a European political foundation has committed concurrent infringements of this Regulation, only the sanction laid down for the most serious infringement shall be imposed, unless otherwise provided in point (a) of paragraph 4.

6. The sanctions laid down in this Regulation shall be subject to a limitation period of five years from the date of commission of the infringement concerned or, in the case of continuing or repeated infringements, from the date on which those infringements ceased.

Article 28

Cooperation between the Authority, the Authorising Officer of the European Parliament and the Member States

1. The Authority, the Authorising Officer of the European Parliament and the Member States via the National Contact Points shall share information and keep each other regularly informed of matters related to funding provisions, controls and sanctions.

2. They shall also agree on practical arrangements for such exchange of information, including the rules regarding the disclosure of confidential information or evidence and the cooperation among Member States.

3. The Authorising Officer of the European Parliament shall inform the Authority of any findings which might give rise to the imposition of sanctions under Article 27(2) to (4), with a view to allowing the Authority to take appropriate measures.

4. The Authority shall inform the Authorising Officer of the European Parliament of any decision it has taken in relation to sanctions, in order to enable him or her to draw the appropriate consequences under the Financial Regulation.

Article 29

Corrective measures and principles of good administration

1. Before taking a final decision relating to any of the sanctions referred to in Article 27, the Authority or the Authorising Officer of the European Parliament shall give the European political party or the European political foundation concerned an opportunity to introduce the measures required to remedy the situation within a reasonable period of time, which shall not normally exceed one month. In particular, the

Authority or the Authorising Officer of the European Parliament shall allow the possibility of correcting clerical and arithmetical errors, providing additional documents or information where necessary or correcting minor mistakes.

2. Where a European political party or a European political foundation has failed to take corrective measures within the period of time referred to in paragraph 1, the appropriate sanctions referred to in Article 27 shall be decided.

3. Paragraphs 1 and 2 shall not apply in relation to the conditions set out in points (b) to (d) of Article 3(1) and in point (c) of Article 3(2).

Article 30
Recovery

1. On the basis of a decision of the Authority removing a European political party or a European political foundation from the Register, the Authorising Officer of the European Parliament shall withdraw or terminate any ongoing decision or agreement on Union funding, except in the cases provided for in point (c) of Article 16(2) and in points (b) and (d) of Article 3(1). He or she shall also recover any Union funding, including any unspent Union funds from previous years.

2. A European political party or European political foundation on which a sanction has been imposed for any of the infringements listed in Article 27(1) and in points (v) and (vi) of Article 27(2)(a) shall for that reason no longer be in compliance with Article 18(2). As a result, the Authorising Officer of the European Parliament shall terminate the contribution or grant agreement or decision on Union funding received under this Regulation and shall recover amounts unduly paid under the contribution or grant agreement or decision, including any unspent Union funds from previous years.

   In the event of such termination, payments by the Authorising Officer of the European Parliament shall be limited to the eligible expenditure actually incurred by the European political party or European political foundation up to the date when the termination decision takes effect.

   This paragraph shall also be applicable to the cases referred to in point (c) of Article 16(2) and in points (b) and (d) of Article 3(1).

Chapter VI Final Provisions

Article 31
Provision of information to citizens

Subject to Articles 21 and 22 and to their own statutes and internal processes, European political parties may, in the context of elections to the European Parliament, take all appropriate measures to inform citizens of the Union of the affiliations between national political parties and candidates and the European political parties concerned.

Article 32
Transparency

1. The European Parliament shall make public, under the authority of its Authorising Officer or under that of the Authority, on a website created for that purpose, the following:

(a) the names and statutes of all registered European political parties and European political foundations, together with the documents submitted as part of their applications for registration in accordance with Article 8, at the latest four weeks after the Authority has adopted its decision and, thereafter, any amendments notified to the Authority pursuant to Article 9(5) and (6);

(b) a list of applications that have not been approved, together with the documents submitted as part thereof, together with the application for registration in accordance with Article 8 and the grounds for rejection, at the latest four weeks after the Authority adopted its decision;

(c) an annual report with a table of the amounts paid to each European political party and European political foundation, for each financial year for which contributions have been received or grants have been paid from the general budget of the European Union;

(d) the annual financial statements and external audit reports referred to in Article 23(1), and, for European political foundations, the final reports on the implementation of the work programmes or actions;

(e) the names of donors and their corresponding donations reported by European political parties and European political foundations in accordance with Article 20(2), (3) and (4), with the exception of donations from natural persons the value of which does not exceed EUR 1 500 per year and per donor, which shall be reported as 'minor donations'. Donations from natural persons the annual value of which exceeds EUR 1 500 and is below or equal to EUR 3 000 shall not be published without the corresponding donor's prior written consent to their publication. If no such prior consent has been given, such donations shall be reported as 'minor donations'. The total amount of minor donations and the number of donors per calendar year shall also be published;

(f) the contributions referred to in Article 20(7) and (8) and reported by European political parties and European political foundations in accordance with Article 20(2), including the identity of the member parties or organisations which made those contributions;

(g) the details of and reasons for any final decisions taken by the Authority pursuant to Article 27, including, where relevant, any opinions adopted by the committee of independent eminent persons in accordance with Articles 10 and 11, having due regard to Regulation (EC) No. 45/2001;

(h) the details of and reasons for any final decision taken by the Authorising Officer of the European Parliament pursuant to Article 27;

(i) a description of the technical support provided to European political parties; and

(j) the evaluation report of the European Parliament on the application of this Regulation and on the funded activities referred to in Article 38.

2. The European Parliament shall make public the list of legal persons who are members of a European political party, as annexed to the party statutes in accordance with Article 4(2) and updated in accordance with Article 9(6), as well as the total number of individual members.

3. Personal data shall be excluded from publication on the website referred to in paragraph 1 unless those personal data are published pursuant to points (a), (e), or (g) of paragraph 1.

4. European political parties and European political foundations shall, in a publicly available privacy statement, provide potential members and donors with the information required by Article 10 of Directive 95/46/EC, and shall inform them that their personal data will be processed for auditing and control purposes by the European Parliament, the Authority, OLAF, the Court of Auditors, Member States, or external bodies or experts authorised thereby, and that their personal data will be made public on the website referred to in paragraph 1 under the conditions set out in this Article. The Authorising Officer of the European Parliament, in application of Article 11 of Regulation (EC) No. 45/2001, shall include the same information in calls for contributions or proposals as referred to in Article 18(1) of this Regulation.

Article 33
Protection of personal data

1. In processing personal data pursuant to this Regulation, the Authority, the European Parliament and the committee of independent eminent persons established by Article 11 shall comply with Regulation (EC) No. 45/2001. For the purposes of the processing of personal data, they shall be considered data controllers in accordance with point (d) of Article 2 of that Regulation.

2. In processing personal data pursuant to this Regulation, European political parties and European political foundations, Member States when exercising control over aspects relating to the financing of European political parties and European political foundations in accordance with Article 24, and the independent bodies or experts authorised to audit accounts in accordance with Article 23(1) shall comply with Directive 95/46/EC and with the national provisions adopted pursuant thereto. For the purposes of the processing of personal data, they shall be considered data controllers in accordance with point (d) of Article 2 of that Directive.

3. The Authority, the European Parliament and the committee of independent eminent persons established by Article 11 shall ensure that personal data collected by them pursuant to this Regulation are not used for any purpose other than to ensure the legality, regularity and transparency of the funding of European political parties and European political foundations and the membership of European political parties. They shall erase all personal data collected for that purpose at the latest 24 months after the publication of the relevant parts in accordance with Article 32.

4. The Member States and independent bodies or experts authorised to audit accounts shall use the personal data they receive only in order to exercise control over the financing of European political parties and European political foundations. They shall erase those personal data in accordance with applicable national law after transmission pursuant to Article 28.

5. Personal data may be retained beyond the time limits laid down in paragraph 3 or provided for by the applicable national law as referred to in paragraph 4 where such retention is necessary for the purposes of legal or administrative proceedings relating to the funding of a European political party or a European political foundation or the membership of a European political party. All such personal data shall be erased at the latest one week after the date of conclusion of the said proceedings by a final decision, or after any audits, appeals, litigation or claims have been disposed of.

6. The data controllers referred to in paragraphs 1 and 2 shall implement appropriate technical and organisational measures to protect personal data against accidental or unlawful destruction, accidental loss, alteration or unauthorised disclosure or access, in particular where the processing of such data involves their transmission over a network, and against all other unlawful forms of processing.

7. The European Data Protection Supervisor shall be responsible for monitoring and ensuring that the Authority, the European Parliament and the committee of independent eminent persons established by Article 11 respect and protect the fundamental rights and freedoms of natural persons in the processing of personal data pursuant to this Regulation. Without prejudice to any judicial remedy, any data subject may lodge a complaint with the European Data Protection Supervisor if he or she considers that his or her right to the protection of his or her personal data has been infringed as a result of the processing thereof by the Authority, the European Parliament or the committee.

8. European political parties and European political foundations, the Member States and the independent bodies or experts authorised to audit accounts under this Regulation shall be liable in accordance with applicable national law for any damage they cause in the processing of personal data pursuant to this Regulation. The Member States shall ensure that effective, proportionate and dissuasive sanctions are applied for infringements of this Regulation, of Directive 95/46/EC and of the national provisions adopted pursuant thereto, and in particular for the fraudulent use of personal data.

Article 34
Right to be heard
Before the Authority or the Authorising Officer of the European Parliament takes a decision which may adversely affect the rights of a European political party, a European political foundation or an applicant as referred to in Article 8, it shall hear the representatives of the European political party, European political foundation or applicant concerned. The Authority or the European Parliament shall duly state the reasons for its decision.

Article 35
Right of appeal
Decisions taken pursuant to this Regulation may be the subject of court proceedings before the Court of Justice of the European Union, in accordance with the relevant provisions of the TFEU.

Article 36
Exercise of the delegation
1. The power to adopt delegated acts is conferred on the Commission subject to the conditions laid down in this Article.
2. The power to adopt delegated acts referred to in Article 7(2) and Article 8(3) shall be conferred on the Commission for a period of five years from 24 November 2014. The Commission shall draw up a report in respect of the delegation of power not later than nine months before the end of the five-year period. The delegation of power shall be tacitly extended for periods of an identical duration, unless the European Parliament

or the Council opposes such extension not later than three months before the end of each period.

3. The delegation of power referred to in Article 7(2) and Article 8(3) may be revoked at any time by the European Parliament or by the Council. A decision to revoke shall put an end to the delegation of the power specified in that decision. It shall take effect the day following the publication of the decision in the *Official Journal of the European Union* or at a later date specified therein. It shall not affect the validity of any delegated acts already in force.

4. As soon as it adopts a delegated act, the Commission shall notify it simultaneously to the European Parliament and to the Council.

5. A delegated act adopted pursuant to Article 7(2) and Article 8(3) shall enter into force only if no objection has been expressed either by the European Parliament or the Council within a period of two months of notification of that act to the European Parliament and the Council or if, before the expiry of that period, the European Parliament and the Council have both informed the Commission that they will not object. That period shall be extended by two months at the initiative of the European Parliament or of the Council.

Article 37
Committee procedure

1. The Commission shall be assisted by a committee. That committee shall be a committee within the meaning of Regulation (EU) No. 182/2011.

2. Where reference is made to this paragraph, Article 5 of Regulation (EU) No. 182/2011 shall apply.

Article 38
Evaluation

The European Parliament shall, after consultation of the Authority, publish by mid-2018 a report on the application of this Regulation and on the activities funded. The report shall indicate, where appropriate, possible amendments to be made to the statute and funding systems.

Before the end of 2018, the Commission shall present a report on the application of this Regulation accompanied, if appropriate, by a legislative proposal to amend this Regulation.

Article 39
Effective application

Member States shall make such provision as is appropriate to ensure the effective application of this Regulation.

Article 40
Repeal

Regulation (EC) No. 2004/2003 is repealed with effect from the date of entry into force of this Regulation. It shall however continue to apply as regards acts and commitments relating to the funding of political parties and political foundations at European level for the 2014, 2015, 2016 and 2017 budget years.

Article 41

Entry into force and application

This Regulation shall enter into force on the twentieth day following that of its publication in the *Official Journal of the European Union*.

The Commission shall adopt delegated acts as referred to in Article 7(2) and in point (a) of Article 8(3) by no later than 1 July 2015.

This Regulation shall apply from 1 January 2017. The Authority referred to in Article 6 shall however be set up by 1 September 2016. European political parties and European political foundations registered after 1 January 2017 may only apply for funding under this Regulation for activities starting in the 2018 budget year or thereafter.

This Regulation shall be binding in its entirety and directly applicable in all Member States.

7

Regulation 182/2011 Laying Down the Rules and General Principles Concerning Mechanisms for Control by Member States of the Commission's Exercise of Implementing Powers (Comitology Regulation)

THE EUROPEAN PARLIAMENT AND THE COUNCIL OF THE EUROPEAN UNION,

Having regard to the Treaty on the Functioning of the European Union, and in particular Article 291(3) thereof,

Having regard to the proposal from the Commission,

After transmission of the draft legislative act to the national parliaments,

Acting in accordance with the ordinary legislative procedure...

HAVE ADOPTED THIS REGULATION:

Article 1

Subject-matter

This Regulation lays down the rules and general principles governing the mechanisms which apply where a legally binding Union act (hereinafter a 'basic act') identifies the need for uniform conditions of implementation and requires that the adoption of implementing acts by the Commission be subject to the control of Member States.

Article 2

Selection of procedures

1. A basic act may provide for the application of the advisory procedure or the examination procedure, taking into account the nature or the impact of the implementing act required.
2. The examination procedure applies, in particular, for the adoption of:
   (a) implementing acts of general scope[;]
   (b) other implementing acts relating to:
       (i) programmes with substantial implications;
       (ii) the common agricultural and common fisheries policies;
       (iii) the environment, security and safety, or protection of the health or safety, of humans, animals or plants;
       (iv) the common commercial policy;
       (v) taxation.
3. The advisory procedure applies, as a general rule, for the adoption of implementing acts not falling within the ambit of paragraph 2. However, the advisory procedure may apply for the adoption of the implementing acts referred to in paragraph 2 in duly justified cases.

Article 3

Common provisions

1. The common provisions set out in this Article shall apply to all the procedures referred to in Articles 4 to 8.

2. The Commission shall be assisted by a committee composed of representatives of the Member States. The committee shall be chaired by a representative of the Commission. The chair shall not take part in the committee vote.

3. The chair shall submit to the committee the draft implementing act to be adopted by the Commission.

   Except in duly justified cases, the chair shall convene a meeting not less than 14 days from submission of the draft implementing act and of the draft agenda to the committee. The committee shall deliver its opinion on the draft implementing act within a time limit which the chair may lay down according to the urgency of the matter. Time limits shall be proportionate and shall afford committee members early and effective opportunities to examine the draft implementing act and express their views.

4. Until the committee delivers an opinion, any committee member may suggest amendments and the chair may present amended versions of the draft implementing act.

   The chair shall endeavour to find solutions which command the widest possible support within the committee. The chair shall inform the committee of the manner in which the discussions and suggestions for amendments have been taken into account, in particular as regards those suggestions which have been largely supported within the committee.

5. In duly justified cases, the chair may obtain the committee's opinion by written procedure. The chair shall send the committee members the draft implementing act and shall lay down a time limit for delivery of an opinion according to the urgency of the matter. Any committee member who does not oppose the draft implementing act or who does not explicitly abstain from voting thereon before the expiry of that time limit shall be regarded as having tacitly agreed to the draft implementing act.

   Unless otherwise provided in the basic act, the written procedure shall be terminated without result where, within the time limit referred to in the first subparagraph, the chair so decides or a committee member so requests. In such a case, the chair shall convene a committee meeting within a reasonable time.

6. The committee's opinion shall be recorded in the minutes. Committee members shall have the right to ask for their position to be recorded in the minutes. The chair shall send the minutes to the committee members without delay.

7. Where applicable, the control mechanism shall include referral to an appeal committee.

   The appeal committee shall adopt its own rules of procedure by a simple majority of its component members, on a proposal from the Commission.

   Where the appeal committee is seised, it shall meet at the earliest 14 days, except in duly justified cases, and at the latest 6 weeks, after the date of referral. Without prejudice to paragraph 3, the appeal committee shall deliver its opinion within 2 months of the date of referral.

   A representative of the Commission shall chair the appeal committee.

   The chair shall set the date of the appeal committee meeting in close cooperation with the members of the committee, in order to enable Member States and the Commission to ensure an appropriate level of representation. By 1 April 2011, the Commission shall convene the first meeting of the appeal committee in order to adopt its rules of procedure.

Article 4

Advisory procedure

1. Where the advisory procedure applies, the committee shall deliver its opinion, if necessary by taking a vote. If the committee takes a vote, the opinion shall be delivered by a simple majority of its component members.
2. The Commission shall decide on the draft implementing act to be adopted, taking the utmost account of the conclusions drawn from the discussions within the committee and of the opinion delivered.

Article 5

Examination procedure

1. Where the examination procedure applies, the committee shall deliver its opinion by the majority laid down in Article 16(4) and (5) of the Treaty on European Union and, where applicable, Article 238(3) TFEU, for acts to be adopted on a proposal from the Commission. The votes of the representatives of the Member States within the committee shall be weighted in the manner set out in those Articles.
2. Where the committee delivers a positive opinion, the Commission shall adopt the draft implementing act.
3. Without prejudice to Article 7, if the committee delivers a negative opinion, the Commission shall not adopt the draft implementing act. Where an implementing act is deemed to be necessary, the chair may either submit an amended version of the draft implementing act to the same committee within 2 months of delivery of the negative opinion, or submit the draft implementing act within 1 month of such delivery to the appeal committee for further deliberation.
4. Where no opinion is delivered, the Commission may adopt the draft implementing act, except in the cases provided for in the second subparagraph. Where the Commission does not adopt the draft implementing act, the chair may submit to the committee an amended version thereof.

   Without prejudice to Article 7, the Commission shall not adopt the draft implementing act where:
   (a) that act concerns taxation, financial services, the protection of the health or safety of humans, animals or plants, or definitive multilateral safeguard measures;
   (b) the basic act provides that the draft implementing act may not be adopted where no opinion is delivered; or
   (c) a simple majority of the component members of the committee opposes it.

   In any of the cases referred to in the second subparagraph, where an implementing act is deemed to be necessary, the chair may either submit an amended version of that act to the same committee within 2 months of the vote, or submit the draft implementing act within 1 month of the vote to the appeal committee for further deliberation.
5. By way of derogation from paragraph 4, the following procedure shall apply for the adoption of draft definitive anti-dumping or countervailing measures, where no opinion is delivered by the committee and a simple majority of its component members opposes the draft implementing act.

   The Commission shall conduct consultations with the Member States. 14 days at the earliest and 1 month at the latest after the committee meeting, the Commission shall inform the committee members of the results of those consultations and submit a draft implementing act to the appeal committee. By way of derogation from Article 3(7), the appeal committee shall meet 14 days at the earliest and 1 month at the latest after the submission of the draft implementing act. The appeal committee shall deliver its opinion in accordance with Article 6. The time limits laid down in this paragraph shall be without prejudice to the need to respect the deadlines laid down in the relevant basic acts.

Article 6
Referral to the appeal committee

1. The appeal committee shall deliver its opinion by the majority provided for in Article 5(1).
2. Until an opinion is delivered, any member of the appeal committee may suggest amendments to the draft implementing act and the chair may decide whether or not to modify it.

   The chair shall endeavour to find solutions which command the widest possible support within the appeal committee.

   The chair shall inform the appeal committee of the manner in which the discussions and suggestions for amendments have been taken into account, in particular as regards suggestions for amendments which have been largely supported within the appeal committee.
3. Where the appeal committee delivers a positive opinion, the Commission shall adopt the draft implementing act.

   Where no opinion is delivered, the Commission may adopt the draft implementing act.

   Where the appeal committee delivers a negative opinion, the Commission shall not adopt the draft implementing act.
4. By way of derogation from paragraph 3, for the adoption of definitive multilateral safeguard measures, in the absence of a positive opinion voted by the majority provided for in Article 5(1), the Commission shall not adopt the draft measures.
5. By way of derogation from paragraph 1, until 1 September 2012, the appeal committee shall deliver its opinion on draft definitive anti-dumping or countervailing measures by a simple majority of its component members.

Article 7
Adoption of implementing acts in exceptional cases

By way of derogation from Article 5(3) and the second subparagraph of Article 5(4), the Commission may adopt a draft implementing act where it needs to be adopted without delay in order to avoid creating a significant disruption of the markets in the area of agriculture or a risk for the financial interests of the Union within the meaning of Article 325 TFEU.

In such a case, the Commission shall immediately submit the adopted implementing act to the appeal committee. Where the appeal committee delivers a negative opinion on the adopted implementing act, the Commission shall repeal that act immediately. Where the appeal committee delivers a positive opinion or no opinion is delivered, the implementing act shall remain in force.

Article 8
Immediately applicable implementing acts

1. By way of derogation from Articles 4 and 5, a basic act may provide that, on duly justified imperative grounds of urgency, this Article is to apply.

2. The Commission shall adopt an implementing act which shall apply immediately, without its prior submission to a committee, and shall remain in force for a period not exceeding 6 months unless the basic act provides otherwise.

3. At the latest 14 days after its adoption, the chair shall submit the act referred to in paragraph 2 to the relevant committee in order to obtain its opinion.

4. Where the examination procedure applies, in the event of the committee delivering a negative opinion, the Commission shall immediately repeal the implementing act adopted in accordance with paragraph 2.

5. Where the Commission adopts provisional anti-dumping or countervailing measures, the procedure provided for in this Article shall apply. The Commission shall adopt such measures after consulting or, in cases of extreme urgency, after informing the Member States. In the latter case, consultations shall take place 10 days at the latest after notification to the Member States of the measures adopted by the Commission.

Article 9
Rules of procedure

1. Each committee shall adopt by a simple majority of its component members its own rules of procedure on the proposal of its chair, on the basis of standard rules to be drawn up by the Commission following consultation with Member States. Such standard rules shall be published by the Commission in the *Official Journal of the European Union*.

   In so far as may be necessary, existing committees shall adapt their rules of procedure to the standard rules.

2. The principles and conditions on public access to documents and the rules on data protection applicable to the Commission shall apply to the committees.

Article 10
Information on committee proceedings

1. The Commission shall keep a register of committee proceedings which shall contain:
   (a) a list of committees;
   (b) the agendas of committee meetings;
   (c) the summary records, together with the lists of the authorities and organisations to which the persons designated by the Member States to represent them belong;
   (d) the draft implementing acts on which the committees are asked to deliver an opinion;
   (e) the voting results;
   (f) the final draft implementing acts following delivery of the opinion of the committees;
   (g) information concerning the adoption of the final draft implementing acts by the Commission; and
   (h) statistical data on the work of the committees.

2. The Commission shall also publish an annual report on the work of the committees.

3. The European Parliament and the Council shall have access to the information referred to in paragraph 1 in accordance with the applicable rules.

4. At the same time as they are sent to the committee members, the Commission shall make available to the European Parliament and the Council the documents referred to

in points (b), (d) and (f) of paragraph 1 whilst also informing them of the availability of such documents.

5. The references of all documents referred to in points (a) to (g) of paragraph 1 as well as the information referred to in paragraph 1(h) shall be made public in the register.

Article 11
Right of scrutiny for the European Parliament and the Council
Where a basic act is adopted under the ordinary legislative procedure, either the European Parliament or the Council may at any time indicate to the Commission that, in its view, a draft implementing act exceeds the implementing powers provided for in the basic act. In such a case, the Commission shall review the draft implementing act, taking account of the positions expressed, and shall inform the European Parliament and the Council whether it intends to maintain, amend or withdraw the draft implementing act.

Article 12
Repeal of Decision 1999/468/EC
Decision 1999/468/EC is hereby repealed.

The effects of Article 5a of Decision 1999/468/EC shall be maintained for the purposes of existing basic acts making reference thereto.

Article 13
Transitional provisions: adaptation of existing basic acts
1. Where basic acts adopted before the entry into force of this Regulation provide for the exercise of implementing powers by the Commission in accordance with Decision 1999/468/EC, the following rules shall apply:
   (a) where the basic act makes reference to Article 3 of Decision 1999/468/EC, the advisory procedure referred to in Article 4 of this Regulation shall apply;
   (b) where the basic act makes reference to Article 4 of Decision 1999/468/EC, the examination procedure referred to in Article 5 of this Regulation shall apply, with the exception of the second and third subparagraphs of Article 5(4);
   (c) where the basic act makes reference to Article 5 of Decision 1999/468/EC, the examination procedure referred to in Article 5 of this Regulation shall apply and the basic act shall be deemed to provide that, in the absence of an opinion, the Commission may not adopt the draft implementing act, as envisaged in point (b) of the second subparagraph of Article 5(4);
   (d) where the basic act makes reference to Article 6 of Decision 1999/468/EC, Article 8 of this Regulation shall apply;
   (e) where the basic act makes reference to Articles 7 and 8 of Decision 1999/468/EC, Articles 10 and 11 of this Regulation shall apply.
2. Articles 3 and 9 of this Regulation shall apply to all existing committees for the purposes of paragraph 1.
3. Article 7 of this Regulation shall apply only to existing procedures which make reference to Article 4 of Decision 1999/468/EC.
4. The transitional provisions laid down in this Article shall not prejudge the nature of the acts concerned.

Article 14
Transitional arrangement
This Regulation shall not affect pending procedures in which a committee has already delivered its opinion in accordance with Decision 1999/468/EC.

Article 15
Review
By 1 March 2016, the Commission shall present a report to the European Parliament and the Council on the implementation of this Regulation, accompanied, if necessary, by appropriate legislative proposals.

Article 16
Entry into force
This Regulation shall enter into force on 1 March 2011.

This Regulation is binding in its entirety and directly applicable in all Member States.
(*Signatures omitted*)

STATEMENT BY THE EUROPEAN PARLIAMENT, THE COUNCIL AND THE COMMISSION

Article 5(2) of this Regulation requires the Commission to adopt a draft implementing act where the committee delivers a positive opinion. This provision does not preclude that Commission may, as is the current practice, in very exceptional cases, take into consideration new circumstances that have arisen after the vote and decide not to adopt a draft implementing act, after having duly informed the committee and the legislator.

STATEMENTS BY THE COMMISSION

The Commission will proceed to an examination of all legislative acts in force which were not adapted to the regulatory procedure with scrutiny before the entry into force of the Lisbon Treaty, in order to assess if those instruments need to be adapted to the regime of delegated acts introduced by Article 290 of the Treaty on the Functioning of the European Union. The Commission will make the appropriate proposals as soon as possible and no later than at the dates mentioned in the indicative calendar annexed to this declaration.

While this alignment exercise is underway, the Commission will keep the European Parliament regularly informed on draft implementing measures related to these instruments which should become, in the future, delegated acts.

As regards legislative acts in force which currently contain references to the regulatory procedure with scrutiny, the Commission will review the provisions attached to this procedure in each instrument it intends to modify, in order to adapt them in due course according to the criteria laid down in the Treaty. In addition, the European Parliament and the Council will be entitled to signal basic acts they consider important to adapt as a matter of priority.

The Commission will assess the results of this process by the end of 2012 in order to estimate how many legislative acts containing references to the regulatory procedure with scrutiny remain in force. The Commission will then prepare the appropriate legislative initiatives to complete the adaptation. The overall objective of the Commission is that, by the end of the 7th term of the Parliament, all provisions referring to the regulatory procedure with scrutiny would have been removed from all legislative instruments.

The Commission notes that it has recently launched a study which will provide a complete and objective review of all aspects of the EU's trade defence policy and practice, including an evaluation of the performance, methods, utilisation and effectiveness of the present TDI scheme in achieving its trade policy objectives, an evaluation of the effectiveness of the existing and potential policy decisions of the European Union (e.g., the Union interest test, the lesser duty rule, the duty collection system) in comparison with the policy decisions made by certain trading partners and an examination of the basic anti-dumping and anti-subsidy regulations in light of the administrative practice of the EU institutions, the judgments of the Court of Justice of the European Union and the recommendations and rulings of the WTO Dispute Settlement Body.

The Commission intends, in the light of the results of the study and of developments in the Doha Development Agenda negotiations to explore whether and how to further update and modernize the EU's trade defence instruments[.]

The Commission also recalls the recent initiatives it has taken to improve the transparency of the operation of trade defence instruments (such as the appointment of a Hearing Officer) and its work with Member States to clarify key elements of trade defence practice. The Commission attaches substantial importance to this work, and will seek to identify, in consultation with the Member States, other initiatives which could be taken in this respect.

Under the comitology rules based on Council Decision 1999/468/EC, where a Common Agricultural Policy (CAP) management committee has delivered an unfavourable opinion, the Commission must submit the draft measure in question to the Council which may take a different decision within a month. However, the Commission is not barred from acting but has the choice to either put the measure in place or defer its application. Hence, the Commission may take the measure where it considers on balance that suspending its application would for instance provoke irreversible negative market effects. When afterwards the Council decides otherwise the measure put in effect by the Commission becomes of course redundant. Thus the current rules equip the Commission with an instrument that allows protecting the common interest of the whole Union by adopting a measure at least on an interim basis.

Article 7 of this Regulation pursues the objective of maintaining this approach within the new comitology arrangements but limited to exceptional situations and on the basis of clearly defined and restrictive criteria. It would allow the Commission to adopt a draft measure despite the unfavourable opinion of the examination committee provided that its 'non adoption within an imperative deadline would create a significant disruption of the markets … or for the financial interests of the Union.' The provision refers to situations where it is not possible to wait until the committee votes again on the same or another draft measure because in the meantime the market would be significantly disrupted e.g. due to the speculative behaviour of operators. To ensure the Union's ability to act it would give Member States and the Commission the opportunity to have another informed discussion on the draft measure without leaving things undecided and open to speculation with the negative consequences for the markets and the budget.

Such situations may namely arise in the context of the day-to-day management of the CAP (e.g. fixing of export refunds, management of licences, special safeguard clause) where decisions need often to be taken quickly and can have significant economic consequences for the markets and thus farmers and operators but also for the budget of the Union.

In cases where the European Parliament or the Council indicate to the Commission that they consider a draft implementing act to exceed the implementing powers provided for in the basic act, the Commission will immediately review the draft implementing act taking into account the positions expressed by the European Parliament or the Council.

The Commission will act in a manner which takes duly into account the urgency of the matter.

Before deciding whether the draft implementing act shall be adopted, amended or withdrawn, the Commission will inform the European Parliament or the Council of the action it intends to take and of its reasons for doing so.

8

Regulation 58/2003 Laying Down the Statute for Executive Agencies to Be Entrusted with Certain Tasks in the Management of Union Programmes

THE COUNCIL OF THE EUROPEAN UNION,

Having regard to the Treaty [on the Functioning of the European Union], and in particular Article [352] thereof,

Having regard to the proposal from the Commission,

Having regard to the opinion of the European Parliament,

Having regard to the opinion of the Court of Auditors ...

HAS ADOPTED THIS REGULATION:

Article 1

Aim

This Regulation lays down the statute of executive agencies to which the Commission, under its own control and responsibility, may entrust certain tasks relating to the management of [Union] programmes.

Article 2

Definitions

For the purpose of this Regulation:

(a) "executive agency" means a legal entity established in accordance with this Regulation;

(b) "[Union] programme" means any activity, set of activities or other initiative which the relevant basic instrument or budgetary authorisation requires the Commission to implement for the benefit of one or more categories of specific beneficiaries, by committing expenditure.

Article 3

Setting-up and winding-up of executive agencies

1. The Commission may decide, after a prior cost-benefit analysis, to set up an executive agency with a view to entrusting it with certain tasks relating to the management of one or more [Union] programmes. It shall determine the lifetime of the executive agency. The cost-benefit analysis shall take into account a number of factors such as identification of the tasks justifying outsourcing, a cost-benefit analysis which includes the costs of coordination and checks, the impact on human resources, possible savings within the general budgetary framework of the European Union, efficiency and flexibility in the implementation of outsourced tasks, simplification of the procedures used, proximity of outsourced activities to final beneficiaries, visibility of the [Union]

as promoter of the [Union] programme concerned and the need to maintain an adequate level of know-how inside the Commission.

2. At the date determined when setting up the executive agency, the Commission may extend the duration of its lifetime for a period not exceeding that originally provided for. Such extension may be renewed. Where the Commission considers that it no longer requires the services of an executive agency which it has set up, or that its existence no longer complies with the principles of sound financial management, it shall decide to wind it up. In that event, it shall appoint two liquidators. The Commission shall determine the conditions for liquidation of the executive agency. The net result after liquidation shall be taken up in the general budget of the European Union. The decision to extend its lifetime, renew such extension or wind up the agency shall be taken on the basis of the cost-benefit analysis referred to in paragraph 1.

3. The Commission shall adopt the decisions referred to in paragraphs 1 and 2 in accordance with the procedure laid down in Article 24(2). They shall be amended in accordance with the same procedure. The Commission shall forward to the Committee referred to in Article 24(1) all the information necessary in this context, in particular the cost-benefit analysis referred to in paragraph 1 of this Article and the evaluation reports referred to in Article 25.

4. When adopting a [Union] programme, the Commission shall inform the budgetary authority of whether it intends to set up an executive agency to implement the programme.

5. All executive agencies set up under paragraph 1 of this Article must comply with this Regulation.

Article 4

Legal status

1. An executive agency is a [Union] body with a public service role.
2. An executive agency shall have legal personality. In each of the Member States, it shall enjoy the most extensive legal capacity accorded to legal persons under national law. It may, in particular, acquire or dispose of movable and immovable property and be a party to legal proceedings. To this end, it shall be represented by its Director.

Article 5

Location

1. An executive agency shall be located at the place where the Commission and its departments are located, in accordance with the Protocol on the location of the seats of the institutions and of certain bodies and departments of the European [Union] and of Europol.
2. It shall organise its departments according to the management needs of the [Union] programmes for which it is responsible and according to the criteria of sound financial management.

Article 6

Tasks

1. To attain the objective set out in Article 3(1), the Commission may entrust an executive agency with any tasks required to implement a [Union] programme, with

the exception of tasks requiring discretionary powers in translating political choices into action.

2. Executive agencies may in particular be entrusted with the following tasks:

(a) managing some or all of the phases in the lifetime of a project, in relation with specific individual projects, in the context of implementing a [Union] programme and carrying out the necessary checks to that end, by adopting the relevant decisions using the powers delegated to it by the Commission;

(b) adopting the instruments of budget implementation for the revenue and expenditure and carrying out all activities required to implement a [Union] programme on the basis of the power delegated by the Commission, and in particular activities linked to the awarding of contracts and grants;

(c) gathering, analysing and transmitting to the Commission all the information needed to guide the implementation of a [Union] programme.3. The terms, criteria, parameters and procedures with which an executive agency must comply when performing the tasks referred to in paragraph 2 and the details of the checks to be performed by the Commission departments responsible for [Union] programmes in the management of which an agency is involved shall be defined by the Commission in the instrument of delegation.

Article 7

Structure

1. An executive agency shall be managed by a Steering Committee and a director.

2. An executive agency's director shall have authority over its staff.

Article 8

Steering Committee

1. The Steering Committee shall consist of five members appointed by the Commission.

2. The term of office of the members of the Steering Committee shall be two years in principle and shall take into account the length of time fixed for implementation of the [Union] programme, management of which has been entrusted to the executive agency. The appointment may be renewed. On expiry of their term of office, or should they resign, the members shall remain in office until their appointment is renewed or they have been replaced.

3. The Steering Committee shall choose a chairperson and deputy-chairperson from among its members.

4. The Steering Committee shall meet when convened by the chairperson, at least four times a year. It may also be convened at the request of its members, by at least a simple majority, or at the request of the director.

5. Any member of the Steering Committee unable to attend a meeting may be represented by another member specially empowered for the meeting concerned. Each member may represent only one other member. Should the chairperson be unable to attend, the Steering Committee shall be chaired by the deputy-chairperson.

6. The Steering Committee's decisions shall be adopted by a simple majority of votes. In the event of a tie, the chair shall have the casting vote.

Article 9

Tasks of the Steering Committee

1. The Steering Committee shall adopt its own rules of procedure.
2. On the basis of a draft submitted by the director and after approval by the Commission, the Steering Committee shall, no later than the beginning of each year, adopt the executive agency's annual work programme comprising detailed objectives and performance indicators. The work programme must comply with the programming defined by the Commission in accordance with the instruments establishing the [Union] programmes in the management of which the executive agency is involved. The annual work programme may be amended during the year following the same procedure, in particular to take account of Commission decisions relating to the [Union] programmes concerned. The projects included in the annual work programme shall be accompanied by an estimate of the necessary expenditure.
3. The Steering Committee shall adopt the executive agency's administrative budget by the procedure laid down in Article 13.
4. The Steering Committee shall obtain the Commission's agreement before deciding to accept any gifts, legacies and grants from sources other than the [Union].
5. The Steering Committee shall decide on the organisation of the departments of the executive agency.
6. The Steering Committee shall adopt any special rules needed to implement the right of access to the executive agency's documents in accordance with Article 23(1).
7. No later than 31 March of each year, the Steering Committee shall adopt and submit to the Commission an annual activity report together with financial and management information. The report shall be drawn up in accordance with Article 60(7) of Regulation (EC, Euratom) No. 1605/2002. The report shall cover both implementation of the operating appropriations corresponding to the [Union] programme managed by the executive agency and the implementation of its administrative budget.

   The Commission shall no later than 15 June each year send to the budgetary authority a summary of executive agencies' annual reports for the previous year, to be attached to that referred to in Article 60(7) of Regulation (EC, Euratom) No. 1605/2002.
8. The Steering Committee shall adopt and apply measures to combat fraud and irregularities.
9. The Steering Committee shall perform the other tasks entrusted to it by this Regulation.

Article 10

Director

1. The director of the executive agency shall be appointed by the Commission, which shall to that end appoint an official within the meaning of the Staff Regulations of officials and the conditions of employment of other servants of the European [Union] laid down by Council Regulation (EEC, Euratom, ECSC) No. 259/68, hereafter referred to as "Staff Regulations".
2. The director shall be appointed for a term of four years in principle and shall take into account the length of time fixed for implementation of the [Union] programme, management of which had been entrusted to the executive agency. This appointment may

be renewed. After receiving the opinion of the Steering Committee, the Commission may remove the director from office before expiry of the term of office.

Article 11
Tasks of the director

1. The director shall represent the executive agency and shall be responsible for its management.

2. The director shall prepare the work of the Steering Committee, in particular the draft annual work programme of the executive agency. The director shall participate, without voting, in the work of the Steering Committee.

3. The director shall ensure that the annual work programme of the executive agency is implemented. In particular, the director shall be responsible for performance of the tasks referred to in Article 6 and shall take the relevant decisions to that effect. The director shall act as the executive agency's authorising officer by delegation as regards implementation of the operational appropriations relating to the [Union] programmes in the management of which the executive agency is involved, where the Commission has delegated powers to the agency to perform budget implementation tasks.

4. The director shall draw up the provisional statement of revenue and expenditure and, as authorising officer, shall implement the executive agency's administrative budget in accordance with the Financial Regulation referred to in Article 15.

5. The director shall be responsible for preparing and publishing the reports which the executive agency must present to the Commission. These are the annual reports on the activities of the executive agency referred to in Article 9(7) and all other reports, of a general or specific nature, which the Commission asks the executive agency to produce.

6. The director shall be empowered under the arrangements applicable to other servants of the European [Union] to conclude employment contracts in respect of staff of the executive agency. The director shall be responsible for all other matters relating to personnel management within the executive agency.

7. In accordance with the financial Regulation applicable to the general budget of the European [Union], the director shall set up management and internal control systems adapted to the tasks entrusted to the executive agency to ensure the operations it performs are lawful, comply with the rules and are effective.

Article 12
Operating budget

1. Forecasts of all the executive agency's revenue and expenditure shall be prepared for each financial year, which shall be the same as the calendar year, and shall be shown in its operating budget. The forecasts, which shall include the establishment plan of the executive agency, shall be sent to the budgetary authority with the documents relating to the preliminary draft general budget of the European Union. The establishment plan, consisting only of temporary posts and specifying the number, grade and category of the staff employed by the executive agency during the financial year concerned, shall be approved by the budgetary authority and published in an annex to Section III – Commission – of the general budget of the European Union.

2. The revenue and expenditure of the executive agency's operating budget shall be in balance.

3. The executive agency's revenue shall include a subsidy entered in the general budget of the European Union, without prejudice to other revenue to be determined by the budgetary authority, drawn from the financial allocation to the [Union] programmes which the agency is involved in the management of.

Article 13

Preparation of the operating budget

1. Each year the director shall draw up a draft operating budget for the executive agency covering the agency's running costs for the following financial year and shall submit it to the Steering Committee.

2. No later than 1 March each year, the Steering Committee shall adopt the draft operating budget, including the establishment plan, for the following financial year and shall submit it to the Commission.

3. On the basis of this draft budget and in the light of the Commission's programming for the [Union] programmes in the management of which the executive agency is involved, the Commission shall propose, as part of the annual budget procedure, the annual subsidy to the executive agency's operating budget.

4. At the beginning of each financial year, the Steering Committee shall adopt the executive agency's operating budget, on the basis of the annual subsidy thus determined by the budgetary authority, at the same time as it adopts the annual work programme, adjusting the budget in accordance with the different contributions granted to the executive agency and any funds from other sources.

5. The operating budget of the agency may not be adopted definitively until the general budget of the European Union has been finally adopted.

6. When the Commission contemplates setting up an executive agency, it shall inform the budgetary authority in accordance with the budgetary procedure and respecting the principle of transparency:
    (a) of the resources in terms of appropriations and jobs required to run the executive agency;
    (b) of planned secondments of officials from the Commission to the executive agency;
    (c) of administrative resources freed by transferring tasks from the Commission departments to the executive agency, and the re-allocation of those freed administrative resources.

7. In accordance with the Financial Regulation referred to in Article 15, all amendments to the operating budget, including the establishment plan, shall be submitted in an amending budget adopted in accordance with the procedure provided for in this Article.

Article 14

Implementation of the operating budget and discharge

1. The director shall implement the executive agency's operating budget.

2. The executive agency's accounts shall be consolidated with those of the Commission in accordance with the procedure laid down in Articles 127 and 128 of Regulation (EC, Euratom) No 1605/2002 and in accordance with the following:

(a) each year, the director shall submit detailed provisional accounts of all revenue and expenditure for the previous financial year to the Steering Committee, which shall forward them, by 1 March at the latest, to the Commission's accounting officer and to the Court of Auditors;

(b) the final accounts shall be sent to the Commission's accounting officer and the Court of Auditors by 1 July of the following year at the latest.

3. The European Parliament, acting on a recommendation from the Council, shall grant a discharge to the executive agency for the implementation of its budget no later than 29 April of year n+2 after examination of the report by the Court of Auditors.

Such discharge shall be granted together with that relating to implementation of the general budget of the European Union.

Article 15

Financial Regulation applicable to the operating budget

The standard financial regulation applicable to the operating budget of an executive agency shall be adopted by the Commission. That standard regulation may deviate from the financial Regulation applicable to the general budget of the European [Union] only if the specific operating requirements of the executive agencies so require.

Article 16

Financial Regulation applicable to the operational appropriations

1. Where the Commission has delegated tasks to the executive agency relating to the budget implementation of operational appropriations for [Union] programmes in accordance with Article 6(2)(b), such appropriations shall be entered in the general budget of the European Union and shall be implemented by direct charging to that budget under the responsibility of the Commission.

2. The director shall act as the executive agency's authorising officer by delegation as regards implementation of these operational appropriations and shall comply to that end with the obligations laid down in the financial Regulation applicable to the general budget of the European [Union].

3. Discharge in respect of implementation of the operational appropriations shall be given within the framework of the discharge given in respect of the general budget of the European Union, in accordance with Article [319], of which it is an integral part.

Article 17

Programmes financed from sources other than the general budget of the European Union

Articles 13 and 16 shall apply without prejudice to specific provisions laid down in the basic instruments relating to programmes financed from sources other than the general budget of the European Union.

Article 18

Staff

1. The executive agency's staff shall consist of [Union] officials seconded as temporary staff members by the institutions to positions of responsibility in the executive agency, and of other temporary staff members directly recruited by the executive agency, as well as

of other servants recruited by the executive agency on renewable contracts. The nature of the contract, governed by either private law or public law, its duration and the extent of the servants' obligations vis-à-vis the agency, and the appropriate eligibility criteria shall be determined on the basis of the specific nature of the tasks to be performed, and shall comply with the Staff Regulations as well as with current national legislation.

2. Subject to permanent activities and regardless of the type of secondment of the official, the institution of origin:

    (a) shall not, for the duration of the secondment, fill the posts vacated by that secondment;

    (b) shall take into account in the standard abatement the expenses of the officials transferred to the executive agencies.

    Nevertheless, the total number of posts concerned by paragraph 1 and the first subparagraph of paragraph 2 shall not exceed the number of posts necessary for performance of the tasks conferred upon the executive agency by the Commission.

3. The Steering Committee, in agreement with the Commission, shall adopt the necessary implementing rules for personnel management within the executive agency, if necessary.

Article 19

Privileges and immunities

The Protocol of 8 April 1965 on the privileges and immunities of the European [Union] shall apply to both the executive agency and its staff, insofar as it is subject to the Staff Regulations.

Article 20

Supervision

1. Implementation of the [Union] programmes entrusted to executive agencies shall be supervised by the Commission. Such supervision shall follow the procedures it shall adopt in accordance with Article 6(3).

2. The function of internal auditor shall be performed in the executive agencies by the internal auditor of the Commission.

3. The Commission and the executive agency shall implement the recommendations of the internal auditors, each according to their respective powers.

4. The European Anti-Fraud Office (OLAF) set up by Commission Decision 1999/352/ EC, ECSC, Euratom of 28 April 1999 shall enjoy the same powers in respect of executive agencies and their staff as it enjoys in respect of Commission departments. As soon as the executive agency is set up, it shall subscribe to the Interinstitutional Agreement of 25 May 1999 between the European Parliament, the Council of the European Union and the Commission of the European [Union] concerning internal investigations by the European Anti-Fraud Office (OLAF). The Steering Committee shall formalise this acceptance and adopt the provisions needed to facilitate internal inquiries conducted by OLAF.

5. The Court of Auditors shall examine the executive agency's accounts in accordance with Article [287] of the Treaty.

6. All acts of the executive agency, and in particular all decisions adopted and contracts concluded by it, must provide explicitly that the Commission's internal auditor, OLAF and the Court of Auditors may conduct on-the-spot inspections of the documents of all contractors and sub-contractors which have received [Union] funds, including at the premises of the final beneficiaries.

Article 21
Liability

1. The contractual liability of the executive agency shall be governed by the law applicable to the contract in question.
2. In the case of non-contractual liability, the executive agency shall make good any damage caused by the agency or its servants in the performance of their duties, in accordance with the general principles common to the laws of the Member States. The Court of Justice shall have jurisdiction in disputes relating to compensation for any such damage.
3. The personal liability of staff towards the executive agency shall be governed by the rules applicable to them.

Article 22
Legality of acts

1. Any act of an executive agency which injures a third party may be referred to the Commission by any person directly or individually concerned or by a Member State for a review of its legality.

   Administrative proceedings shall be referred to the Commission within one month of the day on which the interested party or Member State concerned learnt of the act challenged.

   After hearing the arguments adduced by the interested party or by the Member State concerned and those of the executive agency, the Commission shall take a decision on the administrative proceedings within two months of the date on which proceedings were instituted. Without prejudice to the Commission's obligation to reply in writing giving grounds for its decision, the failure by the Commission to reply within that deadline shall be taken as implicit rejection of the proceedings.
2. On its own initiative the Commission may review any act of an executive agency. It shall decide within two months of the day on which that review, after having heard the arguments adduced by the agency.
3. Where an act is referred to the Commission in accordance with paragraphs 1 or 2, the Commission may suspend implementation of the act at issue or prescribe interim measures. In its final decision the Commission may uphold the executive agency's act or decide that the agency must modify it either in whole or in part.
4. Executive agencies must take the necessary measures within a reasonable period to comply with the Commission's decision.
5. An action for annulment of the Commission's explicit or implicit decision to reject the administrative appeal may be brought before the Court of Justice, in accordance with Article [263] of the Treaty.

Article 23
Access to documents and confidentiality

1. Executive agencies shall be subject to Regulation (EC) No. 1049/2001 of the European Parliament and of the Council of 30 May 2001 on public access to European Parliament, Council and Commission documents when it receives a request for access to a document in its possession.

   The Steering Committee shall adopt any special rules needed to implement these provisions no later than six months after the setting-up of the executive agency.

2. The members of the Steering Committee, the director and members of staff and all persons involved in the activities of the executive agency shall be required, even after their duties have ceased, not to disclose information of the kind covered by the obligation of professional secrecy.

Article 24
Committee
1. The Commission shall be assisted by a committee, hereinafter referred to as the "Committee for Executive Agencies".
2. Where reference is made to this paragraph, Articles 5 and 7 of Decision 1999/468/EC shall apply.
   The period laid down in Article 5(6) of Decision 1999/468/EC shall be set at three months.
3. The Committee shall adopt its rules of procedure.

Article 25
Evaluation
1. An external evaluation report on the first three years of operation of each executive agency shall be drawn up by the Commission and submitted to the steering committee of the executive agency, to the European Parliament, to the Council and to the Court of Auditors. It shall include a cost-benefit analysis as referred to in Article 3(1).
2. The evaluation shall subsequently be repeated every three years under the same conditions.
3. Further to the evaluation reports, the executive agency and the Commission shall take all appropriate steps to resolve any problems identified.
4. If, further to an evaluation, the Commission finds that the very existence of an executive agency is no longer justified with a view to sound financial management, the Commission shall decide to wind up that agency.

Article 26
Interim measures
As far as executive agencies have already been set up:
   (a) the annual activity report referred to in Article 9(7) shall be drawn up for the first time for the 2003 financial year;
   (b) the deadline referred to in Article 14(2)(b) for transmission of the final accounts shall apply for the first time to the 2005 financial year;
   (c) for the financial years prior to 2005 the deadline for transmission of the final accounts shall be 15 September.

Article 27
Entry into force
This Regulation shall enter into force on the 10th day following that of its publication in the Official Journal of the European [Union].

This Regulation shall be binding in its entirety and directly applicable in all Member States. (*Signatures omitted*)

9

Regulation 1215/2012 on Jurisdiction and the Recognition and Enforcement of Judgments in Civil and Commercial Matters (recast)

Contents

THE EUROPEAN PARLIAMENT AND THE COUNCIL OF THE EUROPEAN UNION,

Having regard to the Treaty on the Functioning of the European Union, and in particular Article 67(4) and points (a), (c) and (e) of Article 81(2) thereof...

Acting in accordance with the ordinary legislative procedure...

HAVE ADOPTED THIS REGULATION:

Chapter I Scope and Definitions

Article 1

1. This Regulation shall apply in civil and commercial matters whatever the nature of the court or tribunal. It shall not extend, in particular, to revenue, customs or

administrative matters or to the liability of the State for acts and omissions in the exercise of State authority (*acta iure imperii*).

2. This Regulation shall not apply to:

   (a) the status or legal capacity of natural persons, rights in property arising out of a matrimonial relationship or out of a relationship deemed by the law applicable to such relationship to have comparable effects to marriage;

   (b) bankruptcy, proceedings relating to the winding-up of insolvent companies or other legal persons, judicial arrangements, compositions and analogous proceedings;

   (c) social security;

   (d) arbitration;

   (e) maintenance obligations arising from a family relationship, parentage, marriage or affinity;

   (f) wills and succession, including maintenance obligations arising by reason of death.

Article 2

For the purposes of this Regulation:

   (a) 'judgment' means any judgment given by a court or tribunal of a Member State, whatever the judgment may be called, including a decree, order, decision or writ of execution, as well as a decision on the determination of costs or expenses by an officer of the court.

   For the purposes of Chapter III, 'judgment' includes provisional, including protective, measures ordered by a court or tribunal which by virtue of this Regulation has jurisdiction as to the substance of the matter. It does not include a provisional, including protective, measure which is ordered by such a court or tribunal without the defendant being summoned to appear, unless the judgment containing the measure is served on the defendant prior to enforcement;

   (b) 'court settlement' means a settlement which has been approved by a court of a Member State or concluded before a court of a Member State in the course of proceedings;

   (c) 'authentic instrument' means a document which has been formally drawn up or registered as an authentic instrument in the Member State of origin and the authenticity of which:

   (i) relates to the signature and the content of the instrument; and

   (ii) has been established by a public authority or other authority empowered for that purpose;

   (d) 'Member State of origin' means the Member State in which, as the case may be, the judgment has been given, the court settlement has been approved or concluded, or the authentic instrument has been formally drawn up or registered;

   (e) 'Member State addressed' means the Member State in which the recognition of the judgment is invoked or in which the enforcement of the judgment, the court settlement or the authentic instrument is sought;

   (f) 'court of origin' means the court which has given the judgment the recognition of which is invoked or the enforcement of which is sought.

Article 3

For the purposes of this Regulation, 'court' includes the following authorities to the extent that they have jurisdiction in matters falling within the scope of this Regulation:

   (a) in Hungary, in summary proceedings concerning orders to pay (fizetési meghagyásos eljárás), the notary (közjegyző);

   (b) in Sweden, in summary proceedings concerning orders to pay (betalningsföreläggande) and assistance (handräckning), the Enforcement Authority (Kronofogdemyndigheten).

Chapter II Jurisdiction

SECTION 1 GENERAL PROVISIONS

Article 4

1. Subject to this Regulation, persons domiciled in a Member State shall, whatever their nationality, be sued in the courts of that Member State.
2. Persons who are not nationals of the Member State in which they are domiciled shall be governed by the rules of jurisdiction applicable to nationals of that Member State.

Article 5

1. Persons domiciled in a Member State may be sued in the courts of another Member State only by virtue of the rules set out in Sections 2 to 7 of this Chapter.
2. In particular, the rules of national jurisdiction of which the Member States are to notify the Commission pursuant to point (a) of Article 76(1) shall not be applicable as against the persons referred to in paragraph 1.

Article 6

1. If the defendant is not domiciled in a Member State, the jurisdiction of the courts of each Member State shall, subject to Article 18(1), Article 21(2) and Articles 24 and 25, be determined by the law of that Member State.
2. As against such a defendant, any person domiciled in a Member State may, whatever his nationality, avail himself in that Member State of the rules of jurisdiction there in force, and in particular those of which the Member States are to notify the Commission pursuant to point (a) of Article 76(1), in the same way as nationals of that Member State.

SECTION 2 SPECIAL JURISDICTION

Article 7

A person domiciled in a Member State may be sued in another Member State:

(1)

   (a) in matters relating to a contract, in the courts for the place of performance of the obligation in question;

   (b) for the purpose of this provision and unless otherwise agreed, the place of performance of the obligation in question shall be:

     — in the case of the sale of goods, the place in a Member State where, under the contract, the goods were delivered or should have been delivered,

     — in the case of the provision of services, the place in a Member State where, under the contract, the services were provided or should have been provided;

    (c) if point (b) does not apply then point (a) applies;

(2)   in matters relating to tort, delict or quasi-delict, in the courts for the place where the harmful event occurred or may occur;

(3)   as regards a civil claim for damages or restitution which is based on an act giving rise to criminal proceedings, in the court seised of those proceedings, to the extent that that court has jurisdiction under its own law to entertain civil proceedings;

(4)   as regards a civil claim for the recovery, based on ownership, of a cultural object as defined in point 1 of Article 1 of Directive 93/7/EEC initiated by the person claiming the right to recover such an object, in the courts for the place where the cultural object is situated at the time when the court is seised;

(5)   as regards a dispute arising out of the operations of a branch, agency or other establishment, in the courts for the place where the branch, agency or other establishment is situated;

(6)   as regards a dispute brought against a settlor, trustee or beneficiary of a trust created by the operation of a statute, or by a written instrument, or created orally and evidenced in writing, in the courts of the Member State in which the trust is domiciled;

(7)   as regards a dispute concerning the payment of remuneration claimed in respect of the salvage of a cargo or freight, in the court under the authority of which the cargo or freight in question:

    (a) has been arrested to secure such payment; or

    (b) could have been so arrested, but bail or other security has been given;

    provided that this provision shall apply only if it is claimed that the defendant has an interest in the cargo or freight or had such an interest at the time of salvage.

Article 8

A person domiciled in a Member State may also be sued:

(1)   where he is one of a number of defendants, in the courts for the place where any one of them is domiciled, provided the claims are so closely connected that it is expedient to hear and determine them together to avoid the risk of irreconcilable judgments resulting from separate proceedings;

(2)   as a third party in an action on a warranty or guarantee or in any other third-party proceedings, in the court seised of the original proceedings, unless these were instituted solely with the object of removing him from the jurisdiction of the court which would be competent in his case;

(3)   on a counter-claim arising from the same contract or facts on which the original claim was based, in the court in which the original claim is pending;

(4)   in matters relating to a contract, if the action may be combined with an action against the same defendant in matters relating to rights *in rem* in immovable property, in the court of the Member State in which the property is situated.

Article 9

Where by virtue of this Regulation a court of a Member State has jurisdiction in actions relating to liability from the use or operation of a ship, that court, or any other court substituted for this purpose by the internal law of that Member State, shall also have jurisdiction over claims for limitation of such liability.

SECTION 3 JURISDICTION IN MATTERS RELATING TO INSURANCE

Article 10

In matters relating to insurance, jurisdiction shall be determined by this Section, without prejudice to Article 6 and point 5 of Article 7.

Article 11

1. An insurer domiciled in a Member State may be sued:
   (a) in the courts of the Member State in which he is domiciled;
   (b) in another Member State, in the case of actions brought by the policyholder, the insured or a beneficiary, in the courts for the place where the claimant is domiciled; or
   (c) if he is a co-insurer, in the courts of a Member State in which proceedings are brought against the leading insurer.
2. An insurer who is not domiciled in a Member State but has a branch, agency or other establishment in one of the Member States shall, in disputes arising out of the operations of the branch, agency or establishment, be deemed to be domiciled in that Member State.

Article 12

In respect of liability insurance or insurance of immovable property, the insurer may in addition be sued in the courts for the place where the harmful event occurred. The same applies if movable and immovable property are covered by the same insurance policy and both are adversely affected by the same contingency.

Article 13

1. In respect of liability insurance, the insurer may also, if the law of the court permits it, be joined in proceedings which the injured party has brought against the insured.
2. Articles 10, 11 and 12 shall apply to actions brought by the injured party directly against the insurer, where such direct actions are permitted.
3. If the law governing such direct actions provides that the policyholder or the insured may be joined as a party to the action, the same court shall have jurisdiction over them.

Article 14

1. Without prejudice to Article 13(3), an insurer may bring proceedings only in the courts of the Member State in which the defendant is domiciled, irrespective of whether he is the policyholder, the insured or a beneficiary.
2. The provisions of this Section shall not affect the right to bring a counter-claim in the court in which, in accordance with this Section, the original claim is pending.

Article 15

The provisions of this Section may be departed from only by an agreement:
(1) which is entered into after the dispute has arisen;
(2) which allows the policyholder, the insured or a beneficiary to bring proceedings in courts other than those indicated in this Section;

(3) which is concluded between a policyholder and an insurer, both of whom are at the time of conclusion of the contract domiciled or habitually resident in the same Member State, and which has the effect of conferring jurisdiction on the courts of that Member State even if the harmful event were to occur abroad, provided that such an agreement is not contrary to the law of that Member State;

(4) which is concluded with a policyholder who is not domiciled in a Member State, except in so far as the insurance is compulsory or relates to immovable property in a Member State; or

(5) which relates to a contract of insurance in so far as it covers one or more of the risks set out in Article 16.

Article 16

The following are the risks referred to in point 5 of Article 15:

(1) any loss of or damage to:
   (a) seagoing ships, installations situated offshore or on the high seas, or aircraft, arising from perils which relate to their use for commercial purposes;
   (b) goods in transit other than passengers' baggage where the transit consists of or includes carriage by such ships or aircraft;

(2) any liability, other than for bodily injury to passengers or loss of or damage to their baggage:
   (a) arising out of the use or operation of ships, installations or aircraft as referred to in point 1(a) in so far as, in respect of the latter, the law of the Member State in which such aircraft are registered does not prohibit agreements on jurisdiction regarding insurance of such risks;
   (b) for loss or damage caused by goods in transit as described in point 1(b);

(3) any financial loss connected with the use or operation of ships, installations or aircraft as referred to in point 1(a), in particular loss of freight or charter-hire;

(4) any risk or interest connected with any of those referred to in points 1 to 3;

(5) notwithstanding points 1 to 4, all 'large risks' as defined in Directive 2009/138/EC of the European Parliament and of the Council of 25 November 2009 on the taking-up and pursuit of the business of Insurance and Reinsurance (Solvency II).

SECTION 4 JURISDICTION OVER CONSUMER CONTRACTS

Article 17

1. In matters relating to a contract concluded by a person, the consumer, for a purpose which can be regarded as being outside his trade or profession, jurisdiction shall be determined by this Section, without prejudice to Article 6 and point 5 of Article 7, if:
   (a) it is a contract for the sale of goods on instalment credit terms;
   (b) it is a contract for a loan repayable by instalments, or for any other form of credit, made to finance the sale of goods; or
   (c) in all other cases, the contract has been concluded with a person who pursues commercial or professional activities in the Member State of the consumer's domicile or, by any means, directs such activities to that Member State or to several States including that Member State, and the contract falls within the scope of such activities.

2. Where a consumer enters into a contract with a party who is not domiciled in a Member State but has a branch, agency or other establishment in one of the Member States, that party shall, in disputes arising out of the operations of the branch, agency or establishment, be deemed to be domiciled in that Member State.

3. This Section shall not apply to a contract of transport other than a contract which, for an inclusive price, provides for a combination of travel and accommodation.

Article 18

1. A consumer may bring proceedings against the other party to a contract either in the courts of the Member State in which that party is domiciled or, regardless of the domicile of the other party, in the courts for the place where the consumer is domiciled.

2. Proceedings may be brought against a consumer by the other party to the contract only in the courts of the Member State in which the consumer is domiciled.

3. This Article shall not affect the right to bring a counter-claim in the court in which, in accordance with this Section, the original claim is pending.

Article 19

The provisions of this Section may be departed from only by an agreement:

(1) which is entered into after the dispute has arisen;

(2) which allows the consumer to bring proceedings in courts other than those indicated in this Section; or

(3) which is entered into by the consumer and the other party to the contract, both of whom are at the time of conclusion of the contract domiciled or habitually resident in the same Member State, and which confers jurisdiction on the courts of that Member State, provided that such an agreement is not contrary to the law of that Member State.

SECTION 5 JURISDICTION OVER INDIVIDUAL CONTRACTS OF EMPLOYMENT

Article 20

1. In matters relating to individual contracts of employment, jurisdiction shall be determined by this Section, without prejudice to Article 6, point 5 of Article 7 and, in the case of proceedings brought against an employer, point 1 of Article 8.

2. Where an employee enters into an individual contract of employment with an employer who is not domiciled in a Member State but has a branch, agency or other establishment in one of the Member States, the employer shall, in disputes arising out of the operations of the branch, agency or establishment, be deemed to be domiciled in that Member State.

Article 21

1. An employer domiciled in a Member State may be sued:

(a) in the courts of the Member State in which he is domiciled; or

(b) in another Member State:

(i) in the courts for the place where or from where the employee habitually carries out his work or in the courts for the last place where he did so; or

(ii) if the employee does not or did not habitually carry out his work in any one country, in the courts for the place where the business which engaged the employee is or was situated.

2. An employer not domiciled in a Member State may be sued in a court of a Member State in accordance with point (b) of paragraph 1.

Article 22

1. An employer may bring proceedings only in the courts of the Member State in which the employee is domiciled.
2. The provisions of this Section shall not affect the right to bring a counter-claim in the court in which, in accordance with this Section, the original claim is pending.

Article 23

The provisions of this Section may be departed from only by an agreement:
(1) which is entered into after the dispute has arisen; or
(2) which allows the employee to bring proceedings in courts other than those indicated in this Section.

SECTION 6 EXCLUSIVE JURISDICTION

Article 24

The following courts of a Member State shall have exclusive jurisdiction, regardless of the domicile of the parties:
(1) in proceedings which have as their object rights *in rem* in immovable property or tenancies of immovable property, the courts of the Member State in which the property is situated.

  However, in proceedings which have as their object tenancies of immovable property concluded for temporary private use for a maximum period of six consecutive months, the courts of the Member State in which the defendant is domiciled shall also have jurisdiction, provided that the tenant is a natural person and that the landlord and the tenant are domiciled in the same Member State;
(2) in proceedings which have as their object the validity of the constitution, the nullity or the dissolution of companies or other legal persons or associations of natural or legal persons, or the validity of the decisions of their organs, the courts of the Member State in which the company, legal person or association has its seat. In order to determine that seat, the court shall apply its rules of private international law;
(3) in proceedings which have as their object the validity of entries in public registers, the courts of the Member State in which the register is kept;
(4) in proceedings concerned with the registration or validity of patents, trade marks, designs, or other similar rights required to be deposited or registered, irrespective of whether the issue is raised by way of an action or as a defence, the courts of the Member State in which the deposit or registration has been applied for, has taken place or is under the terms of an instrument of the Union or an international convention deemed to have taken place.

  Without prejudice to the jurisdiction of the European Patent Office under the Convention on the Grant of European Patents, signed at Munich on 5 October 1973, the courts of each Member State shall have exclusive jurisdiction in proceedings concerned with the registration or validity of any European patent granted for that Member State;

(5) in proceedings concerned with the enforcement of judgments, the courts of the Member State in which the judgment has been or is to be enforced.

SECTION 7 PROROGATION OF JURISDICTION

Article 25

1. If the parties, regardless of their domicile, have agreed that a court or the courts of a Member State are to have jurisdiction to settle any disputes which have arisen or which may arise in connection with a particular legal relationship, that court or those courts shall have jurisdiction, unless the agreement is null and void as to its substantive validity under the law of that Member State. Such jurisdiction shall be exclusive unless the parties have agreed otherwise. The agreement conferring jurisdiction shall be either:
   (a) in writing or evidenced in writing;
   (b) in a form which accords with practices which the parties have established between themselves; or
   (d) in international trade or commerce, in a form which accords with a usage of which the parties are or ought to have been aware and which in such trade or commerce is widely known to, and regularly observed by, parties to contracts of the type involved in the particular trade or commerce concerned.

2. Any communication by electronic means which provides a durable record of the agreement shall be equivalent to 'writing'.

3. The court or courts of a Member State on which a trust instrument has conferred jurisdiction shall have exclusive jurisdiction in any proceedings brought against a settlor, trustee or beneficiary, if relations between those persons or their rights or obligations under the trust are involved.

4. Agreements or provisions of a trust instrument conferring jurisdiction shall have no legal force if they are contrary to Articles 15, 19 or 23, or if the courts whose jurisdiction they purport to exclude have exclusive jurisdiction by virtue of Article 24.

5. An agreement conferring jurisdiction which forms part of a contract shall be treated as an agreement independent of the other terms of the contract.

   The validity of the agreement conferring jurisdiction cannot be contested solely on the ground that the contract is not valid.

Article 26

1. Apart from jurisdiction derived from other provisions of this Regulation, a court of a Member State before which a defendant enters an appearance shall have jurisdiction. This rule shall not apply where appearance was entered to contest the jurisdiction, or where another court has exclusive jurisdiction by virtue of Article 24.

2. In matters referred to in Sections 3, 4 or 5 where the policyholder, the insured, a beneficiary of the insurance contract, the injured party, the consumer or the employee is the defendant, the court shall, before assuming jurisdiction under paragraph 1, ensure that the defendant is informed of his right to contest the jurisdiction of the court and of the consequences of entering or not entering an appearance.

SECTION 8 EXAMINATION AS TO JURISDICTION AND ADMISSIBILITY

Article 27

Where a court of a Member State is seised of a claim which is principally concerned with a matter over which the courts of another Member State have exclusive jurisdiction by virtue of Article 24, it shall declare of its own motion that it has no jurisdiction.

Article 28

1. Where a defendant domiciled in one Member State is sued in a court of another Member State and does not enter an appearance, the court shall declare of its own motion that it has no jurisdiction unless its jurisdiction is derived from the provisions of this Regulation.
2. The court shall stay the proceedings so long as it is not shown that the defendant has been able to receive the document instituting the proceedings or an equivalent document in sufficient time to enable him to arrange for his defence, or that all necessary steps have been taken to this end.
3. Article 19 of Regulation (EC) No. 1393/2007 of the European Parliament and of the Council of 13 November 2007 on the service in the Member States of judicial and extrajudicial documents in civil or commercial matters (service of documents) shall apply instead of paragraph 2 of this Article if the document instituting the proceedings or an equivalent document had to be transmitted from one Member State to another pursuant to that Regulation.
4. Where Regulation (EC) No. 1393/2007 is not applicable, Article 15 of the Hague Convention of 15 November 1965 on the Service Abroad of Judicial and Extrajudicial Documents in Civil or Commercial Matters shall apply if the document instituting the proceedings or an equivalent document had to be transmitted abroad pursuant to that Convention.

SECTION 9 LIS PENDENS – RELATED ACTIONS

Article 29

1. Without prejudice to Article 31(2), where proceedings involving the same cause of action and between the same parties are brought in the courts of different Member States, any court other than the court first seised shall of its own motion stay its proceedings until such time as the jurisdiction of the court first seised is established.
2. In cases referred to in paragraph 1, upon request by a court seised of the dispute, any other court seised shall without delay inform the former court of the date when it was seised in accordance with Article 32.
3. Where the jurisdiction of the court first seised is established, any court other than the court first seised shall decline jurisdiction in favour of that court.

Article 30

1. Where related actions are pending in the courts of different Member States, any court other than the court first seised may stay its proceedings.
2. Where the action in the court first seised is pending at first instance, any other court may also, on the application of one of the parties, decline jurisdiction if the court first seised has jurisdiction over the actions in question and its law permits the consolidation thereof.
3. For the purposes of this Article, actions are deemed to be related where they are so closely connected that it is expedient to hear and determine them together to avoid the risk of irreconcilable judgments resulting from separate proceedings.

Article 31

1. Where actions come within the exclusive jurisdiction of several courts, any court other than the court first seised shall decline jurisdiction in favour of that court.
2. Without prejudice to Article 26, where a court of a Member State on which an agreement as referred to in Article 25 confers exclusive jurisdiction is seised, any court of another Member State shall stay the proceedings until such time as the court seised on the basis of the agreement declares that it has no jurisdiction under the agreement.
3. Where the court designated in the agreement has established jurisdiction in accordance with the agreement, any court of another Member State shall decline jurisdiction in favour of that court.
4. Paragraphs 2 and 3 shall not apply to matters referred to in Sections 3, 4 or 5 where the policyholder, the insured, a beneficiary of the insurance contract, the injured party, the consumer or the employee is the claimant and the agreement is not valid under a provision contained within those Sections.

Article 32

1. For the purposes of this Section, a court shall be deemed to be seised:
   (a) at the time when the document instituting the proceedings or an equivalent document is lodged with the court, provided that the claimant has not subsequently failed to take the steps he was required to take to have service effected on the defendant; or
   (b) if the document has to be served before being lodged with the court, at the time when it is received by the authority responsible for service, provided that the claimant has not subsequently failed to take the steps he was required to take to have the document lodged with the court.
   The authority responsible for service referred to in point (b) shall be the first authority receiving the documents to be served.
2. The court, or the authority responsible for service, referred to in paragraph 1, shall note, respectively, the date of the lodging of the document instituting the proceedings or the equivalent document, or the date of receipt of the documents to be served.

Article 33

1. Where jurisdiction is based on Article 4 or on Articles 7, 8 or 9 and proceedings are pending before a court of a third State at the time when a court in a Member State is seised of an action involving the same cause of action and between the same parties as the proceedings in the court of the third State, the court of the Member State may stay the proceedings if:
   (a) it is expected that the court of the third State will give a judgment capable of recognition and, where applicable, of enforcement in that Member State; and
   (b) the court of the Member State is satisfied that a stay is necessary for the proper administration of justice.
2. The court of the Member State may continue the proceedings at any time if:
   (a) the proceedings in the court of the third State are themselves stayed or discontinued;
   (b) it appears to the court of the Member State that the proceedings in the court of the third State are unlikely to be concluded within a reasonable time; or

(c) the continuation of the proceedings is required for the proper administration of justice.

3. The court of the Member State shall dismiss the proceedings if the proceedings in the court of the third State are concluded and have resulted in a judgment capable of recognition and, where applicable, of enforcement in that Member State.

4. The court of the Member State shall apply this Article on the application of one of the parties or, where possible under national law, of its own motion.

Article 34

1. Where jurisdiction is based on Article 4 or on Articles 7, 8 or 9 and an action is pending before a court of a third State at the time when a court in a Member State is seised of an action which is related to the action in the court of the third State, the court of the Member State may stay the proceedings if:
   (a) it is expedient to hear and determine the related actions together to avoid the risk of irreconcilable judgments resulting from separate proceedings;
   (b) it is expected that the court of the third State will give a judgment capable of recognition and, where applicable, of enforcement in that Member State; and
   (c) the court of the Member State is satisfied that a stay is necessary for the proper administration of justice.

2. The court of the Member State may continue the proceedings at any time if:
   (a) it appears to the court of the Member State that there is no longer a risk of irreconcilable judgments;
   (b) the proceedings in the court of the third State are themselves stayed or discontinued;
   (c) it appears to the court of the Member State that the proceedings in the court of the third State are unlikely to be concluded within a reasonable time; or
   (d) the continuation of the proceedings is required for the proper administration of justice.

3. The court of the Member State may dismiss the proceedings if the proceedings in the court of the third State are concluded and have resulted in a judgment capable of recognition and, where applicable, of enforcement in that Member State.

4. The court of the Member State shall apply this Article on the application of one of the parties or, where possible under national law, of its own motion.

SECTION 10 PROVISIONAL, INCLUDING PROTECTIVE, MEASURES

Article 35

Application may be made to the courts of a Member State for such provisional, including protective, measures as may be available under the law of that Member State, even if the courts of another Member State have jurisdiction as to the substance of the matter.

Chapter III Recognition and Enforcement

SECTION 1 RECOGNITION

Article 36

1. A judgment given in a Member State shall be recognised in the other Member States without any special procedure being required.

2. Any interested party may, in accordance with the procedure provided for in Subsection 2 of Section 3, apply for a decision that there are no grounds for refusal of recognition as referred to in Article 45.
3. If the outcome of proceedings in a court of a Member State depends on the determination of an incidental question of refusal of recognition, that court shall have jurisdiction over that question.

Article 37

1. A party who wishes to invoke in a Member State a judgment given in another Member State shall produce:
   (a) a copy of the judgment which satisfies the conditions necessary to establish its authenticity; and
   (b) the certificate issued pursuant to Article 53.
2. The court or authority before which a judgment given in another Member State is invoked may, where necessary, require the party invoking it to provide, in accordance with Article 57, a translation or a transliteration of the contents of the certificate referred to in point (b) of paragraph 1. The court or authority may require the party to provide a translation of the judgment instead of a translation of the contents of the certificate if it is unable to proceed without such a translation.

Article 38

The court or authority before which a judgment given in another Member State is invoked may suspend the proceedings, in whole or in part, if:
   (a) the judgment is challenged in the Member State of origin; or
   (b) an application has been submitted for a decision that there are no grounds for refusal of recognition as referred to in Article 45 or for a decision that the recognition is to be refused on the basis of one of those grounds.

SECTION 2 ENFORCEMENT

Article 39

A judgment given in a Member State which is enforceable in that Member State shall be enforceable in the other Member States without any declaration of enforceability being required.

Article 40

An enforceable judgment shall carry with it by operation of law the power to proceed to any protective measures which exist under the law of the Member State addressed.

Article 41

1. Subject to the provisions of this Section, the procedure for the enforcement of judgments given in another Member State shall be governed by the law of the Member State addressed. A judgment given in a Member State which is enforceable in the Member State addressed shall be enforced there under the same conditions as a judgment given in the Member State addressed.
2. Notwithstanding paragraph 1, the grounds for refusal or of suspension of enforcement under the law of the Member State addressed shall apply in so far as they are not incompatible with the grounds referred to in Article 45.

3. The party seeking the enforcement of a judgment given in another Member State shall not be required to have a postal address in the Member State addressed. Nor shall that party be required to have an authorised representative in the Member State addressed unless such a representative is mandatory irrespective of the nationality or the domicile of the parties.

Article 42

1. For the purposes of enforcement in a Member State of a judgment given in another Member State, the applicant shall provide the competent enforcement authority with:
   (a) a copy of the judgment which satisfies the conditions necessary to establish its authenticity; and
   (b) the certificate issued pursuant to Article 53, certifying that the judgment is enforceable and containing an extract of the judgment as well as, where appropriate, relevant information on the recoverable costs of the proceedings and the calculation of interest.
2. For the purposes of enforcement in a Member State of a judgment given in another Member State ordering a provisional, including a protective, measure, the applicant shall provide the competent enforcement authority with:
   (a) a copy of the judgment which satisfies the conditions necessary to establish its authenticity;
   (b) the certificate issued pursuant to Article 53, containing a description of the measure and certifying that:
      (i) the court has jurisdiction as to the substance of the matter;
      (ii) the judgment is enforceable in the Member State of origin; and
   (c) where the measure was ordered without the defendant being summoned to appear, proof of service of the judgment.
3. The competent enforcement authority may, where necessary, require the applicant to provide, in accordance with Article 57, a translation or a transliteration of the contents of the certificate.
4. The competent enforcement authority may require the applicant to provide a translation of the judgment only if it is unable to proceed without such a translation.

Article 43

1. Where enforcement is sought of a judgment given in another Member State, the certificate issued pursuant to Article 53 shall be served on the person against whom the enforcement is sought prior to the first enforcement measure. The certificate shall be accompanied by the judgment, if not already served on that person.
2. Where the person against whom enforcement is sought is domiciled in a Member State other than the Member State of origin, he may request a translation of the judgment in order to contest the enforcement if the judgment is not written in or accompanied by a translation into either of the following languages:
   (a) a language which he understands; or
   (b) the official language of the Member State in which he is domiciled or, where there are several official languages in that Member State, the official language or one of the official languages of the place where he is domiciled.

Where a translation of the judgment is requested under the first subparagraph, no measures of enforcement may be taken other than protective measures until that translation has been provided to the person against whom enforcement is sought.

This paragraph shall not apply if the judgment has already been served on the person against whom enforcement is sought in one of the languages referred to in the first subparagraph or is accompanied by a translation into one of those languages.

3. This Article shall not apply to the enforcement of a protective measure in a judgment or where the person seeking enforcement proceeds to protective measures in accordance with Article 40.

Article 44

1. In the event of an application for refusal of enforcement of a judgment pursuant to Subsection 2 of Section 3, the court in the Member State addressed may, on the application of the person against whom enforcement is sought:
   (a) limit the enforcement proceedings to protective measures;
   (b) make enforcement conditional on the provision of such security as it shall determine; or
   (c) suspend, either wholly or in part, the enforcement proceedings.
2. The competent authority in the Member State addressed shall, on the application of the person against whom enforcement is sought, suspend the enforcement proceedings where the enforceability of the judgment is suspended in the Member State of origin.

SECTION 3 REFUSAL OF RECOGNITION AND ENFORCEMENT
SUBSECTION 1 REFUSAL OF RECOGNITION

Article 45

1. On the application of any interested party, the recognition of a judgment shall be refused:
   (a) if such recognition is manifestly contrary to public policy (ordre public) in the Member State addressed;
   (b) where the judgment was given in default of appearance, if the defendant was not served with the document which instituted the proceedings or with an equivalent document in sufficient time and in such a way as to enable him to arrange for his defence, unless the defendant failed to commence proceedings to challenge the judgment when it was possible for him to do so;
   (c) if the judgment is irreconcilable with a judgment given between the same parties in the Member State addressed;
   (d) if the judgment is irreconcilable with an earlier judgment given in another Member State or in a third State involving the same cause of action and between the same parties, provided that the earlier judgment fulfils the conditions necessary for its recognition in the Member State addressed; or
   (e) if the judgment conflicts with:
      (i) Sections 3, 4 or 5 of Chapter II where the policyholder, the insured, a beneficiary of the insurance contract, the injured party, the consumer or the employee was the defendant; or
      (ii) Section 6 of Chapter II.

2. In its examination of the grounds of jurisdiction referred to in point (e) of paragraph 1, the court to which the application was submitted shall be bound by the findings of fact on which the court of origin based its jurisdiction.
3. Without prejudice to point (e) of paragraph 1, the jurisdiction of the court of origin may not be reviewed. The test of public policy referred to in point (a) of paragraph 1 may not be applied to the rules relating to jurisdiction.
4. The application for refusal of recognition shall be made in accordance with the procedures provided for in Subsection 2 and, where appropriate, Section 4.

SUBSECTION 2 REFUSAL OF ENFORCEMENT

Article 46
On the application of the person against whom enforcement is sought, the enforcement of a judgment shall be refused where one of the grounds referred to in Article 45 is found to exist.

Article 47
1. The application for refusal of enforcement shall be submitted to the court which the Member State concerned has communicated to the Commission pursuant to point (a) of Article 75 as the court to which the application is to be submitted.
2. The procedure for refusal of enforcement shall, in so far as it is not covered by this Regulation, be governed by the law of the Member State addressed.
3. The applicant shall provide the court with a copy of the judgment and, where necessary, a translation or transliteration of it.
4. The court may dispense with the production of the documents referred to in the first subparagraph if it already possesses them or if it considers it unreasonable to require the applicant to provide them. In the latter case, the court may require the other party to provide those documents.
5. The party seeking the refusal of enforcement of a judgment given in another Member State shall not be required to have a postal address in the Member State addressed. Nor shall that party be required to have an authorised representative in the Member State addressed unless such a representative is mandatory irrespective of the nationality or the domicile of the parties.

Article 48
The court shall decide on the application for refusal of enforcement without delay.

Article 49
1. The decision on the application for refusal of enforcement may be appealed against by either party.
2. The appeal is to be lodged with the court which the Member State concerned has communicated to the Commission pursuant to point (b) of Article 75 as the court with which such an appeal is to be lodged.

Article 50
The decision given on the appeal may only be contested by an appeal where the courts with which any further appeal is to be lodged have been communicated by the Member State concerned to the Commission pursuant to point (c) of Article 75.

Article 51

1. The court to which an application for refusal of enforcement is submitted or the court which hears an appeal lodged under Article 49 or Article 50 may stay the proceedings if an ordinary appeal has been lodged against the judgment in the Member State of origin or if the time for such an appeal has not yet expired. In the latter case, the court may specify the time within which such an appeal is to be lodged.

2. Where the judgment was given in Ireland, Cyprus or the United Kingdom, any form of appeal available in the Member State of origin shall be treated as an ordinary appeal for the purposes of paragraph 1.

SECTION 4 COMMON PROVISIONS

Article 52

Under no circumstances may a judgment given in a Member State be reviewed as to its substance in the Member State addressed.

Article 53

The court of origin shall, at the request of any interested party, issue the certificate using the form set out in Annex I.

Article 54

1. If a judgment contains a measure or an order which is not known in the law of the Member State addressed, that measure or order shall, to the extent possible, be adapted to a measure or an order known in the law of that Member State which has equivalent effects attached to it and which pursues similar aims and interests.

   Such adaptation shall not result in effects going beyond those provided for in the law of the Member State of origin.

2. Any party may challenge the adaptation of the measure or order before a court.

3. If necessary, the party invoking the judgment or seeking its enforcement may be required to provide a translation or a transliteration of the judgment.

Article 55

A judgment given in a Member State which orders a payment by way of a penalty shall be enforceable in the Member State addressed only if the amount of the payment has been finally determined by the court of origin.

Article 56

No security, bond or deposit, however described, shall be required of a party who in one Member State applies for the enforcement of a judgment given in another Member State on the ground that he is a foreign national or that he is not domiciled or resident in the Member State addressed.

Article 57

1. When a translation or a transliteration is required under this Regulation, such translation or transliteration shall be into the official language of the Member State concerned or, where there are several official languages in that Member State, into the official language or one of the official languages of court proceedings of the place where a

judgment given in another Member State is invoked or an application is made, in accordance with the law of that Member State.

2. For the purposes of the forms referred to in Articles 53 and 60, translations or transliterations may also be into any other official language or languages of the institutions of the Union that the Member State concerned has indicated it can accept.

3. Any translation made under this Regulation shall be done by a person qualified to do translations in one of the Member States.

Chapter IV Authentic Instruments and Court Settlements

Article 58

1. An authentic instrument which is enforceable in the Member State of origin shall be enforceable in the other Member States without any declaration of enforceability being required. Enforcement of the authentic instrument may be refused only if such enforcement is manifestly contrary to public policy (ordre public) in the Member State addressed.

    The provisions of Section 2, Subsection 2 of Section 3, and Section 4 of Chapter III shall apply as appropriate to authentic instruments.

2. The authentic instrument produced must satisfy the conditions necessary to establish its authenticity in the Member State of origin.

Article 59

A court settlement which is enforceable in the Member State of origin shall be enforced in the other Member States under the same conditions as authentic instruments.

Article 60

The competent authority or court of the Member State of origin shall, at the request of any interested party, issue the certificate using the form set out in Annex II containing a summary of the enforceable obligation recorded in the authentic instrument or of the agreement between the parties recorded in the court settlement.

Chapter V General Provisions

Article 61

No legalisation or other similar formality shall be required for documents issued in a Member State in the context of this Regulation.

Article 62

1. In order to determine whether a party is domiciled in the Member State whose courts are seised of a matter, the court shall apply its internal law.

2. If a party is not domiciled in the Member State whose courts are seised of the matter, then, in order to determine whether the party is domiciled in another Member State, the court shall apply the law of that Member State.

Article 63

1. For the purposes of this Regulation, a company or other legal person or association of natural or legal persons is domiciled at the place where it has its:

(a) statutory seat;

(b) central administration; or

(c) principal place of business.

2. For the purposes of Ireland, Cyprus and the United Kingdom, 'statutory seat' means the registered office or, where there is no such office anywhere, the place of incorporation or, where there is no such place anywhere, the place under the law of which the formation took place.

3. In order to determine whether a trust is domiciled in the Member State whose courts are seised of the matter, the court shall apply its rules of private international law.

Article 64

Without prejudice to any more favourable provisions of national laws, persons domiciled in a Member State who are being prosecuted in the criminal courts of another Member State of which they are not nationals for an offence which was not intentionally committed may be defended by persons qualified to do so, even if they do not appear in person. However, the court seised of the matter may order appearance in person; in the case of failure to appear, a judgment given in the civil action without the person concerned having had the opportunity to arrange for his defence need not be recognised or enforced in the other Member States.

Article 65

1. The jurisdiction specified in point 2 of Article 8 and Article 13 in actions on a warranty or guarantee or in any other third-party proceedings may be resorted to in the Member States included in the list established by the Commission pursuant to point (b) of Article 76(1) and Article 76(2) only in so far as permitted under national law. A person domiciled in another Member State may be invited to join the proceedings before the courts of those Member States pursuant to the rules on third-party notice referred to in that list.

2. Judgments given in a Member State by virtue of point 2 of Article 8 or Article 13 shall be recognised and enforced in accordance with Chapter III in any other Member State. Any effects which judgments given in the Member States included in the list referred to in paragraph 1 may have, in accordance with the law of those Member States, on third parties by application of paragraph 1 shall be recognised in all Member States.

3. The Member States included in the list referred to in paragraph 1 shall, within the framework of the European Judicial Network in civil and commercial matters established by Council Decision 2001/470/EC ('the European Judicial Network') provide information on how to determine, in accordance with their national law, the effects of the judgments referred to in the second sentence of paragraph 2.

Chapter VI Transitional Provisions

Article 66

1. This Regulation shall apply only to legal proceedings instituted, to authentic instruments formally drawn up or registered and to court settlements approved or concluded on or after 10 January 2015.

2. Notwithstanding Article 80, Regulation (EC) No. 44/2001 shall continue to apply to judgments given in legal proceedings instituted, to authentic instruments formally drawn up or registered and to court settlements approved or concluded before 10 January 2015 which fall within the scope of that Regulation.

Chapter VII Relationship with Other Instruments

Article 67
This Regulation shall not prejudice the application of provisions governing jurisdiction and the recognition and enforcement of judgments in specific matters which are contained in instruments of the Union or in national legislation harmonised pursuant to such instruments.

Article 68
1. This Regulation shall, as between the Member States, supersede the 1968 Brussels Convention, except as regards the territories of the Member States which fall within the territorial scope of that Convention and which are excluded from this Regulation pursuant to Article 355 of the TFEU.
2. In so far as this Regulation replaces the provisions of the 1968 Brussels Convention between the Member States, any reference to that Convention shall be understood as a reference to this Regulation.

Article 69
Subject to Articles 70 and 71, this Regulation shall, as between the Member States, supersede the conventions that cover the same matters as those to which this Regulation applies. In particular, the conventions included in the list established by the Commission pursuant to point (c) of Article 76(1) and Article 76(2) shall be superseded.

Article 70
1. The conventions referred to in Article 69 shall continue to have effect in relation to matters to which this Regulation does not apply.
2. They shall continue to have effect in respect of judgments given, authentic instruments formally drawn up or registered and court settlements approved or concluded before the date of entry into force of Regulation (EC) No. 44/2001.

Article 71
1. This Regulation shall not affect any conventions to which the Member States are parties and which, in relation to particular matters, govern jurisdiction or the recognition or enforcement of judgments.
2. With a view to its uniform interpretation, paragraph 1 shall be applied in the following manner:
   (a) this Regulation shall not prevent a court of a Member State which is party to a convention on a particular matter from assuming jurisdiction in accordance with that convention, even where the defendant is domiciled in another Member State which is not party to that convention. The court hearing the action shall, in any event, apply Article 28 of this Regulation;

(b) judgments given in a Member State by a court in the exercise of jurisdiction provided for in a convention on a particular matter shall be recognised and enforced in the other Member States in accordance with this Regulation.

Where a convention on a particular matter to which both the Member State of origin and the Member State addressed are parties lays down conditions for the recognition or enforcement of judgments, those conditions shall apply. In any event, the provisions of this Regulation on recognition and enforcement of judgments may be applied.

Article 71a

1. For the purposes of this Regulation, a court common to several Member States as specified in paragraph 2 (a 'common court') shall be deemed to be a court of a Member State when, pursuant to the instrument establishing it, such a common court exercises jurisdiction in matters falling within the scope of this Regulation.
2. For the purposes of this Regulation, each of the following courts shall be a common court:
   (a) the Unified Patent Court established by the Agreement on a Unified Patent Court signed on 19 February 2013 (the 'UPC Agreement'); and
   (b) the Benelux Court of Justice established by the Treaty of 31 March 1965 concerning the establishment and statute of a Benelux Court of Justice (the 'Benelux Court of Justice Treaty').

Article 71b

The jurisdiction of a common court shall be determined as follows:

(1) a common court shall have jurisdiction where, under this Regulation, the courts of a Member State party to the instrument establishing the common court would have jurisdiction in a matter governed by that instrument;
(2) where the defendant is not domiciled in a Member State, and this Regulation does not otherwise confer jurisdiction over him, Chapter II shall apply as appropriate regardless of the defendant's domicile.

Application may be made to a common court for provisional, including protective, measures even if the courts of a third State have jurisdiction as to the substance of the matter;
(3) where a common court has jurisdiction over a defendant under point 2 in a dispute relating to an infringement of a European patent giving rise to damage within the Union, that court may also exercise jurisdiction in relation to damage arising outside the Union from such an infringement.

Such jurisdiction may only be established if property belonging to the defendant is located in any Member State party to the instrument establishing the common court and the dispute has a sufficient connection with any such Member State.

Article 71c

1. Articles 29 to 32 shall apply where proceedings are brought in a common court and in a court of a Member State not party to the instrument establishing the common court.
2. Articles 29 to 32 shall apply where, during the transitional period referred to in Article 83 of the UPC Agreement, proceedings are brought in the Unified Patent Court and in a court of a Member State party to the UPC Agreement.

Article 71d

This Regulation shall apply to the recognition and enforcement of:

(a) judgments given by a common court which are to be recognised and enforced in a Member State not party to the instrument establishing the common court; and

(b) judgments given by the courts of a Member State not party to the instrument establishing the common court which are to be recognised and enforced in a Member State party to that instrument.

However, where recognition and enforcement of a judgment given by a common court is sought in a Member State party to the instrument establishing the common court, any rules of that instrument on recognition and enforcement shall apply instead of the rules of this Regulation.

Article 72

This Regulation shall not affect agreements by which Member States, prior to the entry into force of Regulation (EC) No. 44/2001, undertook pursuant to Article 59 of the 1968 Brussels Convention not to recognise judgments given, in particular in other Contracting States to that Convention, against defendants domiciled or habitually resident in a third State where, in cases provided for in Article 4 of that Convention, the judgment could only be founded on a ground of jurisdiction specified in the second paragraph of Article 3 of that Convention.

Article 73

1. This Regulation shall not affect the application of the 2007 Lugano Convention.

2. This Regulation shall not affect the application of the 1958 New York Convention.

3. This Regulation shall not affect the application of bilateral conventions and agreements between a third State and a Member State concluded before the date of entry into force of Regulation (EC) No. 44/2001 which concern matters governed by this Regulation.

Chapter VIII Final Provisions

Article 74

The Member States shall provide, within the framework of the European Judicial Network and with a view to making the information available to the public, a description of national rules and procedures concerning enforcement, including authorities competent for enforcement, and information on any limitations on enforcement, in particular debtor protection rules and limitation or prescription periods.

The Member States shall keep this information permanently updated.

Article 75

By 10 January 2014, the Member States shall communicate to the Commission:

(a) the courts to which the application for refusal of enforcement is to be submitted pursuant to Article 47(1);

(b) the courts with which an appeal against the decision on the application for refusal of enforcement is to be lodged pursuant to Article 49(2);

(c) the courts with which any further appeal is to be lodged pursuant to Article 50; and

(d) the languages accepted for translations of the forms as referred to in Article 57(2).

The Commission shall make the information publicly available through any appropriate means, in particular through the European Judicial Network.

Article 76

1. The Member States shall notify the Commission of:
   (a) the rules of jurisdiction referred to in Articles 5(2) and 6(2);
   (b) the rules on third-party notice referred to in Article 65; and
   (c) the conventions referred to in Article 69.
2. The Commission shall, on the basis of the notifications by the Member States referred to in paragraph 1, establish the corresponding lists.
3. The Member States shall notify the Commission of any subsequent amendments required to be made to those lists. The Commission shall amend those lists accordingly.
4. The Commission shall publish the lists and any subsequent amendments made to them in the *Official Journal of the European Union*.
5. The Commission shall make all information notified pursuant to paragraphs 1 and 3 publicly available through any other appropriate means, in particular through the European Judicial Network.

Article 77

The Commission shall be empowered to adopt delegated acts in accordance with Article 78 concerning the amendment of Annexes I and II.

Article 78

1. The power to adopt delegated acts is conferred on the Commission subject to the conditions laid down in this Article.
2. The power to adopt delegated acts referred to in Article 77 shall be conferred on the Commission for an indeterminate period of time from 9 January 2013.
3. The delegation of power referred to in Article 77 may be revoked at any time by the European Parliament or by the Council. A decision to revoke shall put an end to the delegation of the power specified in that decision. It shall take effect the day following the publication of the decision in the *Official Journal of the European Union* or at a later date specified therein. It shall not affect the validity of any delegated acts already in force.
4. As soon as it adopts a delegated act, the Commission shall notify it simultaneously to the European Parliament and to the Council.
5. A delegated act adopted pursuant to Article 77 shall enter into force only if no objection has been expressed either by the European Parliament or the Council within a period of two months of notification of that act to the European Parliament and the Council or if, before the expiry of that period, the European Parliament and the Council have both informed the Commission that they will not object. That period shall be extended by two months at the initiative of the European Parliament or of the Council.

Article 79

By 11 January 2022 the Commission shall present a report to the European Parliament, to the Council and to the European Economic and Social Committee on the application of this Regulation. That report shall include an evaluation of the possible need for a further extension of the rules on jurisdiction to defendants not domiciled in a Member State, taking into account the operation of this Regulation and possible developments at international level. Where appropriate, the report shall be accompanied by a proposal for amendment of this Regulation.

Article 80

This Regulation shall repeal Regulation (EC) No. 44/2001. References to the repealed Regulation shall be construed as references to this Regulation and shall be read in accordance with the correlation table set out in Annex III.

Article 81

This Regulation shall enter into force on the twentieth day following that of its publication in the *Official Journal of the European Union.*

It shall apply from 10 January 2015, with the exception of Articles 75 and 76, which shall apply from 10 January 2014.

This Regulation shall be binding in its entirety and directly applicable in the Member States in accordance with the Treaties.

9

PART II
Union Secondary Law: Legislation and Other Acts

10

Regulation 492/2011 on Freedom of Movement for Workers within the Union

Contents

THE EUROPEAN PARLIAMENT AND THE COUNCIL OF THE EUROPEAN UNION,

Having regard to the Treaty on the Functioning of the European Union, and in particular Article 46 thereof,

Having regard to the proposal from the European Commission,

After transmission of the draft legislative act to the national parliaments,

Having regard to the opinion of the European Economic and Social Committee,

Acting in accordance with the ordinary legislative procedure ...

HAVE ADOPTED THIS REGULATION:[*]

---

[*] Some provisions within Regulation 492/2011 have subsequently been deleted by Regulation 2016/589 on a European network of employment services (EURES), workers' access to mobility services and the further integration of labour markets [2016] OJ L107/1, art. 39(1) of which states: "Regulation (EU) No. 492/2011 is amended as follows: (a) Articles 11 and 12, Article 13(2), Articles 14 to 20 and Article 38 are deleted; (b) Article 13(1) is deleted with effect from 13 May 2018".

Chapter I Employment, Equal Treatment and Workers' Families

SECTION 1 ELIGIBILITY FOR EMPLOYMENT

Article 1

1. Any national of a Member State shall, irrespective of his place of residence, have the right to take up an activity as an employed person, and to pursue such activity, within the territory of another Member State in accordance with the provisions laid down by law, regulation or administrative action governing the employment of nationals of that State.

2. He shall, in particular, have the right to take up available employment in the territory of another Member State with the same priority as nationals of that State.

Article 2

Any national of a Member State and any employer pursuing an activity in the territory of a Member State may exchange their applications for and offers of employment, and may conclude and perform contracts of employment in accordance with the provisions in force laid down by law, regulation or administrative action, without any discrimination resulting therefrom.

Article 3

1. Under this Regulation, provisions laid down by law, regulation or administrative action or administrative practices of a Member State shall not apply:

   (a) where they limit application for and offers of employment, or the right of foreign nationals to take up and pursue employment or subject these to conditions not applicable in respect of their own nationals; or

   (b) where, though applicable irrespective of nationality, their exclusive or principal aim or effect is to keep nationals of other Member States away from the employment offered.

   The first subparagraph shall not apply to conditions relating to linguistic knowledge required by reason of the nature of the post to be filled.

2. There shall be included in particular among the provisions or practices of a Member State referred to in the first subparagraph of paragraph 1 those which:

   (a) prescribe a special recruitment procedure for foreign nationals;

   (b) limit or restrict the advertising of vacancies in the press or through any other medium or subject it to conditions other than those applicable in respect of employers pursuing their activities in the territory of that Member State;

   (c) subject eligibility for employment to conditions of registration with employment offices or impede recruitment of individual workers, where persons who do not reside in the territory of that State are concerned.

Article 4

1. Provisions laid down by law, regulation or administrative action of the Member States which restrict by number or percentage the employment of foreign nationals in any undertaking, branch of activity or region, or at a national level, shall not apply to nationals of the other Member States.

2. When in a Member State the granting of any benefit to undertakings is subject to a minimum percentage of national workers being employed, nationals of the other

10

Member States shall be counted as national workers, subject to Directive 2005/36/EC of the European Parliament and of the Council of 7 September 2005 on the recognition of professional qualifications.

Article 5

A national of a Member State who seeks employment in the territory of another Member State shall receive the same assistance there as that afforded by the employment offices in that State to their own nationals seeking employment.

Article 6

1. The engagement and recruitment of a national of one Member State for a post in another Member State shall not depend on medical, vocational or other criteria which are discriminatory on grounds of nationality by comparison with those applied to nationals of the other Member State who wish to pursue the same activity.
2. A national who holds an offer in his name from an employer in a Member State other than that of which he is a national may have to undergo a vocational test, if the employer expressly requests this when making his offer of employment.

SECTION 2 EMPLOYMENT AND EQUALITY OF TREATMENT

Article 7

1. A worker who is a national of a Member State may not, in the territory of another Member State, be treated differently from national workers by reason of his nationality in respect of any conditions of employment and work, in particular as regards remuneration, dismissal, and, should he become unemployed, reinstatement or re-employment.
2. He shall enjoy the same social and tax advantages as national workers.
3. He shall also, by virtue of the same right and under the same conditions as national workers, have access to training in vocational schools and retraining centres.
4. Any clause of a collective or individual agreement or of any other collective regulation concerning eligibility for employment, remuneration and other conditions of work or dismissal shall be null and void in so far as it lays down or authorises discriminatory conditions in respect of workers who are nationals of the other Member States.

Article 8

A worker who is a national of a Member State and who is employed in the territory of another Member State shall enjoy equality of treatment as regards membership of trade unions and the exercise of rights attaching thereto, including the right to vote and to be eligible for the administration or management posts of a trade union. He may be excluded from taking part in the management of bodies governed by public law and from holding an office governed by public law. Furthermore, he shall have the right of eligibility for workers' representative bodies in the undertaking.

The first paragraph of this Article shall not affect laws or regulations in certain Member States which grant more extensive rights to workers coming from the other Member States.

Article 9

1. A worker who is a national of a Member State and who is employed in the territory of another Member State shall enjoy all the rights and benefits accorded to national workers in matters of housing, including ownership of the housing he needs.
2. A worker referred to in paragraph 1 may, with the same right as nationals, put his name down on the housing lists in the region in which he is employed, where such lists exist, and shall enjoy the resultant benefits and priorities.

   If his family has remained in the country whence he came, they shall be considered for this purpose as residing in the said region, where national workers benefit from a similar presumption.

SECTION 3 WORKERS' FAMILIES

Article 10

The children of a national of a Member State who is or has been employed in the territory of another Member State shall be admitted to that State's general educational, apprenticeship and vocational training courses under the same conditions as the nationals of that State, if such children are residing in its territory.

Member States shall encourage all efforts to enable such children to attend these courses under the best possible conditions.

Chapter II Clearance of Vacancies and Applications for Employment (repealed)

Chapter III Committees for Ensuring Close Cooperation between the Member States in Matters Concerning the Freedom of Movement of Workers and their Employment

SECTION 1 THE ADVISORY COMMITTEE

Article 21

The Advisory Committee shall be responsible for assisting the Commission in the examination of any questions arising from the application of the Treaty on the Functioning of the European Union and measures taken in pursuance thereof, in matters concerning the freedom of movement of workers and their employment.

Article 22

The Advisory Committee shall be responsible in particular for:

(a) examining problems concerning freedom of movement and employment within the framework of national manpower policies, with a view to coordinating the employment policies of the Member States at Union level, thus contributing to the development of the economies and to an improved balance of the labour market;
(b) making a general study of the effects of implementing this Regulation and any supplementary measures;
(c) submitting to the Commission any reasoned proposals for revising this Regulation;
(d) delivering, either at the request of the Commission or on its own initiative, reasoned opinions on general questions or on questions of principle, in particular on exchange of information concerning developments in the labour market, on the

movement of workers between Member States, on programmes or measures to develop vocational guidance and vocational training which are likely to increase the possibilities of freedom of movement and employment, and on all forms of assistance to workers and their families, including social assistance and the housing of workers.

Article 23

1. The Advisory Committee shall be composed of six members for each Member State, two of whom shall represent the Government, two the trade unions and two the employers' associations.
2. For each of the categories referred to in paragraph 1, one alternate member shall be appointed by each Member State.
3. The term of office of the members and their alternates shall be 2 years. Their appointments shall be renewable.

    On expiry of their term of office, the members and their alternates shall remain in office until replaced or until their appointments are renewed.

Article 24

The members of the Advisory Committee and their alternates shall be appointed by the Council, which shall endeavour, when selecting representatives of trade unions and employers' associations, to achieve adequate representation on the Committee of the various economic sectors concerned.

The list of members and their alternates shall be published by the Council for information in the *Official Journal of the European Union*.

Article 25

The Advisory Committee shall be chaired by a member of the Commission or his representative. The Chairman shall not vote. The Committee shall meet at least twice a year. It shall be convened by its Chairman, either on his own initiative, or at the request of at least one third of the members.

Secretarial services shall be provided for the Committee by the Commission.

Article 26

The Chairman may invite individuals or representatives of bodies with wide experience in the field of employment or movement of workers to take part in meetings as observers or as experts. The Chairman may be assisted by expert advisers.

Article 27

1. An opinion delivered by the Advisory Committee shall not be valid unless two thirds of the members are present.
2. Opinions shall state the reasons on which they are based; they shall be delivered by an absolute majority of the votes validly cast; they shall be accompanied by a written statement of the views expressed by the minority, when the latter so requests.

Article 28

The Advisory Committee shall establish its working methods by rules of procedure which shall enter into force after the Council, having received an opinion from the Commission, has given its approval. The entry into force of any amendment that the Committee decides to make thereto shall be subject to the same procedure.

SECTION 2 THE TECHNICAL COMMITTEE

Article 29

The Technical Committee shall be responsible for assisting the Commission in the preparation, promotion and follow-up of all technical work and measures for giving effect to this Regulation and any supplementary measures.

Article 30

The Technical Committee shall be responsible in particular for:
- (a) promoting and advancing cooperation between the public authorities concerned in the Member States on all technical questions relating to freedom of movement of workers and their employment;
- (b) formulating procedures for the organisation of the joint activities of the public authorities concerned;
- (c) facilitating the gathering of information likely to be of use to the Commission and the undertaking of the studies and research provided for in this Regulation, and encouraging exchange of information and experience between the administrative bodies concerned;
- (d) investigating at a technical level the harmonisation of the criteria by which Member States assess the state of their labour markets.

Article 31

1. The Technical Committee shall be composed of representatives of the Governments of the Member States. Each Government shall appoint as member of the Technical Committee one of the members who represent it on the Advisory Committee.
2. Each Government shall appoint an alternate from among its other representatives – members or alternates – on the Advisory Committee.

Article 32

The Technical Committee shall be chaired by a member of the Commission or his representative. The Chairman shall not vote. The Chairman and the members of the Committee may be assisted by expert advisers.

Secretarial services shall be provided for the Committee by the Commission.

Article 33

The proposals and opinions formulated by the Technical Committee shall be submitted to the Commission, and the Advisory Committee shall be informed thereof. Any such proposals and opinions shall be accompanied by a written statement of the views expressed by the various members of the Technical Committee, when the latter so request.

10

Article 34

The Technical Committee shall establish its working methods by rules of procedure which shall enter into force after the Council, having received an opinion from the Commission, has given its approval. The entry into force of any amendment which the Committee decides to make thereto shall be subject to the same procedure.

Chapter IV Final Provisions

Article 35

The rules of procedure of the Advisory Committee and of the Technical Committee in force on 8 November 1968 shall continue to apply.

Article 36

1. This Regulation shall not affect the provisions of the Treaty establishing the European Atomic Energy Community which deal with eligibility for skilled employment in the field of nuclear energy, nor any measures taken in pursuance of that Treaty.

   Nevertheless, this Regulation shall apply to the category of workers referred to in the first subparagraph and to members of their families in so far as their legal position is not governed by the above-mentioned Treaty or measures.

2. This Regulation shall not affect measures taken in accordance with Article 48 of the Treaty on the Functioning of the European Union.

3. This Regulation shall not affect the obligations of Member States arising out of special relations or future agreements with certain non-European countries or territories, based on institutional ties existing on 8 November 1968, or agreements in existence on 8 November 1968 with certain non-European countries or territories, based on institutional ties between them.

   Workers from such countries or territories who, in accordance with this provision, are pursuing activities as employed persons in the territory of one of those Member States may not invoke the benefit of the provisions of this Regulation in the territory of the other Member States.

Article 37

Member States shall, for information purposes, communicate to the Commission the texts of agreements, conventions or arrangements concluded between them in the manpower field between the date of their being signed and that of their entry into force.

Article 38 (repealed)

Article 39

The administrative expenditure of the Advisory Committee and of the Technical Committee shall be included in the general budget of the European Union in the section relating to the Commission.

Article 40

This Regulation shall apply to the Member States and to their nationals, without prejudice to Articles 2 and 3.

Article 41

Regulation (EEC) No. 1612/68 is hereby repealed.

References to the repealed Regulation shall be construed as references to this Regulation and shall be read in accordance with the correlation table in Annex II.

Article 42

This Regulation shall enter into force on the 20th day following its publication in the *Official Journal of the European Union*.

This Regulation shall be binding in its entirety and directly applicable in all Member States.

(*Signatures omitted*)

Annex II Correlation Table

Regulation (EEC) No. 1612/68	This Regulation
Part I	Chapter I
Title I	Section 1
Article 1	Article 1
Article 2	Article 2
Article 3(1), first subparagraph	Article 3(1), first subparagraph
Article 3(1), first subparagraph, first indent	Article 3(1), first subparagraph, point (a)
Article 3(1), first subparagraph, second indent	Article 3(1), first subparagraph, point (b)
Article 3(1), second subparagraph	Article 3(1), second subparagraph
Article 3(2)	Article 3(2)
Article 4	Article 4
Article 5	Article 5
Article 6	Article 6
Title II	Section 2
Article 7	Article 7
Article 8(1)	Article 8
Article 9	Article 9
Title III	Section 3
Article 12	Article 10
Part II	Chapter II
Title I	Section 1
Article 13	Article 11
Article 14	Article 12
Title II	Section 2
Article 15	Article 13
Article 16	Article 14

10

(cont.)

Regulation (EEC) No. 1612/68	This Regulation
Article 17	Article 15
Article 18	Article 16
Title III	Section 3
Article 19	Article 17
Title IV	Section 4
Article 21	Article 18
Article 22	Article 19
Article 23	Article 20
Part III	Chapter III
Title I	Section 1
Article 24	Article 21
Article 25	Article 22
Article 26	Article 23
Article 27	Article 24
Article 28	Article 25
Article 29	Article 26
Article 30	Article 27
Article 31	Article 28
Title II	Section 2
Article 32	Article 29
Article 33	Article 30
Article 34	Article 31
Article 35	Article 32
Article 36	Article 33
Article 37	Article 34
Part IV	Chapter IV
Title I	–
Article 38	–
Article 39	Article 35
Article 40	–
Article 41	–
Title II	–
Article 42(1)	Article 36(1)
Article 42(2)	Article 36(2)
Article 42(3), first subparagraph, first and second indents	Article 36(3), first subparagraph
Article 42(3), second subparagraph	Article 36(3), second subparagraph

(cont.)

Regulation (EEC) No. 1612/68	This Regulation
Article 43	Article 37
Article 44	Article 38
Article 45	–
Article 46	Article 39
Article 47	Article 40
–	Article 41
Article 48	Article 42
–	Annex I
–	Annex II

10

11

Regulation 883/2004 on the Coordination of Social Security Systems

Contents

THE EUROPEAN PARLIAMENT AND THE COUNCIL OF THE EUROPEAN UNION,

Having regard to the Treaty [on the Functioning of the European Union], and in particular Articles [48] and [352] thereof,

Having regard to the proposal from the Commission presented after consultation with the social partners and the Administrative Commission on Social Security for Migrant Workers,

Having regard to the opinion of the European Economic and Social Committee,

Acting in accordance with the procedure laid down in Article [294] of the Treaty …

HAVE ADOPTED THIS REGULATION:

TITLE I GENERAL PROVISIONS

Article 1

Definitions

For the purposes of this Regulation:

(a) 'activity as an employed person' means any activity or equivalent situation treated as such for the purposes of the social security legislation of the Member State in which such activity or equivalent situation exists;

(b) 'activity as a self-employed person' means any activity or equivalent situation treated as such for the purposes of the social security legislation of the Member State in which such activity or equivalent situation exists;

(c) 'insured person', in relation to the social security branches covered by Title III, Chapters 1 and 3, means any person satisfying the conditions required under the legislation of the Member State competent under Title II to have the right to benefits, taking into account the provisions of this Regulation;

(d) 'civil servant' means a person considered to be such or treated as such by the Member State to which the administration employing him/her is subject;

(e) 'special scheme for civil servants' means any social security scheme which is different from the general social security scheme applicable to employed persons in the Member State concerned and to which all, or certain categories of, civil servants are directly subject;

(f) 'frontier worker' means any person pursuing an activity as an employed or self-employed person in a Member State and who resides in another Member State to which he/she returns as a rule daily or at least once a week;

(g) 'refugee' shall have the meaning assigned to it in Article 1 of the Convention relating to the Status of Refugees, signed in Geneva on 28 July 1951;

(h) 'stateless person' shall have the meaning assigned to it in Article 1 of the Convention relating to the Status of Stateless Persons, signed in New York on 28 September 1954;

(i) 'member of the family' means:

1.

    (i) any person defined or recognised as a member of the family or designated as a member of the household by the legislation under which benefits are provided;

    (ii) with regard to benefits in kind pursuant to Title III, Chapter 1 on sickness, maternity and equivalent paternity benefits, any person defined or recognised as a member of the family or designated as a member of the household by the legislation of the Member State in which he/she resides;

2. if the legislation of a Member State which is applicable under subparagraph 1 does not make a distinction between the members of the family and other persons to whom it is applicable, the spouse, minor children, and dependent children who have reached the age of majority shall be considered members of the family;

3. if, under the legislation which is applicable under subparagraphs 1 and 2, a person is considered a member of the family or member of the household only if he/she lives in the same household as the insured person or pensioner, this condition shall be considered satisfied if the person in question is mainly dependent on the insured person or pensioner;

11

(j) 'residence' means the place where a person habitually resides;

(k) 'stay' means temporary residence;

(l) 'legislation' means, in respect of each Member State, laws, regulations and other statutory provisions and all other implementing measures relating to the social security branches covered by Article 3(1);

This term excludes contractual provisions other than those which serve to implement an insurance obligation arising from the laws and regulations referred to in the preceding subparagraph or which have been the subject of a decision by the public authorities which makes them obligatory or extends their scope, provided that the Member State concerned makes a declaration to that effect, notified to the President of the European Parliament and the President of the Council of the European Union. Such declaration shall be published in the Official Journal of the European Union;

(m) 'competent authority' means, in respect of each Member State, the Minister, Ministers or other equivalent authority responsible for social security schemes throughout or in any part of the Member State in question;

(n) 'Administrative Commission' means the commission referred to in Article 71;

(o) 'Implementing Regulation' means the Regulation referred to in Article 89;

(p) 'institution' means, in respect of each Member State, the body or authority responsible for applying all or part of the legislation;

(q) 'competent institution' means:

(i) the institution with which the person concerned is insured at the time of the application for benefit; or

(ii) the institution from which the person concerned is or would be entitled to benefits if he/she or a member or members of his/her family resided in the Member State in which the institution is situated; or

(iii) the institution designated by the competent authority of the Member State concerned; or

(iv) in the case of a scheme relating to an employer's obligations in respect of the benefits set out in Article 3(1), either the employer or the insurer involved or, in default thereof, the body or authority designated by the competent authority of the Member State concerned;

(r) 'institution of the place of residence' and 'institution of the place of stay' mean respectively the institution which is competent to provide benefits in the place where the person concerned resides and the institution which is competent to provide benefits in the place where the person concerned is staying, in accordance with the legislation administered by that institution or, where no such institution exists, the institution designated by the competent authority of the Member State concerned;

(s) 'competent Member State' means the Member State in which the competent institution is situated;

(t) 'period of insurance' means periods of contribution, employment or self-employment as defined or recognised as periods of insurance by the legislation under which they were completed or considered as completed, and all periods treated as such, where they are regarded by the said legislation as equivalent to periods of insurance;

(u) 'period of employment' or 'period of self-employment' mean periods so defined or recognised by the legislation under which they were completed, and all periods treated as such, where they are regarded by the said legislation as equivalent to periods of employment or to periods of self-employment;

(v) 'period of residence' means periods so defined or recognised by the legislation under which they were completed or considered as completed;

(va) '[b]enefits in kind' means:

    (i) for the purposes of Title III, Chapter 1 (sickness, maternity and equivalent paternity benefits), benefits in kind provided for under the legislation of a Member State which are intended to supply, make available, pay directly or reimburse the cost of medical care and products and services ancillary to that care. This includes long-term care benefits in kind;

    (ii) for the purposes of Title III, Chapter 2 (accidents at work and occupational diseases), all benefits in kind relating to accidents at work and occupational diseases as defined in point (i) above and provided for under the Member States' accidents at work and occupational diseases schemes;

(w) 'pension' covers not only pensions but also lump-sum benefits which can be substituted for them and payments in the form of reimbursement of contributions and, subject to the provisions of Title III, revaluation increases or supplementary allowances;

(x) 'pre-retirement benefit' means: all cash benefits, other than an unemployment benefit or an early old-age benefit, provided from a specified age to workers who have reduced, ceased or suspended their remunerative activities until the age at which they qualify for an old-age pension or an early retirement pension, the receipt of which is not conditional upon the person concerned being available to the employment services of the competent State; 'early old-age benefit' means a benefit provided before the normal pension entitlement age is reached and which either continues to be provided once the said age is reached or is replaced by another oldage benefit;

(y) 'death grant' means any one-off payment in the event of death excluding the lump-sum benefits referred to in subparagraph w;

(z) 'family benefit' means all benefits in kind or in cash intended to meet family expenses, excluding advances of maintenance payments and special childbirth and adoption allowances mentioned in Annex I.

Article 2
Persons covered

1. This Regulation shall apply to nationals of a Member State, stateless persons and refugees residing in a Member State who are or have been subject to the legislation of one or more Member States, as well as to the members of their families and to their survivors.

2. It shall also apply to the survivors of persons who have been subject to the legislation of one or more Member States, irrespective of the nationality of such persons, where their survivors are nationals of a Member State or stateless persons or refugees residing in one of the Member States.

11

Article 3
Matters covered
1. This Regulation shall apply to all legislation concerning the following branches of social security:
   (a) sickness benefits;
   (b) maternity and equivalent paternity benefits;
   (c) invalidity benefits;
   (d) old-age benefits;
   (e) survivors' benefits;
   (f) benefits in respect of accidents at work and occupational diseases;
   (g) death grants;
   (h) unemployment benefits;
   (i) pre-retirement benefits;
   (j) family benefits.
2. Unless otherwise provided for in Annex XI, this Regulation shall apply to general and special social security schemes, whether contributory or non-contributory, and to schemes relating to the obligations of an employer or shipowner.
3. This Regulation shall also apply to the special non-contributory cash benefits covered by Article 70.
4. The provisions of Title III of this Regulation shall not, however, affect the legislative provisions of any Member State concerning a ship owner's obligations.
5. This Regulation shall not apply to:
   (a) social and medical assistance[;] or
   (b) benefits in relation to which a Member State assumes the liability for damages to persons and provides for compensation, such as those for victims of war and military action or their consequences; victims of crime, assassination or terrorist acts; victims of damage occasioned by agents of the Member State in the course of their duties; or victims who have suffered a disadvantage for political or religious reasons or for reasons of descent.

Article 4

Equality of treatment
Unless otherwise provided for by this Regulation, persons to whom this Regulation applies shall enjoy the same benefits and be subject to the same obligations under the legislation of any Member State as the nationals thereof.

Article 5

Equal treatment of benefits, income, facts or events
Unless otherwise provided for by this Regulation and in the light of the special implementing provisions laid down, the following shall apply:
(a) where, under the legislation of the competent Member State, the receipt of social security benefits and other income has certain legal effects, the relevant provisions of that legislation shall also apply to the receipt of equivalent benefits acquired under the legislation of another Member State or to income acquired in another Member State;

(b) where, under the legislation of the competent Member State, legal effects are attributed to the occurrence of certain facts or events, that Member State shall take account of like facts or events occurring in any Member State as though they had taken place in its own territory.

Article 6
Aggregation of periods

Unless otherwise provided for by this Regulation, the competent institution of a Member State whose legislation makes:

— the acquisition, retention, duration or recovery of the right to benefits,
— the coverage by legislation, or
— the access to or the exemption from compulsory, optional continued or voluntary insurance,

conditional upon the completion of periods of insurance, employment, self-employment or residence shall, to the extent necessary, take into account periods of insurance, employment, self-employment or residence completed under the legislation of any other Member State as though they were periods completed under the legislation which it applies.

Article 7
Waiving of residence rules

Unless otherwise provided for by this Regulation, cash benefits payable under the legislation of one or more Member States or under this Regulation shall not be subject to any reduction, amendment, suspension, withdrawal or confiscation on account of the fact that the beneficiary or the members of his/her family reside in a Member State other than that in which the institution responsible for providing benefits is situated.

Article 8
Relations between this Regulation and other coordination instruments

1. This Regulation shall replace any social security convention applicable between Member States falling under its scope. Certain provisions of social security conventions entered into by the Member States before the date of application of this Regulation shall, however, continue to apply provided that they are more favourable to the beneficiaries or if they arise from specific historical circumstances and their effect is limited in time. For these provisions to remain applicable, they shall be included in Annex II. If, on objective grounds, it is not possible to extend some of these provisions to all persons to whom the Regulation applies this shall be specified.

2. Two or more Member States may, as the need arises, conclude conventions with each other based on the principles of this Regulation and in keeping with the spirit thereof.

Article 9
Declarations by the Member States on the scope of this Regulation

1. The Member States shall notify the European Commission in writing of the declarations made in accordance with point (l) of Article 1, the legislation and schemes referred to in Article 3, the conventions entered into as referred to in Article 8(2), the minimum benefits referred to in Article 58, and the lack of an insurance system as

referred to in Article 65a(1), as well as substantive amendments. Such notifications shall indicate the date from which this Regulation will apply to the schemes specified by the Member States therein.

2. These notifications shall be submitted to the European Commission every year and shall be given the necessary publicity.

Article 10
Prevention of overlapping of benefits

Unless otherwise specified, this Regulation shall neither confer nor maintain the right to several benefits of the same kind for one and the same period of compulsory insurance.

TITLE II DETERMINATION OF THE LEGISLATION APPLICABLE

Article 11
General rules

1. Persons to whom this Regulation applies shall be subject to the legislation of a single Member State only. Such legislation shall be determined in accordance with this Title.

2. For the purposes of this Title, persons receiving cash benefits because or as a consequence of their activity as an employed or self-employed person shall be considered to be pursuing the said activity. This shall not apply to invalidity, old-age or survivors' pensions or to pensions in respect of accidents at work or occupational diseases or to sickness benefits in cash covering treatment for an unlimited period.

3. Subject to Articles 12 to 16:
   (a) a person pursuing an activity as an employed or self-employed person in a Member State shall be subject to the legislation of that Member State;
   (b) a civil servant shall be subject to the legislation of the Member State to which the administration employing him/her is subject;
   (c) a person receiving unemployment benefits in accordance with Article 65 under the legislation of the Member State of residence shall be subject to the legislation of that Member State;
   (d) a person called up or recalled for service in the armed forces or for civilian service in a Member State shall be subject to the legislation of that Member State;
   (e) any other person to whom subparagraphs (a) to (d) do not apply shall be subject to the legislation of the Member State of residence, without prejudice to other provisions of this Regulation guaranteeing him/her benefits under the legislation of one or more other Member States.

4. For the purposes of this Title, an activity as an employed or self-employed person normally pursued on board a vessel at sea flying the flag of a Member State shall be deemed to be an activity pursued in the said Member State. However, a person employed on board a vessel flying the flag of a Member State and remunerated for such activity by an undertaking or a person whose registered office or place of business is in another Member State shall be subject to the legislation of the latter Member State if he/she resides in that State. The undertaking or person paying the remuneration shall be considered as the employer for the purposes of the said legislation.

5. An activity as a flight crew or cabin crew member performing air passenger or freight services shall be deemed to be an activity pursued in the Member State where the home base, as defined in Annex III to Regulation (EEC) No. 3922/91, is located.

Article 12

Special rules

1. A person who pursues an activity as an employed person in a Member State on behalf of an employer which normally carries out its activities there and who is posted by that employer to another Member State to perform work on that employer's behalf shall continue to be subject to the legislation of the first Member State, provided that the anticipated duration of such work does not exceed 24 months and that he/she is not sent to replace another posted person.

2. A person who normally pursues an activity as a self-employed person in a Member State who goes to pursue a similar activity in another Member State shall continue to be subject to the legislation of the first Member State, provided that the anticipated duration of such activity does not exceed 24 months.

Article 13

Pursuit of activities in two or more Member States

1. A person who normally pursues an activity as an employed person in two or more Member States shall be subject:
   (a) to the legislation of the Member State of residence if he/she pursues a substantial part of his/her activity in that Member State; or
   (b) if he/she does not pursue a substantial part of his/her activity in the Member State of residence:
       (i) to the legislation of the Member State in which the registered office or place of business of the undertaking or employer is situated if he/she is employed by one undertaking or employer; or
       (ii) to the legislation of the Member State in which the registered office or place of business of the undertakings or employers is situated if he/she is employed by two or more undertakings or employers which have their registered office or place of business in only one Member State; or
       (iii) to the legislation of the Member State in which the registered office or place of business of the undertaking or employer is situated other than the Member State of residence if he/she is employed by two or more undertakings or employers, which have their registered office or place of business in two Member States, one of which is the Member State of residence; or
       (iv) to the legislation of the Member State of residence if he/she is employed by two or more undertakings or employers, at least two of which have their registered office or place of business in different Member States other than the Member State of residence.

2. A person who normally pursues an activity as a self-employed person in two or more Member States shall be subject to:
   (a) the legislation of the Member State of residence if he/she pursues a substantial part of his/her activity in that Member State; or

(b) the legislation of the Member State in which the centre of interest of his/her activities is situated, if he/she does not reside in one of the Member States in which he/she pursues a substantial part of his/her activity.

3. A person who normally pursues an activity as an employed person and an activity as a self-employed person in different Member States shall be subject to the legislation of the Member State in which he/she pursues an activity as an employed person or, if he/she pursues such an activity in two or more Member States, to the legislation determined in accordance with paragraph 1.

4. A person who is employed as a civil servant by one Member State and who pursues an activity as an employed person and/or as a self-employed person in one or more other Member States shall be subject to the legislation of the Member State to which the administration employing him/her is subject.

5. Persons referred to in paragraphs 1 to 4 shall be treated, for the purposes of the legislation determined in accordance with these provisions, as though they were pursuing all their activities as employed or self-employed persons and were receiving all their income in the Member State concerned.

Article 14
Voluntary insurance or optional continued insurance

1. Articles 11 to 13 shall not apply to voluntary insurance or to optional continued insurance unless, in respect of one of the branches referred to in Article 3(1), only a voluntary scheme of insurance exists in a Member State.

2. Where, by virtue of the legislation of a Member State, the person concerned is subject to compulsory insurance in that Member State, he/she may not be subject to a voluntary insurance scheme or an optional continued insurance scheme in another Member State. In all other cases in which, for a given branch, there is a choice between several voluntary insurance schemes or optional continued insurance schemes, the person concerned shall join only the scheme of his/her choice.

3. However, in respect of invalidity, old age and survivors' benefits, the person concerned may join the voluntary or optional continued insurance scheme of a Member State, even if he/she is compulsorily subject to the legislation of another Member State, provided that he/she has been subject, at some stage in his/her career, to the legislation of the first Member State because or as a consequence of an activity as an employed or self-employed person and if such overlapping is explicitly or implicitly allowed under the legislation of the first Member State.

4. Where the legislation of a Member State makes admission to voluntary insurance or optional continued insurance conditional upon residence in that Member State or upon previous activity as an employed or self-employed person, Article 5(b) shall apply only to persons who have been subject, at some earlier stage, to the legislation of that Member State on the basis of an activity as an employed or self-employed person.

Article 15
Contract staff of the European [Union]

Contract staff of the European [Union] may opt to be subject to the legislation of the Member State in which they are employed, to the legislation of the Member State to which they were last subject or to the legislation of the Member State whose nationals they are, in respect of provisions other than those relating to family allowances, provided under the scheme applicable to such staff. This right of option, which may be exercised once only, shall take effect from the date of entry into employment.

Article 16
Exceptions to Articles 11 to 15

1. Two or more Member States, the competent authorities of these Member States or the bodies designated by these authorities may by common agreement provide for exceptions to Articles 11 to 15 in the interest of certain persons or categories of persons.

2. A person who receives a pension or pensions under the legislation of one or more Member States and who resides in another Member State may at his/her request be exempted from application of the legislation of the latter State provided that he/she is not subject to that legislation on account of pursuing an activity as an employed or self-employed person.

TITLE III SPECIAL PROVISIONS CONCERNING THE VARIOUS CATEGORIES OF BENEFITS

Chapter 1 Sickness, Maternity and Equivalent Paternity Benefits

SECTION 1 INSURED PERSONS AND MEMBERS OF THEIR FAMILIES, EXCEPT PENSIONERS AND MEMBERS OF THEIR FAMILIES

Article 17
Residence in a Member State other than the competent Member State

An insured person or members of his/her family who reside in a Member State other than the competent Member State shall receive in the Member State of residence benefits in kind provided, on behalf of the competent institution, by the institution of the place of residence, in accordance with the provisions of the legislation it applies, as though they were insured under the said legislation.

Article 18
Stay in the competent Member State when residence is in another Member State – Special rules for the members of the families of frontier workers

1. Unless otherwise provided for by paragraph 2, the insured person and the members of his/her family referred to in Article 17 shall also be entitled to benefits in kind while staying in the competent Member State. The benefits in kind shall be provided by the competent institution and at its own expense, in accordance with the provisions of the legislation it applies, as though the persons concerned resided in that Member State.

2. The members of the family of a frontier worker shall be entitled to benefits in kind during their stay in the competent Member State.

    Where the competent Member State is listed in Annex III however, the members of the family of a frontier worker who reside in the same Member State as the frontier worker shall be entitled to benefits in kind in the competent Member State only under the conditions laid down in Article 19(1).

11

Article 19
Stay outside the competent Member State

1. Unless otherwise provided for by paragraph 2, an insured person and the members of his/her family staying in a Member State other than the competent Member State shall be entitled to the benefits in kind which become necessary on medical grounds during their stay, taking into account the nature of the benefits and the expected length of the stay. These benefits shall be provided on behalf of the competent institution by the institution of the place of stay, in accordance with the provisions of the legislation it applies, as though the persons concerned were insured under the said legislation.
2. The Administrative Commission shall establish a list of benefits in kind which, in order to be provided during a stay in another Member State, require for practical reasons a prior agreement between the person concerned and the institution providing the care.

Article 20
Travel with the purpose of receiving benefits in kind – authorisation to receive appropriate treatment outside the Member State of residence

1. Unless otherwise provided for by this Regulation, an insured person travelling to another Member State with the purpose of receiving benefits in kind during the stay shall seek authorisation from the competent institution.
2. An insured person who is authorised by the competent institution to go to another Member State with the purpose of receiving the treatment appropriate to his/her condition shall receive the benefits in kind provided, on behalf of the competent institution, by the institution of the place of stay, in accordance with the provisions of the legislation it applies, as though he/she were insured under the said legislation. The authorisation shall be accorded where the treatment in question is among the benefits provided for by the legislation in the Member State where the person concerned resides and where he/she cannot be given such treatment within a time limit which is medically justifiable, taking into account his/her current state of health and the probable course of his/her illness.
3. Paragraphs 1 and 2 shall apply mutatis mutandis to the members of the family of an insured person.
4. If the members of the family of an insured person reside in a Member State other than the Member State in which the insured person resides, and this Member State has opted for reimbursement on the basis of fixed amounts, the cost of the benefits in kind referred to in paragraph 2 shall be borne by the institution of the place of residence of the members of the family. In this case, for the purposes of paragraph 1, the institution of the place of residence of the members of the family shall be considered to be the competent institution.

Article 21
Cash benefits

1. An insured person and members of his/her family residing or staying in a Member State other than the competent Member State shall be entitled to cash benefits provided by the competent institution in accordance with the legislation it applies. By agreement between the competent institution and the institution of the place of residence or stay, such benefits may, however, be provided by the institution of the place

of residence or stay at the expense of the competent institution in accordance with the legislation of the competent Member State.

2. The competent institution of a Member State whose legislation stipulates that the calculation of cash benefits shall be based on average income or on an average contribution basis shall determine such average income or average contribution basis exclusively by reference to the incomes confirmed as having been paid, or contribution bases applied, during the periods completed under the said legislation.

3. The competent institution of a Member State whose legislation provides that the calculation of cash benefits shall be based on standard income shall take into account exclusively the standard income or, where appropriate, the average of standard incomes for the periods completed under the said legislation.

4. Paragraphs 2 and 3 shall apply mutatis mutandis to cases where the legislation applied by the competent institution lays down a specific reference period which corresponds in the case in question either wholly or partly to the periods which the person concerned has completed under the legislation of one or more other Member States.

Article 22
Pension claimants

1. An insured person who, on making a claim for a pension, or during the investigation thereof, ceases to be entitled to benefits in kind under the legislation of the Member State last competent, shall remain entitled to benefits in kind under the legislation of the Member State in which he/she resides, provided that the pension claimant satisfies the insurance conditions of the legislation of the Member State referred to in paragraph 2. The right to benefits in kind in the Member State of residence shall also apply to the members of the family of the pension claimant.

2. The benefits in kind shall be chargeable to the institution of the Member State which, in the event of a pension being awarded, would become competent under Articles 23 to 25.

SECTION 2 PENSIONERS AND MEMBERS OF THEIR FAMILIES

Article 23
Right to benefits in kind under the legislation of the Member State of residence

A person who receives a pension or pensions under the legislation of two or more Member States, of which one is the Member State of residence, and who is entitled to benefits in kind under the legislation of that Member State, shall, with the members of his/her family, receive such benefits in kind from and at the expense of the institution of the place of residence, as though he/she were a pensioner whose pension was payable solely under the legislation of that Member State.

Article 24
No right to benefits in kind under the legislation of the Member State of residence

1. A person who receives a pension or pensions under the legislation of one or more Member States and who is not entitled to benefits in kind under the legislation of the Member State of residence shall nevertheless receive such benefits for himself/herself and the members of his/her family, in so far as he/she would be entitled thereto under

the legislation of the Member State or of at least one of the Member States competent in respect of his/her pensions, if he/she resided in that Member State. The benefits in kind shall be provided at the expense of the institution referred to in paragraph 2 by the institution of the place of residence, as though the person concerned were entitled to a pension and benefits in kind under the legislation of that Member State.

2. In the cases covered by paragraph 1, the cost of benefits in kind shall be borne by the institution as determined in accordance with the following rules:

   (a) where the pensioner is entitled to benefits in kind under the legislation of a single Member State, the cost shall be borne by the competent institution of that Member State;

   (b) where the pensioner is entitled to benefits in kind under the legislation of two or more Member States, the cost thereof shall be borne by the competent institution of the Member State to whose legislation the person has been subject for the longest period of time; should the application of this rule result in several institutions being responsible for the cost of benefits, the cost shall be borne by the institution applying the legislation to which the pensioner was last subject.

Article 25

Pensions under the legislation of one or more Member States other than the Member State of residence, where there is a right to benefits in kind in the latter Member State

Where the person receiving a pension or pensions under the legislation of one or more Member States resides in a Member State under whose legislation the right to receive benefits in kind is not subject to conditions of insurance, or of activity as an employed or self-employed person, and no pension is received from that Member State, the cost of benefits in kind provided to him/her and to members of his/her family shall be borne by the institution of one of the Member States competent in respect of his/her pensions determined in accordance with Article 24(2), to the extent that the pensioner and the members of his/her family would be entitled to such benefits if they resided in that Member State.

Article 26

Residence of members of the family in a Member State other than the one in which the pensioner resides

Members of the family of a person receiving a pension or pensions under the legislation of one or more Member States who reside in a Member State other than the one in which the pensioner resides shall be entitled to receive benefits in kind from the institution of the place of their residence in accordance with the provisions of the legislation it applies, in so far as the pensioner is entitled to benefits in kind under the legislation of a Member State. The costs shall be borne by the competent institution responsible for the costs of the benefits in kind provided to the pensioner in his/her Member State of residence.

Article 27

Stay of the pensioner or the members of his/her family in a Member State other than the Member State in which they reside – stay in the competent Member State – authorisation for appropriate treatment outside the Member State of residence

1. Article 19 shall apply mutatis mutandis to a person receiving a pension or pensions under the legislation of one or more Member States and entitled to benefits in kind

under the legislation of one of the Member States which provide his/her pension(s) or to the members of his/her family who are staying in a Member State other than the one in which they reside.

2. Article 18(1) shall apply mutatis mutandis to the persons described in paragraph 1 when they stay in the Member State in which is situated the competent institution responsible for the cost of the benefits in kind provided to the pensioner in his/her Member State of residence and the said Member State has opted for this and is listed in Annex IV.

3. Article 20 shall apply mutatis mutandis to a pensioner and/or the members of his/ her family who are staying in a Member State other than the one in which they reside with the purpose of receiving there the treatment appropriate to their condition.

4. Unless otherwise provided for by paragraph 5, the cost of the benefits in kind referred to in paragraphs 1 to 3 shall be borne by the competent institution responsible for the cost of benefits in kind provided to the pensioner in his/her Member State of residence.

5. The cost of the benefits in kind referred to in paragraph 3 shall be borne by the institution of the place of residence of the pensioner or of the members of his/her family, if these persons reside in a Member State which has opted for reimbursement on the basis of fixed amounts. In these cases, for the purposes of paragraph 3, the institution of the place of residence of the pensioner or of the members of his/her family shall be considered to be the competent institution.

Article 28
Special rules for retired frontier workers

1. A frontier worker who has retired because of old-age or invalidity is entitled in the event of sickness to continue to receive benefits in kind in the Member State where he/she last pursued his/her activity as an employed or self-employed person, in so far as this is a continuation of treatment which began in that Member State. 'Continuation of treatment' means the continued investigation, diagnosis and treatment of an illness for its entire duration.

   The first subparagraph shall apply mutatis mutandis to the members of the family of the former frontier worker unless the Member State where the frontier worker last pursued his/her activity is listed in Annex III.

2. A pensioner who, in the five years preceding the effective date of an old-age or invalidity pension has been pursuing an activity as an employed or self-employed person for at least two years as a frontier worker shall be entitled to benefits in kind in the Member State in which he/she pursued such an activity as a frontier worker, if this Member State and the Member State in which the competent institution responsible for the costs of the benefits in kind provided to the pensioner in his/ her Member State of residence is situated have opted for this and are both listed in Annex V.

3. Paragraph 2 shall apply mutatis mutandis to the members of the family of a former frontier worker or his/her survivors if, during the periods referred to in paragraph 2, they were entitled to benefits in kind under Article 18(2), even if the frontier worker died before his/her pension commenced, provided he/she had been pursuing an activity as an employed or self-employed person as a frontier worker for at least two years in the five years preceding his/her death.

4. Paragraphs 2 and 3 shall be applicable until the person concerned becomes subject to the legislation of a Member State on the basis of an activity as an employed or self-employed person.

5. The cost of the benefits in kind referred to in paragraphs 1 to 3 shall be borne by the competent institution responsible for the cost of benefits in kind provided to the pensioner or to his/her survivors in their respective Member States of residence.

Article 29
Cash benefits for pensioners

1. Cash benefits shall be paid to a person receiving a pension or pensions under the legislation of one or more Member States by the competent institution of the Member State in which is situated the competent institution responsible for the cost of benefits in kind provided to the pensioner in his/her Member State of residence. Article 21 shall apply mutatis mutandis.

2. Paragraph 1 shall also apply to the members of a pensioner's family.

Article 30
Contributions by pensioners

1. The institution of a Member State which is responsible under the legislation it applies for making deductions in respect of contributions for sickness, maternity and equivalent paternity benefits, may request and recover such deductions, calculated in accordance with the legislation it applies, only to the extent that the cost of the benefits pursuant to Articles 23 to 26 is to be borne by an institution of the said Member State.

2. Where, in the cases referred to in Article 25, the acquisition of sickness, maternity and equivalent paternity benefits is subject to the payment of contributions or similar payments under the legislation of a Member State in which the pensioner concerned resides, these contributions shall not be payable by virtue of such residence.

SECTION 3 COMMON PROVISIONS

Article 31
General provision

Articles 23 to 30 shall not apply to a pensioner or the members of his/her family who are entitled to benefits under the legislation of a Member State on the basis of an activity as an employed or self-employed person. In such a case, the person concerned shall be subject, for the purposes of this Chapter, to Articles 17 to 21.

Article 32
Prioritising of the right to benefits in kind – special rule for the right of members of the family to benefits in the Member State of residence

1. An independent right to benefits in kind based on the legislation of a Member State or on this Chapter shall take priority over a derivative right to benefits for members of a family. A derivative right to benefits in kind shall, however, take priority over independent rights, where the independent right in the Member State of residence exists directly and solely on the basis of the residence of the person concerned in that Member State.

2. Where the members of the family of an insured person reside in a Member State under whose legislation the right to benefits in kind is not subject to conditions of insurance

or activity as an employed or self-employed person, benefits in kind shall be provided at the expense of the competent institution in the Member State in which they reside, if the spouse or the person caring for the children of the insured person pursues an activity as an employed or self-employed person in the said Member State or receives a pension from that Member State on the basis of an activity as an employed or self-employed person.

Article 33
Substantial benefits in kind

1. An insured person or a member of his/her family who has had a right to a prosthesis, a major appliance or other substantial benefits in kind recognised by the institution of a Member State, before he/she became insured under the legislation applied by the institution of another Member State, shall receive such benefits at the expense of the first institution, even if they are awarded after the said person has already become insured under the legislation applied by the second institution.
2. The Administrative Commission shall draw up the list of benefits covered by paragraph 1.

Article 34
Overlapping of long-term care benefits

1. If a recipient of long-term care benefits in cash, which have to be treated as sickness benefits and are therefore provided by the Member State competent for cash benefits under Articles 21 or 29, is, at the same time and under this Chapter, entitled to claim benefits in kind intended for the same purpose from the institution of the place of residence or stay in another Member State, and an institution in the first Member State is also required to reimburse the cost of these benefits in kind under Article 35, the general provision on prevention of overlapping of benefits laid down in Article 10 shall be applicable, with the following restriction only: if the person concerned claims and receives the benefit in kind, the amount of the benefit in cash shall be reduced by the amount of the benefit in kind which is or could be claimed from the institution of the first Member State required to reimburse the cost.
2. The Administrative Commission shall draw up the list of the cash benefits and benefits in kind covered by paragraph 1.
3. Two or more Member States, or their competent authorities, may agree on other or supplementary measures which shall not be less advantageous for the persons concerned than the principles laid down in paragraph 1.

Article 35
Reimbursements between institutions

1. The benefits in kind provided by the institution of a Member State on behalf of the institution of another Member State under this Chapter shall give rise to full reimbursement.
2. The reimbursements referred to in paragraph 1 shall be determined and effected in accordance with the arrangements set out in the Implementing Regulation, either on production of proof of actual expenditure, or on the basis of fixed amounts for Member States the legal or administrative structures of which are such that the use of reimbursement on the basis of actual expenditure is not appropriate.

11

3. Two or more Member States, and their competent authorities, may provide for other methods of reimbursement or waive all reimbursement between the institutions coming under their jurisdiction.

Chapter 2 Benefits in Respect of Accidents at Work and Occupational Diseases

Article 36

Right to benefits in kind and in cash

1. Without prejudice to any more favourable provisions in paragraphs 2 and 2a of this Article, Articles 17, 18(1), 19(1) and 20(1) shall also apply to benefits relating to accidents at work or occupational diseases.
2. A person who has sustained an accident at work or has contracted an occupational disease and who resides or stays in a Member State other than the competent Member State shall be entitled to the special benefits in kind of the scheme covering accidents at work and occupational diseases provided, on behalf of the competent institution, by the institution of the place of residence or stay in accordance with the legislation which it applies, as though he/she were insured under the said legislation.
2a. The competent institution may not refuse to grant the authorisation provided for in Article 20(1) to a person who has sustained an accident at work or who has contracted an occupational disease and who is entitled to benefits chargeable to that institution, where the treatment appropriate to his/her condition cannot be given in the Member State in which he/she resides within a time-limit which is medically justifiable, taking into account his/her current state of health and the probable course of the illness.
3. Article 21 shall also apply to benefits falling within this Chapter.

Article 37

Costs of transport

1. The competent institution of a Member State whose legislation provides for meeting the costs of transporting a person who has sustained an accident at work or is suffering from an occupational disease, either to his/her place of residence or to a hospital, shall meet such costs to the corresponding place in another Member State where the person resides, provided that that institution gives prior authorisation for such transport, duly taking into account the reasons justifying it. Such authorisation shall not be required in the case of a frontier worker.
2. The competent institution of a Member State whose legislation provides for meeting the costs of transporting the body of a person killed in an accident at work to the place of burial shall, in accordance with the legislation it applies, meet such costs to the corresponding place in another Member State where the person was residing at the time of the accident.

Article 38

Benefits for an occupational disease where the person suffering from such a disease has been exposed to the same risk in several Member States

When a person who has contracted an occupational disease has, under the legislation of two or more Member States, pursued an activity which by its nature is likely to cause the said disease, the benefits that he/she or his/her survivors may claim shall be provided exclusively under the legislation of the last of those States whose conditions are satisfied.

Article 39
Aggravation of an occupational disease
In the event of aggravation of an occupational disease for which a person suffering from such a disease has received or is receiving benefits under the legislation of a Member State, the following rules shall apply:

(a) if the person concerned, while in receipt of benefits, has not pursued, under the legislation of another Member State, an activity as an employed or self-employed person likely to cause or aggravate the disease in question, the competent institution of the first Member State shall bear the cost of the benefits under the provisions of the legislation which it applies, taking into account the aggravation;

(b) if the person concerned, while in receipt of benefits, has pursued such an activity under the legislation of another Member State, the competent institution of the first Member State shall bear the cost of the benefits under the legislation it applies without taking the aggravation into account. The competent institution of the second Member State shall grant a supplement to the person concerned, the amount of which shall be equal to the difference between the amount of benefits due after the aggravation and the amount which would have been due prior to the aggravation under the legislation it applies, if the disease in question had occurred under the legislation of that Member State;

(c) the rules concerning reduction, suspension or withdrawal laid down by the legislation of a Member State shall not be invoked against persons receiving benefits provided by institutions of two Member States in accordance with subparagraph (b).

Article 40
Rules for taking into account the special features of certain legislation

1. If there is no insurance against accidents at work or occupational diseases in the Member State in which the person concerned resides or stays, or if such insurance exists but there is no institution responsible for providing benefits in kind, those benefits shall be provided by the institution of the place of residence or stay responsible for providing benefits in kind in the event of sickness.

2. If there is no insurance against accidents at work or occupational diseases in the competent Member State, the provisions of this Chapter concerning benefits in kind shall nevertheless be applied to a person who is entitled to those benefits in the event of sickness, maternity or equivalent paternity under the legislation of that Member State if that person sustains an accident at work or suffers from an occupational disease during a residence or stay in another Member State. Costs shall be borne by the institution which is competent for the benefits in kind under the legislation of the competent Member State.

3. Article 5 shall apply to the competent institution in a Member State as regards the equivalence of accidents at work and occupational diseases which either have occurred or have been confirmed subsequently under the legislation of another Member State when assessing the degree of incapacity, the right to benefits or the amount thereof, on condition that:

(a) no compensation is due in respect of an accident at work or an occupational disease which had occurred or had been confirmed previously under the legislation it applies; and

(b) no compensation is due in respect of an accident at work or an occupational disease which had occurred or had been confirmed subsequently, under the legislation of the other Member State under which the accident at work or the occupational disease had occurred or been confirmed.

Article 41
Reimbursements between institutions

1. Article 35 shall also apply to benefits falling within this Chapter, and reimbursement shall be made on the basis of actual costs.

2. Two or more Member States, or their competent authorities, may provide for other methods of reimbursement or waive all reimbursement between the institutions under their jurisdiction.

Chapter 3 Death Grants

Article 42
Right to grants where death occurs in, or where the person entitled resides in, a Member State other than the competent Member State

1. When an insured person or a member of his/her family dies in a Member State other than the competent Member State, the death shall be deemed to have occurred in the competent Member State.

2. The competent institution shall be obliged to provide death grants payable under the legislation it applies, even if the person entitled resides in a Member State other than the competent Member State.

3. Paragraphs 1 and 2 shall also apply when the death is the result of an accident at work or an occupational disease.

Article 43
Provision of benefits in the event of the death of a pensioner

1. In the event of the death of a pensioner who was entitled to a pension under the legislation of one Member State, or to pensions under the legislations of two or more Member States, when that pensioner was residing in a Member State other than that of the institution responsible for the cost of benefits in kind provided under Articles 24 and 25, the death grants payable under the legislation administered by that institution shall be provided at its own expense as though the pensioner had been residing at the time of his/her death in the Member State in which that institution is situated.

2. Paragraph 1 shall apply mutatis mutandis to the members of the family of a pensioner.

Chapter 4 Invalidity Benefits

Article 44
Persons subject only to type A legislation

1. For the purposes of this Chapter, 'type A legislation' means any legislation under which the amount of invalidity benefits is independent of the duration of the

periods of insurance or residence and which is expressly included by the competent Member State in Annex VI, and 'type B legislation' means any other legislation.

2. A person who has been successively or alternately subject to the legislation of two or more Member States and who has completed periods of insurance or residence exclusively under type A legislations shall be entitled to benefits only from the institution of the Member State whose legislation was applicable at the time when the incapacity for work followed by invalidity occurred, taking into account, where appropriate, Article 45, and shall receive such benefits in accordance with that legislation.

3. A person who is not entitled to benefits under paragraph 2 shall receive the benefits to which he/she is still entitled under the legislation of another Member State, taking into account, where appropriate, Article 45.

4. If the legislation referred to in paragraph 2 or 3 contains rules for the reduction, suspension or withdrawal of invalidity benefits in the case of overlapping with other income or with benefits of a different kind within the meaning of Article 53(2), Articles 53(3) and 55(3) shall apply mutatis mutandis.

Article 45

Special provisions on aggregation of periods

The competent institution of a Member State whose legislation makes the acquisition, retention or recovery of the right to benefits conditional upon the completion of periods of insurance or residence shall, where necessary, apply Article 51(1) mutatis mutandis.

Article 46

Persons subject either only to type B legislation or to type A and B legislation

1. A person who has been successively or alternately subject to the legislation of two or more Member States, of which at least one is not a type A legislation, shall be entitled to benefits under Chapter 5, which shall apply mutatis mutandis taking into account paragraph 3.

2. However, if the person concerned has been previously subject to a type B legislation and suffers incapacity for work leading to invalidity while subject to a type A legislation, he/she shall receive benefits in accordance with Article 44, provided that:
   — he satisfies the conditions of that legislation exclusively or of others of the same type, taking into account, where appropriate, Article 45, but without having recourse to periods of insurance or residence completed under a type B legislation, and
   — he does not assert any claims to old-age benefits, taking into account Article 50(1).

3. A decision taken by an institution of a Member State concerning the degree of invalidity of a claimant shall be binding on the institution of any other Member State concerned, provided that the concordance between the legislation of these Member States on conditions relating to the degree of invalidity is acknowledged in Annex VII.

11

Article 47

Aggravation of invalidity

1. In the case of aggravation of an invalidity for which a person is receiving benefits under the legislation of one or more Member States, the following provisions shall apply, taking the aggravation into account:

   (a) the benefits shall be provided in accordance with Chapter 5, applied mutatis mutandis;

   (b) however, where the person concerned has been subject to two or more type A legislations and since receiving benefit has not been subject to the legislation of another Member State, the benefit shall be provided in accordance with Article 44(2).

2. If the total amount of the benefit or benefits payable under paragraph 1 is lower than the amount of the benefit which the person concerned was receiving at the expense of the institution previously competent for payment, that institution shall pay him/her a supplement equal to the difference between the two amounts.

3. If the person concerned is not entitled to benefits at the expense of an institution of another Member State, the competent institution of the Member State previously competent shall provide the benefits in accordance with the legislation it applies, taking into account the aggravation and, where appropriate, Article 45.

Article 48

Conversion of invalidity benefits into old-age benefits

1. Invalidity benefits shall be converted into old-age benefits, where appropriate, under the conditions laid down by the legislation or legislations under which they are provided and in accordance with Chapter 5.

2. Where a person receiving invalidity benefits can establish a claim to old-age benefits under the legislation of one or more other Member States, in accordance with Article 50, any institution which is responsible for providing invalidity benefits under the legislation of a Member State shall continue to provide such a person with the invalidity benefits to which he/she is entitled under the legislation it applies until paragraph 1 becomes applicable in respect of that institution, or otherwise for as long as the person concerned satisfies the conditions for such benefits.

3. Where invalidity benefits provided under the legislation of a Member State, in accordance with Article 44, are converted into old-age benefits and where the person concerned does not yet satisfy the conditions laid down by the legislation of one or more of the other Member States for receiving those benefits, the person concerned shall receive, from that or those Member States, invalidity benefits from the date of the conversion.

   Those invalidity benefits shall be provided in accordance with Chapter 5 as if that Chapter had been applicable at the time when the incapacity for work leading to invalidity occurred, until the person concerned satisfies the qualifying conditions for old-age benefit laid down by the national legislations concerned or, where such conversion is not provided for, for as long as he/she is entitled to invalidity benefits under the latter legislation or legislations.

4. The invalidity benefits provided under Article 44 shall be recalculated in accordance with Chapter 5 as soon as the beneficiary satisfies the qualifying conditions for invalidity benefits laid down by a type B legislation, or as soon as he/she receives old-age benefits under the legislation of another Member State.

Article 49
Special provisions for civil servants
Articles 6, 44, 46, 47 and 48 and Article 60(2) and (3) shall apply mutatis mutandis to persons covered by a special scheme for civil servants.

Chapter 5 Old-age and Survivors' Pensions

Article 50
General provisions
1. All the competent institutions shall determine entitlement to benefit, under all the legislations of the Member States to which the person concerned has been subject, when a request for award has been submitted, unless the person concerned expressly requests deferment of the award of old-age benefits under the legislation of one or more Member States.
2. If at a given moment the person concerned does not satisfy, or no longer satisfies, the conditions laid down by all the legislations of the Member States to which he/she has been subject, the institutions applying legislation the conditions of which have been satisfied shall not take into account, when performing the calculation in accordance with Article 52(1)(a) or (b), the periods completed under the legislations the conditions of which have not been satisfied, or are no longer satisfied, where this gives rise to a lower amount of benefit.
3. Paragraph 2 shall apply mutatis mutandis when the person concerned has expressly requested deferment of the award of old-age benefits.
4. A new calculation shall be performed automatically as and when the conditions to be fulfilled under the other legislations are satisfied or when a person requests the award of an old-age benefit deferred in accordance with paragraph 1, unless the periods completed under the other legislations have already been taken into account by virtue of paragraph 2 or 3.

Article 51
Special provisions on aggregation of periods
1. Where the legislation of a Member State makes the granting of certain benefits conditional upon the periods of insurance having been completed only in a specific activity as an employed or self-employed person or in an occupation which is subject to a special scheme for employed or self-employed persons, the competent institution of that Member State shall take into account periods completed under the legislation of other Member States only if completed under a corresponding scheme or, failing that, in the same occupation, or where appropriate, in the same activity as an employed or self-employed person.

   If, account having been taken of the periods thus completed, the person concerned does not satisfy the conditions for receipt of the benefits of a special scheme, these periods shall be taken into account for the purposes of providing the benefits of the general scheme or, failing that, of the scheme applicable to manual or clerical workers, as the case may be, provided that the person concerned had been affiliated to one or other of those schemes.

2. The periods of insurance completed under a special scheme of a Member State shall be taken into account for the purposes of providing the benefits of the general scheme or, failing that, of the scheme applicable to manual or clerical workers, as the case may be, of another Member State, provided that the person concerned had been affiliated to one or other of those schemes, even if those periods have already been taken into account in the latter Member State under a special scheme.

3. Where the legislation or specific scheme of a Member State makes the acquisition, retention or recovery of the right to benefits conditional upon the person concerned being insured at the time of the materialisation of the risk, this condition shall be regarded as having been satisfied if that person has been previously insured under the legislation or specific scheme of that Member State and is, at the time of the materialisation of the risk, insured under the legislation of another Member State for the same risk or, failing that, if a benefit is due under the legislation of another Member State for the same risk. The latter condition shall, however, be deemed to be fulfilled in the cases referred to in Article 57.

Article 52
Award of benefits

1. The competent institution shall calculate the amount of the benefit that would be due:
   (a) under the legislation it applies, only where the conditions for entitlement to benefits have been satisfied exclusively under national law (independent benefit);
   (b) by calculating a theoretical amount and subsequently an actual amount (pro rata benefit), as follows:
      (i) the theoretical amount of the benefit is equal to the benefit which the person concerned could claim if all the periods of insurance and/or of residence which have been completed under the legislations of the other Member States had been completed under the legislation it applies on the date of the award of the benefit. If, under this legislation, the amount does not depend on the duration of the periods completed, that amount shall be regarded as being the theoretical amount;
      (ii) the competent institution shall then establish the actual amount of the pro rata benefit by applying to the theoretical amount the ratio between the duration of the periods completed before materialisation of the risk under the legislation it applies and the total duration of the periods completed before materialisation of the risk under the legislations of all the Member States concerned.

2. Where appropriate, the competent institution shall apply, to the amount calculated in accordance with subparagraphs 1(a) and (b), all the rules relating to reduction, suspension or withdrawal, under the legislation it applies, within the limits provided for by Articles 53 to 55.

3. The person concerned shall be entitled to receive from the competent institution of each Member State the higher of the amounts calculated in accordance with subparagraphs 1(a) and (b).

4. Where the calculation pursuant to paragraph 1(a) in one Member State invariably results in the independent benefit being equal to or higher than the pro rata benefit, calculated in accordance with paragraph 1(b), the competent institution shall waive the pro rata calculation, provided that:

      (i)   such a situation is set out in Part 1 of Annex VIII;

      (ii) no legislation containing rules against overlapping, as referred to in Articles 54 and 55, is applicable unless the conditions laid down in Article 55(2) are fulfilled; and

      (iii) Article 57 is not applicable in relation to periods completed under the legislation of another Member State in the specific circumstances of the case.

5. Notwithstanding the provisions of paragraphs 1, 2 and 3, the pro rata calculation shall not apply to schemes providing benefits in respect of which periods of time are of no relevance to the calculation, subject to such schemes being listed in part 2 of Annex VIII. In such cases, the person concerned shall be entitled to the benefit calculated in accordance with the legislation of the Member State concerned.

Article 53

Rules to prevent overlapping

1. Any overlapping of invalidity, old age and survivors' benefits calculated or provided on the basis of periods of insurance and/or residence completed by the same person shall be considered to be overlapping of benefits of the same kind.

2. Overlapping of benefits which cannot be considered to be of the same kind within the meaning of paragraph 1 shall be considered to be overlapping of benefits of a different kind.

3. The following provisions shall be applicable for the purposes of rules to prevent overlapping laid down by the legislation of a Member State in the case of overlapping of a benefit in respect of invalidity, old age or survivors with a benefit of the same kind or a benefit of a different kind or with other income:

    (a) the competent institution shall take into account the benefits or incomes acquired in another Member State only where the legislation it applies provides for benefits or income acquired abroad to be taken into account;

    (b) the competent institution shall take into account the amount of benefits to be paid by another Member State before deduction of tax, social security contributions and other individual levies or deductions, unless the legislation it applies provides for the application of rules to prevent overlapping after such deductions, under the conditions and the procedures laid down in the Implementing Regulation;

    (c) the competent institution shall not take into account the amount of benefits acquired under the legislation of another Member State on the basis of voluntary insurance or continued optional insurance;

    (d) if a single Member State applies rules to prevent overlapping because the person concerned receives benefits of the same or of a different kind under the legislation of other Member States or income acquired in other Member States, the benefit due may be reduced solely by the amount of such benefits or such income.

Article 54

Overlapping of benefits of the same kind

1. Where benefits of the same kind due under the legislation of two or more Member States overlap, the rules to prevent overlapping laid down by the legislation of a Member State shall not be applicable to a pro rata benefit.

2. The rules to prevent overlapping shall apply to an independent benefit only if the benefit concerned is:
   (a) a benefit the amount of which does not depend on the duration of periods of insurance or residence, or
   (b) a benefit the amount of which is determined on the basis of a credited period deemed to have been completed between the date on which the risk materialised and a later date, overlapping with:
       (i) a benefit of the same type, except where an agreement has been concluded between two or more Member States to avoid the same credited period being taken into account more than once, or
       (ii) a benefit referred to in subparagraph (a).
   The benefits and agreements referred to in subparagraphs (a) and (b) are listed in Annex IX.

Article 55
Overlapping of benefits of a different kind
1. If the receipt of benefits of a different kind or other income requires the application of the rules to prevent overlapping provided for by the legislation of the Member States concerned regarding:
   (a) two or more independent benefits, the competent institutions shall divide the amounts of the benefit or benefits or other income, as they have been taken into account, by the number of benefits subject to the said rules; however, the application of this subparagraph cannot deprive the person concerned of his/her status as a pensioner for the purposes of the other chapters of this Title under the conditions and the procedures laid down in the Implementing Regulation;
   (b) one or more pro rata benefits, the competent institutions shall take into account the benefit or benefits or other income and all the elements stipulated for applying the rules to prevent overlapping as a function of the ratio between the periods of insurance and/or residence established for the calculation referred to in Article 52(1)(b)(ii);
   (c) one or more independent benefits and one or more pro-rata benefits, the competent institutions shall apply mutatis mutandis subparagraph (a) as regards independent benefits and subparagraph (b) as regards pro rata benefits.
2. The competent institution shall not apply the division stipulated in respect of independent benefits, if the legislation it applies provides for account to be taken of benefits of a different kind and/or other income and all other elements for calculating part of their amount determined as a function of the ratio between periods of insurance and/or residence referred to in Article 52(1)(b)(ii).
3. Paragraphs 1 and 2 shall apply mutatis mutandis where the legislation of one or more Member States provides that a right to a benefit cannot be acquired in the case where the person concerned is in receipt of a benefit of a different kind, payable under the legislation of another Member State, or of other income.

Article 56
Additional provisions for the calculation of benefits
1. For the calculation of the theoretical and pro rata amounts referred to in Article 52(1)(b), the following rules shall apply:

(a) where the total length of the periods of insurance and/or residence completed before the risk materialised under the legislations of all the Member States concerned is longer than the maximum period required by the legislation of one of these Member States for receipt of full benefit, the competent institution of that Member State shall take into account this maximum period instead of the total length of the periods completed; this method of calculation shall not result in the imposition on that institution of the cost of a benefit greater than the full benefit provided for by the legislation it applies. This provision shall not apply to benefits the amount of which does not depend on the length of insurance;

(b) the procedure for taking into account overlapping periods is laid down in the Implementing Regulation;

(c) if the legislation of a Member State provides that the benefits are to be calculated on the basis of incomes, contributions, bases of contributions, increases, earnings, other amounts or a combination of more than one of them (average, proportional, fixed or credited), the competent institution shall:

(i) determine the basis for calculation of the benefits in accordance only with periods of insurance completed under the legislation it applies;

(ii) use, in order to determine the amount to be calculated in accordance with the periods of insurance and/or residence completed under the legislation of the other Member States, the same elements determined or recorded for the periods of insurance completed under the legislation it applies;

where necessary in accordance with the procedures laid down in Annex XI for the Member State concerned;

(d) [i]n the event that point (c) is not applicable because the legislation of a Member State provides for the benefit to be calculated on the basis of elements other than periods of insurance or residence which are not linked to time, the competent institution shall take into account, in respect of each period of insurance or residence completed under the legislation of any other Member State, the amount of the capital accrued, the capital which is considered as having been accrued or any other element for the calculation under the legislation it administers divided by the corresponding units of periods in the pension scheme concerned.

2. The provisions of the legislation of a Member State concerning the revalorisation of the elements taken into account for the calculation of benefits shall apply, as appropriate, to the elements to be taken into account by the competent institution of that Member State, in accordance with paragraph 1, in respect of the periods of insurance or residence completed under the legislation of other Member States.

Article 57
Periods of insurance or residence of less than one year

1. Notwithstanding Article 52(1)(b), the institution of a Member State shall not be required to provide benefits in respect of periods completed under the legislation it applies which are taken into account when the risk materialises, if:
— the duration of the said periods is less than one year, and
— taking only these periods into account no right to benefit is acquired under that legislation.

For the purposes of this Article, 'periods' shall mean all periods of insurance, employment, self-employment or residence which either qualify for, or directly increase, the benefit concerned.

2. The competent institution of each of the Member States concerned shall take into account the periods referred to in paragraph 1, for the purposes of Article 52(1)(b)(i).

3. If the effect of applying paragraph 1 would be to relieve all the institutions of the Member States concerned of their obligations, benefits shall be provided exclusively under the legislation of the last of those Member States whose conditions are satisfied, as if all the periods of insurance and residence completed and taken into account in accordance with Articles 6 and 51(1) and (2) had been completed under the legislation of that Member State.

4. This Article shall not apply to schemes listed in Part 2 of Annex VIII.

Article 58
Award of a supplement

1. A recipient of benefits to whom this chapter applies may not, in the Member State of residence and under whose legislation a benefit is payable to him/her, be provided with a benefit which is less than the minimum benefit fixed by that legislation for a period of insurance or residence equal to all the periods taken into account for the payment in accordance with this chapter.

2. The competent institution of that Member State shall pay him/her throughout the period of his/her residence in its territory a supplement equal to the difference between the total of the benefits due under this chapter and the amount of the minimum benefit.

Article 59
Recalculation and revaluation of benefits

1. If the method for determining benefits or the rules for calculating benefits are altered under the legislation of a Member State, or if the personal situation of the person concerned undergoes a relevant change which, under that legislation, would lead to an adjustment of the amount of the benefit, a recalculation shall be carried out in accordance with Article 52.

2. On the other hand, if, by reason of an increase in the cost of living or changes in the level of income or other grounds for adjustment, the benefits of the Member State concerned are altered by a percentage or fixed amount, such percentage or fixed amount shall be applied directly to the benefits determined in accordance with Article 52, without the need for a recalculation.

Article 60
Special provisions for civil servants

1. Articles 6, 50, 51(3) and 52 to 59 shall apply mutatis mutandis to persons covered by a special scheme for civil servants.

2. However, if the legislation of a competent Member State makes the acquisition, liquidation, retention or recovery of the right to benefits under a special scheme for civil servants subject to the condition that all periods of insurance be completed under

one or more special schemes for civil servants in that Member State, or be regarded by the legislation of that Member State as equivalent to such periods, the competent institution of that State shall take into account only the periods which can be recognised under the legislation it applies.

If, account having been taken of the periods thus completed, the person concerned does not satisfy the conditions for the receipt of these benefits, these periods shall be taken into account for the award of benefits under the general scheme or, failing that, the scheme applicable to manual or clerical workers, as the case may be.

3. Where, under the legislation of a Member State, benefits under a special scheme for civil servants are calculated on the basis of the last salary or salaries received during a reference period, the competent institution of that State shall take into account, for the purposes of the calculation, only those salaries, duly revalued, which were received during the period or periods for which the person concerned was subject to that legislation.

Chapter 6 Unemployment Benefits

Article 61
Special rules on aggregation of periods of insurance, employment or self-employment

1. The competent institution of a Member State whose legislation makes the acquisition, retention, recovery or duration of the right to benefits conditional upon the completion of either periods of insurance, employment or self-employment shall, to the extent necessary, take into account periods of insurance, employment or self-employment completed under the legislation of any other Member State as though they were completed under the legislation it applies.

However, when the applicable legislation makes the right to benefits conditional on the completion of periods of insurance, the periods of employment or self-employment completed under the legislation of another Member State shall not be taken into account unless such periods would have been considered to be periods of insurance had they been completed in accordance with the applicable legislation.

2. Except in the cases referred to in Article 65(5)(a), the application of paragraph 1 of this Article shall be conditional on the person concerned having the most recently completed, in accordance with the legislation under which the benefits are claimed:
   — periods of insurance, if that legislation requires periods of insurance,
   — periods of employment, if that legislation requires periods of employment, or
   — periods of self-employment, if that legislation requires periods of self-employment.

Article 62
Calculation of benefits

1. The competent institution of a Member State whose legislation provides for the calculation of benefits on the basis of the amount of the previous salary or professional income shall take into account exclusively the salary or professional income received by the person concerned in respect of his/her last activity as an employed or self-employed person under the said legislation.

2. Paragraph 1 shall also apply where the legislation administered by the competent institution provides for a specific reference period for the determination of the

salary which serves as a basis for the calculation of benefits and where, for all or part of that period, the person concerned was subject to the legislation of another Member State.

3. By way of derogation from paragraphs 1 and 2, as far as the unemployed persons covered by Article 65(5)(a) are concerned, the institution of the place of residence shall take into account the salary or professional income received by the person concerned in the Member State to whose legislation he/she was subject during his/her last activity as an employed or self-employed person, in accordance with the Implementing Regulation.

Article 63
Special provisions for the waiving of residence rules
For the purpose of this Chapter, Article 7 shall apply only in the cases provided for by Articles 64, 65 and 65a and within the limits prescribed therein.

Article 64
Unemployed persons going to another Member State
1. A wholly unemployed person who satisfies the conditions of the legislation of the competent Member State for entitlement to benefits, and who goes to another Member State in order to seek work there, shall retain his/her entitlement to unemployment benefits in cash under the following conditions and within the following limits:
   (a) before his/her departure, the unemployed person must have been registered as a person seeking work and have remained available to the employment services of the competent Member State for at least four weeks after becoming unemployed. However, the competent services or institutions may authorise his/her departure before such time has expired;
   (b) the unemployed person must register as a person seeking work with the employment services of the Member State to which he/she has gone, be subject to the control procedure organised there and adhere to the conditions laid down under the legislation of that Member State. This condition shall be considered satisfied for the period before registration if the person concerned registers within seven days of the date on which he/she ceased to be available to the employment services of the Member State which he/she left. In exceptional cases, the competent services or institutions may extend this period;
   (c) entitlement to benefits shall be retained for a period of three months from the date when the unemployed person ceased to be available to the employment services of the Member State which he/she left, provided that the total duration for which the benefits are provided does not exceed the total duration of the period of his/her entitlement to benefits under the legislation of that Member State; the competent services or institutions may extend the period of three months up to a maximum of six months;
   (d) the benefits shall be provided by the competent institution in accordance with the legislation it applies and at its own expense.
2. If the person concerned returns to the competent Member State on or before the expiry of the period during which he/she is entitled to benefits under paragraph 1(c), he/she shall continue to be entitled to benefits under the legislation of that Member

State. He/she shall lose all entitlement to benefits under the legislation of the competent Member State if he/she does not return there on or before the expiry of the said period, unless the provisions of that legislation are more favourable. In exceptional cases the competent services or institutions may allow the person concerned to return at a later date without loss of his/her entitlement.

3. Unless the legislation of the competent Member State is more favourable, between two periods of employment the maximum total period for which entitlement to benefits shall be retained under paragraph 1 shall be three months; the competent services or institutions may extend that period up to a maximum of six months.

4. The arrangements for exchanges of information, cooperation and mutual assistance between the institutions and services of the competent Member State and the Member State to which the person goes in order to seek work shall be laid down in the Implementing Regulation.

Article 65

Unemployed persons who resided in a Member State other than the competent State

1. A person who is partially or intermittently unemployed and who, during his/her last activity as an employed or self-employed person, resided in a Member State other than the competent Member State shall make himself/herself available to his/her employer or to the employment services in the competent Member State. He/she shall receive benefits in accordance with the legislation of the competent Member State as if he/she were residing in that Member State. These benefits shall be provided by the institution of the competent Member State.

2. A wholly unemployed person who, during his/her last activity as an employed or self-employed person, resided in a Member State other than the competent Member State and who continues to reside in that Member State or returns to that Member State shall make himself/herself available to the employment services in the Member State of residence. Without prejudice to Article 64, a wholly unemployed person may, as a supplementary step, make himself/herself available to the employment services of the Member State in which he/she pursued his/her last activity as an employed or self-employed person.

   An unemployed person, other than a frontier worker, who does not return to his/her Member State of residence, shall make himself/herself available to the employment services in the Member State to whose legislation he/she was last subject.

3. The unemployed person referred to in the first sentence of paragraph 2 shall register as a person seeking work with the competent employment services of the Member State in which he/she resides, shall be subject to the control procedure organised there and shall adhere to the conditions laid down under the legislation of that Member State. If he/she chooses also to register as a person seeking work in the Member State in which he/she pursued his/her last activity as an employed or self-employed person, he/she shall comply with the obligations applicable in that State.

4. The implementation of the second sentence of paragraph 2 and of the second sentence of paragraph 3, as well as the arrangements for exchanges of information, cooperation and mutual assistance between the institutions and services of the Member State of residence and the Member State in which he/she pursued his/her last occupation, shall be laid down in the Implementing Regulation.

5.

   (a) The unemployed person referred to in the first and second sentences of paragraph 2 shall receive benefits in accordance with the legislation of the Member State of residence as if he/she had been subject to that legislation during his/her last activity as an employed or self-employed person. Those benefits shall be provided by the institution of the place of residence.

   (b) However, a worker other than a frontier worker who has been provided benefits at the expense of the competent institution of the Member State to whose legislation he/she was last subject shall firstly receive, on his/her return to the Member State of residence, benefits in accordance with Article 64, receipt of the benefits in accordance with (a) being suspended for the period during which he/she receives benefits under the legislation to which he/she was last subject.

6. The benefits provided by the institution of the place of residence under paragraph 5 shall continue to be at its own expense. However, subject to paragraph 7, the competent institution of the Member State to whose legislation he/she was last subject shall reimburse to the institution of the place of residence the full amount of the benefits provided by the latter institution during the first three months. The amount of the reimbursement during this period may not be higher than the amount payable, in the case of unemployment, under the legislation of the competent Member State. In the case referred to in paragraph 5(b), the period during which benefits are provided under Article 64 shall be deducted from the period referred to in the second sentence of this paragraph. The arrangements for reimbursement shall be laid down in the Implementing Regulation.

7. However, the period of reimbursement referred to in paragraph 6 shall be extended to five months when the person concerned has, during the preceding 24 months, completed periods of employment or self-employment of at least 12 months in the Member State to whose legislation he/she was last subject, where such periods would qualify for the purposes of establishing entitlement to unemployment benefits.

8. For the purposes of paragraphs 6 and 7, two or more Member States, or their competent authorities, may provide for other methods of reimbursement or waive all reimbursement between the institutions falling under their jurisdiction.

Article 65a

Special provisions for wholly unemployed self-employed frontier workers where no unemployment benefits system covering self-employed persons exists in the Member State of residence

1. By way of derogation from Article 65, a wholly unemployed person who, as a frontier worker, has most recently completed periods of insurance as a self-employed person or periods of self-employment recognised for the purposes of granting unemployment benefits in a Member State other than his/her Member State of residence and whose Member State of residence has submitted notification that there is no possibility for any category of self-employed persons to be covered by an unemployment benefits system of that Member State, shall register with and make himself/herself available to the employment services in the Member State in which he/she pursued his/her last activity as a self-employed person and, when he/she applies for benefits, shall continuously adhere to the conditions laid down under the legislation of the latter Member

State. The wholly unemployed person may, as a supplementary step, make himself/herself available to the employment services of the Member State of residence.

2. Benefits shall be provided to the wholly unemployed person referred to in paragraph 1 by the Member State to whose legislation he/she was last subject in accordance with the legislation which that Member State applies.

3. If the wholly unemployed person referred to in paragraph 1 does not wish to become or remain available to the employment services of the Member State of last activity after having been registered there, and wishes to seek work in the Member State of residence, Article 64 shall apply mutatis mutandis, except Article 64(1)(a). The competent institution may extend the period referred to in the first sentence of Article 64(1)(c) up to the end of the period of entitlement to benefits.

Chapter 7 Pre-retirement Benefits

Article 66
Benefits
When the applicable legislation makes the right to pre-retirement benefits conditional on the completion of periods of insurance, of employment or of self-employment, Article 6 shall not apply.

Chapter 8 Family Benefits

Article 67
Members of the family residing in another Member State
A person shall be entitled to family benefits in accordance with the legislation of the competent Member State, including for his/her family members residing in another Member State, as if they were residing in the former Member State. However, a pensioner shall be entitled to family benefits in accordance with the legislation of the Member State competent for his/her pension.

Article 68
Priority rules in the event of overlapping
1. Where, during the same period and for the same family members, benefits are provided for under the legislation of more than one Member State the following priority rules shall apply:
   (a) in the case of benefits payable by more than one Member State on different bases, the order of priority shall be as follows: firstly, rights available on the basis of an activity as an employed or self-employed person, secondly, rights available on the basis of receipt of a pension and finally, rights obtained on the basis of residence;
   (b) in the case of benefits payable by more than one Member State on the same basis, the order of priority shall be established by referring to the following subsidiary criteria:
      (i) in the case of rights available on the basis of an activity as an employed or self-employed person: the place of residence of the children, provided that there is such activity, and additionally, where appropriate, the highest amount of the benefits provided for by the conflicting legislations. In the latter case,

the cost of benefits shall be shared in accordance with criteria laid down in the Implementing Regulation;

(ii) in the case of rights available on the basis of receipt of pensions: the place of residence of the children, provided that a pension is payable under its legislation, and additionally, where appropriate, the longest period of insurance or residence under the conflicting legislations;

(iii) in the case of rights available on the basis of residence: the place of residence of the children.

2. In the case of overlapping entitlements, family benefits shall be provided in accordance with the legislation designated as having priority in accordance with paragraph 1. Entitlements to family benefits by virtue of other conflicting legislation or legislations shall be suspended up to the amount provided for by the first legislation and a differential supplement shall be provided, if necessary, for the sum which exceeds this amount. However, such a differential supplement does not need to be provided for children residing in another Member State when entitlement to the benefit in question is based on residence only.

3. If, under Article 67, an application for family benefits is submitted to the competent institution of a Member State whose legislation is applicable, but not by priority right in accordance with paragraphs 1 and 2 of this Article:

(a) that institution shall forward the application without delay to the competent institution of the Member State whose legislation is applicable by priority, inform the person concerned and, without prejudice to the provisions of the Implementing Regulation concerning the provisional award of benefits, provide, if necessary, the differential supplement mentioned in paragraph 2;

(b) the competent institution of the Member State whose legislation is applicable by priority shall deal with this application as though it were submitted directly to itself, and the date on which such an application was submitted to the first institution shall be considered as the date of its claim to the institution with priority.

Article 68a

Provision of benefits

In the event that family benefits are not used by the person to whom they should be provided for the maintenance of the members of the family, the competent institution shall discharge its legal obligations by providing those benefits to the natural or legal person in fact maintaining the members of the family, at the request and through the agency of the institution in their Member State of residence or of the designated institution or body appointed for that purpose by the competent authority of their Member State of residence.

Article 69

Additional provisions

1. If, under the legislation designated by virtue of Articles 67 and 68, no right is acquired to the payment of additional or special family benefits for orphans, such benefits shall be paid by default, and in addition to the other family benefits acquired in accordance with the abovementioned legislation, under the legislation of the Member State to which the deceased worker was subject for the longest period of time, in so far as

the right was acquired under that legislation. If no right was acquired under that legislation, the conditions for the acquisition of such right under the legislations of the other Member States shall be examined and benefits provided in decreasing order of the length of periods of insurance or residence completed under the legislation of those Member States.

2. Benefits paid in the form of pensions or supplements to pensions shall be provided and calculated in accordance with Chapter 5.

Chapter 9 Special Non-contributory Cash Benefits

Article 70
General provision

1. This Article shall apply to special non-contributory cash benefits which are provided under legislation which, because of its personal scope, objectives and/or conditions for entitlement, has characteristics both of the social security legislation referred to in Article 3(1) and of social assistance.

2. For the purposes of this Chapter, 'special non-contributory cash benefits' means those which:
   (a) are intended to provide either:
      (i) supplementary, substitute or ancillary cover against the risks covered by the branches of social security referred to in Article 3(1), and which guarantee the persons concerned a minimum subsistence income having regard to the economic and social situation in the Member State concerned; or
      (ii) solely specific protection for the disabled, closely linked to the said person's social environment in the Member State concerned[;] and
   (b) where the financing exclusively derives from compulsory taxation intended to cover general public expenditure and the conditions for providing and for calculating the benefits are not dependent on any contribution in respect of the beneficiary. However, benefits provided to supplement a contributory benefit shall not be considered to be contributory benefits for this reason alone[;] and
   (c) are listed in Annex X.

3. Article 7 and the other chapters of this Title shall not apply to the benefits referred to in paragraph 2 of this Article.

4. The benefits referred to in paragraph 2 shall be provided exclusively in the Member State in which the persons concerned reside, in accordance with its legislation. Such benefits shall be provided by and at the expense of the institution of the place of residence.

TITLE IV ADMINISTRATIVE COMMISSION AND ADVISORY COMMITTEE

Article 71
Composition and working methods of the Administrative Commission

1. The Administrative Commission for the Coordination of Social Security Systems (hereinafter called the Administrative Commission) attached to the European Commission shall be made up of a government representative from each of the Member States, assisted, where necessary, by expert advisers. A representative of the

European Commission shall attend the meetings of the Administrative Commission in an advisory capacity.

2. The Administrative Commission shall act by a qualified majority as defined by the Treaties, except when adopting its rules which shall be drawn up by mutual agreement among its members.

   Decisions on questions of interpretation referred to in Article 72(a) shall be given the necessary publicity.

3. Secretarial services for the Administrative Commission shall be provided by the European Commission.

Article 72
Tasks of the Administrative Commission

The Administrative Commission shall:

(a) deal with all administrative questions and questions of interpretation arising from the provisions of this Regulation or those of the Implementing Regulation, or from any agreement concluded or arrangement made thereunder, without prejudice to the right of the authorities, institutions and persons concerned to have recourse to the procedures and tribunals provided for by the legislation of the Member States, by this Regulation or by the Treaty;

(b) facilitate the uniform application of [Union] law, especially by promoting exchange of experience and best administrative practices;

(c) foster and develop cooperation between Member States and their institutions in social security matters in order, inter alia, to take into account particular questions regarding certain categories of persons; facilitate realisation of actions of cross border cooperation activities in the area of the coordination of social security systems;

(d) encourage as far as possible the use of new technologies in order to facilitate the free movement of persons, in particular by modernising procedures for exchanging information and adapting the information flow between institutions for the purposes of exchange by electronic means, taking account of the development of data processing in each Member State; the Administrative Commission shall adopt the common structural rules for data processing services, in particular on security and the use of standards, and shall lay down provisions for the operation of the common part of those services;

(e) undertake any other function falling within its competence under this Regulation and the Implementing Regulation or any agreement or arrangement concluded thereunder;

(f) make any relevant proposals to the European Commission concerning the coordination of social security schemes, with a view to improving and modernising the [Union] acquis by drafting subsequent Regulations or by means of other instruments provided for by the Treaty;

(g) establish the factors to be taken into account for drawing up accounts relating to the costs to be borne by the institutions of the Member States under this Regulation and to adopt the annual accounts between those institutions, based on the report of the Audit Board referred to in Article 74.

Article 73

Technical Commission for Data Processing

1. A Technical Commission for Data Processing (hereinafter called the Technical Commission) shall be attached to the Administrative Commission. The Technical Commission shall propose to the Administrative Commission common architecture rules for the operation of data-processing services, in particular on security and the use of standards; it shall deliver reports and a reasoned opinion before decisions are taken by the Administrative Commission pursuant to Article 72(d). The composition and working methods of the Technical Commission shall be determined by the Administrative Commission.
2. To this end, the Technical Commission shall:
    (a) gather together the relevant technical documents and undertake the studies and other work required to accomplish its tasks;
    (b) submit to the Administrative Commission the reports and reasoned opinions referred to in paragraph 1;
    (c) carry out all other tasks and studies on matters referred to it by the Administrative Commission;
    (d) ensure the management of [Union] pilot projects using data-processing services and, for the [Union] part, operational systems using data-processing services.

Article 74

Audit Board

1. An Audit Board shall be attached to the Administrative Commission. The composition and working methods of the Audit Board shall be determined by the Administrative Commission.
    The Audit Board shall:
    (a) verify the method of determining and calculating the annual average costs presented by Member States;
    (b) collect the necessary data and carry out the calculations required for establishing the annual statement of claims of each Member State;
    (c) give the Administrative Commission periodic accounts of the results of the implementation of this Regulation and of the Implementing Regulation, in particular as regards the financial aspect;
    (d) provide the data and reports necessary for decisions to be taken by the Administrative Commission pursuant to Article 72(g);
    (e) make any relevant suggestions it may have to the Administrative Commission, including those concerning this Regulation, in connection with subparagraphs (a), (b) and (c);
    (f) carry out all work, studies or assignments on matters referred to it by the Administrative Commission.

Article 75

Advisory Committee for the Coordination of Social Security Systems

1. An Advisory Committee for the Coordination of Social Security Systems (hereinafter referred to as Advisory Committee) is hereby established, comprising, from each Member State:

(a) one government representative;

(b) one representative from the trade unions;

(c) one representative from the employers' organisations.

For each of the categories referred to above, an alternate member shall be appointed for each Member State.

The members and alternate members of the Advisory Committee shall be appointed by the Council. The Advisory Committee shall be chaired by a representative of the European Commission. The Advisory Committee shall draw up its Rules of Procedure.

2. The Advisory Committee shall be empowered, at the request of the European Commission, the Administrative Commission or on its own initiative:

(a) to examine general questions or questions of principle and problems arising from the implementation of the [Union] provisions on the coordination of social security systems, especially regarding certain categories of persons;

(b) to formulate opinions on such matters for the Administrative Commission and proposals for any revisions of the said provisions.

TITLE V MISCELLANEOUS PROVISIONS

Article 76

Cooperation

1. The competent authorities of the Member States shall communicate to each other all information regarding:

(a) measures taken to implement this Regulation;

(b) changes in their legislation which may affect the implementation of this Regulation.

2. For the purposes of this Regulation, the authorities and institutions of the Member States shall lend one another their good offices and act as though implementing their own legislation. The administrative assistance given by the said authorities and institutions shall, as a rule, be free of charge. However, the Administrative Commission shall establish the nature of reimbursable expenses and the limits above which their reimbursement is due.

3. The authorities and institutions of the Member States may, for the purposes of this Regulation, communicate directly with one another and with the persons involved or their representatives.

4. The institutions and persons covered by this Regulation shall have a duty of mutual information and cooperation to ensure the correct implementation of this Regulation.

The institutions, in accordance with the principle of good administration, shall respond to all queries within a reasonable period of time and shall in this connection provide the persons concerned with any information required for exercising the rights conferred on them by this Regulation.

The persons concerned must inform the institutions of the competent Member State and of the Member State of residence as soon as possible of any change in their personal or family situation which affects their right to benefits under this Regulation.

5. Failure to respect the obligation of information referred to in the third subparagraph of paragraph 4 may result in the application of proportionate measures in accordance with national law. Nevertheless, these measures shall be equivalent to those applicable to similar situations under domestic law and shall not make it impossible or excessively difficult in practice for claimants to exercise the rights conferred on them by this Regulation.

6. In the event of difficulties in the interpretation or application of this Regulation which could jeopardise the rights of a person covered by it, the institution of the competent Member State or of the Member State of residence of the person concerned shall contact the institution(s) of the Member State(s) concerned. If a solution cannot be found within a reasonable period, the authorities concerned may call on the Administrative Commission to intervene.

7. The authorities, institutions and tribunals of one Member State may not reject applications or other documents submitted to them on the grounds that they are written in an official language of another Member State, recognised as an official language of the [Union] institutions in accordance with Article [342] of the Treaty.

Article 77
Protection of personal data

1. Where, according to this Regulation or to the Implementing Regulation, the authorities or institutions of a Member State communicate personal data to the authorities or institutions of another Member State, such communication shall be subject to the data protection legislation of the Member State transmitting them. Any communication from the authority or institution of the receiving Member State as well as the storage, alteration and destruction of the data provided by that Member State shall be subject to the data protection legislation of the receiving Member State.

2. Data required for the application of this Regulation and the Implementing Regulation shall be transmitted by one Member State to another Member State in accordance with [Union] provisions on the protection of natural persons with regard to the processing and free movement of personal data.

Article 78
Data processing

1. Member States shall progressively use new technologies for the exchange, access and processing of the data required to apply this Regulation and the Implementing Regulation. The European Commission shall lend its support to activities of common interest as soon as the Member States have established such data-processing services.

2. Each Member State shall be responsible for managing its own part of the data-processing services in accordance with the [Union] provisions on the protection of natural persons with regard to the processing and the free movement of personal data.

3. An electronic document sent or issued by an institution in conformity with this Regulation and the Implementing Regulation may not be rejected by any authority or institution of another Member State on the grounds that it was received by electronic means, once the receiving institution has declared that it can receive electronic documents. Reproduction and recording of such documents shall be presumed to be a

11

correct and accurate reproduction of the original document or representation of the information it relates to, unless there is proof to the contrary.

4. An electronic document shall be considered valid if the computer system on which the document is recorded contains the safeguards necessary in order to prevent any alteration, disclosure or unauthorised access to the recording. It shall at any time be possible to reproduce the recorded information in an immediately readable form. When an electronic document is transferred from one social security institution to another, appropriate security measures shall be taken in accordance with the [Union] provisions on the protection of natural persons with regard to the processing and the free movement of personal data.

Article 79

Funding of activities in the social security field

In connection with this Regulation and the Implementing Regulation, the European Commission may fund in full or in part:

(a) activities aimed at improving exchanges of information between the social security authorities and institutions of the Member States, particularly the electronic exchange of data;

(b) any other activity aimed at providing information to the persons covered by this Regulation and their representatives about the rights and obligations deriving from this Regulation, using the most appropriate means.

Article 80

Exemptions

1. Any exemption from or reduction of taxes, stamp duty, notarial or registration fees provided for under the legislation of one Member State in respect of certificates or documents required to be produced in application of the legislation of that Member State shall be extended to similar certificates or documents required to be produced in application of the legislation of another Member State or of this Regulation.

2. All statements, documents and certificates of any kind whatsoever required to be produced in application of this Regulation shall be exempt from authentication by diplomatic or consular authorities.

Article 81

Claims, declarations or appeals

Any claim, declaration or appeal which should have been submitted, in application of the legislation of one Member State, within a specified period to an authority, institution or tribunal of that Member State shall be admissible if it is submitted within the same period to a corresponding authority, institution or tribunal of another Member State. In such a case the authority, institution or tribunal receiving the claim, declaration or appeal shall forward it without delay to the competent authority, institution or tribunal of the former Member State either directly or through the competent authorities of the Member States concerned. The date on which such claims, declarations or appeals were submitted to the authority, institution or tribunal of the second Member State shall be considered as the date of their submission to the competent authority, institution or tribunal.

Article 82
Medical examinations

Medical examinations provided for by the legislation of one Member State may be carried out at the request of the competent institution, in another Member State, by the institution of the place of residence or stay of the claimant or the person entitled to benefits, under the conditions laid down in the Implementing Regulation or agreed between the competent authorities of the Member States concerned.

Article 83
Implementation of legislation

Special provisions for implementing the legislation of certain Member States are referred to in Annex XI.

Article 84
Collection of contributions and recovery of benefits

1. Collection of contributions due to an institution of one Member State and recovery of benefits provided by the institution of one Member State but not due may be effected in another Member State in accordance with the procedures and with the guarantees and privileges applicable to the collection of contributions due to the corresponding institution of the latter Member State and the recovery of benefits provided by it but not due.
2. Enforceable decisions of the judicial and administrative authorities relating to the collection of contributions, interest and any other charges or to the recovery of benefits provided but not due under the legislation of one Member State shall be recognised and enforced at the request of the competent institution in another Member State within the limits and in accordance with the procedures laid down by the legislation and any other procedures applicable to similar decisions of the latter Member State. Such decisions shall be declared enforceable in that Member State in so far as the legislation and any other procedures of that Member State so require.
3. Claims of an institution of one Member State shall in enforcement, bankruptcy or settlement proceedings in another Member State enjoy the same privileges as the legislation of the latter Member State accords to claims of the same kind.
4. The procedure for implementing this Article, including costs reimbursement, shall be governed by the Implementing Regulation or, where necessary and as a complementary measure, by means of agreements between Member States.

Article 85
Rights of institutions

1. If a person receives benefits under the legislation of one Member State in respect of an injury resulting from events occurring in another Member State, any rights of the institution responsible for providing benefits against a third party liable to provide compensation for the injury shall be governed by the following rules:
   (a) where the institution responsible for providing benefits is, under the legislation it applies, subrogated to the rights which the beneficiary has against the third party, such subrogation shall be recognised by each Member State;
   (b) where the institution responsible for providing benefits has a direct right against the third party, each Member State shall recognise such rights.

11

2. If a person receives benefits under the legislation of one Member State in respect of an injury resulting from events occurring in another Member State, the provisions of the said legislation which determine the cases in which the civil liability of employers or of their employees is to be excluded shall apply with regard to the said person or to the competent institution.

   Paragraph 1 shall also apply to any rights of the institution responsible for providing benefits against employers or their employees in cases where their liability is not excluded.

3. Where, in accordance with Article 35(3) and/or Article 41(2), two or more Member States or their competent authorities have concluded an agreement to waive reimbursement between institutions under their jurisdiction, or, where reimbursement does not depend on the amount of benefits actually provided, any rights arising against a liable third party shall be governed by the following rules:

   (a) where the institution of the Member State of residence or stay accords benefits to a person in respect of an injury sustained in its territory, that institution, in accordance with the provisions of the legislation it applies, shall exercise the right to subrogation or direct action against the third party liable to provide compensation for the injury;

   (b) for the application of (a):

       (i) the person receiving benefits shall be deemed to be insured with the institution of the place of residence or stay, and

       (ii) that institution shall be deemed to be the institution responsible for providing benefits;

   (c) paragraphs 1 and 2 shall remain applicable in respect of any benefits not covered by the waiver agreement or a reimbursement which does not depend on the amount of benefits actually provided.

Article 86

Bilateral agreements

As far as relations between, on the one hand, Luxembourg and, on the other hand, France, Germany and Belgium are concerned, the application and the duration of the period referred to in Article 65(7) shall be subject to the conclusion of bilateral agreements.

TITLE VI TRANSITIONAL AND FINAL PROVISIONS

Article 87

Transitional provisions

1. No rights shall be acquired pursuant to this Regulation for the period before its date of application.

2. Any period of insurance and, where appropriate, any period of employment, self-employment or residence completed under the legislation of a Member State prior to the date of application of this Regulation in the Member State concerned shall be taken into consideration for the determination of rights acquired under this Regulation.

3. Subject to paragraph 1, a right shall be acquired under this Regulation even if it relates to a contingency arising before its date of application in the Member State concerned.

4. Any benefit which has not been awarded or which has been suspended by reason of the nationality or place of residence of the person concerned shall, at the request of that person, be provided or resumed with effect from the date of application of this Regulation in the Member State concerned, provided that the rights for which benefits were previously provided have not given rise to a lump-sum payment.

5. The rights of a person to whom a pension was provided prior to the date of application of this Regulation in a Member State may, at the request of the person concerned, be reviewed, taking into account this Regulation.

6. If a request referred to in paragraph 4 or 5 is submitted within two years from the date of application of this Regulation in a Member State, the rights acquired in accordance with this Regulation shall have effect from that date, and the legislation of any Member State concerning the forfeiture or limitation of rights may not be invoked against the persons concerned.

7. If a request referred to in paragraph 4 or 5 is submitted after the expiry of the two-year period following the date of application of this Regulation in the Member State concerned, rights not forfeited or not time-barred shall have effect from the date on which the request was submitted, subject to any more favourable provisions under the legislation of any Member State.

8. If, as a result of this Regulation, a person is subject to the legislation of a Member State other than that determined in accordance with Title II of Regulation (EEC) No. 1408/71, that legislation shall continue to apply while the relevant situation remains unchanged and in any case for no longer than 10 years from the date of application of this Regulation unless the person concerned requests that he/she be subject to the legislation applicable under this Regulation. The request shall be submitted within 3 months after the date of application of this Regulation to the competent institution of the Member State whose legislation is applicable under this Regulation if the person concerned is to be subject to the legislation of that Member State as of the date of application of this Regulation. If the request is made after the time limit indicated, the change of applicable legislation shall take place on the first day of the following month.

9. Article 55 of this Regulation shall apply only to pensions not subject to Article 46c of Regulation (EEC) No. 1408/71 on the date of application of this Regulation.

10. The provisions of the second sentences of Article 65(2) and (3) shall be applicable to Luxembourg at the latest two years after the date of application of this Regulation.

10a. The entries in Annex III corresponding to Estonia, Spain, Italy, Lithuania, Hungary and the Netherlands shall cease to have effect 4 years after the date of application of this Regulation.

10b. The list contained in Annex III shall be reviewed no later than 31 October 2014 on the basis of a report by the Administrative Commission. That report shall include an impact assessment of the significance, frequency, scale and costs, both in absolute and in relative terms, of the application of the provisions of Annex III. That report shall also include the possible effects of repealing those provisions for those Member States which continue to be listed in that Annex after the date referred to in paragraph 10a. In the light of that report, the Commission shall decide whether to submit a proposal concerning a review of the list, with the aim in principle of repealing the list unless the report of the Administrative Commission provides compelling reasons not to do so.

11. Member States shall ensure that appropriate information is provided regarding the changes in rights and obligations introduced by this Regulation and the Implementing Regulation.

Article 87a
Transitional provision for application of Regulation (EU) No. 465/2012

1. If as a result of the entry into force of Regulation (EU) No. 465/2012, a person is subject, in accordance with Title II of this Regulation, to the legislation of a different Member State than that to which he/she was subject before that entry into force, the legislation of the Member State applicable before that date shall continue to apply to him/her for a transitional period lasting for as long as the relevant situation remains unchanged and, in any case, for no longer than 10 years from the date of entry into force of Regulation (EU) No. 465/2012. Such a person may request that the transitional period no longer applies to him/her. Such request shall be submitted to the institution designated by the competent authority of the Member State of residence. Requests submitted by 29 September 2012 shall be deemed to take effect on 28 June 2012. Requests submitted after 29 September 2012 shall take effect on the first day of the month following that of their submission.

2. No later than 29 June 2014, the Administrative Commission shall evaluate the implementation of the provisions laid down in Article 65a of this Regulation and present a report on their application. On the basis of this report, the European Commission may, as appropriate, submit proposals to amend those provisions.

Article 88
Updating of the Annexes
The Annexes of this Regulation shall be revised periodically.

Article 89
Implementing Regulation
A further Regulation shall lay down the procedure for implementing this Regulation.

Article 90
Repeal

1. Council Regulation (EEC) No. 1408/71 shall be repealed from the date of application of this Regulation.

    However, Regulation (EEC) No. 1408/71 shall remain in force and shall continue to have legal effect for the purposes of:

    (a) Council Regulation (EC) No. 859/2003 of 14 May 2003 extending the provisions of Regulation (EEC) No 1408/71 and Regulation (EEC) No. 574/72 to nationals of third countries who are not already covered by those provisions solely on the ground of their nationality, for as long as that Regulation has not been repealed or modified;

    (b) Council Regulation (EEC) No. 1661/85 of 13 June 1985 laying down the technical adaptations to the [Union] rules on social security for migrant workers with regard to Greenland, for as long as that Regulation has not been repealed or modified;

(c) the Agreement on the European Economic Area and the Agreement between the European [Union] and its Member States, of the one part, and the Swiss Confederation, of the other part, on the free movement of persons and other agreements which contain a reference to Regulation (EEC) No. 1408/71, for as long as those agreements have not been modified in the light of this Regulation.

2. References to Regulation (EEC) No. 1408/71 in Council Directive 98/49/EC of 29 June 1998 on safeguarding the supplementary pension rights of employed and self-employed persons moving within the [Union] are to be read as referring to this Regulation.

Article 91

Entry into force

This Regulation shall enter into force on the 20th day after its publication in the Official Journal of the European Union.

It shall apply from the date of entry into force of the Implementing Regulation.

This Regulation shall be binding in its entirety and directly applicable in all Member States.

(*Signatures omitted*)

ANNEX X SPECIAL NON-CONTRIBUTORY CASH BENEFITS

(Article 70(2)(c))

BELGIUM

(a) Income replacement allowance (Law of 27 February 1987);

(b) Guaranteed income for elderly persons (Law of 22 March 2001).

BULGARIA

Social Pension for old age (Article 89 of the Social Insurance Code).

CZECH REPUBLIC

Social allowance (State Social Support Act No 117/1995 Sb.).

DENMARK

Accommodation expenses for pensioners (Law on individual accommodation assistance, consolidated by Law No 204 of 29 March 1995).

GERMANY

(a) Basic subsistence income for the elderly and for persons with reduced earning capacity under Chapter 4 of Book XII of the Social Code;

(b) Benefits to cover subsistence costs under the basic provision for jobseekers unless, with respect to these benefits, the eligibility requirements for a temporary supplement following receipt of unemployment benefit (Article 24(1) of Book II of the Social Code) are fulfilled.

ESTONIA
- (a) Disabled adult allowance (Social Benefits for Disabled Persons Act of 27 January 1999);
- (b) State unemployment allowance (Labour Market Services and Support Act of 29 September 2005).

IRELAND
- (a) Jobseekers' allowance (Social Welfare Consolidation Act 2005, Part 3, Chapter 2);
- (b) State pension (non-contributory) (Social Welfare Consolidation Act 2005, Part 3, Chapter 4);
- (c) Widow's (non-contributory) pension and widower's (non-contributory) pension (Social Welfare Consolidation Act 2005, Part 3, Chapter 6);
- (d) Disability allowance (Social Welfare Consolidation Act 2005, Part 3, Chapter 10);
- (e) Mobility allowance (Health Act 1970, Section 61);
- (f) Blind pension (Social Welfare Consolidation Act 2005, Part 3, Chapter 5).

GREECE
Special benefits for the elderly (Law 1296/82).

SPAIN
- (a) Minimum income guarantee (Law No 13/82 of 7 April 1982);
- (b) Cash benefits to assist the elderly and invalids unable to work (Royal Decree No 2620/81 of 24 July 1981);
- (c) (i) Non-contributory invalidity and retirement pensions as provided for in Article 38(1) of the Consolidated Text of the General Law on Social Security, approved by Royal Legislative Decree No 1/1994 of 20 June 1994; and
  - (ii) the benefits which supplement the above pensions, as provided for in the legislation of the Comunidades Autonómas, where such supplements guarantee a minimum subsistence income having regard to the economic and social situation in the Comunidades Autonómas concerned;
- (d) Allowances to promote mobility and to compensate for transport costs (Law No 13/1982 of 7 April 1982).

FRANCE
- (a) Supplementary allowances of:
  - (i) the Special Invalidity Fund; and
  - (ii) the Old Age Solidarity Fund in respect of acquired rights (Law of 30 June 1956, codified in Book VIII of the Social Security Code);
- (b) Disabled adults' allowance (Law of 30 June 1975, codified in Book VIII of the Social Security Code);
- (c) Special allowance (Law of 10 July 1952, codified in Book VIII of the Social Security Code) in respect of acquired rights;
- (d) Old-age solidarity allowance (ordinance of 24 June 2004, codified in Book VIII of the Social Security Code) as of 1 January 2006.

ITALY

(a) Social pensions for persons without means (Law No 153 of 30 April 1969);

(b) Pensions and allowances for the civilian disabled or invalids (Laws No 118 of 30 March 1971, No 18 of 11 February 1980 and No 508 of 23 November 1988);

(c) Pensions and allowances for the deaf and dumb (Laws No 381 of 26 May 1970 and No 508 of 23 November 1988);

(d) Pensions and allowances for the civilian blind (Laws No 382 of 27 May 1970 and No 508 of 23 November 1988);

(e) Benefits supplementing the minimum pensions (Laws No 218 of 4 April 1952, No 638 of 11 November 1983 and No 407 of 29 December 1990);

(f) Benefits supplementing disability allowances (Law No 222 of 12 June 1984);

(g) Social allowance (Law No 335 of 8 August 1995);

(h) Social increase (Article 1(1) and (12) of Law No 544 of 29 December 1988 and successive amendments).

CYPRUS

(a) Social Pension (Social Pension Law of 1995 (Law 25(I)/95), as amended);

(b) Severe motor disability allowance (Council of Ministers' Decisions Nos 38210 of 16 October 1992, 41370 of 1 August 1994, 46183 of 11 June 1997 and 53675 of 16 May 2001);

(c) Special grant to blind persons (Special Grants Law of 1996 (Law 77(I)/96), as amended).

LATVIA

(a) State Social Security Benefit (Law on State Social Benefits of 1 January 2003);

(b) Allowance for the compensation of transportation expenses for disabled persons with restricted mobility (Law on State Social Benefits of 1 January 2003).

LITHUANIA

(a) Social assistance pension (Law of 2005 on State Social Assistance Benefits, Article 5);

(b) Relief compensation (Law of 2005 on State Social Assistance Benefits, Article 15);

(c) Transport compensation for the disabled who have mobility problems (Law of 2000 on Transport Compensation, Article 7).

LUXEMBOURG

Income for the seriously disabled (Article 1(2), Law of 12 September 2003), with the exception of persons recognised as being disabled workers and employed on the mainstream labour market or in a sheltered environment.

HUNGARY

(a) Invalidity annuity (Decree No 83/1987 (XII 27) of the Council of Ministers on Invalidity Annuity);

(b) Non-contributory old age allowance (Act III of 1993 on Social Administration and Social Benefits);

(c) Transport allowance (Government Decree No 164/1995 (XII 27) on Transport Allowances for Persons with Severe Physical Handicap).

MALTA
(a) Supplementary allowance (Section 73 of the Social Security Act (Cap. 318) 1987);
(b) Age pension (Social Security Act (Cap. 318) 1987).

NETHERLANDS
(a) Work and Employment Support for Disabled Young Persons Act of 24 April 1997 (Wet Wajong).
(b) Supplementary Benefits Act of 6 November 1986 (TW).

AUSTRIA
Compensatory supplement (Federal Act of 9 September 1955 on General Social Insurance – ASVG, Federal Act of 11 October 1978 on Social insurance for persons engaged in trade and commerce – GSVG and Federal Act of 11 October 1978 on Social insurance for farmers – BSVG).

POLAND
Social pension (Act of 27 June 2003 on social pensions).

PORTUGAL
(a) Non-contributory State old-age and invalidity pension (Decree-Law No 464/80 of 13 October 1980);
(b) Non-contributory widowhood pension (Regulatory Decree No 52/81 of 11 November 1981);
(c) Solidarity supplement for the elderly (Decree – Law No 232/2005 of 29 December 2005, amended by Decree – Law No 236/2006 of 11 December 2006).

SLOVENIA
(a) State pension (Pension and Disability Insurance Act of 23 December 1999);
(b) Income support for pensioners (Pension and Disability Insurance Act of 23 December 1999);
(c) Maintenance allowance (Pension and Disability Insurance Act of 23 December 1999).

SLOVAKIA
(a) Adjustment awarded before 1 January 2004 to pensions constituting the sole source of income;
(b) Social pension which has been awarded before 1 January 2004.

FINLAND
(a) Housing allowance for pensioners (Act concerning the Housing Allowance for pensioners, 571/2007);
(b) Labour market support (Act on Unemployment Benefits 1290/2002);
(c) Special assistance for immigrants (Act on Special Assistance for Immigrants, 1192/2002).

SWEDEN

  (a) Housing supplements for persons receiving a pension (Law 2001:761);

  (b) Financial support for the elderly (Law 2001:853).

UNITED KINGDOM

  (a) State Pension Credit (State Pension Credit Act 2002 and State Pension Credit Act (Northern Ireland) 2002);

  (b) Income-based allowances for jobseekers (Jobseekers Act 1995 and Jobseekers (Northern Ireland) Order 1995);

  (d) Disability Living Allowance mobility component (Social Security Contributions and Benefits Act 1992 and Social Security Contributions and Benefits (Northern Ireland) Act 1992);

  (e) Employment and Support Allowance Income-related (Welfare Reform Act 2007 and Welfare Reform Act (Northern Ireland) 2007).

11

12

Directive 2005/36 on the Recognition of Professional Qualifications

Contents

THE EUROPEAN PARLIAMENT AND THE COUNCIL OF THE EUROPEAN UNION,

Having regard to the Treaty [on the Functioning of the European Union], and in particular Article [46], Article [53](1), and Article [62] thereof,

Having regard to the proposal from the Commission,

Having regard to the opinion of the European Economic and Social Committee,

Acting in accordance with the procedure laid down in Article [294] of the Treaty …

HAVE ADOPTED THIS DIRECTIVE:

TITLE I GENERAL PROVISIONS

Article 1
Purpose

This Directive establishes rules according to which a Member State which makes access to or pursuit of a regulated profession in its territory contingent upon possession of specific professional qualifications (referred to hereinafter as the host Member State) shall recognise professional qualifications obtained in one or more other Member States (referred to hereinafter as the home Member State) and which allow the holder of the said qualifications to pursue the same profession there, for access to and pursuit of that profession.

This Directive also establishes rules concerning partial access to a regulated profession and recognition of professional traineeships pursued in another Member State.

Article 2
Scope

1. This Directive shall apply to all nationals of a Member State wishing to pursue a regulated profession in a Member State, including those belonging to the liberal professions, other than that in which they obtained their professional qualifications, on either a self-employed or employed basis.

   This Directive shall also apply to all nationals of a Member State who have pursued a professional traineeship outside the home Member State.
2. Each Member State may permit Member State nationals in possession of evidence of professional qualifications not obtained in a Member State to pursue a regulated profession within the meaning of Article 3(1)(a) on its territory in accordance with its rules. In the case of professions covered by Title III, Chapter III, this initial recognition shall respect the minimum training conditions laid down in that Chapter.
3. Where, for a given regulated profession, other specific arrangements directly related to the recognition of professional qualifications are established in a separate instrument of [Union] law, the corresponding provisions of this Directive shall not apply.
4. This Directive shall not apply to notaries who are appointed by an official act of government.

Article 3
Definitions

1. For the purposes of this Directive, the following definitions apply:
   (a) 'regulated profession': a professional activity or group of professional activities, access to which, the pursuit of which, or one of the modes of pursuit of which is subject, directly or indirectly, by virtue of legislative, regulatory or administrative provisions to the possession of specific professional qualifications; in particular, the use of a professional title limited by legislative, regulatory or administrative provisions to holders of a given professional qualification shall constitute a mode of pursuit. Where the first sentence of this definition does not apply, a profession referred to in paragraph 2 shall be treated as a regulated profession;
   (b) 'professional qualifications': qualifications attested by evidence of formal qualifications, an attestation of competence referred to in Article 11, point (a)(i) and/or professional experience;

(c) 'evidence of formal qualifications': diplomas, certificates and other evidence issued by an authority in a Member State designated pursuant to legislative, regulatory or administrative provisions of that Member State and certifying successful completion of professional training obtained mainly in the [Union]. Where the first sentence of this definition does not apply, evidence of formal qualifications referred to in paragraph 3 shall be treated as evidence of formal qualifications;

(d) 'competent authority': any authority or body empowered by a Member State specifically to issue or receive training diplomas and other documents or information and to receive the applications, and take the decisions, referred to in this Directive;

(e) 'regulated education and training': any training which is specifically geared to the pursuit of a given profession and which comprises a course or courses complemented, where appropriate, by professional training, or probationary or professional practice.

The structure and level of the professional training, probationary or professional practice shall be determined by the laws, regulations or administrative provisions of the Member State concerned or monitored or approved by the authority designated for that purpose;

(f) 'professional experience': the actual and lawful full-time or equivalent part-time pursuit of the profession concerned in a Member State;

(g) 'adaptation period': the pursuit of a regulated profession in the host Member State under the responsibility of a qualified member of that profession, such period of supervised practice possibly being accompanied by further training. This period of supervised practice shall be the subject of an assessment. The detailed rules governing the adaptation period and its assessment as well as the status of a migrant under supervision shall be laid down by the competent authority in the host Member State.

The status enjoyed in the host Member State by the person undergoing the period of supervised practice, in particular in the matter of right of residence as well as obligations, social rights and benefits, allowances and remuneration, shall be established by the competent authorities in that Member State in accordance with applicable [Union] law;

(h) 'aptitude test': a test of the professional knowledge, skills and competences of the applicant, carried out or recognised by the competent authorities of the host Member State with the aim of assessing the ability of the applicant to pursue a regulated profession in that Member State.

In order to permit this test to be carried out, the competent authorities shall draw up a list of subjects which, on the basis of a comparison of the education and training required in the host Member State and that received by the applicant, are not covered by the diploma or other evidence of formal qualifications possessed by the applicant.

The aptitude test must take account of the fact that the applicant is a qualified professional in the home Member State or the Member State from which the applicant comes. It shall cover subjects to be selected from those on the list, knowledge of which is essential in order to be able to pursue the profession in question in the host Member State. The test may also cover knowledge of the professional rules applicable to the activities in question in the host Member State.

The detailed application of the aptitude test and the status, in the host Member State, of the applicant who wishes to prepare himself for the aptitude test in that Member State shall be determined by the competent authorities in that Member State;

(i) 'manager of an undertaking': any person who in an undertaking in the occupational field in question has pursued an activity:

(i) as a manager of an undertaking or a manager of a branch of an undertaking; or

(ii) as a deputy to the proprietor or the manager of an undertaking where that post involves responsibility equivalent to that of the proprietor or manager represented; or

(iii) in a managerial post with duties of a commercial and/or technical nature and with responsibility for one or more departments of the undertaking.

(j) 'professional traineeship': without prejudice to Article 46(4), a period of professional practice carried out under supervision provided it constitutes a condition for access to a regulated profession, and which can take place either during or after completion of an education leading to a diploma;

(k) 'European Professional Card': an electronic certificate proving either that the professional has met all the necessary conditions to provide services in a host Member State on a temporary and occasional basis or the recognition of professional qualifications for establishment in a host Member State;

(l) 'lifelong learning': all general education, vocational education and training, non-formal education and informal learning undertaken throughout life, resulting in an improvement in knowledge, skills and competences, which may include professional ethics;

(m) 'overriding reasons of general interest': reasons recognised as such in the case-law of the Court of Justice of the European Union;

(n) 'European Credit Transfer and Accumulation System or ECTS credits': the credit system for higher education used in the European Higher Education Area.

2. A profession practised by the members of an association or organisation listed in Annex I shall be treated as a regulated profession.

The purpose of the associations or organisations referred to in the first subparagraph is, in particular, to promote and maintain a high standard in the professional field concerned. To that end they are recognised in a special form by a Member State and award evidence of formal qualifications to their members, ensure that their members respect the rules of professional conduct which they prescribe, and confer on them the right to use a title or designatory letters or to benefit from a status corresponding to those formal qualifications.

On each occasion that a Member State grants recognition to an association or organisation referred to in the first subparagraph, it shall inform the Commission. The Commission shall examine whether that association or organisation fulfils the conditions provided for in the second subparagraph. In order to take due account of regulatory developments in Member States, the Commission shall be empowered to adopt delegated acts in accordance with Article 57c in order to update Annex I where the conditions provided for in the second subparagraph are satisfied.

12

Where the conditions provided for in the second subparagraph are not satisfied, the Commission shall adopt an implementing act in order to reject the requested update of Annex I.

3. Evidence of formal qualifications issued by a third country shall be regarded as evidence of formal qualifications if the holder has three years' professional experience in the profession concerned on the territory of the Member State which recognised that evidence of formal qualifications in accordance with Article 2(2), certified by that Member State.

Article 4
Effects of recognition

1. The recognition of professional qualifications by the host Member State shall allow beneficiaries to gain access in that Member State to the same profession as that for which they are qualified in the home Member State and to pursue it in the host Member State under the same conditions as its nationals.

2. For the purposes of this Directive, the profession which the applicant wishes to pursue in the host Member State is the same as that for which he is qualified in his home Member State if the activities covered are comparable.

3. By way of derogation from paragraph 1, partial access to a profession in the host Member State shall be granted under the conditions laid down in Article 4f.

Article 4a
European Professional Card

1. Member States shall issue holders of a professional qualification with a European Professional Card upon their request and on condition that the Commission has adopted the relevant implementing acts provided for in paragraph 7.

2. When a European Professional Card has been introduced for a particular profession by means of relevant implementing acts adopted pursuant to paragraph 7, the holder of a professional qualification concerned may choose to apply for such a Card or to make use of the procedures provided for in Titles II and III.

3. Member States shall ensure that the holder of a European Professional Card benefits from all the rights conferred by Articles 4b to 4e.

4. Where the holder of a professional qualification intends to provide services under Title II other than those covered by Article 7(4), the competent authority of the home Member State shall issue the European Professional Card in accordance with Articles 4b and 4c. The European Professional Card shall, where applicable, constitute the declaration under Article 7.

5. Where the holder of a professional qualification intends to establish himself in another Member State under Chapters I to IIIa of Title III or to provide services under Article 7(4), the competent authority of the home Member State shall complete all preparatory steps with regard to the individual file of the applicant created within the Internal Market Information System (IMI) (IMI file) as provided for in Articles 4b and 4d. The competent authority of the host Member State shall issue the European Professional Card in accordance with Articles 4b and 4d.

For the purpose of establishment, the issuance of a European Professional Card shall not provide an automatic right to practise a particular profession if there are registration requirements or other control procedures already in place in the host Member State before a European Professional Card is introduced for that profession.

6. Member States shall designate competent authorities for dealing with IMI files and issuing European Professional Cards. Those authorities shall ensure an impartial, objective and timely processing of applications for European Professional Cards. The assistance centres referred to in Article 57b may also act in the capacity of a competent authority. Member States shall ensure that competent authorities and assistance centres inform citizens, including prospective applicants, about the functioning and the added value of a European Professional Card for the professions for which it is available.

7. The Commission shall, by means of implementing acts, adopt measures necessary to ensure the uniform application of the provisions on the European Professional Cards for those professions that meet the conditions laid down in the second subparagraph of this paragraph, including measures concerning the format of the European Professional Card, the processing of written applications, the translations to be provided by the applicant to support any application for a European Professional Card, details of the documents required pursuant to Article 7(2) or Annex VII to present a complete application and procedures for making and processing payments for a European Professional Card, taking into account the particularities of the profession concerned. The Commission shall also specify, by means of implementing acts, how, when and for which documents competent authorities may request certified copies in accordance with the second subparagraph of Article 4b(3), Articles 4d(2) and 4d(3) for the profession concerned.

The introduction of a European Professional Card for a particular profession by means of the adoption of relevant implementing acts referred to in the first subparagraph shall be subject to all of the following conditions:

(a) there is significant mobility or potential for significant mobility in the profession concerned;

(b) there is sufficient interest expressed by the relevant stakeholders;

(c) the profession or the education and training geared to the pursuit of the profession is regulated in a significant number of Member States.

Those implementing acts shall be adopted in accordance with the examination procedure referred to in Article 58(2).

8. Any fees which applicants may incur in relation to administrative procedures to issue a European Professional Card shall be reasonable, proportionate and commensurate with the costs incurred by the home and the host Member States and shall not act as a disincentive to apply for a European Professional Card.

Article 4b

Application for a European Professional Card and creation of an IMI file

1. The home Member State shall enable a holder of a professional qualification to apply for a European Professional Card through an on-line tool, provided by the Commission, that automatically creates an IMI file for the particular applicant. Where a home Member State allows also for written applications, it shall put in place all necessary arrangements for the creation of the IMI file, any information to be sent to the applicant and the issuance of the European Professional Card.

2. Applications shall be supported by the documents required in the implementing acts to be adopted pursuant to Article 4a(7).

3. Within one week of receipt of the application, the competent authority of the home Member State shall acknowledge receipt of the application and inform the applicant of any missing document.

   Where applicable, the competent authority of the home Member State shall issue any supporting certificate required under this Directive. The competent authority of the home Member State shall verify whether the applicant is legally established in the home Member State and whether all the necessary documents which have been issued in the home Member State are valid and authentic. In the event of duly justified doubts, the competent authority of the home Member State shall consult the relevant body and may request from the applicant certified copies of documents. In case of subsequent applications by the same applicant, the competent authorities of the home and the host Member States may not request the re-submission of documents which are already contained in the IMI file and which are still valid.

4. The Commission may, by means of implementing acts, adopt the technical specifications, the measures necessary to ensure integrity, confidentiality and accuracy of information contained in the European Professional Card and in the IMI file, and the conditions and the procedures for issuing a European Professional Card to its holder, including the possibility of downloading it or submitting updates for the IMI file. Those implementing acts shall be adopted in accordance with the examination procedure referred to in Article 58(2).

Article 4c

European Professional Card for the temporary and occasional provision of services other than those covered by Article 7(4)

1. The competent authority of the home Member State shall verify the application and the supporting documents in the IMI file and issue the European Professional Card for the temporary and occasional provision of services other than those covered by Article 7(4) within three weeks. That time period shall start upon receipt of the missing documents referred to in the first subparagraph of Article 4b(3) or, if no further documents were requested, upon the expiry of the one-week period referred to in that subparagraph. It shall then transmit the European Professional Card immediately to the competent authority of each host Member State concerned and shall inform the applicant accordingly. The host Member State may not require any further declaration under Article 7 for the following 18 months.

2. The decision of the competent authority of the home Member State, or the absence of a decision within the period of three weeks referred to in paragraph 1, shall be subject to appeal under national law.

3. If a holder of a European Professional Card wishes to provide services in Member States other than those initially mentioned in the application referred to in paragraph 1 that holder may apply for such extension. If the holder wishes to continue providing services beyond the period of 18 months referred to in paragraph 1, that holder shall inform the competent authority accordingly. In either case, that holder shall also provide any information on material changes in the situation substantiated in the IMI file that may be required by the competent authority in the home Member State in

accordance with the implementing acts to be adopted pursuant to Article 4a(7). The competent authority of the home Member State shall transmit the updated European Professional Card to the host Member States concerned.

4. The European Professional Card shall be valid in the entire territory of all the host Member States concerned for as long as its holder maintains the right to practice on the basis of the documents and information contained in the IMI file.

Article 4d

European Professional Card for establishment and for the temporary and occasional provision of services under Article 7(4)

1. The competent authority of the home Member State shall, within one month, verify the authenticity and validity of the supporting documents in the IMI file for the purpose of issuing a European Professional Card for establishment or for the temporary and occasional provision of services under Article 7(4). That time period shall start upon receipt of the missing documents referred to in the first subparagraph of Article 4b(3) or, if no further documents were requested, upon the expiry of the one-week period referred to in that subparagraph. It shall then transmit the application immediately to the competent authority of the host Member State. The home Member State shall inform the applicant of the status of the application at the same time as it transmits the application to the host Member State.

2. In the cases referred to in Articles 16, 21, 49a and 49b, a host Member State shall decide whether to issue a European Professional Card under paragraph 1 within one month of receipt of the application transmitted by the home Member State. In the event of duly justified doubts, the host Member State may request additional information from, or the inclusion of a certified copy of a document by, the home Member State, which the latter shall provide no later than two weeks after the submission of the request. Subject to the second subparagraph of paragraph 5, the period of one month shall apply, notwithstanding any such request.

3. In the cases referred to in Articles 7(4) and 14, a host Member State shall decide whether to issue a European Professional Card or to subject the holder of a professional qualification to compensation measures within two months of receipt of the application transmitted by the home Member State. In the event of duly justified doubts, the host Member State may request additional information from, or the inclusion of a certified copy of a document by, the home Member State which the latter shall provide no later than two weeks after the submission of the request. Subject to the second subparagraph of paragraph 5, the period of two months shall apply, notwithstanding any such request.

4. In the event that the host Member State does not receive the necessary information which it may require in accordance with this Directive for taking a decision on the issuance of the European Professional Card from either the home Member State or the applicant, it may refuse to issue the Card. Such refusal shall be duly justified.

5. Where the host Member State fails to take a decision within the time limits set out in paragraphs 2 and 3 of this Article or fails to organise an aptitude test in accordance with Article 7(4), the European Professional Card shall be deemed to be issued and shall be sent automatically, through IMI, to the holder of a professional qualification.

The host Member State shall have the possibility to extend by two weeks the deadlines set out in paragraphs 2 and 3 for the automatic issuance of the European Professional Card. It shall explain the reason for the extension and inform the applicant accordingly. Such an extension may be repeated once and only where it is strictly necessary, in particular for reasons relating to public health or the safety of the service recipients.

6. The actions taken by the home Member State in accordance with paragraph 1 shall replace any application for recognition of professional qualifications under the national law of the host Member State.

7. The decisions of the home and the host Member State adopted under paragraphs 1 to 5 or the absence of decision by the home Member State shall be subject to appeal under the national law of the Member State concerned.

Article 4e
Processing and access to data regarding the European Professional Card

1. Without prejudice to the presumption of innocence, the competent authorities of the home and the host Member States shall update, in a timely manner, the corresponding IMI file with information regarding disciplinary actions or criminal sanctions which relate to a prohibition or restriction and which have consequences for the pursuit of activities by the holder of a European Professional Card under this Directive. In so doing they shall respect personal data protection rules provided for in Directive 95/46/EC of the European Parliament and of the Council of 24 October 1995 on the protection of individuals with regard to the processing of personal data and on the free movement of such data and Directive 2002/58/EC of the European Parliament and of the Council of 12 July 2002 concerning the processing of personal data and the protection of privacy in the electronic communications sector (Directive on privacy and electronic communications). Such updates shall include the deletion of information which is no longer required. The holder of the European Professional Card as well as the competent authorities that have access to the corresponding IMI file shall be informed immediately of any updates. That obligation shall be without prejudice to the alert obligations for Member States under Article 56a.

2. The content of the information updates referred to in paragraph 1 shall be limited to the following:
   (a) the identity of the professional;
   (b) the profession concerned;
   (c) information about the national authority or court which has adopted the decision on restriction or prohibition;
   (d) the scope of the restriction or the prohibition; and
   (e) the period for which the restriction or the prohibition applies.

3. Access to the information in the IMI file shall be limited to the competent authorities of the home and the host Member States, in accordance with Directive 95/46/EC. The competent authorities shall inform the holder of the European Professional Card of the content of the IMI file upon that holder's request.

4. The information included in the European Professional Card shall be limited to the information that is necessary to ascertain its holder's right to exercise the profession for which it has been issued, namely the holder's name, surname, date and place of birth, profession, formal qualifications, and the applicable regime, competent authorities

involved, Card number, security features and reference to a valid proof of identity. Information relating to professional experience acquired, or compensation measures passed, by the holder of the European Professional Card shall be included in the IMI file.

5. The personal data included in the IMI file may be processed for as long as it is needed for the purpose of the recognition procedure as such and as evidence of the recognition or of the transmission of the declaration required under Article 7. Member States shall ensure that the holder of a European Professional Card has the right at any time, and at no cost to that holder, to request the rectification of inaccurate or incomplete data, or the deletion or blocking of the IMI file concerned. The holder shall be informed of this right at the time the European Professional Card is issued, and reminded of it every two years thereafter. The reminder shall be sent automatically via IMI where the initial application for the European Professional Card was submitted online.

In the event of a request for deletion of an IMI file linked to a European Professional Card issued for the purpose of establishment or temporary and occasional provision of services under Article 7(4), the competent authorities of the host Member State concerned shall issue the holder of professional qualifications with evidence attesting to the recognition of his professional qualifications.

6. In relation to the processing of personal data in the European Professional Card and all IMI files, the relevant competent authorities of the Member States shall be regarded as controllers within the meaning of point (d) of Article 2 of Directive 95/46/EC. In relation to its responsibilities under paragraphs 1 to 4 of this Article and the processing of personal data involved therein, the Commission shall be regarded as a controller within the meaning of point (d) of Article 2 of Regulation (EC) No. 45/2001 of the European Parliament and of the Council of 18 December 2000 on the protection of individuals with regard to the processing of personal data by the [Union] institutions and bodies and on the free movement of such data.

7. Without prejudice to paragraph 3, host Member States shall provide that employers, customers, patients, public authorities and other interested parties may verify the authenticity and validity of a European Professional Card presented to them by the Card holder.

The Commission shall, by means of implementing acts, lay down rules concerning access to the IMI file, and the technical means and the procedures for the verification referred to in the first subparagraph. Those implementing acts shall be adopted in accordance with the examination procedure referred to in Article 58(2).

Article 4f
Partial access

1. The competent authority of the host Member State shall grant partial access, on a case-by-case basis, to a professional activity in its territory only when all the following conditions are fulfilled:
   (a) the professional is fully qualified to exercise in the home Member State the professional activity for which partial access is sought in the host Member State;
   (b) differences between the professional activity legally exercised in the home Member State and the regulated profession in the host Member State as such are so large that the application of compensation measures would amount to requiring the

applicant to complete the full programme of education and training required in the host Member State to have access to the full regulated profession in the host Member State;

(c) the professional activity can objectively be separated from other activities falling under the regulated profession in the host Member State.

For the purpose of point (c), the competent authority of the host Member State shall take into account whether the professional activity can be pursued autonomously in the home Member State.

2. Partial access may be rejected if such rejection is justified by overriding reasons of general interest, suitable for securing the attainment of the objective pursued, and does not go beyond what is necessary to attain that objective.

3. Applications for the purpose of establishment in a host Member State shall be examined in accordance with Chapters I and IV of Title III.

4. Applications for the purpose of providing temporary and occasional services in the host Member State concerning professional activities that have public health or safety implications shall be examined in accordance with Title II.

5. By derogation from the sixth subparagraph of Article 7(4) and Article 52(1), the professional activity shall be exercised under the professional title of the home Member State once partial access has been granted. The host Member State may require use of that professional title in the languages of the host Member State. Professionals benefiting from partial access shall clearly indicate to the service recipients the scope of their professional activities.

6. This Article shall not apply to professionals benefiting from automatic recognition of their professional qualifications under Chapters II, III and IIIa of Title III.

TITLE II FREE PROVISION OF SERVICES

Article 5
Principle of the free provision of services

1. Without prejudice to specific provisions of [Union] law, as well as to Articles 6 and 7 of this Directive, Member States shall not restrict, for any reason relating to professional qualifications, the free provision of services in another Member State:

(a) if the service provider is legally established in a Member State for the purpose of pursuing the same profession there (hereinafter referred to as the Member State of establishment), and

(b) where the service provider moves, if he has pursued that profession in one or several Member States for at least one year during the last 10 years preceding the provision of services when the profession is not regulated in the Member State of establishment. The condition of one year's pursuit shall not apply if the profession or the education and training leading to the profession is regulated.

2. The provisions of this title shall only apply where the service provider moves to the territory of the host Member State to pursue, on a temporary and occasional basis, the profession referred to in paragraph 1.

The temporary and occasional nature of the provision of services shall be assessed case by case, in particular in relation to its duration, its frequency, its regularity and its continuity.

3. Where a service provider moves, he shall be subject to professional rules of a professional, statutory or administrative nature which are directly linked to professional qualifications, such as the definition of the profession, the use of titles and serious professional malpractice which is directly and specifically linked to consumer protection and safety, as well as disciplinary provisions which are applicable in the host Member State to professionals who pursue the same profession in that Member State.

Article 6
Exemptions

Pursuant to Article 5(1), the host Member State shall exempt service providers established in another Member State from the requirements which it places on professionals established in its territory relating to:

(a) authorisation by, registration with or membership of a professional organisation or body. In order to facilitate the application of disciplinary provisions in force on their territory according to Article 5(3), Member States may provide either for automatic temporary registration with or for pro forma membership of such a professional organisation or body, provided that such registration or membership does not delay or complicate in any way the provision of services and does not entail any additional costs for the service provider. A copy of the declaration and, where applicable, of the renewal referred to in Article 7(1), accompanied, for professions which have implications for public health and safety referred to in Article 7(4) or which benefit from automatic recognition under Title III Chapter III, by a copy of the documents referred to in Article 7(2) shall be sent by the competent authority to the relevant professional organisation or body, and this shall constitute automatic temporary registration or pro forma membership for this purpose;

(b) registration with a public social security body for the purpose of settling accounts with an insurer relating to activities pursued for the benefit of insured persons.

The service provider shall, however, inform in advance or, in an urgent case, afterwards, the body referred to in point (b) of the services which he has provided.

Article 7
Declaration to be made in advance, if the service provider moves

1. Member States may require that, where the service provider first moves from one Member State to another in order to provide services, he shall inform the competent authority in the host Member State in a written declaration to be made in advance including the details of any insurance cover or other means of personal or collective protection with regard to professional liability. Such declaration shall be renewed once a year if the service provider intends to provide temporary or occasional services in that Member State during that year. The service provider may supply the declaration by any means.

2. Moreover, for the first provision of services or if there is a material change in the situation substantiated by the documents, Member States may require that the declaration be accompanied by the following documents:

(a) proof of the nationality of the service provider;

(b) an attestation certifying that the holder is legally established in a Member State for the purpose of pursuing the activities concerned and that he is not prohibited from practising, even temporarily, at the moment of delivering the attestation;

(c) evidence of professional qualifications;

(d) for cases referred to in point (b) of Article 5(1), any means of proof that the service provider has pursued the activity concerned for at least one year during the previous 10 years;

(e) for professions in the security sector, in the health sector and professions related to the education of minors, including in childcare and early childhood education, where the Member State so requires for its own nationals, an attestation confirming the absence of temporary or final suspensions from exercising the profession or of criminal convictions;

(f) for professions that have patient safety implications, a declaration about the applicant's knowledge of the language necessary for practising the profession in the host Member State;

(g) for professions covering the activities referred to in Article 16 and which were notified by a Member State in accordance with Article 59(2), a certificate concerning the nature and duration of the activity issued by the competent authority or body of the Member State where the service provider is established.

2a. Submission of a required declaration by the service provider in accordance with paragraph 1 shall entitle that service provider to have access to the service activity or to exercise that activity in the entire territory of the Member State concerned. A Member State may require additional information listed in paragraph 2 concerning the professional qualifications of the service provider if:

(a) the profession is regulated in parts of that Member State's territory in a different manner;

(b) such regulation is applicable also to all nationals of that Member State;

(c) the differences in such regulation are justified by overriding reasons of general interest relating to public health or safety of service recipients; and

(d) the Member State has no other means of obtaining such information.

3. The service shall be provided under the professional title of the Member State of establishment, in so far as such a title exists in that Member State for the professional activity in question. That title shall be indicated in the official language or one of the official languages of the Member State of establishment in such a way as to avoid any confusion with the professional title of the host Member State. Where no such professional title exists in the Member State of establishment, the service provider shall indicate his formal qualification in the official language or one of the official languages of that Member State. By way of exception, the service shall be provided under the professional title of the host Member State for cases referred to in Title III Chapter III.

4. For the first provision of services, in the case of regulated professions that have public health or safety implications which do not benefit from automatic recognition under Chapter II, III or IIIa of Title III, the competent authority of the host Member State may check the professional qualifications of the service provider prior to the first provision of services. Such a prior check shall be possible only where the purpose of the check is to avoid serious damage to the health or safety of the service recipient due to a

lack of professional qualification of the service provider and where the check does not go beyond what is necessary for that purpose.

No later than one month after receipt of the declaration and accompanying documents, referred to in paragraphs 1 and 2, the competent authority shall inform the service provider of its decision:

(a) not to check his professional qualifications;

(b) having checked his professional qualifications:

    (i) to require the service provider to take an aptitude test; or

    (ii) to allow the provision of services.

Where there is a difficulty which would result in delay in taking a decision under the second subparagraph, the competent authority shall notify the service provider of the reason for the delay within the same deadline. The difficulty shall be solved within one month of that notification and the decision finalised within two months of resolution of the difficulty.

Where there is a substantial difference between the professional qualifications of the service provider and the training required in the host Member State, to the extent that that difference is such as to be harmful to public health or safety, and that it cannot be compensated by the service provider's professional experience or by knowledge, skills and competences acquired through lifelong learning formally validated to that end by a relevant body, the host Member State shall give that service provider the opportunity to show, by means of an aptitude test, as referred to in point (b) of the second subparagraph, that they have acquired the knowledge, skills or competence that were lacking. The host Member State shall take a decision on that basis on whether to allow the provision of services. In any case, it must be possible to provide the service within one month of the decision taken in accordance with the second subparagraph.

In the absence of a reaction of the competent authority within the deadlines set out in the second and third subparagraphs, the service may be provided.

In cases where professional qualifications have been verified under this paragraph, the service shall be provided under the professional title of the host Member State.

Article 8

Administrative cooperation

1. The competent authorities of the host Member State may ask the competent authorities of the Member State of establishment, in the event of justified doubts, to provide any information relevant to the legality of the service provider's establishment and good conduct, as well as the absence of any disciplinary or criminal sanctions of a professional nature. In the event that the competent authorities of the host Member State decide to check the service provider's professional qualifications, they may ask the competent authorities of the Member State of establishment for information about the service provider's training courses to the extent necessary to assess substantial differences likely to be harmful to public health or safety. The competent authorities of the Member State of establishment shall provide that information in accordance with Article 56. In the case of non-regulated professions in the home Member State, the assistance centres referred to in Article 57b may also provide such information.

2. The competent authorities shall ensure the exchange of all information necessary for complaints by a recipient of a service against a service provider to be correctly pursued. Recipients shall be informed of the outcome of the complaint.

Article 9
Information to be given to the recipients of the service
In cases where the service is provided under the professional title of the Member State of establishment or under the formal qualification of the service provider, in addition to the other requirements relating to information contained in [Union] law, the competent authorities of the host Member State may require the service provider to furnish the recipient of the service with any or all of the following information:

(a) if the service provider is registered in a commercial register or similar public register, the register in which he is registered, his registration number, or equivalent means of identification contained in that register;

(b) if the activity is subject to authorisation in the Member State of establishment, the name and address of the competent supervisory authority;

(c) any professional association or similar body with which the service provider is registered;

(d) the professional title or, where no such title exists, the formal qualification of the service provider and the Member State in which it was awarded;

(e) if the service provider performs an activity which is subject to VAT, the VAT identification number referred to in Article 22(1) of the sixth Council Directive 77/388/EEC of 17 May 1977 on the harmonisation of the laws of the Member States relating to turnover taxes – Common system of value added tax: uniform basis of assessment;

(f) details of any insurance cover or other means of personal or collective protection with regard to professional liability.

TITLE III FREEDOM OF ESTABLISHMENT

Chapter I General System for the Recognition of Evidence of Training

Article 10
Scope
This Chapter applies to all professions which are not covered by Chapters II and III of this Title and in the following cases in which the applicant, for specific and exceptional reasons, does not satisfy the conditions laid down in those Chapters:

(a) for activities listed in Annex IV, when the migrant does not meet the requirements set out in Articles 17, 18 and 19;

(b) for doctors with basic training, specialised doctors, nurses responsible for general care, dental practitioners, specialised dental practitioners, veterinary surgeons, midwives, pharmacists and architects, when the migrant does not meet the requirements of effective and lawful professional practice referred to in Articles 23, 27, 33, 37, 39, 43 and 49;

(c) for architects, when the migrant holds evidence of formal qualification not listed in Annex V, point 5.7;

(d) without prejudice to Article 21(1), 23 and 27, for doctors, nurses, dental practitioners, veterinary surgeons, midwives, pharmacists and architects holding evidence of formal qualifications as a specialist who must have taken part in the training leading to the possession of a title listed in Annex V, points 5.1.1, 5.2.2, 5.3.2, 5.4.2, 5.5.2, 5.6.2 and 5.7.1, and solely for the purpose of the recognition of the relevant specialty;

(e) for nurses responsible for general care and specialised nurses holding evidence of formal qualifications as a specialist who have taken part in the training leading to the possession of a title listed in Annex V, point 5.2.2, when the migrant seeks recognition in another Member State where the relevant professional activities are pursued by specialised nurses without training as general care nurse;

(f) for specialised nurses without training as general care nurse, when the migrant seeks recognition in another Member State where the relevant professional activities are pursued by nurses responsible for general care, specialised nurses without training as general care nurse or specialised nurses holding evidence of formal qualifications as a specialist who have taken part in the training leading to the possession of the titles listed in Annex V, point 5.2.2;

(g) for migrants meeting the requirements set out in Article 3(3).

Article 11
Levels of qualification
For the purposes of Article 13 and Article 14(6), professional qualifications shall be grouped under the following levels:

(a) an attestation of competence issued by a competent authority in the home Member State designated pursuant to legislative, regulatory or administrative provisions of that Member State, on the basis of:

(i) either a training course not forming part of a certificate or diploma within the meaning of points (b), (c), (d) or (e), or a specific examination without prior training, or full-time pursuit of the profession in a Member State for three consecutive years or for an equivalent duration on a part-time basis during the previous 10 years,

(ii) or general primary or secondary education, attesting that the holder has acquired general knowledge;

(b) a certificate attesting to a successful completion of a secondary course[:]

(i) either general in character, supplemented by a course of study or professional training other than those referred to in point (c) and/or by the probationary or professional practice required in addition to that course, or

(ii) technical or professional in character, supplemented where appropriate by a course of study or professional training as referred to in point (i), and/or by the probationary or professional practice required in addition to that course;

(c) a diploma certifying successful completion of[:]

(i) either training at post-secondary level other than that referred to in points (d) and (e) of a duration of at least one year or of an equivalent duration on a part-time basis, one of the conditions of entry of which is, as a general rule, the successful completion of the secondary course required to obtain entry to university or higher education or the completion of equivalent school education of the second secondary level, as well as the professional training which may be required in addition to that post-secondary course; or

(ii) regulated education and training or, in the case of regulated professions, vocational training with a special structure, with competences going beyond what is provided for in level b, equivalent to the level of training provided for under point (i), if such training provides a comparable professional standard and prepares the trainee for a comparable level of responsibilities and functions provided that the diploma is accompanied by a certificate from the home Member State;

(d) a diploma certifying that the holder has successfully completed training at post-secondary level of at least three and not more than four years' duration, or of an equivalent duration on a part-time basis, which may in addition be expressed with an equivalent number of ECTS credits, at a university or establishment of higher education or another establishment of equivalent level and, where appropriate, that he has successfully completed the professional training required in addition to the post-secondary course;

(e) a diploma certifying that the holder has successfully completed a post-secondary course of at least four years' duration, or of an equivalent duration on a part-time basis, which may in addition be expressed with an equivalent number of ECTS credits, at a university or establishment of higher education or another establishment of equivalent level and, where appropriate, that he has successfully completed the professional training required in addition to the post-secondary course.

———————

Article 12
Equal treatment of qualifications

Any evidence of formal qualifications or set of evidence of formal qualifications issued by a competent authority in a Member State, certifying successful completion of training in the Union, on a full or part-time basis, within or outside formal programmes, which is recognised by that Member State as being of an equivalent level and which confers on the holder the same rights of access to or pursuit of a profession or prepares for the pursuit of that profession, shall be treated as evidence of formal qualifications referred to in Article 11, including the level in question.

Any professional qualification which, although not satisfying the requirements contained in the legislative, regulatory or administrative provisions in force in the home Member State for access to or the pursuit of a profession, confers on the holder acquired rights by virtue of these provisions, shall also be treated as such evidence of formal qualifications under the same conditions as set out in the first subparagraph. This applies in particular if the home Member State raises the level of training required for admission to a profession and for its exercise, and if an individual who has undergone former training, which does not meet the requirements of the new qualification, benefits from acquired rights by virtue of national legislative, regulatory or administrative provisions; in such case this former training is considered by the host Member State, for the purposes of the application of Article 13, as corresponding to the level of the new training.

Article 13

Conditions for recognition

1. If access to or pursuit of a regulated profession in a host Member State is contingent upon possession of specific professional qualifications, the competent authority of that Member State shall permit applicants to access and pursue that profession, under the same conditions as apply to its nationals, if they possess an attestation of competence or evidence of formal qualifications referred to in Article 11, required by another Member State in order to gain access to and pursue that profession on its territory.

   Attestations of competence or evidence of formal qualifications shall be issued by a competent authority in a Member State, designated in accordance with the laws, regulations or administrative provisions of that Member State.

2. Access to, and pursuit of, a profession as described in paragraph 1 shall also be granted to applicants who have pursued the profession in question on a full-time basis for one year or for an equivalent overall duration on a part-time basis during the previous 10 years in another Member State which does not regulate that profession, and who possess one or more attestations of competence or evidence of formal qualifications issued by another Member State which does not regulate the profession.

   Attestations of competence and evidence of formal qualifications shall satisfy the following conditions:

   (a) they are issued by a competent authority in a Member State, designated in accordance with the laws, regulations or administrative provisions of that Member State;

   (b) they attest that the holder has been prepared for the pursuit of the profession in question.

   The one year of professional experience referred to in the first subparagraph may not, however, be required if the evidence of formal qualifications which the applicant possesses certifies regulated education and training.

3. The host Member State shall accept the level attested under Article 11 by the home Member State, as well as the certificate by which the home Member State certifies that regulated education and training or vocational training with a special structure referred to in point (c)(ii) of Article 11 is equivalent to the level provided for in point (c)(i) of Article 11.

4. By way of derogation from paragraphs 1 and 2 of this Article and from Article 14, the competent authority of the host Member State may refuse access to, and pursuit of, the profession to holders of an attestation of competence classified under point (a) of Article 11 where the national professional qualification required to exercise the profession on its territory is classified under point (e) of Article 11.

Article 14

Compensation measures

1. Article 13 shall not preclude the host Member State from requiring the applicant to complete an adaptation period of up to three years or to take an aptitude test if:

   (a) the training the applicant has received covers substantially different matters than those covered by the evidence of formal qualifications required in the host Member State;

   (b) the regulated profession in the host Member State comprises one or more regulated professional activities which do not exist in the corresponding profession in the applicant's home Member State, and the training required in the host Member State covers substantially different matters from those covered by the applicant's attestation of competence or evidence of formal qualifications.

2. If the host Member State makes use of the option provided for in paragraph 1, it must offer the applicant the choice between an adaptation period and an aptitude test.

Where a Member State considers, with respect to a given profession, that it is necessary to derogate from the requirement, set out in the previous subparagraph, that it give the applicant a choice between an adaptation period and an aptitude test, it shall inform the other Member States and the Commission in advance and provide sufficient justification for the derogation.

Where the Commission considers that the derogation referred to in the second subparagraph is inappropriate or that it is not in accordance with Union law, it shall adopt an implementing act, within three months of receiving all necessary information, to ask the relevant Member State to refrain from taking the envisaged measure. In the absence of a response from the Commission within that deadline, the derogation may be applied.

3. By way of derogation from the principle of the right of the applicant to choose, as laid down in paragraph 2, for professions whose pursuit requires precise knowledge of national law and in respect of which the provision of advice and/or assistance concerning national law is an essential and constant aspect of the professional activity, the host Member State may stipulate either an adaptation period or an aptitude test.

This applies also to the cases provided for in Article 10 points (b) and (c), in Article 10 point (d) concerning doctors and dental practitioners in Article 10 point (f) when the migrant seeks recognition in another Member State where the relevant professional activities are pursued by nurses responsible for general care or specialised nurses holding evidence of formal qualifications as a specialist who have taken part in the training leading to the possession of the titles listed in Annex V, point 5.2.2 and in Article 10 point (g).

In the cases covered by Article 10 point (a), the host Member State may require an adaptation period or an aptitude test if the migrant envisages pursuing professional activities in a self-employed capacity or as a manager of an undertaking which require the knowledge and the application of the specific national rules in force, provided that knowledge and application of those rules are required by the competent authorities of the host Member State for access to such activities by its own nationals.

By way of derogation from the principle of the right of the applicant to choose, as laid down in paragraph 2, the host Member State may stipulate either an adaptation period or an aptitude test in the case of:

(a) a holder of a professional qualification referred to in point (a) of Article 11, who applies for recognition of his professional qualifications where the national professional qualification required is classified under point (c) of Article 11; or

(b) a holder of a professional qualification referred to in point (b) of Article 11, who applies for recognition of his professional qualifications where the national professional qualification required is classified under point (d) or (e) of Article 11.

In the case of a holder of a professional qualification referred to in point (a) of Article 11 who applies for recognition of his professional qualifications where the national professional qualification required is classified under point (d) of Article 11, the host Member State may impose both an adaptation period and an aptitude test.

4. For the purposes of paragraphs 1 and 5, 'substantially different matters' means matters in respect of which knowledge, skills and competences acquired are essential for pursuing the profession and with regard to which the training received by the migrant shows significant differences in terms of content from the training required by the host Member State.

5. Paragraph 1 shall be applied with due regard to the principle of proportionality. In particular, if the host Member State intends to require the applicant to complete an adaptation period or take an aptitude test, it must first ascertain whether the knowledge, skills and competences acquired by the applicant in the course of his professional experience or through lifelong learning, and formally validated to that end by a relevant body, in any Member State or in a third country, is of such nature as to cover, in full or in part, the substantially different matters defined in paragraph 4.

6. The decision imposing an adaptation period or an aptitude test shall be duly justified. In particular, the applicant shall be provided with the following information:

   (a) the level of the professional qualification required in the host Member State and the level of the professional qualification held by the applicant in accordance with the classification set out in Article 11; and

   (b) the substantial differences referred to in paragraph 4 and the reasons for which those differences cannot be compensated by knowledge, skills and competences acquired in the course of professional experience or through lifelong learning formally validated to that end by a relevant body.

7. Member States shall ensure that an applicant has the possibility of taking the aptitude test referred to in paragraph 1 not later than six months after the initial decision imposing an aptitude test on the applicant.

———————

Chapter II Recognition of Professional Experience

Article 16
Requirements regarding professional experience

If, in a Member State, access to or pursuit of one of the activities listed in Annex IV is contingent upon possession of general, commercial or professional knowledge and aptitudes, that Member State shall recognise previous pursuit of the activity in another Member State as sufficient proof of such knowledge and aptitudes. The activity must have been pursued in accordance with Articles 17, 18 and 19.

Article 17
Activities referred to in list I of Annex IV

1. For the activities in list I of Annex IV, the activity in question must have been previously pursued:

   (a) for six consecutive years on a self-employed basis or as a manager of an undertaking; or

   (b) for three consecutive years on a self-employed basis or as a manager of an undertaking, where the beneficiary proves that he has received previous training of at least three years for the activity in question, evidenced by a certificate recognised by the Member State or judged by a competent professional body to be fully valid; or

12

(c) for four consecutive years on a self-employed basis or as a manager of an undertaking, where the beneficiary can prove that he has received, for the activity in question, previous training of at least two years' duration, attested by a certificate recognised by the Member State or judged by a competent professional body to be fully valid; or

(d) for three consecutive years on a self-employed basis, if the beneficiary can prove that he has pursued the activity in question on an employed basis for at least five years; or

(e) for five consecutive years in an executive position, of which at least three years involved technical duties and responsibility for at least one department of the company, if the beneficiary can prove that he has received, for the activity in question, previous training of at least three years' duration, as attested by a certificate recognised by the Member State or judged by a competent professional body to be fully valid.

2. In cases (a) and (d), the activity must not have finished more than 10 years before the date on which the complete application was submitted by the person concerned to the competent authority referred to in Article 56.

3. Paragraph 1(e) shall not apply to activities in Group ex 855, hairdressing establishments, of the ISIC Nomenclature.

Article 18
Activities referred to in list II of Annex IV

1. For the activities in list II of Annex IV, the activity in question must have been previously pursued:

(a) for five consecutive years on a self-employed basis or as a manager of an undertaking, or

(b) for three consecutive years on a self-employed basis or as a manager of an undertaking, where the beneficiary proves that he has received previous training of at least three years for the activity in question, evidenced by a certificate recognised by the Member State or judged by a competent professional body to be fully valid, or

(c) for four consecutive years on a self-employed basis or as a manager of an undertaking, where the beneficiary can prove that he has received, for the activity in question, previous training of at least two years' duration, attested by a certificate recognised by the Member State or judged by a competent professional body to be fully valid, or

(d) for three consecutive years on a self-employed basis or as a manager of an undertaking, if the beneficiary can prove that he has pursued the activity in question on an employed basis for at least five years, or

(e) for five consecutive years on an employed basis, if the beneficiary can prove that he has received, for the activity in question, previous training of at least three years' duration, as attested by a certificate recognised by the Member State or judged by a competent professional body to be fully valid, or

(f) for six consecutive years on an employed basis, if the beneficiary can prove that he has received previous training in the activity in question of at least two years' duration, as attested by a certificate recognised by the Member State or judged by a competent professional body to be fully valid.

2. In cases (a) and (d), the activity must not have finished more than 10 years before the date on which the complete application was submitted by the person concerned to the competent authority referred to in Article 56.

Article 19
Activities referred to in list III of Annex IV

1. For the activities in list III of Annex IV, the activity in question must have been previously pursued:
   (a) for three consecutive years, either on a self-employed basis or as a manager of an undertaking, or
   (b) for two consecutive years, either on a self-employed basis or as a manager of an undertaking, if the beneficiary can prove that he has received previous training for the activity in question, as attested by a certificate recognised by the Member State or judged by a competent professional body to be fully valid, or
   (c) for two consecutive years, either on a self-employed basis or as a manager of an undertaking, if the beneficiary can prove that he has pursued the activity in question on an employed basis for at least three years, or
   (d) for three consecutive years, on an employed basis, if the beneficiary can prove that he has received previous training for the activity in question, as attested by a certificate recognised by the Member State or judged by a competent professional body to be fully valid.
2. In cases (a) and (c), the activity must not have finished more than 10 years before the date on which the complete application was submitted by the person concerned to the competent authority referred to in Article 56.

Article 20
Adaptation of lists of activities in Annex IV

The Commission shall be empowered to adopt delegated acts in accordance with Article 57c concerning the adaptation of the lists of activities set out in Annex IV which are the subject of recognition of professional experience pursuant to Article 16, with a view to updating or clarifying the activities listed in Annex IV in particular in order to further specify their scope and to take due account of the latest developments in the field of activity-based nomenclatures, provided that this does not involve any narrowing of the scope of the activities related to the individual categories and that there is no shift of activities between the existing lists I, II and III of Annex IV.

> **Chapter III** Recognition on the Basis of Coordination of Minimum Training Conditions

SECTION 1 GENERAL PROVISIONS

Article 21
Principle of automatic recognition

1. Each Member State shall recognise evidence of formal qualifications as doctor giving access to the professional activities of doctor with basic training and specialised doctor, as nurse responsible for general care, as dental practitioner, as specialised dental practitioner, as veterinary surgeon, as pharmacist and as architect, listed in Annex V,

12

points 5.1.1, 5.1.2, 5.2.2, 5.3.2, 5.3.3, 5.4.2, 5.6.2 and 5.7.1 respectively, which satisfy the minimum training conditions referred to in Articles 24, 25, 31, 34, 35, 38, 44 and 46 respectively, and shall, for the purposes of access to and pursuit of the professional activities, give such evidence the same effect on its territory as the evidence of formal qualifications which it itself issues.

Such evidence of formal qualifications must be issued by the competent bodies in the Member States and accompanied, where appropriate, by the certificates listed in Annex V, points 5.1.1, 5.1.2, 5.2.2, 5.3.2, 5.3.3, 5.4.2, 5.6.2 and 5.7.1 respectively.

The provisions of the first and second subparagraphs do not affect the acquired rights referred to in Articles 23, 27, 33, 37, 39 and 49.

2. Each Member State shall recognise, for the purpose of pursuing general medical practice in the framework of its national social security system, evidence of formal qualifications listed in Annex V, point 5.1.4 and issued to nationals of the Member States by the other Member States in accordance with the minimum training conditions laid down in Article 28.

The provisions of the previous subparagraph do not affect the acquired rights referred to in Article 30.

3. Each Member State shall recognise evidence of formal qualifications as a midwife, awarded to nationals of Member States by the other Member States, listed in Annex V, point 5.5.2, which complies with the minimum training conditions referred to in Article 40 and satisfies the criteria set out in Article 41, and shall, for the purposes of access to and pursuit of the professional activities, give such evidence the same effect on its territory as the evidence of formal qualifications which it itself issues. This provision does not affect the acquired rights referred to in Articles 23 and 43.

4. In respect of the operation of pharmacies that are not subject to territorial restrictions, a Member State may, by way of derogation, decide not to give effect to evidence of formal qualifications referred to in point 5.6.2 of Annex V, for the setting up of new pharmacies open to the public. For the purposes of this paragraph, pharmacies which have been open for less than three years shall also be considered as new pharmacies.

That derogation may not be applied in respect of pharmacists whose formal qualifications have already been recognised by the competent authorities of the host Member State for other purposes and who have been effectively and lawfully engaged in the professional activities of a pharmacist for at least three consecutive years in that Member State.

5. Evidence of formal qualifications as an architect referred to in Annex V, point 5.7.1, which is subject to automatic recognition pursuant to paragraph 1, proves completion of a course of training which began not earlier than during the academic reference year referred to in that Annex.

6. Each Member State shall make access to, and pursuit of, the professional activities of doctors, nurses responsible for general care, dental practitioners, veterinary surgeons, midwives and pharmacists subject to possession of evidence of formal qualifications referred to in points 5.1.1, 5.1.2, 5.1.4, 5.2.2, 5.3.2, 5.3.3, 5.4.2, 5.5.2 and 5.6.2 of Annex V respectively, attesting that the professional concerned, over the duration of his training, has acquired, as appropriate, the knowledge, skills and competences referred to in Articles 24(3), 31(6), 31(7), 34(3), 38(3), 40(3) and 44(3).

In order to take account of generally acknowledged scientific and technical progress, the Commission shall be empowered to adopt delegated acts in accordance with Article 57c to update the knowledge and skills referred to in Articles 24(3), 31(6), 34(3), 38(3), 40(3), 44(3) and 46(4) to reflect the evolution of Union law directly affecting the professionals concerned.

Such updates shall not entail an amendment of existing essential legislative principles in Member States regarding the structure of professions as regards training and conditions of access by natural persons. Such updates shall respect the responsibility of the Member States for the organisation of education systems, as set out in Article 165(1) of the Treaty on the Functioning of the European Union (TFEU). —————

Article 21a

Notification procedure

1. Each Member State shall notify the Commission of the laws, regulations and administrative provisions which it adopts with regard to the issuing of evidence of formal qualifications in the professions covered by this Chapter.

    In the case of evidence of formal qualifications referred to in Section 8, notification in accordance with the first subparagraph shall also be addressed to the other Member States.

2. The notification referred to in paragraph 1 shall include information about the duration and content of the training programmes.

3. The notification referred to in paragraph 1 shall be transmitted via IMI.

4. In order to take due account of legislative and administrative developments in the Member States, and on condition that the laws, regulations and administrative provisions notified pursuant to paragraph 1 of this Article are in conformity with the conditions set out in this Chapter, the Commission shall be empowered to adopt delegated acts in accordance with Article 57c in order to amend points 5.1.1 to 5.1.4, 5.2.2, 5.3.2, 5.3.3, 5.4.2, 5.5.2, 5.6.2 and 5.7.1 of Annex V, concerning the updating of the titles adopted by the Member States for evidence of formal qualifications and, where appropriate, the body which issues the evidence of formal qualifications, the certificate which accompanies it and the corresponding professional title.

5. Where the legislative, regulatory and administrative provisions notified pursuant to paragraph 1 are not in conformity with the conditions set out in this Chapter, the Commission shall adopt an implementing act in order to reject the requested amendment of points 5.1.1 to 5.1.4, 5.2.2, 5.3.2, 5.3.3, 5.4.2, 5.5.2, 5.6.2 or 5.7.1 of Annex V.

Article 22

Common provisions on training

With regard to the training referred to in Articles 24, 25, 28, 31, 34, 35, 38, 40, 44 and 46:

(a) Member States may authorise part-time training under conditions laid down by the competent authorities; those authorities shall ensure that the overall duration, level and quality of such training is not lower than that of continuous full-time training;

(b) Member States shall, in accordance with the procedures specific to each Member State, ensure, by encouraging continuous professional development, that professionals whose professional qualification is covered by Chapter III of this Title are

12

able to update their knowledge, skills and competences in order to maintain a safe and effective practice and keep abreast of professional developments.

Member States shall communicate to the Commission the measures taken pursuant to point (b) of the first paragraph by 18 January 2016.

Article 23
Acquired rights

1. Without prejudice to the acquired rights specific to the professions concerned, in cases where the evidence of formal qualifications as doctor giving access to the professional activities of doctor with basic training and specialised doctor, as nurse responsible for general care, as dental practitioner, as specialised dental practitioner, as veterinary surgeon, as midwife and as pharmacist held by Member States nationals does not satisfy all the training requirements referred to in Articles 24, 25, 31, 34, 35, 38, 40 and 44, each Member State shall recognise as sufficient proof evidence of formal qualifications issued by those Member States insofar as such evidence attests successful completion of training which began before the reference dates laid down in Annex V, points 5.1.1, 5.1.2, 5.2.2, 5.3.2, 5.3.3, 5.4.2, 5.5.2 and 5.6.2 and is accompanied by a certificate stating that the holders have been effectively and lawfully engaged in the activities in question for at least three consecutive years during the five years preceding the award of the certificate.

2. The same provisions shall apply to evidence of formal qualifications as doctor giving access to the professional activities of doctor with basic training and specialised doctor, as nurse responsible for general care, as dental practitioner, as specialised dental practitioner, as veterinary surgeon, as midwife and as pharmacist, obtained in the territory of the former German Democratic Republic, which does not satisfy all the minimum training requirements laid down in Articles 24, 25, 31, 34, 35, 38, 40 and 44 if such evidence certifies successful completion of training which began before:
   (a) 3 October 1990 for doctors with basic training, nurses responsible for general care, dental practitioners with basic training, specialised dental practitioners, veterinary surgeons, midwives and pharmacists, and
   (b) 3 April 1992 for specialised doctors.

   The evidence of formal qualifications referred to in the first subparagraph confers on the holder the right to pursue professional activities throughout German territory under the same conditions as evidence of formal qualifications issued by the competent German authorities referred to in Annex V, points 5.1.1, 5.1.2, 5.2.2, 5.3.2, 5.3.3, 5.4.2, 5.5.2 and 5.6.2.

3. Without prejudice to the provisions of Article 37(1), each Member State shall recognise evidence of formal qualifications as doctor giving access to the professional activities of doctor with basic training and specialised doctor, as nurse responsible for general care, as veterinary surgeon, as midwife, as pharmacist and as architect held by Member States nationals and issued by the former Czechoslovakia, or whose training commenced, for the Czech Republic and Slovakia, before 1 January 1993, where the authorities of either of the two aforementioned Member States attest that such evidence of formal qualifications has the same legal validity within their territory as the evidence of formal qualifications which they issue and, with respect to architects, as the evidence of formal qualifications specified for those Member States in Annex VI,

point 6, as regards access to the professional activities of doctor with basic training, specialised doctor, nurse responsible for general care, veterinary surgeon, midwife, pharmacist with respect to the activities referred to in Article 45(2), and architect with respect to the activities referred to in Article 48, and the pursuit of such activities.

Such an attestation must be accompanied by a certificate issued by those same authorities stating that such persons have effectively and lawfully been engaged in the activities in question within their territory for at least three consecutive years during the five years prior to the date of issue of the certificate.

4. Each Member State shall recognise evidence of formal qualifications as doctor giving access to the professional activities of doctor with basic training and specialised doctor, as nurse responsible for general care, as dental practitioner, as specialised dental practitioner, as veterinary surgeon, as midwife, as pharmacist and as architect held by nationals of the Member States and issued by the former Soviet Union, or whose training commenced[:]

(a) for Estonia, before 20 August 1991,

(b) for Latvia, before 21 August 1991,

(c) for Lithuania, before 11 March 1990,

where the authorities of any of the three aforementioned Member States attest that such evidence has the same legal validity within their territory as the evidence which they issue and, with respect to architects, as the evidence of formal qualifications specified for those Member States in Annex VI, point 6, as regards access to the professional activities of doctor with basic training, specialised doctor, nurse responsible for general care, dental practitioner, specialised dental practitioner, veterinary surgeon, midwife, pharmacist with respect to the activities referred to in Article 45(2), and architect with respect to the activities referred to in Article 48, and the pursuit of such activities.

Such an attestation must be accompanied by a certificate issued by those same authorities stating that such persons have effectively and lawfully been engaged in the activities in question within their territory for at least three consecutive years during the five years prior to the date of issue of the certificate.

With regard to evidence of formal qualifications as veterinary surgeons issued by the former Soviet Union or in respect of which training commenced, for Estonia, before 20 August 1991, the attestation referred to in the preceding subparagraph must be accompanied by a certificate issued by the Estonian authorities stating that such persons have effectively and lawfully been engaged in the activities in question within their territory for at least five consecutive years during the seven years prior to the date of issue of the certificate.

5. Without prejudice to Article 43b, each Member State shall recognise evidence of formal qualifications as doctor giving access to the professional activities of doctor with basic training and specialised doctor, as nurse responsible for general care, as dental practitioner, as specialised dental practitioner, as veterinary surgeon, as midwife, as pharmacist and as architect held by nationals of the Member States and issued by the former Yugoslavia, or whose training commenced[:]

(a) for Slovenia, before 25 June 1991; and

(b) for Croatia, before 8 October 1991;

where the authorities of the aforementioned Member States attest that such evidence has the same legal validity within their territory as the evidence which they issue and, with respect to architects, as the evidence of formal qualifications specified for those Member States in Annex VI, point 6, as regards access to the professional activities of doctor with basic training, specialised doctor, nurse responsible for general care, dental practitioner, specialised dental practitioner, veterinary surgeon, midwife, pharmacist with respect to the activities referred to in Article 45(2), and architect with respect to the activities referred to in Article 48, and the pursuit of such activities.

Such an attestation must be accompanied by a certificate issued by those same authorities stating that such persons have effectively and lawfully been engaged in the activities in question within their territory for at least three consecutive years during the five years prior to the date of issue of the certificate.

6. Each Member State shall recognise as sufficient proof for Member State nationals whose evidence of formal qualifications as a doctor, nurse responsible for general care, dental practitioner, veterinary surgeon, midwife and pharmacist does not correspond to the titles given for that Member State in Annex V, points 5.1.1, 5.1.2, 5.1.3, 5.1.4, 5.2.2, 5.3.2, 5.3.3, 5.4.2, 5.5.2 and 5.6.2, evidence of formal qualifications issued by those Member States accompanied by a certificate issued by the competent authorities or bodies.

The certificate referred to in the first subparagraph shall state that the evidence of formal qualifications certifies successful completion of training in accordance with Articles 24, 25, 28, 31, 34, 35, 38, 40 and 44 respectively and is treated by the Member State which issued it in the same way as the qualifications whose titles are listed in Annex V, points 5.1.1, 5.1.2, 5.1.3, 5.1.4, 5.2.2, 5.3.2, 5.3.3, 5.4.2, 5.5.2 and 5.6.2.

Article 23a

Specific circumstances

1. By way of derogation from the present Directive, Bulgaria may authorise the holders of the qualification of 'фелдшер' (feldsher) awarded in Bulgaria before 31 December 1999 and exercising this profession under the Bulgarian national social security scheme on 1 January 2000 to continue to exercise the said profession, even if parts of their activity fall under the provisions of the present Directive concerning doctors of medicine and nurses responsible for general care respectively.

2. The holders of the Bulgarian qualification of 'фелдшер' (feldsher) referred to in paragraph 1 are not entitled to obtain professional recognition in other Member States as doctors of medicine nor as nurses responsible for general care under this Directive.

SECTION 2 DOCTORS OF MEDICINE

Article 24

Basic medical training

1. Admission to basic medical training shall be contingent upon possession of a diploma or certificate providing access, for the studies in question, to universities.

2. Basic medical training shall comprise a total of at least five years of study, which may in addition be expressed with the equivalent ECTS credits, and shall consist of at least 5 500 hours of theoretical and practical training provided by, or under the supervision of, a university.

For professionals who began their studies before 1 January 1972, the course of training referred to in the first subparagraph may comprise six months of full-time practical training at university level under the supervision of the competent authorities.

3. Basic medical training shall provide an assurance that the person in question has acquired the following knowledge and skills:

(a) adequate knowledge of the sciences on which medicine is based and a good understanding of the scientific methods including the principles of measuring biological functions, the evaluation of scientifically established facts and the analysis of data;

(b) sufficient understanding of the structure, functions and behaviour of healthy and sick persons, as well as relations between the state of health and physical and social surroundings of the human being;

(c) adequate knowledge of clinical disciplines and practices, providing him with a coherent picture of mental and physical diseases, of medicine from the points of view of prophylaxis, diagnosis and therapy and of human reproduction;

(d) suitable clinical experience in hospitals under appropriate supervision.

Article 25
Specialist medical training

1. Admission to specialist medical training shall be contingent upon completion and validation of a basic medical training programme as referred to in Article 24(2) in the course of which the trainee has acquired the relevant knowledge of basic medicine.

2. Specialist medical training shall comprise theoretical and practical training at a university or medical teaching hospital or, where appropriate, a medical care establishment approved for that purpose by the competent authorities or bodies.

The Member States shall ensure that the minimum duration of specialist medical training courses referred to in Annex V, point 5.1.3 is not less than the duration provided for in that point. Training shall be given under the supervision of the competent authorities or bodies. It shall include personal participation of the trainee specialised doctor in the activity and responsibilities entailed by the services in question.

3. Training shall be given on a full-time basis at specific establishments which are recognised by the competent authorities. It shall entail participation in the full range of medical activities of the department where the training is given, including duty on call, in such a way that the trainee specialist devotes all his professional activity to his practical and theoretical training throughout the entire working week and throughout the year, in accordance with the procedures laid down by the competent authorities. Accordingly, these posts shall be the subject of appropriate remuneration.

3a. Member States may provide, in national legislation, for partial exemptions from parts of the specialist medical training courses listed in point 5.1.3 of Annex V, to be applied on a case-by-case basis provided that that part of the training has been followed already during another specialist training course listed in point 5.1.3 of Annex V, for which the professional has already obtained the professional qualification in a Member State. Member States shall ensure that the granted exemption equates to not more than half of the minimum duration of the specialist medical training course in question.

Each Member State shall notify the Commission and the other Member States of the national legislation concerned for any such partial exemptions.

4. The Member States shall make the issuance of evidence of specialist medical training contingent upon possession of evidence of basic medical training referred to in Annex V, point 5.1.1.

5. The Commission shall be empowered to adopt delegated acts in accordance with Article 57c concerning the adaptation of the minimum periods of training referred to in point 5.1.3 of Annex V to scientific and technical progress.

Article 26

Types of specialist medical training

Evidence of formal qualifications as a specialised doctor referred to in Article 21 is such evidence awarded by the competent authorities or bodies referred to in Annex V, point 5.1.2 as corresponds, for the specialised training in question, to the titles in use in the various Member States and referred to in Annex V, point 5.1.3.

In order to take due account of changes in national legislation and with a view to updating this Directive, the Commission shall be empowered to adopt delegated acts in accordance with Article 57c concerning the inclusion in point 5.1.3 of Annex V of new medical specialties common to at least two-fifths of the Member States.

Article 27

Acquired rights specific to specialised doctors

1. A host Member State may require of specialised doctors whose part-time specialist medical training was governed by legislative, regulatory and administrative provisions in force as of 20 June 1975 and who began their specialist training no later than 31 December 1983 that their evidence of formal qualifications be accompanied by a certificate stating that they have been effectively and lawfully engaged in the relevant activities for at least three consecutive years during the five years preceding the award of that certificate.

2. Every Member State shall recognise the qualification of specialised doctors awarded in Spain to doctors who completed their specialist training before 1 January 1995, even if that training does not satisfy the minimum training requirements provided for in Article 25, in so far as that qualification is accompanied by a certificate issued by the competent Spanish authorities and attesting that the person concerned has passed the examination in specific professional competence held in the context of exceptional measures concerning recognition laid down in Royal Decree 1497/99, with a view to ascertaining that the person concerned possesses a level of knowledge and skill comparable to that of doctors who possess a qualification as a specialised doctor defined for Spain in Annex V, points 5.1.2 and 5.1.3.

2a. Member States shall recognise the qualifications of specialised doctors awarded in Italy, and listed in points 5.1.2 and 5.1.3 of Annex V, to doctors who started their specialist training after 31 December 1983 and before 1 January 1991, despite the training concerned not satisfying all the training requirements set out in Article 25, if the qualification is accompanied by a certificate issued by the competent Italian authorities stating that the doctor concerned has effectively and lawfully been engaged, in Italy, in the activities of a medical specialist in the same specialist area concerned, for at least seven consecutive years during the 10 years preceding the award of the certificate.

3. Every Member State which has repealed its legislative, regulatory or administrative provisions relating to the award of evidence of formal qualifications as a specialised doctor referred to in Annex V, points 5.1.2 and 5.1.3 and which has adopted measures relating to acquired rights benefiting its nationals, shall grant nationals of other Member States the right to benefit from those measures, in so far as such evidence of formal qualifications was issued before the date on which the host Member State ceased to issue such evidence for the specialty in question.

    The dates on which these provisions were repealed are set out in Annex V, point 5.1.3.

Article 28
Specific training in general medical practice

1. Admission to specific training in general medical practice shall be contingent upon completion and validation of a basic medical training programme as referred to in Article 24(2) in the course of which the trainee has acquired the relevant knowledge of basic medicine.

2. The specific training in general medical practice leading to the award of evidence of formal qualifications issued before 1 January 2006 shall be of a duration of at least two years on a full-time basis. In the case of evidence of formal qualifications issued after that date, the training shall be of a duration of at least three years on a full-time basis.

    Where the training programme referred to in Article 24 comprises practical training given by an approved hospital possessing appropriate general medical equipment and services or as part of an approved general medical practice or an approved centre in which doctors provide primary medical care, the duration of that practical training may, up to a maximum of one year, be included in the duration provided for in the first subparagraph for certificates of training issued on or after 1 January 2006.

    The option provided for in the second subparagraph shall be available only for Member States in which the specific training in general medical practice lasted two years as of 1 January 2001.

3. The specific training in general medical practice shall be carried out on a full-time basis, under the supervision of the competent authorities or bodies. It shall be more practical than theoretical.

    The practical training shall be given, on the one hand, for at least six months in an approved hospital possessing appropriate equipment and services and, on the other hand, for at least six months as part of an approved general medical practice or an approved centre at which doctors provide primary health care.

    The practical training shall take place in conjunction with other health establishments or structures concerned with general medicine. Without prejudice to the minimum periods laid down in the second subparagraph, however, the practical training may be given during a period of not more than six months in other approved establishments or health structures concerned with general medicine.

12

The training shall require the personal participation of the trainee in the professional activity and responsibilities of the persons with whom he is working.

4. Member States shall make the issuance of evidence of formal qualifications in general medical practice subject to possession of evidence of formal qualifications in basic medical training referred to in Annex V, point 5.1.1.

5. Member States may issue evidence of formal qualifications referred to in Annex V, point 5.1.4 to a doctor who has not completed the training provided for in this Article but who has completed a different, supplementary training, as attested by evidence of formal qualifications issued by the competent authorities in a Member State. They may not, however, award evidence of formal qualifications unless it attests knowledge of a level qualitatively equivalent to the knowledge acquired from the training provided for in this Article.

Member States shall determine, *inter alia*, the extent to which the complementary training and professional experience already acquired by the applicant may replace the training provided for in this Article.

The Member States may only issue the evidence of formal qualifications referred to in Annex V, point 5.1.4 if the applicant has acquired at least six months' experience of general medicine in a general medical practice or a centre in which doctors provide primary health care of the types referred to in paragraph 3.

Article 29

Pursuit of the professional activities of general practitioners

Each Member State shall, subject to the provisions relating to acquired rights, make the pursuit of the activities of a general practitioner in the framework of its national social security system contingent upon possession of evidence of formal qualifications referred to in Annex V, point 5.1.4.

Member States may exempt persons who are currently undergoing specific training in general medicine from this condition.

Article 30

Acquired rights specific to general practitioners

1. Each Member State shall determine the acquired rights. It shall, however, confer as an acquired right the right to pursue the activities of a general practitioner in the framework of its national social security system, without the evidence of formal qualifications referred to in Annex V, point 5.1.4, on all doctors who enjoy this right as of the reference date stated in that point by virtue of provisions applicable to the medical profession giving access to the professional activities of doctor with basic training and who are established as of that date on its territory, having benefited from the provisions of Articles 21 or 23.

The competent authorities of each Member State shall, on demand, issue a certificate stating the holder's right to pursue the activities of general practitioner in the framework of their national social security systems, without the evidence of formal qualifications referred to in Annex V, point 5.1.4, to doctors who enjoy acquired rights pursuant to the first subparagraph.

2. Every Member State shall recognise the certificates referred to in paragraph 1, second subparagraph, awarded to nationals of Member States by the other Member States, and

shall give such certificates the same effect on its territory as evidence of formal qualifications which it awards and which permit the pursuit of the activities of a general
practitioner in the framework of its national social security system.

SECTION 3 NURSES RESPONSIBLE FOR GENERAL CARE

Article 31
Training of nurses responsible for general care
1. Admission to training for nurses responsible for general care shall be contingent upon
   either:
   (a) completion of general education of 12 years, as attested by a diploma, certificate or
       other evidence issued by the competent authorities or bodies in a Member State or
       a certificate attesting success in an examination of an equivalent level and giving
       access to universities or to higher education institutions of a level recognised as
       equivalent; or
   (b) completion of general education of at least 10 years, as attested by a diploma,
       certificate or other evidence issued by the competent authorities or bodies in a
       Member State or a certificate attesting success in an examination of an equivalent
       level and giving access to a vocational school or vocational training programme
       for nursing.
2. Training of nurses responsible for general care shall be given on a full-time basis and
   shall include at least the programme described in Annex V, point 5.2.1.

   The Commission shall be empowered to adopt delegated acts in accordance with
   Article 57c concerning amendments to the list set out in point 5.2.1 of Annex V with
   a view to adapting it to scientific and technical progress.

   The amendments referred to in the second subparagraph shall not entail an amendment of existing essential legislative principles in Member States regarding the structure of professions as regards training and conditions of access by natural persons.
   Such amendments shall respect the responsibility of the Member States for the organisation of education systems, asset out in Article 165(1) TFEU.
3. The training of nurses responsible for general care shall comprise a total of at least
   three years of study, which may in addition be expressed with the equivalent ECTS
   credits, and shall consist of at least 4600 hours of theoretical and clinical training, the
   duration of the theoretical training representing at least one third and the duration of
   the clinical training at least one half of the minimum duration of the training. Member
   States may grant partial exemptions to professionals who have received part of their
   training on courses which are of at least an equivalent level.

   The Member States shall ensure that institutions providing nursing training are
   responsible for the coordination of theoretical and clinical training throughout the
   entire study programme.
4. Theoretical education is that part of nurse training from which trainee nurses
   acquire the professional knowledge, skills and competences required under paragraphs 6 and 7. The training shall be given by teachers of nursing care and by
   other competent persons, at universities, higher education institutions of a level
   recognised as equivalent or at vocational schools or through vocational training
   programmes for nursing.

12

5. Clinical training is that part of nurse training in which trainee nurses learn, as part of a team and in direct contact with a healthy or sick individual and/or community, to organise, dispense and evaluate the required comprehensive nursing care, on the basis of the knowledge, skills and competences which they have acquired. The trainee nurse shall learn not only how to work in a team, but also how to lead a team and organise overall nursing care, including health education for individuals and small groups, within health institutes or in the community.

This training shall take place in hospitals and other health institutions and in the community, under the responsibility of nursing teachers, in cooperation with and assisted by other qualified nurses. Other qualified personnel may also take part in the teaching process.

Trainee nurses shall participate in the activities of the department in question insofar as those activities are appropriate to their training, enabling them to learn to assume the responsibilities involved in nursing care.

6. Training for nurses responsible for general care shall provide an assurance that the professional in question has acquired the following knowledge and skills:
   (a) comprehensive knowledge of the sciences on which general nursing is based, including sufficient understanding of the structure, physiological functions and behaviour of healthy and sick persons, and of the relationship between the state of health and the physical and social environment of the human being;
   (b) knowledge of the nature and ethics of the profession and of the general principles of health and nursing;
   (c) adequate clinical experience; such experience, which should be selected for its training value, should be gained under the supervision of qualified nursing staff and in places where the number of qualified staff and equipment are appropriate for the nursing care of the patient;
   (d) the ability to participate in the practical training of health personnel and experience of working with such personnel;
   (e) experience of working together with members of other professions in the health sector.

7. Formal qualifications as a nurse responsible for general care shall provide evidence that the professional in question is able to apply at least the following competences regardless of whether the training took place at universities, higher education institutions of a level recognised as equivalent or at vocational schools or through vocational training programmes for nursing:
   (a) competence to independently diagnose the nursing care required using current theoretical and clinical knowledge and to plan, organise and implement nursing care when treating patients on the basis of the knowledge and skills acquired in accordance with points (a), (b) and (c) of paragraph 6 in order to improve professional practice;
   (b) competence to work together effectively with other actors in the health sector, including participation in the practical training of health personnel on the basis of the knowledge and skills acquired in accordance with points (d) and (e) of paragraph 6;
   (c) competence to empower individuals, families and groups towards healthy lifestyles and self-care on the basis of the knowledge and skills acquired in accordance with points (a) and (b) of paragraph 6;

(d) competence to independently initiate life-preserving immediate measures and to carry out measures in crises and disaster situations;

(e) competence to independently give advice to, instruct and support persons needing care and their attachment figures;

(f) competence to independently assure the quality of, and to evaluate, nursing care;

(g) competence to comprehensively communicate professionally and to cooperate with members of other professions in the health sector;

(h) competence to analyse the care quality to improve his own professional practice as a nurse responsible for general care.

Article 32

Pursuit of the professional activities of nurses responsible for general care

For the purposes of this Directive, the professional activities of nurses responsible for general care are the activities pursued on a professional basis and referred to in Annex V, point 5.2.2.

Article 33

Acquired rights specific to nurses responsible for general care

1. Where the general rules of acquired rights apply to nurses responsible for general care, the activities referred to in Article 23 must have included full responsibility for the planning, organisation and administration of nursing care delivered to the patient.

――――――

3. Member States shall recognise evidence of formal qualifications in nursing that:

(a) were awarded in Poland, to nurses who completed training before 1 May 2004, which did not comply with the minimum training requirements laid down in Article 31; and

(b) are attested by the diploma 'bachelor' which was obtained on the basis of a special upgrading programme contained in:

(i) Article 11 of the Act of 20 April 2004 on the amendment of the Act on professions of nurse and midwife and on some other legal acts (Official Journal of the Republic of Poland of 2004 No. 92, pos. 885 and of 2007, No. 176, pos. 1237) and the Regulation of the Minister of Health of 11 May 2004 on the detailed conditions of delivering studies for nurses and midwives, who hold a certificate of secondary school (final examination – matura) and are graduates of medical lyceum and medical vocational schools teaching in a profession of a nurse and a midwife (Official Journal of the Republic of Poland of 2004 No. 110, pos. 1170 and of 2010 No. 65, pos. 420); or

(ii) Article 52.3 point 2 of the Act of 15 July 2011 on professions of nurse and midwife (Official Journal of the Republic of Poland of 2011 No. 174, pos. 1039) and the Regulation of the Minister of Health of 14 June 2012 on the detailed conditions of delivering higher education courses for nurses and midwives who hold a certificate of secondary school (final examination – matura) and are graduates of a medical secondary school or a post-secondary school teaching in a profession of a nurse and a midwife (Official Journal of the Republic of Poland of 2012, pos. 770),

12

for the purpose of verifying that the nurse concerned has a level of knowledge and competence comparable to that of nurses holding the qualifications listed for Poland in point 5.2.2 of Annex V.

Article 33(a)

As regards the Romanian qualification of nurse responsible for general care, only the following acquired rights provisions shall apply:

In the case of nationals of Member States who were trained as a nurse responsible for general care in Romania and whose training does not satisfy the minimum training requirements laid down in Article 31, Member States shall recognise the following evidence of formal qualifications as a nurse responsible for general care as being sufficient proof, provided that that evidence is accompanied by a certificate stating that those Member State nationals have effectively and lawfully been engaged in the activities of a nurse responsible for general care in Romania, including taking full responsibility for the planning, organisation and carrying out of the nursing care of patients, for a period of at least three consecutive years during the five years prior to the date of issue of the certificate:

(a) Certificat de competențe profesionale de asistent medical generalist with post-secondary education obtained from a școală postliceală, attesting to training started before 1 January 2007;

(b) Diplomă de absolvire de asistent medical generalist with short-time higher education studies, attesting to training started before 1 October 2003;

(c) Diplomă de licență de asistent medical generalist with long-time higher education studies, attesting to training started before 1 October 2003.

SECTION 4 DENTAL PRACTITIONERS

Article 34
Basic dental training

1. Admission to basic dental training presupposes possession of a diploma or certificate giving access, for the studies in question, to universities or higher institutes of a level recognised as equivalent, in a Member State.

2. Basic dental training shall comprise a total of at least five years of study, which may in addition be expressed with the equivalent ECTS credits, and shall consist of at least 5000 hours of full-time theoretical and practical training that comprises at least the programme described in point 5.3.1 of Annex V and that is provided in a university, in a higher institute providing training recognised as being of an equivalent level or under the supervision of a university.

The Commission shall be empowered to adopt delegated acts in accordance with Article 57c concerning the amendment of the list set out in point 5.3.1 of Annex V with a view to adapting it to scientific and technical progress.

The amendments referred to in the second subparagraph shall not entail an amendment of existing essential legislative principles in Member States regarding the structure of professions as regards training and conditions of access by natural persons. Such amendments shall respect the responsibility of the Member States for the organisation of education systems, as set out in Article 165(1) TFEU.

3. Basic dental training shall provide an assurance that the person in question has acquired the following knowledge and skills:

   (a) adequate knowledge of the sciences on which dentistry is based and a good understanding of scientific methods, including the principles of measuring biological functions, the evaluation of scientifically established facts and the analysis of data;

   (b) adequate knowledge of the constitution, physiology and behaviour of healthy and sick persons as well as the influence of the natural and social environment on the state of health of the human being, in so far as these factors affect dentistry;

   (c) adequate knowledge of the structure and function of the teeth, mouth, jaws and associated tissues, both healthy and diseased, and their relationship to the general state of health and to the physical and social well-being of the patient;

   (d) adequate knowledge of clinical disciplines and methods, providing the dentist with a coherent picture of anomalies, lesions and diseases of the teeth, mouth, jaws and associated tissues and of preventive, diagnostic and therapeutic dentistry;

   (e) suitable clinical experience under appropriate supervision.

This training shall provide him with the skills necessary for carrying out all activities involving the prevention, diagnosis and treatment of anomalies and diseases of the teeth, mouth, jaws and associated tissues.

Article 35
Specialist dental training

1. Admission to specialist dental training shall be contingent upon completion and validation of basic dental training referred to in Article 34, or possession of the documents referred to in Articles 23 and 37.

2. Specialist dental training shall comprise theoretical and practical instruction in a university centre, in a treatment teaching and research centre or, where appropriate, in a health establishment approved for that purpose by the competent authorities or bodies.

Full-time specialist dental courses shall be of a minimum of three years' duration and shall be supervised by the competent authorities or bodies. They shall involve the personal participation of the dental practitioner training to be a specialist in the activity and in the responsibilities of the establishment concerned.

————

3. The Member States shall make the issuance of evidence of specialist dental training contingent upon possession of evidence of basic dental training referred to in Annex V, point 5.3.2.

4. The Commission shall be empowered to adopt delegated acts in accordance with Article 57c concerning the adaptation of the minimum period of training referred to in paragraph 2 to scientific and technical progress.

5. In order to take due account of changes in national legislation, and with a view to updating this Directive, the Commission shall be empowered to adopt delegated acts in accordance with Article 57c concerning the inclusion in point 5.3.3 of Annex V of new dental specialties common to at least two-fifths of the Member States.

Article 36
Pursuit of the professional activities of dental practitioners

1. For the purposes of this Directive, the professional activities of dental practitioners are the activities defined in paragraph 3 and pursued under the professional qualifications

listed in Annex V, point 5.3.2.2. The profession of dental practitioner shall be based on dental training referred to in Article 34 and shall constitute a specific profession which is distinct from other general or specialised medical professions. Pursuit of the activities of a dental practitioner requires the possession of evidence of formal qualifications referred to in Annex V, point 5.3.

2. Holders of such evidence of formal qualifications shall be treated in the same way as those to whom Articles 23 or 37 apply.

3. The Member States shall ensure that dental practitioners are generally able to gain access to and pursue the activities of prevention, diagnosis and treatment of anomalies and diseases affecting the teeth, mouth, jaws and adjoining tissue, having due regard to the regulatory provisions and rules of professional ethics on the reference dates referred to in Annex V, point 5.3.2.

Article 37
Acquired rights specific to dental practitioners

1. Every Member State shall, for the purposes of the pursuit of the professional activities of dental practitioners under the qualifications listed in Annex V, point 5.3.2, recognise evidence of formal qualifications as a doctor issued in Italy, Spain, Austria, the Czech Republic, Slovakia and Romania to persons who began their medical training on or before the reference date stated in that Annex for the Member State concerned, accompanied by a certificate issued by the competent authorities of that Member State.

   The certificate must show that the two following conditions are met:

   (a) that the persons in question have been effectively, lawfully and principally engaged in that Member State in the activities referred to in Article 36 for at least three consecutive years during the five years preceding the award of the certificate;

   (b) that those persons are authorised to pursue the said activities under the same conditions as holders of evidence of formal qualifications listed for that Member State in Annex V, point 5.3.2.

   Persons who have successfully completed at least three years of study, certified by the competent authorities in the Member State concerned as being equivalent to the training referred to in Article 34, shall be exempt from the three-year practical work experience referred to in the second subparagraph, point (a).

   With regard to the Czech Republic and Slovakia, evidence of formal qualifications obtained in the former Czechoslovakia shall be accorded the same level of recognition as Czech and Slovak evidence of formal qualifications and under the same conditions as set out in the preceding subparagraphs.

2. Each Member State shall recognise evidence of formal qualifications as a doctor issued in Italy to persons who began their university medical training after 28 January 1980 and no later than 31 December 1984, accompanied by a certificate issued by the competent Italian authorities.

   The certificate must show that the three following conditions are met:

   (a) that the persons in question passed the relevant aptitude test held by the competent Italian authorities with a view to establishing that those persons possess a level of knowledge and skills comparable to that of persons possessing evidence of formal qualifications listed for Italy in Annex V, point 5.3.2;

(b) that they have been effectively, lawfully and principally engaged in the activities referred to in Article 36 in Italy for at least three consecutive years during the five years preceding the award of the certificate;

(c) that they are authorised to engage in or are effectively, lawfully and principally engaged in the activities referred to in Article 36, under the same conditions as the holders of evidence of formal qualifications listed for Italy in Annex V, point 5.3.2.

Persons who have successfully completed at least three years of study certified by the competent authorities as being equivalent to the training referred to in Article 34 shall be exempt from the aptitude test referred to in the second subparagraph, point (a).

Persons who began their university medical training after 31 December 1984 shall be treated in the same way as those referred to above, provided that the abovementioned three years of study began before 31 December 1994.

3. As regards evidence of formal qualifications of dental practitioners, Member States shall recognise such evidence pursuant to Article 21 in cases where the applicants began their training on or before 18 January 2016.

4. Each Member State shall recognise evidence of formal qualifications as a doctor issued in Spain to professionals who began their university medical training between 1 January 1986 and 31 December 1997, accompanied by a certificate issued by the Spanish competent authorities.

The certificate shall confirm that the following conditions have been met:

(a) the professional in question has successfully completed at least three years of study, certified by the Spanish competent authorities as being equivalent to the training referred to in Article 34;

(b) the professional in question was effectively, lawfully and principally engaged in the activities referred to in Article 36 in Spain for at least three consecutive years during the five years preceding the award of the certificate;

(c) the professional in question is authorised to engage in or is effectively, lawfully and principally engaged in the activities referred to in Article 36, under the same conditions as the holders of evidence of formal qualifications listed for Spain in point 5.3.2 of Annex V.

SECTION 5 VETERINARY SURGEONS

Article 38
The training of veterinary surgeons

1. The training of veterinary surgeons shall comprise a total of at least five years of full-time theoretical and practical study, which may in addition be expressed with the equivalent ECTS credits, at a university or at a higher institute providing training recognised as being of an equivalent level, or under the supervision of a university, covering at least the study programme referred to in point 5.4.1 of Annex V.

The Commission shall be empowered to adopt delegated acts in accordance with Article 57c concerning the amendment of the list set out in point 5.4.1 of Annex V with a view to adapting it to scientific and technical progress.

The amendments referred to in the second subparagraph shall not entail an amendment of existing essential legislative principles in Member States regarding the structure of professions as regards training and conditions of access by natural persons. Such amendments shall respect the responsibility of the Member States for the organisation of education systems, as set out in Article 165(1) TFEU.

2. Admission to veterinary training shall be contingent upon possession of a diploma or certificate entitling the holder to enter, for the studies in question, university establishments or institutes of higher education recognised by a Member State to be of an equivalent level for the purpose of the relevant study.

3. Training as a veterinary surgeon shall provide an assurance that the professional in question has acquired the following knowledge and skills:

(a) adequate knowledge of the sciences on which the activities of a veterinary surgeon are based and of the Union law relating to those activities;

(b) adequate knowledge of the structure, functions, behaviour and physiological needs of animals, as well as the skills and competences needed for their husbandry, feeding, welfare, reproduction and hygiene in general;

(c) the clinical, epidemiological and analytical skills and competences required for the prevention, diagnosis and treatment of the diseases of animals, including anaesthesia, aseptic surgery and painless death, whether considered individually or in groups, including specific knowledge of the diseases which may be transmitted to humans;

(d) adequate knowledge, skills and competences for preventive medicine, including competences relating to inquiries and certification;

(e) adequate knowledge of the hygiene and technology involved in the production, manufacture and putting into circulation of animal feedstuffs or foodstuffs of animal origin intended for human consumption, including the skills and competences required to understand and explain good practice in this regard;

(f) the knowledge, skills and competences required for the responsible and sensible use of veterinary medicinal products, in order to treat the animals and to ensure the safety of the food chain and the protection of the environment.

Article 39

Acquired rights specific to veterinary surgeons

Without prejudice to Article 23(4), with regard to nationals of Member States whose evidence of formal qualifications as a veterinary surgeon was issued by, or whose training commenced in, Estonia before 1 May 2004, Member States shall recognise such evidence of formal qualifications as a veterinary surgeon if it is accompanied by a certificate stating that such persons have effectively and lawfully been engaged in the activities in question in Estonia for at least five consecutive years during the seven years prior to the date of issue of the certificate.

SECTION 6 MIDWIVES

Article 40

The training of midwives

1. The training of midwives shall comprise a total of at least:

(a) specific full-time training as a midwife comprising at least three years of theoretical and practical study (route I) comprising at least the programme described in Annex V, point 5.5.1, or

(b) specific full-time training as a midwife of 18 months' duration (route II), comprising at least the study programme described in Annex V, point 5.5.1, which was not the subject of equivalent training of nurses responsible for general care.

The Member States shall ensure that institutions providing midwife training are responsible for coordinating theory and practice throughout the programme of study.

The Commission shall be empowered to adopt delegated acts in accordance with Article 57c concerning the amendment of the list set out in point 5.5.1 of Annex V with a view to adapting it to scientific and technical progress.

The amendments referred to in the third subparagraph shall not entail an amendment of existing essential legislative principles in Member States regarding the structure of professions as regards training and conditions of access by natural persons. Such amendments shall respect the responsibility of the Member States for the organisation of education systems, asset out in Article 165(1) TFEU.

2. Admission to training as a midwife shall be contingent upon one of the following conditions:

(a) completion of at least 12 years of general school education or possession of a certificate attesting success in an examination, of an equivalent level, for admission to a midwifery school for route I;

(b) possession of evidence of formal qualifications as a nurse responsible for general care referred to in point 5.2.2 of Annex V for route II.

3. Training as a midwife shall provide an assurance that the professional in question has acquired the following knowledge and skills:

(a) detailed knowledge of the sciences on which the activities of midwives are based, particularly midwifery, obstetrics and gynaecology;

(b) adequate knowledge of the ethics of the profession and the legislation relevant for the practice of the profession;

(c) adequate knowledge of general medical knowledge (biological functions, anatomy and physiology) and of pharmacology in the field of obstetrics and of the newly born, and also knowledge of the relationship between the state of health and the physical and social environment of the human being, and of his behaviour;

(d) adequate clinical experience gained in approved institutions allowing the midwife to be able, independently and under his own responsibility, to the extent necessary and excluding pathological situations, to manage the antenatal care, to conduct the delivery and its consequences in approved institutions, and to supervise labour and birth, postnatal care and neonatal resuscitation while awaiting a medical practitioner;

(e) adequate understanding of the training of health personnel and experience of working with such personnel.

Article 41

Procedures for the recognition of evidence of formal qualifications as a midwife

1. The evidence of formal qualifications as a midwife referred to in point 5.5.2 of Annex V shall be subject to automatic recognition pursuant to Article 21 in so far as they satisfy one of the following criteria:

(a) full-time training of at least three years as a midwife, which may in addition be expressed with the equivalent ECTS credits, consisting of at least 4600 hours of theoretical and practical training, with at least one third of the minimum duration representing clinical training;

(b) full-time training as a midwife of at least two years, which may in addition be expressed with the equivalent ECTS credits, consisting of at least 3600 hours, contingent upon possession of evidence of formal qualifications as a nurse responsible for general care referred to in point 5.2.2 of Annex V;

(c) full-time training as a midwife of at least 18 months, which may in addition be expressed with the equivalent ECTS credits, consisting of at least 3000 hours, contingent upon possession of evidence of formal qualifications as a nurse responsible for general care referred to in point 5.2.2 of Annex V, and followed by one year's professional practice for which a certificate has been issued in accordance with paragraph 2.

2. The certificate referred to in paragraph 1 shall be issued by the competent authorities in the home Member State. It shall certify that the holder, after obtaining evidence of formal qualifications as a midwife, has satisfactorily pursued all the activities of a midwife for a corresponding period in a hospital or a health care establishment approved for that purpose.

Article 42

Pursuit of the professional activities of a midwife

1. The provisions of this section shall apply to the activities of midwives as defined by each Member State, without prejudice to paragraph 2, and pursued under the professional titles set out in Annex V, point 5.5.2.

2. The Member States shall ensure that midwives are able to gain access to and pursue at least the following activities:

(a) provision of sound family planning information and advice;

(b) diagnosis of pregnancies and monitoring normal pregnancies; carrying out the examinations necessary for the monitoring of the development of normal pregnancies;

(c) prescribing or advising on the examinations necessary for the earliest possible diagnosis of pregnancies at risk;

(d) provision of programmes of parenthood preparation and complete preparation for childbirth including advice on hygiene and nutrition;

(e) caring for and assisting the mother during labour and monitoring the condition of the foetus in utero by the appropriate clinical and technical means;

(f) conducting spontaneous deliveries including where required episiotomies and in urgent cases breech deliveries;

(g) recognising the warning signs of abnormality in the mother or infant which necessitate referral to a doctor and assisting the latter where appropriate; taking the necessary emergency measures in the doctor's absence, in particular the manual removal of the placenta, possibly followed by manual examination of the uterus;

(h) examining and caring for the new-born infant; taking all initiatives which are necessary in case of need and carrying out where necessary immediate resuscitation;

(i) caring for and monitoring the progress of the mother in the post-natal period and giving all necessary advice to the mother on infant care to enable her to ensure the optimum progress of the new-born infant;

(j) carrying out treatment prescribed by doctors;

(k) drawing up the necessary written reports.

Article 43

Acquired rights specific to midwives

1. Every Member State shall, in the case of Member State nationals whose evidence of formal qualifications as a midwife satisfies all the minimum training requirements laid down in Article 40 but, by virtue of Article 41, is not recognised unless it is accompanied by a certificate of professional practice referred to in Article 41(2), recognise as sufficient proof evidence of formal qualifications issued by those Member States before the reference date referred to in Annex V, point 5.5.2, accompanied by a certificate stating that those nationals have been effectively and lawfully engaged in the activities in question for at least two consecutive years during the five years preceding the award of the certificate.

1a. As regards evidence of formal qualifications of midwives, Member States shall recognise automatically those qualifications where the applicant started the training before 18 January 2016, and the admission requirement for such training was 10 years of general education or an equivalent level for route I, or completed training as a nurse responsible for general care as attested by evidence of formal qualification referred to in point 5.2.2 of Annex V before starting a midwifery training falling under route II.

2. The conditions laid down in paragraph 1 shall apply to the nationals of Member States whose evidence of formal qualifications as a midwife certifies completion of training received in the territory of the former German Democratic Republic and satisfying all the minimum training requirements laid down in Article 40 but where the evidence of formal qualifications, by virtue of Article 41, is not recognised unless it is accompanied by the certificate of professional experience referred to in Article 41(2), where it attests a course of training which began before 3 October 1990.

------

4. Member States shall recognise evidence of formal qualifications in midwifery that:

(a) were awarded in Poland, to midwives who completed training before 1 May 2004, which did not comply with the minimum training requirements laid down in Article 40; and

(b) are attested by the diploma 'bachelor' which was obtained on the basis of a special upgrading programme contained in:

(i) Article 11 of the Act of 20 April 2004 on the amendment of the Act on professions of nurse and midwife and on some other legal acts (Official Journal of the Republic of Poland of 2004 No 92, pos. 885 and of 2007 No 176, pos. 1237) and the Regulation of the Minister of Health of 11 May 2004 on the detailed conditions of delivering studies for nurses and midwives, who hold a certificate of secondary school (final examination – matura) and are graduates of medical lyceum and medical vocational schools teaching in a profession of a nurse and a midwife (Official

Journal of the Republic of Poland of 2004 No 110, pos. 1170 and of 2010 No 65, pos. 420); or

(ii) Article 53.3 point 3 of the Act of 15 July 2011 on professions of nurse and midwife (Official Journal of the Republic of Poland of 2011 No 174, pos. 1039) and the Regulation of the Minister of Health of 14 June 2012 on the detailed conditions of delivering higher education courses for nurses and midwives who hold a certificate of secondary school (final examination – matura) and are graduates of a medical secondary school or a post-secondary school teaching in a profession of a nurse and a midwife (Official Journal of the Republic of Poland of 2012, pos. 770),

for the purpose of verifying that the midwife concerned has a level of knowledge and competence comparable to that of midwives holding the qualifications listed for Poland in point 5.5.2 of Annex V.

Article 43(a)

As regards the Romanian qualifications in midwifery, only the following acquired rights provisions will apply:

In the case of nationals of the Member States whose evidence of formal qualifications as a midwife (asistent medical obstetrică-ginecologie/obstetrics-gynecology nurse) were awarded by Romania before the date of accession and which do not satisfy the minimum training requirements laid down in Article 40, Member States shall recognise the said evidence of formal qualifications as being sufficient proof for the purposes of carrying out the activities of midwife, if they are accompanied by a certificate stating that those Member State nationals have effectively and lawfully been engaged in the activities of midwife in Romania, for at least five consecutive years during the seven years prior to the issue of the certificate.

Article 43b

Acquired rights in midwifery shall not apply to the following qualifications which were obtained in Croatia before 1 July 2013: viša medicinska sestra ginekološko-opstetričkog smjera (High Gynaecology-Obstetrical Nurse), medicinska sestra ginekološko-opstetričkog smjera (Gynaecology-Obstetrical Nurse), višamedicinska sestra primaljskog smjera (High Nurse with Midwifery Degree), medicinska sestra primaljskog smjera (Nurse with Midwifery Degree), ginekološko-opstetrička primalja (Gynaecology-Obstetrical Midwife) and primalja (Midwife).

SECTION 7 PHARMACIST

Article 44
Training as a pharmacist

1. Admission to a course of training as a pharmacist shall be contingent upon possession of a diploma or certificate giving access, in a Member State, to the studies in question, at universities or higher institutes of a level recognised as equivalent.

2. Evidence of formal qualifications as a pharmacist shall attest to training of at least five years' duration, which may in addition be expressed with the equivalent ECTS credits, comprising at least:

(a) four years of full-time theoretical and practical training at a university or at a higher institute of a level recognised as equivalent, or under the supervision of a university;

(b) during or at the end of the theoretical and practical training, six-month trainee-ship in a pharmacy which is open to the public or in a hospital under the supervision of that hospital's pharmaceutical department.

The training cycle referred to in this paragraph shall include at least the programme described in point 5.6.1 of Annex V. The Commission shall be empowered to adopt delegated acts in accordance with Article 57c concerning the amendment of the list set out in point 5.6.1 of Annex V with a view to adapting it to scientific and technical progress, including the evolution of pharmacological practice.

The amendments referred to in the second subparagraph shall not entail an amendment of existing essential legislative principles in Member States regarding the structure of professions as regards training and conditions of access by natural persons. Such amendments shall respect the responsibility of the Member States for the organisation of education systems, as set out in Article 165(1) TFEU.

3. Training for pharmacists shall provide an assurance that the person concerned has acquired the following knowledge and skills:

(a) adequate knowledge of medicines and the substances used in the manufacture of medicines;

(b) adequate knowledge of pharmaceutical technology and the physical, chemical, biological and microbiological testing of medicinal products;

(c) adequate knowledge of the metabolism and the effects of medicinal products and of the action of toxic substances, and of the use of medicinal products;

(d) adequate knowledge to evaluate scientific data concerning medicines in order to be able to supply appropriate information on the basis of this knowledge;

(e) adequate knowledge of the legal and other requirements associated with the pursuit of pharmacy.

Article 45
Pursuit of the professional activities of a pharmacist

1. For the purposes of this Directive, the activities of a pharmacist are those, access to which and pursuit of which are contingent, in one or more Member States, upon professional qualifications and which are open to holders of evidence of formal qualifications of the types listed in Annex V, point 5.6.2.

2. The Member States shall ensure that the holders of evidence of formal qualifications in pharmacy at university level or a level recognised as equivalent, which satisfies the requirements of Article 44, are able to gain access to and pursueat least the following activities, subject to the requirement, where appropriate, of supplementary professional experience:

(a) preparation of the pharmaceutical form of medicinal products;

(b) manufacture and testing of medicinal products;

(c) testing of medicinal products in a laboratory for the testing of medicinal products;

(d) storage, preservation and distribution of medicinal products at the wholesale stage;

(e) supply, preparation, testing, storage, distribution and dispensing of safe and efficacious medicinal products of the required quality in pharmacies open to the public;

(f) preparation, testing, storage and dispensing of safe and efficacious medicinal products of the required quality in hospitals;

(g) provision of information and advice on medicinal products as such, including on their appropriate use;

(h) reporting of adverse reactions of pharmaceutical products to the competent authorities;

(i) personalised support for patients who administer their medication;

(j) contribution to local or national public health campaigns.

3. If a Member State makes access to or pursuit of one of the activities of a pharmacist contingent upon supplementary professional experience, in addition to possession of evidence of formal qualifications referred to in Annex V, point 5.6.2, that Member State shall recognise as sufficient proof in this regard a certificate issued by the competent authorities in the home Member State stating that the person concerned has been engaged in those activities in the home Member State for a similar period.

4. The recognition referred to in paragraph 3 shall not apply with regard to the two-year period of professional experience required by the Grand Duchy of Luxembourg for the grant of a State public pharmacy concession.

5. If, on 16 September 1985, a Member State had a competitive examination in place designed to select from among the holders referred to in paragraph 2, those who are to be authorised to become owners of new pharmacies whose creation has been decided on as part of a national system of geographical division, that Member State may, by way of derogation from paragraph 1, proceed with that examination and require nationals of Member States who possess evidence of formal qualifications as a pharmacist referred to in Annex V, point 5.6.2 or who benefit from the provisions of Article 23 to take part in it.

SECTION 8 ARCHITECT

Article 46
Training of architects

1. Training as an architect shall comprise:
   (a) a total of at least five years of full-time study at a university or a comparable teaching institution, leading to successful completion of a university-level examination; or
   (b) not less than four years of full-time study at a university or a comparable teaching institution leading to successful completion of a university-level examination, accompanied by a certificate attesting to the completion of two years of professional traineeship in accordance with paragraph 4.

2. Architecture must be the principal component of the study referred to in paragraph 1. The study shall maintain a balance between theoretical and practical aspects of architectural training and shall guarantee at least the acquisition of the following knowledge, skills and competences:

(a) the ability to create architectural designs that satisfy both aesthetic and technical requirements;

(b) adequate knowledge of the history and theories of architecture and the related arts, technologies and human sciences;

(c) knowledge of the fine arts as an influence on the quality of architectural design;

(d) adequate knowledge of urban design, planning and the skills involved in the planning process;

(e) understanding of the relationship between people and buildings, and between buildings and their environment, and of the need to relate buildings and the spaces between them to human needs and scale;

(f) understanding of the profession of architect and the role of the architect in society, in particular in preparing briefs that take account of social factors;

(g) understanding of the methods of investigation and preparation of the brief for a design project;

(h) understanding of the structural design, and constructional and engineering problems associated with building design;

(i) adequate knowledge of physical problems and technologies and of the function of buildings so as to provide them with internal conditions of comfort and protection against the climate, in the framework of sustainable development;

(j) the necessary design skills to meet building users' requirements within the constraints imposed by cost factors and building regulations;

(k) adequate knowledge of the industries, organisations, regulations and procedures involved in translating design concepts into buildings and integrating plans into overall planning.

3. The number of years of academic study referred to in paragraphs 1 and 2 may in addition be expressed with the equivalent ECTS credits.

4. The professional traineeship referred to in point (b) of paragraph 1 shall take place only after completion of the first three years of the study. At least one year of the professional traineeship shall build up on knowledge, skills and competences acquired during the study referred to in paragraph 2. To that end, the professional traineeship shall be carried out under the supervision of a person or body that has been authorised by the competent authority in the home Member State. Such supervised traineeship may take place in any country. The professional traineeship shall be evaluated by the competent authority in the home Member State.

Article 47

Derogations from the conditions for the training of architects

By way of derogation from Article 46, the following shall also be recognised as complying with Article 21: training as part of social betterment schemes or part-time university studies which satisfies the requirements set out in Article 46(2), as attested by an examination in architecture passed by a professional who has been working for seven years or more in the field of architecture under the supervision of an architect or architectural bureau. The examination must be of university level and be equivalent to the final examination referred to in point (b) of Article 46(1).

Article 48
Pursuit of the professional activities of architects

1. For the purposes of this Directive, the professional activities of an architect are the activities regularly carried out under the professional title of 'architect'.

2. Nationals of a Member State who are authorised to use that title pursuant to a law which gives the competent authority of a Member State the power to award that title to Member States nationals who are especially distinguished by the quality of their work in the field of architecture shall be deemed to satisfy the conditions required for the pursuit of the activities of an architect, under the professional title of 'architect'. The architectural nature of the activities of the persons concerned shall be attested by a certificate awarded by their home Member State.

Article 49
Acquired rights specific to architects

1. Each Member State shall accept evidence of formal qualifications as an architect listed in Annex VI, awarded by the other Member States, and attesting a course of training which began no later than the reference academic year referred to in that Annex, even if they do not satisfy the minimum requirements laid down in Article 46, and shall, for the purposes of access to and pursuit of the professional activities of an architect, give such evidence the same effect on its territory as evidence of formal qualifications as an architect which it itself issues.

   Under these circumstances, certificates issued by the competent authorities of the Federal Republic of Germany attesting that evidence of formal qualifications issued on or after 8 May 1945 by the competent authorities of the German Democratic Republic is equivalent to such evidence listed in that Annex, shall be recognised.

1a. Paragraph 1 shall also apply to evidence of formal qualifications as an architect listed in Annex V, where the training started before 18 January 2016.

2. Without prejudice to paragraph 1, every Member State shall recognise the following evidence of formal qualifications and shall, for the purposes of access to and pursuit of the professional activities of an architect performed, give them the same effect on its territory as evidence of formal qualifications which it itself issues: certificates issued to nationals of Member States by the Member States which have enacted rules governing the access to and pursuit of the activities of an architect as of the following dates:

   (a) 1 January 1995 for Austria, Finland and Sweden;

   (b) 1 May 2004 for the Czech Republic, Estonia, Cyprus, Latvia, Lithuania, Hungary, Malta, Poland, Slovenia and Slovakia;

   (ba) 1 July 2013 for Croatia;

   (c) 5 August 1987 for the other Member States.

   The certificates referred to in the first subparagraph shall certify that the holder was authorized, no later than the respective date, to use the professional title of architect, and that he has been effectively engaged, in the context of those rules, in the activities in question for at least three consecutive years during the five years preceding the award of the certificate.

3. Each Member State shall give the following evidence the same effect on its territory as evidence of formal qualifications it itself issues for the purposes of access to

and pursuit of the professional activities of an architect: evidence of completion of training existing as of 5 August 1985 and commenced no later than 17 January 2014, provided by 'Fachhochschulen' in the Federal Republic of Germany over a period of three years, satisfying the requirements set out in Article 46(2) and giving access to the activities referred to in Article 48 in that Member State under the professional title of 'architect', in so far as the training was followed by a four-year period of professional experience in the Federal Republic of Germany, as attested by a certificate issued by the competent authority in whose roll the name of the architect wishing to benefit from the provisions of this Directive appears.

Chapter IIIA Automatic Recognition on the Basis of Common Training Principles

Article 49a

Common training framework

1. For the purpose of this Article, 'common training framework' means a common set of minimum knowledge, skills and competences necessary for the pursuit of a specific profession. A common training framework shall not replace national training programmes unless a Member State decides otherwise under national law. For the purpose of access to and pursuit of a profession in Member States which regulate that profession, a Member State shall give evidence of professional qualifications acquired on the basis of such a framework the same effect in its territory as the evidence of formal qualifications which it itself issues, on condition that such framework fulfils the conditions laid down in paragraph 2.

2. A common training framework shall comply with the following conditions:
   (a) the common training framework enables more professionals to move across Member States;
   (b) the profession to which the common training framework applies is regulated, or the education and training leading to the profession is regulated in at least one third of the Member States;
   (c) the common set of knowledge, skills and competences combines the knowledge, skills and competences required in the systems of education and training applicable in at least one third of the Member States; it shall be irrelevant whether the knowledge, skills and competences have been acquired as part of a general training course at a university or higher education institution or as part of a vocational training course;
   (d) the common training framework shall be based on levels of the EQF, as defined in Annex II of the Recommendation of the European Parliament and of the Council of 23 April 2008 on the establishment of the European Qualifications Framework for lifelong learning;
   (e) the profession concerned is neither covered by another common training framework nor subject to automatic recognition under Chapter III of Title III;
   (f) the common training framework has been prepared following a transparent due process, including the relevant stakeholders from Member States where the profession is not regulated;
   (g) the common training framework permits nationals from any Member State to be eligible for acquiring the professional qualification under such framework without

first being required to be a member of any professional organisation or to be registered with such organisation.

3. Representative professional organisations at Union level, as well as national professional organisations or competent authorities from at least one third of the Member States, may submit to the Commission suggestions for common training frameworks which meet the conditions laid down in paragraph 2.

4. The Commission shall be empowered to adopt delegated acts in accordance with Article 57c to establish a common training framework for a given profession based on the conditions laid down in paragraph 2 of this Article.

5. A Member State shall be exempted from the obligation of introducing the common training framework referred to in paragraph 4 on its territory and from the obligation of granting automatic recognition to the professional qualifications acquired under that common training framework if one of the following conditions is fulfilled:

   (a) there are no education or training institutions available in its territory to offer such training for the profession concerned;

   (b) the introduction of the common training framework would adversely affect the organisation of its system of education and professional training;

   (c) there are substantial differences between the common training framework and the training required in its territory, which entail serious risks for public policy, public security, public health or for the safety of the service recipients or the protection of the environment.

6. Member States shall, within six months of the entry into force of the delegated act referred to in paragraph 4, notify to the Commission and to the other Member States:

   (a) the national qualifications, and where applicable the national professional titles, that comply with the common training framework; or

   (b) any use of the exemption referred to in paragraph 5, along with a justification of which conditions under that paragraph were fulfilled. The Commission may, within three months, request further clarification if it considers that a Member State has provided no or insufficient justification that one of these conditions has been fulfilled. The Member State shall reply within three months of any such request.

   The Commission may adopt an implementing act to list the national professional qualifications and national professional titles benefiting from automatic recognition under the common training framework adopted in accordance with paragraph 4.

7. This Article also applies to specialties of a profession, provided such specialties concern professional activities the access to and the pursuit of which are regulated in Member States, where the profession is already subject to automatic recognition under Chapter III of Title III, but not the specialty concerned.

Article 49b

Common training tests

1. For the purpose of this Article, a 'common training test' means a standardised aptitude test available across participating Member States and reserved to holders of a particular professional qualification. Passing such a test in a Member State shall entitle the

holder of a particular professional qualification to pursue the profession in any host Member State concerned under the same conditions as the holders of professional qualifications acquired in that Member State.

2. The common training test shall comply with the following conditions:

(a) the common training test enables more professionals to move across Member States;

(b) the profession to which the common training test applies is regulated, or the education and training leading to the profession concerned is regulated in at least one third of the Member States;

(c) the common training test has been prepared following a transparent due process, including the relevant stakeholders from Member States where the profession is not regulated;

(d) the common training test permits nationals from any Member State to participate in such a test and in the practical organisation of such tests in Member States without first being required to be a member of any professional organisation or to be registered with such organisation.

3. Representative professional organisations at Union level, as well as national professional organisations or competent authorities from at least one third of the Member States, may submit to the Commission suggestions for common training tests which meet the conditions laid down in paragraph 2.

4. The Commission shall be empowered to adopt delegated acts in accordance with Article 57c to establish the contents of a common training test, and the conditions required for taking and passing the test.

5. A Member State shall be exempted from the obligation of organising the common training test referred to in paragraph 4 on its territory and from the obligation of granting automatic recognition to professionals who have passed the common training test if one of the following conditions is fulfilled:

(a) the profession concerned is not regulated on its territory;

(b) the contents of the common training test will not sufficiently mitigate serious risks for public health or the safety of the service recipients, which are relevant on its territory;

(c) the contents of the common training test would render access to the profession significantly less attractive compared to national requirements.

6. Member States shall, within six months of the entry into force of the delegated act referred to in paragraph 4, notify to the Commission and to the other Member States:

(a) the available capacity for organising such tests; or

(b) any use of the exemption referred to in paragraph 5, along with the justification of which conditions under that paragraph were fulfilled. The Commission may, within three months, request further clarification, if it considers that a Member State has provided no or insufficient justification that one of these conditions has been fulfilled. The Member State shall reply within three months of any such request.

The Commission may adopt an implementing act to list the Member States in which the common training tests adopted in accordance with paragraph 4 are to be organised, the frequency during a calendar year and other arrangements necessary for organising common training tests across Member States.

Chapter IV Common Provisions on Establishment

Article 50
Documentation and formalities

1. Where the competent authorities of the host Member State decide on an application for authorisation to pursue the regulated profession in question by virtue of this Title, those authorities may demand the documents and certificates listed in Annex VII.

   The documents referred to in Annex VII, point 1(d), (e) and (f), shall not be more than three months old by the date on which they are submitted.

   The Member States, bodies and other legal persons shall guarantee the confidentiality of the information which they receive.

2. In the event of justified doubts, the host Member State may require from the competent authorities of a Member State confirmation of the authenticity of the attestations and evidence of formal qualifications awarded in that other Member State, as well as, where applicable, confirmation of the fact that the beneficiary fulfils, for the professions referred to in Chapter III of this Title, the minimum training conditions set out respectively in Articles 24, 25, 28, 31, 34, 35, 38, 40, 44 and 46.

3. In cases of justified doubt, where evidence of formal qualifications, as defined in Article 3(1)(c), has been issued by a competent authority in a Member State and includes training received in whole or in part in an establishment legally established in the territory of another Member State, the host Member State shall be entitled to verify with the competent body in the Member State of origin of the award:

   (a) whether the training course at the establishment which gave the training has been formally certified by the educational establishment based in the Member State of origin of the award;

   (b) whether the evidence of formal qualifications issued is the same as that which would have been awarded if the course had been followed entirely in the Member State of origin of the award; and

   (c) whether the evidence of formal qualifications confers the same professional rights in the territory of the Member State of origin of the award.

3a. In the event of justified doubts, the host Member State may require from the competent authorities of a Member State confirmation of the fact that the applicant is not suspended or prohibited from the pursuit of the profession as a result of serious professional misconduct or conviction of criminal offences relating to the pursuit of any of his professional activities.

3b. Exchange of information between competent authorities of different Member States under this Article shall take place via IMI.

4. Where a host Member State requires its nationals to swear a solemn oath or make a sworn statement in order to gain access to a regulated profession, and where the wording of that oath or statement cannot be used by nationals of the other Member States, the host Member State shall ensure that the persons concerned can use an appropriate equivalent wording.

Article 51
Procedure for the mutual recognition of professional qualifications

1. The competent authority of the host Member State shall acknowledge receipt of the application within one month of receipt and inform the applicant of any missing document.

2. The procedure for examining an application for authorisation to practise a regulated profession must be completed as quickly as possible and lead to a duly substantiated decision by the competent authority in the host Member State in any case within three months after the date on which the applicant's complete file was submitted. However, this deadline may be extended by one month in cases falling under Chapters I and II of this Title.

3. The decision, or failure to reach a decision within the deadline, shall be subject to appeal under national law.

Article 52
Use of professional titles

1. If, in a host Member State, the use of a professional title relating to one of the activities of the profession in question is regulated, nationals of the other Member States who are authorised to practise a regulated profession on the basis of Title III shall use the professional title of the host Member State, which corresponds to that profession in that Member State, and make use of any associated initials.

2. Where a profession is regulated in the host Member State by an association or organisation within the meaning of Article 3(2), nationals of Member States shall not be authorised to use the professional title issued by that organisation or association, or its abbreviated form, unless they furnish proof that they are members of that association or organisation.

   If the association or organisation makes membership contingent upon certain qualifications, it may do so, only under the conditions laid down in this Directive, in respect of nationals of other Member States who possess professional qualifications.

3. A Member State may not reserve the use of the professional title to the holders of professional qualifications if it has not notified the association or organisation to the Commission and to the other Member States in accordance with Article 3(2).

TITLE IV DETAILED RULES FOR PURSUING THE PROFESSION

Article 53
Knowledge of languages

1. Professionals benefiting from the recognition of professional qualifications shall have a knowledge of languages necessary for practising the profession in the host Member State.

2. A Member State shall ensure that any controls carried out by, or under the supervision of, the competent authority for controlling compliance with the obligation under paragraph 1 shall be limited to the knowledge of one official language of the host Member State, or one administrative language of the host Member State provided that it is also an official language of the Union.

3. Controls carried out in accordance with paragraph 2 may be imposed if the profession to be practised has patient safety implications. Controls may be imposed in respect of other professions in cases where there is a serious and concrete doubt about the sufficiency of the professional's language knowledge in respect of the professional activities that that professional intends to pursue.

   Controls may be carried out only after the issuance of a European Professional Card in accordance with Article 4d or after the recognition of a professional qualification, as the case may be.

4. Any language controls shall be proportionate to the activity to be pursued. The professional concerned shall be allowed to appeal such controls under national law.

Article 54
Use of academic titles
Without prejudice to Articles 7 and 52, the host Member State shall ensure that the right shall be conferred on the persons concerned to use academic titles conferred on them in the home Member State, and possibly an abbreviated form thereof, in the language of the home Member State. The host Member State may require that title to be followed by the name and address of the establishment or examining board which awarded it. Where an academic title of the home Member State is liable to be confused in the host Member State with a title which, in the latter Member State, requires supplementary training not acquired by the beneficiary, the host Member State may require the beneficiary to use the academic title of the home Member State in an appropriate form, to be laid down by the host Member State.

Article 55
Approval by health insurance funds
Without prejudice to Article 5(1) and Article 6, first subparagraph, point (b), Member States which require persons who acquired their professional qualifications in their territory to complete a preparatory period of in-service training and/or a period of professional experience in order to be approved by a health insurance fund, shall waive this obligation for the holders of evidence of professional qualifications of doctor and dental practitioner acquired in other Member States.

Article 55a
Recognition of professional traineeship
1. If access to a regulated profession in the home Member State is contingent upon completion of a professional traineeship, the competent authority of the home Member State shall, when considering a request for authorisation to exercise the regulated profession, recognise professional traineeships carried out in another Member State provided the traineeship is in accordance with the published guidelines referred to in paragraph 2, and shall take into account professional traineeships carried out in a third country. However, Member States may, in national legislation, set a reasonable limit on the duration of the part of the professional traineeship which can be carried out abroad.

2. Recognition of the professional traineeship shall not replace any requirements in place to pass an examination in order to gain access to the profession in question.

The competent authorities shall publish guidelines on the organisation and recognition of professional traineeships carried out in another Member State or in a third country, in particular on the role of the supervisor of the professional traineeship.

TITLE V ADMINISTRATIVE COOPERATION AND RESPONSIBILITY TOWARDS CITIZENS FOR IMPLEMENTATION

Article 56
Competent authorities

1. The competent authorities of the host Member State and of the home Member State shall work in close collaboration and shall provide mutual assistance in order to facilitate application of this Directive. They shall ensure the confidentiality of the information which they exchange.

2. The competent authorities of the home and the host Member States shall exchange information regarding disciplinary action or criminal sanctions taken or any other serious, specific circumstances which are likely to have consequences for the pursuit of activities under this Directive. In so doing, they shall respect personal data protection rules provided for in Directives 95/46/EC and 2002/58/EC.

   The home Member State shall examine the veracity of the circumstances and its authorities shall decide on the nature and scope of the investigations which need to be carried out and shall inform the host Member State of the conclusions which it draws from the information available to it.

2a. For the purposes of paragraphs 1 and 2, the competent authorities shall use IMI.

3. Each Member State shall, no later than 20 October 2007, designate the authorities and bodies competent to award or receive evidence of formal qualifications and other documents or information, and those competent to receive applications and take the decisions referred to in this Directive, and shall forthwith inform the other Member States and the Commission thereof.

4. Each Member State shall designate a coordinator for the activities of the competent authorities referred to in paragraph 1 and shall inform other Member States and the Commission thereof.

   The coordinators' tasks shall be:
   (a) to promote uniform application of this Directive;
   (b) to collect all the information which is relevant for application of this Directive, such as on the conditions for access to regulated professions in the Member States;
   (c) to examine suggestions for common training frameworks and common training tests;
   (d) to exchange information and best practice for the purpose of optimising continuous professional development in Member States;
   (e) to exchange information and best practice on the application of compensation measures referred to in Article 14.

   For the purpose of carrying out the task set out in point (b) of this paragraph, the coordinators may solicit the help of the assistance centres referred to in Article 57b.

12

Article 56a
Alert mechanism

1. The competent authorities of a Member State shall inform the competent authorities of all other Member States about a professional whose pursuit on the territory of that Member State of the following professional activities in their entirety or parts thereof has been restricted or prohibited, even temporarily, by national authorities or courts:

    (a) doctor of medicine and of general practice possessing evidence of a formal qualification referred to in points 5.1.1 and 5.1.4 of Annex V;

    (b) specialist doctor of medicine possessing a title referred to in point 5.1.3 of Annex V;

    (c) nurse responsible for general care possessing evidence of a formal qualification referred to in point 5.2.2 of Annex V;

    (d) dental practitioner possessing evidence of a formal qualification referred to in point 5.3.2 of Annex V;

    (e) specialist dentists possessing evidence of a formal qualification referred to in point 5.3.3 of Annex V;

    (f) veterinary surgeon possessing evidence of a formal qualification referred to in point 5.4.2 of Annex V;

    (g) midwife possessing evidence of a formal qualification referred to in point 5.5.2 of Annex V;

    (h) pharmacist possessing evidence of a formal qualification listed in point 5.6.2 of Annex V;

    (i) holders of certificates mentioned in point 2 of Annex VII attesting that the holder completed a training which satisfies the minimum requirements listed in Articles 24, 25, 31, 34, 35, 38, 40, or 44 respectively, but which started earlier than the reference dates of the qualifications listed in points 5.1.3, 5.1.4, 5.2.2, 5.3.2, 5.3.3, 5.4.2, 5.5.2, 5.6.2 of Annex V;

    (j) holders of certificates of acquired rights as referred to in Articles 23, 27, 29, 33, 33a, 37, 43 and 43a;

    (k) other professionals exercising activities that have patient safety implications, where the professional is pursuing a profession regulated in that Member State;

    (l) professionals exercising activities relating to the education of minors, including in childcare and early childhood education, where the professional is pursuing a profession regulated in that Member State.

2. Competent authorities shall send the information referred to in paragraph 1 by way of alert via IMI at the latest within three days from the date of adoption of the decision restricting or prohibiting pursuit of the professional activity in its entirety or in part by the professional concerned. That information shall be limited to the following:

    (a) the identity of the professional;

    (b) the profession concerned;

    (c) information about the national authority or court adopting the decision on restriction or prohibition;

    (d) the scope of the restriction or the prohibition; and

    (e) the period during which the restriction or the prohibition applies.

3. The competent authorities of a Member State concerned shall, at the latest within three days from the date of adoption of the court decision, inform the competent authorities

of all other Member States, by way of alert via IMI, about the identity of professionals who have applied for the recognition of a qualification under this Directive and who have subsequently been found by courts to have used falsified evidence of professional qualifications in this context.

4. The processing of personal data for the purpose of the exchange of information referred to in paragraphs 1 and 3 shall be carried out in accordance with Directives 95/46/EC and 2002/58/EC. The processing of personal data by the Commission shall be carried out in accordance with Regulation (EC) No. 45/2001.

5. The competent authorities of all Member States shall be informed without delay when a prohibition or a restriction referred to in paragraph 1 has expired. For that purpose, the competent authority of the Member State which provides the information in accordance with paragraph 1 shall also be required to provide the date of expiry as well as any subsequent change to that date.

6. Member States shall provide that professionals, in respect of whom alerts are sent to other Member States, are informed in writing of decisions on alerts at the same time as the alert itself, may appeal under national law against the decision or apply for rectification of such decisions and shall have access to remedies in respect of any damage caused by false alerts sent to other Member States, and in such cases the decision on the alert shall be qualified to indicate that it is subject to proceedings by the professional.

7. Data regarding alerts may be processed within IMI for as long as they are valid. Alerts shall be deleted within three days from the date of adoption of the revoking decision or from the expiry of the prohibition or the restriction referred to in paragraph 1.

8. The Commission shall adopt implementing acts for the application of the alert mechanism. Those implementing acts shall include provisions on the authorities entitled to send or receive alerts and on the withdrawal and closure of alerts, and measures to ensure the security of processing. Those implementing acts shall be adopted in accordance with the examination procedure referred to in Article 58(2).

Article 57
Central online access to information

1. Member States shall ensure that the following information is available online through the points of single contact, referred to in Article 6 of Directive 2006/123/EC of the European Parliament and of the Council of 12 December 2006 on services in the internal market, and regularly updated:

   (a) a list of all regulated professions in the Member State including contact details of the competent authorities for each regulated profession and the assistance centres referred to in Article 57b;

   (b) a list of the professions for which a European Professional Card is available, the functioning of that Card, including all related fees to be paid by professionals, and the competent authorities for issuing that Card;

   (c) a list of all professions for which the Member State applies Article 7(4) under national laws, regulations and administrative provisions;

   (d) a list of regulated education and training, and training with a special structure, referred to in point (c)(ii) of Article 11;

12

(e) the requirements and procedures referred to in Articles 7, 50, 51 and 53 for the professions regulated in the Member State, including all related fees to be paid by citizens and documents to be submitted by citizens to competent authorities;

(f) details on how to appeal, under national laws, regulations and administrative provisions, decisions of competent authorities adopted under this Directive.

2. Member States shall ensure that the information referred to in paragraph 1 is provided in a clear and comprehensive way for users, that it is easily accessible remotely and by electronic means and that it is kept up to date.

3. Member States shall ensure that any request for information addressed to the point of single contact is replied to as soon as possible.

4. Member States and the Commission shall take accompanying measures in order to encourage points of single contact to make the information provided for in paragraph 1 available in other official languages of the Union. This shall not affect the legislation of Member States on the use of languages in their territory.

5. Member States shall cooperate with each other and the Commission for the purpose of implementing paragraphs 1, 2 and 4.

Article 57a
Procedures by electronic means

1. Member States shall ensure that all requirements, procedures and formalities relating to matters covered by this Directive may be easily completed, remotely and by electronic means, through the relevant point of single contact or the relevant competent authorities. This shall not prevent competent authorities of Member States from requesting certified copies at a later stage in the event of justified doubts and where strictly necessary.

2. Paragraph 1 shall not apply to the carrying out of an adaptation period or aptitude test.

3. Where it is justified for Member States to ask for advanced electronic signatures, as defined in point 2 of Article 2 of Directive 1999/93/EC of the European Parliament and of the Council of 13 December 1999 on a [Union] framework for electronic signatures, for the completion of procedures referred to in paragraph 1 of this Article, Member States shall accept electronic signatures in compliance with Commission Decision 2009/767/EC of 16 October 2009 setting out measures facilitating the use of procedures by electronic means through the points of single contact under Directive 2006/123/EC of the European Parliament and of the Council on services in the internal market and provide for technical means to process documents with advanced electronic signature in formats defined by Commission Decision 2011/130/EU of 25 February 2011 establishing minimum requirements for the cross-border processing of documents signed electronically by competent authorities under Directive 2006/123/EC of the European Parliament and of the Council on services in the internal market.

4. All procedures shall be carried out in accordance with Article 8 of Directive 2006/123/EC relating to the points of single contact. The procedural time limits set out in Article 7(4) and Article 51 of this Directive shall commence at the point when an application or any missing document has been submitted by a citizen to a point of single contact or directly to the relevant competent authority. Any request for certified copies referred to in paragraph 1 of this Article shall not be considered as a request for missing documents.

Article 57b
Assistance centres

1. Each Member State shall designate, no later than 18 January 2016, an assistance centre whose remit shall be to provide citizens, as well as assistance centres of the other Member States, with assistance concerning the recognition of professional qualifications provided for in this Directive, including information on the national legislation governing the professions and the pursuit of those professions, social legislation, and, where appropriate, the rules of ethics.

2. The assistance centres in host Member States shall assist citizens in exercising the rights conferred on them by this Directive, in cooperation, where appropriate, with the assistance centre in the home Member State and the competent authorities and the points of single contact in the host Member State.

3. Any competent authority in the home or host Member State shall be required to fully cooperate with the assistance centre in the host Member State and where appropriate the home Member State,and provide all relevant information about individual cases to such assistance centres upon their request and subject to data protection rules in accordance with Directives 95/46/EC and 2002/58/EC.

4. At the Commission's request, the assistance centres shall inform the Commission of the result of enquiries with which they are dealing within two months after receiving such a request.

Article 57c
Exercise of the delegation

1. The power to adopt delegated acts is conferred on the Commission subject to the conditions laid down in this Article.

2. The power to adopt delegated acts referred to in the third subparagraph of Article 3(2), Article 20, the second subparagraph of Article 21(6), Article 21a(4), Article 25(5), the second paragraph of Article 26, the second subparagraph of Article 31(2), the second subparagraph of Article 34(2), Article 35(4) and (5), the second subparagraph of Article 38(1), the third subparagraph of Article 40(1), the second subparagraph of Article 44(2), Article 49a(4) and Article 49b(4) shall be conferred on the Commission for a period of five years from 17 January 2014. The Commission shall draw up a report in respect of the delegation of power not later than nine months before the end of the five-year period. The delegation of power shall be tacitly extended for periods of an identical duration, unless the European Parliament or the Council opposes such extension not later than three months before the end of each period.

3. The power to adopt delegated acts referred to in the third subparagraph of Article 3(2), Article 20, the second subparagraph of Article 21(6), Article 21a(4), Article 25(5), the second paragraph of Article 26, the second subparagraph of Article 31(2), the second subparagraph of Article 34(2), Article 35(4) and (5), the second subparagraph of Article 38(1), the third subparagraph of Article 40(1), the second subparagraph of Article 44(2), Article 49a(4) and Article 49b(4) may be revoked at any time by the European Parliament or by the Council. A decision to revoke shall put an end to the delegation of the power specified in that decision. It shall take effect the day following the publication of the decision in the *Official Journal of the European Union* or at a later date specified therein. It shall not affect the validity of any delegated acts already in force.

12

4. As soon as it adopts a delegated act, the Commission shall notify it simultaneously to the European Parliament and to the Council.

5. A delegated act adopted pursuant to the third subparagraph of Article 3(2), Article 20, the second subparagraph of Article 21(6), Article 21a(4), Article 25(5), the second paragraph of Article 26, the second subparagraph of Article 31(2), the second subparagraph of Article 34(2), Article 35(4) and (5), the second subparagraph of Article 38(1), the third subparagraph of Article 40(1), the second subparagraph of Article 44(2), Article 49a(4) and Article 49b(4) shall enter into force only if no objection has been expressed either by the European Parliament or the Council within a period of two months of notification of that act to the European Parliament and the Council or if, before the expiry of that period, the European Parliament and the Council have both informed the Commission that they will not object. That period shall be extended by two months at the initiative of the European Parliament or of the Council.

Article 58
Committee procedure

1. The Commission shall be assisted by a Committee on the recognition of professional qualifications. That committee shall be a committee within the meaning of Regulation (EU) No. 182/2011.

2. Where reference is made to this paragraph, Article 5 of Regulation (EU) No. 182/2011 shall apply.

Article 59
Transparency

1. Member States shall notify to the Commission a list of existing regulated professions, specifying the activities covered by each profession, and a list of regulated education and training, and training with a special structure, referred to in point(c)(ii) of Article 11, in their territory by 18 January 2016. Any change to those lists shall also be notified to the Commission without undue delay. The Commission shall set up and maintain a publicly available database of regulated professions, including a general description of activities covered by each profession.

2. By 18 January 2016, Member States shall notify to the Commission the list of professions for which a prior check of qualifications is necessary under Article 7(4). Member States shall provide the Commission with a specific justification for the inclusion of each of those professions on that list.

3. Member States shall examine whether requirements under their legal system restricting the access to a profession or its pursuit to the holders of a specific professional qualification, including the use of professional titles and the professional activities allowed under such title, referred to in this Article as 'requirements' are compatible with the following principles:
   (a) requirements must be neither directly nor indirectly discriminatory on the basis of nationality or residence;
   (b) requirements must be justified by overriding reasons of general interest;
   (c) requirements must be suitable for securing the attainment of the objective pursued and must not go beyond what is necessary to attain that objective.

4. Paragraph 1 shall also apply to professions regulated in a Member State by an association or organisation within the meaning of Article 3(2) and any requirements for membership of those associations or organisations.

5. By 18 January 2016, Member States shall provide the Commission with information on the requirements they intend to maintain and the reasons for considering that those requirements comply with paragraph 3. Member States shall provide information on the requirements they subsequently introduced, and the reasons for considering that those requirements comply with paragraph 3, within six months of the adoption of the measure.

6. By 18 January 2016, and every two years thereafter, Member States shall also submit a report to the Commission about the requirements which have been removed or made less stringent.

7. The Commission shall forward the reports referred to in paragraph 6 to the other Member States which shall submit their observations within six months. Within the same period of six months, the Commission shall consult interested parties, including the professions concerned.

8. The Commission shall provide a summary report based on the information provided by Member States to the Group of Coordinators established under Commission Decision 2007/172/EC of 19 March 2007 setting up the group of coordinators for the recognition of professional qualifications, which may make observations.

9. In light of the observations provided for in paragraphs 7 and 8, the Commission shall, by 18 January 2017, submit its final findings to the European Parliament and the Council, accompanied where appropriate by proposals for further initiatives.

TITLE VI OTHER PROVISIONS

Article 60

Reports

1. As from 20 October 2007, Member States shall, every two years, send a report to the Commission on the application of the system. In addition to general observations, the report shall contain a statistical summary of decisions taken and a description of the main problems arising from the application of this Directive.

   As from 18 January 2016 the statistical summary of decisions taken referred to in the first subparagraph shall contain detailed information on the number and types of decisions taken in accordance with this Directive, including the types of decisions on partial access taken by competent authorities in accordance with Article 4f, and a description of the main problems arising from application of this Directive.

2. By 18 January 2019, and every five years thereafter, the Commission shall publish a report on the implementation of this Directive.

   The first such report shall focus in particular on the new elements introduced in this Directive and consider in particular the following issues:

   (a) the functioning of the European Professional Card;

   (b) the modernisation of the knowledge, skills and competences for the professions covered by Chapter III of Title III, including the list of competences referred to in Article 31(7);

   (c) the functioning of the common training frameworks and common training tests;

(d) the results of the special upgrading programme laid down under Romanian laws, regulations and administrative provisions for holders of the evidence of formal qualifications mentioned in Article 33a, as well as for holders of evidence of formal qualifications of post-secondary level, with a view to assessing the need to review the current provisions governing the acquired rights regime applicable to the Romanian evidence of formal qualifications as nurse responsible for general care.

Member States shall provide all necessary information for the preparation of that report.

Article 61

Derogation clause

If, for the application of one of the provisions of this Directive, a Member State encounters major difficulties in a particular area, the Commission shall examine those difficulties in collaboration with the Member State concerned.

Where appropriate, the Commission shall adopt an implementing act to permit the Member State in question to derogate from the relevant provision for a limited period of time.

Article 62

Repeal

Directives 77/452/EEC, 77/453/EEC, 78/686/EEC, 78/687/EEC, 78/1026/EEC, 78/1027/EEC, 80/154/EEC, 80/155/EEC, 85/384/EEC, 85/432/EEC, 85/433/EEC, 89/48/EEC, 92/51/EEC, 93/16/EEC and 1999/42/EC are repealed with effect from 20 October 2007. References to the repealed Directives shall be understood as references to this Directive and the acts adopted on the basis of those Directives shall not be affected by the repeal.

Article 63

Transposition

Member States shall bring into force the laws, regulations and administrative provisions necessary to comply with this Directive by 20 October 2007 at the latest. They shall forthwith inform the Commission thereof.

When Member States adopt these measures, they shall contain a reference to this Directive or be accompanied by such a reference on the occasion of their official publication. Member States shall determine how such reference is to be made.

Article 64

Entry into force

This Directive shall enter into force on the 20th day following its publication in the *Official Journal of the European Union*.

Article 65

Addressees

This Directive is addressed to the Member States.

13

Directive 2004/38 on the Right of Citizens of the Union and their Family Members to Move and Reside Freely within the Territory of the Member States

Contents

THE EUROPEAN PARLIAMENT AND THE COUNCIL OF THE EUROPEAN UNION,

Having regard to the Treaty [on the Functioning of the European Union], and in particular Articles [18, 21, 46, 50 and 59] thereof,

Having regard to the proposal from the Commission,

Having regard to the opinion of the European Economic and Social Committee,

Having regard to the opinion of the Committee of the Regions,

Acting in accordance with the procedure laid down in Article [294] of the Treaty ...

HAVE ADOPTED THIS DIRECTIVE:

Chapter I General Provisions

Article 1

Subject

This Directive lays down:

(a) the conditions governing the exercise of the right of free movement and residence within the territory of the Member States by Union citizens and their family members;

(b) the right of permanent residence in the territory of the Member States for Union citizens and their family members;

(c) the limits placed on the rights set out in (a) and (b) on grounds of public policy, public security or public health.

Article 2
Definitions

For the purposes of this Directive:

1. 'Union citizen' means any person having the nationality of a Member State;
2. 'family member' means:
    (a) the spouse;
    (b) the partner with whom the Union citizen has contracted a registered partnership, on the basis of the legislation of a Member State, if the legislation of the host Member State treats registered partnerships as equivalent to marriage and in accordance with the conditions laid down in the relevant legislation of the host Member State;
    (c) the direct descendants who are under the age of 21 or are dependants and those of the spouse or partner as defined in point (b);
    (d) the dependent direct relatives in the ascending line and those of the spouse or partner as defined in point (b);
3. 'host Member State' means the Member State to which a Union citizen moves in order to exercise his/her right of free movement and residence.

Article 3
Beneficiaries

1. This Directive shall apply to all Union citizens who move to or reside in a Member State other than that of which they are a national, and to their family members as defined in point 2 of Article 2 who accompany or join them.
2. Without prejudice to any right to free movement and residence the persons concerned may have in their own right, the host Member State shall, in accordance with its national legislation, facilitate entry and residence for the following persons:
    (a) any other family members, irrespective of their nationality, not falling under the definition in point 2 of Article 2 who, in the country from which they have come, are dependants or members of the household of the Union citizen having the primary right of residence, or where serious health grounds strictly require the personal care of the family member by the Union citizen;
    (b) the partner with whom the Union citizen has a durable relationship, duly attested. The host Member State shall undertake an extensive examination of the personal circumstances and shall justify any denial of entry or residence to these people.

Chapter II Right of Exit and Entry

Article 4
Right of exit

1. Without prejudice to the provisions on travel documents applicable to national border controls, all Union citizens with a valid identity card or passport and their family members who are not nationals of a Member State and who hold a valid passport shall

have the right to leave the territory of a Member State to travel to another Member State.

2. No exit visa or equivalent formality may be imposed on the persons to whom paragraph 1 applies.

3. Member States shall, acting in accordance with their laws, issue to their own nationals, and renew, an identity card or passport stating their nationality.

4. The passport shall be valid at least for all Member States and for countries through which the holder must pass when travelling between Member States. Where the law of a Member State does not provide for identity cards to be issued, the period of validity of any passport on being issued or renewed shall be not less than five years.

Article 5
Right of entry

1. Without prejudice to the provisions on travel documents applicable to national border controls, Member States shall grant Union citizens leave to enter their territory with a valid identity card or passport and shall grant family members who are not nationals of a Member State leave to enter their territory with a valid passport.

   No entry visa or equivalent formality may be imposed on Union citizens.

2. Family members who are not nationals of a Member State shall only be required to have an entry visa in accordance with Regulation (EC) No. 539/2001 or, where appropriate, with national law. For the purposes of this Directive, possession of the valid residence card referred to in Article 10 shall exempt such family members from the visa requirement.

   Member States shall grant such persons every facility to obtain the necessary visas. Such visas shall be issued free of charge as soon as possible and on the basis of an accelerated procedure.

3. The host Member State shall not place an entry or exit stamp in the passport of family members who are not nationals of a Member State provided that they present the residence card provided for in Article 10.

4. Where a Union citizen, or a family member who is not a national of a Member State, does not have the necessary travel documents or, if required, the necessary visas, the Member State concerned shall, before turning them back, give such persons every reasonable opportunity to obtain the necessary documents or have them brought to them within a reasonable period of time or to corroborate or prove by other means that they are covered by the right of free movement and residence.

5. The Member State may require the person concerned to report his/her presence within its territory within a reasonable and non-discriminatory period of time. Failure to comply with this requirement may make the person concerned liable to proportionate and non-discriminatory sanctions.

Chapter III Right of Residence

Article 6
Right of residence for up to three months

1. Union citizens shall have the right of residence on the territory of another Member State for a period of up to three months without any conditions or any formalities other than the requirement to hold a valid identity card or passport.

13

2. The provisions of paragraph 1 shall also apply to family members in possession of a valid passport who are not nationals of a Member State, accompanying or joining the Union citizen.

Article 7
Right of residence for more than three months
1. All Union citizens shall have the right of residence on the territory of another Member State for a period of longer than three months if they:
    (a) are workers or self-employed persons in the host Member State; or
    (b) have sufficient resources for themselves and their family members not to become a burden on the social assistance system of the host Member State during their period of residence and have comprehensive sickness insurance cover in the host Member State; or
    (c) — are enrolled at a private or public establishment, accredited or financed by the host Member State on the basis of its legislation or administrative practice, for the principal purpose of following a course of study, including vocational training; and
    — have comprehensive sickness insurance cover in the host Member State and assure the relevant national authority, by means of a declaration or by such equivalent means as they may choose, that they have sufficient resources for themselves and their family members not to become a burden on the social assistance system of the host Member State during their period of residence; or
    (d) are family members accompanying or joining a Union citizen who satisfies the conditions referred to in points (a), (b) or (c).
2. The right of residence provided for in paragraph 1 shall extend to family members who are not nationals of a Member State, accompanying or joining the Union citizen in the host Member State, provided that such Union citizen satisfies the conditions referred to in paragraph 1(a), (b) or (c).
3. For the purposes of paragraph 1(a), a Union citizen who is no longer a worker or self-employed person shall retain the status of worker or self-employed person in the following circumstances:
    (a) he/she is temporarily unable to work as the result of an illness or accident;
    (b) he/she is in duly recorded involuntary unemployment after having been employed for more than one year and has registered as a job-seeker with the relevant employment office;
    (c) he/she is in duly recorded involuntary unemployment after completing a fixed-term employment contract of less than a year or after having become involuntarily unemployed during the first twelve months and has registered as a job-seeker with the relevant employment office. In this case, the status of worker shall be retained for no less than six months;
    (d) he/she embarks on vocational training. Unless he/she is involuntarily unemployed, the retention of the status of worker shall require the training to be related to the previous employment.
4. By way of derogation from paragraphs 1(d) and 2 above, only the spouse, the registered partner provided for in Article 2(2)(b) and dependent children shall have the right of residence as family members of a Union citizen meeting the conditions

13

under 1(c) above. Article 3(2) shall apply to his/her dependent direct relatives in the ascending lines and those of his/her spouse or registered partner.

Article 8
Administrative formalities for Union citizens

1. Without prejudice to Article 5(5), for periods of residence longer than three months, the host Member State may require Union citizens to register with the relevant authorities.

2. The deadline for registration may not be less than three months from the date of arrival. A registration certificate shall be issued immediately, stating the name and address of the person registering and the date of the registration. Failure to comply with the registration requirement may render the person concerned liable to proportionate and non-discriminatory sanctions.

3. For the registration certificate to be issued, Member States may only require that[:]
   — Union citizens to whom point (a) of Article 7(1) applies present a valid identity card or passport, a confirmation of engagement from the employer or a certificate of employment, or proof that they are self-employed persons,
   — Union citizens to whom point (b) of Article 7(1) applies present a valid identity card or passport and provide proof that they satisfy the conditions laid down therein,
   — Union citizens to whom point (c) of Article 7(1) applies present a valid identity card or passport, provide proof of enrolment at an accredited establishment and of comprehensive sickness insurance cover and the declaration or equivalent means referred to in point (c) of Article 7(1). Member States may not require this declaration to refer to any specific amount of resources.

4. Member States may not lay down a fixed amount which they regard as 'sufficient resources', but they must take into account the personal situation of the person concerned. In all cases this amount shall not be higher than the threshold below which nationals of the host Member State become eligible for social assistance, or, where this criterion is not applicable, higher than the minimum social security pension paid by the host Member State.

5. For the registration certificate to be issued to family members of Union citizens, who are themselves Union citizens, Member States may require the following documents to be presented:
   (a) a valid identity card or passport;
   (b) a document attesting to the existence of a family relationship or of a registered partnership;
   (c) where appropriate, the registration certificate of the Union citizen whom they are accompanying or joining;
   (d) in cases falling under points (c) and (d) of Article 2(2), documentary evidence that the conditions laid down therein are met;
   (e) in cases falling under Article 3(2)(a), a document issued by the relevant authority in the country of origin or country from which they are arriving certifying that they are dependants or members of the household of the Union citizen, or proof of the existence of serious health grounds which strictly require the personal care of the family member by the Union citizen;

13

(f) in cases falling under Article 3(2)(b), proof of the existence of a durable relation-
     ship with the Union citizen.

Article 9
Administrative formalities for family members who are not nationals of a Member State

1. Member States shall issue a residence card to family members of a Union citizen who are not nationals of a Member State, where the planned period of residence is for more than three months.
2. The deadline for submitting the residence card application may not be less than three months from the date of arrival.
3. Failure to comply with the requirement to apply for a residence card may make the person concerned liable to proportionate and non-discriminatory sanctions.

Article 10
Issue of residence cards

1. The right of residence of family members of a Union citizen who are not nationals of a Member State shall be evidenced by the issuing of a document called 'Residence card of a family member of a Union citizen' no later than six months from the date on which they submit the application. A certificate of application for the residence card shall be issued immediately.
2. For the residence card to be issued, Member States shall require presentation of the following documents:
   (a) a valid passport;
   (b) a document attesting to the existence of a family relationship or of a registered partnership;
   (c) the registration certificate or, in the absence of a registration system, any other proof of residence in the host Member State of the Union citizen whom they are accompanying or joining;
   (d) in cases falling under points (c) and (d) of Article 2(2), documentary evidence that the conditions laid down therein are met;
   (e) in cases falling under Article 3(2)(a), a document issued by the relevant authority in the country of origin or country from which they are arriving certifying that they are dependants or members of the household of the Union citizen, or proof of the existence of serious health grounds which strictly require the personal care of the family member by the Union citizen;
   (f) in cases falling under Article 3(2)(b), proof of the existence of a durable relation-ship with the Union citizen.

Article 11
Validity of the residence card

1. The residence card provided for by Article 10(1) shall be valid for five years from the date of issue or for the envisaged period of residence of the Union citizen, if this period is less than five years.
2. The validity of the residence card shall not be affected by temporary absences not exceeding six months a year, or by absences of a longer duration for compulsory

military service or by one absence of a maximum of 12 consecutive months for important reasons such as pregnancy and childbirth, serious illness, study or vocational training, or a posting in another Member State or a third country.

Article 12

Retention of the right of residence by family members in the event of death or departure of the Union citizen

1. Without prejudice to the second subparagraph, the Union citizen's death or departure from the host Member State shall not affect the right of residence of his/her family members who are nationals of a Member State.

    Before acquiring the right of permanent residence, the persons concerned must meet the conditions laid down in points (a), (b), (c) or (d) of Article 7(1).

2. Without prejudice to the second subparagraph, the Union citizen's death shall not entail loss of the right of residence of his/her family members who are not nationals of a Member State and who have been residing in the host Member State as family members for at least one year before the Union citizen's death.

    Before acquiring the right of permanent residence, the right of residence of the persons concerned shall remain subject to the requirement that they are able to show that they are workers or self-employed persons or that they have sufficient resources for themselves and their family members not to become a burden on the social assistance system of the host Member State during their period of residence and have comprehensive sickness insurance cover in the host Member State, or that they are members of the family, already constituted in the host Member State, of a person satisfying these requirements. 'Sufficient resources' shall be as defined in Article 8(4).

    Such family members shall retain their right of residence exclusively on a personal basis.

3. The Union citizen's departure from the host Member State or his/her death shall not entail loss of the right of residence of his/her children or of the parent who has actual custody of the children, irrespective of nationality, if the children reside in the host Member State and are enrolled at an educational establishment, for the purpose of studying there, until the completion of their studies.

Article 13

Retention of the right of residence by family members in the event of divorce, annulment of marriage or termination of registered partnership

1. Without prejudice to the second subparagraph, divorce, annulment of the Union citizen's marriage or termination of his/her registered partnership, as referred to in point 2(b) of Article 2 shall not affect the right of residence of his/her family members who are nationals of a Member State.

    Before acquiring the right of permanent residence, the persons concerned must meet the conditions laid down in points (a), (b), (c) or (d) of Article 7(1).

2. Without prejudice to the second subparagraph, divorce, annulment of marriage or termination of the registered partnership referred to in point 2(b) of Article 2 shall not entail loss of the right of residence of a Union citizen's family members who are not nationals of a Member State where:

13

(a) prior to initiation of the divorce or annulment proceedings or termination of the registered partnership referred to in point 2(b) of Article 2, the marriage or registered partnership has lasted at least three years, including one year in the host Member State; or

(b) by agreement between the spouses or the partners referred to in point 2(b) of Article 2 or by court order, the spouse or partner who is not a national of a Member State has custody of the Union citizen's children; or

(c) this is warranted by particularly difficult circumstances, such as having been a victim of domestic violence while the marriage or registered partnership was subsisting; or

(d) by agreement between the spouses or partners referred to in point 2(b) of Article 2 or by court order, the spouse or partner who is not a national of a Member State has the right of access to a minor child, provided that the court has ruled that such access must be in the host Member State, and for as long as is required.

Before acquiring the right of permanent residence, the right of residence of the persons concerned shall remain subject to the requirement that they are able to show that they are workers or self-employed persons or that they have sufficient resources for themselves and their family members not to become a burden on the social assistance system of the host Member State during their period of residence and have comprehensive sickness insurance cover in the host Member State, or that they are members of the family, already constituted in the host Member State, of a person satisfying these requirements. 'Sufficient resources' shall be as defined in Article 8(4).

Such family members shall retain their right of residence exclusively on [a] personal basis.

Article 14
Retention of the right of residence

1. Union citizens and their family members shall have the right of residence provided for in Article 6, as long as they do not become an unreasonable burden on the social assistance system of the host Member State.

2. Union citizens and their family members shall have the right of residence provided for in Articles 7, 12 and 13 as long as they meet the conditions set out therein.

   In specific cases where there is a reasonable doubt as to whether a Union citizen or his/her family members satisfies the conditions set out in Articles 7, 12 and 13, Member States may verify if these conditions are fulfilled. This verification shall not be carried out systematically.

3. An expulsion measure shall not be the automatic consequence of a Union citizen's or his or her family member's recourse to the social assistance system of the host Member State.

4. By way of derogation from paragraphs 1 and 2 and without prejudice to the provisions of Chapter VI, an expulsion measure may in no case be adopted against Union citizens or their family members if:

   (a) the Union citizens are workers or self-employed persons, or

   (b) the Union citizens entered the territory of the host Member State in order to seek employment. In this case, the Union citizens and their family members may not be expelled for as long as the Union citizens can provide evidence that they are continuing to seek employment and that they have a genuine chance of being engaged.

Article 15
Procedural safeguards

1. The procedures provided for by Articles 30 and 31 shall apply by analogy to all decisions restricting free movement of Union citizens and their family members on grounds other than public policy, public security or public health.
2. Expiry of the identity card or passport on the basis of which the person concerned entered the host Member State and was issued with a registration certificate or residence card shall not constitute a ground for expulsion from the host Member State.
3. The host Member State may not impose a ban on entry in the context of an expulsion decision to which paragraph 1 applies.

Chapter IV Right of Permanent Residence

SECTION I ELIGIBILITY

Article 16
General rule for Union citizens and their family members

1. Union citizens who have resided legally for a continuous period of five years in the host Member State shall have the right of permanent residence there. This right shall not be subject to the conditions provided for in Chapter III.
2. Paragraph 1 shall apply also to family members who are not nationals of a Member State and have legally resided with the Union citizen in the host Member State for a continuous period of five years.
3. Continuity of residence shall not be affected by temporary absences not exceeding a total of six months a year, or by absences of a longer duration for compulsory military service, or by one absence of a maximum of 12 consecutive months for important reasons such as pregnancy and childbirth, serious illness, study or vocational training, or a posting in another Member State or a third country.
4. Once acquired, the right of permanent residence shall be lost only through absence from the host Member State for a period exceeding two consecutive years.

Article 17
Exemptions for persons no longer working in the host Member State and their family members

1. By way of derogation from Article 16, the right of permanent residence in the host Member State shall be enjoyed before completion of a continuous period of five years of residence by:
   (a) workers or self-employed persons who, at the time they stop working, have reached the age laid down by the law of that Member State for entitlement to an old age pension or workers who cease paid employment to take early retirement, provided that they have been working in that Member State for at least the preceding twelve months and have resided there continuously for more than three years.

If the law of the host Member State does not grant the right to an old age pension to certain categories of self-employed persons, the age condition shall be deemed to have been met once the person concerned has reached the age of 60;

(b) workers or self-employed persons who have resided continuously in the host Member State for more than two years and stop working there as a result of permanent incapacity to work.

If such incapacity is the result of an accident at work or an occupational disease entitling the person concerned to a benefit payable in full or in part by an institution in the host Member State, no condition shall be imposed as to length of residence;

(c) workers or self-employed persons who, after three years of continuous employment and residence in the host Member State, work in an employed or self-employed capacity in another Member State, while retaining their place of residence in the host Member State, to which they return, as a rule, each day or at least once a week.

For the purposes of entitlement to the rights referred to in points (a) and (b), periods of employment spent in the Member State in which the person concerned is working shall be regarded as having been spent in the host Member State.

Periods of involuntary unemployment duly recorded by the relevant employment office, periods not worked for reasons not of the person's own making and absences from work or cessation of work due to illness or accident shall be regarded as periods of employment.

2. The conditions as to length of residence and employment laid down in point (a) of paragraph 1 and the condition as to length of residence laid down in point (b) of paragraph 1 shall not apply if the worker's or the self-employed person's spouse or partner as referred to in point 2(b) of Article 2 is a national of the host Member State or has lost the nationality of that Member State by marriage to that worker or self-employed person.

3. Irrespective of nationality, the family members of a worker or a self-employed person who are residing with him in the territory of the host Member State shall have the right of permanent residence in that Member State, if the worker or self-employed person has acquired himself the right of permanent residence in that Member State on the basis of paragraph 1.

4. If, however, the worker or self-employed person dies while still working but before acquiring permanent residence status in the host Member State on the basis of paragraph 1, his family members who are residing with him in the host Member State shall acquire the right of permanent residence there, on condition that:

(a) the worker or self-employed person had, at the time of death, resided continuously on the territory of that Member State for two years; or

(b) the death resulted from an accident at work or an occupational disease; or

(c) the surviving spouse lost the nationality of that Member State following marriage to the worker or self-employed person.

Article 18
Acquisition of the right of permanent residence by certain family members who are not nationals of a Member State

Without prejudice to Article 17, the family members of a Union citizen to whom Articles 12(2) and 13(2) apply, who satisfy the conditions laid down therein, shall acquire the right of permanent residence after residing legally for a period of five consecutive years in the host Member State.

SECTION II ADMINISTRATIVE FORMALITIES

Article 19

Document certifying permanent residence for Union citizens

1. Upon application Member States shall issue Union citizens entitled to permanent residence, after having verified duration of residence, with a document certifying permanent residence.
2. The document certifying permanent residence shall be issued as soon as possible.

Article 20

Permanent residence card for family members who are not nationals of a Member State

1. Member States shall issue family members who are not nationals of a Member State entitled to permanent residence with a permanent residence card within six months of the submission of the application. The permanent residence card shall be renewable automatically every 10 years.
2. The application for a permanent residence card shall be submitted before the residence card expires. Failure to comply with the requirement to apply for a permanent residence card may render the person concerned liable to proportionate and non-discriminatory sanctions.
3. Interruption in residence not exceeding two consecutive years shall not affect the validity of the permanent residence card.

Article 21

Continuity of residence

For the purposes of this Directive, continuity of residence may be attested by any means of proof in use in the host Member State. Continuity of residence is broken by any expulsion decision duly enforced against the person concerned.

Chapter V Provisions Common to the Right of Residence and the Right of Permanent Residence

Article 22

Territorial scope

The right of residence and the right of permanent residence shall cover the whole territory of the host Member State. Member States may impose territorial restrictions on the right of residence and the right of permanent residence only where the same restrictions apply to their own nationals.

Article 23

Related rights

Irrespective of nationality, the family members of a Union citizen who have the right of residence or the right of permanent residence in a Member State shall be entitled to take up employment or self-employment there.

13

Article 24
Equal treatment

1. Subject to such specific provisions as are expressly provided for in the Treaty and secondary law, all Union citizens residing on the basis of this Directive in the territory of the host Member State shall enjoy equal treatment with the nationals of that Member State within the scope of the Treaty. The benefit of this right shall be extended to family members who are not nationals of a Member State and who have the right of residence or permanent residence.

2. By way of derogation from paragraph 1, the host Member State shall not be obliged to confer entitlement to social assistance during the first three months of residence or, where appropriate, the longer period provided for in Article 14(4)(b), nor shall it be obliged, prior to acquisition of the right of permanent residence, to grant maintenance aid for studies, including vocational training, consisting in student grants or student loans to persons other than workers, self-employed persons, persons who retain such status and members of their families.

Article 25
General provisions concerning residence documents

1. Possession of a registration certificate as referred to in Article 8, of a document certifying permanent residence, of a certificate attesting submission of an application for a family member residence card, of a residence card or of a permanent residence card, may under no circumstances be made a precondition for the exercise of a right or the completion of an administrative formality, as entitlement to rights may be attested by any other means of proof.

2. All documents mentioned in paragraph 1 shall be issued free of charge or for a charge not exceeding that imposed on nationals for the issuing of similar documents.

Article 26
Checks

Member States may carry out checks on compliance with any requirement deriving from their national legislation for non-nationals always to carry their registration certificate or residence card, provided that the same requirement applies to their own nationals as regards their identity card. In the event of failure to comply with this requirement, Member States may impose the same sanctions as those imposed on their own nationals for failure to carry their identity card.

Chapter VI Restrictions on the Right of Entry and the Right of Residence on Grounds of Public Policy, Public Security or Public Health

Article 27
General principles

1. Subject to the provisions of this Chapter, Member States may restrict the freedom of movement and residence of Union citizens and their family members, irrespective of nationality, on grounds of public policy, public security or public health. These grounds shall not be invoked to serve economic ends.

2. Measures taken on grounds of public policy or public security shall comply with the principle of proportionality and shall be based exclusively on the personal conduct of the individual concerned. Previous criminal convictions shall not in themselves constitute grounds for taking such measures.

   The personal conduct of the individual concerned must represent a genuine, present and sufficiently serious threat affecting one of the fundamental interests of society. Justifications that are isolated from the particulars of the case or that rely on considerations of general prevention shall not be accepted.

3. In order to ascertain whether the person concerned represents a danger for public policy or public security, when issuing the registration certificate or, in the absence of a registration system, not later than three months from the date of arrival of the person concerned on its territory or from the date of reporting his/her presence within the territory, as provided for in Article 5(5), or when issuing the residence card, the host Member State may, should it consider this essential, request the Member State of origin and, if need be, other Member States to provide information concerning any previous police record the person concerned may have. Such enquiries shall not be made as a matter of routine. The Member State consulted shall give its reply within two months.

4. The Member State which issued the passport or identity card shall allow the holder of the document who has been expelled on grounds of public policy, public security, or public health from another Member State to re-enter its territory without any formality even if the document is no longer valid or the nationality of the holder is in dispute.

Article 28
Protection against expulsion

1. Before taking an expulsion decision on grounds of public policy or public security, the host Member State shall take account of considerations such as how long the individual concerned has resided on its territory, his/her age, state of health, family and economic situation, social and cultural integration into the host Member State and the extent of his/her links with the country of origin.

2. The host Member State may not take an expulsion decision against Union citizens or their family members, irrespective of nationality, who have the right of permanent residence on its territory, except on serious grounds of public policy or public security.

3. An expulsion decision may not be taken against Union citizens, except if the decision is based on imperative grounds of public security, as defined by Member States, if they:
   (a) have resided in the host Member State for the previous 10 years; or
   (b) are a minor, except if the expulsion is necessary for the best interests of the child, as provided for in the United Nations Convention on the Rights of the Child of 20 November 1989.

Article 29
Public health

1. The only diseases justifying measures restricting freedom of movement shall be the diseases with epidemic potential as defined by the relevant instruments of the World Health Organisation and other infectious diseases or contagious parasitic diseases if

they are the subject of protection provisions applying to nationals of the host Member State.

2. Diseases occurring after a three-month period from the date of arrival shall not constitute grounds for expulsion from the territory.

3. Where there are serious indications that it is necessary, Member States may, within three months of the date of arrival, require persons entitled to the right of residence to undergo, free of charge, a medical examination to certify that they are not suffering from any of the conditions referred to in paragraph 1. Such medical examinations may not be required as a matter of routine.

Article 30
Notification of decisions

1. The persons concerned shall be notified in writing of any decision taken under Article 27(1), in such a way that they are able to comprehend its content and the implications for them.

2. The persons concerned shall be informed, precisely and in full, of the public policy, public security or public health grounds on which the decision taken in their case is based, unless this is contrary to the interests of State security.

3. The notification shall specify the court or administrative authority with which the person concerned may lodge an appeal, the time limit for the appeal and, where applicable, the time allowed for the person to leave the territory of the Member State. Save in duly substantiated cases of urgency, the time allowed to leave the territory shall be not less than one month from the date of notification.

Article 31
Procedural safeguards

1. The persons concerned shall have access to judicial and, where appropriate, administrative redress procedures in the host Member State to appeal against or seek review of any decision taken against them on the grounds of public policy, public security or public health.

2. Where the application for appeal against or judicial review of the expulsion decision is accompanied by an application for an interim order to suspend enforcement of that decision, actual removal from the territory may not take place until such time as the decision on the interim order has been taken, except:
   — where the expulsion decision is based on a previous judicial decision; or
   — where the persons concerned have had previous access to judicial review; or
   — where the expulsion decision is based on imperative grounds of public security under Article 28(3).

3. The redress procedures shall allow for an examination of the legality of the decision, as well as of the facts and circumstances on which the proposed measure is based. They shall ensure that the decision is not disproportionate, particularly in view of the requirements laid down in Article 28.

4. Member States may exclude the individual concerned from their territory pending the redress procedure, but they may not prevent the individual from submitting his/her defence in person, except when his/her appearance may cause serious troubles to public policy or public security or when the appeal or judicial review concerns a denial of entry to the territory.

Article 32
Duration of exclusion orders

1. Persons excluded on grounds of public policy or public security may submit an application for lifting of the exclusion order after a reasonable period, depending on the circumstances, and in any event after three years from enforcement of the final exclusion order which has been validly adopted in accordance with [Union] law, by putting forward arguments to establish that there has been a material change in the circumstances which justified the decision ordering their exclusion.

   The Member State concerned shall reach a decision on this application within six months of its submission.

2. The persons referred to in paragraph 1 shall have no right of entry to the territory of the Member State concerned while their application is being considered.

Article 33
Expulsion as a penalty or legal consequence

1. Expulsion orders may not be issued by the host Member State as a penalty or legal consequence of a custodial penalty, unless they conform to the requirements of Articles 27, 28 and 29.

2. If an expulsion order, as provided for in paragraph 1, is enforced more than two years after it was issued, the Member State shall check that the individual concerned is currently and genuinely a threat to public policy or public security and shall assess whether there has been any material change in the circumstances since the expulsion order was issued.

Chapter VII Final Provisions

Article 34
Publicity

Member States shall disseminate information concerning the rights and obligations of Union citizens and their family members on the subjects covered by this Directive, particularly by means of awareness-raising campaigns conducted through national and local media and other means of communication.

Article 35
Abuse of rights

Member States may adopt the necessary measures to refuse, terminate or withdraw any right conferred by this Directive in the case of abuse of rights or fraud, such as marriages of convenience. Any such measure shall be proportionate and subject to the procedural safeguards provided for in Articles 30 and 31.

Article 36
Sanctions

Member States shall lay down provisions on the sanctions applicable to breaches of national rules adopted for the implementation of this Directive and shall take the measures required for their application. The sanctions laid down shall be effective and proportionate. Member States shall notify the Commission of these provisions not later than 30 April 2006 and as promptly as possible in the case of any subsequent changes.

13

Article 37

More favourable national provisions

The provisions of this Directive shall not affect any laws, regulations or administrative provisions laid down by a Member State which would be more favourable to the persons covered by this Directive.

Article 38

Repeals

— — — — —

2. Directives 64/221/EEC, 68/360/EEC, 72/194/EEC, 73/148/EEC, 75/34/EEC, 75/35/EEC, 90/364/EEC, 90/365/EEC and 93/96/EEC shall be repealed with effect from 30 April 2006.
3. References made to the repealed provisions and Directives shall be construed as being made to this Directive.

Article 39

Report

No later than 30 April 2008 the Commission shall submit a report on the application of this Directive to the European Parliament and the Council, together with any necessary proposals, notably on the opportunity to extend the period of time during which Union citizens and their family members may reside in the territory of the host Member State without any conditions. The Member States shall provide the Commission with the information needed to produce the report.

Article 40

Transposition

1. Member States shall bring into force the laws, regulations and administrative provisions necessary to comply with this Directive by 30 April 2006.

   When Member States adopt those measures, they shall contain a reference to this Directive or shall be accompanied by such a reference on the occasion of their official publication. The methods of making such reference shall be laid down by the Member States.
2. Member States shall communicate to the Commission the text of the provisions of national law which they adopt in the field covered by this Directive together with a table showing how the provisions of this Directive correspond to the national provisions adopted.

Article 41

Entry into force

This Directive shall enter into force on the day of its publication in the Official Journal of the European Union.

Article 42

Addressees

This Directive is addressed to the Member States.

14

Directive 2006/123 on Services in the Internal Market

Contents

THE EUROPEAN PARLIAMENT AND THE COUNCIL OF THE EUROPEAN UNION,

Having regard to the Treaty [on the Functioning of the European Union], and in particular the first and third sentence of Article [53(1)] and Article [62] thereof,

Having regard to the proposal from the Commission,

Having regard to the Opinion of the European Economic and Social Committee,

Having regard to the opinion of the Committee of the Regions, Acting in accordance with the procedure laid down in Article [294] of the Treaty ...

HAVE ADOPTED THIS DIRECTIVE:

Chapter I General Provisions

14

Article 1

Subject matter

1. This Directive establishes general provisions facilitating the exercise of the freedom of establishment for service providers and the free movement of services, while maintaining a high quality of services.
2. This Directive does not deal with the liberalisation of services of general economic interest, reserved to public or private entities, nor with the privatisation of public entities providing services.
3. This Directive does not deal with the abolition of monopolies providing services nor with aids granted by Member States which are covered by [Union] rules on competition.

This Directive does not affect the freedom of Member States to define, in conformity with [Union] law, what they consider to be services of general economic interest, how those services should be organised and financed, in compliance with the State aid rules, and what specific obligations they should be subject to.

4. This Directive does not affect measures taken at [Union] level or at national level, in conformity with [Union] law, to protect or promote cultural or linguistic diversity or media pluralism.

5. This Directive does not affect Member States' rules of criminal law. However, Member States may not restrict the freedom to provide services by applying criminal law provisions which specifically regulate or affect access to or exercise of a service activity in circumvention of the rules laid down in this Directive.

6. This Directive does not affect labour law, that is any legal or contractual provision concerning employment conditions, working conditions, including health and safety at work and the relationship between employers and workers, which Member States apply in accordance with national law which respects [Union] law. Equally, this Directive does not affect the social security legislation of the Member States.

7. This Directive does not affect the exercise of fundamental rights as recognised in the Member States and by [Union] law. Nor does it affect the right to negotiate, conclude and enforce collective agreements and to take industrial action in accordance with national law and practices which respect [Union] law.

Article 2
Scope
1. This Directive shall apply to services supplied by providers established in a Member State.

2. This Directive shall not apply to the following activities:
   (a) non-economic services of general interest;
   (b) financial services, such as banking, credit, insurance and re-insurance, occupational or personal pensions, securities, investment funds, payment and investment advice, including the services listed in Annex I to Directive 2006/48/EC;
   (c) electronic communications services and networks, and associated facilities and services, with respect to matters covered by Directives 2002/19/EC, 2002/20/EC, 2002/21/EC, 2002/22/EC and 2002/58/EC;
   (d) services in the field of transport, including port services, falling within the scope of Title [VI] of [Part Three] the [FEU] Treaty;
   (e) services of temporary work agencies;
   (f) healthcare services whether or not they are provided via healthcare facilities, and regardless of the ways in which they are organised and financed at national level or whether they are public or private;
   (g) audiovisual services, including cinematographic services, whatever their mode of production, distribution and transmission, and radio broadcasting;
   (h) gambling activities which involve wagering a stake with pecuniary value in games of chance, including lotteries, gambling in casinos and betting transactions;
   (i) activities which are connected with the exercise of official authority as set out in Article [51] of the Treaty;

(j) social services relating to social housing, childcare and support of families and persons permanently or temporarily in need which are provided by the State, by providers mandated by the State or by charities recognised as such by the State;

(k) private security services;

(l) services provided by notaries and bailiffs, who are appointed by an official act of government.

3. This Directive shall not apply to the field of taxation.

Article 3

Relationship with other provisions of [Union] law

1. If the provisions of this Directive conflict with a provision of another [Union] act governing specific aspects of access to or exercise of a service activity in specific sectors or for specific professions, the provision of the other [Union] act shall prevail and shall apply to those specific sectors or professions. These include:

(a) Directive 96/71/EC;

(b) Regulation (EEC) No. 1408/71;

(c) Council Directive 89/552/EEC of 3 October 1989 on the coordination of certain provisions laid down by law, regulation or administrative action in Member States concerning the pursuit of television broadcasting activities[;]

(d) Directive 2005/36/EC.

2. This Directive does not concern rules of private international law, in particular rules governing the law applicable to contractual and non contractual obligations, including those which guarantee that consumers benefit from the protection granted to them by the consumer protection rules laid down in the consumer legislation in force in their Member State.

3. Member States shall apply the provisions of this Directive in compliance with the rules of the Treaty on the right of establishment and the free movement of services.

Article 4

Definitions

For the purposes of this Directive, the following definitions shall apply:

(1) 'service' means any self-employed economic activity, normally provided for remuneration, as referred to in Article [57] of the Treaty;

(2) 'provider' means any natural person who is a national of a Member State, or any legal person as referred to in Article [54] of the Treaty and established in a Member State, who offers or provides a service;

(3) 'recipient' means any natural person who is a national of a Member State or who benefits from rights conferred upon him by [Union] acts, or any legal person as referred to in Article [54] of the Treaty and established in a Member State, who, for professional or non-professional purposes, uses, or wishes to use, a service;

(4) 'Member State of establishment' means the Member State in whose territory the provider of the service concerned is established;

(5) 'establishment' means the actual pursuit of an economic activity, as referred to in Article [49] of the Treaty, by the provider for an indefinite period and through a stable infrastructure from where the business of providing services is actually carried out;

14

(6) 'authorisation scheme' means any procedure under which a provider or recipient is in effect required to take steps in order to obtain from a competent authority a formal decision, or an implied decision, concerning access to a service activity or the exercise thereof;

(7) 'requirement' means any obligation, prohibition, condition or limit provided for in the laws, regulations or administrative provisions of the Member States or in consequence of case-law, administrative practice, the rules of professional bodies, or the collective rules of professional associations or other professional organisations, adopted in the exercise of their legal autonomy; rules laid down in collective agreements negotiated by the social partners shall not as such be seen as requirements within the meaning of this Directive;

(8) 'overriding reasons relating to the public interest' means reasons recognised as such in the case law of the Court of Justice, including the following grounds: public policy; public security; public safety; public health; preserving the financial equilibrium of the social security system; the protection of consumers, recipients of services and workers; fairness of trade transactions; combating fraud; the protection of the environment and the urban environment; the health of animals; intellectual property; the conservation of the national historic and artistic heritage; social policy objectives and cultural policy objectives;

(9) 'competent authority' means anybody or authority which has a supervisory or regulatory role in a Member State in relation to service activities, including, in particular, administrative authorities, including courts acting as such, professional bodies, and those professional associations or other professional organisations which, in the exercise of their legal autonomy, regulate in a collective manner access to service activities or the exercise thereof;

(10) 'Member State where the service is provided' means the Member State where the service is supplied by a provider established in another Member State;

(11) 'regulated profession' means a professional activity or a group of professional activities as referred to in Article 3(1)(a) of Directive 2005/36/EC;

(12) 'commercial communication' means any form of communication designed to promote, directly or indirectly, the goods, services or image of an undertaking, organisation or person engaged in commercial, industrial or craft activity or practising a regulated profession. The following do not in themselves constitute commercial communications:

(a) information enabling direct access to the activity of the undertaking, organisation or person, including in particular a domain name or an electronic-mailing address;

(b) communications relating to the goods, services or image of the undertaking, organisation or person, compiled in an independent manner, particularly when provided for no financial consideration.

Chapter II Administrative Simplification

Article 5
Simplification of procedures

1. Member States shall examine the procedures and formalities applicable to access to a service activity and to the exercise thereof. Where procedures and formalities

examined under this paragraph are not sufficiently simple, Member States shall simplify them.

2. The Commission may introduce harmonised forms at [Union] level, in accordance with the procedure referred to in Article 40(2). These forms shall be equivalent to certificates, attestations and any other documents required of a provider.

3. Where Member States require a provider or recipient to supply a certificate, attestation or any other document proving that a requirement has been satisfied, they shall accept any document from another Member State which serves an equivalent purpose or from which it is clear that the requirement in question has been satisfied. They may not require a document from another Member State to be produced in its original form, or as a certified copy or as a certified translation, save in the cases provided for in other [Union] instruments or where such a requirement is justified by an overriding reason relating to the public interest, including public order and security.

The first subparagraph shall not affect the right of Member States to require noncertified translations of documents in one of their official languages.

4. Paragraph 3 shall not apply to the documents referred to in Article 7(2) and 50 of Directive 2005/36/EC, in Articles 45(3), 46, 49 and 50 of Directive 2004/18/EC of the European Parliament and of the Council of 31 March 2004 on the coordination of procedures for the award of public works contracts, public supply contracts and public service contracts, in Article 3(2) of Directive 98/5/EC of the European Parliament and of the Council of 16 February 1998 to facilitate practice of the profession of lawyer on a permanent basis in a Member State other than that in which the qualification was obtained, in the First Council Directive 68/151/EEC of 9 March 1968 on coordination of safeguards which, for the protection of the interests of members and others, are required by Member States of companies within the meaning of the second paragraph of Article [65] of the Treaty, with a view to making such safeguards equivalent throughout the [Union] and in the Eleventh Council Directive 89/666/EECof 21 December 1989 concerning disclosure requirements in respect of branches opened in a Member State by certain types of company governed by the law of another State.

Article 6
Points of single contact

1. Member States shall ensure that it is possible for providers to complete the following procedures and formalities through points of single contact:
    (a) all procedures and formalities needed for access to his service activities, in particular, all declarations, notifications or applications necessary for authorisation from the competent authorities, including applications for inclusion in a register, a roll or a database, or for registration with a professional body or association;
    (b) any applications for authorisation needed to exercise his service activities.
2. The establishment of points of single contact shall be without prejudice to the allocation of functions and powers among the authorities within national systems.

Article 7
Right to information

1. Member States shall ensure that the following information is easily accessible to providers and recipients through the points of single contact:

(a) requirements applicable to providers established in their territory, in particular those requirements concerning the procedures and formalities to be completed in order to access and to exercise service activities;

(b) the contact details of the competent authorities enabling the latter to be contacted directly, including the details of those authorities responsible for matters concerning the exercise of service activities;

(c) the means of, and conditions for, accessing public registers and databases on providers and services;

(d) the means of redress which are generally available in the event of dispute between the competent authorities and the provider or the recipient, or between a provider and a recipient or between providers;

(e) the contact details of the associations or organisations, other than the competent authorities, from which providers or recipients may obtain practical assistance.

2. Member States shall ensure that it is possible for providers and recipients to receive, at their request, assistance from the competent authorities, consisting in information on the way in which the requirements referred to in point (a) of paragraph 1 are generally interpreted and applied. Where appropriate, such advice shall include a simple step-by-step guide. The information shall be provided in plain and intelligible language.

3. Member States shall ensure that the information and assistance referred to in paragraphs 1 and 2 are provided in a clear and unambiguous manner, that they are easily accessible at a distance and by electronic means and that they are kept up to date.

4. Member States shall ensure that the points of single contact and the competent authorities respond as quickly as possible to any request for information or assistance as referred to in paragraphs 1 and 2 and, in cases where the request is faulty or unfounded, inform the applicant accordingly without delay.

5. Member States and the Commission shall take accompanying measures in order to encourage points of single contact to make the information provided for in this Article available in other [Union] languages. This does not interfere with Member States' legislation on the use of languages.

6. The obligation for competent authorities to assist providers and recipients does not require those authorities to provide legal advice in individual cases but concerns only general information on the way in which requirements are usually interpreted or applied.

Article 8

Procedures by electronic means

1. Member States shall ensure that all procedures and formalities relating to access to a service activity and to the exercise thereof may be easily completed, at a distance and by electronic means, through the relevant point of single contact and with the relevant competent authorities.

2. Paragraph 1 shall not apply to the inspection of premises on which the service is provided or of equipment used by the provider or to physical examination of the capability or of the personal integrity of the provider or of his responsible staff.

3. The Commission shall, in accordance with the procedure referred to in Article 40(2), adopt detailed rules for the implementation of paragraph 1 of this Article with a view to facilitating the interoperability of information systems and use of procedures by

electronic means between Member States, taking into account common standards developed at [Union] level.

Chapter III Freedom of Establishment for Providers

SECTION 1 AUTHORISATIONS

Article 9

Authorisation schemes

1. Member States shall not make access to a service activity or the exercise thereof subject to an authorisation scheme unless the following conditions are satisfied:
   (a) the authorisation scheme does not discriminate against the provider in question;
   (b) the need for an authorisation scheme is justified by an overriding reason relating to the public interest;
   (c) the objective pursued cannot be attained by means of a less restrictive measure, in particular because an a posteriori inspection would take place too late to be genuinely effective.
2. In the report referred to in Article 39(1), Member States shall identify their authorisation schemes and give reasons showing their compatibility with paragraph 1 of this Article.
3. This section shall not apply to those aspects of authorisation schemes which are governed directly or indirectly by other [Union] instruments.

Article 10

Conditions for the granting of authorisation

1. Authorisation schemes shall be based on criteria which preclude the competent authorities from exercising their power of assessment in an arbitrary manner.
2. The criteria referred to in paragraph 1 shall be:
   (a) non-discriminatory;
   (b) justified by an overriding reason relating to the public interest;
   (c) proportionate to that public interest objective;
   (d) clear and unambiguous;
   (e) objective;
   (f) made public in advance;
   (g) transparent and accessible.
3. The conditions for granting authorisation for a new establishment shall not duplicate requirements and controls which are equivalent or essentially comparable as regards their purpose to which the provider is already subject in another Member State or in the same Member State. The liaison points referred to in Article 28(2) and the provider shall assist the competent authority by providing any necessary information regarding those requirements.
4. The authorisation shall enable the provider to have access to the service activity, or to exercise that activity, throughout the national territory, including by means of setting up agencies, subsidiaries, branches or offices, except where an authorisation for each individual establishment or a limitation of the authorisation to a certain part of the territory is justified by an overriding reason relating to the public interest.

14

5. The authorisation shall be granted as soon as it is established, in the light of an appropriate examination, that the conditions for authorisation have been met.

6. Except in the case of the granting of an authorisation, any decision from the competent authorities, including refusal or withdrawal of an authorisation, shall be fully reasoned and shall be open to challenge before the courts or other instances of appeal.

7. This Article shall not call into question the allocation of the competences, at local or regional level, of the Member States' authorities granting authorisations.

Article 11
Duration of authorisation

1. An authorisation granted to a provider shall not be for a limited period, except where:
   (a) the authorisation is being automatically renewed or is subject only to the continued fulfilment of requirements;
   (b) the number of available authorisations is limited by an overriding reason relating to the public interest; or
   (c) a limited authorisation period can be justified by an overriding reason relating to the public interest.

2. Paragraph 1 shall not concern the maximum period before the end of which the provider must actually commence his activity after receiving authorisation.

3. Member States shall require a provider to inform the relevant point of single contact provided for in Article 6 of the following changes:
   (a) the creation of subsidiaries whose activities fall within the scope of the authorisation scheme;
   (b) changes in his situation which result in the conditions for authorisation no longer being met.

4. This Article shall be without prejudice to the Member States' ability to revoke authorisations, when the conditions for authorisation are no longer met.

Article 12
Selection from among several candidates

1. Where the number of authorisations available for a given activity is limited because of the scarcity of available natural resources or technical capacity, Member States shall apply a selection procedure to potential candidates which provides full guarantees of impartiality and transparency, including, in particular, adequate publicity about the launch, conduct and completion of the procedure.

2. In the cases referred to in paragraph 1, authorisation shall be granted for an appropriate limited period and may not be open to automatic renewal nor confer any other advantage on the provider whose authorisation has just expired or on any person having any particular links with that provider.

3. Subject to paragraph 1 and to Articles 9 and 10, Member States may take into account, in establishing the rules for the selection procedure, considerations of public health, social policy objectives, the health and safety of employees or self-employed persons, the protection of the environment, the preservation of cultural heritage and other overriding reasons relating to the public interest, in conformity with [Union] law.

Article 13
Authorisation procedures

1. Authorisation procedures and formalities shall be clear, made public in advance and be such as to provide the applicants with a guarantee that their application will be dealt with objectively and impartially.

2. Authorisation procedures and formalities shall not be dissuasive and shall not unduly complicate or delay the provision of the service. They shall be easily accessible and any charges which the applicants may incur from their application shall be reasonable and proportionate to the cost of the authorisation procedures in question and shall not exceed the cost of the procedures.

3. Authorisation procedures and formalities shall provide applicants with a guarantee that their application will be processed as quickly as possible and, in any event, within a reasonable period which is fixed and made public in advance. The period shall run only from the time when all documentation has been submitted. When justified by the complexity of the issue, the time period may be extended once, by the competent authority, for a limited time. The extension and its duration shall be duly motivated and shall be notified to the applicant before the original period has expired.

4. Failing a response within the time period set or extended in accordance with paragraph 3, authorisation shall be deemed to have been granted. Different arrangements may nevertheless be put in place, where justified by overriding reasons relating to the public interest, including a legitimate interest of third parties.

5. All applications for authorisation shall be acknowledged as quickly as possible. The acknowledgement must specify the following:
   (a) the period referred to in paragraph 3;
   (b) the available means of redress;
   (c) where applicable, a statement that in the absence of a response within the period specified, the authorisation shall be deemed to have been granted.

6. In the case of an incomplete application, the applicant shall be informed as quickly as possible of the need to supply any additional documentation, as well as of any possible effects on the period referred to in paragraph 3.

7. When a request is rejected because it fails to comply with the required procedures or formalities, the applicant shall be informed of the rejection as quickly as possible.

SECTION 2 REQUIREMENTS PROHIBITED OR SUBJECT TO EVALUATION

Article 14
Prohibited requirements

Member States shall not make access to, or the exercise of, a service activity in their territory subject to compliance with any of the following:

(1) discriminatory requirements based directly or indirectly on nationality or, in the case of companies, the location of the registered office, including in particular:
   (a) nationality requirements for the provider, his staff, persons holding the share capital or members of the provider's management or supervisory bodies;
   (b) a requirement that the provider, his staff, persons holding the share capital or members of the provider's management or supervisory bodies be resident within the territory;

(2) a prohibition on having an establishment in more than one Member State or on being entered in the registers or enrolled with professional bodies or associations of more than one Member State;

(3) restrictions on the freedom of a provider to choose between a principal or a secondary establishment, in particular an obligation on the provider to have its principal establishment in their territory, or restrictions on the freedom to choose between establishment in the form of an agency, branch or subsidiary;

(4) conditions of reciprocity with the Member State in which the provider already has an establishment, save in the case of conditions of reciprocity provided for in [Union] instruments concerning energy;

(5) the case-by-case application of an economic test making the granting of authorisation subject to proof of the existence of an economic need or market demand, an assessment of the potential or current economic effects of the activity or an assessment of the appropriateness of the activity in relation to the economic planning objectives set by the competent authority; this prohibition shall not concern planning requirements which do not pursue economic aims but serve overriding reasons relating to the public interest;

(6) the direct or indirect involvement of competing operators, including within consultative bodies, in the granting of authorisations or in the adoption of other decisions of the competent authorities, with the exception of professional bodies and associations or other organisations acting as the competent authority; this prohibition shall not concern the consultation of organisations, such as chambers of commerce or social partners, on matters other than individual applications for authorisation, or a consultation of the public at large;

(7) an obligation to provide or participate in a financial guarantee or to take out insurance from a provider or body established in their territory. This shall not affect the possibility for Member States to require insurance or financial guarantees as such, nor shall it affect requirements relating to the participation in a collective compensation fund, for instance for members of professional bodies or organisations;

(8) an obligation to have been pre-registered, for a given period, in the registers held in their territory or to have previously exercised the activity for a given period in their territory.

Article 15
Requirements to be evaluated

1. Member States shall examine whether, under their legal system, any of the requirements listed in paragraph 2 are imposed and shall ensure that any such requirements are compatible with the conditions laid down in paragraph 3. Member States shall adapt their laws, regulations or administrative provisions so as to make them compatible with those conditions.

2. Member States shall examine whether their legal system makes access to a service activity or the exercise of it subject to compliance with any of the following non-discriminatory requirements:

   (a) quantitative or territorial restrictions, in particular in the form of limits fixed according to population or of a minimum geographical distance between providers;

(b) an obligation on a provider to take a specific legal form;

(c) requirements which relate to the shareholding of a company;

(d) requirements, other than those concerning matters covered by Directive 2005/36/EC or provided for in other [Union] instruments, which reserve access to the service activity in question to particular providers by virtue of the specific nature of the activity;

(e) a ban on having more than one establishment in the territory of the same State;

(f) requirements fixing a minimum number of employees;

(g) fixed minimum and/or maximum tariffs with which the provider must comply;

(h) an obligation on the provider to supply other specific services jointly with his service.

3. Member States shall verify that the requirements referred to in paragraph 2 satisfy the following conditions:

(a) non-discrimination: requirements must be neither directly nor indirectly discriminatory according to nationality nor, with regard to companies, according to the location of the registered office;

(b) necessity: requirements must be justified by an overriding reason relating to the public interest;

(c) proportionality: requirements must be suitable for securing the attainment of the objective pursued; they must not go beyond what is necessary to attain that objective and it must not be possible to replace those requirements with other, less restrictive measures which attain the same result.

4. Paragraphs 1, 2 and 3 shall apply to legislation in the field of services of general economic interest only insofar as the application of these paragraphs does not obstruct the performance, in law or in fact, of the particular task assigned to them.

5. In the mutual evaluation report provided for in Article 39(1), Member States shall specify the following:

(a) the requirements that they intend to maintain and the reasons why they consider that those requirements comply with the conditions set out in paragraph 3;

(b) the requirements which have been abolished or made less stringent.

6. From 28 December 2006 Member States shall not introduce any new requirement of a kind listed in paragraph 2, unless that requirement satisfies the conditions laid down in paragraph 3.

7. Member States shall notify the Commission of any new laws, regulations or administrative provisions which set requirements as referred to in paragraph 6, together with the reasons for those requirements. The Commission shall communicate the provisions concerned to the other Member States. Such notification shall not prevent Member States from adopting the provisions in question.

Within a period of 3 months from the date of receipt of the notification, the Commission shall examine the compatibility of any new requirements with [Union] law and, where appropriate, shall adopt a decision requesting the Member State in question to refrain from adopting them or to abolish them.

The notification of a draft national law in accordance with Directive 98/34/EC shall fulfil the obligation of notification provided for in this Directive.

14

Chapter IV Free Movement of Services

SECTION 1 FREEDOM TO PROVIDE SERVICES AND RELATED DEROGATIONS

Article 16
Freedom to provide services

1. Member States shall respect the right of providers to provide services in a Member State other than that in which they are established.

   The Member State in which the service is provided shall ensure free access to and free exercise of a service activity within its territory.

   Member States shall not make access to or exercise of a service activity in their territory subject to compliance with any requirements which do not respect the following principles:

   (a) non-discrimination: the requirement may be neither directly nor indirectly discriminatory with regard to nationality or, in the case of legal persons, with regard to the Member State in which they are established;

   (b) necessity: the requirement must be justified for reasons of public policy, public security, public health or the protection of the environment;

   (c) proportionality: the requirement must be suitable for attaining the objective pursued, and must not go beyond what is necessary to attain that objective.

2. Member States may not restrict the freedom to provide services in the case of a provider established in another Member State by imposing any of the following requirements:

   (a) an obligation on the provider to have an establishment in their territory;

   (b) an obligation on the provider to obtain an authorisation from their competent authorities including entry in a register or registration with a professional body or association in their territory, except where provided for in this Directive or other instruments of [Union] law;

   (c) a ban on the provider setting up a certain form or type of infrastructure in their territory, including an office or chambers, which the provider needs in order to supply the services in question;

   (d) the application of specific contractual arrangements between the provider and the recipient which prevent or restrict service provision by the self-employed;

   (e) an obligation on the provider to possess an identity document issued by its competent authorities specific to the exercise of a service activity;

   (f) requirements, except for those necessary for health and safety at work, which affect the use of equipment and material which are an integral part of the service provided;

   (g) restrictions on the freedom to provide the services referred to in Article 19.

3. The Member State to which the provider moves shall not be prevented from imposing requirements with regard to the provision of a service activity, where they are justified for reasons of public policy, public security, public health or the protection of the environment and in accordance with paragraph 1. Nor shall that Member State be prevented from applying, in accordance with [Union] law, its rules on employment conditions, including those laid down in collective agreements.

4. By 28 December 2011 the Commission shall, after consultation of the Member States and the social partners at [Union] level, submit to the European Parliament and the

Council a report on the application of this Article, in which it shall consider the need to propose harmonisation measures regarding service activities covered by this Directive.

Article 17
Additional derogations from the freedom to provide services
Article 16 shall not apply to:

(1) services of general economic interest which are provided in another Member State, inter alia:

    (a) in the postal sector, services covered by Directive 97/67/EC of the European Parliament and of the Council of 15 December 1997 on common rules for the development of the internal market of [Union] postal services and the improvement of quality of service;

    (b) in the electricity sector, services covered by Directive 2003/54/EC of the European Parliament and of the Council of 26 June 2003 concerning common rules for the internal market in electricity;

    (c) in the gas sector, services covered by Directive 2003/55/EC of the European Parliament and of the Council of 26 June 2003 concerning common rules for the internal market in natural gas;

    (d) water distribution and supply services and waste water services;

    (e) treatment of waste;

(2) matters covered by Directive 96/71/EC;

(3) matters covered by Directive 95/46/EC of the European Parliament and of the Council of 24 October 1995 on the protection of individuals with regard to the processing of personal data and on the free movement of such data;

(4) matters covered by Council Directive 77/249/EEC of 22 March 1977 to facilitate the effective exercise by lawyers of freedom to provide services;

(5) the activity of judicial recovery of debts;

(6) matters covered by Title II of Directive 2005/36/EC, as well as requirements in the Member State where the service is provided which reserve an activity to a particular profession;

(7) matters covered by Regulation (EEC) No. 1408/71;

(8) as regards administrative formalities concerning the free movement of persons and their residence, matters covered by the provisions of Directive 2004/38/EC that lay down administrative formalities of the competent authorities of the Member State where the service is provided with which beneficiaries must comply;

(9) as regards third country nationals who move to another Member State in the context of the provision of a service, the possibility for Member States to require visa or residence permits for third country nationals who are not covered by the mutual recognition regime provided for in Article 21 of the Convention implementing the Schengen Agreement of 14 June 1985 on the gradual abolition of checks at the common borders or the possibility to oblige third country nationals to report to the competent authorities of the Member State in which the service is provided on or after their entry;

(10) as regards the shipment of waste, matters covered by Council Regulation (EEC) No. 259/93 of 1 February 1993 on the supervision and control of shipments of waste within, into and out of the European [Union];

14

(11) copyright, neighbouring rights and rights covered by Council Directive 87/54/EEC of 16 December 1986 on the legal protection of topographies of semiconductor products and by Directive 96/9/EC of the European Parliament and of the Council of 11 March 1996 on the legal protection of databases as well as industrial property rights;

(12) acts requiring by law the involvement of a notary;

(13) matters covered by Directive 2006/43/EC of the European Parliament and of the Council of 17 May 2006 on statutory audit of annual accounts and consolidated accounts;

(14) the registration of vehicles leased in another Member State;

(15) provisions regarding contractual and non-contractual obligations, including the form of contracts, determined pursuant to the rules of private international law.

Article 18
Case-by-case derogations

1. By way of derogation from Article 16, and in exceptional circumstances only, a Member State may, in respect of a provider established in another Member State, take measures relating to the safety of services.

2. The measures provided for in paragraph 1 may be taken only if the mutual assistance procedure laid down in Article 35 is complied with and the following conditions are fulfilled:

   (a) the national provisions in accordance with which the measure is taken have not been subject to [Union] harmonisation in the field of the safety of services;

   (b) the measures provide for a higher level of protection of the recipient than would be the case in a measure taken by the Member State of establishment in accordance with its national provisions;

   (c) the Member State of establishment has not taken any measures or has taken measures which are insufficient as compared with those referred to in Article 35(2);

   (d) the measures are proportionate.

3. Paragraphs 1 and 2 shall be without prejudice to provisions, laid down in [Union] instruments, which guarantee the freedom to provide services or which allow derogations therefrom.

SECTION 2 RIGHTS OF RECIPIENTS OF SERVICES

Article 19
Prohibited restrictions

Member States may not impose on a recipient requirements which restrict the use of a service supplied by a provider established in another Member State, in particular the following requirements:

   (a) an obligation to obtain authorisation from or to make a declaration to their competent authorities;

   (b) discriminatory limits on the grant of financial assistance by reason of the fact that the provider is established in another Member State or by reason of the location of the place at which the service is provided.

Article 20
Non-discrimination

1. Member States shall ensure that the recipient is not made subject to discriminatory requirements based on his nationality or place of residence.
2. Member States shall ensure that the general conditions of access to a service, which are made available to the public at large by the provider, do not contain discriminatory provisions relating to the nationality or place of residence of the recipient, but without precluding the possibility of providing for differences in the conditions of access where those differences are directly justified by objective criteria.

Article 21
Assistance for recipients

1. Member States shall ensure that recipients can obtain, in their Member State of residence, the following information:
   (a) general information on the requirements applicable in other Member States relating to access to, and exercise of, service activities, in particular those relating to consumer protection;
   (b) general information on the means of redress available in the case of a dispute between a provider and a recipient;
   (c) the contact details of associations or organisations, including the centres of the European Consumer Centres Network, from which providers or recipients may obtain practical assistance.

   Where appropriate, advice from the competent authorities shall include a simple step-by-step guide. Information and assistance shall be provided in a clear and unambiguous manner, shall be easily accessible at a distance, including by electronic means, and shall be kept up to date.
2. Member States may confer responsibility for the task referred to in paragraph 1 on points of single contact or on any other body, such as the centres of the European Consumer Centres Network, consumer associations or Euro Info Centres. Member States shall communicate to the Commission the names and contact details of the designated bodies. The Commission shall transmit them to all Member States.
3. In fulfilment of the requirements set out in paragraphs 1 and 2, the body approached by the recipient shall, if necessary, contact the relevant body for the Member State concerned. The latter shall send the information requested as soon as possible to the requesting body which shall forward the information to the recipient. Member States shall ensure that those bodies give each other mutual assistance and shall put in place all possible measures for effective cooperation. Together with the Commission, Member States shall put in place practical arrangements necessary for the implementation of paragraph 1.
4. The Commission shall, in accordance with the procedure referred to in Article 40(2), adopt measures for the implementation of paragraphs 1, 2 and 3 of this Article, specifying the technical mechanisms for the exchange of information between the bodies of the various Member States and, in particular, the interoperability of information systems, taking into account common standards.

14

Chapter V Quality of Services

Article 22
Information on providers and their services

1. Member States shall ensure that providers make the following information available to the recipient:

   (a) the name of the provider, his legal status and form, the geographic address at which he is established and details enabling him to be contacted rapidly and communicated with directly and, as the case may be, by electronic means;

   (b) where the provider is registered in a trade or other similar public register, the name of that register and the provider's registration number, or equivalent means of identification in that register;

   (c) where the activity is subject to an authorisation scheme, the particulars of the relevant competent authority or the single point of contact;

   (d) where the provider exercises an activity which is subject to VAT, the identification number referred to in Article 22(1) of Sixth Council Directive 77/388/EEC of 17 May 1977 on the harmonisation of the laws of the Member States relating to turnover taxes – Common system of value added tax: uniform basis of assessment;

   (e) in the case of the regulated professions, any professional body or similar institution with which the provider is registered, the professional title and the Member State in which that title has been granted;

   (f) the general conditions and clauses, if any, used by the provider;

   (g) the existence of contractual clauses, if any, used by the provider concerning the law applicable to the contract and/or the competent courts;

   (h) the existence of an after-sales guarantee, if any, not imposed by law;

   (i) the price of the service, where a price is pre-determined by the provider for a given type of service;

   (j) the main features of the service, if not already apparent from the context;

   (k) the insurance or guarantees referred to in Article 23(1), and in particular the contact details of the insurer or guarantor and the territorial coverage.

2. Member States shall ensure that the information referred to in paragraph 1, according to the provider's preference:

   (a) is supplied by the provider on his own initiative;

   (b) is easily accessible to the recipient at the place where the service is provided or the contract concluded;

   (c) can be easily accessed by the recipient electronically by means of an address supplied by the provider;

   (d) appears in any information documents supplied to the recipient by the provider which set out a detailed description of the service he provides.

3. Member States shall ensure that, at the recipient's request, providers supply the following additional information:

   (a) where the price is not pre-determined by the provider for a given type of service, the price of the service or, if an exact price cannot be given, the method for calculating the price so that it can be checked by the recipient, or a sufficiently detailed estimate;

14

(b) as regards the regulated professions, a reference to the professional rules applicable in the Member State of establishment and how to access them;

(c) information on their multidisciplinary activities and partnerships which are directly linked to the service in question and on the measures taken to avoid conflicts of interest. That information shall be included in any information document in which providers give a detailed description of their services;

(d) any codes of conduct to which the provider is subject and the address at which these codes may be consulted by electronic means, specifying the language version available;

(e) where a provider is subject to a code of conduct, or member of a trade association or professional body which provides for recourse to a non-judicial means of dispute settlement, information in this respect. The provider shall specify how to access detailed information on the characteristics of, and conditions for, the use of non-judicial means of dispute settlement.

4. Member States shall ensure that the information which a provider must supply in accordance with this Chapter is made available or communicated in a clear and unambiguous manner, and in good time before conclusion of the contract or, where there is no written contract, before the service is provided.

5. The information requirements laid down in this Chapter are in addition to requirements already provided for in [Union] law and do not prevent Member States from imposing additional information requirements applicable to providers established in their territory.

6. The Commission may, in accordance with the procedure referred to in Article 40(2), specify the content of the information provided for in paragraphs 1 and 3 of this Article according to the specific nature of certain activities and may specify the practical means of implementing paragraph 2 of this Article.

Article 23
Professional liability insurance and guarantees

1. Member States may ensure that providers whose services present a direct and particular risk to the health or safety of the recipient or a third person, or to the financial security of the recipient, subscribe to professional liability insurance appropriate to the nature and extent of the risk, or provide a guarantee or similar arrangement which is equivalent or essentially comparable as regards its purpose.

2. When a provider establishes himself in their territory, Member States may not require professional liability insurance or a guarantee from the provider where he is already covered by a guarantee which is equivalent, or essentially comparable as regards its purpose and the cover it provides in terms of the insured risk, the insured sum or a ceiling for the guarantee and possible exclusions from the cover, in another Member State in which the provider is already established. Where equivalence is only partial, Member States may require a supplementary guarantee to cover those aspects not already covered.

When a Member State requires a provider established in its territory to subscribe to professional liability insurance or to provide another guarantee, that Member State shall accept as sufficient evidence attestations of such insurance cover issued by credit institutions and insurers established in other Member States.

3. Paragraphs 1 and 2 shall not affect professional insurance or guarantee arrangements provided for in other [Union] instruments.

4. For the implementation of paragraph 1, the Commission may, in accordance with the regulatory procedure referred to in Article 40(2), establish a list of services which exhibit the characteristics referred to in paragraph 1 of this Article. The Commission may also, in accordance with the procedure referred to in Article 40(3), adopt measures designed to amend non-essential elements of this Directive by supplementing it by establishing common criteria for defining, for the purposes of the insurance or guarantees referred to in paragraph 1 of this Article, what is appropriate to the nature and extent of the risk.

5. For the purpose of this Article[:]
   — 'direct and particular risk' means a risk arising directly from the provision of the service,
   — 'health and safety' means, in relation to a recipient or a third person, the prevention of death or serious personal injury,
   — 'financial security' means, in relation to a recipient, the prevention of substantial losses of money or of value of property,
   — 'professional liability insurance' means insurance taken out by a provider in respect of potential liabilities to recipients and, where applicable, third parties arising out of the provision of the service.

Article 24

Commercial communications by the regulated professions

1. Member States shall remove all total prohibitions on commercial communications by the regulated professions.

2. Member States shall ensure that commercial communications by the regulated professions comply with professional rules, in conformity with [Union] law, which relate, in particular, to the independence, dignity and integrity of the profession, as well as to professional secrecy, in a manner consistent with the specific nature of each profession. Professional rules on commercial communications shall be non-discriminatory, justified by an overriding reason relating to the public interest and proportionate.

Article 25

Multidisciplinary activities

1. Member States shall ensure that providers are not made subject to requirements which oblige them to exercise a given specific activity exclusively or which restrict the exercise jointly or in partnership of different activities.

   However, the following providers may be made subject to such requirements:
   (a) the regulated professions, in so far as is justified in order to guarantee compliance with the rules governing professional ethics and conduct, which vary according to the specific nature of each profession, and is necessary in order to ensure their independence and impartiality;
   (b) providers of certification, accreditation, technical monitoring, test or trial services, in so far as is justified in order to ensure their independence and impartiality.

2. Where multidisciplinary activities between providers referred to in points (a) and (b) of paragraph 1 are authorised, Member States shall ensure the following:

(a) that conflicts of interest and incompatibilities between certain activities are prevented;

(b) that the independence and impartiality required for certain activities is secured;

(c) that the rules governing professional ethics and conduct for different activities are compatible with one another, especially as regards matters of professional secrecy.

3. In the report referred to in Article 39(1), Member States shall indicate which providers are subject to the requirements laid down in paragraph 1 of this Article, the content of those requirements and the reasons for which they consider them to be justified.

Article 26

Policy on quality of services

1. Member States shall, in cooperation with the Commission, take accompanying measures to encourage providers to take action on a voluntary basis in order to ensure the quality of service provision, in particular through use of one of the following methods:

   (a) certification or assessment of their activities by independent or accredited bodies;

   (b) drawing up their own quality charter or participation in quality charters or labels drawn up by professional bodies at [Union] level.

2. Member States shall ensure that information on the significance of certain labels and the criteria for applying labels and other quality marks relating to services can be easily accessed by providers and recipients.

3. Member States shall, in cooperation with the Commission, take accompanying measures to encourage professional bodies, as well as chambers of commerce and craft associations and consumer associations, in their territory to cooperate at [Union] level in order to promote the quality of service provision, especially by making it easier to assess the competence of a provider.

4. Member States shall, in cooperation with the Commission, take accompanying measures to encourage the development of independent assessments, notably by consumer associations, in relation to the quality and defects of service provision, and, in particular, the development at [Union] level of comparative trials or testing and the communication of the results.

5. Member States, in cooperation with the Commission, shall encourage the development of voluntary European standards with the aim of facilitating compatibility between services supplied by providers in different Member States, information to the recipient and the quality of service provision.

Article 27

Settlement of disputes

1. Member States shall take the general measures necessary to ensure that providers supply contact details, in particular a postal address, fax number or e-mail address and telephone number to which all recipients, including those resident in another Member State, can send a complaint or a request for information about the service provided. Providers shall supply their legal address if this is not their usual address for correspondence.

   Member States shall take the general measures necessary to ensure that providers respond to the complaints referred to in the first subparagraph in the shortest possible time and make their best efforts to find a satisfactory solution.

14

2. Member States shall take the general measures necessary to ensure that providers are obliged to demonstrate compliance with the obligations laid down in this Directive as to the provision of information and to demonstrate that the information is accurate.

3. Where a financial guarantee is required for compliance with a judicial decision, Member States shall recognise equivalent guarantees lodged with a credit institution or insurer established in another Member State. Such credit institutions must be authorised in a Member State in accordance with Directive 2006/48/EC and such insurers in accordance, as appropriate, with First Council Directive 73/239/EEC of 24 July 1973 on the coordination of laws, regulations and administrative provisions relating to the taking-up and pursuit of the business of direct insurance other than life assurance and Directive 2002/83/EC of the European Parliament and of the Council of 5 November 2002 concerning life assurance.

4. Member States shall take the general measures necessary to ensure that providers who are subject to a code of conduct, or are members of a trade association or professional body, which provides for recourse to a non-judicial means of dispute settlement inform the recipient thereof and mention that fact in any document which presents their services in detail, specifying how to access detailed information on the characteristics of, and conditions for, the use of such a mechanism.

Chapter VI Administrative Cooperation

Article 28
Mutual assistance – general obligations

1. Member States shall give each other mutual assistance, and shall put in place measures for effective cooperation with one another, in order to ensure the supervision of providers and the services they provide.

2. For the purposes of this Chapter, Member States shall designate one or more liaison points, the contact details of which shall be communicated to the other Member States and the Commission. The Commission shall publish and regularly update the list of liaison points.

3. Information requests and requests to carry out any checks, inspections and investigations under this Chapter shall be duly motivated, in particular by specifying the reason for the request. Information exchanged shall be used only in respect of the matter for which it was requested.

4. In the event of receiving a request for assistance from competent authorities in another Member State, Member States shall ensure that providers established in their territory supply their competent authorities with all the information necessary for supervising their activities in compliance with their national laws.

5. In the event of difficulty in meeting a request for information or in carrying out checks, inspections or investigations, the Member State in question shall rapidly inform the requesting Member State with a view to finding a solution.

6. Member States shall supply the information requested by other Member States or the Commission by electronic means and within the shortest possible period of time.

7. Member States shall ensure that registers in which providers have been entered, and which may be consulted by the competent authorities in their territory, may also

be consulted, in accordance with the same conditions, by the equivalent competent authorities of the other Member States.

8. Member States shall communicate to the Commission information on cases where other Member States do not fulfil their obligation of mutual assistance. Where necessary, the Commission shall take appropriate steps, including proceedings provided for in Article [258] of the Treaty, in order to ensure that the Member States concerned comply with their obligation of mutual assistance. The Commission shall periodically inform Member States about the functioning of the mutual assistance provisions.

Article 29

Mutual assistance – general obligations for the Member State of establishment

1. With respect to providers providing services in another Member State, the Member State of establishment shall supply information on providers established in its territory when requested to do so by another Member State and, in particular, confirmation that a provider is established in its territory and, to its knowledge, is not exercising his activities in an unlawful manner.

2. The Member State of establishment shall undertake the checks, inspections and investigations requested by another Member State and shall inform the latter of the results and, as the case may be, of the measures taken. In so doing, the competent authorities shall act to the extent permitted by the powers vested in them in their Member State. The competent authorities can decide on the most appropriate measures to be taken in each individual case in order to meet the request by another Member State.

3. Upon gaining actual knowledge of any conduct or specific acts by a provider established in its territory which provides services in other Member States, that, to its knowledge, could cause serious damage to the health or safety of persons or to the environment, the Member State of establishment shall inform all other Member States and the Commission within the shortest possible period of time.

Article 30

Supervision by the Member State of establishment in the event of the temporary movement of a provider to another Member State

1. With respect to cases not covered by Article 31(1), the Member State of establishment shall ensure that compliance with its requirements is supervised in conformity with the powers of supervision provided for in its national law, in particular through supervisory measures at the place of establishment of the provider.

2. The Member State of establishment shall not refrain from taking supervisory or enforcement measures in its territory on the grounds that the service has been provided or caused damage in another Member State.

3. The obligation laid down in paragraph 1 shall not entail a duty on the part of the Member State of establishment to carry out factual checks and controls in the territory of the Member State where the service is provided. Such checks and controls shall be carried out by the authorities of the Member State where the provider is temporarily operating at the request of the authorities of the Member State of establishment, in accordance with Article 31.

14

Article 31

Supervision by the Member State where the service is provided in the event of the temporary movement of the provider

1. With respect to national requirements which may be imposed pursuant to Articles 16 or 17, the Member State where the service is provided is responsible for the supervision of the activity of the provider in its territory. In conformity with [Union] law, the Member State where the service is provided:

    (a) shall take all measures necessary to ensure the provider complies with those requirements as regards the access to and the exercise of the activity;

    (b) shall carry out the checks, inspections and investigations necessary to supervise the service provided.

2. With respect to requirements other than those referred to in paragraph 1, where a provider moves temporarily to another Member State in order to provide a service without being established there, the competent authorities of that Member State shall participate in the supervision of the provider in accordance with paragraphs 3 and 4.

3. At the request of the Member State of establishment, the competent authorities of the Member State where the service is provided shall carry out any checks, inspections and investigations necessary for ensuring the effective supervision by the Member State of establishment. In so doing, the competent authorities shall act to the extent permitted by the powers vested in them in their Member State. The competent authorities may decide on the most appropriate measures to be taken in each individual case in order to meet the request by the Member State of establishment.

4. On their own initiative, the competent authorities of the Member State where the service is provided may conduct checks, inspections and investigations on the spot, provided that those checks, inspections or investigations are not discriminatory, are not motivated by the fact that the provider is established in another Member State and are proportionate.

Article 32

Alert mechanism

1. Where a Member State becomes aware of serious specific acts or circumstances relating to a service activity that could cause serious damage to the health or safety of persons or to the environment in its territory or in the territory of other Member States, that Member State shall inform the Member State of establishment, the other Member States concerned and the Commission within the shortest possible period of time.

2. The Commission shall promote and take part in the operation of a European network of Member States' authorities in order to implement paragraph 1.

3. The Commission shall adopt and regularly update, in accordance with the procedure referred to in Article 40(2), detailed rules concerning the management of the network referred to in paragraph 2 of this Article.

Article 33

Information on the good repute of providers

1. Member States shall, at the request of a competent authority in another Member State, supply information, in conformity with their national law, on disciplinary or administrative actions or criminal sanctions and decisions concerning insolvency or bankruptcy involving fraud taken by their competent authorities in respect of the provider

which are directly relevant to the provider's competence or professional reliability. The Member State which supplies the information shall inform the provider thereof.

A request made pursuant to the first subparagraph must be duly substantiated, in particular as regards the reasons for the request for information.

2. Sanctions and actions referred to in paragraph 1 shall only be communicated if a final decision has been taken. With regard to other enforceable decisions referred to in paragraph 1, the Member State which supplies the information shall specify whether a particular decision is final or whether an appeal has been lodged in respect of it, in which case the Member State in question should provide an indication of the date when the decision on appeal is expected.

Moreover, that Member State shall specify the provisions of national law pursuant to which the provider was found guilty or penalised.

3. Implementation of paragraphs 1 and 2 must comply with rules on the provision of personal data and with rights guaranteed to persons found guilty or penalised in the Member States concerned, including by professional bodies. Any information in question which is public shall be accessible to consumers.

Article 34

Accompanying measures

1. The Commission, in cooperation with Member States, shall establish an electronic system for the exchange of information between Member States, taking into account existing information systems.

2. Member States shall, with the assistance of the Commission, take accompanying measures to facilitate the exchange of officials in charge of the implementation of mutual assistance and training of such officials, including language and computer training.

3. The Commission shall assess the need to establish a multi-annual programme in order to organise relevant exchanges of officials and training.

Article 35

Mutual assistance in the event of case-by-case derogations

1. Where a Member State intends to take a measure pursuant to Article 18, the procedure laid down in paragraphs 2 to 6 of this Article shall apply without prejudice to court proceedings, including preliminary proceedings and acts carried out in the framework of a criminal investigation.

2. The Member State referred to in paragraph 1 shall ask the Member State of establishment to take measures with regard to the provider, supplying all relevant information on the service in question and the circumstances of the case.

The Member State of establishment shall check, within the shortest possible period of time, whether the provider is operating lawfully and verify the facts underlying the request. It shall inform the requesting Member State within the shortest possible period of time of the measures taken or envisaged or, as the case may be, the reasons why it has not taken any measures.

3. Following communication by the Member State of establishment as provided for in the second subparagraph of paragraph 2, the requesting Member State shall notify the Commission and the Member State of establishment of its intention to take measures, stating the following:

14

(a) the reasons why it believes the measures taken or envisaged by the Member State of establishment are inadequate;

(b) the reasons why it believes the measures it intends to take fulfil the conditions laid down in Article 18.

4. The measures may not be taken until fifteen working days after the date of notification provided for in paragraph 3.

5. Without prejudice to the possibility for the requesting Member State to take the measures in question upon expiry of the period specified in paragraph 4, the Commission shall, within the shortest possible period of time, examine the compatibility with [Union] law of the measures notified.

Where the Commission concludes that the measure is incompatible with [Union] law, it shall adopt a decision asking the Member State concerned to refrain from taking the proposed measures or to put an end to the measures in question as a matter of urgency.

6. In the case of urgency, a Member State which intends to take a measure may derogate from paragraphs 2, 3 and 4. In such cases, the measures shall be notified within the shortest possible period of time to the Commission and the Member State of establishment, stating the reasons for which the Member State considers that there is urgency.

Article 36
Implementing measures

In accordance with the procedure referred to in Article 40(3), the Commission shall adopt the implementing measures designed to amend non-essential elements of this Chapter by supplementing it by specifying the time-limits provided for in Articles 28 and 35. The Commission shall also adopt, in accordance with the procedure referred to in Article 40(2), the practical arrangements for the exchange of information by electronic means between Member States, and in particular the interoperability provisions for information systems.

Chapter VII Convergence Programme

Article 37
Codes of conduct at [Union] level

1. Member States shall, in cooperation with the Commission, take accompanying measures to encourage the drawing up at [Union] level, particularly by professional bodies, organisations and associations, of codes of conduct aimed at facilitating the provision of services or the establishment of a provider in another Member State, in conformity with [Union] law.

2. Member States shall ensure that the codes of conduct referred to in paragraph 1 are accessible at a distance, by electronic means.

Article 38
Additional harmonisation

The Commission shall assess, by 28 December 2010 the possibility of presenting proposals for harmonisation instruments on the following subjects:

(a) access to the activity of judicial recovery of debts;

(b) private security services and transport of cash and valuables.

Article 39
Mutual evaluation
1. By 28 December 2009 at the latest, Member States shall present a report to the Commission, containing the information specified in the following provisions:
   (a) Article 9(2), on authorisation schemes;
   (b) Article 15(5), on requirements to be evaluated;
   (c) Article 25(3), on multidisciplinary activities.
2. The Commission shall forward the reports provided for in paragraph 1 to the Member States, which shall submit their observations on each of the reports within six months of receipt. Within the same period, the Commission shall consult interested parties on those reports.
3. The Commission shall present the reports and the Member States' observations to the Committee referred to in Article 40(1), which may make observations.
4. In the light of the observations provided for in paragraphs 2 and 3, the Commission shall, by 28 December 2010 at the latest, present a summary report to the European Parliament and to the Council, accompanied where appropriate by proposals for additional initiatives.
5. By 28 December 2009 at the latest, Member States shall present a report to the Commission on the national requirements whose application could fall under the third subparagraph of Article 16(1) and the first sentence of Article 16(3), providing reasons why they consider that the application of those requirements fulfil the criteria referred to in the third subparagraph of Article 16(1) and the first sentence of Article 16(3).

   Thereafter, Member States shall transmit to the Commission any changes in their requirements, including new requirements, as referred to above, together with the reasons for them.

   The Commission shall communicate the transmitted requirements to other Member States. Such transmission shall not prevent the adoption by Member States of the provisions in question. The Commission shall on an annual basis thereafter provide analyses and orientations on the application of these provisions in the context of this Directive.

Article 40
Committee procedure
1. The Commission shall be assisted by a Committee.
2. Where reference is made to this paragraph, Articles 5 and 7 of Decision 1999/468/EC shall apply, having regard to the provisions of Article 8 thereof. The period laid down in Article 5(6) of Decision 1999/468/EC shall be set at three months.
3. Where reference is made to this paragraph, Article 5a(1) to (4), and Article 7 of Decision 1999/468/EC shall apply, having regard to the provisions of Article 8 thereof.

Article 41
Review clause
The Commission, by 28 December 2011 and every three years thereafter, shall present to the European Parliament and to the Council a comprehensive report on the application of this Directive. This report shall, in accordance with Article 16(4), address in particular the application of Article 16. It shall also consider the need for additional measures for

matters excluded from the scope of application of this Directive. It shall be accompanied, where appropriate, by proposals for amendment of this Directive with a view to completing the Internal Market for services.

Article 42
Amendment of Directive 98/27/EC
In the Annex to Directive 98/27/EC of the European Parliament and of the Council of 19 May 1998 on injunctions for the protection of consumers' interests, the following point shall be added:

'13. Directive 2006/123/EC of the European Parliament and of the Council of 12 December 2006 on services in the internal market (OJ L 376, 27.12.2006, p. 36)'.

Article 43
Protection of personal data
The implementation and application of this Directive and, in particular, the provisions on supervision shall respect the rules on the protection of personal data as provided for in Directives 95/46/EC and 2002/58/EC.

Chapter VIII Final Provisions

Article 44
Transposition
1. Member States shall bring into force the laws, regulations and administrative provisions necessary to comply with this Directive before 28 December 2009.
   They shall forthwith communicate to the Commission the text of those measures. When Member States adopt these measures, they shall contain a reference to this Directive or shall be accompanied by such a reference on the occasion of their official publication. The methods of making such reference shall be laid down by Member States.
2. Member States shall communicate to the Commission the text of the main provisions of national law which they adopt in the field covered by this Directive.

Article 45
Entry into force
This Directive shall enter into force on the day following that of its publication in the *Official Journal of the European Union*.

Article 46
Addressees
This Directive is addressed to the Member States.

(*Signatures omitted*)

15

Directive 96/71 on the Posting of Workers in the Framework of the Provision of Services

THE EUROPEAN PARLIAMENT AND THE COUNCIL OF THE EUROPEAN UNION,

Having regard to the Treaty [on the Functioning of the European Union], and in particular Articles [53(1)] and [62] thereof,

Having regard to the proposal from the Commission,

Having regard to the opinion of the Economic and Social Committee,

Acting in accordance with the procedure laid down in Article [294] of the Treaty ...

HAVE ADOPTED THIS DIRECTIVE:

Article 1

Scope

1. This Directive shall apply to undertakings established in a Member State which, in the framework of the transnational provision of services, post workers, in accordance with paragraph 3, to the territory of a Member State.
2. This Directive shall not apply to merchant navy undertakings as regards seagoing personnel.
3. This Directive shall apply to the extent that the undertakings referred to in paragraph 1 take one of the following transnational measures:
   (a) post workers to the territory of a Member State on their account and under their direction, under a contract concluded between the undertaking making the posting and the party for whom the services are intended, operating in that Member State, provided there is an employment relationship between the undertaking making the posting and the worker during the period of posting; or
   (b) post workers to an establishment or to an undertaking owned by the group in the territory of a Member State, provided there is an employment relationship between the undertaking making the posting and the worker during the period of posting; or
   (c) being a temporary employment undertaking or placement agency, hire out a worker to a user undertaking established or operating in the territory of a Member State, provided there is an employment relationship between the temporary employment undertaking or placement agency and the worker during the period of posting.
4. Undertakings established in a non-member State must not be given more favourable treatment than undertakings established in a Member State.

Article 2

Definition

1. For the purposes of this Directive, 'posted worker' means a worker who, for a limited period, carries out his work in the territory of a Member State other than the State in which he normally works.

2. For the purposes of this Directive, the definition of a worker is that which applies in the law of the Member State to whose territory the worker is posted.

Article 3
Terms and conditions of employment

1. Member States shall ensure that, whatever the law applicable to the employment relationship, the undertakings referred to in Article 1(1) guarantee workers posted to their territory the terms and conditions of employment covering the following matters which, in the Member State where the work is carried out, are laid down:
   — by law, regulation or administrative provision, and/or
   — by collective agreements or arbitration awards which have been declared universally applicable within the meaning of paragraph 8, insofar as they concern the activities referred to in the Annex:
     (a) maximum work periods and minimum rest periods;
     (b) minimum paid annual holidays;
     (c) the minimum rates of pay, including overtime rates; this point does not apply to supplementary occupational retirement pension schemes;
     (d) the conditions of hiring-out of workers, in particular the supply of workers by temporary employment undertakings;
     (e) health, safety and hygiene at work;
     (f) protective measures with regard to the terms and conditions of employment of pregnant women or women who have recently given birth, of children and of young people;
     (g) equality of treatment between men and women and other provisions on non-discrimination.
   For the purposes of this Directive, the concept of minimum rates of pay referred to in paragraph 1(c) is defined by the national law and/or practice of the Member State to whose territory the worker is posted.

2. In the case of initial assembly and/or first installation of goods where this is an integral part of a contract for the supply of goods and necessary for taking the goods supplied into use and carried out by the skilled and/or specialist workers of the supplying undertaking, the first subparagraph of paragraph 1(b) and (c) shall not apply, if the period of posting does not exceed eight days.
   This provision shall not apply to activities in the field of building work listed in the Annex.

3. Member States may, after consulting employers and labour, in accordance with the traditions and practices of each Member State, decide not to apply the first subparagraph of paragraph 1(c) in the cases referred to in Article 1(3)(a) and (b) when the length of the posting does not exceed one month.

4. Member States may, in accordance with national laws and/or practices, provide that exemptions may be made from the first subparagraph of paragraph 1(c) in the cases referred to in Article 1(3)(a) and (b) and from a decision by a Member State within the meaning of paragraph 3 of this Article, by means of collective agreements within the meaning of paragraph 8 of this Article, concerning one or more sectors of activity, where the length of the posting does not exceed one month.

5. Member States may provide for exemptions to be granted from the first subparagraph of paragraph 1(b) and (c) in the cases referred to in Article 1(3)(a) and (b) on the grounds that the amount of work to be done is not significant.

Member States availing themselves of the option referred to in the first subparagraph shall lay down the criteria which the work to be performed must meet in order to be considered as 'non-significant'.

6. The length of the posting shall be calculated on the basis of a reference period of one year from the beginning of the posting.

For the purpose of such calculations, account shall be taken of any previous periods for which the post has been filled by a posted worker.

7. Paragraphs 1 to 6 shall not prevent application of terms and conditions of employment which are more favourable to workers.

Allowances specific to the posting shall be considered to be part of the minimum wage, unless they are paid in reimbursement of expenditure actually incurred on account of the posting, such as expenditure on travel, board and lodging.

8. 'Collective agreements or arbitration awards which have been declared universally applicable' means collective agreements or arbitration awards which must be observed by all undertakings in the geographical area and in the profession or industry concerned.

In the absence of a system for declaring collective agreements or arbitration awards to be of universal application within the meaning of the first subparagraph, Member States may, if they so decide, base themselves on:

— collective agreements or arbitration awards which are generally applicable to all similar undertakings in the geographical area and in the profession or industry concerned, and/or

— collective agreements which have been concluded by the most representative employers' and labour organizations at national level and which are applied throughout national territory,

provided that their application to the undertakings referred to in Article 1(1) ensures equality of treatment on matters listed in the first subparagraph of paragraph 1 of this Article between those undertakings and the other undertakings referred to in this subparagraph which are in a similar position.

Equality of treatment, within the meaning of this Article, shall be deemed to exist where national undertakings in a similar position:

— are subject, in the place in question or in the sector concerned, to the same obligations as posting undertakings as regards the matters listed in the first subparagraph of paragraph 1, and

— are required to fulfil such obligations with the same effects.

9. Member States may provide that the undertakings referred to in Article 1(1) must guarantee workers referred to in Article 1(3)(c) the terms and conditions which apply to temporary workers in the Member State where the work is carried out.

10. This Directive shall not preclude the application by Member States, in compliance with the Treaty, to national undertakings and to the undertakings of other States, on a basis of equality of treatment, of:

— terms and conditions of employment on matters other than those referred to in the first subparagraph of paragraph 1 in the case of public policy provisions,

15

— terms and conditions of employment laid down in the collective agreements or arbitration awards within the meaning of paragraph 8 and concerning activities other than those referred to in the Annex.

Article 4

Cooperation on information

1. For the purposes of implementing this Directive, Member States shall, in accordance with national legislation and/or practice, designate one or more liaison offices or one or more competent national bodies.

2. Member States shall make provision for cooperation between the public authorities which, in accordance with national legislation, are responsible for monitoring the terms and conditions of employment referred to in Article 3. Such cooperation shall in particular consist in replying to reasoned requests from those authorities for information on the transnational hiring-out of workers, including manifest abuses or possible cases of unlawful transnational activities.

   The Commission and the public authorities referred to in the first subparagraph shall cooperate closely in order to examine any difficulties which might arise in the application of Article 3(10).

   Mutual administrative assistance shall be provided free of charge.

3. Each Member State shall take the appropriate measures to make the information on the terms and conditions of employment referred to in Article 3 generally available.

4. Each Member State shall notify the other Member States and the Commission of the liaison offices and/or competent bodies referred to in paragraph 1.

Article 5

Measures

Member States shall take appropriate measures in the event of failure to comply with this Directive.

They shall in particular ensure that adequate procedures are available to workers and/or their representatives for the enforcement of obligations under this Directive.

Article 6

Jurisdiction

In order to enforce the right to the terms and conditions of employment guaranteed in Article 3, judicial proceedings may be instituted in the Member State in whose territory the worker is or was posted, without prejudice, where applicable, to the right, under existing international conventions on jurisdiction, to institute proceedings in another State.

Article 7

Implementation

Member States shall adopt the laws, regulations and administrative provisions necessary to comply with this Directive by 16 December 1999 at the latest. They shall forthwith inform the Commission thereof.

When Member States adopt these provisions, they shall contain a reference to this Directive or shall be accompanied by such reference on the occasion of their official publication. The methods of making such reference shall be laid down by Member States.

Article 8

Commission review

By 16 December 2001 at the latest, the Commission shall review the operation of this Directive with a view to proposing the necessary amendments to the Council where appropriate.

Article 9

This Directive is addressed to the Member States.

(*Signatures omitted*)

ANNEX

The activities mentioned in Article 3(1), second indent, include all building work relating to the construction, repair, upkeep, alteration or demolition of buildings, and in particular the following work:

1. excavation
2. earthmoving
3. actual building work
4. assembly and dismantling of prefabricated elements
5. fitting out or installation
6. Alterations
7. Renovation
8. Repairs
9. dismantling
10. demolition
11. maintenance
12. upkeep, painting and cleaning work
13. improvements.

15

PART II
Union Secondary Law: Legislation and Other Acts

16

Regulation 330/2010 on the Application of Article 101(3) to Categories of Vertical Agreements and Concerted Practices

THE EUROPEAN COMMISSION,

Having regard to the Treaty on the Functioning of the European Union,

Having regard to Regulation No 19/65/EEC of the Council of 2 March 1965 on the application of Article [101(3)] of the Treaty to certain categories of agreements and concerted practices, and in particular Article 1 thereof,

Having published a draft of this Regulation,

After consulting the Advisory Committee on Restrictive Practices and Dominant Positions …

HAS ADOPTED THIS REGULATION:

Article 1
Definitions

1. For the purposes of this Regulation, the following definitions shall apply:
   (a) 'vertical agreement' means an agreement or concerted practice entered into between two or more undertakings each of which operates, for the purposes of the agreement or the concerted practice, at a different level of the production or distribution chain, and relating to the conditions under which the parties may purchase, sell or resell certain goods or services;
   (b) 'vertical restraint' means a restriction of competition in a vertical agreement falling within the scope of Article 101(1) of the Treaty;
   (c) 'competing undertaking' means an actual or potential competitor; 'actual competitor' means an undertaking that is active on the same relevant market; 'potential competitor' means an undertaking that, in the absence of the vertical agreement, would, on realistic grounds and not just as a mere theoretical possibility, in case of a small but permanent increase in relative prices be likely to undertake, within a short period of time, the necessary additional investments or other necessary switching costs to enter the relevant market;
   (d) 'non-compete obligation' means any direct or indirect obligation causing the buyer not to manufacture, purchase, sell or resell goods or services which compete with the contract goods or services, or any direct or indirect obligation on the buyer to purchase from the supplier or from another undertaking designated by the supplier more than 80% of the buyer's total purchases of the contract goods or services and their substitutes on the relevant market, calculated on the basis of the value or, where such is standard industry practice, the volume of its purchases in the preceding calendar year;
   (e) 'selective distribution system' means a distribution system where the supplier undertakes to sell the contract goods or services, either directly or indirectly, only

to distributors selected on the basis of specified criteria and where these distributors undertake not to sell such goods or services to unauthorised distributors within the territory reserved by the supplier to operate that system;

(f) 'intellectual property rights' includes industrial property rights, know-how, copyright and neighbouring rights;

(g) 'know-how' means a package of non-patented practical information, resulting from experience and testing by the supplier, which is secret, substantial and identified: in this context, 'secret' means that the know-how is not generally known or easily accessible; 'substantial' means that the know-how is significant and useful to the buyer for the use, sale or resale of the contract goods or services; 'identified' means that the know-how is described in a sufficiently comprehensive manner so as to make it possible to verify that it fulfils the criteria of secrecy and substantiality;

(h) 'buyer' includes an undertaking which, under an agreement falling within Article 101(1) of the Treaty, sells goods or services on behalf of another undertaking;

(i) 'customer of the buyer' means an undertaking not party to the agreement which purchases the contract goods or services from a buyer which is party to the agreement.

2. For the purposes of this Regulation, the terms 'undertaking', 'supplier' and 'buyer' shall include their respective connected undertakings.

'Connected undertakings' means:

(a) undertakings in which a party to the agreement, directly or indirectly:
   (i) has the power to exercise more than half the voting rights, or
   (ii) has the power to appoint more than half the members of the supervisory board, board of management or bodies legally representing the undertaking, or
   (iii) has the right to manage the undertaking's affairs;

(b) undertakings which directly or indirectly have, over a party to the agreement, the rights or powers listed in point (a);

(c) undertakings in which an undertaking referred to in point (b) has, directly or indirectly, the rights or powers listed in point (a);

(d) undertakings in which a party to the agreement together with one or more of the undertakings referred to in points (a), (b) or (c), or in which two or more of the latter undertakings, jointly have the rights or powers listed in point (a);

(e) undertakings in which the rights or the powers listed in point (a) are jointly held by:
   (i) parties to the agreement or their respective connected undertakings referred to in points (a) to (d), or
   (ii) one or more of the parties to the agreement or one or more of their connected undertakings referred to in points (a) to (d) and one or more third parties.

Article 2

Exemption

1. Pursuant to Article 101(3) of the Treaty and subject to the provisions of this Regulation, it is hereby declared that Article 101(1) of the Treaty shall not apply to vertical agreements.

   This exemption shall apply to the extent that such agreements contain vertical restraints.

2. The exemption provided for in paragraph 1 shall apply to vertical agreements entered into between an association of undertakings and its members, or between

such an association and its suppliers, only if all its members are retailers of goods and if no individual member of the association, together with its connected undertakings, has a total annual turnover exceeding EUR 50 million. Vertical agreements entered into by such associations shall be covered by this Regulation without prejudice to the application of Article 101 of the Treaty to horizontal agreements concluded between the members of the association or decisions adopted by the association.

3. The exemption provided for in paragraph 1 shall apply to vertical agreements containing provisions which relate to the assignment to the buyer or use by the buyer of intellectual property rights, provided that those provisions do not constitute the primary object of such agreements and are directly related to the use, sale or resale of goods or services by the buyer or its customers. The exemption applies on condition that, in relation to the contract goods or services, those provisions do not contain restrictions of competition having the same object as vertical restraints which are not exempted under this Regulation.

4. The exemption provided for in paragraph 1 shall not apply to vertical agreements entered into between competing undertakings. However, it shall apply where competing undertakings enter into a non-reciprocal vertical agreement and:
   (a) the supplier is a manufacturer and a distributor of goods, while the buyer is a distributor and not a competing undertaking at the manufacturing level; or
   (b) the supplier is a provider of services at several levels of trade, while the buyer provides its goods or services at the retail level and is not a competing undertaking at the level of trade where it purchases the contract services.

5. This Regulation shall not apply to vertical agreements the subject matter of which falls within the scope of any other block exemption regulation, unless otherwise provided for in such a regulation.

Article 3
Market share threshold

1. The exemption provided for in Article 2 shall apply on condition that the market share held by the supplier does not exceed 30% of the relevant market on which it sells the contract goods or services and the market share held by the buyer does not exceed 30% of the relevant market on which it purchases the contract goods or services.

2. For the purposes of paragraph 1, where in a multi party agreement an undertaking buys the contract goods or services from one undertaking party to the agreement and sells the contract goods or services to another undertaking party to the agreement, the market share of the first undertaking must respect the market share threshold provided for in that paragraph both as a buyer and a supplier in order for the exemption provided for in Article 2 to apply.

Article 4
Restrictions that remove the benefit of the block exemption – hardcore restrictions

The exemption provided for in Article 2 shall not apply to vertical agreements which, directly or indirectly, in isolation or in combination with other factors under the control of the parties, have as their object:

(a) the restriction of the buyer's ability to determine its sale price, without prejudice to the possibility of the supplier to impose a maximum sale price or recommend a sale price, provided that they do not amount to a fixed or minimum sale price as a result of pressure from, or incentives offered by, any of the parties;

(b) the restriction of the territory into which, or of the customers to whom, a buyer party to the agreement, without prejudice to a restriction on its place of establishment, may sell the contract goods or services, except:

(i) the restriction of active sales into the exclusive territory or to an exclusive customer group reserved to the supplier or allocated by the supplier to another buyer, where such a restriction does not limit sales by the customers of the buyer,

(ii) the restriction of sales to end users by a buyer operating at the wholesale level of trade,

(iii) the restriction of sales by the members of a selective distribution system to unauthorised distributors within the territory reserved by the supplier to operate that system, and

(iv) the restriction of the buyer's ability to sell components, supplied for the purposes of incorporation, to customers who would use them to manufacture the same type of goods as those produced by the supplier;

(c) the restriction of active or passive sales to end users by members of a selective distribution system operating at the retail level of trade, without prejudice to the possibility of prohibiting a member of the system from operating out of an unauthorised place of establishment;

(d) the restriction of cross-supplies between distributors within a selective distribution system, including between distributors operating at different level[s] of trade;

(e) the restriction, agreed between a supplier of components and a buyer who incorporates those components, of the supplier's ability to sell the components as spare parts to end-users or to repairers or other service providers not entrusted by the buyer with the repair or servicing of its goods.

Article 5
Excluded restrictions

1. The exemption provided for in Article 2 shall not apply to the following obligations contained in vertical agreements:

(a) any direct or indirect non-compete obligation, the duration of which is indefinite or exceeds five years;

(b) any direct or indirect obligation causing the buyer, after termination of the agreement, not to manufacture, purchase, sell or resell goods or services;

(c) any direct or indirect obligation causing the members of a selective distribution system not to sell the brands of particular competing suppliers.

For the purposes of point (a) of the first subparagraph, a non-compete obligation which is tacitly renewable beyond a period of five years shall be deemed to have been concluded for an indefinite duration.

2. By way of derogation from paragraph 1(a), the time limitation of five years shall not apply where the contract goods or services are sold by the buyer from premises and land owned by the supplier or leased by the supplier from third parties not connected

16

with the buyer, provided that the duration of the non-compete obligation does not exceed the period of occupancy of the premises and land by the buyer.

3. By way of derogation from paragraph 1(b), the exemption provided for in Article 2 shall apply to any direct or indirect obligation causing the buyer, after termination of the agreement, not to manufacture, purchase, sell or resell goods or services where the following conditions are fulfilled:

   (a) the obligation relates to goods or services which compete with the contract goods or services;

   (b) the obligation is limited to the premises and land from which the buyer has operated during the contract period;

   (c) the obligation is indispensable to protect know-how transferred by the supplier to the buyer;

   (d) the duration of the obligation is limited to a period of one year after termination of the agreement.

   Paragraph 1(b) is without prejudice to the possibility of imposing a restriction which is unlimited in time on the use and disclosure of know-how which has not entered the public domain.

Article 6

Non-application of this Regulation

Pursuant to Article 1a of Regulation No. 19/65/EEC, the Commission may by regulation declare that, where parallel networks of similar vertical restraints cover more than 50% of a relevant market, this Regulation shall not apply to vertical agreements containing specific restraints relating to that market.

Article 7

Application of the market share threshold

For the purposes of applying the market share thresholds provided for in Article 3 the following rules shall apply:

   (a) the market share of the supplier shall be calculated on the basis of market sales value data and the market share of the buyer shall be calculated on the basis of market purchase value data. If market sales value or market purchase value data are not available, estimates based on other reliable market information, including market sales and purchase volumes, may be used to establish the market share of the undertaking concerned;

   (b) the market shares shall be calculated on the basis of data relating to the preceding calendar year;

   (c) the market share of the supplier shall include any goods or services supplied to vertically integrated distributors for the purposes of sale;

   (d) if a market share is initially not more than 30% but subsequently rises above that level without exceeding 35%, the exemption provided for in Article 2 shall continue to apply for a period of two consecutive calendar years following the year in which the 30% market share threshold was first exceeded;

   (e) if a market share is initially not more than 30% but subsequently rises above 35%, the exemption provided for in Article 2 shall continue to apply for one calendar year following the year in which the level of 35% was first exceeded;

(f) the benefit of points (d) and (e) may not be combined so as to exceed a period of two calendar years;

(g) the market share held by the undertakings referred to in point (e) of the second subparagraph of Article 1(2) shall be apportioned equally to each undertaking having the rights or the powers listed in point (a) of the second subparagraph of Article 1(2).

Article 8

Application of the turnover threshold

1. For the purpose of calculating total annual turnover within the meaning of Article 2(2), the turnover achieved during the previous financial year by the relevant party to the vertical agreement and the turnover achieved by its connected undertakings in respect of all goods and services, excluding all taxes and other duties, shall be added together. For this purpose, no account shall be taken of dealings between the party to the vertical agreement and its connected undertakings or between its connected undertakings.

2. The exemption provided for in Article 2 shall remain applicable where, for any period of two consecutive financial years, the total annual turnover threshold is exceeded by no more than 10%.

Article 9

Transitional period

The prohibition laid down in Article 101(1) of the Treaty shall not apply during the period from 1 June 2010 to 31 May 2011 in respect of agreements already in force on 31 May 2010 which do not satisfy the conditions for exemption provided for in this Regulation but which, on 31 May 2010, satisfied the conditions for exemption provided for in Regulation (EC) No. 2790/1999.

Article 10

Period of validity

This Regulation shall enter into force on 1 June 2010.

It shall expire on 31 May 2022.

This Regulation shall be binding in its entirety and directly applicable in all Member States.

(*Signatures omitted*)

16

17

Regulation 139/2004 on the Control of Concentrations between Undertakings (EU Merger Regulation)

THE COUNCIL OF THE EUROPEAN UNION,

Having regard to the Treaty [on the Functioning of the European Union], and in particular Articles [103] and [352] thereof,

Having regard to the proposal from the Commission,

Having regard to the opinion of the European Parliament,

Having regard to the opinion of the European Economic and Social Committee ...

HAS ADOPTED THIS REGULATION:

Article 1

Scope

1. Without prejudice to Article 4(5) and Article 22, this Regulation shall apply to all concentrations with a [Union] dimension as defined in this Article.
2. A concentration has a [Union] dimension where:
   (a) the combined aggregate worldwide turnover of all the undertakings concerned is more than EUR 5000 million; and
   (b) the aggregate [Union]-wide turnover of each of at least two of the undertakings concerned is more than EUR 250 million, unless each of the undertakings concerned achieves more than two-thirds of its aggregate [Union]-wide turnover within one and the same Member State.
3. A concentration that does not meet the thresholds laid down in paragraph 2 has a [Union] dimension where:
   (a) the combined aggregate worldwide turnover of all the undertakings concerned is more than EUR 2500 million;
   (b) in each of at least three Member States, the combined aggregate turnover of all the undertakings concerned is more than EUR 100 million;
   (c) in each of at least three Member States included for the purpose of point (b), the aggregate turnover of each of at least two of the undertakings concerned is more than EUR 25 million; and
   (d) the aggregate [Union]-wide turnover of each of at least two of the undertakings concerned is more than EUR 100 million, unless each of the undertakings concerned achieves more than two-thirds of its aggregate [Union]-wide turnover within one and the same Member State.
4. On the basis of statistical data that may be regularly provided by the Member States, the Commission shall report to the Council on the operation of the thresholds and criteria set out in paragraphs 2 and 3 by 1 July 2009 and may present proposals pursuant to paragraph 5.5. Following the report referred to in paragraph 4 and on a proposal

from the Commission, the Council, acting by a qualified majority, may revise the thresholds and criteria mentioned in paragraph 3.

Article 2
Appraisal of concentrations

1. Concentrations within the scope of this Regulation shall be appraised in accordance with the objectives of this Regulation and the following provisions with a view to establishing whether or not they are compatible with the common market.

   In making this appraisal, the Commission shall take into account:

   (a) the need to maintain and develop effective competition within the common market in view of, among other things, the structure of all the markets concerned and the actual or potential competition from undertakings located either within or outwith the [Union];

   (b) the market position of the undertakings concerned and their economic and financial power, the alternatives available to suppliers and users, their access to supplies or markets, any legal or other barriers to entry, supply and demand trends for the relevant goods and services, the interests of the intermediate and ultimate consumers, and the development of technical and economic progress provided that it is to consumers' advantage and does not form an obstacle to competition.

2. A concentration which would not significantly impede effective competition in the common market or in a substantial part of it, in particular as a result of the creation or strengthening of a dominant position, shall be declared compatible with the common market.

3. A concentration which would significantly impede effective competition, in the common market or in a substantial part of it, in particular as a result of the creation or strengthening of a dominant position, shall be declared incompatible with the common market.

4. To the extent that the creation of a joint venture constituting a concentration pursuant to Article 3 has as its object or effect the coordination of the competitive behaviour of undertakings that remain independent, such coordination shall be appraised in accordance with the criteria of Article [101](1) and (3) of the Treaty, with a view to establishing whether or not the operation is compatible with the common market.

5. In making this appraisal, the Commission shall take into account in particular:

   — whether two or more parent companies retain, to a significant extent, activities in the same market as the joint venture or in a market which is downstream or upstream from that of the joint venture or in a neighbouring market closely related to this market,

   — whether the coordination which is the direct consequence of the creation of the joint venture affords the undertakings concerned the possibility of eliminating competition in respect of a substantial part of the products or services in question.

Article 3
Definition of concentration

1. A concentration shall be deemed to arise where a change of control on a lasting basis results from:

   (a) the merger of two or more previously independent undertakings or parts of undertakings, or

17

(b) the acquisition, by one or more persons already controlling at least one undertaking, or by one or more undertakings, whether by purchase of securities or assets, by contract or by any other means, of direct or indirect control of the whole or parts of one or more other undertakings.

2. Control shall be constituted by rights, contracts or any other means which, either separately or in combination and having regard to the considerations of fact or law involved, confer the possibility of exercising decisive influence on an undertaking, in particular by:

(a) ownership or the right to use all or part of the assets of an undertaking;

(b) rights or contracts which confer decisive influence on the composition, voting or decisions of the organs of an undertaking.

3. Control is acquired by persons or undertakings which:

(a) are holders of the rights or entitled to rights under the contracts concerned; or

(b) while not being holders of such rights or entitled to rights under such contracts, have the power to exercise the rights deriving therefrom.

4. The creation of a joint venture performing on a lasting basis all the functions of an autonomous economic entity shall constitute a concentration within the meaning of paragraph 1(b).

5. A concentration shall not be deemed to arise where:

(a) credit institutions or other financial institutions or insurance companies, the normal activities of which include transactions and dealing in securities for their own account or for the account of others, hold on a temporary basis securities which they have acquired in an undertaking with a view to reselling them, provided that they do not exercise voting rights in respect of those securities with a view to determining the competitive behaviour of that undertaking or provided that they exercise such voting rights only with a view to preparing the disposal of all or part of that undertaking or of its assets or the disposal of those securities and that any such disposal takes place within one year of the date of acquisition; that period may be extended by the Commission on request where such institutions or companies can show that the disposal was not reasonably possible within the period set;

(b) control is acquired by an office-holder according to the law of a Member State relating to liquidation, winding up, insolvency, cessation of payments, compositions or analogous proceedings;

(c) the operations referred to in paragraph 1(b) are carried out by the financial holding companies referred to in Article 5(3) of Fourth Council Directive 78/660/EEC of 25 July 1978 based on Article [50(2)](g) of the Treaty on the annual accounts of certain types of companies provided however that the voting rights in respect of the holding are exercised, in particular in relation to the appointment of members of the management and supervisory bodies of the undertakings in which they have holdings, only to maintain the full value of those investments and not to determine directly or indirectly the competitive conduct of those undertakings.

Article 4

Prior notification of concentrations and pre-notification referral at the request of the notifying parties

1. Concentrations with a [Union] dimension defined in this Regulation shall be notified to the Commission prior to their implementation and following the conclusion of the

agreement, the announcement of the public bid, or the acquisition of a controlling interest.

Notification may also be made where the undertakings concerned demonstrate to the Commission a good faith intention to conclude an agreement or, in the case of a public bid, where they have publicly announced an intention to make such a bid, provided that the intended agreement or bid would result in a concentration with a [Union] dimension.

For the purposes of this Regulation, the term "notified concentration" shall also cover intended concentrations notified pursuant to the second subparagraph. For the purposes of paragraphs 4 and 5 of this Article, the term "concentration" includes intended concentrations within the meaning of the second subparagraph.

2. A concentration which consists of a merger within the meaning of Article 3(1)(a) or in the acquisition of joint control within the meaning of Article 3(1)(b) shall be notified jointly by the parties to the merger or by those acquiring joint control as the case may be. In all other cases, the notification shall be effected by the person or undertaking acquiring control of the whole or parts of one or more undertakings.

3. Where the Commission finds that a notified concentration falls within the scope of this Regulation, it shall publish the fact of the notification, at the same time indicating the names of the undertakings concerned, their country of origin, the nature of the concentration and the economic sectors involved. The Commission shall take account of the legitimate interest of undertakings in the protection of their business secrets.

4. Prior to the notification of a concentration within the meaning of paragraph 1, the persons or undertakings referred to in paragraph 2 may inform the Commission, by means of a reasoned submission, that the concentration may significantly affect competition in a market within a Member State which presents all the characteristics of a distinct market and should therefore be examined, in whole or in part, by that Member State.

The Commission shall transmit this submission to all Member States without delay. The Member State referred to in the reasoned submission shall, within 15 working days of receiving the submission, express its agreement or disagreement as regards the request to refer the case. Where that Member State takes no such decision within this period, it shall be deemed to have agreed.

Unless that Member State disagrees, the Commission, where it considers that such a distinct market exists, and that competition in that market may be significantly affected by the concentration, may decide to refer the whole or part of the case to the competent authorities of that Member State with a view to the application of that State's national competition law.

The decision whether or not to refer the case in accordance with the third subparagraph shall be taken within 25 working days starting from the receipt of the reasoned submission by the Commission. The Commission shall inform the other Member States and the persons or undertakings concerned of its decision. If the Commission does not take a decision within this period, it shall be deemed to have adopted a decision to refer the case in accordance with the submission made by the persons or undertakings concerned.

If the Commission decides, or is deemed to have decided, pursuant to the third and fourth subparagraphs, to refer the whole of the case, no notification shall be made pursuant to paragraph 1 and national competition law shall apply. Article 9(6) to (9) shall apply mutatis mutandis.

5. With regard to a concentration as defined in Article 3 which does not have a [Union] dimension within the meaning of Article 1 and which is capable of being reviewed under the national competition laws of at least three Member States, the persons or undertakings referred to in paragraph 2 may, before any notification to the competent authorities, inform the Commission by means of a reasoned submission that the concentration should be examined by the Commission.

The Commission shall transmit this submission to all Member States without delay. Any Member State competent to examine the concentration under its national competition law may, within 15 working days of receiving the reasoned submission, express its disagreement as regards the request to refer the case.

Where at least one such Member State has expressed its disagreement in accordance with the third subparagraph within the period of 15 working days, the case shall not be referred. The Commission shall, without delay, inform all Member States and the persons or undertakings concerned of any such expression of disagreement.

Where no Member State has expressed its disagreement in accordance with the third subparagraph within the period of 15 working days, the concentration shall be deemed to have a [Union] dimension and shall be notified to the Commission in accordance with paragraphs 1 and 2. In such situations, no Member State shall apply its national competition law to the concentration.

6. The Commission shall report to the Council on the operation of paragraphs 4 and 5 by 1 July 2009. Following this report and on a proposal from the Commission, the Council, acting by a qualified majority, may revise paragraphs 4 and 5.

Article 5
Calculation of turnover

1. Aggregate turnover within the meaning of this Regulation shall comprise the amounts derived by the undertakings concerned in the preceding financial year from the sale of products and the provision of services falling within the undertakings' ordinary activities after deduction of sales rebates and of value added tax and other taxes directly related to turnover. The aggregate turnover of an undertaking concerned shall not include the sale of products or the provision of services between any of the undertakings referred to in paragraph 4.

Turnover, in the [Union] or in a Member State, shall comprise products sold and services provided to undertakings or consumers, in the [Union] or in that Member State as the case may be.

2. By way of derogation from paragraph 1, where the concentration consists of the acquisition of parts, whether or not constituted as legal entities, of one or more undertakings, only the turnover relating to the parts which are the subject of the concentration shall be taken into account with regard to the seller or sellers.

However, two or more transactions within the meaning of the first subparagraph which take place within a two-year period between the same persons or undertakings shall be treated as one and the same concentration arising on the date of the last transaction.

3. In place of turnover the following shall be used:

(a) for credit institutions and other financial institutions, the sum of the following income items as defined in Council Directive 86/635/EEC, after deduction of value added tax and other taxes directly related to those items, where appropriate:

(i) interest income and similar income;

(ii) income from securities:

— income from shares and other variable yield securities,

— income from participating interests,

— income from shares in affiliated undertakings;

(iii) commissions receivable;

(iv) net profit on financial operations;

(v) other operating income.

The turnover of a credit or financial institution in the [Union] or in a Member State shall comprise the income items, as defined above, which are received by the branch or division of that institution established in the [Union] or in the Member State in question, as the case may be;

(b) for insurance undertakings, the value of gross premiums written which shall comprise all amounts received and receivable in respect of insurance contracts issued by or on behalf of the insurance undertakings, including also outgoing reinsurance premiums, and after deduction of taxes and parafiscal contributions or levies charged by reference to the amounts of individual premiums or the total volume of premiums; as regards Article 1(2)(b) and (3)(b), (c) and (d) and the final part of Article 1(2) and (3), gross premiums received from [Union] residents and from residents of one Member State respectively shall be taken into account.

4. Without prejudice to paragraph 2, the aggregate turnover of an undertaking concerned within the meaning of this Regulation shall be calculated by adding together the respective turnovers of the following:

(a) the undertaking concerned;

(b) those undertakings in which the undertaking concerned, directly or indirectly:

(i) owns more than half the capital or business assets, or

(ii) has the power to exercise more than half the voting rights, or

(iii) has the power to appoint more than half the members of the supervisory board, the administrative board or bodies legally representing the undertakings, or

(iv) has the right to manage the undertakings' affairs;

(c) those undertakings which have in the undertaking concerned the rights or powers listed in (b);

(d) those undertakings in which an undertaking as referred to in (c) has the rights or powers listed in (b);

(e) those undertakings in which two or more undertakings as referred to in (a) to (d) jointly have the rights or powers listed in (b).

5. Where undertakings concerned by the concentration jointly have the rights or powers listed in paragraph 4(b), in calculating the aggregate turnover of the undertakings concerned for the purposes of this Regulation:

(a) no account shall be taken of the turnover resulting from the sale of products or the provision of services between the joint undertaking and each of the undertakings concerned or any other undertaking connected with any one of them, as set out in paragraph 4(b) to (e);

(b) account shall be taken of the turnover resulting from the sale of products and the provision of services between the joint undertaking and any third undertakings. This turnover shall be apportioned equally amongst the undertakings concerned.

Article 6

Examination of the notification and initiation of proceedings

1. The Commission shall examine the notification as soon as it is received.

   (a) Where it concludes that the concentration notified does not fall within the scope of this Regulation, it shall record that finding by means of a decision.

   (b) Where it finds that the concentration notified, although falling within the scope of this Regulation, does not raise serious doubts as to its compatibility with the common market, it shall decide not to oppose it and shall declare that it is compatible with the common market.

   A decision declaring a concentration compatible shall be deemed to cover restrictions directly related and necessary to the implementation of the concentration.

   (c) Without prejudice to paragraph 2, where the Commission finds that the concentration notified falls within the scope of this Regulation and raises serious doubts as to its compatibility with the common market, it shall decide to initiate proceedings. Without prejudice to Article 9, such proceedings shall be closed by means of a decision as provided for in Article 8(1) to (4), unless the undertakings concerned have demonstrated to the satisfaction of the Commission that they have abandoned the concentration.

2. Where the Commission finds that, following modification by the undertakings concerned, a notified concentration no longer raises serious doubts within the meaning of paragraph 1(c), it shall declare the concentration compatible with the common market pursuant to paragraph 1(b).

   The Commission may attach to its decision under paragraph 1(b) conditions and obligations intended to ensure that the undertakings concerned comply with the commitments they have entered into vis-à-vis the Commission with a view to rendering the concentration compatible with the common market.

3. The Commission may revoke the decision it took pursuant to paragraph 1(a) or (b) where:

   (a) the decision is based on incorrect information for which one of the undertakings is responsible or where it has been obtained by deceit, or

   (b) the undertakings concerned commit a breach of an obligation attached to the decision.

4. In the cases referred to in paragraph 3, the Commission may take a decision under paragraph 1, without being bound by the time limits referred to in Article 10(1).

5. The Commission shall notify its decision to the undertakings concerned and the competent authorities of the Member States without delay.

Article 7

Suspension of concentrations

1. A concentration with a [Union] dimension as defined in Article 1, or which is to be examined by the Commission pursuant to Article 4(5), shall not be implemented

either before its notification or until it has been declared compatible with the common market pursuant to a decision under Articles 6(1)(b), 8(1) or 8(2), or on the basis of a presumption according to Article 10(6).

2. Paragraph 1 shall not prevent the implementation of a public bid or of a series of transactions in securities including those convertible into other securities admitted to trading on a market such as a stock exchange, by which control within the meaning of Article 3 is acquired from various sellers, provided that:

(a) the concentration is notified to the Commission pursuant to Article 4 without delay; and

(b) the acquirer does not exercise the voting rights attached to the securities in question or does so only to maintain the full value of its investments based on a derogation granted by the Commission under paragraph 3.

3. The Commission may, on request, grant a derogation from the obligations imposed in paragraphs 1 or 2. The request to grant a derogation must be reasoned. In deciding on the request, the Commission shall take into account inter alia the effects of the suspension on one or more undertakings concerned by the concentration or on a third party and the threat to competition posed by the concentration. Such a derogation may be made subject to conditions and obligations in order to ensure conditions of effective competition. A derogation may be applied for and granted at any time, be it before notification or after the transaction.

4. The validity of any transaction carried out in contravention of paragraph 1 shall be dependent on a decision pursuant to Article 6(1)(b) or Article 8(1), (2) or (3) or on a presumption pursuant to Article 10(6).

This Article shall, however, have no effect on the validity of transactions in securities including those convertible into other securities admitted to trading on a market such as a stock exchange, unless the buyer and seller knew or ought to have known that the transaction was carried out in contravention of paragraph 1.

Article 8
Powers of decision of the Commission

1. Where the Commission finds that a notified concentration fulfils the criterion laid down in Article 2(2) and, in the cases referred to in Article 2(4), the criteria laid down in Article [101](3) of the Treaty, it shall issue a decision declaring the concentration compatible with the common market.

A decision declaring a concentration compatible shall be deemed to cover restrictions directly related and necessary to the implementation of the concentration.

2. Where the Commission finds that, following modification by the undertakings concerned, a notified concentration fulfils the criterion laid down in Article 2(2) and, in the cases referred to in Article 2(4), the criteria laid down in Article [101](3) of the Treaty, it shall issue a decision declaring the concentration compatible with the common market.

The Commission may attach to its decision conditions and obligations intended to ensure that the undertakings concerned comply with the commitments they have entered into vis-à-vis the Commission with a view to rendering the concentration compatible with the common market.

A decision declaring a concentration compatible shall be deemed to cover restrictions directly related and necessary to the implementation of the concentration.

17

3. Where the Commission finds that a concentration fulfils the criterion defined in Article 2(3) or, in the cases referred to in Article 2(4), does not fulfil the criteria laid down in Article [101](3) of the Treaty, it shall issue a decision declaring that the concentration is incompatible with the common market.

4. Where the Commission finds that a concentration:
   (a) has already been implemented and that concentration has been declared incompatible with the common market, or
   (b) has been implemented in contravention of a condition attached to a decision taken under paragraph 2, which has found that, in the absence of the condition, the concentration would fulfil the criterion laid down in Article 2(3) or, in the cases referred to in Article 2(4), would not fulfil the criteria laid down in Article [101](3) of the Treaty, the Commission may:
   — require the undertakings concerned to dissolve the concentration, in particular through the dissolution of the merger or the disposal of all the shares or assets acquired, so as to restore the situation prevailing prior to the implementation of the concentration; in circumstances where restoration of the situation prevailing before the implementation of the concentration is not possible through dissolution of the concentration, the Commission may take any other measure appropriate to achieve such restoration as far as possible,
   — order any other appropriate measure to ensure that the undertakings concerned dissolve the concentration or take other restorative measures as required in its decision.

   In cases falling within point (a) of the first subparagraph, the measures referred to in that subparagraph may be imposed either in a decision pursuant to paragraph 3 or by separate decision.

5. The Commission may take interim measures appropriate to restore or maintain conditions of effective competition where a concentration:
   (a) has been implemented in contravention of Article 7, and a decision as to the compatibility of the concentration with the common market has not yet been taken;
   (b) has been implemented in contravention of a condition attached to a decision under Article 6(1)(b) or paragraph 2 of this Article;
   (c) has already been implemented and is declared incompatible with the common market.

6. The Commission may revoke the decision it has taken pursuant to paragraphs 1 or 2 where:
   (a) the declaration of compatibility is based on incorrect information for which one of the undertakings is responsible or where it has been obtained by deceit; or
   (b) the undertakings concerned commit a breach of an obligation attached to the decision.

7. The Commission may take a decision pursuant to paragraphs 1 to 3 without being bound by the time limits referred to in Article 10(3), in cases where:
   (a) it finds that a concentration has been implemented
      (i) in contravention of a condition attached to a decision under Article 6(1)(b), or
      (ii) in contravention of a condition attached to a decision taken under paragraph 2 and in accordance with Article 10(2), which has found that, in the absence

of the condition, the concentration would raise serious doubts as to its compatibility with the common market; or

(b) a decision has been revoked pursuant to paragraph 6.

8. The Commission shall notify its decision to the undertakings concerned and the competent authorities of the Member States without delay.

Article 9
Referral to the competent authorities of the Member States

1. The Commission may, by means of a decision notified without delay to the undertakings concerned and the competent authorities of the other Member States, refer a notified concentration to the competent authorities of the Member State concerned in the following circumstances.

2. Within 15 working days of the date of receipt of the copy of the notification, a Member State, on its own initiative or upon the invitation of the Commission, may inform the Commission, which shall inform the undertakings concerned, that:

(a) a concentration threatens to affect significantly competition in a market within that Member State, which presents all the characteristics of a distinct market, or

(b) a concentration affects competition in a market within that Member State, which presents all the characteristics of a distinct market and which does not constitute a substantial part of the common market.

3. If the Commission considers that, having regard to the market for the products or services in question and the geographical reference market within the meaning of paragraph 7, there is such a distinct market and that such a threat exists, either:

(a) it shall itself deal with the case in accordance with this Regulation; or

(b) it shall refer the whole or part of the case to the competent authorities of the Member State concerned with a view to the application of that State's national competition law.

If, however, the Commission considers that such a distinct market or threat does not exist, it shall adopt a decision to that effect which it shall address to the Member State concerned, and shall itself deal with the case in accordance with this Regulation.

In cases where a Member State informs the Commission pursuant to paragraph 2(b) that a concentration affects competition in a distinct market within its territory that does not form a substantial part of the common market, the Commission shall refer the whole or part of the case relating to the distinct market concerned, if it considers that such a distinct market is affected.

4. A decision to refer or not to refer pursuant to paragraph 3 shall be taken:

(a) as a general rule within the period provided for in Article 10(1), second subparagraph, where the Commission, pursuant to Article 6(1)(b), has not initiated proceedings; or

(b) within 65 working days at most of the notification of the concentration concerned where the Commission has initiated proceedings under Article 6(1)(c), without taking the preparatory steps in order to adopt the necessary measures under Article 8(2), (3) or (4) to maintain or restore effective competition on the market concerned.

17

5. If within the 65 working days referred to in paragraph 4(b) the Commission, despite a reminder from the Member State concerned, has not taken a decision on referral in accordance with paragraph 3 nor has taken the preparatory steps referred to in paragraph 4(b), it shall be deemed to have taken a decision to refer the case to the Member State concerned in accordance with paragraph 3(b).

6. The competent authority of the Member State concerned shall decide upon the case without undue delay.

   Within 45 working days after the Commission's referral, the competent authority of the Member State concerned shall inform the undertakings concerned of the result of the preliminary competition assessment and what further action, if any, it proposes to take. The Member State concerned may exceptionally suspend this time limit where necessary information has not been provided to it by the undertakings concerned as provided for by its national competition law.

   Where a notification is requested under national law, the period of 45 working days shall begin on the working day following that of the receipt of a complete notification by the competent authority of that Member State.

7. The geographical reference market shall consist of the area in which the undertakings concerned are involved in the supply and demand of products or services, in which the conditions of competition are sufficiently homogeneous and which can be distinguished from neighbouring areas because, in particular, conditions of competition are appreciably different in those areas. This assessment should take account in particular of the nature and characteristics of the products or services concerned, of the existence of entry barriers or of consumer preferences, of appreciable differences of the undertakings' market shares between the area concerned and neighbouring areas or of substantial price differences.

8. In applying the provisions of this Article, the Member State concerned may take only the measures strictly necessary to safeguard or restore effective competition on the market concerned.

9. In accordance with the relevant provisions of the Treaty, any Member State may appeal to the Court of Justice, and in particular request the application of Article [279] of the Treaty, for the purpose of applying its national competition law.

Article 10
Time limits for initiating proceedings and for decisions

1. Without prejudice to Article 6(4), the decisions referred to in Article 6(1) shall be taken within 25 working days at most. That period shall begin on the working day following that of the receipt of a notification or, if the information to be supplied with the notification is incomplete, on the working day following that of the receipt of the complete information.

   That period shall be increased to 35 working days where the Commission receives a request from a Member State in accordance with Article 9(2) or where the undertakings concerned offer commitments pursuant to Article 6(2) with a view to rendering the concentration compatible with the common market.

2. Decisions pursuant to Article 8(1) or (2) concerning notified concentrations shall be taken as soon as it appears that the serious doubts referred to in Article 6(1)(c) have been removed, particularly as a result of modifications made by the undertakings concerned, and at the latest by the time limit laid down in paragraph 3.

3. Without prejudice to Article 8(7), decisions pursuant to Article 8(1) to (3) concerning notified concentrations shall be taken within not more than 90 working days of the date on which the proceedings are initiated. That period shall be increased to 105 working days where the undertakings concerned offer commitments pursuant to Article 8(2), second subparagraph, with a view to rendering the concentration compatible with the common market, unless these commitments have been offered less than 55 working days after the initiation of proceedings.

The periods set by the first subparagraph shall likewise be extended if the notifying parties make a request to that effect not later than 15 working days after the initiation of proceedings pursuant to Article 6(1)(c). The notifying parties may make only one such request. Likewise, at any time following the initiation of proceedings, the periods set by the first subparagraph may be extended by the Commission with the agreement of the notifying parties. The total duration of any extension or extensions effected pursuant to this subparagraph shall not exceed 20 working days.

4. The periods set by paragraphs 1 and 3 shall exceptionally be suspended where, owing to circumstances for which one of the undertakings involved in the concentration is responsible, the Commission has had to request information by decision pursuant to Article 11 or to order an inspection by decision pursuant to Article 13.

The first subparagraph shall also apply to the period referred to in Article 9(4)(b).

5. Where the Court of Justice gives a judgment which annuls the whole or part of a Commission decision which is subject to a time limit set by this Article, the concentration shall be re-examined by the Commission with a view to adopting a decision pursuant to Article 6(1).

The concentration shall be re-examined in the light of current market conditions.

The notifying parties shall submit a new notification or supplement the original notification, without delay, where the original notification becomes incomplete by reason of intervening changes in market conditions or in the information provided. Where there are no such changes, the parties shall certify this fact without delay.

The periods laid down in paragraph 1 shall start on the working day following that of the receipt of complete information in a new notification, a supplemented notification, or a certification within the meaning of the third subparagraph.

The second and third subparagraphs shall also apply in the cases referred to in Article 6(4) and Article 8(7).

6. Where the Commission has not taken a decision in accordance with Article 6(1)(b), (c), 8(1), (2) or (3) within the time limits set in paragraphs 1 and 3 respectively, the concentration shall be deemed to have been declared compatible with the common market, without prejudice to Article 9.

Article 11

Requests for information

1. In order to carry out the duties assigned to it by this Regulation, the Commission may, by simple request or by decision, require the persons referred to in Article 3(1)(b), as well as undertakings and associations of undertakings, to provide all necessary information.

2. When sending a simple request for information to a person, an undertaking or an association of undertakings, the Commission shall state the legal basis and the purpose of

17

the request, specify what information is required and fix the time limit within which the information is to be provided, as well as the penalties provided for in Article 14 for supplying incorrect or misleading information.

3. Where the Commission requires a person, an undertaking or an association of undertakings to supply information by decision, it shall state the legal basis and the purpose of the request, specify what information is required and fix the time limit within which it is to be provided. It shall also indicate the penalties provided for in Article 14 and indicate or impose the penalties provided for in Article 15. It shall further indicate the right to have the decision reviewed by the Court of Justice.

4. The owners of the undertakings or their representatives and, in the case of legal persons, companies or firms, or associations having no legal personality, the persons authorised to represent them by law or by their constitution, shall supply the information requested on behalf of the undertaking concerned. Persons duly authorised to act may supply the information on behalf of their clients. The latter shall remain fully responsible if the information supplied is incomplete, incorrect or misleading.

5. The Commission shall without delay forward a copy of any decision taken pursuant to paragraph 3 to the competent authorities of the Member State in whose territory the residence of the person or the seat of the undertaking or association of undertakings is situated, and to the competent authority of the Member State whose territory is affected. At the specific request of the competent authority of a Member State, the Commission shall also forward to that authority copies of simple requests for information relating to a notified concentration.

6. At the request of the Commission, the governments and competent authorities of the Member States shall provide the Commission with all necessary information to carry out the duties assigned to it by this Regulation.

7. In order to carry out the duties assigned to it by this Regulation, the Commission may interview any natural or legal person who consents to be interviewed for the purpose of collecting information relating to the subject matter of an investigation. At the beginning of the interview, which may be conducted by telephone or other electronic means, the Commission shall state the legal basis and the purpose of the interview.

   Where an interview is not conducted on the premises of the Commission or by telephone or other electronic means, the Commission shall inform in advance the competent authority of the Member State in whose territory the interview takes place. If the competent authority of that Member State so requests, officials of that authority may assist the officials and other persons authorised by the Commission to conduct the interview.

Article 12
Inspections by the authorities of the Member States

1. At the request of the Commission, the competent authorities of the Member States shall undertake the inspections which the Commission considers to be necessary under Article 13(1), or which it has ordered by decision pursuant to Article 13(4). The officials of the competent authorities of the Member States who are responsible for conducting these inspections as well as those authorised or appointed by them shall exercise their powers in accordance with their national law.

2. If so requested by the Commission or by the competent authority of the Member State within whose territory the inspection is to be conducted, officials and other accompanying persons authorised by the Commission may assist the officials of the authority concerned.

Article 13
The Commission's powers of inspection

1. In order to carry out the duties assigned to it by this Regulation, the Commission may conduct all necessary inspections of undertakings and associations of undertakings.

2. The officials and other accompanying persons authorised by the Commission to conduct an inspection shall have the power:
   (a) to enter any premises, land and means of transport of undertakings and associations of undertakings;
   (b) to examine the books and other records related to the business, irrespective of the medium on which they are stored;
   (c) to take or obtain in any form copies of or extracts from such books or records;
   (d) to seal any business premises and books or records for the period and to the extent necessary for the inspection;
   (e) to ask any representative or member of staff of the undertaking or association of undertakings for explanations on facts or documents relating to the subject matter and purpose of the inspection and to record the answers.

3. Officials and other accompanying persons authorised by the Commission to conduct an inspection shall exercise their powers upon production of a written authorisation specifying the subject matter and purpose of the inspection and the penalties provided for in Article 14, in the production of the required books or other records related to the business which is incomplete or where answers to questions asked under paragraph 2 of this Article are incorrect or misleading. In good time before the inspection, the Commission shall give notice of the inspection to the competent authority of the Member State in whose territory the inspection is to be conducted.

4. Undertakings and associations of undertakings are required to submit to inspections ordered by decision of the Commission. The decision shall specify the subject matter and purpose of the inspection, appoint the date on which it is to begin and indicate the penalties provided for in Articles 14 and 15 and the right to have the decision reviewed by the Court of Justice. The Commission shall take such decisions after consulting the competent authority of the Member State in whose territory the inspection is to be conducted.

5. Officials of, and those authorised or appointed by, the competent authority of the Member State in whose territory the inspection is to be conducted shall, at the request of that authority or of the Commission, actively assist the officials and other accompanying persons authorised by the Commission. To this end, they shall enjoy the powers specified in paragraph 2.

6. Where the officials and other accompanying persons authorised by the Commission find that an undertaking opposes an inspection, including the sealing of business premises, books or records, ordered pursuant to this Article, the Member State concerned shall afford them the necessary assistance, requesting where appropriate the

assistance of the police or of an equivalent enforcement authority, so as to enable them to conduct their inspection.

7. If the assistance provided for in paragraph 6 requires authorisation from a judicial authority according to national rules, such authorisation shall be applied for. Such authorisation may also be applied for as a precautionary measure.

8. Where authorisation as referred to in paragraph 7 is applied for, the national judicial authority shall ensure that the Commission decision is authentic and that the coercive measures envisaged are neither arbitraryn or excessive having regard to the subject matter of the inspection. In its control of proportionlity of the coercive measures, the national judicial authority may ask the Commission, directly or through the competent authority of that Member State, for detailed explanations relating to the subject matter of the inspection. However, the national judicial authority may not call into question the necessity for the inspection nor demand that it be provided with the information in the Commission's file. The lawfulness of the Commission's decision shall be subject to review only by the Court of Justice.

Article 14
Fines

1. The Commission may by decision impose on the persons referred to in Article 3(1) (b), undertakings or associations of undertakings, fines not exceeding 1% of the aggregate turnover of the undertaking or association of undertakings concerned within the meaning of Article 5 where, intentionally or negligently:

   (a) they supply incorrect or misleading information in a submission, certification, notification or supplement thereto, pursuant to Article 4, Article 10(5) or Article 22(3);

   (b) they supply incorrect or misleading information in response to a request made pursuant to Article 11(2);

   (c) in response to a request made by decision adopted pursuant to Article 11(3), they supply incorrect, incomplete or misleading information or do not supply information within the required time limit;

   (d) they produce the required books or other records related to the business in incomplete form during inspections under Article 13, or refuse to submit to an inspection ordered by decision taken pursuant to Article 13(4);

   (e) in response to a question asked in accordance with Article 13(2)(e),
   — they give an incorrect or misleading answer,
   — they fail to rectify within a time limit set by the Commission an incorrect, incomplete or misleading answer given by a member of staff, or
   — they fail or refuse to provide a complete answer on facts relating to the subject matter and purpose of an inspection ordered by a decision adopted pursuant to Article 13(4);

   (f) seals affixed by officials or other accompanying persons authorised by the Commission in accordance with Article 13(2)(d) have been broken.

2. The Commission may by decision impose fines not exceeding 10% of the aggregate turnover of the undertaking concerned within the meaning of Article 5 on the persons referred to in Article 3(1)b or the undertakings concerned where, either intentionally or negligently, they:

(a) fail to notify a concentration in accordance with Articles 4 or 22(3) prior to its implementation, unless they are expressly authorised to do so by Article 7(2) or by a decision taken pursuant to Article 7(3);

(b) implement a concentration in breach of Article 7;

(c) implement a concentration declared incompatible with the common market by decision pursuant to Article 8(3) or do not comply with any measure ordered by decision pursuant to Article 8(4) or (5);

(d) fail to comply with a condition or an obligation imposed by decision pursuant to Articles 6(1)(b), Article 7(3) or Article 8(2), second subparagraph.

3. In fixing the amount of the fine, regard shall be had to the nature, gravity and duration of the infringement.4. Decisions taken pursuant to paragraphs 1, 2 and 3 shall not be of a criminal law nature.

Article 15
Periodic penalty payments

1. The Commission may by decision impose on the persons referred to in Article 3(1)b, undertakings or associations of undertakings, periodic penalty payments not exceeding 5% of the average daily aggregate turnover of the undertaking or association of undertakings concerned within the meaning of Article 5 for each working day of delay, calculated from the date set in the decision, in order to compel them:

(a) to supply complete and correct information which it has requested by decision taken pursuant to Article 11(3);

(b) to submit to an inspection which it has ordered by decision taken pursuant to Article 13(4);

(c) to comply with an obligation imposed by decision pursuant to Article 6(1)(b), Article 7(3) or Article 8(2), second subparagraph; or

(d) to comply with any measures ordered by decision pursuant to Article 8(4) or (5).

2. Where the persons referred to in Article 3(1)(b), undertakings or associations of undertakings have satisfied the obligation which the periodic penalty payment was intended to enforce, the Commission may fix the definitive amount of the periodic penalty payments at a figure lower than that which would arise under the original decision.

Article 16
Review by the Court of Justice

The Court of Justice shall have unlimited jurisdiction within the meaning of Article [261] of the Treaty to review decisions whereby the Commission has fixed a fine or periodic penalty payments; it may cancel, reduce or increase the fine or periodic penalty payment imposed.

Article 17
Professional secrecy

1. Information acquired as a result of the application of this Regulation shall be used only for the purposes of the relevant request, investigation or hearing.

2. Without prejudice to Article 4(3), Articles 18 and 20, the Commission and the competent authorities of the Member States, their officials and other servants and other

persons working under the supervision of these authorities as well as officials and civil servants of other authorities of the Member States shall not disclose information they have acquired through the application of this Regulation of the kind covered by the obligation of professional secrecy.

3. Paragraphs 1 and 2 shall not prevent publication of general information or of surveys which do not contain information relating to particular undertakings or associations of undertakings.

Article 18
Hearing of the parties and of third persons

1. Before taking any decision provided for in Article 6(3), Article 7(3), Article 8(2) to (6), and Articles 14 and 15, the Commission shall give the persons, undertakings and associations of undertakings concerned the opportunity, at every stage of the procedure up to the consultation of the Advisory Committee, of making known their views on the objections against them.

2. By way of derogation from paragraph 1, a decision pursuant to Articles 7(3) and 8(5) may be taken provisionally, without the persons, undertakings or associations of undertakings concerned being given the opportunity to make known their views beforehand, provided that the Commission gives them that opportunity as soon as possible after having taken its decision.

3. The Commission shall base its decision only on objections on which the parties have been able to submit their observations. The rights of the defence shall be fully respected in the proceedings. Access to the file shall be open at least to the parties directly involved, subject to the legitimate interest of undertakings in the protection of their business secrets.

4. In so far as the Commission or the competent authorities of the Member States deem it necessary, they may also hear other natural or legal persons. Natural or legal persons showing a sufficient interest and especially members of the administrative or management bodies of the undertakings concerned or the recognised representatives of their employees shall be entitled, upon application, to be heard.

Article 19
Liaison with the authorities of the Member States

1. The Commission shall transmit to the competent authorities of the Member States copies of notifications within three working days and, as soon as possible, copies of the most important documents lodged with or issued by the Commission pursuant to this Regulation. Such documents shall include commitments offered by the undertakings concerned vis-à-vis the Commission with a view to rendering the concentration compatible with the common market pursuant to Article 6(2) or Article 8(2), second subparagraph.

2. The Commission shall carry out the procedures set out in this Regulation in close and constant liaison with the competent authorities of the Member States, which may express their views upon those procedures. For the purposes of Article 9 it shall obtain information from the competent authority of the Member State as referred to in paragraph 2 of that Article and give it the opportunity to make known its views at every

stage of the procedure up to the adoption of a decision pursuant to paragraph 3 of that Article; to that end it shall give it access to the file.

3. An Advisory Committee on concentrations shall be consulted before any decision is taken pursuant to Article 8(1) to (6), Articles 14 or 15 with the exception of provisional decisions taken in accordance with Article 18(2).

4. The Advisory Committee shall consist of representatives of the competent authorities of the Member States. Each Member State shall appoint one or two representatives; if unable to attend, they may be replaced by other representatives. At least one of the representatives of a Member State shall be competent in matters of restrictive practices and dominant positions.

5. Consultation shall take place at a joint meeting convened at the invitation of and chaired by the Commission. A summary of the case, together with an indication of the most important documents and a preliminary draft of the decision to be taken for each case considered, shall be sent with the invitation. The meeting shall take place not less than 10 working days after the invitation has been sent. The Commission may in exceptional cases shorten that period as appropriate in order to avoid serious harm to one or more of the undertakings concerned by a concentration.

6. The Advisory Committee shall deliver an opinion on the Commission's draft decision, if necessary by taking a vote. The Advisory Committee may deliver an opinion even if some members are absent and unrepresented. The opinion shall be delivered in writing and appended to the draft decision. The Commission shall take the utmost account of the opinion delivered by the Committee. It shall inform the Committee of the manner in which its opinion has been taken into account.

7. The Commission shall communicate the opinion of the Advisory Committee, together with the decision, to the addressees of the decision. It shall make the opinion public together with the decision, having regard to the legitimate interest of undertakings in the protection of their business secrets.

Article 20
Publication of decisions

1. The Commission shall publish the decisions which it takes pursuant to Article 8(1) to(6), Articles 14 and 15 with the exception of provisional decisions taken in accordance with Article 18(2) together with the opinion of the Advisory Committee in the Official Journal of the European Union.

2. The publication shall state the names of the parties and the main content of the decision; it shall have regard to the legitimate interest of undertakings in the protection of their business secrets.

Article 21
Application of the Regulation and jurisdiction

1. This Regulation alone shall apply to concentrations as defined in Article 3, and Council Regulations (EC) No. 1/2003, (EEC) No. 1017/68, (EEC) No. 4056/86 and (EEC) No. 3975/87 shall not apply, except in relation to joint ventures that do not have a [Union] dimension and which have as their object or effect the coordination of the competitive behaviour of undertakings that remain independent.

17

2. Subject to review by the Court of Justice, the Commission shall have sole jurisdiction to take the decisions provided for in this Regulation.

3. No Member State shall apply its national legislation on competition to any concentration that has a [Union] dimension.

   The first subparagraph shall be without prejudice to any Member State's power to carry out any enquiries necessary for the application of Articles 4(4), 9(2) or after referral, pursuant to Article 9(3), first subparagraph, indent (b), or Article 9(5), to take the measures strictly necessary for the application of Article 9(8).

4. Notwithstanding paragraphs 2 and 3, Member States may take appropriate measures to protect legitimate interests other than those taken into consideration by this Regulation and compatible with the general principles and other provisions of [Union] law.

   Public security, plurality of the media and prudential rules shall be regarded as legitimate interests within the meaning of the first subparagraph.

   Any other public interest must be communicated to the Commission by the Member State concerned and shall be recognised by the Commission after an assessment of its compatibility with the general principles and other provisions of [Union] law before the measures referred to above may be taken. The Commission shall inform the Member State concerned of its decision within 25 working days of that communication.

Article 22
Referral to the Commission

1. One or more Member States may request the Commission to examine any concentration as defined in Article 3 that does not have a [Union] dimension within the meaning of Article 1 but affects trade between Member States and threatens to significantly affect competition within the territory of the Member State or States making the request.

   Such a request shall be made at most within 15 working days of the date on which the concentration was notified, or if no notification is required, otherwise made known to the Member State concerned.

2. The Commission shall inform the competent authorities of the Member States and the undertakings concerned of any request received pursuant to paragraph 1 without delay.

   Any other Member State shall have the right to join the initial request within a period of 15 working days of being informed by the Commission of the initial request.

   All national time limits relating to the concentration shall be suspended until, in accordance with the procedure set out in this Article, it has been decided where the concentration shall be examined. As soon as a Member State has informed the Commission and the undertakings concerned that it does not wish to join the request, the suspension of its national time limits shall end.

3. The Commission may, at the latest 10 working days after the expiry of the period set in paragraph 2, decide to examine, the concentration where it considers that it affects trade between Member States and threatens to significantly affect competition within the territory of the Member State or States making the request. If the Commission does not take a decision within this period, it shall be deemed to have adopted a decision to examine the concentration in accordance with the request.

The Commission shall inform all Member States and the undertakings concerned of its decision. It may request the submission of a notification pursuant to Article 4.

The Member State or States having made the request shall no longer apply their national legislation on competition to the concentration.

4. Article 2, Article 4(2) to (3), Articles 5, 6, and 8 to 21 shall apply where the Commission examines a concentration pursuant to paragraph 3. Article 7 shall apply to the extent that the concentration has not been implemented on the date on which the Commission informs the undertakings concerned that a request has been made.

Where a notification pursuant to Article 4 is not required, the period set in Article 10(1) within which proceedings may be initiated shall begin on the working day following that on which the Commission informs the undertakings concerned that it has decided to examine the concentration pursuant to paragraph 3.

5. The Commission may inform one or several Member States that it considers a concentration fulfils the criteria in paragraph 1. In such cases, the Commission may invite that Member State or those Member States to make a request pursuant to paragraph 1.

Article 23
Implementing provisions

1. The Commission shall have the power to lay down in accordance with the procedure referred to in paragraph 2:
   (a) implementing provisions concerning the form, content and other details of notifications and submissions pursuant to Article 4;
   (b) implementing provisions concerning time limits pursuant to Article 4(4), (5)[,] Articles 7, 9, 10 and 22;
   (c) the procedure and time limits for the submission and implementation of commitments pursuant to Article 6(2) and Article 8(2);
   (d) implementing provisions concerning hearings pursuant to Article 18.

2. The Commission shall be assisted by an Advisory Committee, composed of representatives of the Member States.
   (a) Before publishing draft implementing provisions and before adopting such provisions, the Commission shall consult the Advisory Committee.
   (b) Consultation shall take place at a meeting convened at the invitation of and chaired by the Commission. A draft of the implementing provisions to be taken shall be sent with the invitation. The meeting shall take place not less than 10 working days after the invitation has been sent.
   (c) The Advisory Committee shall deliver an opinion on the draft implementing provisions, if necessary by taking a vote. The Commission shall take the utmost account of the opinion delivered by the Committee.

Article 24
Relations with third countries

1. The Member States shall inform the Commission of any general difficulties encountered by their undertakings with concentrations as defined in Article 3 in a third country.

2. Initially not more than one year after the entry into force of this Regulation and, thereafter periodically, the Commission shall draw up a report examining the treatment

accorded to undertakings having their seat or their principal fields of activity in the [Union], in the terms referred to in paragraphs 3 and 4, as regards concentrations in third countries. The Commission shall submit those reports to the Council, together with any recommendations.

3. Whenever it appears to the Commission, either on the basis of the reports referred to in paragraph 2 or on the basis of other information, that a third country does not grant undertakings having their seat or their principal fields of activity in the [Union], treatment comparable to that granted by the [Union] to undertakings from that country, the Commission may submit proposals to the Council for an appropriate mandate for negotiation with a view to obtaining comparable treatment for undertakings having their seat or their principal fields of activity in the [Union].

4. Measures taken under this Article shall comply with the obligations of the [Union] or of the Member States, without prejudice to Article [351] of the Treaty, under international agreements, whether bilateral or multilateral.

Article 25

Repeal

1. Without prejudice to Article 26(2), Regulations (EEC) No. 4064/89 and (EC) No. 1310/97 shall be repealed with effect from 1 May 2004.

2. References to the repealed Regulations shall be construed as references to this Regulation and shall be read in accordance with the correlation table in the Annex.

Article 26

Entry into force and transitional provisions

1. This Regulation shall enter into force on the 20th day following that of its publication in the Official Journal of the European Union.

    It shall apply from 1 May 2004.

2. Regulation (EEC) No. 4064/89 shall continue to apply to any concentration which was the subject of an agreement or announcement or where control was acquired within the meaning of Article 4(1) of that Regulation before the date of application of this Regulation, subject, in particular, to the provisions governing applicability set out in Article 25(2) and (3) of Regulation (EEC) No. 4064/89 and Article 2 of Regulation (EEC) No. 1310/97.

3. As regards concentrations to which this Regulation applies by virtue of accession, the date of accession shall be substituted for the date of application of this Regulation.

    This Regulation shall be binding in its entirety and directly applicable in all Member States.

    (*Signatures omitted*)

18

Regulation 651/2014 Declaring Certain Categories of Aid Compatible with the Internal Market in Application of Articles 107 and 108 of the Treaty

Contents

18

THE EUROPEAN COMMISSION,

Having regard to the Treaty on the Functioning of the European Union, and in particular Article 108(4) thereof,

Having regard to Council Regulation [2015/1588 on the application of Articles 107 and 108 of the Treaty on the Functioning of the European Union to certain categories of horizontal State aid] …

HAS ADOPTED THIS REGULATION:

Chapter I Common Provisions

Article 1

Scope

1. This Regulation shall apply to the following categories of aid:
    (a) regional aid;
    (b) aid to SMEs in the form of investment aid, operating aid and SMEs' access to finance;
    (c) aid for environmental protection;
    (d) aid for research and development and innovation;
    (e) training aid;
    (f) recruitment and employment aid for disadvantaged workers and workers with disabilities;
    (g) aid to make good the damage caused by certain natural disasters;
    (h) social aid for transport for residents of remote regions;
    (i) aid for broadband infrastructures;
    (j) aid for culture and heritage conservation;
    (k) aid for sport and multifunctional recreational infrastructure;
    (l) aid for local infrastructures;
    (m) aid for regional airports; and
    (n) aid for ports.

2. This Regulation shall not apply to:
    (a) schemes under Sections 1 (with the exception of Article 15), 2, 3, 4, 7 (with the exception of Article 44), and 10 of Chapter III of this Regulation, if the average annual State aid budget exceeds EUR 150 million, from six months after their entry into force. The Commission may decide that this Regulation shall continue to apply for a longer period to any of these aid schemes after having assessed the relevant evaluation plan notified by the Member State to the Commission, within 20 working days from the scheme's entry into force;
    (b) any alterations of schemes referred to in Article 1(2)(a), other than modifications which cannot affect the compatibility of the aid scheme under this Regulation or cannot significantly affect the content of the approved evaluation plan;
    (c) aid to export-related activities towards third countries or Member States, namely aid directly linked to the quantities exported, to the establishment and operation of a distribution network or to other current costs linked to the export activity;
    (d) aid contingent upon the use of domestic over imported goods.

3. This Regulation shall not apply to:
    (a) aid granted in the fishery and aquaculture sector, as covered by Regulation (EU) No. 1379/2013 of the European Parliament and of the Council with the exception of training aid, aid for SMEs' access to finance, aid in the field of research and development, innovation aid for SMEs, aid for disadvantaged workers and workers with disabilities, regional investment aid in outermost regions and regional operating aid schemes;
    (b) aid granted in the primary agricultural production sector, with the exception of regional investment aid in outermost regions, regional operating aid schemes, aid for consultancy in favour of SMEs, risk finance aid, aid for research and

development, innovation aid for SMEs, environmental aid, training aid and aid for disadvantaged workers and workers with disabilities;

(c) aid granted in the sector of processing and marketing of agricultural products, in the following cases:

(i) where the amount of the aid is fixed on the basis of the price or quantity of such products purchased from primary producers or put on the market by the undertakings concerned;

(ii) where the aid is conditional on being partly or entirely passed on to primary producers;

(d) aid to facilitate the closure of uncompetitive coal mines, as covered by Council Decision 2010/787/EU;

(e) the categories of regional aid referred to in Article 13.

Where an undertaking is active in the excluded sectors as referred to in points (a), (b) or (c) of the first subparagraph and in sectors which fall within the scope of this Regulation, this Regulation applies to aid granted in respect of the latter sectors or activities, provided that Member States ensure by appropriate means, such as separation of activities or distinction of costs, that the activities in the excluded sectors do not benefit from the aid granted in accordance with this Regulation.

4. This Regulation shall not apply to:

(a) aid schemes which do not explicitly exclude the payment of individual aid in favour of an undertaking which is subject to an outstanding recovery order following a previous Commission decision declaring an aid granted by the same Member State illegal and incompatible with the internal market, with the exception of aid schemes to make good the damage caused by certain natural disasters;

(b) ad hoc aid in favour of an undertaking as referred to in point (a);

(c) aid to undertakings in difficulty, with the exception of aid schemes to make good the damage caused by certain natural disasters, start-up aid schemes and regional operating aid schemes, provided those schemes do not treat undertakings in difficulty more favourably than other undertakings.

5. This Regulation shall not apply to State aid measures, which entail, by themselves, by the conditions attached to them or by their financing method a non-severable violation of Union law, in particular:

(a) aid measures where the grant of aid is subject to the obligation for the beneficiary to have its headquarters in the relevant Member State or to be predominantly established in that Member State; [h]owever, the requirement to have an establishment or branch in the aid granting Member State at the moment of payment of the aid is allowed;

(b) aid measures where the grant of aid is subject to the obligation for the beneficiary to use nationally produced goods or national services;

(c) aid measures restricting the possibility for the beneficiaries to exploit the research, development and innovation results in other Member States.

Article 2

Definitions

For the purposes of this Regulation the following definitions shall apply:

(1) 'aid' means any measure fulfilling all the criteria laid down in Article 107(1) of the Treaty;

(2) 'small and medium-sized enterprises' or 'SMEs' means undertakings fulfilling the criteria laid down in Annex I;

(3) 'worker with disabilities' means any person who:
   (a) is recognised as worker with disabilities under national law; or
   (b) has long-term physical, mental, intellectual or sensory impairment(s) which, in interaction with various barriers, may hinder their full and effective participation in a work environment on an equal basis with other workers;

(4) 'disadvantaged worker' means any person who:
   (a) has not been in regular paid employment for the previous 6 months; or
   (b) is between 15 and 24 years of age; or
   (c) has not attained an upper secondary educational or vocational qualification (International Standard Classification of Education 3) or is within two years after completing full-time education and who has not previously obtained his or her first regular paid employment; or
   (d) is over the age of 50 years; or
   (e) lives as a single adult with one or more dependants; or
   (f) works in a sector or profession in a Member State where the gender imbalance is at least 25% higher than the average gender imbalance across all economic sectors in that Member State, and belongs to that underrepresented gender group; or
   (g) is a member of an ethnic minority within a Member State and who requires development of his or her linguistic, vocational training or work experience profile to enhance prospects of gaining access to stable employment;

(5) 'transport' means transport of passengers by aircraft, maritime transport, road, rail, or by inland waterway or freight transport services for hire or reward;

(6) 'transport costs' means the costs of transport for hire or reward actually paid by the beneficiaries per journey, comprising:
   (a) freight charges, handling costs and temporary stocking costs, in so far as these costs relate to the journey;
   (b) insurance costs applied to the cargo;
   (c) taxes, duties or levies applied to the cargo and, if applicable, to the deadweight, both at point of origin and point of destination; and
   (d) safety and security control costs, surcharges for increased fuel costs;

(7) 'remote regions' means outermost regions, Malta, Cyprus, Ceuta and Melilla, islands which are part of the territory of a Member State and sparsely populated areas;

(8) 'marketing of agricultural products' means holding or display with a view to sale, offering for sale, delivery or any other manner of placing on the market, except the first sale by a primary producer to resellers or processors and any activity preparing a product for such first sale; a sale by a primary producer to final consumers shall be considered to be marketing if it takes place in separate premises reserved for that purpose;

(9) 'primary agricultural production' means production of products of the soil and of stock farming, listed in Annex I to the Treaty, without performing any further operation changing the nature of such products;

(10) 'processing of agricultural products' means any operation on an agricultural product resulting in a product which is also an agricultural product, except on-farm activities necessary for preparing an animal or plant product for the first sale;

(11) 'agricultural product' means the products listed in Annex I to the Treaty, except fishery and aquaculture products listed in Annex I to Regulation (EU) No. 1379/2013 of the European Parliament and of the Council of 11 December 2013;

(12) 'outermost regions' means regions as defined in Article 349 of the Treaty. In accordance with European Council Decision 2010/718/EU, from 1 January 2012, Saint-Barthélemy ceased to be an outermost region. In accordance with European Council Decision 2012/419/EU on 1 January 2014, Mayotte became an outermost region;

(13) 'coal' means high-grade, medium-grade and low-grade category A and B coal within the meaning of the international codification system for coal established by the United Nations Economic Commission for Europe and clarified in the Council Decision of 10 December 2010 on State aid to facilitate the closure of uncompetitive coal mines;

(14) 'individual aid' means:
   (i) ad hoc aid; and
   (ii) awards of aid to individual beneficiaries on the basis of an aid scheme;

(15) 'aid scheme' means any act on the basis of which, without further implementing measures being required, individual aid awards may be made to undertakings defined within the act in a general and abstract manner and any act on the basis of which aid which is not linked to a specific project may be granted to one or several undertakings for an indefinite period of time and/or for an indefinite amount;

(16) 'evaluation plan' means a document containing at least the following minimum elements: the objectives of the aid scheme to be evaluated, the evaluation questions, the result indicators, the envisaged methodology to conduct the evaluation, the data collection requirements, the proposed timing of the evaluation including the date of submission of the final evaluation report, the description of the independent body conducting the evaluation or the criteria that will be used for its selection and the modalities for ensuring the publicity of the evaluation;

(17) 'ad hoc aid' means aid not granted on the basis of an aid scheme;

(18) 'undertaking in difficulty' means an undertaking in respect of which at least one of the following circumstances occurs:
   (a) In the case of a limited liability company (other than an SME that has been in existence for less than three years or, for the purposes of eligibility for risk finance aid, an SME within 7 years from its first commercial sale that qualifies for risk finance investments following due diligence by the selected financial intermediary), where more than half of its subscribed share capital has disappeared as a result of accumulated losses. This is the case when deduction of accumulated losses from reserves (and all other elements generally considered as part of the own funds of the company) leads to a negative cumulative amount that exceeds half of the subscribed share capital. For the purposes of this provision, 'limited liability company' refers in particular to the types of company mentioned in Annex I of Directive 2013/34/EU and 'share capital' includes, where relevant, any share premium;

18

(b) In the case of a company where at least some members have unlimited liability for the debt of the company (other than an SME that has been in existence for less than three years or, for the purposes of eligibility for risk finance aid, an SME within 7 years from its first commercial sale that qualifies for risk finance investments following due diligence by the selected financial intermediary), where more than half of its capital as shown in the company accounts has disappeared as a result of accumulated losses. For the purposes of this provision, 'a company where at least some members have unlimited liability for the debt of the company' refers in particular to the types of company mentioned in Annex II of Directive 2013/34/EU;

(c) Where the undertaking is subject to collective insolvency proceedings or fulfils the criteria under its domestic law for being placed in collective insolvency proceedings at the request of its creditors;

(d) Where the undertaking has received rescue aid and has not yet reimbursed the loan or terminated the guarantee, or has received restructuring aid and is still subject to a restructuring plan;

(e) In the case of an undertaking that is not an SME, where, for the past two years:
(1) the undertaking's book debt to equity ratio has been greater than 7,5 and
(2) the undertaking's EBITDA interest coverage ratio has been below 1,0;

(19) 'territorial spending obligations': mean the obligations imposed by the authority granting the aid on beneficiaries to spend a minimum amount and/or conduct a minimum level of production activity in a particular territory;

(20) 'adjusted aid amount' means the maximum permissible aid amount for a large investment project, calculated according to the following formula:

$$\text{maximum aid amount} = R \times (A + 0{,}50 \times B + 0 \times C)$$

where: R is the maximum aid intensity applicable in the area concerned established in an approved regional map and which is in force on the date of granting the aid, excluding the increased aid intensity for SMEs; A is the initial EUR 50 million of eligible costs, B is the part of eligible costs between EUR 50 million and EUR 100 million and C is the part of eligible costs above EUR 100 million;

(21) 'repayable advance' means a loan for a project which is paid in one or more instalments and the conditions for the reimbursement of which depend on the outcome of the project;

(22) 'gross grant equivalent' means the amount of the aid if it had been provided in the form of a grant to the beneficiary, before any deduction of tax or other charge;

(23) 'start of works' means the earlier of either the start of construction works relating to the investment, or the first legally binding commitment to order equipment or any other commitment that makes the investment irreversible. Buying land and preparatory works such as obtaining permits and conducting feasibility studies are not considered start of works. For take-overs, 'start of works' means the moment of acquiring the assets directly linked to the acquired establishment;

(24) 'large enterprises' means undertakings not fulfilling the criteria laid down in Annex I;

(25) 'fiscal successor scheme' means a scheme in the form of tax advantages which constitutes an amended version of a previously existing scheme in the form of tax advantages and which replaces it;

(26) 'aid intensity' means the gross aid amount expressed as a percentage of the eligible costs, before any deduction of tax or other charge;

(27) 'assisted areas' means areas designated in an approved regional aid map for the period 1.7.2014–31.12.2020 in application of Articles 107(3)(a) and (c) of the Treaty;

(28) 'date of granting of the aid' means the date when the legal right to receive the aid is conferred on the beneficiary under the applicable national legal regime;

(29) 'tangible assets' means assets consisting of land, buildings and plant, machinery and equipment;

(30) 'intangible assets' means assets that do not have a physical or financial embodiment such as patents, licences, know-how or other intellectual property;

(31) 'wage cost' means the total amount actually payable by the beneficiary of the aid in respect of the employment concerned, comprising over a defined period of time the gross wage before tax and compulsory contributions such as social security, child care and parent care costs;

(32) 'net increase in the number of employees' means a net increase in the number of employees in the establishment concerned compared with the average over a given period in time, and that any posts lost during that period must therefore be deducted and that the number of persons employed full-time, part-time and seasonal has to be considered with their annual labour unit fractions;

(33) 'dedicated infrastructure' means infrastructure that is built for *ex-ante* identifiable undertaking(s) and tailored to their needs[;]

(34) 'financial intermediary' means any financial institution regardless of its form and ownership, including fund-of-funds, private equity investment funds, public investment funds, banks, micro-finance institutions and guarantee societies;

(35) 'journey' means the movement of goods from the point of origin to the point of destination, including any intermediary sections or stages within or outside the Member State concerned, made using one or more means of transport;

(36) 'fair rate of return (FRR)' means the expected rate of return equivalent to a risk-adjusted discount rate which reflects the level of risk of a project and the nature and level of capital the private investors plan to invest;

(37) 'total financing' means the overall investment amount made into an eligible undertaking or project under Section 3 or under Articles 16 or 39 of this Regulation to the exclusion of entirely private investments provided on market terms and outside the scope of the relevant State aid measure;

(38) 'competitive bidding process' means a non-discriminatory bidding process that provides for the participation of a sufficient number of undertakings and where the aid is granted on the basis of either the initial bid submitted by the bidder or a clearing price. In addition, the budget or volume related to the bidding process is a binding constraint leading to a situation where not all bidders can receive aid;

(39) 'operating profit' means the difference between the discounted revenues and the discounted operating costs over the economic lifetime of the investment, where this difference is positive. The operating costs include costs such as personnel costs, materials, contracted services, communications, energy, maintenance, rent, administration, but exclude depreciation charges and the costs of financing if

these have been covered by investment aid. Discounting revenues and operating costs using an appropriate discount rate allows a reasonable profit to be made;

Definitions applying to regional aid

(40) Definitions applying to aid for broadband infrastructures (Section 10) are applicable to the relevant regional aid provisions;

(41) 'regional investment aid' means regional aid granted for an initial investment or an initial investment in favour of a new economic activity;

(42) 'regional operating aid' means aid to reduce an undertaking's current expenditure. This includes cost categories such as personnel costs, materials, contracted services, communications, energy, maintenance, rent, administration, but excludes depreciation charges and the costs of financing if these have been included in the eligible costs when granting investment aid;

(43) 'steel sector' means all activities related to the production of one or more of the following products:

(a) pig iron and ferro-alloys:
pig iron for steelmaking, foundry and other pig iron, spiege-leisen and high-carbon ferro-manganese, not including other ferro-alloys;

(b) crude and semi-finished products of iron, ordinary steel or special steel:
liquid steel whether or not cast into ingots, including ingots for forging semi-finished products: blooms, billets and slabs; sheet bars and tinplate bars; hot-rolled wide coils, with the exception of production of liquid steel for castings from small and medium-sized foundries;

(c) hot finished products of iron, ordinary steel or special steel:
rails, sleepers, fishplates, soleplates, joists, heavy sections of 80 mm and over, sheet piling, bars and sections of less than 80 mm and flats of less than 150 mm, wire rod, tube rounds and squares, hot-rolled hoop and strip (including tube strip), hot-rolled sheet (coated or uncoated), plates and sheets of 3 mm thickness and over, universal plates of 150 mm and over, with the exception of wire and wire products, bright bars and iron castings;

(d) cold finished products:
tinplate, terneplate, blackplate, galvanised sheets, other coated sheets, cold-rolled sheets, electrical sheets and strip for tinplate, cold-rolled plate, in coil and in strip;

(e) tubes:
all seamless steel tubes, welded steel tubes with a diameter of over 406.4 mm;

(44) 'synthetic fibres sector' means:

(a) extrusion/texturisation of all generic types of fibre and yarn based on polyester, polyamide, acrylic or polypropylene, irrespective of their end-uses; or

(b) polymerisation (including polycondensation) where it is integrated with extrusion in terms of the machinery used; or

(c) any ancillary process linked to the contemporaneous installation of extrusion/texturisation capacity by the prospective beneficiary or by another company in the group to which it belongs and which, in the specific business activity concerned, is normally integrated with such capacity in terms of the machinery used;

18

(45)   'transport sector' means the transport of passengers by aircraft, maritime transport, road or rail and by inland waterway or freight transport services for hire or reward; more specifically, the 'transport sector' means the following activities in terms of NACE Rev. 2:

   (a) NACE 49: Land transport and transport via pipelines, excluding NACE 49.32 Taxi operation, 49.42 Removal services, 49.5 Transport via pipeline;

   (b) NACE 50: Water transport;

   (c) NACE 51: Air transport, excluding NACE 51.22 Space transport;

(46)   'scheme targeted at a limited number of specific sectors of economic activity' means a scheme which covers activities falling within the scope of less than five classes (four-digit numerical code) of the NACE Rev. 2 statistical classification;

(47)   'tourism activity' means the following activities in terms of NACE Rev. 2:

   (a) NACE 55: Accommodation;

   (b) NACE 56: Food and beverage service activities;

   (c) NACE 79: Travel agency, tour operator reservation service and related activities;

   (d) NACE 90: Creative, arts and entertainment activities;

   (e) NACE 91: Libraries, archives, museums and other cultural activities;

   (f) NACE 93: Sports activities and amusement and recreation activities;

(48)   'sparsely populated areas' means NUTS 2 regions with less than 8 inhabitants per km2 or NUTS 3 regions with less than 12,5 inhabitants per km2 or areas which are recognized by the Commission as such in an individual decision on a regional aid map in force at the time the aid is granted;

(48a) 'very sparsely populated areas' means NUTS 2 regions with less than 8 inhabitants per km2 or areas which are recognized by the Commission as such in an individual decision on a regional aid map in force at the time the aid is granted;

(49)   'initial investment' means:

   (a) an investment in tangible and intangible assets related to the setting-up of a new establishment, extension of the capacity of an existing establishment, diversification of the output of an establishment into products not previously produced in the establishment or a fundamental change in the overall production process of an existing establishment; or

   (b) an acquisition of assets belonging to an establishment that has closed or would have closed had it not been purchased, and is bought by an investor unrelated to the seller and excludes sole acquisition of the shares of an undertaking;

(50)   'the same or a similar activity' means an activity falling under the same class (four-digit numerical code) of the NACE Rev. 2 statistical classification of economic activities as laid down in Regulation (EC) No. 1893/2006 of the European Parliament and of the Council of 20 December 2006 establishing the statistical classification of economic activities NACE Revision 2 and amending Council Regulation (EEC) No. 3037/90 as well as certain EC Regulations on specific statistical domains;

(51)   'initial investment in favour of new economic activity' means:

   (a) an investment in tangible and intangible assets related to the setting up of a new establishment, or to the diversification of the activity of an establishment, under the condition that the new activity is not the same or a similar activity to the activity previously performed in the establishment;

18

(b) the acquisition of the assets belonging to an establishment that has closed or would have closed had it not been purchased, and is bought by an investor unrelated to the seller, under the condition that the new activity to be performed using the acquired assets is not the same or a similar activity to the activity performed in the establishment prior to the acquisition;

(52) 'large investment project' means an initial investment with eligible costs exceeding EUR 50 million, calculated at prices and exchange rates on the date of granting the aid;

(53) 'point of destination' means the place where the goods are unloaded;

(54) 'point of origin' means the place where the goods are loaded for transport;

(55) 'areas eligible for operating aid' means an outermost region referred to in Article 349 of the Treaty, a sparsely populated area or a very sparsely populated area;

(56) 'means of transport' means rail transport, road freight transport, inland waterway transport, maritime transport, air transport, and intermodal transport;

(57) 'urban development fund' ('UDF') means a specialised investment vehicle set up for the purpose of investing in urban development projects under an urban development aid measure. UDFs are managed by an urban development fund manager;

(58) 'urban development fund manager' means a professional management company with legal personality, selecting and making investments in eligible urban development projects;

(59) 'urban development project' ('UDP') means an investment project that has the potential to support the implementation of interventions envisaged by an integrated approach to sustainable urban development and contribute to achieving of the objectives defined therein, including projects with an internal rate of return which may not be sufficient to attract financing on a purely commercial basis. An urban development project may be organised as a separate block of finance within the legal structures of the beneficiary private investor or as a separate legal entity, e.g. a special purpose vehicle;

(60) 'integrated sustainable urban development strategy' means a strategy officially proposed and certified by a relevant local authority or public sector agency, defined for a specific urban geographic area and period, that set out integrated actions to tackle the economic, environmental, climate, demographic and social challenges affecting urban areas;

(61) 'in-kind contribution' means the contribution of land or real estate where the land or real estate forms part of the urban development project;

(61a) 'relocation' means a transfer of the same or similar activity or part thereof from an establishment in one contracting party to the EEA Agreement (initial establishment) to the establishment in which the aided investment takes place in another contracting party to the EEA Agreement (aided establishment). There is a transfer if the product or service in the initial and in the aided establishments serves at least partly the same purposes and meets the demands or needs of the same type of customers and jobs are lost in the same or similar activity in one of the initial establishments of the beneficiary in the EEA;

Definitions for aid to SMEs

(62) 'employment directly created by an investment project' means employment concerning the activity to which the investment relates, including employment

created following an increase in the utilisation rate of the capacity created by the investment;

(63) 'organisational cooperation' means the development of joint business strategies or management structures, the provision of common services or services to facilitate cooperation, coordinated activities such as research or marketing, the support of networks and clusters, the improvement of accessibility and communication, the use of joint instruments to encourage entrepreneurship and trade with SMEs;

(64) 'advisory services linked to cooperation' means consulting, assistance and training for the exchange of knowledge and experiences and for improvement of cooperation;

(65) 'support services linked to cooperation' means the provision of office space, websites, data banks, libraries, market research, handbooks, working and model documents;

Definitions for aid for access to finance for SMEs

(66) 'quasi-equity investment' means a type of financing that ranks between equity and debt, having a higher risk than senior debt and a lower risk than common equity and whose return for the holder is predominantly based on the profits or losses of the underlying target undertaking and which are unsecured in the event of default. Quasi-equity investments can be structured as debt, unsecured and subordinated, including mezzanine debt, and in some cases convertible into equity, or as preferred equity;

(67) 'guarantee' in the context of sections 1, 3 and 7 of the Regulation means a written commitment to assume responsibility for all or part of a third party's newly originated loan transactions such as debt or lease instruments, as well as quasi-equity instruments;

(68) 'guarantee rate' means the percentage of loss coverage by a public investor of each and every transaction eligible under the relevant State aid measure;

(69) 'exit' means the liquidation of holdings by a financial intermediary or investor, including trade sale, write-offs, repayment of shares/loans, sale to another financial intermediary or another investor, sale to a financial institution and sale by public offering, including an initial public offering (IPO);

(70) 'financial endowment' means a repayable public investment made to a financial intermediary for the purposes of making investments under a risk finance measure, and where all the proceeds shall be returned to the public investor;

(71) 'risk finance investment' means equity and quasi-equity investments, loans including leases, guarantees, or a mix thereof to eligible undertakings for the purposes of making new investments;

(72) 'independent private investor' means a private investor who is not a shareholder of the eligible undertaking in which it invests, including business angels and financial institutions, irrespective of their ownership, to the extent that they bear the full risk in respect of their investment. Upon the creation of a new company, private investors, including the founders, are considered to be independent from that company;

(73) 'natural person' for the purpose of Articles 21 and 23 means a person other than a legal entity who is not an undertaking for the purposes of Article 107(1) of the Treaty;

(74) 'equity investment' means the provision of capital to an undertaking, invested directly or indirectly in return for the ownership of a corresponding share of that undertaking;

(75) 'first commercial sale' means the first sale by a company on a product or service market, excluding limited sales to test the market;

(76) 'unlisted SME' means an SME which is not listed on the official list of a stock exchange, except for alternative trading platforms;

(77) 'follow-on investment' means additional risk finance investment in a company subsequent to one or more previous risk finance investment rounds;

(78) 'replacement capital' means the purchase of existing shares in a company from an earlier investor or shareholder;

(79) 'entrusted entity' means the European Investment Bank and the European Investment Fund, an international financial institution in which a Member State is a shareholder, or a financial institution established in a Member State aiming at the achievement of public interest under the control of a public authority, a public law body, or a private law body with a public service mission: the entrusted entity can be selected or directly appointed in accordance with the provisions of Directive 2004/18/EC on the coordination of procedures for the award of public works contracts, public supply contracts and public service contracts, or any subsequent legislation replacing that Directive in full or in part;

(80) 'innovative enterprise' means an enterprise:
   (a) that can demonstrate, by means of an evaluation carried out by an external expert that it will in the foreseeable future develop products, services or processes which are new or substantially improved compared to the state of the art in its industry, and which carry a risk of technological or industrial failure[;] or
   (b) the research and development costs of which represent at least 10% of its total operating costs in at least one of the three years preceding the granting of the aid or, in the case of a start-up enterprise without any financial history, in the audit of its current fiscal period, as certified by an external auditor;

(81) 'alternative trading platform' means a multilateral trading facility as defined in Article 4(1)(15) of Directive 2004/39/EC where the majority of the financial instruments admitted to trading are issued by SMEs;

(82) 'loan' means an agreement which obliges the lender to make available to the borrower an agreed amount of money for an agreed period of time and under which the borrower is obliged to repay the amount within the agreed period. It may take the form of a loan, or another funding instrument, including a lease, which provides the lender with a predominant component of minimum yield. The refinancing of existing loans shall not be an eligible loan[;]

Definitions for aid for research and development and innovation

(83) 'research and knowledge-dissemination organisation' means an entity (such as universities or research institutes, technology transfer agencies, innovation intermediaries, research-oriented physical or virtual collaborative entities), irrespective of its legal status (organised under public or private law) or way of financing, whose primary goal is to independently conduct fundamental research, industrial research or experimental development or to widely disseminate the results of such

activities by way of teaching, publication or knowledge transfer. Where such entity also pursues economic activities the financing, the costs and the revenues of those economic activities must be accounted for separately. Undertakings that can exert a decisive influence upon such an entity, in the quality of, for example, shareholders or members, may not enjoy preferential access to the results generated by it;

(84) 'fundamental research' means experimental or theoretical work undertaken primarily to acquire new knowledge of the underlying foundations of phenomena and observable facts, without any direct commercial application or use in view;

(85) 'industrial research' means the planned research or critical investigation aimed at the acquisition of new knowledge and skills for developing new products, processes or services or for bringing about a significant improvement in existing products, processes or services. It comprises the creation of components parts of complex systems, and may include the construction of prototypes in a laboratory environment or in an environment with simulated interfaces to existing systems as well as of pilot lines, when necessary for the industrial research and notably for generic technology validation;

(86) 'experimental development' means acquiring, combining, shaping and using existing scientific, technological, business and other relevant knowledge and skills with the aim of developing new or improved products, processes or services. This may also include, for example, activities aiming at the conceptual definition, planning and documentation of new products, processes or services;

Experimental development may comprise prototyping, demonstrating, piloting, testing and validation of new or improved products, processes or services in environments representative of real life operating conditions where the primary objective is to make further technical improvements on products, processes or services that are not substantially set. This may include the development of a commercially usable prototype or pilot which is necessarily the final commercial product and which is too expensive to produce for it to be used only for demonstration and validation purposes.

Experimental development does not include routine or periodic changes made to existing products, production lines, manufacturing processes, services and other operations in progress, even if those changes may represent improvements;

(87) 'feasibility study' means the evaluation and analysis of the potential of a project, which aims at supporting the process of decision-making by objectively and rationally uncovering its strengths and weaknesses, opportunities and threats, as well as identifying the resources required to carry it through and ultimately its prospects for success;

(88) 'personnel costs' means the costs of researchers, technicians and other supporting staff to the extent employed on the relevant project or activity;

(89) 'arm's length' means that the conditions of the transaction between the contracting parties do not differ from those which would be stipulated between independent enterprises and contain no element of collusion. Any transaction that results from an open, transparent and non-discriminatory procedure is considered as meeting the arm's length principle;

(90) 'effective collaboration' means collaboration between at least two independent parties to exchange knowledge or technology, or to achieve a common objective based on the division of labour where the parties jointly define the scope of

the collaborative project, contribute to its implementation and share its risks, as well as its results. One or several parties may bear the full costs of the project and thus relieve other parties of its financial risks. Contract research and provision of research services are not considered forms of collaboration[;]

(91) 'research infrastructure' means facilities, resources and related services that are used by the scientific community to conduct research in their respective fields and covers scientific equipment or sets of instruments, knowledge-based resources such as collections, archives or structured scientific information, enabling information and communication technology-based infrastructures such as grid, computing, software and communication, or any other entity of a unique nature essential to conduct research. Such infrastructures may be 'single-sited' or 'distributed' (an organised network of resources) in accordance with Article 2(a) of Council Regulation (EC) No. 723/2009 of 25 June 2009 on the Community legal framework for a European Research Infrastructure Consortium (ERIC);

(92) 'innovation clusters' means structures or organised groups of independent parties (such as innovative start-ups, small, medium and large enterprises, as well as research and knowledge dissemination organisations, non-for-profit organisations and other related economic actors) designed to stimulate innovative activity through promotion, sharing of facilities and exchange of knowledge and expertise and by contributing effectively to knowledge transfer, networking, information dissemination and collaboration among the undertakings and other organisations in the cluster;

(93) 'highly qualified personnel' means staff having a tertiary education degree and at least 5 years of relevant professional experience which may also include doctoral training;

(94) 'innovation advisory services' means consultancy, assistance and training in the fields of knowledge transfer, acquisition, protection and exploitation of intangible assets, use of standards and regulations embedding them;

(95) 'innovation support services' means the provision of office space, data banks, libraries, market research, laboratories, quality labelling, testing and certification for the purpose of developing more effective products, processes or services;

(96) 'organisational innovation' means the implementation of a new organisational method in an undertaking's business practices, workplace organisation or external relations, excluding changes that are based on organisational methods already in use in the undertaking, changes in management strategy, mergers and acquisitions, ceasing to use a process, simple capital replacement or extension, changes resulting purely from changes in factor prices, customisation, localisation, regular, seasonal and other cyclical changes and trading of new or significantly improved products;

(97) 'process innovation' means the implementation of a new or significantly improved production or delivery method (including significant changes in techniques, equipment or software), excluding minor changes or improvements, increases in production or service capabilities through the addition of manufacturing or logistical systems which are very similar to those already in use, ceasing to use a process, simple capital replacement or extension, changes resulting purely from changes in factor prices, customisation, localisation, regular, seasonal and other cyclical changes and trading of new or significantly improved products;

(98) 'secondment' means temporary employment of staff by a beneficiary with the right for the staff to return to the previous employer;

Definitions for aid for disadvantaged workers and for workers with disabilities

(99) 'severely disadvantaged worker' means any person who:
(a) has not been in regular paid employment for at least 24 months; or
(b) has not been in regular paid employment for at least 12 months and belongs to one of the categories (b) to (g) mentioned under the definition of 'disadvantaged worker'[;]

(100) 'sheltered employment' means employment in an undertaking where at least 30% of workers are workers with disabilities;

Definitions applying to aid for environmental protection

(101) 'environmental protection' means any action designed to remedy or prevent damage to physical surroundings or natural resources by a beneficiary's own activities, to reduce risk of such damage or to lead to a more efficient use of natural resources, including energy-saving measures and the use of renewable sources of energy;

(102) 'Union standard' means:
(a) a mandatory Union standard setting the levels to be attained in environmental terms by individual undertakings; or
(b) the obligation under Directive 2010/75/EU of the European Parliament and of the Council to use the best available techniques (BAT) and ensure that emission levels of pollutants are not higher than they would be when applying BAT; for the cases where emission levels associated with the BAT have been defined in implementing acts adopted under Directive 2010/75/EU, those levels will be applicable for the purpose of this Regulation; where those levels are expressed as a range, the limit where the BAT is first achieved will be applicable;

(103) 'energy efficiency' means an amount of saved energy determined by measuring and/or estimating consumption before and after implementation of an energy-efficiency improvement measure, whilst ensuring normalisation for external conditions that affect energy consumption;

(104) 'energy efficiency project' means an investment project that increases the energy efficiency of a building;

(105) 'energy efficiency fund (EEF)' means a specialised investment vehicle set up for the purpose of investing in energy efficiency projects aimed at improving the energy efficiency of buildings in both the domestic and non-domestic sectors. EEFs are managed by an energy efficiency fund manager;

(106) 'energy efficiency fund manager' means a professional management company with a legal personality, selecting and making investments in eligible energy efficiency projects;

(107) 'high-efficiency cogeneration' means cogeneration which satisfies the definition of high efficiency cogeneration as set out in Article 2(34) of Directive 2012/27/EU of the European Parliament and of the Council of 25 October 2012 on energy efficiency, amending Directives 2009/125/EC and 2010/30/EU and repealing Directives 2004/8/EC and 2006/32/EC;

(108) 'cogeneration' or combined heat and power (CHP) means the simultaneous generation in one process of thermal energy and electrical and/or mechanical energy;

(109) 'energy from renewable energy sources' means energy produced by plants using only renewable energy sources, as well as the share in terms of calorific value of energy produced from renewable energy sources in hybrid plants which also use conventional energy sources. It includes renewable electricity used for filling storage systems, but excludes electricity produced as a result of storage systems;

(110) 'renewable energy sources' means the following renewable non-fossil energy sources: wind, solar, aerothermal, geothermal, hydrothermal and ocean energy, hydropower, biomass, landfill gas, sewage treatment plant gas and biogases;

(111) 'biofuel' means liquid or gaseous fuel for transport produced from biomass;

(112) 'sustainable biofuel' means a biofuel fulfilling the sustainability criteria set out in Article 17 of Directive 2009/28/EC;

(113) 'food based biofuel' means a biofuel produced from cereal and other starch rich crops, sugars and oil crops as defined in the Commission's Proposal for a Directive of the European Parliament and of the Council amending Directive 98/70/EC relating to the quality of petrol and diesel fuels and amending Directive 2009/28/EC on the promotion of the use of energy from renewable sources;

(114) 'new and innovative technology' means a new and unproven technology compared to the state of the art in the industry, which carries a risk of technological or industrial failure and is not an optimisation or scaling up of an existing technology;

(115) 'balancing responsibilities' means responsibility for imbalances (deviations between generation, consumption and commercial transactions) of a market participant or its chosen representative, referred to as the 'Balance Responsible Party', within a given period of time, referred to as the 'Imbalance Settlement Period';

(116) 'standard balancing responsibilities' means non-discriminatory balancing responsibilities across technologies which do not exempt any generator from those responsibilities;

(117) 'biomass' means the biodegradable fraction of products, waste and residues from agriculture (including vegetal and animal substances), forestry and related industries including fisheries and aquaculture, as well as biogases and the biodegradable fraction of industrial and municipal waste;

(118) 'total levelized costs of producing energy' is a calculation of the cost of generating electricity at the point of connection to a load or electricity grid. It includes the initial capital, discount rate, as well as the costs of continuous operation, fuel, and maintenance;

(119) 'environmental tax' means a tax with a specific tax base that has a clear negative effect on the environment or which seeks to tax certain activities, goods or services so that the environmental costs may be included in their price and/or so that producers and consumers are oriented towards activities which better respect the environment;

(120) 'Union minimum tax level' means the minimum level of taxation provided for in the Union legislation; for energy products and electricity it means the minimum level of taxation laid down in Annex I to Council Directive 2003/96/EC of 27 October 2003 restructuring the Community framework for the taxation of energy products and electricity;

(121) 'contaminated site' means a site where there is a confirmed presence, caused by man, of hazardous substances of such a level that they pose a significant risk to

human health or the environment taking into account current and approved future use of the land;

(122) 'polluter pays principle' or 'PPP' means that the costs of measures to deal with pollution should be borne by the polluter who causes the pollution;

(123) 'pollution' means the damage caused by a polluter directly or indirectly damaging the environment, or by creating conditions leading to such damage to physical surroundings or natural resources;

(124) 'energy efficient district heating and cooling' means a district heating and cooling system which satisfies the definition of efficient district heating and cooling system set out in Article 2(41) and (42) of Directive 2012/27/EU. The definition includes the heating/cooling production plants and the network (including related facilities) necessary to distribute the heat/ cooling from the production units to the customer premises;

(125) 'polluter' means someone who directly or indirectly damages the environment or who creates conditions leading to such damage[;]

(126) 're-use' means any operation by which products or components that are not waste are used again for the same purpose for which they were conceived;

(127) 'preparing for re-use' means checking, cleaning or repairing recovery operations, by which products or components of products that have become waste are prepared so that they can be re-used without any other pre-processing;

(128) 'recycling' means any recovery operation by which waste materials are reprocessed into products, materials or substances whether for the original or other purposes. It includes the reprocessing of organic material but does not include energy recovery and the reprocessing into materials that are to be used as fuels or for backfilling operations;

(129) 'state of the art' means a process in which the re-use of a waste product to manufacture an end product is economically profitable normal practice. Where appropriate, the concept of state of the art must be interpreted from a Union technological and internal market perspective;

(130) 'energy infrastructure' means any physical equipment or facility which is located within the Union or linking the Union to one or more third countries and falling under the following categories:

(a) concerning electricity:

(i) infrastructure for transmission, as defined in Article 2(3) by Directive 2009/72/EC of 13 July 2009 concerning common rules for internal market in electricity;

(ii) infrastructure for distribution, as defined in Article 2(5) by Directive 2009/72/EC;

(iii) electricity storage, defined as facilities used for storing electricity on a permanent or temporary basis in above-ground or underground infrastructure or geological sites, provided they are directly connected to high-voltage transmission lines designed for a voltage of 110 kV or more;

(iv) any equipment or installation essential for the systems defined in points (i) to (iii) to operate safely, securely and efficiently, including protection, monitoring and control systems at all voltage levels and substations; and

18

(v) smart grids, defined as any equipment, line, cable or installation, both at transmission and low and medium voltage distribution level, aiming at two-way digital communication, real-time or close to real-time, interactive and intelligent monitoring and management of electricity generation, transmission, distribution and consumption within an electricity network in view of developing a network efficiently integrating the behaviour and actions of all users connected to it – generators, consumers and those that do both – in order to ensure an economically efficient, sustainable electricity system with low losses and high quality and security of supply and safety;

(b) concerning gas:

   (i) transmission and distribution pipelines for the transport of natural gas and bio gas that form part of a network, excluding high-pressure pipelines used for upstream distribution of natural gas;

   (ii) underground storage facilities connected to the high-pressure gas pipelines mentioned in point (i);

   (iii) reception, storage and regasification or decompression facilities for liquefied natural gas ('LNG') or compressed natural gas ('CNG'); and

   (iv) any equipment or installation essential for the system to operate safely, securely and efficiently or to enable bi-directional capacity, including compressor stations;

(c) concerning oil:

   (i) pipelines used to transport crude oil;

   (ii) pumping stations and storage facilities necessary for the operation of crude oil pipelines; and

   (iii) any equipment or installation essential for the system in question to operate properly, securely and efficiently, including protection, monitoring and control systems and reverse-flow devices;

(d) concerning CO_2: networks of pipelines, including associated booster stations, for the transport of CO_2 to storage sites, with the aim to inject the CO_2 in suitable underground geological formations for permanent storage;

(131) 'internal energy market legislation' includes Directive 2009/72/EC of the European Parliament and of the Council of 13 July 2009 concerning common rules for the internal market in electricity, Directive 2009/73/EC of the European Parliament and of the Council of 13 July 2009 concerning common rules for the internal market in natural gas, Regulation (EC) No. 713/2009 of the European Parliament and of the Council of 13 July 2009 establishing an Agency for the Cooperation of Energy Regulators; Regulation (EC) No. 714/2009 of the European Parliament and of the Council of 13 July 2009 on conditions for access to the network for cross-border exchanges and Regulation (EC) No. 715/2009 of the European Parliament and of the Council of 13 July 2009 on conditions for access to the natural gas transmission networks or any subsequent legislation replacing these acts in full or in part;

Definitions applying to social aid for transport for residents of remote regions

(132) 'normal residence' means the place where a natural person lives for at least 185 days, in each calendar year, because of personal and occupational ties; in the case of a

person whose occupational ties are in a different place from his/her personal ties and who lives in two or more Member States, the place of normal residence is regarded as the place of his/her personal ties provided that he/she returns there regularly; where a person is living in a Member State in order to carry out a task of a set duration, the place of residence is still regarded as being the place of his/her personal ties, irrespective of whether he/she returns there during the course of this activity; attendance at a university or school in another Member State does not constitute a transfer of normal residence; alternatively, 'normal residence' shall have the meaning attributed to it in Member States' national law[;]

Definitions for aid for broadband infrastructures

(133) 'basic broadband' 'Basic broadband networks' means networks with basic functionalities which are based on technology platforms such as asymmetric digital subscriber lines (up to ADSL2+ networks), non-enhanced cable (e.g. DOCSIS 2.0), mobile networks of third generation (UMTS) and satellite systems;

(134) 'broadband-related civil engineering works' means the civil engineering works which are necessary for the deployment of a broadband network, such as digging up a road in order to enable the placement of (broadband) ducts[;]

(135) 'ducts' means underground pipes or conduits used to house (fibre, copper or coax) cables of a broadband network[;]

(136) 'physical unbundling' grants access to the end-consumer access line and allows competitors' own transmission systems to directly transmit over it[;]

(137) 'passive broadband infrastructure' means a broadband network without any active component. It typically comprises civil engineering infrastructure, ducts and dark fibre and street cabinets[;]

(138) 'next generation access (NGA) networks' means advanced networks which have at least the following characteristics: (a) deliver services reliably at a very high speed per subscriber through optical (or equivalent technology) backhaul sufficiently close to user premises to guarantee the actual delivery of the very high speed; (b) support a variety of advanced digital services including converged all-IP services, and (c) have substantially higher upload speeds (compared to basic broadband networks). At the current stage of market and technological development, NGA networks are: (a) fibre-based access networks (FTTx), (b) advanced upgraded cable networks and (c) certain advanced wireless access networks capable of delivering reliable high-speeds per subscriber[;]

(139) 'wholesale access' means access which enables an operator to utilise the facilities of another operator. The widest possible access to be provided over the relevant network shall include, on the basis of the current technological developments, at least the following access products. For FTTH/FTTB networks: ducts access, access to dark fibre, unbundled access to the local loop, and bitstream access. For cable networks: duct access and bit-stream access. For FTTC networks: duct access, sub-loop unbundling and bit-stream access. For passive network infrastructure: duct access, access to dark fibre and/or unbundled access to the local loop. For ADSL-based broadband networks: unbundled access to the local loop, bit-stream access. For mobile or wireless networks: bit-stream, sharing of physical masts and access to the backhaul networks. For satellite platforms: bit-stream access[;]

18

Definitions for aid for culture and heritage conservation

(140) 'difficult audiovisual works': means the works identified as such by Member States on the basis of pre-defined criteria when setting up schemes or granting the aid and may include films whose sole original version is in a language of a Member State with a limited territory, population or language area, short films, films by first-time and second-time directors, documentaries, or low budget or otherwise commercially difficult works[;]

(141) Development Assistance Committee (DAC) List of the OECD: means all countries and territories that are eligible to receive official development assistance and included in the list compiled by the Organisation for Economic Cooperation and Development (OECD);

(142) 'reasonable profit' shall be determined with respect to the typical profit for the sector concerned. In any event, a rate of return on capital that does not exceed the relevant swap rate plus a premium of 100 basis points will be considered to be reasonable[;]

Definitions for aid for sport and multifunctional recreational infrastructures

(143) 'professional sport' means the practice of sport in the nature of gainful employment or remunerated service, irrespective of whether or not a formal labour contract has been established between the professional sportsperson and the relevant sport organisation, where the compensation exceeds the cost of participation and constitutes a significant part of the income for the sportsperson. Travel and accommodation expenses to participate to the sport event shall not be considered as compensation for the purposes of this Regulation[;]

Definitions for aid for regional airports

(144) 'airport infrastructure' means infrastructure and equipment for the provision of airport services by the airport to airlines and the various service providers, including runways, terminals, aprons, taxiways, centralised ground handling infrastructure and any other facilities that directly support the airport services, excluding infrastructure and equipment which is primarily necessary for pursuing non-aeronautical activities;

(145) 'airline' means any airline with a valid operating licence issued by a Member State or a Member of the Common European Aviation Area pursuant to Regulation (EC) No. 1008/2008 of the European Parliament and of the Council;

(146) 'airport' means an entity or group of entities performing the economic activity of providing airport services to airlines;

(147) 'airport services' means services provided to airlines by an airport or any of its subsidiaries, to ensure the handling of aircraft, from landing to take-off, and of passengers and freight, so as to enable airlines to provide air transport services, including the provision of ground handling services and the provision of centralised ground handling infrastructure;

(148) 'average annual passenger traffic' means a figure determined on the basis of the inbound and outbound passenger traffic during the two financial years preceding that in which the aid is granted;

(149) 'centralised ground handling infrastructure' means infrastructure which is normally operated by the airport manager and put at the disposal of the various providers of

ground handling services active at the airport in exchange for remuneration, excluding equipment owned or operated by the providers of ground handling services;

(150) 'high-speed train' means a train capable of reaching speeds of over 200 km/h;

(151) 'ground handling services' means services provided to airport users at airports as described in the Annex to Council Directive 96/67/EC;

(152) 'non-aeronautical activities' means commercial services to airlines or other users of the airport, including ancillary services to passengers, freight forwarders or other service providers, renting out of offices and shops, car parking and hotels;

(153) 'regional airport' means an airport with average annual passenger traffic of up to 3 million passengers;

Definitions for aid for ports

(154) 'port' means an area of land and water made up of such infrastructure and equipment, so as to permit the reception of waterborne vessels, their loading and unloading, the storage of goods, the receipt and delivery of those goods and the embarkation and disembarkation of passengers, crew and other persons and any other infrastructure necessary for transport operators in the port;

(155) 'maritime port' means a port for, principally, the reception of sea-going vessels;

(156) 'inland port' means a port other than a maritime port, for the reception of inland waterway vessels;

(157) 'port infrastructure' means infrastructure and facilities for the provision of transport related port services, for example berths used for the mooring of ships, quay walls, jetties and floating pontoon ramps in tidal areas, internal basins, backfills and land reclamation, alternative fuel infrastructure and infrastructure for the collection of ship-generated waste and cargo residues;

(158) 'port superstructure' means surface arrangements (such as for storage), fixed equipment (such as warehouses and terminal buildings) as well as mobile equipment (such as cranes) located in a port for the provision of transport related port services;

(159) 'access infrastructure' means any type of infrastructure necessary to ensure access and entry from land or sea and river by users to a port, or in a port, such as roads, rail tracks, channels and locks;

(160) 'dredging' means the removal of sediments from the bottom of the waterway access to a port, or in a port;

(161) 'alternative fuel infrastructure' means a fixed, mobile or offshore port infrastructure allowing a port to supply vessels with energy sources such as electricity, hydrogen, biofuels as defined in point (i) of Article 2 of Directive 2009/28/EC, synthetic and paraffinic fuels, natural gas, including biomethane, in gaseous form (compressed natural gas (CNG)) and liquefied form (liquefied natural gas (LNG)), and liquefied petroleum gas (LPG) which serve, at least partly, as a substitute for fossil oil sources in the energy supply to transport and which have the potential to contribute to its decarbonisation and enhance the environmental performance of the transport sector;

(162) 'vessels' mean floating structures, whether self-propelled or not, with one or more surface displacement hulls;

(163) 'sea-going vessels' mean vessels other than those which navigate solely or mainly in inland waterways or in waters within, or closely adjacent to, sheltered waters;

(164) 'inland waterway vessels' mean vessels intended solely or mainly for navigation on inland waterways or in waters within, or closely adjacent to, sheltered waters;

(165) 'infrastructure for the collection of ship-generated waste and cargo residues' means fixed, floating or mobile port facilities capable of receiving ship-generated waste or cargo residues as defined in Directive 2000/59/EC of the European Parliament and of the Council.

Article 3

Conditions for exemption

Aid schemes, individual aid granted under aid schemes and ad hoc aid shall be compatible with the internal market within the meaning of Article 107(2) or (3) of the Treaty and shall be exempted from the notification requirement of Article 108(3) of the Treaty provided that such aid fulfils all the conditions laid down in Chapter I of this Regulation, as well as the specific conditions for the relevant category of aid laid down in Chapter III of this Regulation.

Article 4

Notification thresholds

1. This Regulation shall not apply to aid which exceeds the following thresholds:
    (a) for regional investment aid: the 'adjusted aid amount' of aid, as calculated in accordance with the mechanism defined in Article 2, point 20 for an investment with eligible costs of EUR 100 million;
    (b) for regional urban development aid, EUR 20 million as laid down in Article 16(3);
    (c) for investment aid to SMEs: EUR 7,5 million per undertaking per investment project;
    (d) for aid for consultancy in favour of SMEs: EUR 2 million per undertaking, per project;
    (e) for aid to SMEs for participation in fairs: EUR 2 million per undertaking, per year;
    (f) for aid to SMEs for cooperation costs incurred by participating in European Territorial Cooperation projects: EUR 2 million per undertaking, per project;
    (g) for risk finance aid: EUR 15 million per eligible undertaking as laid down in Article 21(9);
    (h) for aid for start-ups: the amounts laid down per undertaking in Article 22(3), (4) and (5);
    (i) for aid for research and development:
        (i) if the project is predominantly fundamental research: EUR 40 million per undertaking, per project; that is the case where more than half of the eligible costs of the project are incurred through activities which fall within the category of fundamental research;
        (ii) if the project is predominantly industrial research: EUR 20 million per undertaking, per project; that is the case where more than half of the eligible costs of the project are incurred through activities which fall within the category of industrial research or within the categories of industrial research and fundamental research taken together;
        (iii) if the project is predominantly experimental development: EUR 15 million per undertaking, per project; that is the case where more than half of the

eligible costs of the project are incurred through activities which fall within the category of experimental development;

(iv) if the project is a Eureka project or is implemented by a Joint Undertaking established on the basis of Article 185 or of Article 187 of the Treaty, the amounts referred to in points (i) to (iii) are doubled[;]

(v) if the aid for research and development projects is granted in the form of repayable advances which, in the absence of an accepted methodology to calculate their gross grant equivalent, are expressed as a percentage of the eligible costs and the measure provides that in case of a successful outcome of the project, as defined on the basis of a reasonable and prudent hypothesis, the advances will be repaid with an interest rate at least equal to the discount rate applicable at the time of grant, the amounts referred to in points (i) to (iv) are increased by 50%;

(vi) aid for feasibility studies in preparation for research activities: EUR 7,5 million per study;

(j) for investment aid for research infrastructures: EUR 20 million per infrastructure;

(k) for aid for innovation clusters: EUR 7,5 million per cluster;

(l) innovation aid for SMEs: EUR 5 million per undertaking, per project;

(m) for aid for process and organisational innovation: EUR 7,5 million per undertaking, per project;

(n) for training aid: EUR 2 million per training project;

(o) for aid for the recruitment of disadvantaged workers: EUR 5 million per undertaking, per year;

(p) for aid for the employment of workers with disabilities in the form of wage subsidies: EUR 10 million per undertaking, per year;

(q) for aid for compensating the additional costs of employing workers with disabilities: EUR 10 million per undertaking, per year;

(r) for aid for compensating the costs of assistance provided to disadvantaged workers: EUR 5 million per undertaking, per year;

(s) for investment aid for environmental protection, excluding investment aid for the remediation of contaminated sites and aid for the distribution network part of the energy efficient district heating and cooling installation: EUR 15 million per undertaking per investment project;

(t) for investment aid for energy efficiency projects: EUR 10 million as laid down in Article 39(5);

(u) for investment aid for remediation of contaminated sites: EUR 20 million per undertaking per investment project;

(v) for operating aid for the production of electricity from renewable sources and operating aid for the promotion of energy from renewable sources in small scale installations: EUR 15 million per undertaking per project. When the aid is granted on the basis of a competitive bidding process under Article 42: EUR 150 million per year taking into account the combined budget of all schemes falling under Article 42;

(w) for investment aid for the district heating or cooling distribution network: EUR 20 million per undertaking per investment project;

(x) for investment aid for energy infrastructure: EUR 50 million per undertaking, per investment project;

18

(y) for aid for broadband infrastructures: EUR 70 million total costs per project;

(z) for investment aid for culture and heritage conservation: EUR 150 million per project; operating aid for culture and heritage conservation: EUR 75 million per undertaking per year;

(aa) for aid schemes for audiovisual works: EUR 50 million per scheme per year;

(bb) for investment aid for sport and multifunctional recreational infrastructures: EUR 30 million or the total costs exceeding EUR 100 million per project; operating aid for sport infrastructure: EUR 2 million per infrastructure per year;

(cc) for investment aid for local infrastructures: EUR 10 million or the total costs exceeding EUR 20 million for the same infrastructure;

(dd) for aid for regional airports: the aid intensities and aid amounts laid down in Article 56a;

(ee) for aid for maritime ports: eligible costs of EUR 130 million per project (or EUR 150 million per project in a maritime port included in the work plan of a Core Network Corridor as referred to in Article 47 of Regulation (EU) No 1315/2013 of the European Parliament and of the Council); as regards dredging a project is defined as all dredging carried out within one calendar year; and

(ff) for aid for inland ports: eligible costs of EUR 40 million per project (or EUR 50 million per project in an inland port included in the work plan of a Core Network Corridor as referred to in Article 47 of Regulation (EU) No. 1315/2013); as regards dredging a project is defined as all dredging carried out within one calendar year.

2. The thresholds set out or referred to in paragraph 1 shall not be circumvented by artificially splitting up the aid schemes or aid projects.

Article 5
Transparency of aid

1. This Regulation shall apply only to aid in respect of which it is possible to calculate precisely the gross grant equivalent of the aid ex ante without any need to undertake a risk assessment ('transparent aid').

2. The following categories of aid shall be considered to be transparent:

(a) aid comprised in grants and interest rate subsidies;

(b) aid comprised in loans, where the gross grant equivalent has been calculated on the basis of the reference rate prevailing at the time of the grant;

(c) aid comprised in guarantees:

(i) where the gross grant equivalent has been calculated on the basis of safe-harbour premiums laid down in a Commission notice; or

(ii) where before the implementation of the measure, the methodology to calculate the gross grant equivalent of the guarantee has been accepted on the basis of the Commission Notice on the application of Articles 87 and 88 of the EC Treaty to State aid in the form of guarantees, or any successor notice, following notification of that methodology to the Commission under any regulation adopted by the Commission in the State aid area applicable at the time, and the approved methodology explicitly addresses the type of guarantee and the type of underlying transaction at stake in the context of the application of this Regulation;

(d) aid in the form of tax advantages, where the measure provides for a cap ensuring that the applicable threshold is not exceeded;

(e) aid for regional urban development if the conditions laid down in Article 16 are fulfilled;

(f) aid comprised in risk finance measures if the conditions laid down in Article 21 are fulfilled;

(g) aid for start-ups if the conditions laid down in Article 22 are fulfilled;

(h) aid for energy efficiency projects if the conditions laid down in Article 39 are fulfilled;

(i) aid in the form of premiums in addition to the market price if the conditions laid down in Article 42 are fulfilled;

(j) aid in the form of repayable advances, if the total nominal amount of the repayable advance does not exceed the thresholds applicable under this Regulation or if, before implementation of the measure, the methodology to calculate the gross grant equivalent of the repayable advance has been accepted following its notification to the Commission;

(k) aid in the form of the sale or the lease of tangible assets below market rates where the value is established either by an independent expert evaluation prior to the transaction or by reference to a publicly available, regularly updated and generally accepted benchmark.

Article 6
Incentive effect

1. This Regulation shall apply only to aid which has an incentive effect.

2. Aid shall be considered to have an incentive effect if the beneficiary has submitted a written application for the aid to the Member State concerned before work on the project or activity starts. The application for the aid shall contain at least the following information:

(a) undertaking's name and size;

(b) description of the project, including its start and end dates;

(c) location of the project;

(d) list of project costs;

(e) type of aid (grant, loan, guarantee, repayable advance, equity injection or other) and amount of public funding needed for the project[.]

3. Ad hoc aid granted to large enterprises shall be considered to have an incentive effect if, in addition to ensuring that the condition laid down in paragraph 2 is fulfilled, the Member State has verified, before granting the aid concerned, that documentation prepared by the beneficiary establishes that the aid will result in one or more of the following:

(a) in the case of regional investment aid: that a project is carried out, which would not have been carried out in the area concerned or would not have been sufficiently profitable for the beneficiary in the area concerned in the absence of the aid.

(b) in all other cases, that there is:
— a material increase in the scope of the project/activity due to the aid, or
— a material increase in the total amount spent by the beneficiary on the project/activity due to the aid, or

— a material increase in the speed of completion of the project/ activity concerned[.]

4. By way of derogation from paragraphs 2 and 3, measures in the form of tax advantages shall be deemed to have an incentive effect if the following conditions are fulfilled:

    (a) the measure establishes a right to aid in accordance with objective criteria and without further exercise of discretion by the Member State; and

    (b) the measure has been adopted and is in force before work on the aided project or activity has started, except in the case of fiscal successor schemes, where the activity was already covered by the previous schemes in the form of tax advantages.

5. By way of derogation from paragraphs 2, 3 and 4, the following categories of aid are not required to have or shall be deemed to have an incentive effect:

    (a) regional operating aid and regional urban development aid, where the relevant conditions laid down in Articles 15 and 16 are fulfilled[;]

    (b) aid for access to finance for SMEs, if the relevant conditions laid down in Articles 21 and 22 are fulfilled[;]

    (c) aid for the recruitment of disadvantaged workers in the form of wage subsidies and aid for the employment of workers with disabilities in the form of wage subsidies, if the relevant conditions laid down in Articles 32 and 33 respectively are fulfilled[;]

    (d) aid compensating for the additional costs of employing workers with disabilities and aid for compensating the costs of assistance provided to disadvantaged workers, where the relevant conditions laid down in Articles 34 and 35 are fulfilled;

    (e) aid in the form of reductions in environmental taxes under Directive 2003/96/EC, if the conditions laid down in Article 44 of this Regulation are fulfilled;

    (f) aid to make good the damage caused by certain natural disasters, if the conditions laid down in Article 50 are fulfilled;

    (g) social aid for transport for residents of remote regions, if the conditions laid down in Article 51 are fulfilled;

    (h) aid for culture and heritage conservation, if the conditions laid down in Article 53 are fulfilled.

Article 7

Aid intensity and eligible costs

1. For the purposes of calculating aid intensity and eligible costs, all figures used shall be taken before any deduction of tax or other charge. The eligible costs shall be supported by documentary evidence which shall be clear, specific and contemporary.

    The amounts of eligible costs may be calculated in accordance with the simplified cost options set out in Regulation (EU) No. 1303/2013 of the European Parliament and of the Council, provided that the operation is at least partly financed through a Union fund that allows the use of those simplified cost options and that the category of costs is eligible according to the relevant exemption provision.

2. Where aid is granted in a form other than a grant, the aid amount shall be the gross grant equivalent of the aid.

3. Aid payable in several instalments shall be discounted to its value at the moment it is granted. The eligible costs shall be discounted to their value at the moment the aid is

granted. The interest rate to be used for discounting purposes shall be the discount rate applicable at the moment the aid is granted.

––––––

5. Where aid is granted in the form of repayable advances which, in the absence of an accepted methodology to calculate their gross grant equivalent, are expressed as a percentage of the eligible costs and the measure provides that in case of a successful outcome of the project, as defined on the basis of a reasonable and prudent hypothesis, the advances will be repaid with an interest rate at least equal to the discount rate applicable at the moment the aid is granted, the maximum aid intensities laid down in Chapter III may be increased by 10 percentage points.

6. Where regional aid is granted in the form of repayable advances, the maximum aid intensities established in a regional aid map in force at the moment the aid is granted may not be increased.

Article 8
Cumulation

1. In determining whether the notification thresholds in Article 4 and the maximum aid intensities in Chapter III are respected, the total amount of State aid for the aided activity or project or undertaking shall be taken into account.

2. Where Union funding centrally managed by the institutions, agencies, joint undertakings or other bodies of the Union that is not directly or indirectly under the control of the Member State is combined with State aid, only the latter shall be considered for determining whether notification thresholds and maximum aid intensities or maximum aid amounts are respected, provided that the total amount of public funding granted in relation to the same eligible costs does not exceed the most favourable funding rate laid down in the applicable rules of Union law.

3. Aid with identifiable eligible costs exempted by this Regulation may be cumulated with:
   (a) any other State aid, as long as those measures concern different identifiable eligible costs[;]
   (b) any other State aid, in relation to the same eligible costs, partly or fully overlapping, only if such cumulation does not result in exceeding the highest aid intensity or aid amount applicable to this aid under this Regulation.

4. Aid without identifiable eligible costs exempted under Articles 21, 22 and 23 of this Regulation may be cumulated with any other State aid with identifiable eligible costs. Aid without identifiable eligible costs may be cumulated with any other State aid without identifiable eligible costs, up to the highest relevant total financing threshold fixed in the specific circumstances of each case by this or another block exemption regulation or decision adopted by the Commission.

5. State aid exempted under this Regulation shall not be cumulated with any de minimis aid in respect of the same eligible costs if such cumulation would result in an aid intensity exceeding those laid down in Chapter III of this Regulation.

6. By way of derogation from paragraph 3(b), aid in favour of workers with disabilities, as provided for in Articles 33 and 34 may be cumulated with other aid exempted under this Regulation in relation to the same eligible costs above the highest applicable threshold under this Regulation, provided that such cumulation does not result in an aid intensity exceeding 100% of the relevant costs over any period for which the workers concerned are employed.

18

7. By way of derogation from paragraphs 1 to 6, in determining whether the ceilings for regional operating aid in outermost regions, as set out in Article 15(4), are respected, only regional operating aid in outermost regions implemented under this Regulation shall be taken into account.

Article 9
Publication and information

1. The Member State concerned shall ensure the publication on a comprehensive State aid website, at national or regional level of:
   (a) the summary information referred to in Article 11 in the standardised format laid down in Annex II or a link providing access to it;
   (b) the full text of each aid measure, as referred to in Article 11 or a link providing access to the full text;
   (c) the information referred to in Annex III on each individual aid award exceeding EUR 500 000.

   As regards aid granted to European Territorial Cooperation projects, the information referred to in this paragraph shall be placed on the website of the Member State in which the Managing Authority concerned, as defined in Article 21 of Regulation (EC) No. 1299/2013 of the European Parliament and of the Council, is located. Alternatively, the participating Member States may also decide that each of them shall provide the information relating to the aid measures within their territory on the respective websites.

2. For schemes in the form of tax advantages, and for schemes covered by Article 16 and 21 the conditions set out in paragraph 1(c) of this Article shall be considered fulfilled if Member States publish the required information on individual aid amounts in the following ranges (in EUR million):
   0,5–1;
   1–2;
   2–5;
   5–10;
   10–30; and
   30 and more.

3. For schemes under Article 51 of this Regulation, the publication obligations laid down in this article shall not apply to final consumers.

4. The information referred to in paragraph 1(c) of this Article shall be organised and accessible in a standardised manner, as described in Annex III, and shall allow for effective search and download functions. The information referred to in paragraph 1 shall be published within 6 months from the date the aid was granted, or for aid in the form of tax advantage, within 1 year from the date the tax declaration is due, and shall be available for at least 10 years from the date on which the aid was granted.

5. The Commission shall publish on its website:
   (a) the links to the State aid websites referred to in paragraph 1 of this Article;
   (b) the summary information referred to in Article 11.

6. Member States shall comply with the provisions of this Article at the latest within two years after the entry into force of this Regulation.

Chapter II Monitoring

Article 10

Withdrawal of the benefit of the Block Exemption

Where a Member State grants aid allegedly exempted from the notification requirement under this Regulation without fulfilling the conditions set out in Chapters I to III, the Commission may, after having provided the Member State concerned with the possibility to make its views known, adopt a decision stating that all or some of the future aid measures adopted by the Member State concerned which would otherwise fulfil the requirements of this Regulation, are to be notified to the Commission in accordance with Article 108(3) of the Treaty. The measures to be notified may be limited to the measures granting certain types of aid or in favour of certain beneficiaries or aid measures adopted by certain authorities of the Member State concerned.

Article 11

Reporting

Member States, or in the case of aid granted to European Territorial Cooperation projects, alternatively the Member State in which the Managing Authority, as defined in Article 21 of Regulation (EC) No. 1299/2013 of the European Parliament and of the Council, is located, shall transmit to the Commission:

(a) via the Commission's electronic notification system, the summary information about each aid measure exempted under this Regulation in the standardised format laid down in Annex II, together with a link providing access to the full text of the aid measure, including its amendments, within 20 working days following its entry into force;

(b) an annual report, as referred to in the Commission Regulation (EC) No. 794/2004 of 21 April 2004 implementing Council Regulation (EC) No. 659/1999 of 22 March 1999 laying down detailed rules for the application of Article 93 of the EC Treaty as amended, in electronic form, on the application of this Regulation, containing the information indicated in the Implementing Regulation, in respect of each whole year or each part of the year during which this Regulation applies.

Article 12

Monitoring

1. In order to enable the Commission to monitor the aid exempted from notification by this Regulation, Member States, or alternatively, in the case of aid granted to European Territorial Cooperation projects, the Member State in which the Managing Authority is located, shall maintain detailed records with the information and supporting documentation necessary to establish that all the conditions laid down in this Regulation are fulfilled. Such records shall be kept for 10 years from the date on which the ad hoc aid was granted or the last aid was granted under the scheme.

2. In the case of schemes under which fiscal aid is granted automatically, such as those based on tax declarations of the beneficiaries, and where there is no ex ante verification that all compatibility conditions are met for each beneficiary, Member States shall regularly verify, at least ex post and on a sample basis, that all compatibility conditions

18

are met, and draw the necessary conclusions. Member States shall maintain detailed records of the verifications for at least 10 years from the date of the controls.

3. The Commission may request, from each Member State, all the information and supporting documentation which the Commission considers necessary to monitor the application of this Regulation, including the information mentioned in paragraphs 1 and 2. The Member State concerned shall provide the Commission with the requested information and supporting documents within a period of 20 working days from receipt of the request or such longer period as may be fixed in the request.

Chapter III Specific Provisions for Different Categories of Aid

SECTION 1 REGIONAL AID
SUBSECTION A REGIONAL INVESTMENT AND OPERATING AID

Article 13
Scope of regional aid

This Section shall not apply to:
   (a) aid which favours activities in the steel sector, the coal sector, the shipbuilding sector or the synthetic fibres sector;
   (b) aid to the transport sector as well as the related infrastructure, and aid for energy generation, distribution and infrastructure, except for regional investment aid in outermost regions and regional operating aid schemes;
   (c) regional aid in the form of schemes which are targeted at a limited number of specific sectors of economic activity; schemes aimed at tourism activities, broadband infrastructures or processing and marketing of agricultural products are not considered to be targeted at specific sectors of economic activity;
   (d) regional operating aid granted to undertakings whose principal activities fall under Section K 'Financial and insurance activities' of the NACE Rev. 2 or to undertakings that perform intra-group activities whose principal activities fall under classes 70.10 'Activities of head offices' or 70.22 'Business and other management consultancy activities' of NACE Rev. 2.

Article 14
Regional investment aid

1. Regional investment aid measures shall be compatible with the internal market within the meaning of Article 107(3) of the Treaty and shall be exempted from the notification requirement of Article 108(3) of the Treaty, provided that the conditions laid down in this Article and in Chapter I are fulfilled.
2. The aid shall be granted in assisted areas.
3. In assisted areas fulfilling the conditions of Article 107(3)(a) of the Treaty, the aid may be granted for an initial investment regardless of the size of the beneficiary. In assisted areas fulfilling the conditions of Article 107(3)(c) of the Treaty, the aid may be granted to SMEs for any form of initial investment. Aid to large enterprises shall only be granted for an initial investment in favour of new economic activity in the area concerned.
4. The eligible costs shall be as follows:
   (a) investment costs in tangible and intangible assets;

(b) the estimated wage costs arising from job creation as a result of an initial invest-ment, calculated over a period of two years; or

(c) a combination of points (a) and (b) not exceeding the amount of (a) or (b), which-ever is higher.

5. The investment shall be maintained in the recipient area for at least five years, or at least three years in the case of SMEs, after completion of the investment. This shall not prevent the replacement of plant or equipment that has become outdated or broken within this period, provided that the economic activity is retained in the area con-cerned for the relevant minimum period.

6. The assets acquired shall be new except for SMEs and for the acquisition of an estab-lishment. Costs related to the lease of tangible assets may be taken into account under the following conditions:

(a) for land and buildings, the lease must continue for at least five years after the expected date of completion of the investment project for large undertakings or three years in the case of SMEs;

(b) for plant or machinery, the lease must take the form of financial leasing and must contain an obligation for the beneficiary of the aid to purchase the asset upon expiry of the term of the lease.

In the case of acquisition of the assets of an establishment within the meaning of point 49 or point 51 of Article 2, only the costs of buying the assets from third parties unre-lated to the buyer shall be taken into consideration. The transaction shall take place under market conditions. If aid has already been granted for the acquisition of assets prior to their purchase, the costs of those assets shall be deducted from the eligible costs related to the acquisition of an establishment. Where a member of the family of the original owner, or an employee, takes over a small enterprise, the condition that the assets be bought from third parties unrelated to the buyer shall be waived. The acquisition of shares does not constitute initial investment.

7. For aid granted to large undertakings for a fundamental change in the production pro-cess, the eligible costs must exceed the depreciation of the assets linked to the activity to be modernised in the course of the preceding three fiscal years. For aid granted for a diversification of an existing establishment, the eligible costs must exceed by at least 200% the book value of the assets that are reused, as registered in the fiscal year preceding the start of works.

8. Intangible assets are eligible for the calculation of investment costs if they fulfil the following conditions:

(a) they must be used exclusively in the establishment receiving the aid;

(b) they must be amortisable;

(c) they must be purchased under market conditions from third parties unrelated to the buyer; and

(d) they must be included in the assets of the undertaking receiving the aid and must remain associated with the project for which the aid is granted for at least five years or three years in the case of SMEs.

For large undertakings, costs of intangible assets are eligible only up to a limit of 50% of the total eligible investment costs for the initial investment.

9. Where eligible costs are calculated by reference to the estimated wage costs as referred to in paragraph 4(b), the following conditions shall be fulfilled:

(a) the investment project shall lead to a net increase in the number of employees in the establishment concerned, compared with the average over the previous 12 months, meaning that any job lost shall be deducted from the apparent created number of jobs during that period;

(b) each post shall be filled within three years of completion of works; and

(c) each job created through the investment shall be maintained in the area concerned for a period of at least five years from the date the post was first filled, or three years in the case of SMEs.

10. Regional aid for broadband network development shall fulfil the following conditions:

(a) aid shall be granted only in areas where there is no network of the same category (either basic broadband or NGA) and where no such network is likely to be developed on commercial terms within three years from the decision to grant the aid; and

(b) the subsidised network operator must offer active and passive wholesale access under fair and non-discriminatory conditions including physical unbundling in the case of NGA networks; and

(c) aid shall be allocated on the basis of a competitive selection process.

11. Regional aid for research infrastructures shall be granted only if the aid is made conditional on giving transparent and non-discriminatory access to the aided infrastructure.

12. The aid intensity in gross grant equivalent shall not exceed the maximum aid intensity established in the regional aid map which is in force at the time the aid is granted in the area concerned. Where the aid intensity is calculated on the basis of paragraph 4(c), the maximum aid intensity shall not exceed the most favourable amount resulting from the application of that intensity on the basis of investment costs or wage costs. For large investment projects the aid amount shall not exceed the adjusted aid amount calculated in accordance with the mechanism defined in Article 2, point 20[.]

13. Any initial investment started by the same beneficiary (at group level) within a period of three years from the date of start of works on another aided investment in the same level 3 region of the Nomenclature of Territorial Units for Statistics shall be considered to be part of a single investment project. Where such single investment project is a large investment project, the total aid amount for the single investment project shall not exceed the adjusted aid amount for large investment projects.

14. The aid beneficiary must provide a financial contribution of at least 25% of the eligible costs, either through its own resources or by external financing, in a form, which is free of any public support. In the outermost regions an investment made by an SME may receive an aid with a maximum aid intensity above 75%, in such situations the remainder shall be provided by way of a financial contribution from the aid beneficiary.

15. For an initial investment linked to European territorial cooperation projects covered by Regulation (EU) No. 1299/2013, the aid intensity of the area in which the initial investment is located shall apply to all beneficiaries participating in the project. If the initial investment is located in two or more assisted areas, the maximum aid intensity shall be the one applicable in the assisted area where the highest amount of eligible costs is incurred. In assisted areas eligible for aid under Article 107(3)(c) of the Treaty, this provision shall apply to large undertakings only if the initial investment concerns a new economic activity.

16. The beneficiary shall confirm that it has not carried out a relocation to the establishment in which the initial investment for which aid is requested is to take place, in the two years preceding the application for aid and give a commitment that it will not do so up to a period of two years after the initial investment for which aid is requested is completed.

17. In the fisheries and aquaculture sector, aid shall not be granted to undertakings that have committed one or more of the infringements set out in Article 10(1)(a) to (d) and Article 10(3) of Regulation (EU) No. 508/2014 of the European Parliament and of the Council and for operations of Article 11 of that Regulation.

Article 15
Regional operating aid

1. Regional operating aid schemes in outermost regions, sparsely populated areas and very sparsely populated areas shall be compatible with the internal market within the meaning of Article 107(3) of the Treaty and shall be exempted from the notification requirement of Article 108(3) of the Treaty, provided that the conditions laid down in this Article and in Chapter I are fulfilled.

2. In sparsely populated areas, the regional operating aid schemes shall compensate for the additional transport costs of goods which have been produced in areas eligible for operating aid, as well as additional transport costs of goods that are further processed in those areas, under the following conditions:
   (a) the aid is objectively quantifiable in advance on the basis of a fixed sum or per tonne/kilometre ratio or any other relevant unit;
   (b) the additional transport costs are calculated on the basis of the journey of the goods inside the national border of the Member State concerned using the means of transport which results in the lowest costs for the beneficiary.
   The aid intensity shall not exceed 100% of the additional transport costs as set out in this paragraph.

3. In very sparsely populated areas, the regional operating aid schemes shall prevent or reduce depopulation under the following conditions:
   (a) the beneficiaries have their economic activity in the area concerned;
   (b) the annual aid amount per beneficiary under all operating aid schemes does not exceed 20% of the annual labour costs incurred by the beneficiary in the area concerned.

4. In outermost regions, the operating aid schemes shall compensate for the additional operating costs incurred in those regions as a direct result of one or several of the permanent handicaps referred to in Article 349 of the Treaty, where the beneficiaries have their economic activity in an outermost region provided that the annual aid amount per beneficiary under all operating aid schemes implemented under this Regulation does not exceed any of the following percentages:
   (a) 35% of the gross value added annually created by the beneficiary in the outermost region concerned;
   (b) 40% of the annual labour costs incurred by the beneficiary in the outermost region concerned;
   (c) 30% of the annual turnover of the beneficiary realised in the outermost region concerned.

18

SUBSECTION B URBAN DEVELOPMENT AID

Article 16
Regional urban development aid

1. Regional urban development aid shall be compatible with the internal market within the meaning of Article 107(3) of the Treaty and shall be exempted from the notification requirement of Article 108(3) of the Treaty, provided that the conditions laid down in this Article and in Chapter I are fulfilled.

2. Urban development projects shall fulfil the following criteria:
   (a) they are implemented via urban development funds in assisted areas;
   (b) they are co-financed by the European Structural and Investment Funds;
   (c) they support the implementation of an 'integrated sustainable urban development strategy';

3. The total investment in an urban development project under any urban development aid measure shall not exceed EUR 20 million.

4. The eligible costs shall be the overall costs of the urban development project to the extent that they comply with Articles 65 and 37 of Regulation (EU) No. 1303/2013 of the European Parliament and of the Council.

5. Aid granted by an urban development fund to the eligible urban development projects may take the form of equity, quasi-equity, loans, guarantees, or a mix thereof.

6. The urban development aid shall leverage additional investment from private investors at the level of the urban development funds or the urban development projects, so as to achieve an aggregate amount reaching minimum 30% of the total financing provided to an urban development project.

7. Private and public investors may provide cash or an in-kind contribution or a combination of those for the implementation of an urban development project. An in-kind contribution shall be taken into account at its market value, as certified by an independent qualified expert or duly authorised official body.

8. The urban development measures shall fulfil the following conditions:
   (a) urban development fund managers shall be selected through an open, transparent and non-discriminatory call in accordance with the applicable Union and national laws. In particular, there shall be no discrimination between urban development fund managers on the basis of their place of establishment or incorporation in any Member State. Urban development fund managers may be required to fulfil predefined criteria objectively justified by the nature of the investments;
   (b) the independent private investors shall be selected through an open, transparent and non-discriminatory call in accordance with applicable Union and national laws aimed at establishing the appropriate risk-reward sharing arrangements whereby, for investments other than guarantees, asymmetric profit-sharing shall be given preference over downside protection. If the private investors are not selected by such a call, the fair rate of return to the private investors shall be established by an independent expert selected via an open, transparent and non-discriminatory call;
   (c) in the case of asymmetric loss-sharing between public and private investors, the first loss assumed by the public investor shall be capped at 25% of the total investment;

(d) in the case of guarantees to private investors in urban development projects, the guarantee rate shall be limited to 80% and total losses assumed by a Member State shall be capped at 25% of the underlying guaranteed portfolio;

(e) the investors shall be allowed to be represented in the governance bodies of the urban development fund, such as the supervisory board or the advisory committee;

(f) the urban development fund shall be established according to the applicable laws. The Member State shall provide for a due diligence process in order to ensure a commercially sound investment strategy for the purpose of implementing the urban development aid measure.

9. Urban development funds shall be managed on a commercial basis and shall ensure profit-driven financing decisions. This is considered to be the case when the managers of the urban development fund fulfill the following conditions:

(a) the managers of urban development funds shall be obliged by law or contract to act with the diligence of a professional manager in good faith and avoiding conflicts of interest; best practices and regulatory supervision shall apply;

(b) the remuneration of the managers of urban development funds shall conform to market practices. This requirement is considered to be met where a manager is selected through an open, transparent and non-discriminatory call, based on objective criteria linked to experience, expertise and operational and financial capacity;

(c) the managers of urban development funds shall receive a remuneration linked to performance, or shall share part of the investment risks by co-investing own resources so as to ensure that their interests are permanently aligned with the interests of the public investors;

(d) the managers of urban development funds shall set out an investment strategy, criteria and the proposed timing of investments in urban development projects, establishing the ex ante financial viability and their expected impact on urban development;

(e) a clear and realistic exit strategy shall exist for each equity and quasi-equity investment.

10. Where an urban development fund provides loans or guarantees to urban development projects, the following conditions shall be fulfilled:

(a) in the case of loans, the nominal amount of the loan is taken into account in calculating the maximum investment amount for the purposes of paragraph 3 of this Article;

(b) in the case of guarantees, the nominal amount of the underlying loan is taken into account in calculating the maximum investment amount for the purposes of paragraph 3 of this Article.

11. The Member State may assign the implementation of the urban development aid measure to an entrusted entity.

SECTION 2 AID TO SMES

Article 17
Investment aid to SMEs

1. Investment aid to SMEs operating inside or outside the territory of the Union shall be compatible with the internal market within the meaning of Article 107(3) of the Treaty and shall be exempted from the notification requirement of Article 108(3) of the Treaty, provided that the conditions laid down in this Article and in Chapter I are fulfilled.

2. The eligible costs shall be either or both of the following:
   (a) the costs of investment in tangible and intangible assets;
   (b) the estimated wage costs of employment directly created by the investment project, calculated over a period of two years.

3. In order to be considered an eligible cost for the purposes of this Article, an investment shall consist of the following:
   (a) an investment in tangible and/or intangible assets relating to the setting-up of a new establishment, the extension of an existing establishment, diversification of the output of an establishment into new additional products or a fundamental change in the overall production process of an existing establishment; or
   (b) the acquisition of the assets belonging to an establishment, where the following conditions are fulfilled:
   — the establishment has closed or would have closed had it not been purchased;
   — the assets are purchased from third parties unrelated to the buyer;
   — the transaction takes place under market conditions.

   Where a member of the family of the original owner, or an employee, takes over a small enterprise, the condition that the assets shall be bought from third parties unrelated to the buyer shall be waived. The sole acquisition of the shares of an undertaking shall not constitute investment.

4. Intangible assets shall fulfil all of the following conditions:
   (a) they shall be used exclusively in the establishment receiving the aid;
   (b) they shall be regarded as amortizable assets;
   (c) they shall be purchased under market conditions from third parties unrelated to the buyer;
   (d) they shall be included in the assets of the undertaking for at least three years[.]

5. Employment directly created by an investment project shall fulfil the following conditions:
   (a) it shall be created within three years of completion of the investment;
   (b) there shall be a net increase in the number of employees in the establishment concerned, compared with the average over the previous 12 months;
   (c) it shall be maintained during a minimum period of three years from the date the post was first filled.

6. The aid intensity shall not exceed:
   (a) 20% of the eligible costs in the case of small enterprises;
   (b) 10% of the eligible costs in the case of medium-sized enterprises.

Article 18
Aid for consultancy in favour of SMEs

1. Aid for consultancy in favour of SMEs shall be compatible with the internal market within the meaning of Article 107(3) of the Treaty and shall be exempted from the

notification requirement of Article 108(3) of the Treaty, provided that the conditions laid down in this Article and in Chapter I are fulfilled.

2. The aid intensity shall not exceed 50% of the eligible costs.

3. The eligible costs shall be the costs of consultancy services provided by external consultants.

4. The services concerned shall not be a continuous or periodic activity nor relate to the undertaking's usual operating costs, such as routine tax consultancy services, regular legal services or advertising.

Article 19

Aid to SMEs for participation in fairs

1. Aid to SMEs for participation in fairs shall be compatible with the internal market within the meaning of Article 107(3) of the Treaty and shall be exempted from the notification requirement of Article 108(3) of the Treaty, provided that the conditions laid down in this Article and in Chapter I are fulfilled.

2. The eligible costs shall be the costs incurred for renting, setting up and running the stand for the participation of an undertaking in any particular fair or exhibition.

3. The aid intensity shall not exceed 50% of the eligible costs.

Article 20

Aid for cooperation costs incurred by SMEs participating in European territorial co-operation projects

1. Aid for cooperation costs incurred by SMEs participating in the European Territorial Cooperation projects covered by Regulation (EC) No. 1299/2013 of the European Parliament and of the Council shall be compatible with the internal market within the meaning of Article 107(3) of the Treaty and shall be exempted from the notification requirement of Article 108(3) of the Treaty, provided the conditions laid down in this Article and in Chapter I are fulfilled.

2. The eligible costs shall be the following:
   (a) costs for organisational cooperation including the cost of staff and offices to the extent that it is linked to the cooperation project;
   (b) costs of advisory and support services linked to cooperation and delivered by external consultants and service providers;
   (c) travel expenses, costs of equipment and investment expenditure directly related to the project and depreciation of tools and equipment used directly for the project.

3. The services referred to in paragraph 2(b) shall not be a continuous or periodic activity nor relate to the undertaking's usual operating costs, such as routine tax consultancy services, regular legal services or routine advertising.

4. The aid intensity shall not exceed 50% of the eligible costs.

SECTION 3 AID FOR ACCESS TO FINANCE FOR SMES

Article 21

Risk finance aid

1. Risk finance aid schemes in favour of SMEs shall be compatible with the internal market within the meaning of Article 107(3) of the Treaty and shall be exempted from the notification requirement of Article 108(3) of the Treaty, provided the conditions laid down in this Article and in Chapter I are fulfilled.

2. At the level of financial intermediaries, risk finance aid to independent private investors may take one of the following forms:
    (a) equity or quasi-equity, or financial endowment to provide risk finance investments directly or indirectly to eligible undertakings;
    (b) loans to provide risk finance investments directly or indirectly to eligible undertakings;
    (c) guarantees to cover losses from risk finance investments directly or indirectly to eligible undertakings.
3. At the level of independent private investors, risk finance aid may take the forms mentioned in paragraph 2 of this Article, or be in the form of tax incentives to private investors who are natural persons providing risk finance directly or indirectly to eligible undertakings.
4. At the level of eligible undertakings, risk finance aid may take the form of equity, quasi-equity investments, loans, guarantees, or a mix thereof.
5. Eligible undertakings shall be undertakings which at the time of the initial risk finance investment are unlisted SMEs and fulfil at least one of the following conditions:
    (a) they have not been operating in any market;
    (b) they have been operating in any market for less than 7 years following their first commercial sale;
    (c) they require an initial risk finance investment which, based on a business plan prepared in view of entering a new product or geographical market, is higher than 50% of their average annual turnover in the preceding 5 years.
6. The risk finance aid may also cover follow-on investments made in eligible undertakings, including after the 7[-]year period mentioned in paragraph 5(b), if the following cumulative conditions are fulfilled:
    (a) the total amount of risk finance mentioned in paragraph 9 is not exceeded;
    (b) the possibility of follow-on investments was foreseen in the original business plan;
    (c) the undertaking receiving follow-on investments has not become linked, within the meaning of Article 3(3) of Annex I with another undertaking other than the financial intermediary or the independent private investor providing risk finance under the measure, unless the new entity fulfils the conditions of the SME definition.
7. For equity and quasi-equity investments in eligible undertakings, a risk finance measure may provide support for replacement capital only if the latter is combined with new capital representing at least 50% of each investment round into the eligible undertakings.
8. For equity and quasi-equity investments as referred to in paragraph 2(a), no more than 30% of the financial intermediary's aggregate capital contributions and uncalled committed capital may be used for liquidity management purposes.
9. The total amount of risk finance referred to in paragraph 4 shall not exceed EUR 15 million per eligible undertaking under any risk finance measure.
10. For risk finance measures providing equity, quasi-equity or loan investments to eligible undertakings, the risk finance measure shall leverage additional finance from independent private investors at the level of the financial intermediaries or the eligible undertakings, so as to achieve an aggregate private participation rate reaching the following minimum thresholds:

(a) 10% of the risk finance provided to the eligible undertakings prior to their first commercial sale on any market;

(b) 40% of the risk finance provided to the eligible undertakings referred to in paragraph 5(b) of this Article;

(c) 60% of the risk finance for investment provided to eligible undertakings mentioned in paragraph 5(c) and for follow-on investments in eligible undertakings after the 7-year period mentioned in paragraph 5(b).

11. Where a risk finance measure is implemented through a financial intermediary targeting eligible undertakings at different development stages as referred to in paragraph 10 and does not provide for private capital participation at the level of the eligible undertakings the financial intermediary shall achieve a private participation rate that represents at least the weighted average based on the volume of the individual investments in the underlying portfolio and resulting from the application of the minimum participation rates to such investments as referred to in paragraph 10.

12. A risk finance measure shall not discriminate between financial intermediaries on the basis of their place of establishment or incorporation in any Member State. Financial intermediaries may be required to fulfil predefined criteria objectively justified by the nature of the investments.

13. A risk finance measure shall fulfil the following conditions:

(a) it shall be implemented via one or more financial intermediaries, except for tax incentives to private investors in respect of their direct investments into eligible undertakings;

(b) financial intermediaries, as well as investors or fund managers shall be selected through an open, transparent and non-discriminatory call which is made in accordance with applicable Union and national laws and aimed at establishing appropriate risk-reward sharing arrangements whereby, for investments other than guarantees, asymmetric profit sharing shall be given preference over downside protection;

(c) in the case of asymmetric loss-sharing between public and private investors, the first loss assumed by the public investor shall be capped at 25% of the total investment;

(d) in the case of guarantees falling under point 2(c), the guarantee rate shall be limited to 80% and total losses assumed by a Member State shall be capped at a maximum of 25% of the underlying guaranteed portfolio. Only guarantees covering expected losses of the underlying guaranteed portfolio can be provided for free. If a guarantee also comprises coverage of unexpected losses, the financial intermediary shall pay, for the part of the guarantee covering unexpected losses, a market-conform guarantee premium.

14. Risk finance measures shall ensure profit-driven financing decisions. This is considered to be the case where all of the following conditions are fulfilled:

(a) financial intermediaries shall be established according to the applicable laws[;]

(b) the Member State, or the entity entrusted with the implementation of the measure, shall provide for a due diligence process in order to ensure a commercially sound investment strategy for the purpose of implementing the risk finance measure, including an appropriate risk diversification policy aimed at achieving economic viability and efficient scale in terms of size and territorial scope of the relevant portfolio of investments;

(c) risk finance provided to the eligible undertakings shall be based on a viable business plan, containing details of product, sales and profitability development, establishing ex-ante financial viability;

(d) a clear and realistic exit strategy shall exist for each equity and quasi-equity investment.

15. Financial intermediaries shall be managed on a commercial basis. This requirement is considered to be fulfilled where the financial intermediary and, depending on the type of risk finance measure, the fund manager, fulfil the following conditions:

(a) they shall be obliged by law or contract to act with the diligence of a professional manager in good faith and avoiding conflicts of interest; best practices and regulatory supervision shall apply;

(b) their remuneration shall conform to market practices. This requirement is presumed to be met where the manager or the financial intermediary is selected through an open, transparent and non-discriminatory selection call, based on objective criteria linked to experience, expertise and operational and financial capacity;

(c) they shall receive a remuneration linked to performance, or shall share part of the investment risks by co-investing own resources so as to ensure that their interests are permanently aligned with the interests of the public investor;

(d) they shall set out an investment strategy, criteria and the proposed timing of investments;

(e) investors shall be allowed to be represented in the governance bodies of the investment fund, such as the supervisory board or the advisory committee.

16. A risk finance measure providing guarantees or loans to eligible undertakings or providing quasi-equity investments structured as debt in eligible undertakings, shall fulfil the following conditions:

(a) as a result of the measure, the financial intermediary shall undertake investments that would not have been carried out or would have been carried out in a restricted or different manner without the aid. The financial intermediary shall be able to demonstrate that it operates a mechanism that ensures that all the advantages are passed on to the largest extent to the final beneficiaries in the form of higher volumes of financing, riskier portfolios, lower collateral requirements, lower guarantee premiums or lower interest rates;

(b) in the case of loans and quasi-equity investments structured as debt, the nominal amount of the instrument is taken into account in calculating the maximum investment amount for the purposes of paragraph 9;

(c) in the case of guarantees, the nominal amount of the underlying loan is taken into account in calculating the maximum investment amount for the purposes of paragraph 9. The guarantee shall not exceed 80% of the underlying loan.

17. A Member State may assign the implementation of a risk finance measure to an entrusted entity.

18. Risk finance aid for SMEs that do not fulfil the conditions laid down in paragraph 5 shall be compatible with the internal market within the meaning of Article 107(3) of

the Treaty and shall be exempted from the notification requirement of Article 108(3) of the Treaty, provided that[:]

(a) at the level of the SMEs, the aid fulfils the conditions laid down in Regulation (EU) No. 1407/2013; and

(b) all the conditions laid down in the present Article, with the exception of those set out in paragraphs 5, 6, 9, 10, and 11, are fulfilled; and

(c) for risk finance measures providing equity, quasi-equity or loan investments to eligible undertakings, the measure shall leverage additional financing from independent private investors at the level of the financial intermediaries or the SMEs, so as to achieve an aggregate private participation rate reaching at least 60% of the risk finance provided to the SMEs.

Article 22

Aid for start-ups

1. Start-up aid schemes shall be compatible with the internal market within the meaning of Article 107(3) of the Treaty and shall be exempted from the notification requirement of Article 108(3) of the Treaty, provided the conditions laid down in this Article and in Chapter I are fulfilled.

2. Eligible undertakings shall be any unlisted small enterprise up to five years following its registration, which fulfils the following conditions:

(a) it has not taken over the activity of another enterprise;

(b) it has not yet distributed profits;

(c) it has not been formed through a merger.

For eligible undertakings that are not subject to registration, the five year eligibility period may be considered to start from the moment when the enterprise either starts its economic activity or is liable to tax for its economic activity.

By way of derogation from point (c) of the first subparagraph, enterprises formed through a merger between undertakings eligible for aid under this Article shall also be considered eligible undertakings up to five years from the date of registration of the oldest enterprise participating in the merger.

3. Start-up aid shall take the form of:

(a) loans with interest rates which are not conform with market conditions, with a duration of 10 years and up to a maximum nominal amount of EUR 1 million, or EUR 1,5 million for undertakings established in assisted areas fulfilling the conditions of Article 107(3)(c) of the Treaty, or EUR 2 million for undertakings established in assisted areas fulfilling the conditions of Article 107(3)(a) of the Treaty. For loans with a duration comprised between 5 and 10 years the maximum amounts may be adjusted by multiplying the amounts above by the ratio between 10 years and the actual duration of the loan. For loans with a duration of less than 5 years, the maximum amount shall be the same as for loans with a duration of 5 years;

(b) guarantees with premiums which are not conform with market conditions, with a duration of 10 years and up to maximum EUR 1,5 million of amount guaranteed, or EUR 2,25 million for undertakings established in assisted areas fulfilling the conditions of Article 107(3)(c) of the Treaty, or EUR 3 million for undertakings established in assisted areas fulfilling the conditions of Article 107(3)(a) of the

18

Treaty. For guarantees with a duration comprised between 5 and 10 years the maximum amount guaranteed amounts may be adjusted by multiplying the amounts above by the ratio between 10 years and the actual duration of the guarantee. For guarantees with a duration of less than 5 years, the maximum amount guaranteed shall be the same as for guarantees with a duration of 5 years. The guarantee shall not exceed 80% of the underlying loan[;]

   (c) grants, including equity or quasi equity investment, interests rate and guarantee premium reductions up to EUR 0,4 million gross grant equivalent or EUR 0,6 million for undertakings established in assisted areas fulfilling the conditions of Article 107(3)(c) of the Treaty, or EUR 0,8 million for undertakings established in assisted areas fulfilling the conditions of Article 107(3)(a) of the Treaty.

4. A beneficiary can receive support through a mix of the aid instruments referred to in paragraph 3 of this Article, provided that the proportion of the amount granted through one aid instrument, calculated on the basis of the maximum aid amount allowed for that instrument, is taken into account in order to determine the residual proportion of the maximum aid amount allowed for the other instruments forming part of such a mixed instrument.

5. For small and innovative enterprises, the maximum amounts set out in paragraph 3 may be doubled.

Article 23
Aid to alternative trading platforms specialised in SMEs

1. Aid in favour of alternative trading platforms specialised in SMEs shall be compatible with the internal market within the meaning of Article 107(3) of the Treaty and shall be exempted from the notification requirement of Article 108(3) of the Treaty, provided the conditions laid down in this Article and in Chapter I are fulfilled.

2. Where the platform operator is a small enterprise, the aid measure may take the form of start-up aid to the platform operator, in which case the conditions laid down in Article 22 shall apply.

    The aid measure may take the form of tax incentives to independent private investors that are natural persons in respect of their risk finance investments made through an alternative trading platform into undertakings eligible under the conditions laid down in Article 21.

Article 24
Aid for scouting costs

1. Aid for scouting costs shall be compatible with the internal market within the meaning of Article 107(3) of the Treaty and shall be exempted from the notification requirement of Article 108(3) of the Treaty, provided the conditions laid down in this Article and in Chapter I are fulfilled.

2. The eligible costs shall be the costs for initial screening and formal due diligence undertaken by managers of financial intermediaries or investors to identify eligible undertakings pursuant to Articles 21 and 22.

3. The aid intensity shall not exceed 50% of the eligible costs.

SECTION 4 AID FOR RESEARCH AND DEVELOPMENT AND INNOVATION

Article 25
Aid for research and development projects

1. Aid for research and development projects, including projects having received a Seal of Excellence quality label under the Horizon 2020 SME-instrument, shall be compatible with the internal market within the meaning of Article 107(3) of the Treaty and shall be exempted from the notification requirement of Article 108(3) of the Treaty provided that the conditions laid down in this Article and in Chapter I are fulfilled.

2. The aided part of the research and development project shall completely fall within one or more of the following categories:
   (a) fundamental research;
   (b) industrial research;
   (c) experimental development;
   (d) feasibility studies.

3. The eligible costs of research and development projects shall be allocated to a specific category of research and development and shall be the following:
   (a) personnel costs: researchers, technicians and other supporting staff to the extent employed on the project;
   (b) costs of instruments and equipment to the extent and for the period used for the project. Where such instruments and equipment are not used for their full life for the project, only the depreciation costs corresponding to the life of the project, as calculated on the basis of generally accepted accounting principles are considered as eligible;
   (c) [c]osts for of buildings and land, to the extent and for the duration period used for the project. With regard to buildings, only the depreciation costs corresponding to the life of the project, as calculated on the basis of generally accepted accounting principles are considered as eligible. For land, costs of commercial transfer or actually incurred capital costs are eligible[;]
   (d) costs of contractual research, knowledge and patents bought or licensed from outside sources at arm's length conditions, as well as costs of consultancy and equivalent services used exclusively for the project;
   (e) additional overheads and other operating expenses, including costs of materials, supplies and similar products, incurred directly as a result of the project.

4. The eligible costs for feasibility studies shall be the costs of the study.

5. The aid intensity for each beneficiary shall not exceed:
   (a) 100% of the eligible costs for fundamental research;
   (b) 50% of the eligible costs for industrial research;
   (c) 25% of the eligible costs for experimental development;
   (d) 50% of the eligible costs for feasibility studies.

6. The aid intensities for industrial research and experimental development may be increased up to a maximum aid intensity of 80% of the eligible costs as follows:
   (a) by 10 percentage points for medium-sized enterprises and by 20 percentage points for small enterprises;
   (b) by 15 percentage points if one of the following conditions is fulfilled:
      (i) the project involves effective collaboration:

- between undertakings among which at least one is an SME, or is carried out in at least two Member States, or in a Member State and in a Contracting Party of the EEA Agreement, and no single undertaking bears more than 70% of the eligible costs; or
- between an undertaking and one or more research and knowledge-dissemination organisations, where the latter bear at least 10% of the eligible costs and have the right to publish their own research results;

(ii) the results of the project are widely disseminated through conferences, publication, open access repositories, or free or open source software.

7. The aid intensities for feasibility studies may be increased by 10 percentage points for medium-sized enterprises and by 20 percentage points for small enterprises[.]

Article 26
Investment aid for research infrastructures

1. Aid for the construction or upgrade of research infrastructures that perform economic activities shall be compatible with the internal market within the meaning of Article 107(3) of the Treaty and shall be exempted from the notification requirement of Article 108(3) of the Treaty, provided that the conditions laid down in this Article and in Chapter I are fulfilled.

2. Where a research infrastructure pursues both economic and non-economic activities, the financing, costs and revenues of each type of activity shall be accounted for separately on the basis of consistently applied and objectively justifiable cost accounting principles.

3. The price charged for the operation or use of the infrastructure shall correspond to a market price.

4. Access to the infrastructure shall be open to several users and be granted on a transparent and non-discriminatory basis. Undertakings which have financed at least 10% of the investment costs of the infrastructure may be granted preferential access under more favourable conditions. In order to avoid overcompensation, such access shall be proportional to the undertaking's contribution to the investment costs and these conditions shall be made publicly available.

5. The eligible costs shall be the investment costs in intangible and tangible assets.

6. The aid intensity shall not exceed 50% of the eligible costs.

7. Where a research infrastructure receives public funding for both economic and non-economic activities, Member States shall put in place a monitoring and clawback mechanism in order to ensure that the applicable aid intensity is not exceeded as a result of an increase in the share of economic activities compared to the situation envisaged at the time of awarding the aid.

Article 27
Aid for innovation clusters

1. Aid for innovation clusters shall be compatible with the internal market within the meaning of Article 107(3) of the Treaty and shall be exempted from the notification requirement of Article 108(3) of the Treaty, provided that the conditions laid down in this Article and in Chapter I are fulfilled.

2. Aid for innovation clusters shall be granted exclusively to the legal entity operating the innovation cluster (cluster organisation).

3. Access to the cluster's premises, facilities and activities shall be open to several users and be granted on a transparent and non-discriminatory basis. Undertakings which have financed at least 10% of the investment costs of the innovation cluster may be granted preferential access under more favourable conditions. In order to avoid over-compensation, such access shall be proportional to the undertaking's contribution to the investment costs and these conditions shall be made publicly available.

4. The fees charged for using the cluster's facilities and for participating in the cluster's activities shall correspond to the market price or reflect their costs.

5. Investment aid may be granted for the construction or upgrade of innovation clusters. The eligible costs shall be the investment costs in intangible and tangible assets.

6. The aid intensity of investment aid for innovation clusters shall not exceed 50% of the eligible costs. The aid intensity may be increased by 15 percentage points for innovation clusters located in assisted areas fulfilling the conditions of Article 107(3)(a) of the Treaty and by 5 percentage points for innovation clusters located in assisted areas fulfilling the conditions of Article 107(3)(c) of the Treaty[.]

7. Operating aid may be granted for the operation of innovation clusters. It shall not exceed 10 years.

8. The eligible costs of operating aid for innovation clusters shall be the personnel and administrative costs (including overhead costs) relating to:
   (a) animation of the cluster to facilitate collaboration, information sharing and the provision or channelling of specialised and customised business support services;
   (b) marketing of the cluster to increase participation of new undertakings or organisations and to increase visibility;
   (c) management of the cluster's facilities; organisation of training programmes, workshops and conferences to support knowledge sharing and networking and transnational cooperation.

9. The aid intensity of operating aid shall not exceed 50% of the total eligible costs during the period over which the aid is granted.

Article 28
Innovation aid for SMEs

1. Innovation aid for SMEs shall be compatible with the internal market within the meaning of Article 107(3) of the Treaty and shall be exempted from the notification requirement of Article 108(3) of the Treaty, provided the conditions laid down in this Article and in Chapter I are fulfilled:

2. The eligible costs shall be the following:
   (a) costs for obtaining, validating and defending patents and other intangible assets;
   (b) costs for secondment of highly qualified personnel from a research and knowledge-dissemination organization or a large enterprise, working on research, development and innovation activities in a newly created function within the beneficiary and not replacing other personnel;
   (c) costs for innovation advisory and support services[.]

3. The aid intensity shall not exceed 50% of the eligible costs.

18

4. In the particular case of aid for innovation advisory and support services the aid intensity can be increased up to 100% of the eligible costs provided that the total amount of aid for innovation advisory and support services does not exceed EUR 200 000 per undertaking within any three year period.

Article 29
Aid for process and organisational innovation

1. Aid for process and organisational innovation shall be compatible with the internal market within the meaning of Article 107(3) of the Treaty and shall be exempted from the notification requirement of Article 108(3) of the Treaty, provided the conditions laid down in this Article and in Chapter I are fulfilled.
2. Aid to large undertakings shall only be compatible if they effectively collaborate with SMEs in the aided activity and the collaborating SMEs incur at least 30% of the total eligible costs.
3. The eligible costs shall be the following:
   (a) personnel costs;
   (b) costs of instruments, equipment, buildings and land to the extent and for the period used for the project;
   (c) costs of contractual research, knowledge and patents bought or licensed from outside sources at arm's length conditions;
   (d) additional overheads and other operating costs, including costs of materials, supplies and similar products, incurred directly as a result of the project.
4. The aid intensity shall not exceed 15% of the eligible costs for large undertakings and 50% of the eligible costs for SMEs.

Article 30
Aid for research and development in the fishery and aquaculture sector

1. Aid for research and development in the fishery and aquaculture sector shall be compatible with the internal market within the meaning of Article 107(3) of the Treaty and shall be exempted from the notification requirement of Article 108(3) of the Treaty, provided that the conditions laid down in this Article and in Chapter I are fulfilled.
2. The aided project shall be of interest to all undertakings in the particular sector or sub-sector concerned.
3. Prior to the date of the start of the aided project the following information shall be published on the internet:
   (a) that the aided project will be carried out;
   (b) the goals of the aided project;
   (c) the approximate date for the publication of the results expected from the aided project and its place of publication on the internet;
   (d) a reference that the results of the aided project will be available to all undertakings active in the particular sector or sub-sector concerned at no cost.
4. The results of the aided project shall be made available on internet from the end date of the aided project or the date on which any information concerning those results is given to members of any particular organisation, whatever comes first. The results shall remain available on internet for a period of at least 5 years starting from the end date of the aided project.

5. Aid shall be granted directly to the research and knowledge-dissemination organisation and shall not involve the direct granting of non-research related aid to an undertaking producing, processing or marketing fishery or aquaculture products.
6. The eligible costs shall be those provided in Article 25(3).
7. The aid intensity shall not exceed 100% of the eligible costs.

SECTION 5 TRAINING AID

Article 31

Training aid

1. Training aid shall be compatible with the internal market within the meaning of Article 107(3) of the Treaty and shall be exempted from the notification requirement of Article 108(3) of the Treaty, provided that the conditions laid down in this Article and in Chapter I are fulfilled.
2. Aid shall not be granted for training which undertakings carry out to comply with national mandatory standards on training.
3. The eligible costs shall be the following:
   (a) trainers' personnel costs, for the hours during which the trainers participate in the training;
   (b) trainers' and trainees' operating costs directly relating to the training project such as travel expenses, accommodation costs, materials and supplies directly related to the project, depreciation of tools and equipment, to the extent that they are used exclusively for the training project;
   (c) costs of advisory services linked to the training project;
   (d) trainees' personnel costs and general indirect costs (administrative costs, rent, overheads) for the hours during which the trainees participate in the training.
4. The aid intensity shall not exceed 50% of the eligible costs. It may be increased, up to a maximum aid intensity of 70% of the eligible costs, as follows:
   (a) by 10 percentage points if the training is given to workers with disabilities or disadvantaged workers;
   (b) by 10 percentage points if the aid is granted to medium-sized enterprises and by 20 percentage points if the aid is granted to small enterprises.
5. Where the aid is granted in the maritime transport sector, the aid intensity may be increased to 100% of the eligible costs provided that the following conditions are met:
   (a) the trainees are not active members of the crew but are supernumerary on board; and
   (b) the training is carried out on board of ships entered in Union registers.

SECTION 6 AID FOR DISADVANTAGED WORKERS AND FOR WORKERS WITH DISABILITIES

Article 32

Aid for the recruitment of disadvantaged workers in the form of wage subsidies

1. Aid schemes for the recruitment of disadvantaged workers shall be compatible with the internal market within the meaning of Article 107(3) of the Treaty and shall be exempted from the notification requirement of Article 108(3) of the Treaty, provided the conditions laid down in this Article and in Chapter I are fulfilled.

2. Eligible costs shall be the wage costs over a maximum period of 12 months following recruitment of a disadvantaged worker. Where the worker concerned is a severely disadvantaged worker, eligible costs shall be the wage costs over a maximum period of 24 months following recruitment.

3. Where the recruitment does not represent a net increase, compared with the average over the previous 12 months, in the number of employees in the undertaking concerned, the post or posts shall have fallen vacant following voluntary departure, disability, retirement on grounds of age, voluntary reduction of working time or lawful dismissal for misconduct and not as a result of redundancy.

4. Except in the case of lawful dismissal for misconduct, the disadvantaged workers shall be entitled to continuous employment for a minimum period consistent with the national legislation concerned or any collective agreements governing employment contracts.

5. If the period of employment is shorter than 12 months, or 24 months in the case of severely disadvantaged workers, the aid shall be reduced pro rata accordingly.

6. The aid intensity shall not exceed 50% of the eligible costs.

Article 33
Aid for the employment of workers with disabilities in the form of wage subsidies

1. Aid for the employment of workers with disabilities shall be compatible with the internal market within the meaning of Article 107(3) of the Treaty and shall be exempted from the notification requirement of Article 108(3) of the Treaty, provided the conditions laid down in this Article and in Chapter I are fulfilled.

2. Eligible costs shall be the wage costs over any given period during which the worker with disabilities is employed.

3. Where the recruitment does not represent a net increase, compared with the average over the previous 12 months, in the number of employees in the undertaking concerned, the post or posts shall have fallen vacant following voluntary departure, disabilities, retirement on grounds of age, voluntary reduction of working time or lawful dismissal for misconduct and not as a result of redundancy.

4. Except in the case of lawful dismissal for misconduct, the workers with disabilities shall be entitled to continuous employment for a minimum period consistent with the national legislation concerned or any collective agreements which are legally binding for the undertaking and governing employment contracts.

5. The aid intensity shall not exceed 75% of the eligible costs.

Article 34
Aid for compensating the additional costs of employing workers with disabilities

1. Aid for compensating the additional costs of employing workers with disabilities shall be compatible with the internal market within the meaning of Article 107(3) of the Treaty and shall be exempted from the notification requirement of Article 108(3) of the Treaty, provided the conditions laid down in this Article and in Chapter I are fulfilled.

2. The eligible costs shall be the following:
   (a) costs of adapting the premises;
   (b) costs of employing staff solely for time spent on the assistance of the workers with disabilities and of training such staff to assist workers with disabilities;

(c) costs of adapting or acquiring equipment, or acquiring and validating software for use by workers with disabilities, including adapted or assistive technology facilities, which are additional to those which the beneficiary would have incurred had it employed workers who are not workers with disabilities;

(d) costs directly linked to transport of workers with disabilities to the working place and for work related activities;

(e) wage costs for the hours spent by a worker with disabilities on rehabilitation;

(f) where the beneficiary provides sheltered employment, the costs of constructing, installing or modernising the production units of the undertaking concerned, and any costs of administration and transport, provided that such costs result directly from the employment of workers with disabilities.

3. The aid intensity shall not exceed 100% of the eligible costs.

Article 35

Aid for compensating the costs of assistance provided to disadvantaged workers

1. Aid for compensating the costs of assistance provided to disadvantaged workers shall be compatible with the internal market within the meaning of Article 107(3) of the Treaty and shall be exempt from the notification requirement of Article 108(3) of the Treaty, provided the conditions laid down in this Article and in Chapter I are fulfilled.

2. The eligible costs shall be the costs of:

(a) employing staff solely for time spent on the assistance of the disadvantaged workers over a maximum period of 12 months following recruitment of a disadvantaged worker or over a maximum period of 24 months following recruitment of a severely disadvantaged worker;

(b) of training such staff to assist disadvantaged workers.

3. The assistance provided shall consist of measures to support the disadvantaged worker's autonomy and adaptation to the work environment, in accompanying the worker in social and administrative procedures, facilitation of communication with the entrepreneur and managing conflicts.

4. The aid intensity shall not exceed 50% of the eligible costs.

SECTION 7 AID FOR ENVIRONMENTAL PROTECTION

Article 36

Investment aid enabling undertakings to go beyond union standards for environmental protection or to increase the level of environmental protection in the absence of Union standards

1. Investment aid enabling undertakings to go beyond Union standards for environmental protection or to increase the level of environmental protection in the absence of Union standards shall be compatible with the internal market within the meaning of Article 107(3) of the Treaty and shall be exempted from the notification requirement of Article 108(3) of the Treaty, provided that the conditions laid down in this Article and in Chapter I are fulfilled.

2. The investment shall fulfil one of the following conditions:

(a) it shall enable the beneficiary to increase the level of environmental protection resulting from its activities by going beyond the applicable Union standards,

irrespective of the presence of mandatory national standards that are more stringent than the Union standards;

(b) it shall enable the beneficiary to increase the level of environmental protection
resulting from its activities in the absence of Union standards.

3. Aid shall not be granted where investments are undertaken to ensure that undertakings comply with Union standards already adopted and not yet in force.

4. By way of derogation from paragraph 3, aid may be granted for

(a) the acquisition of new transport vehicles for road, railway, inland waterway and
maritime transport complying with adopted Union standards, provided that the
acquisition occurs before those standards enter into force and that, once mandatory, they do not apply to vehicles already purchased before that date[;]

(b) retrofitting of existing transport vehicles for road, railway, inland waterway and
maritime transport, provided that the Union standards were not yet in force at the
date of entry into operation of those vehicles and that, once mandatory, they do
not apply retroactively to those vehicles.

5. The eligible costs shall be the extra investment costs necessary to go beyond the applicable Union standards or to increase the level of environmental protection in the
absence of Union standards. They shall be determined as follows:

(a) where the costs of investing in environmental protection can be identified in the
total investment cost as a separate investment, this environmental protection-related cost shall constitute the eligible costs;

(b) in all other cases, the costs of investing in environmental protection are identified
by reference to a similar, less environmentally friendly investment that would have
been credibly carried out without the aid. The difference between the costs of both
investments identifies the environmental protection-related cost and constitutes
the eligible costs.

The costs not directly linked to the achievement of a higher level of environmental
protection shall not be eligible.

6. The aid intensity shall not exceed 40% of the eligible costs.

7. The aid intensity may be increased by 10 percentage points for aid granted to medium
sized undertakings and by 20 percentage points for aid granted to small undertakings.

8. The aid intensity may be increased by 15 percentage points for investments located
in assisted areas fulfilling the conditions of Article 107(3)(a) of the Treaty and by 5
percentage points for investments located in assisted areas fulfilling the conditions of
Article 107(3)(c) of the Treaty.

Article 37
Investment aid for early adaptation to future Union standards

1. Aid encouraging undertakings to comply with new Union standards which increase
the level of environmental protection and are not yet in force shall be compatible with
the internal market within the meaning of Article 107(3) of the Treaty and shall be
exempted from the notification requirement of Article 108(3) of the Treaty, provided
that the conditions laid down in this Article and in Chapter I are fulfilled.

2. The Union standards shall have been adopted and the investment shall be implemented and finalised at least one year before the date of entry into force of the standard
concerned.

3. The eligible costs shall be the extra investment costs necessary to go beyond the applicable Union standards. They shall be determined as follows:

(a) where the costs of investing in environmental protection can be identified in the total investment cost as a separate investment, this environmental protection-related cost shall constitute the eligible costs;

(b) in all other cases, the costs of investing in environmental protection are identified by reference to a similar, less environmentally friendly investment that would have been credibly carried out without the aid. The difference between the costs of both investments identifies the environmental protection-related cost and constitutes the eligible costs.

The costs not directly linked to the achievement of a higher level of environmental protection shall not be eligible.

4. The aid intensity shall not exceed the following:

(a) 20% of the eligible costs for small undertakings, 15% of the eligible costs for medium-sized undertakings and 10% of the eligible costs for large undertakings if the implementation and finalisation of the investment take place more than three years before the date of entry into force of the new Union standard;

(b) 15% of the eligible costs for small undertakings, 10% of the eligible costs for medium-sized undertakings and 5% of the eligible costs for large undertakings if the implementation and finalisation of the investment take place between one and three years before the date of entry into force of the new Union standard.

5. The aid intensity may be increased by 15 percentage points for investments located in assisted areas fulfilling the conditions of Article 107(3)(a) of the Treaty and by 5 percentage points for investments located in assisted areas fulfilling the conditions of Article 107(3)(c) of the Treaty.

Article 38
Investment aid for energy efficiency measures

1. Investment aid enabling undertakings to achieve energy efficiency shall be compatible with the internal market within the meaning of Article 107(3) of the Treaty and shall be exempted from the notification requirement of Article 108(3) of the Treaty, provided that the conditions laid down in this Article and in Chapter I are fulfilled.

2. Aid shall not be granted under this Article where improvements are undertaken to ensure that undertakings comply with Union standards already adopted, even if they are not yet in force.

3. The eligible costs shall be the extra investment costs necessary to achieve the higher level of energy efficiency. They shall be determined as follows:

(a) where the costs of investing in energy efficiency can be identified in the total investment cost as a separate investment, this energy efficiency-related cost shall constitute the eligible costs;

(b) in all other cases, the costs of investing in energy efficiency are identified by reference to a similar, less energy efficient investment that would have been credibly carried out without the aid. The difference between the costs of both investments identifies the energy efficiency-related cost and constitutes the eligible costs.

The costs not directly linked to the achievement of a higher level of energy efficiency shall not be eligible.

18

4. The aid intensity shall not exceed 30% of the eligible costs.

5. The aid intensity may be increased by 20 percentage points for aid granted to small undertakings and by 10 percentage points for aid granted to medium-sized undertakings.

6. The aid intensity may be increased by 15 percentage points for investments located in assisted areas fulfilling the conditions of Article 107(3)(a) of the Treaty and by 5 percentage points for investments located in assisted areas fulfilling the conditions of Article 107(3)(c) of the Treaty.

Article 39
Investment aid for energy efficiency projects in buildings

1. Investment aid for energy efficiency projects in buildings shall be compatible with the internal market within the meaning of Article 107(3) of the Treaty and shall be exempted from the notification requirement of Article 108(3) of the Treaty, provided that the conditions laid down in this Article and in Chapter I are fulfilled.

2. Eligible for aid under the present Article are energy efficiency projects relating to buildings.

3. The eligible costs shall be the overall costs of the energy efficiency project.

4. The aid shall be granted in the form of an endowment, equity, a guarantee or loan to an energy efficiency fund or other financial intermediary, which shall fully pass it on to the final beneficiaries being the building owners or tenants.

5. The aid granted by the energy efficiency fund or other financial intermediary to the eligible energy efficiency projects may take the form of loans or guarantees. The nominal value of the loan or the amount guaranteed shall not exceed EUR 10 million per project at the level of the final beneficiaries. The guarantee should not exceed 80% of the underlying loan.

6. The repayment by the building owners to the energy efficiency fund or other financial intermediary shall not be less than the nominal value of the loan.

7. The energy efficiency aid shall leverage additional investment from private investors reaching at minimum 30% of the total financing provided to an energy efficiency project. When the aid is provided by an energy efficiency fund, the leverage of private investment can be done at the level of the energy efficiency fund and/or at the level of the energy efficiency projects, so as to achieve an aggregate minimum 30% of the total financing provided to an energy efficiency project.

8. Member States can set up energy efficiency funds and/or can use financial intermediaries when providing energy efficiency aid. The following conditions must then be fulfilled:

   (a) [f]inancial intermediary managers, as well as energy efficiency fund managers shall be selected through an open, transparent and non-discriminatory call in accordance with applicable Union and national laws. In particular, there shall be no discrimination on the basis of their place of establishment or incorporation in any Member State. Financial intermediaries and energy efficiency fund managers may be required to fulfil predefined criteria objectively justified by the nature of the investments;

   (b) [t]he independent private investors shall be selected through an open, transparent and non-discriminatory call in accordance with applicable Union and national laws aimed at establishing the appropriate risk-reward sharing arrangements whereby, for investments other than guarantees, asymmetric profit-sharing shall be given preference over downside protection. If the private investors are not selected by such a call, the fair rate of return to the private investors shall be established by an independent expert selected via an open, transparent and non-discriminatory call;

(c) [i]n the case of asymmetric loss-sharing between public and private investors, the first loss assumed by the public investor shall be capped at 25% of the total investment;

(d) [i]n the case of guarantees, the guarantee rate shall be limited to 80% and total losses assumed by a Member State shall be capped at 25% of the underlying guaranteed portfolio. Only guarantees covering the expected losses of the underlying guaranteed portfolio can be provided for free. If a guarantee also comprises coverage of unexpected losses, the financial intermediary shall pay, for the part of the guarantee covering unexpected losses, a market-conform guarantee premium;

(e) [t]he investors shall be allowed to be represented in the governance bodies of the energy efficiency fund or financial intermediary, such as the supervisory board or the advisory committee;

(f) [t]he energy efficiency fund or financial intermediary shall be established according to the applicable laws and the Member State shall provide for a due diligence process in order to ensure a commercially sound investment strategy for the purpose of implementing the energy efficiency aid measure.

9. Financial intermediaries, including energy efficiency funds shall be managed on a commercial basis and shall ensure profit-driven financing decisions. This is considered to be the case when the financial intermediary and, as the case may be, the managers of the energy efficiency fund fulfil the following conditions:

(a) they are obliged by law or contract to act with the diligence of a professional manager in good faith and avoiding conflicts of interest; best practices and regulatory supervision shall apply;

(b) their remuneration conforms with market practices. This requirement is considered to be met where the manager is selected through an open, transparent and non-discriminatory call, based on objective criteria linked to experience, expertise and operational and financial capacity;

(c) they shall receive a remuneration linked to performance, or shall share part of the investment risks by co-investing own resources so as to ensure that their interests are permanently aligned with the interests of the public investor;

(d) they shall set out an investment strategy, criteria and the proposed timing of investments in energy efficiency projects, establishing the ex-ante financial viability and their expected impact on energy efficiency[;]

(e) a clear and realistic exit strategy shall exist for the public funds invested in the energy efficiency fund or granted to the financial intermediary, allowing the market to finance energy efficiency projects when the market is ready to do so.

10. Energy efficiency improvements undertaken to ensure that the beneficiary complies with Union standards which have already been adopted shall not be exempted from the notification requirement under this Article.

18

Article 40
Investment aid for high-efficiency cogeneration

1. Investment aid for high-efficiency cogeneration shall be compatible with the internal market within the meaning of Article 107(3) of the Treaty and shall be exempted from the notification requirement of Article 108(3) of the Treaty, provided that the conditions laid down in this Article and in Chapter I are fulfilled.

2. The investment aid shall be granted in respect of newly installed or refurbished capacities only.

3. The new cogeneration unit shall provide overall primary energy savings compared to separate production of heat and electricity as provided for by Directive 2012/27/EU of the European Parliament and of the Council of 25 October 2012 on energy efficiency, amending Directives 2009/125/EC and 2010/30/EU and repealing Directives 2004/8/EC and 2006/32/EC. The improvement of an existing cogeneration unit or conversion of an existing power generation unit into a cogeneration unit shall result in primary energy savings compared to the original situation.

4. The eligible costs shall be the extra investment costs for the equipment needed for the installation to operate as a high-efficiency cogeneration installation, compared to conventional electricity or heating installations of the same capacity or the extra investment cost to upgrade to a higher efficiency when an existing installation already meets the high-efficiency threshold.

5. The aid intensity shall not exceed 45% of the eligible costs. The aid intensity may be increased by 20 percentage points for aid granted to small undertakings and by 10 percentage points for aid granted to medium-sized undertakings.

6. The aid intensity may be increased by 15 percentage points for investments located in assisted areas fulfilling the conditions of Article 107(3)(a) of the Treaty and by 5 percentage points for investments located in assisted areas fulfilling the conditions of Article 107(3)(c) of the Treaty.

Article 41
Investment aid for the promotion of energy from renewable sources

1. Investment aid for the promotion of energy from renewable energy sources shall be compatible with the internal market within the meaning of Article 107(3) of the Treaty and shall be exempted from the notification requirement of Article 108(3) of the Treaty, provided that the conditions laid down in this Article and in Chapter I are fulfilled.

2. Investment aid for the production of biofuels shall be exempted from the notification requirement only to the extent that the aided investments are used for the production of sustainable biofuels other than food-based biofuels. However, investment aid to convert existing food-based biofuel plants into advanced biofuel plants shall be exempted under this Article, provided that the food-based production would be reduced commensurate to the new capacity.

3. Aid shall not be granted for biofuels which are subject to a supply or blending obligation.

4. Aid shall not be granted for hydropower installations that do not comply with Directive 2000/60/EC of the European Parliament.

18

5. The investment aid shall be granted to new installations only. No aid shall be granted or paid out after the installation started operations and aid shall be independent from the output.

6. The eligible costs shall be the extra investment costs necessary to promote the production of energy from renewable sources. They shall be determined as follows:

   (a) where the costs of investing in the production of energy from renewable sources can be identified in the total investment cost as a separate investment, for instance as a readily identifiable add-on component to a pre-existing facility, this renewable energy-related cost shall constitute the eligible costs;

   (b) where the costs of investing in the production of energy from renewable sources can be identified by reference to a similar, less environmentally friendly investment that would have been credibly carried out without the aid, this difference between the costs of both investments identifies the renewable energy-related cost and constitutes the eligible costs;

   (c) for certain small installations where a less environmentally friendly investment cannot be established as plants of a limited size do not exist, the total investment costs to achieve a higher level of environmental protection shall constitute the eligible costs.

   The costs not directly linked to the achievement of a higher level of environmental protection shall not be eligible.

7. The aid intensity shall not exceed:

   (a) 45% of the eligible costs if the eligible costs are calculated on the basis of point (6)(a) or point (6)(b);

   (b) 30% of the eligible cost if the eligible costs are calculated on the basis of point (6)(c).

8. The aid intensity may be increased by 20 percentage points for aid granted to small undertakings and by 10 percentage points for aid granted to medium-sized undertakings.

9. The aid intensity may be increased by 15 percentage points for investments located in assisted areas fulfilling the conditions of Article 107(3)(a) of the Treaty and by 5 percentage points for investments located in assisted areas fulfilling the conditions of Article 107(3)(c) of the Treaty.

10. Where aid is granted in a competitive bidding process on the basis of clear, transparent and non-discriminatory criteria, the aid intensity may reach 100% of the eligible costs. Such a bidding process shall be non-discriminatory and provide for the participation of all interested undertakings. The budget related to the bidding process shall be a binding constraint in the sense that not all participants can receive aid and the aid shall be granted on the basis of the initial bid submitted by the bidder, therefore excluding subsequent negotiations.

Article 42
Operating aid for the promotion of electricity from renewable sources

1. Operating aid for the promotion of electricity from renewable energy sources shall be compatible with the internal market within the meaning of Article 107(3) of the Treaty and shall be exempted from the notification requirement of Article 108(3) of

18

the Treaty, provided that the conditions laid down in this Article and in Chapter I are fulfilled.

2. Aid shall be granted in a competitive bidding process on the basis of clear, transparent and non-discriminatory criteria which shall be open to all generators producing electricity from renewable energy sources on a non-discriminatory basis.

3. The bidding process can be limited to specific technologies where a process open to all generators would lead to a suboptimal result which cannot be addressed in the process design in view of in particular:

   (i) the longer-term potential of a given new and innovative technology; or

   (ii) the need to achieve diversification; or

   (iii) network constraints and grid stability; or

   (iv) system (integration) costs; or

   (v) the need to avoid distortions on the raw material markets from biomass support[.]

   Member States shall carry out a detailed assessment of the applicability of such conditions and report it to the Commission according to the modalities described in Article 11(a).

4. Aid shall be granted to new and innovative renewable energy technologies in a competitive bidding process open to at least one such technology on the basis of clear, transparent and non-discriminatory criteria. Such aid shall not be granted for more than 5% of the planned new electricity capacity from renewable energy sources per year in total.

5. Aid shall be granted as a premium in addition to the market price whereby the generators sell their electricity directly in the market.

6. Aid beneficiaries shall be subject to standard balancing responsibilities. Beneficiaries may outsource balancing responsibilities to other undertakings on their behalf, such as aggregators.

7. Aid shall not be granted when prices are negative.

8. Aid may be granted in the absence of a competitive bidding process as described in paragraph 2 to installations with an installed electricity capacity of less than 1 MW for the production of electricity from all renewable sources except for wind energy, where aid may be granted in the absence of a competitive bidding process as described in paragraph 2 to installations with an installed electricity capacity of less than 6 MW or to installations with less than 6 generation units. Without prejudice to paragraph 9, when aid is granted in the absence of a competitive bidding process, the conditions under paragraphs 5, 6 and 7 shall be respected. In addition, when aid is granted in the absence of a competitive bidding process, the conditions under Article 43 paragraphs 5, 6 and 7 shall be applicable.

9. The conditions under paragraphs 5, 6 and 7 shall not apply to operating aid granted to installations with an installed electricity capacity of less than 500 kW for the production of electricity from all renewable sources except for wind energy, where these conditions shall not apply to operating aid granted to installations with an installed electricity capacity of less than 3 MW or to installations with less than 3 generation units.

10. For the purpose of calculating the above maximum capacities referred to in paragraphs 8 and 9, installations with a common connection point to the electricity grid shall be considered as one installation.

11. Aid shall only be granted until the plant generating the electricity from renewable sources has been fully depreciated according to generally accepted accounting principles. Any investment aid previously received must be deducted from the operating aid.

Article 43

Operating aid for the promotion of energy from renewable sources in small scale installations

1. Operating aid for the promotion of energy from renewable energy sources in small scale installations shall be compatible with the internal market within the meaning of Article 107(3) of the Treaty and shall be exempted from the notification requirement of Article 108(3) of the Treaty, provided that the conditions laid down in this Article and in Chapter I are fulfilled.

2. Aid shall only be granted to installations with an installed capacity of less than 500 kW for the production of energy from all renewable sources except for wind energy, for which aid shall be granted to installations with an installed capacity of less than 3 MW or with less than 3 generation units and for biofuels, for which aid shall be granted to installations with an installed capacity of less than 50 000 tonnes/year. For the purpose of calculating those maximum capacities, small scale installations with a common connection point to the electricity grid shall be considered as one installation.

3. Aid shall only be granted to installations producing sustainable biofuels other than food-based biofuels. However, operating aid to plants producing food-based biofuels that have started operation before 31 December 2013 and are not yet fully depreciated shall be exempted under this Article but in any event no later than 2020.

4. Aid shall not be granted for biofuels which are subject to a supply or blending obligation.

5. The aid per unit of energy shall not exceed the difference between the total levelized costs of producing energy from the renewable source in question and the market price of the form of energy concerned. The levelized costs shall be updated regularly and at least every year.

6. The maximum rate of return used in the levelized cost calculation shall not exceed the relevant swap rate plus a premium of 100 basis points. The relevant swap rate shall be the swap rate of the currency in which the aid is granted for a maturity that reflects the depreciation period of the installations supported.

7. Aid shall only be granted until the installation has been fully depreciated according to generally accepted accounting principles. Any investment aid granted to an installation shall be deducted from the operating aid.

Article 44

Aid in the form of reductions in environmental taxes under Directive 2003/96/EC

1. Aid schemes in the form of reductions in environmental taxes fulfilling the conditions of Council Directive 2003/96/EC of 27 October 2003 restructuring the Community framework for the taxation of energy products and electricity shall be compatible with the internal market within the meaning of Article 107(3) of the Treaty and shall be exempted from the notification requirement of Article 108(3) of the Treaty, provided that the conditions laid down in this Article and in Chapter I are fulfilled.

2. The beneficiaries of the tax reduction shall be selected on the basis of transparent and objective criteria and shall pay at least the respective minimum level of taxation set by Directive 2003/96/EC.

3. Aid schemes in the form of tax reductions shall be based on a reduction of the applicable environmental tax rate or on the payment of a fixed compensation amount or on a combination of these mechanisms.

4. Aid shall not be granted for biofuels which are subject to a supply or blending obligation.

Article 45
Investment aid for remediation of contaminated sites

1. Investment aid to undertakings repairing environmental damage by remediating contaminated sites shall be compatible with the internal market within the meaning of Article 107(3) of the Treaty and shall be exempted from the notification requirement of Article 108(3) of the Treaty, provided that the conditions laid down in this Article and in Chapter I are fulfilled.

2. The investment shall lead to the repair of the environmental damage, including damage to the quality of the soil or of surface water or groundwater.

3. Where the legal or physical person liable for the environmental damage under the law applicable in each Member State without prejudice to the Union rules in this matter – in particular Directive 2004/35/EC of the European Parliament and of the Council of 21 April 2004 on environmental liability with regard to the prevention and remedying of environmental damage as amended by Directive 2006/21/EC of the European Parliament and of the Council of 15 March 2006 on the management of waste from extractive industries, Directive 2009/31/EC of the European Parliament and of the Council of 23 April 2009 on the geological storage of carbon dioxide and amending Council Directive 85/337/EEC, European Parliament and Council Directives 2000/60/EC, 2001/80/EC, 2004/35/EC, 2006/12/EC, 2008/1/EC and Regulation (EC) No 1013/2006 and Directive 2013/30/EU of the European Parliament and of the Council of 12 June 2013 on safety of offshore oil and gas operations and amending Directive 2004/35/EC – is identified, that person must finance the remediation in accordance with the 'polluter pays' principle, and no State aid shall be granted. Where the person liable under the applicable law is not identified or cannot be made to bear the costs, the person responsible for the remediation or decontamination work may receive State aid.

4. The eligible costs shall be the costs incurred for the remediation work, less the increase in the value of the land. All expenditure incurred by an undertaking in remediating its site, whether or not such expenditure can be shown as a fixed asset on its balance sheet, may be considered as eligible investment in the case of the remediation of contaminated sites.

5. Evaluations of the increase in value of the land resulting from remediation shall be carried out by an independent expert.

6. The aid intensity shall not exceed 100% of the eligible costs.

Article 46
Investment aid for energy efficient district heating and cooling

1. Investment aid for the installation of energy efficient district heating and cooling system shall be compatible with the internal market within the meaning of Article 107(3) of the

Treaty and shall be exempted from the notification requirement of Article 108(3) of the Treaty, provided that the conditions laid down in this Article and in Chapter I are fulfilled.

2. The eligible costs for the production plant shall be the extra costs needed for the construction, expansion and refurbishment of one or more generation units to operate as an energy efficient district heating and cooling system compared to a conventional production plant. The investment shall be an integral part of the energy efficient district heating and cooling system.

3. The aid intensity for the production plant shall not exceed 45% of the eligible costs. The aid intensity may be increased by 20 percentage points for aid granted to small undertakings and by 10 percentage points for aid granted to medium-sized undertakings.

4. The aid intensity for the production plant may be increased by 15 percentage points for investments located in assisted areas fulfilling the conditions of Article 107(3)(a) of the Treaty and by 5 percentage points for investments located in assisted areas fulfilling the conditions of Article 107(3)(c) of the Treaty.

5. The eligible costs for the distribution network shall be the investment costs.

6. The aid amount for the distribution network shall not exceed the difference between the eligible costs and the operating profit. The operating profit shall be deducted from the eligible costs ex ante or through a claw-back mechanism.

Article 47
Investment aid for waste recycling and re-utilisation

1. Investment aid for waste recycling and re-utilisation shall be compatible with the internal market within the meaning of Article 107(3) of the Treaty and shall be exempted from the notification requirement of Article 108(3) of the Treaty, provided that the conditions laid down in this Article and in Chapter I are fulfilled.

2. The investment aid shall be granted for the recycling and re-utilisation of waste generated by other undertakings.

3. The recycled or re-used materials treated would otherwise be disposed of, or be treated in a less environmentally friendly manner. Aid to waste recovery operations other than recycling shall not be block exempted under this Article.

4. The aid shall not indirectly relieve the polluters from a burden that should be borne by them under Union law, or from a burden that should be considered a normal company cost.

5. The investment shall not merely increase demand for the materials to be recycled without increasing collection of those materials.

6. The investment shall go beyond the state of the art.

7. The eligible costs shall be the extra investment costs necessary to realise an investment leading to better or more efficient recycling or re-use activities compared to a conventional process of re-use and recycling activities with the same capacity that would be constructed in the absence the aid.

8. The aid intensity shall not exceed 35% of the eligible costs. The aid intensity may be increased by 20 percentage points for aid granted to small undertakings and by 10 percentage points for aid granted to medium-sized undertakings.

9. The aid intensity may be increased by 15 percentage points for investments located in assisted areas fulfilling the conditions of Article 107(3)(a) of the Treaty and by 5

percentage points for investments located in assisted areas fulfilling the conditions of Article 107(3)(c) of the Treaty.

10. Aid for investments relating to the recycling and re-utilisation of the beneficiary's own waste shall not be exempt from the notification requirement under this Article.

Article 48
Investment aid for energy infrastructure

1. Investment aid for the construction or upgrade of energy infrastructure shall be compatible with the internal market within the meaning of Article 107(3) of the Treaty and shall be exempted from the notification requirement of Article 108(3) of the Treaty, provided that the conditions laid down in this Article and in Chapter I are fulfilled.
2. Aid shall be granted for energy infrastructure located in assisted areas.
3. The energy infrastructure shall be subject to full tariff and access regulation according to internal energy market legislation.
4. The eligible costs shall be the investment costs.
5. The aid amount shall not exceed the difference between the eligible costs and the operating profit of the investment. The operating profit shall be deducted from the eligible costs ex ante or through a claw-back mechanism.
6. Aid for investments in electricity and gas storage projects and oil infrastructure shall not be exempt from the notification requirement under this Article.

Article 49
Aid for environmental studies

1. Aid for studies, including energy audits, directly linked to investments referred to in this Section shall be compatible with the internal market within the meaning of Article 107(3) of the Treaty and shall be exempted from the notification requirement of Article 108(3) of the Treaty, provided that the conditions laid down in this Article and in Chapter I are fulfilled.
2. The eligible costs shall be the costs of the studies referred to in paragraph 1.
3. The aid intensity shall not exceed 50% of the eligible costs.
4. The aid intensity may be increased by 20 percentage points for studies undertaken on behalf of small enterprises and by 10 percentage points for studies undertaken on behalf of medium size enterprises.
5. Aid shall not be granted to large undertakings for energy audits carried out under Article 8(4) of the Directive 2012/27/EU, unless the energy audit is carried out in addition to the mandatory energy audit under that Directive.

SECTION 8 AID TO MAKE GOOD THE DAMAGE CAUSED BY CERTAIN NATURAL DISASTERS

Article 50
Aid schemes to make good the damage caused by certain natural disasters

1. Aid schemes to make good the damage caused by earthquakes, avalanches, landslides, floods, tornadoes, hurricanes, volcanic eruptions and wild fires of natural origin shall be compatible with the internal market within the meaning of Article 107(2)(b) of the Treaty and shall be exempted from the notification requirement of Article 108(3) of

18

the Treaty, provided that the conditions laid down in this Article and in Chapter I are fulfilled.

2. Aid shall be granted subject to the following conditions:

   (a) the competent public authorities of a Member State have formally recognised the character of the event as a natural disaster; and

   (b) there is a direct causal link between the natural disaster and the damages suffered by the affected undertaking.

3. Aid schemes related to a specific natural disaster shall be introduced within three years following the occurrence of the event. Aid on the basis of such schemes shall be granted within four years following the occurrence.

4. The costs arising from the damage incurred as a direct consequence of the natural disaster, as assessed by an independent expert recognised by the competent national authority or by an insurance undertaking shall be eligible costs. Such damage may include material damage to assets such as buildings, equipment, machinery or stocks and loss of income due to the full or partial suspension of activity for a period not exceeding six months from the occurrence of the disaster. The calculation of the material damage shall be based on the repair cost or economic value of the affected asset before the disaster. It shall not exceed the repair cost or the decrease in fair market value caused by the disaster, that is to say the difference between the property's value immediately before and immediately after the occurrence of the disaster. Loss of income shall be calculated on the basis of financial data of the affected undertaking (earnings before interest and taxes (EBIT), depreciation and labour costs related only to the establishment affected by the natural disaster) by comparing the financial data for the six months after the occurrence of the disaster with the average of three years chosen among the five years preceding the occurrence of the disaster (by excluding the two years giving the best and the worst financial result) and calculated for the same six months period of the year. The damage shall be calculated at the level of the individual beneficiary.

5. The aid and any other payments received to compensate for the damage, including payments under insurance policies, shall not exceed 100% of the eligible costs.

SECTION 9 SOCIAL AID FOR TRANSPORT FOR RESIDENTS OF REMOTE REGIONS

Article 51
Social aid for transport for residents of remote regions

1. Aid for air and maritime passenger transport shall be compatible with the internal market pursuant to Article 107(2)(a) of the Treaty and shall be exempted from the notification requirement of Article 108(3) of the Treaty, provided that the conditions laid down in this Article and in Chapter I are fulfilled.

2. The entire aid shall be for the benefit of final consumers who have their normal residence in remote regions.

3. The aid shall be granted for passenger transport on a route linking an airport or port in a remote region with another airport or port within the European Economic Area.

4. The aid shall be granted without discrimination as to the identity of the carrier or type of service and without limitation as to the precise route to or from the remote region.

5. The eligible costs shall be the price of a return ticket from or to the remote region, including all taxes and charges invoiced by the carrier to the consumer.

6. The aid intensity shall not exceed 100% of the eligible costs.

SECTION 10 AID FOR BROADBAND INFRASTRUCTURES

Article 52
Aid for broadband infrastructures

1. Investment aid for broadband network development shall be compatible with the internal market pursuant to Article 107(3) of the Treaty and shall be exempted from the notification requirement of Article 108(3) of the Treaty, provided that the conditions laid down in this Article and in Chapter I are fulfilled.

2. The eligible costs shall be the following:
   (a) investment costs for the deployment of a passive broadband infrastructure;
   (b) investment costs of broadband-related civil engineering works;
   (c) investment costs for the deployment of basic broadband networks; and
   (d) investment costs for the deployment of next generation access (NGA) networks.

2a. As an alternative to establishing the eligible costs as provided for in paragraph 2, the maximum amount of aid for a project may be established on the basis of the competitive selection process as required by paragraph 4.

3. The investment shall be located in areas where there is no infrastructure of the same category (either basic broadband or NGA network) and where no such infrastructure is likely to be developed on commercial terms within three years from the moment of publication of the planned aid measure, which shall also be verified through an open public consultation.

4. The aid shall be allocated on the basis of an open, transparent and non-discriminatory competitive selection process respecting the principle of technology neutrality.

5. The network operator shall offer the widest possible active and passive wholesale access, according to Article 2, point 139 of this Regulation, under fair and non-discriminatory conditions, including physical unbundling in the case of NGA networks. Such wholesale access shall be granted for at least seven years and the right of access to ducts or poles shall not be limited in time. In the case of aid for the construction of ducts, the ducts shall be large enough to cater for several cable networks and different network topologies.

6. The wholesale access price shall be based on the pricing principles set by the national regulatory authority and on benchmarks that prevail in other comparable, more competitive areas of the Member State or the Union taking into account the aid received by the network operator. The national regulatory authority shall be consulted on access conditions, including pricing, and in the event of dispute between access seekers and the subsidised infrastructure operator.

7. Member States shall put in place a monitoring and claw-back mechanism if the amount of aid granted to the project exceeds EUR 10 million.

SECTION 11 AID FOR CULTURE AND HERITAGE CONSERVATION

Article 53
Aid for culture and heritage conservation

1. Aid for culture and heritage conservation shall be compatible with the internal market within the meaning of Article 107(3) of the Treaty and shall be exempted from the notification requirement of Article 108(3) of the Treaty, provided the conditions laid down in this Article and in Chapter I are fulfilled.

2. The aid shall be granted for the following cultural purposes and activities:
    (a) museums, archives, libraries, artistic and cultural centres or spaces, theatres, cinemas, opera houses, concert halls, other live performance organisations, film heritage institutions and other similar artistic and cultural infrastructures, organisations and institutions;
    (b) tangible heritage including all forms of movable or immovable cultural heritage and archaeological sites, monuments, historical sites and buildings; natural heritage linked to cultural heritage or if formally recognized as cultural or natural heritage by the competent public authorities of a Member State;
    (c) intangible heritage in any form, including folklorist customs and crafts;
    (d) art or cultural events and performances, festivals, exhibitions and other similar cultural activities;
    (e) cultural and artistic education activities as well as promotion of the understanding of the importance of protection and promotion of the diversity of cultural expressions through educational and greater public awareness programs, including with the use of new technologies;
    (f) writing, editing, production, distribution, digitisation and publishing of music and literature, including translations.
3. The aid may take the form of:
    (a) investment aid, including aid for the construction or upgrade of culture infrastructure;
    (b) operating aid.
4. For investment aid, the eligible costs shall be the investment costs in tangible and intangible assets, including:
    (a) costs for the construction, upgrade, acquisition, conservation or improvement of infrastructure, if at least 80% of either the time or the space capacity per year is used for cultural purposes;
    (b) costs for the acquisition, including leasing, transfer of possession or physical relocation of cultural heritage;
    (c) costs for safeguarding, preservation, restoration and rehabilitation of tangible and intangible cultural heritage, including extra costs for storage under appropriate conditions, special tools, materials and costs for documentation, research, digitalisation and publication;
    (d) costs for improving the accessibility of cultural heritage to the public, including costs for digitisation and other new technologies, costs to improve accessibility for persons with special needs (in particular, ramps and lifts for disabled persons, braille indications and hands-on exhibits in museums) and for promoting cultural diversity with respect to presentations, programmes and visitors;
    (e) costs for cultural projects and activities, cooperation and exchange programmes and grants including costs for selection procedures, costs for promotion and costs incurred directly as a result of the project[.]
5. For operating aid, the eligible costs shall be the following:
    (a) the cultural institution's or heritage site's costs linked to continuous or periodic activities including exhibitions, performances and events and similar cultural activities that occur in the ordinary course of business;
    (b) costs of cultural and artistic education activities as well as promotion of the understanding of the importance of protection and promotion of the diversity

of cultural expressions through educational and greater public awareness programs, including with the use of new technologies;

(c) costs of the improvement of public access to the cultural institution or heritage sites and activities including costs of digitisation and of use of new technologies as well as costs of improving accessibility for persons with disabilities;

(d) operating costs directly relating to the cultural project or activity, such as rent or lease of real estate and cultural venues, travel expenses, materials and supplies directly related to the cultural project or activity, architectural structures for exhibitions and stage sets, loan, lease and depreciation of tools, software and equipment, costs for access rights to copyright works and other related intellectual property rights protected contents, costs for promotion and costs incurred directly as a result of the project or activity; depreciation charges and the costs of financing are only eligible if they have not been covered by investment aid;

(e) costs for personnel working for the cultural institution or heritage site or for a project;

(f) costs for advisory and support services provided by outside consultants and service providers, incurred directly as a result of the project.

6. For investment aid, the aid amount shall not exceed the difference between the eligible costs and the operating profit of the investment[.] The operating profit shall be deducted from the eligible costs ex ante, on the basis of reasonable projections, or through a claw-back mechanism. The operator of the infrastructure is allowed to keep a reasonable profit over the relevant period.

7. For operating aid, the aid amount shall not exceed what is necessary to cover the operating losses and a reasonable profit over the relevant period. This shall be ensured ex ante, on the basis of reasonable projections, or through a claw-back mechanism.

8. For aid not exceeding EUR 2 million, the maximum amount of aid may be set at 80% of eligible costs, as an alternative to application of the method referred to in paragraphs 6 and 7.

9. For the activities defined in paragraph 2(f), the maximum aid amount shall not exceed either the difference between the eligible costs and the project's discounted revenues or 70% of the eligible costs. The revenues shall be deducted from the eligible costs ex ante or through a clawback mechanism. The eligible costs shall be the costs for publishing of music and literature, including the authors' fees (copyright costs), translators' fees, editors' fees, other editorial costs (proofreading, correcting, reviewing), layout and pre-press costs and printing or e-publication costs.

10. Aid to press and magazines, whether they are published in print or electronically, shall not be eligible under this Article.

Article 54
Aid schemes for audiovisual works

1. Aid schemes to support the script-writing, development, production, distribution and promotion of audiovisual works shall be compatible with the internal market pursuant to Article 107(3) of the Treaty and shall be exempted from the notification requirement of Article 108(3) of the Treaty, provided the conditions laid down in this Article and in Chapter I are fulfilled.

2. Aid shall support a cultural product. To avoid manifest errors in the qualification of a product as cultural, each Member State shall establish effective processes, such as selection of proposals by one or more persons entrusted with the selection or verification against a predetermined list of cultural criteria.

3. Aid may take the form of:
   (a) aid to the production of audiovisual works;
   (b) pre-production aid; and
   (c) distribution aid.

4. Where a Member States makes the aid subject to territorial spending obligations, aid schemes for the production of audiovisual works may either:
   (a) require that up to 160% of the aid granted to the production of a given audiovisual work is spent in the territory of the Member State granting the aid; or
   (b) calculate the aid granted to the production of a given audiovisual work as a percentage of the expenditure on production activities in the granting Member State, typically in case of aid schemes in the form of tax incentives.

   In both cases, the maximum expenditure subject to territorial spending obligations shall in no case exceed 80% of the overall production budget.

   For projects to be eligible for aid, a Member State may also require a minimum level of production activity in the territory concerned, but that level shall not exceed 50% of the overall production budget.

5. The eligible costs shall be the following:
   (a) for production aid: the overall costs of production of audiovisual works including costs to improve accessibility for persons with disabilities[;]
   (b) for pre-production aid: the costs of script-writing and the development of audiovisual works[;]
   (c) for distribution aid: the costs of distribution and promotion of audiovisual works.

6. The aid intensity for the production of audiovisual works shall not exceed 50% of the eligible costs.

7. The aid intensity may be increased as follows:
   (a) to 60% of the eligible costs for cross-border productions funded by more than one Member State and involving producers from more than one Member State;
   (b) to 100% of the eligible costs for difficult audiovisual works and co-productions involving countries from the Development Assistance Committee (DAC) List of the OECD.

8. The aid intensity for pre-production shall not exceed 100% of the eligible costs. If the resulting script or project is made into an audiovisual work such as a film, the pre-production costs shall be incorporated in the overall budget and taken into account when calculating the aid intensity. The aid intensity for distribution shall be the same as the aid intensity for production.

9. Aid shall not be reserved for specific production activities or individual parts of the production value chain. Aid for film studio infrastructures shall not be eligible under this Article.

10. Aid shall not be reserved exclusively for nationals and beneficiaries shall not be required to have the status of undertaking established under national commercial law.

18

SECTION 12 AID FOR SPORT AND MULTIFUNCTIONAL RECREATIONAL INFRASTRUCTURES

Article 55
Aid for sport and multifunctional recreational infrastructures

1. Aid for sport and multifunctional recreational infrastructures shall be compatible with the internal market within the meaning of Article 107(3) of the Treaty and shall be exempted from the notification requirement of Article 108(3) of the Treaty, provided that the conditions laid down in this Article and in Chapter I are fulfilled.

2. Sport infrastructure shall not be used exclusively by a single professional sport user. Use of the sport infrastructure by other professional or non-professional sport users shall annually account for at least 20% of time capacity. If the infrastructure is used by several users simultaneously, corresponding fractions of time capacity usage shall be calculated.

3. Multifunctional recreational infrastructure shall consist of recreational facilities with a multifunctional character offering, in particular, cultural and recreational services with the exception of leisure parks and hotel facilities.

4. Access to the sport or multifunctional recreational infrastructures shall be open to several users and be granted on a transparent and non-discriminatory basis. Undertakings which have financed at least 30% of the investment costs of the infrastructure may be granted preferential access under more favourable conditions, provided those conditions are made publicly available.

5. If sport infrastructure is used by professional sport clubs, Member States shall ensure that the pricing conditions for its use are made publicly available.

6. Any concession or other entrustment to a third party to construct, upgrade and/or operate the sport or multifunctional recreational infrastructure shall be assigned on a open, transparent and non-discriminatory basis, having due regard to the applicable procurement rules.

7. The aid may take the form of:
    (a) investment aid, including aid for the construction or upgrade of sport and multi-functional recreational infrastructure;
    (b) operating aid for sport infrastructure[.]

8. For investment aid for sport and multifunctional recreational infrastructure the eligible costs shall be the investment costs in tangible and intangible assets.

9. For operating aid for sport infrastructure the eligible costs shall be the operating costs of the provision of services by the infrastructure. Those operating costs include costs such as personnel costs, materials, contracted services, communications, energy, maintenance, rent, administration, etc., but exclude depreciation charges and the costs of financing if these have been covered by investment aid.

10. For investment aid for sport and multifunctional recreational infrastructure, the aid amount shall not exceed the difference between the eligible costs and the operating profit of the investment. The operating profit shall be deducted from the eligible costs ex ante, on the basis of reasonable projections, or through a claw-back mechanism.

11. For operating aid for sport infrastructure, the aid amount shall not exceed the operating losses over the relevant period. This shall be ensured ex ante, on the basis of reasonable projections, or through a claw-back mechanism.

12. For aid not exceeding EUR 2 million, the maximum amount of aid may be set at 80% of eligible costs, as an alternative to application of the method referred to in paragraphs 10 and 11.

SECTION 13 AID FOR LOCAL INFRASTRUCTURES

Article 56
Investment aid for local infrastructures

1. Financing for the construction or upgrade of local infrastructures which concerns infrastructure that contribute at a local level to improving the business and consumer environment and modernising and developing the industrial base shall be compatible with the internal market within the meaning of Article 107(3) of the Treaty and shall be exempt from the notification requirement of Article 108(3) of the Treaty, provided that the conditions laid down in this Article and in Chapter I are fulfilled.
2. This Article shall not apply to aid for infrastructures that is covered by other sections of Chapter III of this Regulation with the exception of Section 1 – Regional Aid. This Article shall also not apply to airport infrastructure and port infrastructure.
3. The infrastructure shall be made available to interested users on an open, transparent and non-discriminatory basis. The price charged for the use or the sale of the infrastructure shall correspond to market price.
4. Any concession or other entrustment to a third party to operate the infrastructure shall be assigned on an open, transparent and non-discriminatory basis, having due regard to the applicable procurement rules.
5. The eligible costs shall be the investment costs in tangible and intangible assets.
6. The aid amount shall not exceed the difference between the eligible costs and the operating profit of the investment. The operating profit shall be deducted from the eligible costs ex ante, on the basis of reasonable projections, or through a claw-back mechanism.
7. Dedicated infrastructure shall not be exempted under this Article.

SECTION 14 AID FOR REGIONAL AIRPORTS

Article 56a
Aid for regional airports

1. Investment aid to an airport shall be compatible with the internal market within the meaning of Article 107(3) of the Treaty and shall be exempted from the notification requirement of Article 108(3) of the Treaty, provided that the conditions laid down in paragraphs 3 to 14 of this Article and in Chapter I are fulfilled.
2. Operating aid to an airport shall be compatible with the internal market within the meaning of Article 107(3) of the Treaty and shall be exempted from the notification requirement of Article 108(3) of the Treaty, provided that the conditions laid down in paragraphs 3, 4, 10 and 15 to 18 of this Article and in Chapter I are fulfilled.
3. The airport shall be open to all potential users. In the case of physical limitation of capacity, the allocation shall take place on the basis of pertinent, objective, transparent and non-discriminatory criteria.
4. The aid shall not be granted for the relocation of existing airports or for the creation of a new passenger airport, including the conversion of an existing airfield into a passenger airport.

5. The investment concerned shall not exceed what is necessary to accommodate the medium-term expected traffic on the basis of reasonable traffic forecasts.

6. The investment aid shall not be granted to an airport located within 100 kilometres or 60 minutes travelling time by car, bus, train or high-speed train from an existing airport from which scheduled air services, within the meaning of Article 2(16) of Regulation (EC) No. 1008/2008, are operated.

7. Paragraphs 5 and 6 shall not apply to airports with average annual passenger traffic of up to 200 000 passengers during the two financial years preceding the year in which aid is actually granted if the investment aid is not expected to result in the airport increasing its average annual passenger traffic to above 200 000 passengers within two financial years following the granting of the aid. Investment aid granted to such airports shall comply either with paragraph 11 or with paragraphs 13 and 14.

8. Paragraph 6 shall not apply where the investment aid is granted to an airport situated within 100 kilometres from existing airports from which scheduled air services, within the meaning of Article 2(16) of Regulation (EC) No. 1008/2008, are operated, provided the route between each of these other existing airports and the airport receiving the aid necessarily involves either a total travelling time by maritime transportation of at least 90 minutes or air transportation.

9. The investment aid shall not be granted to airports with average annual passenger traffic of more than three million passengers during the two financial years preceding the year in which aid is actually granted. The investment aid shall not be expected to result in the airport increasing its average annual traffic to above three million passengers within two financial years following the granting of the aid.

10. The aid shall not be granted to airports with average annual freight traffic of more than 200 000 tonnes during the two financial years preceding the year in which aid is actually granted. The aid shall not be expected to result in the airport increasing its average annual freight traffic to above 200 000 tonnes within two financial years following the granting of the aid.

11. The investment aid amount shall not exceed the difference between the eligible costs and the operating profit of the investment. The operating profit shall be deducted from the eligible costs ex ante, on the basis of reasonable projections, or through a claw-back mechanism.

12. The eligible costs shall be the costs relating to the investments in airport infrastructure, including planning costs.

13. The investment aid amount shall not exceed:
    (a) 50% of eligible costs for airports with an average annual passenger traffic of one to three million passengers during the two financial years preceding the year in which aid is actually granted;
    (b) 75% of the eligible costs for airports with average annual passenger traffic of up to one million passengers during the two financial years preceding the year in which aid is actually granted.

14. The maximum aid intensities set out in paragraph 13 may be increased by 20 percentage points for airports located in remote regions.

15. Operating aid shall not be granted to airports with average annual passenger traffic of more than 200 000 passengers during the two financial years preceding the year in which aid is actually granted.

16. The amount of operating aid shall not exceed what is necessary to cover the operating losses and a reasonable profit over the relevant period. The aid shall be granted either in the form of periodic instalments fixed ex ante, which shall not be increased during the period for which the aid is granted, or in the form of amounts defined ex post based on the observed operating losses.

17. Operating aid shall not be paid out in respect of any calendar year during which the annual passenger traffic of the airport exceeds 200 000 passengers.

18. The granting of the operating aid shall not be made conditional upon the conclusion of arrangements with specific airlines relating to airport charges, marketing payments or other financial aspects of the airlines' operations at the airport concerned.

SECTION 15 AID FOR PORTS

Article 56b
Aid for maritime ports

1. Aid for maritime ports shall be compatible with the internal market within the meaning of Article 107(3) of the Treaty and shall be exempted from the notification requirement of Article 108(3) of the Treaty, provided that the conditions laid down in this Article and in Chapter I are fulfilled.

2. The eligible costs shall be the costs, including planning costs, of:
   (a) investments for the construction, replacement or upgrade of port infrastructures;
   (b) investments for the construction, replacement or upgrade of access infrastructure;
   (c) dredging.

3. Costs relating to non-transport related activities, including industrial production facilities active in a port, offices or shops, as well as for port superstructures shall not be eligible costs.

4. The aid amount shall not exceed the difference between the eligible costs and the operating profit of the investment or dredging. The operating profit shall be deducted from the eligible costs ex ante, on the basis of reasonable projections, or through a claw-back mechanism.

5. The aid intensity per investment referred to in point (a) of paragraph 2 shall not exceed:
   (a) 100% of the eligible costs where total eligible costs of the project are up to EUR 20 million;
   (b) 80% of the eligible costs where total eligible costs of the project are above EUR 20 million and up to EUR 50 million;
   (c) 60% of the eligible costs where total eligible costs of the project are above EUR 50 million and up to the amount laid down in point (ee) of Article 4(1).
   The aid intensity shall not exceed 100% of the eligible costs determined in point (b) of paragraph 2 and point (c) of paragraph 2 up to the amount laid down in point (ee) of Article 4(1).

6. The aid intensities laid down in points (b) and (c) of the first subparagraph of paragraph 5 may be increased by 10 percentage points for investments located in assisted areas fulfilling the conditions of point (a) of Article 107(3) of the Treaty and by 5 percentage points for investments located in assisted areas fulfilling the conditions of point (c) of Article 107(3) of the Treaty.

18

7. Any concession or other entrustment to a third party to construct, upgrade, operate or rent aided port infrastructure shall be assigned on a competitive, transparent, non-discriminatory and unconditional basis.

8. The aided port infrastructure shall be made available to interested users on an equal and non-discriminatory basis on market terms.

9. For aid not exceeding EUR 5 million, the maximum amount of aid may be set at 80% of eligible costs, as an alternative to application of the method referred to in paragraphs 4, 5 and 6.

Article 56c
Aid for inland ports

1. Aid for inland ports shall be compatible with the internal market within the meaning of Article 107(3) of the Treaty and shall be exempted from the notification requirement of Article 108(3) of the Treaty, provided that the conditions laid down in this Article and in Chapter I are fulfilled.

2. The eligible costs shall be the costs, including planning costs, of:
   (a) investments for the construction, replacement or upgrade of port infrastructures;
   (b) investments for the construction, replacement or upgrade of access infrastructure;
   (c) dredging.

3. Costs relating to non-transport related activities, including industrial production facilities active in a port, offices or shops, as well as for port superstructures shall not be eligible costs.

4. The aid amount shall not exceed the difference between the eligible costs and the operating profit of the investment or dredging. The operating profit shall be deducted from the eligible costs ex ante, on the basis of reasonable projections, or through a claw-back mechanism.

5. The maximum aid intensity shall not exceed 100% of the eligible costs up to the amount laid down in point (ff) of Article 4(1).

6. Any concession or other entrustment to a third party to construct, upgrade, operate or rent aided port infrastructure shall be assigned on a competitive, transparent, non-discriminatory and unconditional basis.

7. The aided port infrastructure shall be made available to interested users on an equal and non-discriminatory basis on market terms.

8. For aid not exceeding EUR 2 million, the maximum amount of aid may be set at 80% of eligible costs, as an alternative to application of the method referred to in paragraphs 4 and 5.

Chapter IV Final Provisions

Article 57
Repeal

Regulation (EC) No. 800/2008 shall be repealed.

Article 58
Transitional provisions

1. This Regulation shall apply to individual aid granted before the respective provisions of this Regulation have entered into force where the aid fulfils all the conditions laid down in this Regulation, with the exception of Article 9.

2. Any aid not exempted from the notification requirement of Article 108(3) of the Treaty by virtue of this Regulation or other regulations adopted pursuant to Article 1 of Regulation (EC) No. 994/98 previously in force shall be assessed by the Commission in accordance with the relevant frameworks, guidelines, communications and notices.

3. Any individual aid granted before 1 January 2015 by virtue of any regulation adopted pursuant to Article 1 of Regulation (EC) No. 994/98 in force at the time of granting the aid shall be compatible with the internal market and exempted from the notification requirement of Article 108(3) of the Treaty with the exclusion of regional aid. Risk capital aid schemes in favour of SMEs set up before 1 July 2014 and exempted from the notification requirement of Article 108(3) of the Treaty under Regulation (EC) No. 800/2008, shall remain exempted and compatible with the internal market until the termination of the funding agreement, provided the commitment of the public funding into the supported private equity investment fund, on the basis of such agreement, was made before 1 January 2015 and the other conditions for exemption remain fulfilled.

3a. Any individual aid granted between 1 July 2014 and 9 July 2017 in accordance with the provisions of this Regulation as applicable at the time of granting the aid shall be compatible with the internal market and exempted from the notification requirement of Article 108(3) of the Treaty. Any individual aid granted before 1 July 2014 in accordance with the provisions of this Regulation, with the exception of Article 9, as applicable either before or after 10 July 2017 shall be compatible with the internal market and exempted from the notification requirement of Article 108(3) of the Treaty.

4. At the end of the period of validity of this Regulation, any aid schemes exempted under this Regulation shall remain exempted during an adjustment period of six months, with the exception of regional aid schemes. The exemption of regional aid schemes shall expire on the date of expiry of the approved regional aid maps. The exemption of risk finance aid exempted pursuant to Article 21(2)(a) shall expire at the end of the period foreseen in the funding agreement, provided the commitment of public funding to the supported private equity investment fund was made on the basis of such agreement within 6 months from the end of the period of validity of this Regulation and all other conditions for exemption remain fulfilled.

5. If this Regulation is amended, any aid scheme exempted under this Regulation as applicable at the time of the entry into force of the scheme shall remain exempted during an adjustment period of six months.

Article 59
This Regulation shall enter into force on 1 July 2014.
   It shall apply until 31 December 2020.

   This Regulation shall be binding in its entirety and directly applicable in all Member States.

18

19

Regulation 1/2003 on the Implementation of the Rules on Competition Laid Down in Articles 101 and 102 of the Treaty

Contents

THE COUNCIL OF THE EUROPEAN UNION,

Having regard to the Treaty [on the Functioning of the European Union] and in particular Article [103] thereof,

Having regard to the proposal from the Commission,

Having regard to the opinion of the European Parliament,

Having regard to the opinion of the European Economic and Social Committee ...

HAS ADOPTED THIS REGULATION:

Chapter I Principles

Article 1

Application of Articles [101] and [102] of the Treaty

1. Agreements, decisions and concerted practices caught by Article [101](1) of the Treaty which do not satisfy the conditions of Article [101](3) of the Treaty shall be prohibited, no prior decision to that effect being required.
2. Agreements, decisions and concerted practices caught by Article [101](1) of the Treaty which satisfy the conditions of Article [101](3) of the Treaty shall not be prohibited, no prior decision to that effect being required.
3. The abuse of a dominant position referred to in Article [102] of the Treaty shall be prohibited, no prior decision to that effect being required.

Article 2

Burden of proof

In any national or [Union] proceedings for the application of Articles [101] and [102] of the Treaty, the burden of proving an infringement of Article[101](1) or of Article [102] of the Treaty shall rest on the party or the authority alleging the infringement. The undertaking or association of undertakings claiming the benefit of Article[101](3) of the Treaty shall bear the burden of proving that the conditions of that paragraph are fulfilled.

Article 3

Relationship between Articles [101] and [102] of the Treaty and national competition laws

1. Where the competition authorities of the Member States or national courts apply national competition law to agreements, decisions by associations of undertakings or concerted practices within the meaning of Article [101](1) of the Treaty which may affect trade between Member States within the meaning of that provision, they shall also apply Article [101] of the Treaty to such agreements, decisions or concerted practices. Where the competition authorities of the Member States or national courts apply national competition law to any abuse prohibited by Article [102] of the Treaty, they shall also apply Article [102] of the Treaty.

2. The application of national competition law may not lead to the prohibition of agreements, decisions by associations of undertakings or concerted practices which may affect trade between Member States but which do not restrict competition within the meaning of Article [101](1) of the Treaty, or which fulfil the conditions of Article [101](3) of the Treaty or which are covered by a Regulation for the application of Article [101](3) of the Treaty. Member States shall not under this Regulation be precluded from adopting and applying on their territory stricter national laws which prohibit or sanction unilateral conduct engaged in by undertakings.

3. Without prejudice to general principles and other provisions of [Union] law, paragraphs 1 and 2 do not apply when the competition authorities and the courts of the Member States apply national merger control laws nor do they preclude the application of provisions of national law that predominantly pursue an objective different from that pursued by Articles [101] and [102] of the Treaty.

Chapter II Powers

Article 4

Powers of the Commission

For the purpose of applying Articles [101] and [102] of the Treaty, the Commission shall have the powers provided for by this Regulation.

Article 5

Powers of the competition authorities of the Member States

The competition authorities of the Member States shall have the power to apply Articles [101] and [102] of the Treaty in individual cases. For this purpose, acting on their own initiative or on a complaint, they may take the following decisions:

— requiring that an infringement be brought to an end,

— ordering interim measures,
— accepting commitments,
— imposing fines, periodic penalty payments or any other penalty provided for in their national law.

Where on the basis of the information in their possession the conditions for prohibition are not met they may likewise decide that there are no grounds for action on their part.

Article 6
Powers of the national courts

National courts shall have the power to apply Articles [101] and [102] of the Treaty.

Chapter III Commission Decisions

Article 7
Finding and termination of infringement

1. Where the Commission, acting on a complaint or on its own initiative, finds that there is an infringement of Article [101] or of Article [102] of the Treaty, it may by decision require the undertakings and associations of undertakings concerned to bring such infringement to an end. For this purpose, it may impose on them any behavioural or structural remedies which are proportionate to the infringement committed and necessary to bring the infringement effectively to an end. Structural remedies can only be imposed either where there is no equally effective behavioural remedy or where any equally effective behavioural remedy would be more burdensome for the undertaking concerned than the structural remedy. If the Commission has a legitimate interest in doing so, it may also find that an infringement has been committed in the past.
2. Those entitled to lodge a complaint for the purposes of paragraph 1 are natural or legal persons who can show a legitimate interest and Member States.

Article 8
Interim measures

1. In cases of urgency due to the risk of serious and irreparable damage to competition, the Commission, acting on its own initiative may by decision, on the basis of a prima facie finding of infringement, order interim measures.
2. A decision under paragraph 1 shall apply for a specified period of time and may be renewed in so far as this is necessary and appropriate.

Article 9
Commitments

1. Where the Commission intends to adopt a decision requiring that an infringement be brought to an end and the undertakings concerned offer commitments to meet the concerns expressed to them by the Commission in its preliminary assessment, the Commission may by decision make those commitments binding on the undertakings. Such a decision may be adopted for a specified period and shall conclude that there are no longer grounds for action by the Commission.
2. The Commission may, upon request or on its own initiative, reopen the proceedings:
   (a) where there has been a material change in any of the facts on which the decision was based;

(b) where the undertakings concerned act contrary to their commitments; or

(c) where the decision was based on incomplete, incorrect or misleading information provided by the parties.

Article 10

Finding of inapplicability

Where the [Union] public interest relating to the application of Articles [101] and [102] of the Treaty so requires, the Commission, acting on its own initiative, may by decision find that Article [101] of the Treaty is not applicable to an agreement, a decision by an association of undertakings or a concerted practice, either because the conditions of Article [101](1) of the Treaty are not fulfilled, or because the conditions of Article [101](3) of the Treaty are satisfied.

The Commission may likewise make such a finding with reference to Article [102] of the Treaty.

Chapter IV Cooperation

Article 11

Cooperation between the Commission and the competition authorities of the Member States

1. The Commission and the competition authorities of the Member States shall apply the [Union] competition rules in close cooperation.

2. The Commission shall transmit to the competition authorities of the Member States copies of the most important documents it has collected with a view to applying Articles 7, 8, 9, 10 and Article 29(1). At the request of the competition authority of a Member State, the Commission shall provide it with a copy of other existing documents necessary for the assessment of the case.

3. The competition authorities of the Member States shall, when acting under Article [101] or Article [102] of the Treaty, inform the Commission in writing before or without delay after commencing the first formal investigative measure. This information may also be made available to the competition authorities of the other Member States.

4. No later than 30 days before the adoption of a decision requiring that an infringement be brought to an end, accepting commitments or withdrawing the benefit of a block exemption Regulation, the competition authorities of the Member States shall inform the Commission. To that effect, they shall provide the Commission with a summary of the case, the envisaged decision or, in the absence thereof, any other document indicating the proposed course of action. This information may also be made available to the competition authorities of the other Member States. At the request of the Commission, the acting competition authority shall make available to the Commission other documents it holds which are necessary for the assessment of the case. The information supplied to the Commission may be made available to the competition authorities of the other Member States. National competition authorities may also exchange between themselves information necessary for the assessment of a case that they are dealing with under Article [101] or Article [102] of the Treaty.

5. The competition authorities of the Member States may consult the Commission on any case involving the application of [Union] law.

6. The initiation by the Commission of proceedings for the adoption of a decision under Chapter III shall relieve the competition authorities of the Member States of their competence to apply Articles [101] and [102] of the Treaty. If a competition authority of a Member State is already acting on a case, the Commission shall only initiate proceedings after consulting with that national competition authority.

Article 12
Exchange of information

1. For the purpose of applying Articles [101] and [102] of the Treaty the Commission and the competition authorities of the Member States shall have the power to provide one another with and use in evidence any matter of fact or of law, including confidential information.
2. Information exchanged shall only be used in evidence for the purpose of applying Article [101] or Article [102] of the Treaty and in respect of the subject-matter for which it was collected by the transmitting authority. However, where national competition law is applied in the same case and in parallel to [Union] competition law and does not lead to a different outcome, information exchanged under this Article may also be used for the application of national competition law.
3. Information exchanged pursuant to paragraph 1 can only be used in evidence to impose sanctions on natural persons where:
   — the law of the transmitting authority foresees sanctions of a similar kind in relation to an infringement of Article [101] or Article [102] of the Treaty or, in the absence thereof,
   — the information has been collected in a way which respects the same level of protection of the rights of defence of natural persons as provided for under the national rules of the receiving authority. However, in this case, the information exchanged cannot be used by the receiving authority to impose custodial sanctions.

Article 13
Suspension or termination of proceedings

1. Where competition authorities of two or more Member States have received a complaint or are acting on their own initiative under Article [101] or Article [102] of the Treaty against the same agreement, decision of an association or practice, the fact that one authority is dealing with the case shall be sufficient grounds for the others to suspend the proceedings before them or to reject the complaint. The Commission may likewise reject a complaint on the ground that a competition authority of a Member State is dealing with the case.
2. Where a competition authority of a Member State or the Commission has received a complaint against an agreement, decision of an association or practice which has already been dealt with by another competition authority, it may reject it.

Article 14
Advisory Committee

1. The Commission shall consult an Advisory Committee on Restrictive Practices and Dominant Positions prior to the taking of any decision under Articles 7, 8, 9, 10, 23, Article 24(2) and Article 29(1).

2. For the discussion of individual cases, the Advisory Committee shall be composed of representatives of the competition authorities of the Member States. For meetings in which issues other than individual cases are being discussed, an additional Member State representative competent in competition matters may be appointed. Representatives may, if unable to attend, be replaced by other representatives.

3. The consultation may take place at a meeting convened and chaired by the Commission, held not earlier than 14 days after dispatch of the notice convening it, together with a summary of the case, an indication of the most important documents and a preliminary draft decision. In respect of decisions pursuant to Article 8, the meeting may be held seven days after the dispatch of the operative part of a draft decision. Where the Commission dispatches a notice convening the meeting which gives a shorter period of notice than those specified above, the meeting may take place on the proposed date in the absence of an objection by any Member State. The Advisory Committee shall deliver a written opinion on the Commission's preliminary draft decision. It may deliver an opinion even if some members are absent and are not represented. At the request of one or several members, the positions stated in the opinion shall be reasoned.

4. Consultation may also take place by written procedure. However, if any Member State so requests, the Commission shall convene a meeting. In case of written procedure, the Commission shall determine a time-limit of not less than 14 days within which the Member States are to put forward their observations for circulation to all other Member States. In case of decisions to be taken pursuant to Article 8, the time-limit of 14 days is replaced by seven days. Where the Commission determines a time-limit for the written procedure which is shorter than those specified above, the proposed time-limit shall be applicable in the absence of an objection by any Member State.

5. The Commission shall take the utmost account of the opinion delivered by the Advisory Committee. It shall inform the Committee of the manner in which its opinion has been taken into account.

6. Where the Advisory Committee delivers a written opinion, this opinion shall be appended to the draft decision. If the Advisory Committee recommends publication of the opinion, the Commission shall carry out such publication taking into account the legitimate interest of undertakings in the protection of their business secrets.

7. At the request of a competition authority of a Member State, the Commission shall include on the agenda of the Advisory Committee cases that are being dealt with by a competition authority of a Member State under Article [101] or Article [102] of the Treaty. The Commission may also do so on its own initiative. In either case, the Commission shall inform the competition authority concerned.

   A request may in particular be made by a competition authority of a Member State in respect of a case where the Commission intends to initiate proceedings with the effect of Article 11(6).

   The Advisory Committee shall not issue opinions on cases dealt with by competition authorities of the Member States. The Advisory Committee may also discuss general issues of [Union] competition law.

Article 15
Cooperation with national courts

1. In proceedings for the application of Article [101] or Article [102] of the Treaty, courts of the Member States may ask the Commission to transmit to them information in

its possession or its opinion on questions concerning the application of the [Union] competition rules.

2. Member States shall forward to the Commission a copy of any written judgment of national courts deciding on the application of Article [101] or Article [102] of the Treaty. Such copy shall be forwarded without delay after the full written judgment is notified to the parties.

3. Competition authorities of the Member States, acting on their own initiative, may submit written observations to the national courts of their Member State on issues relating to the application of Article [101] or Article [102] of the Treaty. With the permission of the court in question, they may also submit oral observations to the national courts of their Member State. Where the coherent application of Article [101] or Article [102] of the Treaty so requires, the Commission, acting on its own initiative, may submit written observations to courts of the Member States. With the permission of the court in question, it may also make oral observations.

For the purpose of the preparation of their observations only, the competition authorities of the Member States and the Commission may request the relevant court of the Member State to transmit or ensure the transmission to them of any documents necessary for the assessment of the case.

4. This Article is without prejudice to wider powers to make observations before courts conferred on competition authorities of the Member States under the law of their Member State.

Article 16
Uniform application of [Union] competition law

1. When national courts rule on agreements, decisions or practices under Article [101] or Article [102] of the Treaty which are already the subject of a Commission decision, they cannot take decisions running counter to the decision adopted by the Commission. They must also avoid giving decisions which would conflict with a decision contemplated by the Commission in proceedings it has initiated. To that effect, the national court may assess whether it is necessary to stay its proceedings. This obligation is without prejudice to the rights and obligations under Article [267] of the Treaty.

2. When competition authorities of the Member States rule on agreements, decisions or practices under Article [101] or Article [102] of the Treaty which are already the subject of a Commission decision, they cannot take decisions which would run counter to the decision adopted by the Commission.

Chapter V Powers of Investigation

Article 17
Investigations into sectors of the economy and into types of agreements

1. Where the trend of trade between Member States, the rigidity of prices or other circumstances suggest that competition may be restricted or distorted within the common market, the Commission may conduct its inquiry into a particular sector of the economy or into a particular type of agreements across various sectors. In the course of that inquiry, the Commission may request the undertakings or associations

of undertakings concerned to supply the information necessary for giving effect to Articles [101] and [102] of the Treaty and may carry out any inspections necessary for that purpose.

The Commission may in particular request the undertakings or associations of undertakings concerned to communicate to it all agreements, decisions and concerted practices.

The Commission may publish a report on the results of its inquiry into particular sectors of the economy or particular types of agreements across various sectors and invite comments from interested parties.

2. Articles 14, 18, 19, 20, 22, 23 and 24 shall apply mutatis mutandis.

Article 18
Requests for information

1. In order to carry out the duties assigned to it by this Regulation, the Commission may, by simple request or by decision, require undertakings and associations of undertakings to provide all necessary information.

2. When sending a simple request for information to an undertaking or association of undertakings, the Commission shall state the legal basis and the purpose of the request, specify what information is required and fix the time-limit within which the information is to be provided, and the penalties provided for in Article 23 for supplying incorrect or misleading information.

3. Where the Commission requires undertakings and associations of undertakings to supply information by decision, it shall state the legal basis and the purpose of the request, specify what information is required and fix the time-limit within which it is to be provided. It shall also indicate the penalties provided for in Article 23 and indicate or impose the penalties provided for in Article 24. It shall further indicate the right to have the decision reviewed by the Court of Justice.

4. The owners of the undertakings or their representatives and, in the case of legal persons, companies or firms, or associations having no legal personality, the persons authorised to represent them by law or by their constitution shall supply the information requested on behalf of the undertaking or the association of undertakings concerned. Lawyers duly authorised to act may supply the information on behalf of their clients. The latter shall remain fully responsible if the information supplied is incomplete, incorrect or misleading.

5. The Commission shall without delay forward a copy of the simple request or of the decision to the competition authority of the Member State in whose territory the seat of the undertaking or association of undertakings is situated and the competition authority of the Member State whose territory is affected.

6. At the request of the Commission the governments and competition authorities of the Member States shall provide the Commission with all necessary information to carry out the duties assigned to it by this Regulation.

Article 19
Power to take statements

1. In order to carry out the duties assigned to it by this Regulation, the Commission may interview any natural or legal person who consents to be interviewed for the purpose of collecting information relating to the subject-matter of an investigation.

2. Where an interview pursuant to paragraph 1 is conducted in the premises of an under-taking, the Commission shall inform the competition authority of the Member State in whose territory the interview takes place. If so requested by the competition authority of that Member State, its officials may assist the officials and other accompanying persons authorised by the Commission to conduct the interview.

Article 20
The Commission's powers of inspection

1. In order to carry out the duties assigned to it by this Regulation, the Commission may conduct all necessary inspections of undertakings and associations of undertakings.
2. The officials and other accompanying persons authorised by the Commission to conduct an inspection are empowered:
   (a) to enter any premises, land and means of transport of undertakings and associations of undertakings;
   (b) to examine the books and other records related to the business, irrespective of the medium on which they are stored;
   (c) to take or obtain in any form copies of or extracts from such books or records;
   (d) to seal any business premises and books or records for the period and to the extent necessary for the inspection;
   (e) to ask any representative or member of staff of the undertaking or association of undertakings for explanations on facts or documents relating to the subject-matter and purpose of the inspection and to record the answers.
3. The officials and other accompanying persons authorised by the Commission to conduct an inspection shall exercise their powers upon production of a written authorisation specifying the subject matter and purpose of the inspection and the penalties provided for in Article 23 in case the production of the required books or other records related to the business is incomplete or where the answers to questions asked under paragraph 2 of the present Article are incorrect or misleading. In good time before the inspection, the Commission shall give notice of the inspection to the competition authority of the Member State in whose territory it is to be conducted.
4. Undertakings and associations of undertakings are required to submit to inspections ordered by decision of the Commission. The decision shall specify the subject matter and purpose of the inspection, appoint the date on which it is to begin and indicate the penalties provided for in Articles 23 and 24 and the right to have the decision reviewed by the Court of Justice. The Commission shall take such decisions after consulting the competition authority of the Member State in whose territory the inspection is to be conducted.
5. Officials of as well as those authorised or appointed by the competition authority of the Member State in whose territory the inspection is to be conducted shall, at the request of that authority or of the Commission, actively assist the officials and other accompanying persons authorised by the Commission. To this end, they shall enjoy the powers specified in paragraph 2.
6. Where the officials and other accompanying persons authorised by the Commission find that an undertaking opposes an inspection ordered pursuant to this Article, the Member State concerned shall afford them the necessary assistance, requesting where appropriate the assistance of the police or of an equivalent enforcement authority, so as to enable them to conduct their inspection.

7. If the assistance provided for in paragraph 6 requires authorisation from a judicial authority according to national rules, such authorisation shall be applied for. Such authorisation may also be applied for as a precautionary measure.

8. Where authorisation as referred to in paragraph 7 is applied for, the national judicial authority shall control that the Commission decision is authentic and that the coercive measures envisaged are neither arbitrary nor excessive having regard to the subject matter of the inspection. In its control of the proportionality of the coercive measures, the national judicial authority may ask the Commission, directly or through the Member State competition authority, for detailed explanations in particular on the grounds the Commission has for suspecting infringement of Articles [101] and [102] of the Treaty, as well as on the seriousness of the suspected infringement and on the nature of the involvement of the undertaking concerned. However, the national judicial authority may not call into question the necessity for the inspection nor demand that it be provided with the information in the Commission's file. The lawfulness of the Commission decision shall be subject to review only by the Court of Justice.

Article 21
Inspection of other premises

1. If a reasonable suspicion exists that books or other records related to the business and to the subject-matter of the inspection, which may be relevant to prove a serious violation of Article [101] or Article [102] of the Treaty, are being kept in any other premises, land and means of transport, including the homes of directors, managers and other members of staff of the undertakings and associations of undertakings concerned, the Commission can by decision order an inspection to be conducted in such other premises, land and means of transport.

2. The decision shall specify the subject matter and purpose of the inspection, appoint the date on which it is to begin and indicate the right to have the decision reviewed by the Court of Justice. It shall in particular state the reasons that have led the Commission to conclude that a suspicion in the sense of paragraph 1 exists. The Commission shall take such decisions after consulting the competition authority of the Member State in whose territory the inspection is to be conducted.

3. A decision adopted pursuant to paragraph 1 cannot be executed without prior authorisation from the national judicial authority of the Member State concerned. The national judicial authority shall control that the Commission decision is authentic and that the coercive measures envisaged are neither arbitrary nor excessive having regard in particular to the seriousness of the suspected infringement, to the importance of the evidence sought, to the involvement of the undertaking concerned and to the reasonable likelihood that business books and records relating to the subject matter of the inspection are kept in the premises for which the authorisation is requested. The national judicial authority may ask the Commission, directly or through the Member State competition authority, for detailed explanations on those elements which are necessary to allow its control of the proportionality of the coercive measures envisaged. However, the national judicial authority may not call into question the necessity for the inspection nor demand that it be provided with information in the Commission's file. The lawfulness of the Commission decision shall be subject to review only by the Court of Justice.

19

4. The officials and other accompanying persons authorised by the Commission to conduct an inspection ordered in accordance with paragraph 1 of this Article shall have the powers set out in Article 20(2)(a), (b) and (c). Article 20(5) and (6) shall apply mutatis mutandis.

Article 22
Investigations by competition authorities of Member States

1. The competition authority of a Member State may in its own territory carry out any inspection or other fact-finding measure under its national law on behalf and for the account of the competition authority of another Member State in order to establish whether there has been an infringement of Article [101] or Article [102] of the Treaty. Any exchange and use of the information collected shall be carried out in accordance with Article 12.

2. At the request of the Commission, the competition authorities of the Member States shall undertake the inspections which the Commission considers to be necessary under Article 20(1) or which it has ordered by decision pursuant to Article 20(4). The officials of the competition authorities of the Member States who are responsible for conducting these inspections as well as those authorised or appointed by them shall exercise their powers in accordance with their national law.

   If so requested by the Commission or by the competition authority of the Member State in whose territory the inspection is to be conducted, officials and other accompanying persons authorised by the Commission may assist the officials of the authority concerned.

Chapter VI Penalties

Article 23
Fines

1. The Commission may by decision impose on undertakings and associations of undertakings fines not exceeding 1% of the total turnover in the preceding business year where, intentionally or negligently:

   (a) they supply incorrect or misleading information in response to a request made pursuant to Article 17 or Article 18(2);

   (b) in response to a request made by decision adopted pursuant to Article 17 or Article 18(3), they supply incorrect, incomplete or misleading information or do not supply information within the required time-limit;

   (c) they produce the required books or other records related to the business in incomplete form during inspections under Article 20 or refuse to submit to inspections ordered by a decision adopted pursuant to Article 20(4);

   (d) in response to a question asked in accordance with Article 20(2)(e),

   — they give an incorrect or misleading answer,

   — they fail to rectify within a time-limit set by the Commission an incorrect, incomplete or misleading answer given by a member of staff, or

   — they fail or refuse to provide a complete answer on facts relating to the subject-matter and purpose of an inspection ordered by a decision adopted pursuant to Article 20(4);

(e) seals affixed in accordance with Article 20(2)(d) by officials or other accompanying persons authorised by the Commission have been broken.

2. The Commission may by decision impose fines on undertakings and associations of undertakings where, either intentionally or negligently:

(a) they infringe Article [101] or Article [102] of the Treaty; or

(b) they contravene a decision ordering interim measures under Article 8; or

(c) they fail to comply with a commitment made binding by a decision pursuant to Article 9.

For each undertaking and association of undertakings participating in the infringement, the fine shall not exceed 10% of its total turnover in the preceding business year.

Where the infringement of an association relates to the activities of its members, the fine shall not exceed 10% of the sum of the total turnover of each member active on the market affected by the infringement of the association.

3. In fixing the amount of the fine, regard shall be had both to the gravity and to the duration of the infringement.

4. When a fine is imposed on an association of undertakings taking account of the turnover of its members and the association is not solvent, the association is obliged to call for contributions from its members to cover the amount of the fine.

Where such contributions have not been made to the association within a time-limit fixed by the Commission, the Commission may require payment of the fine directly by any of the undertakings whose representatives were members of the decision-making bodies concerned of the association.

After the Commission has required payment under the second subparagraph, where necessary to ensure full payment of the fine, the Commission may require payment of the balance by any of the members of the association which were active on the market on which the infringement occurred.

However, the Commission shall not require payment under the second or the third subparagraph from undertakings which show that they have not implemented the infringing decision of the association and either were not aware of its existence or have actively distanced themselves from it before the Commission started investigating the case.

The financial liability of each undertaking in respect of the payment of the fine shall not exceed 10% of its total turnover in the preceding business year.

5. Decisions taken pursuant to paragraphs 1 and 2 shall not be of a criminal law nature.

Article 24
Periodic penalty payments

1. The Commission may, by decision, impose on undertakings or associations of undertakings periodic penalty payments not exceeding 5% of the average daily turnover in the preceding business year per day and calculated from the date appointed by the decision, in order to compel them:

(a) to put an end to an infringement of Article [101] or Article [102] of the Treaty, in accordance with a decision taken pursuant to Article 7;

(b) to comply with a decision ordering interim measures taken pursuant to Article 8;

(c) to comply with a commitment made binding by a decision pursuant to Article 9;

(d) to supply complete and correct information which it has requested by decision taken pursuant to Article 17 or Article 18(3);

(e) to submit to an inspection which it has ordered by decision taken pursuant to Article 20(4).

2. Where the undertakings or associations of undertakings have satisfied the obligation which the periodic penalty payment was intended to enforce, the Commission may fix the definitive amount of the periodic penalty payment at a figure lower than that which would arise under the original decision. Article 23(4) shall apply correspondingly.

Chapter VII Limitation Periods

Article 25
Limitation periods for the imposition of penalties

1. The powers conferred on the Commission by Articles 23 and 24 shall be subject to the following limitation periods:
   (a) three years in the case of infringements of provisions concerning requests for information or the conduct of inspections;
   (b) five years in the case of all other infringements.

2. Time shall begin to run on the day on which the infringement is committed. However, in the case of continuing or repeated infringements, time shall begin to run on the day on which the infringement ceases.

3. Any action taken by the Commission or by the competition authority of a Member State for the purpose of the investigation or proceedings in respect of an infringement shall interrupt the limitation period for the imposition of fines or periodic penalty payments. The limitation period shall be interrupted with effect from the date on which the action is notified to at least one undertaking or association of undertakings which has participated in the infringement. Actions which interrupt the running of the period shall include in particular the following:
   (a) written requests for information by the Commission or by the competition authority of a Member State;
   (b) written authorisations to conduct inspections issued to its officials by the Commission or by the competition authority of a Member State;
   (c) the initiation of proceedings by the Commission or by the competition authority of a Member State;
   (d) notification of the statement of objections of the Commission or of the competition authority of a Member State.

4. The interruption of the limitation period shall apply for all the undertakings or associations of undertakings which have participated in the infringement.

5. Each interruption shall start time running afresh. However, the limitation period shall expire at the latest on the day on which a period equal to twice the limitation period has elapsed without the Commission having imposed a fine or a periodic penalty payment. That period shall be extended by the time during which limitation is suspended pursuant to paragraph 6.

6. The limitation period for the imposition of fines or periodic penalty payments shall be suspended for as long as the decision of the Commission is the subject of proceedings pending before the Court of Justice.

Article 26

Limitation period for the enforcement of penalties

1. The power of the Commission to enforce decisions taken pursuant to Articles 23 and 24 shall be subject to a limitation period of five years.
2. Time shall begin to run on the day on which the decision becomes final.
3. The limitation period for the enforcement of penalties shall be interrupted:
   (a) by notification of a decision varying the original amount of the fine or periodic penalty payment or refusing an application for variation;
   (b) by any action of the Commission or of a Member State, acting at the request of the Commission, designed to enforce payment of the fine or periodic penalty payment.
4. Each interruption shall start time running afresh.
5. The limitation period for the enforcement of penalties shall be suspended for so long as:
   (a) time to pay is allowed;
   (b) enforcement of payment is suspended pursuant to a decision of the Court of Justice.

Chapter VIII Hearings and Professional Secrecy

Article 27

Hearing of the parties, complainants and others

1. Before taking decisions as provided for in Articles 7, 8, 23 and Article 24(2), the Commission shall give the undertakings or associations of undertakings which are the subject of the proceedings conducted by the Commission the opportunity of being heard on the matters to which the Commission has taken objection. The Commission shall base its decisions only on objections on which the parties concerned have been able to comment. Complainants shall be associated closely with the proceedings.
2. The rights of defence of the parties concerned shall be fully respected in the proceedings. They shall be entitled to have access to the Commission's file, subject to the legitimate interest of undertakings in the protection of their business secrets. The right of access to the file shall not extend to confidential information and internal documents of the Commission or the competition authorities of the Member States. In particular, the right of access shall not extend to correspondence between the Commission and the competition authorities of the Member States, or between the latter, including documents drawn up pursuant to Articles 11 and 14. Nothing in this paragraph shall prevent the Commission from disclosing and using information necessary to prove an infringement.
3. If the Commission considers it necessary, it may also hear other natural or legal persons. Applications to be heard on the part of such persons shall, where they show a sufficient interest, be granted. The competition authorities of the Member States may also ask the Commission to hear other natural or legal persons.
4. Where the Commission intends to adopt a decision pursuant to Article 9 or Article 10, it shall publish a concise summary of the case and the main content of the commitments or of the proposed course of action. Interested third parties may submit their observations within a time limit which is fixed by the Commission in its publication

and which may not be less than one month. Publication shall have regard to the legitimate interest of undertakings in the protection of their business secrets.

Article 28
Professional secrecy

1. Without prejudice to Articles 12 and 15, information collected pursuant to Articles 17 to 22 shall be used only for the purpose for which it was acquired.
2. Without prejudice to the exchange and to the use of information foreseen in Articles 11, 12, 14, 15 and 27, the Commission and the competition authorities of the Member States, their officials, servants and other persons working under the supervision of these authorities as well as officials and civil servants of other authorities of the Member States shall not disclose information acquired or exchanged by them pursuant to this Regulation and of the kind covered by the obligation of professional secrecy. This obligation also applies to all representatives and experts of Member States attending meetings of the Advisory Committee pursuant to Article 14.

Chapter IX Exemption Regulations

Article 29
Withdrawal in individual cases

1. Where the Commission, empowered by a Council Regulation, such as Regulations 19/65/EEC, (EEC) No. 2[102]1/71, (EEC) No. 3976/87, (EEC) No. 1534/91 or (EEC) No. 479/92, to apply Article [101](3) of the Treaty by regulation, has declared Article [101](1) of the Treaty inapplicable to certain categories of agreements, decisions by associations of undertakings or concerted practices, it may, acting on its own initiative or on a complaint, withdraw the benefit of such an exemption Regulation when it finds that in any particular case an agreement, decision or concerted practice to which the exemption Regulation applies has certain effects which are incompatible with Article [101](3) of the Treaty.
2. Where, in any particular case, agreements, decisions by associations of undertakings or concerted practices to which a Commission Regulation referred to in paragraph 1 applies have effects which are incompatible with Article [101](3) of the Treaty in the territory of a Member State, or in a part thereof, which has all the characteristics of a distinct geographic market, the competition authority of that Member State may withdraw the benefit of the Regulation in question in respect of that territory.

Chapter X General Provisions

Article 30
Publication of decisions

1. The Commission shall publish the decisions, which it takes pursuant to Articles 7 to 10, 23 and 24.
2. The publication shall state the names of the parties and the main content of the decision, including any penalties imposed. It shall have regard to the legitimate interest of undertakings in the protection of their business secrets.

Article 31

Review by the Court of Justice

The Court of Justice shall have unlimited jurisdiction to review decisions whereby the Commission has fixed a fine or periodic penalty payment. It may cancel, reduce or increase the fine or periodic penalty payment imposed.

––––––––

Article 33

Implementing provisions

1. The Commission shall be authorised to take such measures as may be appropriate in order to apply this Regulation. The measures may concern, inter alia:
   (a) the form, content and other details of complaints lodged pursuant to Article 7 and the procedure for rejecting complaints;
   (b) the practical arrangements for the exchange of information and consultations provided for in Article 11;
   (c) the practical arrangements for the hearings provided for in Article 27.
2. Before the adoption of any measures pursuant to paragraph 1, the Commission shall publish a draft thereof and invite all interested parties to submit their comments within the time-limit it lays down, which may not be less than one month. Before publishing a draft measure and before adopting it, the Commission shall consult the Advisory Committee on Restrictive Practices and Dominant Positions.

Chapter XI Transitional, Amending and Final Provisions

Article 34

Transitional provisions

1. Applications made to the Commission under Article 2 of Regulation No. 17, notifications made under Articles 4 and 5 of that Regulation and the corresponding applications and notifications made under Regulations (EEC) No. 1017/68, (EEC) No. 4056/86 and (EEC) No. 3975/87 shall lapse as from the date of application of this Regulation.
2. Procedural steps taken under Regulation No. 17 and Regulations (EEC) No. 1017/68, (EEC) No. 4056/86 and (EEC) No. 3975/87 shall continue to have effect for the purposes of applying this Regulation.

Article 35

Designation of competition authorities of Member States

1. The Member States shall designate the competition authority or authorities responsible for the application of Articles [101] and [102] of the Treaty in such a way that the provisions of this regulation are effectively complied with. The measures necessary to empower those authorities to apply those Articles shall be taken before 1 May 2004. The authorities designated may include courts.
2. When enforcement of [Union] competition law is entrusted to national administrative and judicial authorities, the Member States may allocate different powers and functions to those different national authorities, whether administrative or judicial.
3. The effects of Article 11(6) apply to the authorities designated by the Member States including courts that exercise functions regarding the preparation and the adoption of

the types of decisions foreseen in Article 5. The effects of Article 11(6) do not extend to courts insofar as they act as review courts in respect of the types of decisions foreseen in Article 5.

4. Notwithstanding paragraph 3, in the Member States where, for the adoption of certain types of decisions foreseen in Article 5, an authority brings an action before a judicial authority that is separate and different from the prosecuting authority and provided that the terms of this paragraph are complied with, the effects of Article 11(6) shall be limited to the authority prosecuting the case which shall withdraw its claim before the judicial authority when the Commission opens proceedings and this withdrawal shall bring the national proceedings effectively to an end.

———————

Article 43

Repeal of Regulations No. 17 and No. 141

1. Regulation No. 17 is repealed with the exception of Article 8(3) which continues to apply to decisions adopted pursuant to Article [101](3) of the Treaty prior to the date of application of this Regulation until the date of expiration of those decisions.

2. Regulation No. 141 is repealed.

3. References to the repealed Regulations shall be construed as references to this Regulation.

Article 44

Report on the application of the present Regulation

Five years from the date of application of this Regulation, the Commission shall report to the European Parliament and the Council on the functioning of this Regulation, in particular on the application of Article 11(6) and Article 17.

On the basis of this report, the Commission shall assess whether it is appropriate to propose to the Council a revision of this Regulation.

Article 45

Entry into force

This Regulation shall enter into force on the 20th day following that of its publication in the Official Journal of the European [Union].

It shall apply from 1 May 2004.

This Regulation shall be binding in its entirety and directly applicable in all Member States.

20

Directive 2014/104 on Certain Rules Governing Actions for Damages under National Law for Infringements of the Competition Law Provisions of the Member States and of the European Union

Contents

THE EUROPEAN PARLIAMENT AND THE COUNCIL OF THE EUROPEAN UNION,
  Having regard to the Treaty on the Functioning of the European Union, and in particular Articles 103 and 114 thereof…
  Acting in accordance with the ordinary legislative procedure…
  HAVE ADOPTED THIS DIRECTIVE:

Chapter I Subject Matter, Scope and Definitions

Article 1

Subject matter and scope

1. This Directive sets out certain rules necessary to ensure that anyone who has suffered harm caused by an infringement of competition law by an undertaking or by an association of undertakings can effectively exercise the right to claim full compensation for that harm from that undertaking or association. It sets out rules fostering undistorted competition in the internal market and removing obstacles to its proper functioning, by ensuring equivalent protection throughout the Union for anyone who has suffered such harm.

2. This Directive sets out rules coordinating the enforcement of the competition rules by competition authorities and the enforcement of those rules in damages actions before national courts.

Article 2

Definitions

For the purposes of this Directive, the following definitions apply:

(1) 'infringement of competition law' means an infringement of Article 101 or 102 TFEU, or of national competition law;

(2) 'infringer' means an undertaking or association of undertakings which has committed an infringement of competition law;

(3) 'national competition law' means provisions of national law that predominantly pursue the same objective as Articles 101 and 102 TFEU and that are applied to the same case and in parallel to Union competition law pursuant to Article 3(1) of Regulation (EC) No. 1/2003, excluding provisions of national law which impose criminal penalties on natural persons, except to the extent that such criminal penalties are the means whereby competition rules applying to undertakings are enforced;

(4) 'action for damages' means an action under national law by which a claim for damages is brought before a national court by an alleged injured party, or by someone acting on behalf of one or more alleged injured parties where Union or national law provides for that possibility, or by a natural or legal person that succeeded in the right of the alleged injured party, including the person that acquired the claim;

(5) 'claim for damages' means a claim for compensation for harm caused by an infringement of competition law;

(6) 'injured party' means a person that has suffered harm caused by an infringement of competition law;

(7) 'national competition authority' means an authority designated by a Member State pursuant to Article 35 of Regulation (EC) No. 1/2003, as being responsible for the application of Articles 101 and 102 TFEU;

(8) 'competition authority' means the Commission or a national competition authority or both, as the context may require;

(9) 'national court' means a court or tribunal of a Member State within the meaning of Article 267 TFEU;

(10) 'review court' means a national court that is empowered by ordinary means of appeal to review decisions of a national competition authority or to review judgments pronouncing on those decisions, irrespective of whether that court itself has the power to find an infringement of competition law;

(11) 'infringement decision' means a decision of a competition authority or review court that finds an infringement of competition law;

(12) 'final infringement decision' means an infringement decision that cannot be, or that can no longer be, appealed by ordinary means;

(13) 'evidence' means all types of means of proof admissible before the national court seized, in particular documents and all other objects containing information, irrespective of the medium on which the information is stored;

(14) 'cartel' means an agreement or concerted practice between two or more competitors aimed at coordinating their competitive behaviour on the market or influencing the relevant parameters of competition through practices such as, but not limited to, the fixing or coordination of purchase or selling prices or other trading conditions, including in relation to intellectual property rights, the allocation of production or sales quotas, the sharing of markets and customers, including bid-rigging, restrictions of imports or exports or anti-competitive actions against other competitors;

(15) 'leniency programme' means a programme concerning the application of Article 101 TFEU or a corresponding provision under national law on the basis of which a participant in a secret cartel, independently of the other undertakings involved in the cartel, cooperates with an investigation of the competition authority, by voluntarily providing presentations regarding that participant's knowledge of, and role in, the cartel in return for which that participant receives, by decision or by a discontinuation of proceedings, immunity from, or a reduction in, fines for its involvement in the cartel;

(16) 'leniency statement' means an oral or written presentation voluntarily provided by, or on behalf of, an undertaking or a natural person to a competition authority or a record thereof, describing the knowledge of that undertaking or natural person of a cartel and describing its role therein, which presentation was drawn up specifically for submission to the competition authority with a view to obtaining immunity or a reduction of fines under a leniency programme, not including pre-existing information;

(17) 'pre-existing information' means evidence that exists irrespective of the proceedings of a competition authority, whether or not such information is in the file of a competition authority;

(18) 'settlement submission' means a voluntary presentation by, or on behalf of, an undertaking to a competition authority describing the undertaking's acknowledgement of, or its renunciation to dispute, its participation in an infringement of competition law and its responsibility for that infringement of competition law, which was drawn up specifically to enable the competition authority to apply a simplified or expedited procedure;

(19) 'immunity recipient' means an undertaking which, or a natural person who, has been granted immunity from fines by a competition authority under a leniency programme;

(20) 'overcharge' means the difference between the price actually paid and the price that would otherwise have prevailed in the absence of an infringement of competition law;

(21) 'consensual dispute resolution' means any mechanism enabling parties to reach the out-of-court resolution of a dispute concerning a claim for damages;

(22) 'consensual settlement' means an agreement reached through consensual dispute resolution[;]

(23) 'direct purchaser' means a natural or legal person who acquired, directly from an infringer, products or services that were the object of an infringement of competition law;

(24) 'indirect purchaser' means a natural or legal person who acquired, not directly from an infringer, but from a direct purchaser or a subsequent purchaser, products or services that were the object of an infringement of competition law, or products or services containing them or derived therefrom.

Article 3
Right to full compensation

1. Member States shall ensure that any natural or legal person who has suffered harm caused by an infringement of competition law is able to claim and to obtain full compensation for that harm.

2. Full compensation shall place a person who has suffered harm in the position in which that person would have been had the infringement of competition law not been committed. It shall therefore cover the right to compensation for actual loss and for loss of profit, plus the payment of interest.

3. Full compensation under this Directive shall not lead to overcompensation, whether by means of punitive, multiple or other types of damages.

Article 4
Principles of effectiveness and equivalence

In accordance with the principle of effectiveness, Member States shall ensure that all national rules and procedures relating to the exercise of claims for damages are designed and applied in such a way that they do not render practically impossible or excessively difficult the exercise of the Union right to full compensation for harm caused by an infringement of competition law. In accordance with the principle of equivalence, national rules and procedures relating to actions for damages resulting from infringements of Article 101 or 102 TFEU shall not be less favourable to the alleged injured parties than those governing similar actions for damages resulting from infringements of national law.

Chapter II Disclosure of Evidence

Article 5
Disclosure of evidence

1. Member States shall ensure that in proceedings relating to an action for damages in the Union, upon request of a claimant who has presented a reasoned justification containing reasonably available facts and evidence sufficient to support the plausibility of its claim for damages, national courts are able to order the defendant or a third party to disclose relevant evidence which lies in their control, subject to the conditions set out in this Chapter. Member States shall ensure that national courts are able, upon request of the defendant, to order the claimant or a third party to disclose relevant evidence.

   This paragraph is without prejudice to the rights and obligations of national courts under Regulation (EC) No. 1206/2001.

2. Member States shall ensure that national courts are able to order the disclosure of specified items of evidence or relevant categories of evidence circumscribed as precisely and as narrowly as possible on the basis of reasonably available facts in the reasoned justification.

3. Member States shall ensure that national courts limit the disclosure of evidence to that which is proportionate. In determining whether any disclosure requested by a party is proportionate, national courts shall consider the legitimate interests of all parties and third parties concerned. They shall, in particular, consider:

   (a) the extent to which the claim or defence is supported by available facts and evidence justifying the request to disclose evidence;

   (b) the scope and cost of disclosure, especially for any third parties concerned, including preventing non-specific searches for information which is unlikely to be of relevance for the parties in the procedure;

   (c) whether the evidence the disclosure of which is sought contains confidential information, especially concerning any third parties, and what arrangements are in place for protecting such confidential information.

4. Member States shall ensure that national courts have the power to order the disclosure of evidence containing confidential information where they consider it relevant to the action for damages. Member States shall ensure that, when ordering the disclosure of such information, national courts have at their disposal effective measures to protect such information.

5. The interest of undertakings to avoid actions for damages following an infringement of competition law shall not constitute an interest that warrants protection.

6. Member States shall ensure that national courts give full effect to applicable legal professional privilege under Union or national law when ordering the disclosure of evidence.

7. Member States shall ensure that those from whom disclosure is sought are provided with an opportunity to be heard before a national court orders disclosure under this Article.

8. Without prejudice to paragraphs 4 and 7 and to Article 6, this Article shall not prevent Member States from maintaining or introducing rules which would lead to wider disclosure of evidence.

Article 6
Disclosure of evidence included in the file of a competition authority

1. Member States shall ensure that, for the purpose of actions for damages, where national courts order the disclosure of evidence included in the file of a competition authority, this Article applies in addition to Article 5.

2. This Article is without prejudice to the rules and practices on public access to documents under Regulation (EC) No. 1049/2001.

3. This Article is without prejudice to the rules and practices under Union or national law on the protection of internal documents of competition authorities and of correspondence between competition authorities.

4. When assessing, in accordance with Article 5(3), the proportionality of an order to disclose information, national courts shall, in addition, consider the following:
   (a) whether the request has been formulated specifically with regard to the nature, subject matter or contents of documents submitted to a competition authority or held in the file thereof, rather than by a non-specific application concerning documents submitted to a competition authority;
   (b) whether the party requesting disclosure is doing so in relation to an action for damages before a national court; and
   (c) in relation to paragraphs 5 and 10, or upon request of a competition authority pursuant to paragraph 11, the need to safeguard the effectiveness of the public enforcement of competition law.

5. National courts may order the disclosure of the following categories of evidence only after a competition authority, by adopting a decision or otherwise, has closed its proceedings:
   (a) information that was prepared by a natural or legal person specifically for the proceedings of a competition authority;
   (b) information that the competition authority has drawn up and sent to the parties in the course of its proceedings; and
   (c) settlement submissions that have been withdrawn.

6. Member States shall ensure that, for the purpose of actions for damages, national courts cannot at any time order a party or a third party to disclose any of the following categories of evidence:

(a) leniency statements; and

(b) settlement submissions.

7. A claimant may present a reasoned request that a national court access the evidence referred to in point (a) or (b) of paragraph 6 for the sole purpose of ensuring that their contents correspond to the definitions in points (16) and (18) of Article 2. In that assessment, national courts may request assistance only from the competent competition authority. The authors of the evidence in question may also have the possibility to be heard. In no case shall the national court permit other parties or third parties access to that evidence.

8. If only parts of the evidence requested are covered by paragraph 6, the remaining parts thereof shall, depending on the category under which they fall, be released in accordance with the relevant paragraphs of this Article.

9. The disclosure of evidence in the file of a competition authority that does not fall into any of the categories listed in this Article may be ordered in actions for damages at any time, without prejudice to this Article.

10. Member States shall ensure that national courts request the disclosure from a competition authority of evidence included in its file only where no party or third party is reasonably able to provide that evidence.

11. To the extent that a competition authority is willing to state its views on the proportionality of disclosure requests, it may, acting on its own initiative, submit observations to the national court before which a disclosure order is sought.

Article 7

Limits on the use of evidence obtained solely through access to the file of a competition authority

1. Member States shall ensure that evidence in the categories listed in Article 6(6) which is obtained by a natural or legal person solely through access to the file of a competition authority is either deemed to be inadmissible in actions for damages or is otherwise protected under the applicable national rules to ensure the full effect of the limits on the disclosure of evidence set out in Article 6.

2. Member States shall ensure that, until a competition authority has closed its proceedings by adopting a decision or otherwise, evidence in the categories listed in Article 6(5) which is obtained by a natural or legal person solely through access to the file of that competition authority is either deemed to be inadmissible in actions for damages or is otherwise protected under the applicable national rules to ensure the full effect of the limits on the disclosure of evidence set out in Article 6.

3. Member States shall ensure that evidence which is obtained by a natural or legal person solely through access to the file of a competition authority and which does not fall under paragraph 1 or 2, can be used in an action for damages only by that person or by a natural or legal person that succeeded to that person's rights, including a person that acquired that person's claim.

Article 8

Penalties

1. Member States shall ensure that national courts are able effectively to impose penalties on parties, third parties and their legal representatives in the event of any of the following:

(a) their failure or refusal to comply with the disclosure order of any national court;

(b) their destruction of relevant evidence;

(c) their failure or refusal to comply with the obligations imposed by a national court order protecting confidential information;

(d) their breach of the limits on the use of evidence provided for in this Chapter.

2. Member States shall ensure that the penalties that can be imposed by national courts are effective, proportionate and dissuasive. The penalties available to national courts shall include, with regard to the behaviour of a party to proceedings for an action for damages, the possibility to draw adverse inferences, such as presuming the relevant issue to be proven or dismissing claims and defences in whole or in part, and the possibility to order the payment of costs.

Chapter III Effect of National Decisions, Limitation Periods, Joint and Several Liability

Article 9
Effect of national decisions

1. Member States shall ensure that an infringement of competition law found by a final decision of a national competition authority or by a review court is deemed to be irrefutably established for the purposes of an action for damages brought before their national courts under Article 101 or 102 TFEU or under national competition law.

2. Member States shall ensure that where a final decision referred to in paragraph 1 is taken in another Member State, that final decision may, in accordance with national law, be presented before their national courts as at least prima facie evidence that an infringement of competition law has occurred and, as appropriate, may be assessed along with any other evidence adduced by the parties.

3. This Article is without prejudice to the rights and obligations of national courts under Article 267 TFEU.

Article 10
Limitation periods

1. Member States shall, in accordance with this Article, lay down rules applicable to limitation periods for bringing actions for damages. Those rules shall determine when the limitation period begins to run, the duration thereof and the circumstances under which it is interrupted or suspended.

2. Limitation periods shall not begin to run before the infringement of competition law has ceased and the claimant knows, or can reasonably be expected to know:

(a) of the behaviour and the fact that it constitutes an infringement of competition law;

(b) of the fact that the infringement of competition law caused harm to it; and

(c) the identity of the infringer.

3. Member States shall ensure that the limitation periods for bringing actions for damages are at least five years.

4. Member States shall ensure that a limitation period is suspended or, depending on national law, interrupted, if a competition authority takes action for the purpose of the investigation or its proceedings in respect of an infringement of competition law to which the action for damages relates. The suspension shall end at the earliest one year

20

after the infringement decision has become final or after the proceedings are otherwise terminated.

Article 11
Joint and several liability

1. Member States shall ensure that undertakings which have infringed competition law through joint behaviour are jointly and severally liable for the harm caused by the infringement of competition law; with the effect that each of those undertakings is bound to compensate for the harm in full, and the injured party has the right to require full compensation from any of them until he has been fully compensated.

2. By way of derogation from paragraph 1, Member States shall ensure that, without prejudice to the right of full compensation as laid down in Article 3, where the infringer is a small or medium-sized enterprise (SME) as defined in Commission Recommendation 2003/361/EC, the infringer is liable only to its own direct and indirect purchasers where:
    (a) its market share in the relevant market was below 5% at any time during the infringement of competition law; and
    (b) the application of the normal rules of joint and several liability would irretrievably jeopardise its economic viability and cause its assets to lose all their value.

3. The derogation laid down in paragraph 2 shall not apply where:
    (a) the SME has led the infringement of competition law or has coerced other undertakings to participate therein; or
    (b) the SME has previously been found to have infringed competition law.

4. By way of derogation from paragraph 1, Member States shall ensure that an immunity recipient is jointly and severally liable as follows:
    (a) to its direct or indirect purchasers or providers; and
    (b) to other injured parties only where full compensation cannot be obtained from the other undertakings that were involved in the same infringement of competition law.
    Member States shall ensure that any limitation period applicable to cases under this paragraph is reasonable and sufficient to allow injured parties to bring such actions.

5. Member States shall ensure that an infringer may recover a contribution from any other infringer, the amount of which shall be determined in the light of their relative responsibility for the harm caused by the infringement of competition law. The amount of contribution of an infringer which has been granted immunity from fines under a leniency programme shall not exceed the amount of the harm it caused to its own direct or indirect purchasers or providers.

6. Member States shall ensure that, to the extent the infringement of competition law caused harm to injured parties other than the direct or indirect purchasers or providers of the infringers, the amount of any contribution from an immunity recipient to other infringers shall be determined in the light of its relative responsibility for that harm.

Chapter IV The Passing-on of Overcharges

Article 12
Passing-on of overcharges and the right to full compensation

1. To ensure the full effectiveness of the right to full compensation as laid down in Article 3, Member States shall ensure that, in accordance with the rules laid down in this

Chapter, compensation of harm can be claimed by anyone who suffered it, irrespective of whether they are direct or indirect purchasers from an infringer, and that compensation of harm exceeding that caused by the infringement of competition law to the claimant, as well as the absence of liability of the infringer, are avoided.

2. In order to avoid overcompensation, Member States shall lay down procedural rules appropriate to ensure that compensation for actual loss at any level of the supply chain does not exceed the overcharge harm suffered at that level.

3. This Chapter shall be without prejudice to the right of an injured party to claim and obtain compensation for loss of profits due to a full or partial passing-on of the overcharge.

4. Member States shall ensure that the rules laid down in this Chapter apply accordingly where the infringement of competition law relates to a supply to the infringer.

5. Member States shall ensure that the national courts have the power to estimate, in accordance with national procedures, the share of any overcharge that was passed on.

Article 13

Passing-on defence

Member States shall ensure that the defendant in an action for damages can invoke as a defence against a claim for damages the fact that the claimant passed on the whole or part of the overcharge resulting from the infringement of competition law. The burden of proving that the overcharge was passed on shall be on the defendant, who may reasonably require disclosure from the claimant or from third parties.

Article 14

Indirect purchasers

1. Member States shall ensure that, where in an action for damages the existence of a claim for damages or the amount of compensation to be awarded depends on whether, or to what degree, an overcharge was passed on to the claimant, taking into account the commercial practice that price increases are passed on down the supply chain, the burden of proving the existence and scope of such a passing-on shall rest with the claimant, who may reasonably require disclosure from the defendant or from third parties.

2. In the situation referred to in paragraph 1, the indirect purchaser shall be deemed to have proven that a passing-on to that indirect purchaser occurred where that indirect purchaser has shown that:

   (a) the defendant has committed an infringement of competition law;

   (b) the infringement of competition law has resulted in an overcharge for the direct purchaser of the defendant; and

   (c) the indirect purchaser has purchased the goods or services that were the object of the infringement of competition law, or has purchased goods or services derived from or containing them.

   This paragraph shall not apply where the defendant can demonstrate credibly to the satisfaction of the court that the overcharge was not, or was not entirely, passed on to the indirect purchaser.

Article 15

Actions for damages by claimants from different levels in the supply chain

1. To avoid that actions for damages by claimants from different levels in the supply chain lead to a multiple liability or to an absence of liability of the infringer, Member States

shall ensure that in assessing whether the burden of proof resulting from the application of Articles 13 and 14 is satisfied, national courts seized of an action for damages are able, by means available under Union or national law, to take due account of any of the following:

(a) actions for damages that are related to the same infringement of competition law, but that are brought by claimants from other levels in the supply chain;

(b) judgments resulting from actions for damages as referred to in point (a);

(c) relevant information in the public domain resulting from the public enforcement of competition law.

2. This Article shall be without prejudice to the rights and obligations of national courts under Article 30 of Regulation (EU) No. 1215/2012.

Article 16
Guidelines for national courts
The Commission shall issue guidelines for national courts on how to estimate the share of the overcharge which was passed on to the indirect purchaser.

Chapter V Quantification of Harm

Article 17
Quantification of harm

1. Member States shall ensure that neither the burden nor the standard of proof required for the quantification of harm renders the exercise of the right to damages practically impossible or excessively difficult. Member States shall ensure that the national courts are empowered, in accordance with national procedures, to estimate the amount of harm if it is established that a claimant suffered harm but it is practically impossible or excessively difficult precisely to quantify the harm suffered on the basis of the evidence available.

2. It shall be presumed that cartel infringements cause harm. The infringer shall have the right to rebut that presumption.

3. Member States shall ensure that, in proceedings relating to an action for damages, a national competition authority may, upon request of a national court, assist that national court with respect to the determination of the quantum of damages where that national competition authority considers such assistance to be appropriate.

Chapter VI Consensual Dispute Resolution

Article 18
Suspensive and other effects of consensual dispute resolution

1. Member States shall ensure that the limitation period for bringing an action for damages is suspended for the duration of any consensual dispute resolution process. The suspension of the limitation period shall apply only with regard to those parties that are or that were involved or represented in the consensual dispute resolution.

2. Without prejudice to provisions of national law in matters of arbitration, Member States shall ensure that national courts seized of an action for damages may suspend their proceedings for up to two years where the parties thereto are involved

in consensual dispute resolution concerning the claim covered by that action for damages.

3. A competition authority may consider compensation paid as a result of a consensual settlement and prior to its decision imposing a fine to be a mitigating factor.

Article 19
Effect of consensual settlements on subsequent actions for damages

1. Member States shall ensure that, following a consensual settlement, the claim of the settling injured party is reduced by the settling co-infringer's share of the harm that the infringement of competition law inflicted upon the injured party.

2. Any remaining claim of the settling injured party shall be exercised only against non-settling co-infringers. Non-settling co-infringers shall not be permitted to recover contribution for the remaining claim from the settling co-infringer.

3. By way of derogation from paragraph 2, Member States shall ensure that where the non-settling co-infringers cannot pay the damages that correspond to the remaining claim of the settling injured party, the settling injured party may exercise the remaining claim against the settling co-infringer.

   The derogation referred to in the first subparagraph may be expressly excluded under the terms of the consensual settlement.

4. When determining the amount of contribution that a co-infringer may recover from any other co-infringer in accordance with their relative responsibility for the harm caused by the infringement of competition law, national courts shall take due account of any damages paid pursuant to a prior consensual settlement involving the relevant co-infringer.

Chapter VII Final Provisions

Article 20
Review

1. The Commission shall review this Directive and shall submit a report thereon to the European Parliament and the Council by 27 December 2020.

2. The report referred to in paragraph 1 shall, inter alia, include information on all of the following:

   (a) the possible impact of financial constraints flowing from the payment of fines imposed by a competition authority for an infringement of competition law on the possibility for injured parties to obtain full compensation for the harm caused by that infringement of competition law;

   (b) the extent to which claimants for damages caused by an infringement of competition law established in an infringement decision adopted by a competition authority of a Member State are able to prove before the national court of another Member State that such an infringement of competition law has occurred;

   (c) the extent to which compensation for actual loss exceeds the overcharge harm caused by the infringement of competition law or suffered at any level of the supply chain.

3. If appropriate, the report referred to in paragraph 1 shall be accompanied by a legislative proposal.

Article 21

Transposition

1. Member States shall bring into force the laws, regulations and administrative provisions necessary to comply with this Directive by 27 December 2016. They shall forthwith communicate to the Commission the text thereof.

   When Member States adopt those measures, they shall contain a reference to this Directive or be accompanied by such a reference on the occasion of their official publication. Member States shall determine how such reference is to be made.

2. Member States shall communicate to the Commission the text of the main provisions of national law which they adopt in the field covered by this Directive.

Article 22

Temporal application

1. Member States shall ensure that the national measures adopted pursuant to Article 21 in order to comply with substantive provisions of this Directive do not apply retroactively.

2. Member States shall ensure that any national measures adopted pursuant to Article 21, other than those referred to in paragraph 1, do not apply to actions for damages of which a national court was seized prior to 26 December 2014.

Article 23

Entry into force

This Directive shall enter into force on the twentieth day following that of its publication in the *Official Journal of the European Union*.

Article 24

Addressees

This Directive is addressed to the Member States.

PART II
Union Secondary Law: Legislation and Other Acts

21

Directive 89/391 on the Introduction of Measures to Encourage Improvements in the Safety and Health of Workers at Work

Contents

THE COUNCIL OF THE EUROPEAN [UNION],

Having regard to the Treaty [on the Functioning of the European Union], and in particular Article [153] thereof,

Having regard to the proposal from the Commission, drawn up after consultation with the Advisory Committee on Safety, Hygiene and Health Protection at Work,

In cooperation with the European Parliament,

Having regard to the opinion of the Economic and Social Committee ...

HAS ADOPTED THIS DIRECTIVE:

SECTION I GENERAL PROVISIONS

Article 1
Object

1. The object of this Directive is to introduce measures to encourage improvements in the safety and health of workers at work.
2. To that end it contains general principles concerning the prevention of occupational risks, the protection of safety and health, the elimination of risk and accident factors, the informing, consultation, balanced participation in accordance with national laws and/or practices and training of workers and their representatives, as well as general guidelines for the implementation of the said principles.
3. This Directive shall be without prejudice to existing or future national and [Union] provisions which are more favourable to protection of the safety and health of workers at work.

Article 2
Scope

1. This Directive shall apply to all sectors of activity, both public and private (industrial, agricultural, commercial, administrative, service, educational, cultural, leisure, etc.).

21

2. This Directive shall not be applicable where characteristics peculiar to certain specific public service activities, such as the armed forces or the police, or to certain specific activities in the civil protection services inevitably conflict with it.

In that event, the safety and health of workers must be ensured as far as possible in the light of the objectives of this Directive.

Article 3

Definitions

For the purposes of this Directive, the following terms shall have the following meanings:

(a) worker: any person employed by an employer, including trainees and apprentices but excluding domestic servants;

(b) employer: any natural or legal person who has an employment relationship with the worker and has responsibility for the undertaking and/or establishment;

(c) workers' representative with specific responsibility for the safety and health of workers: any person elected, chosen or designated in accordance with national laws and/or practices to represent workers where problems arise relating to the safety and health protection of workers at work;

(d) prevention: all the steps or measures taken or planned at all stages of work in the undertaking to prevent or reduce occupational risks.

Article 4

1. Member States shall take the necessary steps to ensure that employers, workers and workers' representatives are subject to the legal provisions necessary for the implementation of this Directive.

2. In particular, Member States shall ensure adequate controls and supervision.

SECTION II EMPLOYERS' OBLIGATIONS

Article 5

General provision

1. The employer shall have a duty to ensure the safety and health of workers in every aspect related to the work.

2. Where, pursuant to Article 7(3), an employer enlists competent external services or persons, this shall not discharge him from his responsibilities in this area.

3. The workers' obligations in the field of safety and health at work shall not affect the principle of the responsibility of the employer.

4. This Directive shall not restrict the option of Member States to provide for the exclusion or the limitation of employers' responsibility where occurrences are due to unusual and unforeseeable circumstances, beyond the employers' control, or to exceptional events, the consequences of which could not have been avoided despite the exercise of all due care. Member States need not exercise the option referred to in the first subparagraph.

Article 6

General obligations on employers

1. Within the context of his responsibilities, the employer shall take the measures necessary for the safety and health protection of workers, including prevention of occupational

risks and provision of information and training, as well as provision of the necessary organization and means.

The employer shall be alert to the need to adjust these measures to take account of changing circumstances and aim to improve existing situations.

2. The employer shall implement the measures referred to in the first subparagraph of paragraph 1 on the basis of the following general principles of prevention:

(a) avoiding risks;

(b) evaluating the risks which cannot be avoided[;]

(c) combating the risks at source;

(d) adapting the work to the individual, especially as regards the design of work places, the choice of work equipment and the choice of working and production methods, with a view, in particular, to alleviating monotonous work and work at a predetermined work-rate and to reducing their effect on health[;]

(e) adapting to technical progress;

(f) replacing the dangerous by the non-dangerous or the less dangerous;

(g) developing a coherent overall prevention policy which covers technology, organization of work, working conditions, social relationships and the influence of factors related to the working environment;

(h) giving collective protective measures priority over individual protective measures;

(i) giving appropriate instructions to the workers.

3. Without prejudice to the other provisions of this Directive, the employer shall, taking into account the nature of the activities of the enterprise and/or establishment:

(a) evaluate the risks to the safety and health of workers, inter alia in the choice of work equipment, the chemical substances or preparations used, and the fitting-out of work places.

Subsequent to this evaluation and as necessary, the preventive measures and the working and production methods implemented by the employer must:

— assure an improvement in the level of protection afforded to workers with regard to safety and health,

— be integrated into all the activities of the undertaking and/or establishment and at all hierarchical levels;

(b) where he entrusts tasks to a worker, take into consideration the worker's capabilities as regards health and safety;

(c) ensure that the planning and introduction of new technologies are the subject of consultation with the workers and/or their representatives, as regards the consequences of the choice of equipment, the working conditions and the working environment for the safety and health of workers;

(d) take appropriate steps to ensure that only workers who have received adequate instructions may have access to areas where there is serious and specific danger.

4. Without prejudice to the other provisions of this Directive, where several undertakings share a work place, the employers shall cooperate in implementing the safety, health and occupational hygiene provisions and, taking into account the nature of the activities, shall coordinate their actions in matters of the protection and prevention of occupational risks, and shall inform one another and their respective workers and/or workers' representatives of these risks.

5. Measures related to safety, hygiene and health at work may in no circumstances involve the workers in financial cost.

Article 7
Protective and preventive services

1. Without prejudice to the obligations referred to in Articles 5 and 6, the employer shall designate one or more workers to carry out activities related to the protection and prevention of occupational risks for the undertaking and/or establishment.

2. Designated workers may not be placed at any disadvantage because of their activities related to the protection and prevention of occupational risks.

   Designated workers shall be allowed adequate time to enable them to fulfil their obligations arising from this Directive.

3. If such protective and preventive measures cannot be organized for lack of competent personnel in the undertaking and/or establishment, the employer shall enlist competent external services or persons.

4. Where the employer enlists such services or persons, he shall inform them of the factors known to affect, or suspected of affecting, the safety and health of the workers and they must have access to the information referred to in Article 10(2).

5. In all cases:
   — the workers designated must have the necessary capabilities and the necessary means,
   — the external services or persons consulted must have the necessary aptitudes and the necessary personal and professional means, and
   — the workers designated and the external services or persons consulted must be sufficient in number

   to deal with the organization of protective and preventive measures, taking into account the size of the undertaking and/or establishment and/or the hazards to which the workers are exposed and their distribution throughout the entire undertaking and/or establishment.

6. The protection from, and prevention of, the health and safety risks which form the subject of this Article shall be the responsibility of one or more workers, of one service or of separate services whether from inside or outside the undertaking and/or establishment.

   The worker(s) and/or agency(ies) must work together whenever necessary.

7. Member States may define, in the light of the nature of the activities and size of the undertakings, the categories of undertakings in which the employer, provided he is competent, may himself take responsibility for the measures referred to in paragraph 1.

8. Member States shall define the necessary capabilities and aptitudes referred to in paragraph 5.

   They may determine the sufficient number referred to in paragraph 5.

Article 8
First aid, fire-fighting and evacuation of workers, serious and imminent danger

1. The employer shall:
   — take the necessary measures for first aid, fire-fighting and evacuation of workers, adapted to the nature of the activities and the size of the undertaking and/or establishment and taking into account other persons present,
   — arrange any necessary contacts with external services, particularly as regards first aid, emergency medical care, rescue work and fire-fighting.

21

2. Pursuant to paragraph 1, the employer shall, inter alia, for first aid, fire-fighting and the evacuation of workers, designate the workers required to implement such measures.

   The number of such workers, their training and the equipment available to them shall be adequate, taking account of the size and/or specific hazards of the undertaking and/or establishment.

3. The employer shall:

   (a) as soon as possible, inform all workers who are, or may be, exposed to serious and imminent danger of the risk involved and of the steps taken or to be taken as regards protection;

   (b) take action and give instructions to enable workers in the event of serious, imminent and unavoidable danger to stop work and/or immediately to leave the work place and proceed to a place of safety;

   (c) save in exceptional cases for reasons duly substantiated, refrain from asking workers to resume work in a working situation where there is still a serious and imminent danger.

4. Workers who, in the event of serious, imminent and unavoidable danger, leave their workstation and/or a dangerous area may not be placed at any disadvantage because of their action and must be protected against any harmful and unjustified consequences, in accordance with national laws and/or practices.

5. The employer shall ensure that all workers are able, in the event of serious and imminent danger to their own safety and/or that of other persons, and where the immediate superior responsible cannot be contacted, to take the appropriate steps in the light of their knowledge and the technical means at their disposal, to avoid the consequences of such danger.

   Their actions shall not place them at any disadvantage, unless they acted carelessly or there was negligence on their part.

Article 9
Various obligations on employers

1. The employer shall:

   (a) be in possession of an assessment of the risks to safety and health at work, including those facing groups of workers exposed to particular risks;

   (b) decide on the protective measures to be taken and, if necessary, the protective equipment to be used;

   (c) keep a list of occupational accidents resulting in a worker being unfit for work for more than three working days;

   (d) draw up, for the responsible authorities and in accordance with national laws and/or practices, reports on occupational accidents suffered by his workers.

2. Member States shall define, in the light of the nature of the activities and size of the undertakings, the obligations to be met by the different categories of undertakings in respect of the drawing-up of the documents provided for in paragraph 1(a) and (b) and when preparing the documents provided for in paragraph 1(c) and (d).

Article 10
Worker information

1. The employer shall take appropriate measures so that workers and/or their representatives in the undertaking and/or establishment receive, in accordance with national

laws and/or practices which may take account, inter alia, of the size of the undertaking and/or establishment, all the necessary information concerning:

(a) the safety and health risks and protective and preventive measures and activities in respect of both the undertaking and/or establishment in general and each type of workstation and/or job;

(b) the measures taken pursuant to Article 8(2).

2. The employer shall take appropriate measures so that employers of workers from any outside undertakings and/or establishments engaged in work in his undertaking and/or establishment receive, in accordance with national laws and/or practices, adequate information concerning the points referred to in paragraph 1(a) and (b) which is to be provided to the workers in question.

3. The employer shall take appropriate measures so that workers with specific functions in protecting the safety and health of workers, or workers' representatives with specific responsibility for the safety and health of workers shall have access, to carry out their functions and in accordance with national laws and/or practices, to:

(a) the risk assessment and protective measures referred to in Article 9(1)(a) and (b);

(b) the list and reports referred to in Article 9(1)(c) and (d);

(c) the information yielded by protective and preventive measures, inspection agencies and bodies responsible for safety and health.

Article 11
Consultation and participation of workers

1. Employers shall consult workers and/or their representatives and allow them to take part in discussions on all questions relating to safety and health at work.

This presupposes:
— the consultation of workers,
— the right of workers and/or their representatives to make proposals,
— balanced participation in accordance with national laws and/or practices.

2. Workers or workers' representatives with specific responsibility for the safety and health of workers shall take part in a balanced way, in accordance with national laws and/or practices, or shall be consulted in advance and in good time by the employer with regard to:

(a) any measure which may substantially affect safety and health;

(b) the designation of workers referred to in Articles 7(1) and 8(2) and the activities referred to in Article 7(1);

(c) the information referred to in Articles 9(1) and 10;

(d) the enlistment, where appropriate, of the competent services or persons outside the undertaking and/or establishment, as referred to in Article 7(3);

(e) the planning and organization of the training referred to in Article 12.

3. Workers' representatives with specific responsibility for the safety and health of workers shall have the right to ask the employer to take appropriate measures and to submit proposals to him to that end to mitigate hazards for workers and/or to remove sources of danger.

4. The workers referred to in paragraph 2 and the workers' representatives referred to in paragraphs 2 and 3 may not be placed at a disadvantage because of their respective activities referred to in paragraphs 2 and 3.

21

5. Employers must allow workers' representatives with specific responsibility for the safety and health of workers adequate time off work, without loss of pay, and provide them with the necessary means to enable such representatives to exercise their rights and functions deriving from this Directive.

6. Workers and/or their representatives are entitled to appeal, in accordance with national law and/or practice, to the authority responsible for safety and health protection at work if they consider that the measures taken and the means employed by the employer are inadequate for the purposes of ensuring safety and health at work.

Workers' representatives must be given the opportunity to submit their observations during inspection visits by the competent authority.

Article 12
Training of workers

1. The employer shall ensure that each worker receives adequate safety and health training, in particular in the form of information and instructions specific to his workstation or job:
   — on recruitment,
   — in the event of a transfer or a change of job,
   — in the event of the introduction of new work equipment or a change in equipment,
   — in the event of the introduction of any new technology.
   The training shall be:
   — adapted to take account of new or changed risks, and
   — repeated periodically if necessary.

2. The employer shall ensure that workers from outside undertakings and/or establishments engaged in work in his undertaking and/or establishment have in fact received appropriate instructions regarding health and safety risks during their activities in his undertaking and/or establishment.

3. Workers' representatives with a specific role in protecting the safety and health of workers shall be entitled to appropriate training.

4. The training referred to in paragraphs 1 and 3 may not be at the workers' expense or at that of the workers' representatives.

The training referred to in paragraph 1 must take place during working hours.

The training referred to in paragraph 3 must take place during working hours or in accordance with national practice either within or outside the undertaking and/or the establishment.

SECTION III WORKERS' OBLIGATIONS

Article 13

1. It shall be the responsibility of each worker to take care as far as possible of his own safety and health and that of other persons affected by his acts or omissions at work in accordance with his training and the instructions given by his employer.

2. To this end, workers must in particular, in accordance with their training and the instructions given by their employer:
   (a) make correct use of machinery, apparatus, tools, dangerous substances, transport equipment and other means of production;

(b) make correct use of the personal protective equipment supplied to them and, after use, return it to its proper place;

(c) refrain from disconnecting, changing or removing arbitrarily safety devices fitted, e.g. to machinery, apparatus, tools, plant and buildings, and use such safety devices correctly;

(d) immediately inform the employer and/or the workers with specific responsibility for the safety and health of workers of any work situation they have reasonable grounds for considering represents a serious and immediate danger to safety and health and of any shortcomings in the protection arrangements;

(e) cooperate, in accordance with national practice, with the employer and/or workers with specific responsibility for the safety and health of workers, for as long as may be necessary to enable any tasks or requirements imposed by the competent authority to protect the safety and health of workers at work to be carried out;

(f) cooperate, in accordance with national practice, with the employer and/or workers with specific responsibility for the safety and health of workers, for as long as may be necessary to enable the employer to ensure that the working environment and working conditions are safe and pose no risk to safety and health within their field of activity.

SECTION IV MISCELLANEOUS PROVISIONS

Article 14
Health surveillance
1. To ensure that workers receive health surveillance appropriate to the health and safety risks they incur at work, measures shall be introduced in accordance with national law and/or practices.
2. The measures referred to in paragraph 1 shall be such that each worker, if he so wishes, may receive health surveillance at regular intervals.
3. Health surveillance may be provided as part of a national health system.

Article 15
Risk groups
Particularly sensitive risk groups must be protected against the dangers which specifically affect them.

Article 16
Individual Directives – Amendments – General scope of this Directive
1. The Council, acting on a proposal from the Commission based on Article [153] of the Treaty, shall adopt individual Directives, inter alia, in the areas listed in the Annex.
2. This Directive and, without prejudice to the procedure referred to in Article 17 concerning technical adjustments, the individual Directives may be amended in accordance with the procedure provided for in Article [153] of the Treaty.
3. The provisions of this Directive shall apply in full to all the areas covered by the individual Directives, without prejudice to more stringent and/or specific provisions contained in these individual Directives.

21

Article 17
Committee procedure
1. The Commission shall be assisted by a committee to make purely technical adjustments to the individual directives provided for in Article 16(1) in order to take account of:
    (a) the adoption of directives in the field of technical harmonisation and standardisation;
    (b) technical progress, changes in international regulations or specifications and new findings.

    Those measures, designed to amend non-essential elements of the individual directives, shall be adopted in accordance with the regulatory procedure with scrutiny referred to in paragraph 2. On imperative grounds of urgency, the Commission may have recourse to the urgency procedure referred to in paragraph 3.
2. Where reference is made to this paragraph, Article 5a(1) to (4) and Article 7 of Decision 1999/468/EC shall apply, having regard to the provisions of Article 8 thereof.
3. Where reference is made to this paragraph, Article 5a(1), (2), (4) and (6) and Article 7 of Decision 1999/468/EC shall apply, having regard to the provisions of Article 8 thereof.

Article 17a
Implementation reports
1. Every five years, the Member States shall submit a single report to the Commission on the practical implementation of this Directive and individual Directives within the meaning of Article 16(1), indicating the points of view of the social partners. The report shall assess the various points related to the practical implementation of the different Directives and, where appropriate and available, provide data disaggregated by gender.
2. The structure of the report, together with a questionnaire specifying its content, shall be defined by the Commission, in cooperation with the Advisory Committee on Safety and Health at Work.

    The report shall include a general part on the provisions of this Directive relating to the common principles and points applicable to all of the Directives referred to in paragraph 1.

    To complement the general part, specific chapters shall deal with implementation of the particular aspects of each Directive, including specific indicators, where available.
3. The Commission shall submit the structure of the report, together with the abovementioned questionnaire specifying its content, to the Member States at least six months before the end of the period covered by the report. The report shall be transmitted to the Commission within 12 months of the end of the five-year period that it covers.
4. Using these reports as a basis, the Commission shall evaluate the implementation of the Directives concerned in terms of their relevance, of research and of new scientific knowledge in the various fields in question. It shall, within 36 months of the end of the five-year period, inform the European Parliament, the Council, the European Economic and Social Committee and the Advisory Committee on Safety and Health

21

at Work of the results of this evaluation and, if necessary, of any initiatives to improve the operation of the regulatory framework.

5. The first report shall cover the period 2007 to 2012.

Article 18
Final provisions

1. Member States shall bring into force the laws, regulations and administrative provisions necessary to comply with this Directive by 31 December 1992. They shall forthwith inform the Commission thereof.

2. Member States shall communicate to the Commission the texts of the provisions of national law which they have already adopted or adopt in the field covered by this Directive.

————————

Article 19

This Directive is addressed to the Member States.

ANNEX

List of areas referred to in Article 16(1)
— Work places
— Work equipment
— Personal protective equipment
— Work with visual display units
— Handling of heavy loads involving risk of back injury
— Temporary or mobile work sites
— Fisheries and agriculture

21

22

Directive 2003/88 Concerning Certain Aspects of the Organisation of Working Time

Contents

THE EUROPEAN PARLIAMENT AND THE COUNCIL OF THE EUROPEAN UNION,
    Having regard to the Treaty [on the Functioning of the European Union], and in particular Article [153](2) thereof,
    Having regard to the proposal from the Commission,
    Having regard to the opinion of the European Economic and Social Committee,
    Having consulted the Committee of the Regions,
    Acting in accordance with the procedure referred to in Article [294] of the Treaty ...
HAVE ADOPTED THIS DIRECTIVE:

Chapter 1 Scope and Definitions

Article 1

Purpose and scope

1. This Directive lays down minimum safety and health requirements for the organisation of working time.
2. This Directive applies to:
   (a) minimum periods of daily rest, weekly rest and annual leave, to breaks and maximum weekly working time; and
   (b) certain aspects of night work, shift work and patterns of work.
3. This Directive shall apply to all sectors of activity, both public and private, within the meaning of Article 2 of Directive 89/391/EEC, without prejudice to Articles 14, 17, 18 and 19 of this Directive.
   This Directive shall not apply to seafarers, as defined in Directive 1999/63/EC without prejudice to Article 2(8) of this Directive.
4. The provisions of Directive 89/391/EEC are fully applicable to the matters referred to in paragraph 2, without prejudice to more stringent and/or specific provisions contained in this Directive.

Article 2
Definitions

For the purposes of this Directive, the following definitions shall apply:

1. "working time" means any period during which the worker is working, at the employer's disposal and carrying out his activity or duties, in accordance with national laws and/or practice;
2. "rest period" means any period which is not working time;
3. "night time" means any period of not less than seven hours, as defined by national law, and which must include, in any case, the period between midnight and 5.00;
4. "night worker" means:
   (a) on the one hand, any worker, who, during night time, works at least three hours of his daily working time as a normal course; and
   (b) on the other hand, any worker who is likely during night time to work a certain proportion of his annual working time, as defined at the choice of the Member State concerned:
      (i) by national legislation, following consultation with the two sides of industry; or
      (ii) by collective agreements or agreements concluded between the two sides of industry at national or regional level;
5. "shift work" means any method of organising work in shifts whereby workers succeed each other at the same work stations according to a certain pattern, including a rotating pattern, and which may be continuous or discontinuous, entailing the need for workers to work at different times over a given period of days or weeks;
6. "shift worker" means any worker whose work schedule is part of shift work;
7. "mobile worker" means any worker employed as a member of travelling or flying personnel by an undertaking which operates transport services for passengers or goods by road, air or inland waterway;
8. "offshore work" means work performed mainly on or from offshore installations (including drilling rigs), directly or indirectly in connection with the exploration, extraction or exploitation of mineral resources, including hydrocarbons, and diving in connection with such activities, whether performed from an offshore installation or a vessel;
9. "adequate rest" means that workers have regular rest periods, the duration of which is expressed in units of time and which are sufficiently long and continuous to ensure that, as a result of fatigue or other irregular working patterns, they do not cause injury to themselves, to fellow workers or to others and that they do not damage their health, either in the short term or in the longer term.

Chapter 2 Minimum Rest Periods – Other Aspects of the Organisation of Working Time

Article 3
Daily rest

Member States shall take the measures necessary to ensure that every worker is entitled to a minimum daily rest period of 11 consecutive hours per 24-hour period.

Article 4
Breaks

Member States shall take the measures necessary to ensure that, where the working day is longer than six hours, every worker is entitled to a rest break, the details of which, including

22

duration and the terms on which it is granted, shall be laid down in collective agreements or agreements between the two sides of industry or, failing that, by national legislation.

Article 5
Weekly rest period

Member States shall take the measures necessary to ensure that, per each seven-day period, every worker is entitled to a minimum uninterrupted rest period of 24 hours plus the 11 hours' daily rest referred to in Article 3.

If objective, technical or work organisation conditions so justify, a minimum rest period of 24 hours may be applied.

Article 6
Maximum weekly working time

Member States shall take the measures necessary to ensure that, in keeping with the need to protect the safety and health of workers:
  (a) the period of weekly working time is limited by means of laws, regulations or administrative provisions or by collective agreements or agreements between the two sides of industry;
  (b) the average working time for each seven-day period, including overtime, does not exceed 48 hours.

Article 7
Annual leave

1. Member States shall take the measures necessary to ensure that every worker is entitled to paid annual leave of at least four weeks in accordance with the conditions for entitlement to, and granting of, such leave laid down by national legislation and/or practice.
2. The minimum period of paid annual leave may not be replaced by an allowance in lieu, except where the employment relationship is terminated.

Chapter 3 Night Work – Shift Work – Patterns of Work

Article 8
Length of night work

Member States shall take the measures necessary to ensure that:
  (a) normal hours of work for night workers do not exceed an average of eight hours in any 24-hour period;
  (b) night workers whose work involves special hazards or heavy physical or mental strain do not work more than eight hours in any period of 24 hours during which they perform night work.

For the purposes of point (b), work involving special hazards or heavy physical or mental strain shall be defined by national legislation and/or practice or by collective agreements or agreements concluded between the two sides of industry, taking account of the specific effects and hazards of night work.

Article 9
Health assessment and transfer of night workers to day work

1. Member States shall take the measures necessary to ensure that:

(a) night workers are entitled to a free health assessment before their assignment and thereafter at regular intervals;

(b) night workers suffering from health problems recognised as being connected with the fact that they perform night work are transferred whenever possible to day work to which they are suited.

2. The free health assessment referred to in paragraph 1(a) must comply with medical confidentiality.

3. The free health assessment referred to in paragraph 1(a) may be conducted within the national health system.

Article 10

Guarantees for night-time working

Member States may make the work of certain categories of night workers subject to certain guarantees, under conditions laid down by national legislation and/or practice, in the case of workers who incur risks to their safety or health linked to night-time working.

Article 11

Notification of regular use of night workers

Member States shall take the measures necessary to ensure that an employer who regularly uses night workers brings this information to the attention of the competent authorities if they so request.

Article 12

Safety and health protection

Member States shall take the measures necessary to ensure that:

(a) night workers and shift workers have safety and health protection appropriate to the nature of their work;

(b) appropriate protection and prevention services or facilities with regard to the safety and health of night workers and shift workers are equivalent to those applicable to other workers and are available at all times.

Article 13

Pattern of work

Member States shall take the measures necessary to ensure that an employer who intends to organise work according to a certain pattern takes account of the general principle of adapting work to the worker, with a view, in particular, to alleviating monotonous work and work at a predetermined work-rate, depending on the type of activity, and of safety and health requirements, especially as regards breaks during working time.

Chapter 4 Miscellaneous Provisions

22

Article 14

More specific [Union] provisions

This Directive shall not apply where other [Union] instruments contain more specific requirements relating to the organisation of working time for certain occupations or occupational activities.

Article 15
More favourable provisions
This Directive shall not affect Member States' right to apply or introduce laws, regulations or administrative provisions more favourable to the protection of the safety and health of workers or to facilitate or permit the application of collective agreements or agreements concluded between the two sides of industry which are more favourable to the protection of the safety and health of workers.

Article 16
Reference periods
Member States may lay down:
   (a) for the application of Article 5 (weekly rest period), a reference period not exceeding 14 days;
   (b) for the application of Article 6 (maximum weekly working time), a reference period not exceeding four months.

   The periods of paid annual leave, granted in accordance with Article 7, and the periods of sick leave shall not be included or shall be neutral in the calculation of the average;
   (c) for the application of Article 8 (length of night work), a reference period defined after consultation of the two sides of industry or by collective agreements or agreements concluded between the two sides of industry at national or regional level.

   If the minimum weekly rest period of 24 hours required by Article 5 falls within that reference period, it shall not be included in the calculation of the average.

Chapter 5 Derogations and Exceptions

Article 17
Derogations
1. With due regard for the general principles of the protection of the safety and health of workers, Member States may derogate from Articles 3 to 6, 8 and 16 when, on account of the specific characteristics of the activity concerned, the duration of the working time is not measured and/or predetermined or can be determined by the workers themselves, and particularly in the case of:
   (a) managing executives or other persons with autonomous decision-taking powers;
   (b) family workers; or
   (c) workers officiating at religious ceremonies in churches and religious communities.
2. Derogations provided for in paragraphs 3, 4 and 5 may be adopted by means of laws, regulations or administrative provisions or by means of collective agreements or agreements between the two sides of industry provided that the workers concerned are afforded equivalent periods of compensatory rest or that, in exceptional cases in which it is not possible, for objective reasons, to grant such equivalent periods of compensatory rest, the workers concerned are afforded appropriate protection.
3. In accordance with paragraph 2 of this Article derogations may be made from Articles 3, 4, 5, 8 and 16:
   (a) in the case of activities where the worker's place of work and his place of residence are distant from one another, including offshore work, or where the worker's different places of work are distant from one another;

(b) in the case of security and surveillance activities requiring a permanent presence in order to protect property and persons, particularly security guards and caretakers or security firms;

(c) in the case of activities involving the need for continuity of service or production, particularly:
   (i) services relating to the reception, treatment and/or care provided by hospitals or similar establishments, including the activities of doctors in training, residential institutions and prisons;
   (ii) dock or airport workers;
   (iii) press, radio, television, cinematographic production, postal and telecommunications services, ambulance, fire and civil protection services;
   (iv) gas, water and electricity production, transmission and distribution, household refuse collection and incineration plants;
   (v) industries in which work cannot be interrupted on technical grounds;
   (vi) research and development activities;
   (vii) agriculture;
   (viii) workers concerned with the carriage of passengers on regular urban transport services;

(d) where there is a foreseeable surge of activity, particularly in:
   (i) agriculture;
   (ii) tourism;
   (iii) postal services;

(e) in the case of persons working in railway transport:
   (i) whose activities are intermittent;
   (ii) who spend their working time on board trains; or
   (iii) whose activities are linked to transport timetables and to ensuring the continuity and regularity of traffic;

(f) in the circumstances described in Article 5(4) of Directive 89/391/EEC;

(g) in cases of accident or imminent risk of accident.

4. In accordance with paragraph 2 of this Article derogations may be made from Articles 3 and 5:

(a) in the case of shift work activities, each time the worker changes shift and cannot take daily and/or weekly rest periods between the end of one shift and the start of the next one;

(b) in the case of activities involving periods of work split up over the day, particularly those of cleaning staff.

5. In accordance with paragraph 2 of this Article, derogations may be made from Article 6 and Article 16(b), in the case of doctors in training, in accordance with the provisions set out in the second to the seventh subparagraphs of this paragraph.

With respect to Article 6 derogations referred to in the first subparagraph shall be permitted for a transitional period of five years from 1 August 2004.

Member States may have up to two more years, if necessary, to take account of difficulties in meeting the working time provisions with respect to their responsibilities for the organisation and delivery of health services and medical care. At least six months before the end of the transitional period, the Member State concerned shall inform the Commission giving its reasons, so that the Commission can give an opinion, after appropriate consultations, within the three months following receipt of such information. If the Member State does not follow the opinion of the Commission, it will justify its decision. The notification and justification of the Member State and the opinion of the Commission shall be published in the Official Journal of the European Union and forwarded to the European Parliament.

Member States may have an additional period of up to one year, if necessary, to take account of special difficulties in meeting the responsibilities referred to in the third subparagraph. They shall follow the procedure set out in that subparagraph.

Member States shall ensure that in no case will the number of weekly working hours exceed an average of 58 during the first three years of the transitional period, an average of 56 for the following two years and an average of 52 for any remaining period.

The employer shall consult the representatives of the employees in good time with a view to reaching an agreement, wherever possible, on the arrangements applying to the transitional period. Within the limits set out in the fifth subparagraph, such an agreement may cover:

(a) the average number of weekly hours of work during the transitional period; and

(b) the measures to be adopted to reduce weekly working hours to an average of 48 by the end of the transitional period.

With respect to Article 16(b) derogations referred to in the first subparagraph shall be permitted provided that the reference period does not exceed 12 months, during the first part of the transitional period specified in the fifth subparagraph, and six months thereafter.

Article 18
Derogations by collective agreements

Derogations may be made from Articles 3, 4, 5, 8 and 16 by means of collective agreements or agreements concluded between the two sides of industry at national or regional level or, in conformity with the rules laid down by them, by means of collective agreements or agreements concluded between the two sides of industry at a lower level.

Member States in which there is no statutory system ensuring the conclusion of collective agreements or agreements concluded between the two sides of industry at national or regional level, on the matters covered by this Directive, or those Member States in which there is a specific legislative framework for this purpose and within the limits thereof, may, in accordance with national legislation and/or practice, allow derogations from Articles 3, 4, 5, 8 and 16 by way of collective agreements or agreements concluded between the two sides of industry at the appropriate collective level.

The derogations provided for in the first and second subparagraphs shall be allowed on condition that equivalent compensating rest periods are granted to the workers concerned or, in exceptional cases where it is not possible for objective reasons to grant such periods, the workers concerned are afforded appropriate protection.

Member States may lay down rules:

(a) for the application of this Article by the two sides of industry; and

(b) for the extension of the provisions of collective agreements or agreements concluded in conformity with this Article to other workers in accordance with national legislation and/or practice.

Article 19
Limitations to derogations from reference periods
The option to derogate from Article 16(b), provided for in Article 17(3) and in Article 18, may not result in the establishment of a reference period exceeding six months.

However, Member States shall have the option, subject to compliance with the general principles relating to the protection of the safety and health of workers, of allowing, for objective or technical reasons or reasons concerning the organisation of work, collective agreements or agreements concluded between the two sides of industry to set reference periods in no event exceeding 12 months.

Before 23 November 2003, the Council shall, on the basis of a Commission proposal accompanied by an appraisal report, re-examine the provisions of this Article and decide what action to take.

Article 20
Mobile workers and offshore work
1. Articles 3, 4, 5 and 8 shall not apply to mobile workers.

   Member States shall, however, take the necessary measures to ensure that such mobile workers are entitled to adequate rest, except in the circumstances laid down in Article 17(3)(f) and (g).
2. Subject to compliance with the general principles relating to the protection of the safety and health of workers, and provided that there is consultation of representatives of the employer and employees concerned and efforts to encourage all relevant forms of social dialogue, including negotiation if the parties so wish, Member States may, for objective or technical reasons or reasons concerning the organisation of work, extend the reference period referred to in Article 16(b) to 12 months in respect of workers who mainly perform offshore work.
3. Not later than 1 August 2005 the Commission shall, after consulting the Member States and management and labour at European level, review the operation of the provisions with regard to offshore workers from a health and safety perspective with a view to presenting, if need be, the appropriate modifications.

Article 21
Workers on board seagoing fishing vessels
1. Articles 3 to 6 and 8 shall not apply to any worker on board a seagoing fishing vessel flying the flag of a Member State.

   Member States shall, however, take the necessary measures to ensure that any worker on board a seagoing fishing vessel flying the flag of a Member State is entitled to adequate rest and to limit the number of hours of work to 48 hours a week on average calculated over a reference period not exceeding 12 months.
2. Within the limits set out in paragraph 1, second subparagraph, and paragraphs 3 and 4 Member States shall take the necessary measures to ensure that, in keeping with the need to protect the safety and health of such workers:
   (a) the working hours are limited to a maximum number of hours which shall not be exceeded in a given period of time; or
   (b) a minimum number of hours of rest are provided within a given period of time.

22

The maximum number of hours of work or minimum number of hours of rest shall be specified by law, regulations, administrative provisions or by collective agreements or agreements between the two sides of the industry.

3. The limits on hours of work or rest shall be either:
   (a) maximum hours of work which shall not exceed:
       (i) 14 hours in any 24-hour period; and
       (ii) 72 hours in any seven-day period;
   or
   (b) minimum hours of rest which shall not be less than:
       (i) 10 hours in any 24-hour period; and
       (ii) 77 hours in any seven-day period.

4. Hours of rest may be divided into no more than two periods, one of which shall be at least six hours in length, and the interval between consecutive periods of rest shall not exceed 14 hours.

5. In accordance with the general principles of the protection of the health and safety of workers, and for objective or technical reasons or reasons concerning the organisation of work, Member States may allow exceptions, including the establishment of reference periods, to the limits laid down in paragraph 1, second subparagraph, and paragraphs 3 and 4. Such exceptions shall, as far as possible, comply with the standards laid down but may take account of more frequent or longer leave periods or the granting of compensatory leave for the workers. These exceptions may be laid down by means of:
   (a) laws, regulations or administrative provisions provided there is consultation, where possible, of the representatives of the employers and workers concerned and efforts are made to encourage all relevant forms of social dialogue; or
   (b) collective agreements or agreements between the two sides of industry.

6. The master of a seagoing fishing vessel shall have the right to require workers on board to perform any hours of work necessary for the immediate safety of the vessel, persons on board or cargo, or for the purpose of giving assistance to other vessels or persons in distress at sea.

7. Members States may provide that workers on board seagoing fishing vessels for which national legislation or practice determines that these vessels are not allowed to operate in a specific period of the calendar year exceeding one month, shall take annual leave in accordance with Article 7 within that period.

Article 22
Miscellaneous provisions

1. A Member State shall have the option not to apply Article 6, while respecting the general principles of the protection of the safety and health of workers, and provided it takes the necessary measures to ensure that:
   (a) no employer requires a worker to work more than 48 hours over a seven-day period, calculated as an average for the reference period referred to in Article 16(b), unless he has first obtained the worker's agreement to perform such work;
   (b) no worker is subjected to any detriment by his employer because he is not willing to give his agreement to perform such work;
   (c) the employer keeps up-to-date records of all workers who carry out such work;

(d) the records are placed at the disposal of the competent authorities, which may, for reasons connected with the safety and/or health of workers, prohibit or restrict the possibility of exceeding the maximum weekly working hours;

(e) the employer provides the competent authorities at their request with information on cases in which agreement has been given by workers to perform work exceeding 48 hours over a period of seven days, calculated as an average for the reference period referred to in Article 16(b).

Before 23 November 2003, the Council shall, on the basis of a Commission proposal accompanied by an appraisal report, re-examine the provisions of this paragraph and decide on what action to take.

2. Member States shall have the option, as regards the application of Article 7, of making use of a transitional period of not more than three years from 23 November 1996, provided that during that transitional period:

(a) every worker receives three weeks' paid annual leave in accordance with the conditions for the entitlement to, and granting of, such leave laid down by national legislation and/or practice; and

(b) the three-week period of paid annual leave may not be replaced by an allowance in lieu, except where the employment relationship is terminated.

3. If Member States avail themselves of the options provided for in this Article, they shall forthwith inform the Commission thereof.

Chapter 6 Final Provisions

Article 23
Level of Protection

Without prejudice to the right of Member States to develop, in the light of changing circumstances, different legislative, regulatory or contractual provisions in the field of working time, as long as the minimum requirements provided for in this Directive are complied with, implementation of this Directive shall not constitute valid grounds for reducing the general level of protection afforded to workers.

Article 24
Reports

1. Member States shall communicate to the Commission the texts of the provisions of national law already adopted or being adopted in the field governed by this Directive.

2. Member States shall report to the Commission every five years on the practical implementation of the provisions of this Directive, indicating the viewpoints of the two sides of industry.

   The Commission shall inform the European Parliament, the Council, the European Economic and Social Committee and the Advisory Committee on Safety, Hygiene and Health Protection at Work thereof.

3. Every five years from 23 November 1996 the Commission shall submit to the European Parliament, the Council and the European Economic and Social Committee a report on the application of this Directive taking into account Articles 22 and 23 and paragraphs 1 and 2 of this Article.

22

Article 25

Review of the operation of the provisions with regard to workers on board seagoing fishing vessels

Not later than 1 August 2009 the Commission shall, after consulting the Member States and management and labour at European level, review the operation of the provisions with regard to workers on board seagoing fishing vessels, and, in particular examine whether these provisions remain appropriate, in particular, as far as health and safety are concerned with a view to proposing suitable amendments, if necessary.

Article 26

Review of the operation of the provisions with regard to workers concerned with the carriage of passengers

Not later than 1 August 2005 the Commission shall, after consulting the Member States and management and labour at European level, review the operation of the provisions with regard to workers concerned with the carriage of passengers on regular urban transport services, with a view to presenting, if need be, the appropriate modifications to ensure a coherent and suitable approach in the sector.

Article 27

Repeal

1. Directive 93/104/EC, as amended by the Directive referred to in Annex I, part A, shall be repealed, without prejudice to the obligations of the Member States in respect of the deadlines for transposition laid down in Annex I, part B.
2. The references made to the said repealed Directive shall be construed as references to this Directive and shall be read in accordance with the correlation table set out in Annex II.

Article 28

Entry into force

This Directive shall enter into force on 2 August 2004.

Article 29

Addressees

This Directive is addressed to the Member States.

(Signatures omitted)

22

23

Directive 1999/70 Concerning the Framework Agreement on Fixed-term Work Concluded by ETUC, UNICE and CEEP

THE COUNCIL OF THE EUROPEAN UNION,

Having regard to the Treaty [on the Functioning of the European Union], and in particular Article [155(2)] thereof,

Having regard to the proposal from the Commission …

HAS ADOPTED THIS DIRECTIVE:

Article 1

The purpose of the Directive is to put into effect the framework agreement on fixed-term contracts concluded on 18 March 1999 between the general cross-industry organisations (ETUC, UNICE and CEEP) annexed hereto.

Article 2

Member States shall bring into force the laws, regulations and administrative provisions necessary to comply with this Directive by 10 July 2001, or shall ensure that, by that date at the latest, management and labour have introduced the necessary measures by agreement, the Member States being required to take any necessary measures to enable them at any time to be in a position to guarantee the results imposed by this Directive. They shall forthwith inform the Commission thereof.

Member States may have a maximum of one more year, if necessary, and following consultation with management and labour, to take account of special difficulties or implementation by a collective agreement. They shall inform the Commission forthwith in such circumstances.

When Member States adopt the provisions referred to in the first paragraph, these shall contain a reference to this Directive or shall be accompanied by such reference at the time of their official publication. The procedure for such reference shall be adopted by the Member States.

Article 3

This Directive shall enter into force on the day of its publication in the Official Journal of the European [Union].

Article 4

This Directive is addressed to the Member States.

(*Signatures omitted*)

ANNEX ETUC–UNICE–CEEP FRAMEWORK AGREEMENT ON FIXED-TERM WORK

Preamble

This framework agreement illustrates the role that the social partners can play in the European employment strategy agreed at the 1997 Luxembourg extraordinary summit and, following the framework agreement on part-time work, represents a further contribution towards achieving a better balance between "flexibility in working time and security for workers".

The parties to this agreement recognise that contracts of an indefinite duration are, and will continue to be, the general form of employment relationship between employers and workers. They also recognise that fixed-term employment contracts respond, in certain circumstances, to the needs of both employers and workers.

This agreement sets out the general principles and minimum requirements relating to fixed-term work, recognising that their detailed application needs to take account of the realities of specific national, sectoral and seasonal situations. It illustrates the willingness of the Social Partners to establish a general framework for ensuring equal treatment for fixed-term workers by protecting them against discrimination and for using fixed-term employment contracts on a basis acceptable to employers and workers.

This agreement applies to fixed-term workers with the exception of those placed by a temporary work agency at the disposition of a user enterprise. It is the intention of the parties to consider the need for a similar agreement relating to temporary agency work.

This agreement relates to the employment conditions of fixed-term workers, recognising that matters relating to statutory social security are for decision by the Member States. In this respect the Social Partners note the Employment Declaration of the Dublin European Council in 1996 which emphasised inter alia, the need to develop more employment-friendly social security systems by "developing social protection systems capable of adapting to new patterns of work and providing appropriate protection to those engaged in such work". The parties to this agreement reiterate the view expressed in the 1997 part-time agreement that Member States should give effect to this Declaration without delay.

In addition, it is also recognised that innovations in occupational social protection systems are necessary in order to adapt them to current conditions, and in particular to provide for the transferability of rights.

The ETUC, UNICE and CEEP request the Commission to submit this framework agreement to the Council for a decision making these requirements binding in the Member States which are party to the Agreement on social policy annexed to the Protocol (No 14) on social policy annexed to the Treaty establishing the European Community.[1]

The parties to this agreement ask the Commission, in its proposal to implement the agreement, to request Member States to adopt the laws, regulations and administrative provisions necessary to comply with the Council Decision within two years from its adoption or ensure that the social partners establish the necessary measures by way of agreement by the end of this period. Member States may, if necessary and following consultation with the social partners, and in order to take account of particular difficulties or

---

[1] The Agreement and the Protocol were, following the Amsterdam Treaty, incorporated into what is now Title X on "Social Policy" of Part Three of the Treaty on the Functioning of the European Union.

implementation by collective agreement have up to a maximum of one additional year to comply with this provision.

The parties to this agreement request that the social partners are consulted prior to any legislative, regulatory or administrative initiative taken by a Member State to conform to the present agreement.

Without prejudice to the role of national courts and the Court of Justice, the parties to this agreement request that any matter relating to the interpretation of this agreement at European level should in the first instance be referred by the Commission to them for an opinion.

General considerations

1. Having regard to the Agreement on social policy annexed to the Protocol (No. 14) on social policy annexed to the Treaty establishing the European Community, and in particular Article[s] 3.4 and 4.2 thereof;

2. Whereas Article 4.2 of the Agreement on social policy provides that agreements concluded at [Union] level may be implemented, at the joint request of the signatory parties, by a Council decision on a proposal from the Commission;

3. Whereas, in its second consultation document on flexibility in working time and security for workers, the Commission announced its intention to propose a legally binding [Union] measure;

4. Whereas in its opinion on the proposal for a Directive on part-time work, the European Parliament invited the Commission to submit immediately proposals for directives on other forms of flexible work, such as fixed-term work and temporary agency work;

5. Whereas in the conclusions of the extraordinary summit on employment adopted in Luxembourg, the European Council invited the social partners to negotiate agreements to "modernise the organisation of work, including flexible working arrangements, with the aim of making undertakings productive and competitive and achieving the required balance between flexibility and security";

6. Whereas employment contracts of an indefinite duration are the general form of employment relationships and contribute to the quality of life of the workers concerned and improve performance;

7. Whereas the use of fixed-term employment contracts based on objective reasons is a way to prevent abuse;

8. Whereas fixed-term employment contracts are a feature of employment in certain sectors, occupations and activities which can suit both employers and workers;

9. Whereas more than half of fixed-term workers in the European Union are women and this agreement can therefore contribute to improving equality of opportunities between women and men;

10. Whereas this agreement refers back to Member States and social partners for the arrangements for the application of its general principles, minimum requirements and provisions, in order to take account of the situation in each Member State and the circumstances of particular sectors and occupations, including the activities of a seasonal nature;

11. Whereas this agreement takes into consideration the need to improve social policy requirements, to enhance the competitiveness of the [Union] economy and to avoid imposing administrative, financial and legal constraints in a way which

23

would hold back the creation and development of small and medium-sized undertakings;

12. Whereas the social partners are best placed to find solutions that correspond to the needs of both employers and workers and shall therefore be given a special role in the implementation and application of this agreement.

THE SIGNATORY PARTIES HAVE AGREED THE FOLLOWING

Purpose (clause 1)

The purpose of this framework agreement is to:

  (a) improve the quality of fixed-term work by ensuring the application of the principle of non-discrimination;

  (b) establish a framework to prevent abuse arising from the use of successive fixed-term employment contracts or relationships.

Scope (clause 2)

1. This agreement applies to fixed-term workers who have an employment contract or employment relationship as defined in law, collective agreements or practice in each Member State.

2. Member States after consultation with the social partners and/or the social partners may provide that this agreement does not apply to:

  (a) initial vocational training relationships and apprenticeship schemes;

  (b) employment contracts and relationships which have been concluded within the framework of a specific public or publicly-supported training, integration and vocational retraining programme.

Definitions (clause 3)

1. For the purpose of this agreement the term "fixed-term worker" means a person having an employment contract or relationship entered into directly between an employer and a worker where the end of the employment contract or relationship is determined by objective conditions such as reaching a specific date, completing a specific task, or the occurrence of a specific event.

2. For the purpose of this agreement, the term "comparable permanent worker" means a worker with an employment contract or relationship of indefinite duration, in the same establishment, engaged in the same or similar work/occupation, due regard being given to qualifications/skills.

  Where there is no comparable permanent worker in the same establishment, the comparison shall be made by reference to the applicable collective agreement, or where there is no applicable collective agreement, in accordance with national law, collective agreements or practice.

Principle of non-discrimination (clause 4)

1. In respect of employment conditions, fixed-term workers shall not be treated in a less favourable manner than comparable permanent workers solely because they have a fixed-term contract or relation unless different treatment is justified on objective grounds.

2. Where appropriate, the principle of pro rata temporis shall apply.

3. The arrangements for the application of this clause shall be defined by the Member States after consultation with the social partners and/or the social partners, having regard to [Union] law and national law, collective agreements and practice.

4. Period-of-service qualifications relating to particular conditions of employment shall be the same for fixed-term workers as for permanent workers except where different length-of-service qualifications are justified on objective grounds.

Measures to prevent abuse (clause 5)

1. To prevent abuse arising from the use of successive fixed-term employment contracts or relationships, Member States, after consultation with social partners in accordance with national law, collective agreements or practice, and/or the social partners, shall, where there are no equivalent legal measures to prevent abuse, introduce in a manner which takes account of the needs of specific sectors and/or categories of workers, one or more of the following measures:

   (a) objective reasons justifying the renewal of such contracts or relationships;

   (b) the maximum total duration of successive fixed-term employment contracts or relationships;

   (c) the number of renewals of such contracts or relationships.

2. Member States after consultation with the social partners and/or the social partners shall, where appropriate, determine under what conditions fixed-term employment contracts or relationships:

   (a) shall be regarded as "successive"[;]

   (b) shall be deemed to be contracts or relationships of indefinite duration.

Information and employment opportunities (clause 6)

1. Employers shall inform fixed-term workers about vacancies which become available in the undertaking or establishment to ensure that they have the same opportunity to secure permanent positions as other workers. Such information may be provided by way of a general announcement at a suitable place in the undertaking or establishment.

2. As far as possible, employers should facilitate access by fixed-term workers to appropriate training opportunities to enhance their skills, career development and occupational mobility.

Information and consultation (clause 7)

1. Fixed-term workers shall be taken into consideration in calculating the threshold above which workers' representative bodies provided for in national and [Union] law may be constituted in the undertaking as required by national provisions.

2. The arrangements for the application of clause 7.1 shall be defined by Member States after consultation with the social partners and/or the social partners in accordance with national law, collective agreements or practice and having regard to clause 4.1.

3. As far as possible, employers should give consideration to the provision of appropriate information to existing workers' representative bodies about fixed-term work in the undertaking.

23

Provisions on implementation (clause 8)

1. Member States and/or the social partners can maintain or introduce more favourable provisions for workers than set out in this agreement.

2. This agreement shall be without prejudice to any more specific [Union] provisions, and in particular [Union] provisions concerning equal treatment or opportunities for men and women.

3. Implementation of this agreement shall not constitute valid grounds for reducing the general level of protection afforded to workers in the field of the agreement.

4. The present agreement does not prejudice the right of the social partners to conclude at the appropriate level, including European level, agreements adapting and/or complementing the provisions of this agreement in a manner which will take note of the specific needs of the social partners concerned.

5. The prevention and settlement of disputes and grievances arising from the application of this agreement shall be dealt with in accordance with national law, collective agreements and practice.

6. The signatory parties shall review the application of this agreement five years after the date of the Council decision if requested by one of the parties to this agreement.

(*Signatures omitted*)

23

24

Directive 2001/23 on the Approximation of the Laws of the Member States Relating to the Safeguarding of Employees' Rights in the Event of Transfers of Undertakings, Businesses or Parts of Undertakings or Businesses

Contents

THE COUNCIL OF THE EUROPEAN UNION,

Having regard to the Treaty [on the Functioning of the European Union], and in particular Article [115] thereof,

Having regard to the proposal from the Commission,

Having regard to the opinion of the European Parliament,

Having regard to the opinion of the Economic and Social Committee …

HAS ADOPTED THIS DIRECTIVE:

Chapter I Scope and Definitions

Article 1

1. (a) This Directive shall apply to any transfer of an undertaking, business, or part of an undertaking or business to another employer as a result of a legal transfer or merger.

   (b) Subject to subparagraph (a) and the following provisions of this Article, there is a transfer within the meaning of this Directive where there is a transfer of an economic entity which retains its identity, meaning an organised grouping of resources which has the objective of pursuing an economic activity, whether or not that activity is central or ancillary.

   (c) This Directive shall apply to public and private undertakings engaged in economic activities whether or not they are operating for gain. An administrative reorganisation of public administrative authorities, or the transfer of administrative functions between public administrative authorities, is not a transfer within the meaning of this Directive.

2. This Directive shall apply where and in so far as the undertaking, business or part of the undertaking or business to be transferred is situated within the territorial scope of the Treaty.

3. This Directive shall apply to a transfer of a seagoing vessel that is part of a transfer of an undertaking, business or part of an undertaking or business within the meaning of paragraphs 1 and 2, provided that the transferee is situated, or the transferred undertaking, business, or part of an undertaking or business remains, within the territorial scope of the Treaty.

   This Directive shall not apply where the object of the transfer consists exclusively of one or more seagoing vessels.

Article 2

1. For the purposes of this Directive:
   (a) "transferor" shall mean any natural or legal person who, by reason of a transfer within the meaning of Article 1(1), ceases to be the employer in respect of the undertaking, business or part of the undertaking or business;
   (b) "transferee" shall mean any natural or legal person who, by reason of a transfer within the meaning of Article 1(1), becomes the employer in respect of the undertaking, business or part of the undertaking or business;
   (c) "representatives of employees" and related expressions shall mean the representatives of the employees provided for by the laws or practices of the Member States;
   (d) "employee" shall mean any person who, in the Member State concerned, is protected as an employee under national employment law.

2. This Directive shall be without prejudice to national law as regards the definition of contract of employment or employment relationship.

   However, Member States shall not exclude from the scope of this Directive contracts of employment or employment relationships solely because:
   (a) of the number of working hours performed or to be performed,
   (b) they are employment relationships governed by a fixed-duration contract of employment within the meaning of Article 1(1) of Council Directive 91/383/ EEC of 25 June 1991 supplementing the measures to encourage improvements in the safety and health at work of workers with a fixed-duration employment relationship or a temporary employment relationship, or
   (c) they are temporary employment relationships within the meaning of Article 1(2) of Directive 91/383/EEC, and the undertaking, business or part of the undertaking or business transferred is, or is part of, the temporary employment business which is the employer.

Chapter II Safeguarding of Employees' Rights

Article 3

1. The transferor's rights and obligations arising from a contract of employment or from an employment relationship existing on the date of a transfer shall, by reason of such transfer, be transferred to the transferee.

   Member States may provide that, after the date of transfer, the transferor and the transferee shall be jointly and severally liable in respect of obligations which arose before the date of transfer from a contract of employment or an employment relationship existing on the date of the transfer.

2. Member States may adopt appropriate measures to ensure that the transferor notifies the transferee of all the rights and obligations which will be transferred to the transferee under this Article, so far as those rights and obligations are or ought to have been known to the transferor at the time of the transfer. A failure by the transferor to notify the transferee of any such right or obligation shall not affect the transfer of that right or obligation and the rights of any employees against the transferee and/or transferor in respect of that right or obligation.

3. Following the transfer, the transferee shall continue to observe the terms and conditions agreed in any collective agreement on the same terms applicable to the transferor under that agreement, until the date of termination or expiry of the collective agreement or the entry into force or application of another collective agreement.

   Member States may limit the period for observing such terms and conditions with the proviso that it shall not be less than one year.

4. (a) Unless Member States provide otherwise, paragraphs 1 and 3 shall not apply in relation to employees' rights to old-age, invalidity or survivors' benefits under supplementary company or intercompany pension schemes outside the statutory social security schemes in Member States.

   (b) Even where they do not provide in accordance with subparagraph (a) that paragraphs 1 and 3 apply in relation to such rights, Member States shall adopt the measures necessary to protect the interests of employees and of persons no longer employed in the transferor's business at the time of the transfer in respect of rights conferring on them immediate or prospective entitlement to old age benefits, including survivors' benefits, under supplementary schemes referred to in sub-paragraph (a).

Article 4

1. The transfer of the undertaking, business or part of the undertaking or business shall not in itself constitute grounds for dismissal by the transferor or the transferee. This provision shall not stand in the way of dismissals that may take place for economic, technical or organisational reasons entailing changes in the workforce.

   Member States may provide that the first subparagraph shall not apply to certain specific categories of employees who are not covered by the laws or practice of the Member States in respect of protection against dismissal.

2. If the contract of employment or the employment relationship is terminated because the transfer involves a substantial change in working conditions to the detriment of the employee, the employer shall be regarded as having been responsible for termination of the contract of employment or of the employment relationship.

Article 5

1. Unless Member States provide otherwise, Articles 3 and 4 shall not apply to any transfer of an undertaking, business or part of an undertaking or business where the transferor is the subject of bankruptcy proceedings or any analogous insolvency proceedings which have been instituted with a view to the liquidation of

24

the assets of the transferor and are under the supervision of a competent public authority (which may be an insolvency practioner authorised by a competent public authority).

2. Where Articles 3 and 4 apply to a transfer during insolvency proceedings which have been opened in relation to a transferor (whether or not those proceedings have been instituted with a view to the liquidation of the assets of the transferor) and provided that such proceedings are under the supervision of a competent public authority (which may be an insolvency practioner determined by national law) a Member State may provide that:

    (a) notwithstanding Article 3(1), the transferor's debts arising from any contracts of employment or employment relationships and payable before the transfer or before the opening of the insolvency proceedings shall not be transferred to the transferee, provided that such proceedings give rise, under the law of that Member State, to protection at least equivalent to that provided for in situations covered by Council Directive 80/987/EEC of 20 October 1980 on the approximation of the laws of the Member States relating to the protection of employees in the event of the insolvency of their employer, and, or alternatively, that,

    (b) the transferee, transferor or person or persons exercising the transferor's functions, on the one hand, and the representatives of the employees on the other hand may agree alterations, in so far as current law or practice permits, to the employees' terms and conditions of employment designed to safeguard employment opportunities by ensuring the survival of the undertaking, business or part of the undertaking or business.

3. A Member State may apply paragraph 20(b) to any transfers where the transferor is in a situation of serious economic crisis, as defined by national law, provided that the situation is declared by a competent public authority and open to judicial supervision, on condition that such provisions already existed in national law on 17 July 1998.

    The Commission shall present a report on the effects of this provision before 17 July 2003 and shall submit any appropriate proposals to the Council.

4. Member States shall take appropriate measures with a view to preventing misuse of insolvency proceedings in such a way as to deprive employees of the rights provided for in this Directive.

Article 6

1. If the undertaking, business or part of an undertaking or business preserves its autonomy, the status and function of the representatives or of the representation of the employees affected by the transfer shall be preserved on the same terms and subject to the same conditions as existed before the date of the transfer by virtue of law, regulation, administrative provision or agreement, provided that the conditions necessary for the constitution of the employee's representation are fulfilled.

    The first subparagraph shall not [a]pply if, under the laws, regulations, administrative provisions or practice in the Member States, or by agreement with the representatives of the employees, the conditions necessary for the reappointment of the representatives of the employees or for the reconstitution of the representation of the employees are fulfilled.

Where the transferor is the subject of bankruptcy proceedings or any analogous insolvency proceedings which have been instituted with a view to the liquidation of the assets of the transferor and are under the supervision of a competent public authority (which may be an insolvency practitioner authorised by a competent public authority), Member States may take the necessary measures to ensure that the transferred employees are properly represented until the new election or designation of representatives of the employees.

If the undertaking, business or part of an undertaking or business does not preserve its autonomy, the Member States shall take the necessary measures to ensure that the employees transferred who were represented before the transfer continue to be properly represented during the period necessary for the reconstitution or reappointment of the representation of employees in accordance with national law or practice.

2. If the term of office of the representatives of the employees affected by the transfer expires as a result of the transfer, the representatives shall continue to enjoy the protection provided by the laws, regulations, administrative provisions or practice of the Member States.

Chapter III Information and Consultation

Article 7

1. The transferor and transferee shall be required to inform the representatives of their respective employees affected by the transfer of the following:
   — the date or proposed date of the transfer,
   — the reasons for the transfer,
   — the legal, economic and social implications of the transfer for the employees,
   — any measures envisaged in relation to the employees.

   The transferor must give such information to the representatives of his employees in good time, before the transfer is carried out.

   The transferee must give such information to the representatives of his employees in good time, and in any event before his employees are directly affected by the transfer as regards their conditions of work and employment.

2. Where the transferor or the transferee envisages measures in relation to his employees, he shall consult the representatives of his employees in good time on such measures with a view to reaching an agreement.

3. Member States whose laws, regulations or administrative provisions provide that representatives of the employees may have recourse to an arbitration board to obtain a decision on the measures to be taken in relation to employees may limit the obligations laid down in paragraphs 1 and 2 to cases where the transfer carried out gives rise to a change in the business likely to entail serious disadvantages for a considerable number of the employees.

   The information and consultations shall cover at least the measures envisaged in relation to the employees.

   The information must be provided and consultations take place in good time before the change in the business as referred to in the first subparagraph is effected.

4. The obligations laid down in this Article shall apply irrespective of whether the decision resulting in the transfer is taken by the employer or an undertaking controlling the employer.

24

In considering alleged breaches of the information and consultation requirements laid down by this Directive, the argument that such a breach occurred because the information was not provided by an undertaking controlling the employer shall not be accepted as an excuse.

5. Member States may limit the obligations laid down in paragraphs 1, 2 and 3 to undertakings or businesses which, in terms of the number of employees, meet the conditions for the election or nomination of a collegiate body representing the employees.

6. Member States shall provide that, where there are no representatives of the employees in an undertaking or business through no fault of their own, the employees concerned must be informed in advance of:
— the date or proposed date of the transfer,
— the reason for the transfer,
— the legal, economic and social implications of the transfer for the employees,
— any measures envisaged in relation to the employees.

Chapter IV Final Provisions

Article 8
This Directive shall not affect the right of Member States to apply or introduce laws, regulations or administrative provisions which are more favourable to employees or to promote or permit collective agreements or agreements between social partners more favourable to employees.

Article 9
Member States shall introduce into their national legal systems such measures as are necessary to enable all employees and representatives of employees who consider themselves wronged by failure to comply with the obligations arising from this Directive to pursue their claims by judicial process after possible recourse to other competent authorities.

Article 10
The Commission shall submit to the Council an analysis of the effect of the provisions of this Directive before 17 July 2006. It shall propose any amendment which may seem necessary.

Article 11
Member States shall communicate to the Commission the texts of the laws, regulations and administrative provisions which they adopt in the field covered by this Directive.

Article 12
Directive 77/187/EEC, as amended by the Directive referred to in Annex I, Part A, is repealed, without prejudice to the obligations of the Member States concerning the time limits for implementation set out in Annex I, Part B.

References to the repealed Directive shall be construed as references to this Directive and shall be read in accordance with the correlation table in Annex II.

Article 13

This Directive shall enter into force on the 20th day following its publication in the Official Journal of the European [Union].

Article 14

This Directive is addressed to the Member States.

(*Signatures omitted*)

24

25

Directive 2006/54 on the Implementation of the Principle of Equal Opportunities and Equal Treatment of Men and Women in Matters of Employment and Occupation

Contents

THE EUROPEAN PARLIAMENT AND THE COUNCIL OF THE EUROPEAN UNION,

Having regard to the Treaty [on the Functioning of the European Union], and in particular Article [157](3) thereof,

Having regard to the proposal from the Commission,

Having regard to the opinion of the European Economic and Social Committee, Acting in accordance with the procedure laid down in Article [294] of the Treaty …

HAVE ADOPTED THIS DIRECTIVE:

TITLE I GENERAL PROVISIONS

Article 1

Purpose

The purpose of this Directive is to ensure the implementation of the principle of equal opportunities and equal treatment of men and women in matters of employment and occupation.

To that end, it contains provisions to implement the principle of equal treatment in relation to:

(a) access to employment, including promotion, and to vocational training;

(b) working conditions, including pay;

(c) occupational social security schemes. It also contains provisions to ensure that such implementation is made more effective by the establishment of appropriate procedures.

Article 2

Definitions

1. For the purposes of this Directive, the following definitions shall apply:

   (a) 'direct discrimination': where one person is treated less favourably on grounds of sex than another is, has been or would be treated in a comparable situation;

   (b) 'indirect discrimination': where an apparently neutral provision, criterion or practice would put persons of one sex at a particular disadvantage compared with persons of the other sex, unless that provision, criterion or practice is objectively justified by a legitimate aim, and the means of achieving that aim are appropriate and necessary;

   (c) 'harassment': where unwanted conduct related to the sex of a person occurs with the purpose or effect of violating the dignity of a person, and of creating an intimidating, hostile, degrading, humiliating or offensive environment;

   (d) 'sexual harassment': where any form of unwanted verbal, non-verbal or physical conduct of a sexual nature occurs, with the purpose or effect of violating the dignity of a person, in particular when creating an intimidating, hostile, degrading, humiliating or offensive environment;

   (e) 'pay': the ordinary basic or minimum wage or salary and any other consideration, whether in cash or in kind, which the worker receives directly or indirectly, in respect of his/her employment from his/her employer;

   (f) 'occupational social security schemes': schemes not governed by Council Directive 79/7/EEC of 19 December 1978 on the progressive implementation of the principle of equal treatment for men and women in matters of social security whose purpose is to provide workers, whether employees or self-employed, in an undertaking or group of undertakings, area of economic activity, occupational sector or group of sectors with benefits intended to supplement the benefits provided by statutory social security schemes or to replace them, whether membership of such schemes is compulsory or optional.

2. For the purposes of this Directive, discrimination includes:

   (a) harassment and sexual harassment, as well as any less favourable treatment based on a person's rejection of or submission to such conduct;

   (b) instruction to discriminate against persons on grounds of sex;

   (c) any less favourable treatment of a woman related to pregnancy or maternity leave within the meaning of Directive 92/85/EEC.

Article 3

Positive action

Member States may maintain or adopt measures within the meaning of Article [157](4) of the Treaty with a view to ensuring full equality in practice between men and women in working life.

25

TITLE II SPECIFIC PROVISIONS

Chapter 1 Equal Pay

Article 4
Prohibition of discrimination

For the same work or for work to which equal value is attributed, direct and indirect discrimination on grounds of sex with regard to all aspects and conditions of remuneration shall be eliminated.

In particular, where a job classification system is used for determining pay, it shall be based on the same criteria for both men and women and so drawn up as to exclude any discrimination on grounds of sex.

Chapter 2 Equal Treatment in Occupational Social Security Schemes

Article 5
Prohibition of discrimination

Without prejudice to Article 4, there shall be no direct or indirect discrimination on grounds of sex in occupational social security schemes, in particular as regards:
  (a) the scope of such schemes and the conditions of access to them;
  (b) the obligation to contribute and the calculation of contributions;
  (c) the calculation of benefits, including supplementary benefits due in respect of a spouse or dependants, and the conditions governing the duration and retention of entitlement to benefits.

Article 6
Personal scope

This Chapter shall apply to members of the working population, including self-employed persons, persons whose activity is interrupted by illness, maternity, accident or involuntary unemployment and persons seeking employment and to retired and disabled workers, and to those claiming under them, in accordance with national law and/or practice.

Article 7
Material scope

1. This Chapter applies to:
  (a) occupational social security schemes which provide protection against the following risks:
    (i) sickness,
    (ii) invalidity,
    (iii) old age, including early retirement,
    (iv) industrial accidents and occupational diseases,
    (v) unemployment;
  (b) occupational social security schemes which provide for other social benefits, in cash or in kind, and in particular survivors' benefits and family allowances, if such benefits constitute a consideration paid by the employer to the worker by reason of the latter's employment.

25

2. This Chapter also applies to pension schemes for a particular category of worker such as that of public servants if the benefits payable under the scheme are paid by reason of the employment relationship with the public employer. The fact that such a scheme forms part of a general statutory scheme shall be without prejudice in that respect.

Article 8
Exclusions from the material scope
1. This Chapter does not apply to:
   - (a) individual contracts for self-employed persons;
   - (b) single-member schemes for self-employed persons;
   - (c) insurance contracts to which the employer is not a party, in the case of workers;
   - (d) optional provisions of occupational social security schemes offered to participants individually to guarantee them:
     - (i) either additional benefits,
     - (ii) or a choice of date on which the normal benefits for self-employed persons will start, or a choice between several benefits;
   - (e) occupational social security schemes in so far as benefits are financed by contributions paid by workers on a voluntary basis.
2. This Chapter does not preclude an employer granting to persons who have already reached the retirement age for the purposes of granting a pension by virtue of an occupational social security scheme, but who have not yet reached the retirement age for the purposes of granting a statutory retirement pension, a pension supplement, the aim of which is to make equal or more nearly equal the overall amount of benefit paid to these persons in relation to the amount paid to persons of the other sex in the same situation who have already reached the statutory retirement age, until the persons benefiting from the supplement reach the statutory retirement age.

Article 9
Examples of discrimination
1. Provisions contrary to the principle of equal treatment shall include those based on sex, either directly or indirectly, for:
   - (a) determining the persons who may participate in an occupational social security scheme;
   - (b) fixing the compulsory or optional nature of participation in an occupational social security scheme;
   - (c) laying down different rules as regards the age of entry into the scheme or the minimum period of employment or membership of the scheme required to obtain the benefits thereof;
   - (d) laying down different rules, except as provided for in points (h) and (j), for the reimbursement of contributions when a worker leaves a scheme without having fulfilled the conditions guaranteeing a deferred right to long-term benefits;
   - (e) setting different conditions for the granting of benefits or restricting such benefits to workers of one or other of the sexes;
   - (f) fixing different retirement ages;

25

(g) suspending the retention or acquisition of rights during periods of maternity leave or leave for family reasons which are granted by law or agreement and are paid by the employer;

(h) setting different levels of benefit, except in so far as may be necessary to take account of actuarial calculation factors which differ according to sex in the case of defined-contribution schemes; in the case of funded defined-benefit schemes, certain elements may be unequal where the inequality of the amounts results from the effects of the use of actuarial factors differing according to sex at the time when the scheme's funding is implemented;

(i) setting different levels for workers' contributions;

(j) setting different levels for employers' contributions, except:

   (i) in the case of defined-contribution schemes if the aim is to equalise the amount of the final benefits or to make them more nearly equal for both sexes,

   (ii) in the case of funded defined-benefit schemes where the employer's contributions are intended to ensure the adequacy of the funds necessary to cover the cost of the benefits defined;

(k) laying down different standards or standards applicable only to workers of a specified sex, except as provided for in points (h) and (j), as regards the guarantee or retention of entitlement to deferred benefits when a worker leaves a scheme.

2. Where the granting of benefits within the scope of this Chapter is left to the discretion of the scheme's management bodies, the latter shall comply with the principle of equal treatment.

Article 10
Implementation as regards self-employed persons

1. Member States shall take the necessary steps to ensure that the provisions of occupational social security schemes for self-employed persons contrary to the principle of equal treatment are revised with effect from 1 January 1993 at the latest or for Member States whose accession took place after that date, at the date that Directive 86/378/EEC became applicable in their territory.

2. This Chapter shall not preclude rights and obligations relating to a period of membership of an occupational social security scheme for self-employed persons prior to revision of that scheme from remaining subject to the provisions of the scheme in force during that period.

Article 11
Possibility of deferral as regards self-employed persons

As regards occupational social security schemes for self-employed persons, Member States may defer compulsory application of the principle of equal treatment with regard to:

   (a) determination of pensionable age for the granting of old-age or retirement pensions, and the possible implications for other benefits:

      (i) either until the date on which such equality is achieved in statutory schemes,

      (ii) or, at the latest, until such equality is prescribed by a directive;

   (b) survivors' pensions until [Union] law establishes the principle of equal treatment in statutory social security schemes in that regard;

(c) the application of Article 9(1)(i) in relation to the use of actuarial calculation factors, until 1 January 1999 or for Member States whose accession took place after that date until the date that Directive 86/378/EEC became applicable in their territory.

Article 12
Retroactive effect

1. Any measure implementing this Chapter, as regards workers, shall cover all benefits under occupational social security schemes derived from periods of employment subsequent to 17 May 1990 and shall apply retroactively to that date, without prejudice to workers or those claiming under them who have, before that date, initiated legal proceedings or raised an equivalent claim under national law. In that event, the implementation measures shall apply retroactively to 8 April 1976 and shall cover all the benefits derived from periods of employment after that date. For Member States which acceded to the [Union] after 8 April 1976, and before 17 May 1990, that date shall be replaced by the date on which Article [157] of the Treaty became applicable in their territory.

2. The second sentence of paragraph 1 shall not prevent national rules relating to time limits for bringing actions under national law from being relied on against workers or those claiming under them who initiated legal proceedings or raised an equivalent claim under national law before 17 May 1990, provided that they are not less favourable for that type of action than for similar actions of a domestic nature and that they do not render the exercise of rights conferred by [Union] law impossible in practice.

3. For Member States whose accession took place after 17 May 1990 and which were on 1 January 1994 Contracting Parties to the Agreement on the European Economic Area, the date of 17 May 1990 in the first sentence of paragraph 1 shall be replaced by 1 January 1994.

4. For other Member States whose accession took place after 17 May 1990, the date of 17 May 1990 in paragraphs 1 and 2 shall be replaced by the date on which Article [157] of the Treaty became applicable in their territory.

Article 13
Flexible pensionable age

Where men and women may claim a flexible pensionable age under the same conditions, this shall not be deemed to be incompatible with this Chapter.

Chapter 3 Equal Treatment as Regards Access to Employment, Vocational Training and Promotion and Working Conditions

Article 14
Prohibition of discrimination

1. There shall be no direct or indirect discrimination on grounds of sex in the public or private sectors, including public bodies, in relation to:
   (a) conditions for access to employment, to self-employment or to occupation, including selection criteria and recruitment conditions, whatever the branch of activity and at all levels of the professional hierarchy, including promotion;

25

(b) access to all types and to all levels of vocational guidance, vocational training, advanced vocational training and retraining, including practical work experience;

(c) employment and working conditions, including dismissals, as well as pay as provided for in Article [157] of the Treaty;

(d) membership of, and involvement in, an organisation of workers or employers, or any organisation whose members carry on a particular profession, including the benefits provided for by such organisations.

2. Member States may provide, as regards access to employment including the training leading thereto, that a difference of treatment which is based on a characteristic related to sex shall not constitute discrimination where, by reason of the nature of the particular occupational activities concerned or of the context in which they are carried out, such a characteristic constitutes a genuine and determining occupational requirement, provided that its objective is legitimate and the requirement is proportionate.

Article 15

Return from maternity leave

A woman on maternity leave shall be entitled, after the end of her period of maternity leave, to return to her job or to an equivalent post on terms and conditions which are no less favourable to her and to benefit from any improvement in working conditions to which she would have been entitled during her absence.

Article 16

Paternity and adoption leave

This Directive is without prejudice to the right of Member States to recognise distinct rights to paternity and/or adoption leave. Those Member States which recognise such rights shall take the necessary measures to protect working men and women against dismissal due to exercising those rights and ensure that, at the end of such leave, they are entitled to return to their jobs or to equivalent posts on terms and conditions which are no less favourable to them, and to benefit from any improvement in working conditions to which they would have been entitled during their absence.

TITLE III HORIZONTAL PROVISIONS

Chapter 1 Remedies and Enforcement

SECTION 1 REMEDIES

Article 17

Defence of rights

1. Member States shall ensure that, after possible recourse to other competent authorities including where they deem it appropriate conciliation procedures, judicial procedures for the enforcement of obligations under this Directive are available to all persons who consider themselves wronged by failure to apply the principle of equal treatment to them, even after the relationship in which the discrimination is alleged to have occurred has ended.

2. Member States shall ensure that associations, organisations or other legal entities which have, in accordance with the criteria laid down by their national law, a legitimate interest

in ensuring that the provisions of this Directive are complied with, may engage, either on behalf or in support of the complainant, with his/her approval, in any judicial and/or administrative procedure provided for the enforcement of obligations under this Directive.

3. Paragraphs 1 and 2 are without prejudice to national rules relating to time limits for bringing actions as regards the principle of equal treatment.

Article 18

Compensation or reparation

Member States shall introduce into their national legal systems such measures as are necessary to ensure real and effective compensation or reparation as the Member States so determine for the loss and damage sustained by a person injured as a result of discrimination on grounds of sex, in a way which is dissuasive and proportionate to the damage suffered. Such compensation or reparation may not be restricted by the fixing of a prior upper limit, except in cases where the employer can prove that the only damage suffered by an applicant as a result of discrimination within the meaning of this Directive is the refusal to take his/her job application into consideration.

SECTION 2 BURDEN OF PROOF

Article 19

Burden of proof

1. Member States shall take such measures as are necessary, in accordance with their national judicial systems, to ensure that, when persons who consider themselves wronged because the principle of equal treatment has not been applied to them establish, before a court or other competent authority, facts from which it may be presumed that there has been direct or indirect discrimination, it shall be for the respondent to prove that there has been no breach of the principle of equal treatment.

2. Paragraph 1 shall not prevent Member States from introducing rules of evidence which are more favourable to plaintiffs.

3. Member States need not apply paragraph 1 to proceedings in which it is for the court or competent body to investigate the facts of the case.

4. Paragraphs 1, 2 and 3 shall also apply to:

    (a) the situations covered by Article [157] of the Treaty and, insofar as discrimination based on sex is concerned, by Directives 92/85/EEC and 96/34/EC;

    (b) any civil or administrative procedure concerning the public or private sector which provides for means of redress under national law pursuant to the measures referred to in (a) with the exception of out-of-court procedures of a voluntary nature or provided for in national law.

5. This Article shall not apply to criminal procedures, unless otherwise provided by the Member States.

Chapter 2 Promotion of Equal Treatment – Dialogue

25

Article 20

Equality bodies

1. Member States shall designate and make the necessary arrangements for a body or bodies for the promotion, analysis, monitoring and support of equal treatment of all

persons without discrimination on grounds of sex. These bodies may form part of agencies with responsibility at national level for the defence of human rights or the safeguard of individuals' rights.

2. Member States shall ensure that the competences of these bodies include:
   (a) without prejudice to the right of victims and of associations, organisations or other legal entities referred to in Article 17(2), providing independent assistance to victims of discrimination in pursuing their complaints about discrimination;
   (b) conducting independent surveys concerning discrimination;
   (c) publishing independent reports and making recommendations on any issue relating to such discrimination;
   (d) at the appropriate level exchanging available information with corresponding European bodies such as any future European Institute for Gender Equality.

Article 21
Social dialogue

1. Member States shall, in accordance with national traditions and practice, take adequate measures to promote social dialogue between the social partners with a view to fostering equal treatment, including, for example, through the monitoring of practices in the workplace, in access to employment, vocational training and promotion, as well as through the monitoring of collective agreements, codes of conduct, research or exchange of experience and good practice.

2. Where consistent with national traditions and practice, Member States shall encourage the social partners, without prejudice to their autonomy, to promote equality between men and women, and flexible working arrangements, with the aim of facilitating the reconciliation of work and private life, and to conclude, at the appropriate level, agreements laying down anti-discrimination rules in the fields referred to in Article 1 which fall within the scope of collective bargaining. These agreements shall respect the provisions of this Directive and the relevant national implementing measures.

3. Member States shall, in accordance with national law, collective agreements or practice, encourage employers to promote equal treatment for men and women in a planned and systematic way in the workplace, in access to employment, vocational training and promotion.

4. To this end, employers shall be encouraged to provide at appropriate regular intervals employees and/or their representatives with appropriate information on equal treatment for men and women in the undertaking.

   Such information may include an overview of the proportions of men and women at different levels of the organisation; their pay and pay differentials; and possible measures to improve the situation in cooperation with employees' representatives.

Article 22
Dialogue with non-governmental organisations

Member States shall encourage dialogue with appropriate non-governmental organisations which have, in accordance with their national law and practice, a legitimate interest in contributing to the fight against discrimination on grounds of sex with a view to promoting the principle of equal treatment.

Chapter 3 General Horizontal Provisions

Article 23
Compliance

Member States shall take all necessary measures to ensure that:

(a) any laws, regulations and administrative provisions contrary to the principle of equal treatment are abolished;

(b) provisions contrary to the principle of equal treatment in individual or collective contracts or agreements, internal rules of undertakings or rules governing the independent occupations and professions and workers' and employers' organisations or any other arrangements shall be, or may be, declared null and void or are amended;

(c) occupational social security schemes containing such provisions may not be approved or extended by administrative measures.

Article 24
Victimisation

Member States shall introduce into their national legal systems such measures as are necessary to protect employees, including those who are employees' representatives provided for by national laws and/or practices, against dismissal or other adverse treatment by the employer as a reaction to a complaint within the undertaking or to any legal proceedings aimed at enforcing compliance with the principle of equal treatment.

Article 25
Penalties

Member States shall lay down the rules on penalties applicable to infringements of the national provisions adopted pursuant to this Directive, and shall take all measures necessary to ensure that they are applied. The penalties, which may comprise the payment of compensation to the victim, must be effective, proportionate and dissuasive. The Member States shall notify those provisions to the Commission by 5 October 2005 at the latest and shall notify it without delay of any subsequent amendment affecting them.

Article 26
Prevention of discrimination

Member States shall encourage, in accordance with national law, collective agreements or practice, employers and those responsible for access to vocational training to take effective measures to prevent all forms of discrimination on grounds of sex, in particular harassment and sexual harassment in the workplace, in access to employment, vocational training and promotion.

Article 27
Minimum requirements

1. Member States may introduce or maintain provisions which are more favourable to the protection of the principle of equal treatment than those laid down in this Directive.

2. Implementation of this Directive shall under no circumstances be sufficient grounds for a reduction in the level of protection of workers in the areas to which it applies,

25

without prejudice to the Member States' right to respond to changes in the situation by introducing laws, regulations and administrative provisions which differ from those in force on the notification of this Directive, provided that the provisions of this Directive are complied with.

Article 28
Relationship to [Union] and national provisions
1. This Directive shall be without prejudice to provisions concerning the protection of women, particularly as regards pregnancy and maternity.
2. This Directive shall be without prejudice to the provisions of Directive 96/34/EC and Directive 92/85/EEC.

Article 29
Gender mainstreaming
Member States shall actively take into account the objective of equality between men and women when formulating and implementing laws, regulations, administrative provisions, policies and activities in the areas referred to in this Directive.

Article 30
Dissemination of information
Member States shall ensure that measures taken pursuant to this Directive, together with the provisions already in force, are brought to the attention of all the persons concerned by all suitable means and, where appropriate, at the workplace.

TITLE IV FINAL PROVISIONS

Article 31
Reports
1. By 15 February 2011, the Member States shall communicate to the Commission all the information necessary for the Commission to draw up a report to the European Parliament and the Council on the application of this Directive.
2. Without prejudice to paragraph 1, Member States shall communicate to the Commission, every four years, the texts of any measures adopted pursuant to Article [157](4) of the Treaty, as well as reports on these measures and their implementation. On the basis of that information, the Commission will adopt and publish every four years a report establishing a comparative assessment of any measures in the light of Declaration No 28 annexed to the Final Act of the Treaty of Amsterdam.
3. Member States shall assess the occupational activities referred to in Article 14(2), in order to decide, in the light of social developments, whether there is justification for maintaining the exclusions concerned. They shall notify the Commission of the results of this assessment periodically, but at least every 8 years.

Article 32
Review
By 15 February 2011 at the latest, the Commission shall review the operation of this Directive and if appropriate, propose any amendments it deems necessary.

25

Article 33

Implementation

Member States shall bring into force the laws, regulations and administrative provisions necessary to comply with this Directive by 15 August 2008 at the latest or shall ensure, by that date, that management and labour introduce the requisite provisions by way of agreement. Member States may, if necessary to take account of particular difficulties, have up to one additional year to comply with this Directive. Member States shall take all necessary steps to be able to guarantee the results imposed by this Directive. They shall forthwith communicate to the Commission the texts of those measures.

When Member States adopt these measures, they shall contain a reference to this Directive or be accompanied by such reference on the occasion of their official publication. They shall also include a statement that references in existing laws, regulations and administrative provisions to the Directives repealed by this Directive shall be construed as references to this Directive. Member States shall determine how such reference is to be made and how that statement is to be formulated.

The obligation to transpose this Directive into national law shall be confined to those provisions which represent a substantive change as compared with the earlier Directives. The obligation to transpose the provisions which are substantially unchanged arises under the earlier Directives.

Member States shall communicate to the Commission the text of the main provisions of national law which they adopt in the field covered by this Directive.

Article 34

Repeal

1. With effect from 15 August 2009 Directives 75/117/EEC, 76/207/EEC, 86/378/EEC and 97/80/EC shall be repealed without prejudice to the obligations of the Member States relating to the time-limits for transposition into national law and application of the Directives set out in Annex I, Part B.
2. References made to the repealed Directives shall be construed as being made to this Directive and should be read in accordance with the correlation table in Annex II.

Article 35

Entry into force

This Directive shall enter into force on the 20th day following its publication in the *Official Journal of the European Union.*

Article 36

Addressees

This Directive is addressed to the Member States.

(*Signatures omitted*)

25

PART II
Union Secondary Law: Legislation and Other Acts

26

Directive 2011/83 on Consumer Rights

Contents

THE EUROPEAN PARLIAMENT AND THE COUNCIL OF THE EUROPEAN UNION,
    Having regard to the Treaty on the Functioning of the European Union, and in particular Article 114 thereof,
    Having regard to the proposal from the European Commission,
    Having regard to the opinion of the European Economic and Social Committee,
    Having regard to the opinion of the Committee of the Regions,
    Acting in accordance with the ordinary legislative procedure …
    HAVE ADOPTED THIS DIRECTIVE:

Chapter I Subject Matter, Definitions and Scope

Article 1
Subject matter
The purpose of this Directive is, through the achievement of a high level of consumer protection, to contribute to the proper functioning of the internal market by approximating certain aspects of the laws, regulations and administrative provisions of the Member States concerning contracts concluded between consumers and traders.

Article 2
Definitions
For the purpose of this Directive, the following definitions shall apply:
(1) 'consumer' means any natural person who, in contracts covered by this Directive, is acting for purposes which are outside his trade, business, craft or profession;

(2) 'trader' means any natural person or any legal person, irrespective of whether privately or publicly owned, who is acting, including through any other person acting in his name or on his behalf, for purposes relating to his trade, business, craft or profession in relation to contracts covered by this Directive;

(3) 'goods' means any tangible movable items, with the exception of items sold by way of execution or otherwise by authority of law; water, gas and electricity shall be considered as goods within the meaning of this Directive where they are put up for sale in a limited volume or a set quantity;

(4) 'goods made to the consumer's specifications' means non-prefabricated goods made on the basis of an individual choice of or decision by the consumer;

(5) 'sales contract' means any contract under which the trader transfers or undertakes to transfer the ownership of goods to the consumer and the consumer pays or undertakes to pay the price thereof, including any contract having as its object both goods and services;

(6) 'service contract' means any contract other than a sales contract under which the trader supplies or undertakes to supply a service to the consumer and the consumer pays or undertakes to pay the price thereof;

(7) 'distance contract' means any contract concluded between the trader and the consumer under an organised distance sales or service-provision scheme without the simultaneous physical presence of the trader and the consumer, with the exclusive use of one or more means of distance communication up to and including the time at which the contract is concluded;

(8) 'off-premises contract' means any contract between the trader and the consumer:
   (a) concluded in the simultaneous physical presence of the trader and the consumer, in a place which is not the business premises of the trader;
   (b) for which an offer was made by the consumer in the same circumstances as referred to in point (a);
   (c) concluded on the business premises of the trader or through any means of distance communication immediately after the consumer was personally and individually addressed in a place which is not the business premises of the trader in the simultaneous physical presence of the trader and the consumer; or
   (d) concluded during an excursion organised by the trader with the aim or effect of promoting and selling goods or services to the consumer;

(9) 'business premises' means:
   (a) any immovable retail premises where the trader carries out his activity on a permanent basis; or
   (b) any movable retail premises where the trader carries out his activity on a usual basis;

(10) 'durable medium' means any instrument which enables the consumer or the trader to store information addressed personally to him in a way accessible for future reference for a period of time adequate for the purposes of the information and which allows the unchanged reproduction of the information stored;

(11) 'digital content' means data which are produced and supplied in digital form;

(12) 'financial service' means any service of a banking, credit, insurance, personal pension, investment or payment nature;

26

(13) 'public auction' means a method of sale where goods or services are offered by the trader to consumers, who attend or are given the possibility to attend the auction in person, through a transparent, competitive bidding procedure run by an auctioneer and where the successful bidder is bound to purchase the goods or services;

(14) 'commercial guarantee' means any undertaking by the trader or a producer (the guarantor) to the consumer, in addition to his legal obligation relating to the guarantee of conformity, to reimburse the price paid or to replace, repair or service goods in any way if they do not meet the specifications or any other requirements not related to conformity set out in the guarantee statement or in the relevant advertising available at the time of, or before the conclusion of the contract;

(15) 'ancillary contract' means a contract by which the consumer acquires goods or services related to a distance contract or an off-premises contract and where those goods are supplied or those services are provided by the trader or by a third party on the basis of an arrangement between that third party and the trader.

Article 3
Scope

1. This Directive shall apply, under the conditions and to the extent set out in its provisions, to any contract concluded between a trader and a consumer. It shall also apply to contracts for the supply of water, gas, electricity or district heating, including by public providers, to the extent that these commodities are provided on a contractual basis.

2. If any provision of this Directive conflicts with a provision of another Union act governing specific sectors, the provision of that other Union act shall prevail and shall apply to those specific sectors.

3. This Directive shall not apply to contracts:

   (a) for social services, including social housing, childcare and support of families and persons permanently or temporarily in need, including long-term care;

   (b) for healthcare as defined in point (a) of Article 3 of Directive 2011/24/EU, whether or not they are provided via healthcare facilities;

   (c) for gambling, which involves wagering a stake with pecuniary value in games of chance, including lotteries, casino games and betting transactions;

   (d) for financial services;

   (e) for the creation, acquisition or transfer of immovable property or of rights in immovable property;

   (f) for the construction of new buildings, the substantial conversion of existing buildings and for rental of accommodation for residential purposes;

   (g) on packages as defined in point 2 of Article 3 of Directive (EU) 2015/2302 of the European Parliament and of the Council.

   Article 6(7), Article 8(2) and (6) and Articles 19, 21 and 22 of this Directive shall apply *mutatis mutandis* to packages as defined in point 2 of Article 3 of Directive (EU) 2015/2302 in relation to travellers as defined in point 6 of Article 3 of that Directive[;]

   (h) which fall within the scope of Directive 2008/122/EC of the European Parliament and of the Council of 14 January 2009 on the protection of consumers in respect of certain aspects of timeshare, long-term holiday product, resale and exchange contracts;

(i) which, in accordance with the laws of Member States, are established by a public office-holder who has a statutory obligation to be independent and impartial and who must ensure, by providing comprehensive legal information, that the consumer only concludes the contract on the basis of careful legal consideration and with knowledge of its legal scope;

(j) for the supply of foodstuffs, beverages or other goods intended for current consumption in the household, and which are physically supplied by a trader on frequent and regular rounds to the consumer's home, residence or workplace;

(k) for passenger transport services, with the exception of Article 8(2) and Articles 19 and 22;

(l) concluded by means of automatic vending machines or automated commercial premises;

(m) concluded with telecommunications operators through public payphones for their use or concluded for the use of one single connection by telephone, Internet or fax established by a consumer.

4. Member States may decide not to apply this Directive or not to maintain or introduce corresponding national provisions to off-premises contracts for which the payment to be made by the consumer does not exceed EUR 50. Member States may define a lower value in their national legislation.

5. This Directive shall not affect national general contract law such as the rules on the validity, formation or effect of a contract, in so far as general contract law aspects are not regulated in this Directive.

6. This Directive shall not prevent traders from offering consumers contractual arrangements which go beyond the protection provided for in this Directive.

Article 4

Level of harmonisation

Member States shall not maintain or introduce, in their national law, provisions diverging from those laid down in this Directive, including more or less stringent provisions to ensure a different level of consumer protection, unless otherwise provided for in this Directive.

Chapter II Consumer Information for Contracts other than Distance or Off-premises Contracts

Article 5

Information requirements for contracts other than distance or off-premises contracts

1. Before the consumer is bound by a contract other than a distance or an off-premises contract, or any corresponding offer, the trader shall provide the consumer with the following information in a clear and comprehensible manner, if that information is not already apparent from the context:

(a) the main characteristics of the goods or services, to the extent appropriate to the medium and to the goods or services;

(b) the identity of the trader, such as his trading name, the geographical address at which he is established and his telephone number;

(c) the total price of the goods or services inclusive of taxes, or where the nature of the goods or services is such that the price cannot reasonably be calculated in advance, the manner in which the price is to be calculated, as well as, where applicable, all additional freight, delivery or postal charges or, where those charges cannot reasonably be calculated in advance, the fact that such additional charges may be payable;

(d) where applicable, the arrangements for payment, delivery, performance, the time by which the trader undertakes to deliver the goods or to perform the service, and the trader's complaint handling policy;

(e) in addition to a reminder of the existence of a legal guarantee of conformity for goods, the existence and the conditions of after-sales services and commercial guarantees, where applicable;

(f) the duration of the contract, where applicable, or, if the contract is of indeterminate duration or is to be extended automatically, the conditions for terminating the contract;

(g) where applicable, the functionality, including applicable technical protection measures, of digital content;

(h) where applicable, any relevant interoperability of digital content with hardware and software that the trader is aware of or can reasonably be expected to have been aware of.

2. Paragraph 1 shall also apply to contracts for the supply of water, gas or electricity, where they are not put up for sale in a limited volume or set quantity, of district heating or of digital content which is not supplied on a tangible medium.

3. Member States shall not be required to apply paragraph 1 to contracts which involve day-to-day transactions and which are performed immediately at the time of their conclusion.

4. Member States may adopt or maintain additional pre-contractual information requirements for contracts to which this Article applies.

Chapter III Consumer Information and Right of Withdrawal for Distance and Off-premises Contracts

Article 6
Information requirements for distance and off-premises contracts

1. Before the consumer is bound by a distance or off-premises contract, or any corresponding offer, the trader shall provide the consumer with the following information in a clear and comprehensible manner:

(a) the main characteristics of the goods or services, to the extent appropriate to the medium and to the goods or services;

(b) the identity of the trader, such as his trading name;

(c) the geographical address at which the trader is established and the trader's telephone number, fax number and e-mail address, where available, to enable the consumer to contact the trader quickly and communicate with him efficiently and, where applicable, the geographical address and identity of the trader on whose behalf he is acting;

(d) if different from the address provided in accordance with point (c), the geographical address of the place of business of the trader, and, where applicable, that of the trader on whose behalf he is acting, where the consumer can address any complaints;

(e) the total price of the goods or services inclusive of taxes, or where the nature of the goods or services is such that the price cannot reasonably be calculated in advance, the manner in which the price is to be calculated, as well as, where applicable, all additional freight, delivery or postal charges and any other costs or, where those charges cannot reasonably be calculated in advance, the fact that such additional charges may be payable. In the case of a contract of indeterminate duration or a contract containing a subscription, the total price shall include the total costs per billing period. Where such contracts are charged at a fixed rate, the total price shall also mean the total monthly costs. Where the total costs cannot be reasonably calculated in advance, the manner in which the price is to be calculated shall be provided;

(f) the cost of using the means of distance communication for the conclusion of the contract where that cost is calculated other than at the basic rate;

(g) the arrangements for payment, delivery, performance, the time by which the trader undertakes to deliver the goods or to perform the services and, where applicable, the trader's complaint handling policy;

(h) where a right of withdrawal exists, the conditions, time limit and procedures for exercising that right in accordance with Article 11(1), as well as the model withdrawal form set out in Annex I(B);

(i) where applicable, that the consumer will have to bear the cost of returning the goods in case of withdrawal and, for distance contracts, if the goods, by their nature, cannot normally be returned by post, the cost of returning the goods;

(j) that, if the consumer exercises the right of withdrawal after having made a request in accordance with Article 7(3) or Article 8(8), the consumer shall be liable to pay the trader reasonable costs in accordance with Article 14(3);

(k) where a right of withdrawal is not provided for in accordance with Article 16, the information that the consumer will not benefit from a right of withdrawal or, where applicable, the circumstances under which the consumer loses his right of withdrawal;

(l) a reminder of the existence of a legal guarantee of conformity for goods;

(m) where applicable, the existence and the conditions of after sale customer assistance, after-sales services and commercial guarantees;

(n) the existence of relevant codes of conduct, as defined in point (f) of Article 2 of Directive 2005/29/EC, and how copies of them can be obtained, where applicable;

(o) the duration of the contract, where applicable, or, if the contract is of indeterminate duration or is to be extended automatically, the conditions for terminating the contract;

(p) where applicable, the minimum duration of the consumer's obligations under the contract;

(q) where applicable, the existence and the conditions of deposits or other financial guarantees to be paid or provided by the consumer at the request of the trader;

(r) where applicable, the functionality, including applicable technical protection measures, of digital content;

(s) where applicable, any relevant interoperability of digital content with hardware and software that the trader is aware of or can reasonably be expected to have been aware of;

26

(t) where applicable, the possibility of having recourse to an out-of-court complaint and redress mechanism, to which the trader is subject, and the methods for having access to it.

2. Paragraph 1 shall also apply to contracts for the supply of water, gas or electricity, where they are not put up for sale in a limited volume or set quantity, of district heating or of digital content which is not supplied on a tangible medium.

3. In the case of a public auction, the information referred to in points (b), (c) and (d) of paragraph 1 may be replaced by the equivalent details for the auctioneer.

4. The information referred to in points (h), (i) and (j) of paragraph 1 may be provided by means of the model instructions on withdrawal set out in Annex I(A). The trader shall have fulfilled the information requirements laid down in points (h), (i) and (j) of paragraph 1 if he has supplied these instructions to the consumer, correctly filled in.

5. The information referred to in paragraph 1 shall form an integral part of the distance or off-premises contract and shall not be altered unless the contracting parties expressly agree otherwise.

6. If the trader has not complied with the information requirements on additional charges or other costs as referred to in point (e) of paragraph 1, or on the costs of returning the goods as referred to in point (i) of paragraph 1, the consumer shall not bear those charges or costs.

7. Member States may maintain or introduce in their national law language requirements regarding the contractual information, so as to ensure that such information is easily understood by the consumer.

8. The information requirements laid down in this Directive are in addition to information requirements contained in Directive 2006/123/EC and Directive 2000/31/EC and do not prevent Member States from imposing additional information requirements in accordance with those Directives.

    Without prejudice to the first subparagraph, if a provision of Directive 2006/123/ EC or Directive 2000/31/EC on the content and the manner in which the information is to be provided conflicts with a provision of this Directive, the provision of this Directive shall prevail.

9. As regards compliance with the information requirements laid down in this Chapter, the burden of proof shall be on the trader.

Article 7
Formal requirements for off-premises contracts

1. With respect to off-premises contracts, the trader shall give the information provided for in Article 6(1) to the consumer on paper or, if the consumer agrees, on another durable medium. That information shall be legible and in plain, intelligible language.

2. The trader shall provide the consumer with a copy of the signed contract or the confirmation of the contract on paper or, if the consumer agrees, on another durable medium, including, where applicable, the confirmation of the consumer's prior express consent and acknowledgement in accordance with point (m) of Article 16.

3. Where a consumer wants the performance of services or the supply of water, gas or electricity, where they are not put up for sale in a limited volume or set quantity, or of district heating to begin during the withdrawal period provided for in Article 9(2), the trader shall require that the consumer makes such an express request on a durable medium.

4. With respect to off-premises contracts where the consumer has explicitly requested the services of the trader for the purpose of carrying out repairs or maintenance for which the trader and the consumer immediately perform their contractual obligations and where the payment to be made by the consumer does not exceed EUR 200:

   (a) the trader shall provide the consumer with the information referred to in points (b) and (c) of Article 6(1) and information about the price or the manner in which the price is to be calculated together with an estimate of the total price, on paper or, if the consumer agrees, on another durable medium. The trader shall provide the information referred to in points (a), (h) and (k) of Article 6(1), but may choose not to provide it on paper or another durable medium if the consumer expressly agrees;

   (b) the confirmation of the contract provided in accordance with paragraph 2 of this Article shall contain the information provided for in Article 6(1). Member States may decide not to apply this paragraph.

5. Member States shall not impose any further formal pre-contractual information requirements for the fulfilment of the information obligations laid down in this Directive.

Article 8
Formal requirements for distance contracts

1. With respect to distance contracts, the trader shall give the information provided for in Article 6(1) or make that information available to the consumer in a way appropriate to the means of distance communication used in plain and intelligible language. In so far as that information is provided on a durable medium, it shall be legible.

2. If a distance contract to be concluded by electronic means places the consumer under an obligation to pay, the trader shall make the consumer aware in a clear and prominent manner, and directly before the consumer places his order, of the information provided for in points (a), (e), (o) and (p) of Article 6(1).

   The trader shall ensure that the consumer, when placing his order, explicitly acknowledges that the order implies an obligation to pay. If placing an order entails activating a button or a similar function, the button or similar function shall be labelled in an easily legible manner only with the words 'order with obligation to pay' or a corresponding unambiguous formulation indicating that placing the order entails an obligation to pay the trader. If the trader has not complied with this subparagraph, the consumer shall not bebound by the contract or order.

3. Trading websites shall indicate clearly and legibly at the latest at the beginning of the ordering process whether any delivery restrictions apply and which means of payment are accepted.

4. If the contract is concluded through a means of distance communication which allows limited space or time to display the information, the trader shall provide, on that particular means prior to the conclusion of such a contract, at least the pre-contractual information regarding the main characteristics of the goods or services, the identity of the trader, the total price, the right of withdrawal, the duration of the contract and, if the contract is of indeterminate duration, the conditions for terminating the contract, as referred to in points (a), (b), (e), (h) and (o) of Article 6(1). The other information referred to in Article 6(1) shall be provided by the trader to the consumer in an appropriate way in accordance with paragraph 1 of this Article.

26

5. Without prejudice to paragraph 4, if the trader makes a telephone call to the consumer with a view to concluding a distance contract, he shall, at the beginning of the conversation with the consumer, disclose his identity and, where applicable, the identity of the person on whose behalf he makes that call, and the commercial purpose of the call.

6. Where a distance contract is to be concluded by telephone, Member States may provide that the trader has to confirm the offer to the consumer who is bound only once he has signed the offer or has sent his written consent. Member States may also provide that such confirmations have to be made on a durable medium.

7. The trader shall provide the consumer with the confirmation of the contract concluded, on a durable medium within a reasonable time after the conclusion of the distance contract, and at the latest at the time of the delivery of the goods or before the performance of the service begins. That confirmation shall include:

   (a) all the information referred to in Article 6(1) unless the trader has already provided that information to the consumer on a durable medium prior to the conclusion of the distance contract; and

   (b) where applicable, the confirmation of the consumer's prior express consent and acknowledgment in accordance with point (m) of Article 16.

8. Where a consumer wants the performance of services, or the supply of water, gas or electricity, where they are not put up for sale in a limited volume or set quantity, or of district heating, to begin during the withdrawal period provided for in Article 9(2), the trader shall require that the consumer make an express request.

9. This Article shall be without prejudice to the provisions on the conclusion of e-contracts and the placing of e-orders set out in Articles 9 and 11 of Directive 2000/31/EC.

10. Member States shall not impose any further formal pre-contractual information requirements for the fulfilment of the information obligations laid down in this Directive.

Article 9
Right of withdrawal

1. Save where the exceptions provided for in Article 16 apply, the consumer shall have a period of 14 days to withdraw from a distance or off-premises contract, without giving any reason, and without incurring any costs other than those provided for in Article 13(2) and Article 14.

2. Without prejudice to Article 10, the withdrawal period referred to in paragraph 1 of this Article shall expire after 14 days from:

   (a) in the case of service contracts, the day of the conclusion of the contract;

   (b) in the case of sales contracts, the day on which the consumer or a third party other than the carrier and indicated by the consumer acquires physical possession of the goods or:

      (i) in the case of multiple goods ordered by the consumer in one order and delivered separately, the day on which the consumer or a third party other than the carrier and indicated by the consumer acquires physical possession of the last good;

      (ii) in the case of delivery of a good consisting of multiple lots or pieces, the day on which the consumer or a third party other than the carrier and indicated by the consumer acquires physical possession of the last lot or piece;

(iii) in the case of contracts for regular delivery of goods during a defined period of time, the day on which the consumer or a third party other than the carrier and indicated by the consumer acquires physical possession of the first good;

(c) in the case of contracts for the supply of water, gas or electricity, where they are not put up for sale in a limited volume or set quantity, of district heating or of digital content which is not supplied on a tangible medium, the day of the conclusion of the contract.

3. The Member States shall not prohibit the contracting parties from performing their contractual obligations during the withdrawal period. Nevertheless, in the case of off-premises contracts, Member States may maintain existing national legislation prohibiting the trader from collecting the payment from the consumer during the given period after the conclusion of the contract.

Article 10
Omission of information on the right of withdrawal

1. If the trader has not provided the consumer with the information on the right of withdrawal as required by point (h) of Article 6(1), the withdrawal period shall expire 12 months from the end of the initial withdrawal period, as determined in accordance with Article 9(2).

2. If the trader has provided the consumer with the information provided for in paragraph 1 of this Article within 12 months from the day referred to in Article 9(2), the withdrawal period shall expire 14 days after the day upon which the consumer receives that information.

Article 11
Exercise of the right of withdrawal

1. Before the expiry of the withdrawal period, the consumer shall inform the trader of his decision to withdraw from the contract. For this purpose, the consumer may either:

    (a) use the model withdrawal form as set out in Annex I(B); or

    (b) make any other unequivocal statement setting out his decision to withdraw from the contract.

    Member States shall not provide for any formal requirements applicable to the model withdrawal form other than those set out in Annex I(B).

2. The consumer shall have exercised his right of withdrawal within the withdrawal period referred to in Article 9(2) and Article 10 if the communication concerning the exercise of the right of withdrawal is sent by the consumer before that period has expired.

3. The trader may, in addition to the possibilities referred to in paragraph 1, give the option to the consumer to electronically fill in and submit either the model withdrawal form set out in Annex I(B) or any other unequivocal statement on the trader's website. In those cases the trader shall communicate to the consumer an acknowledgement of receipt of such a withdrawal on a durable medium without delay.

4. The burden of proof of exercising the right of withdrawal in accordance with this Article shall be on the consumer.

26

Article 12

Effects of withdrawal

The exercise of the right of withdrawal shall terminate the obligations of the parties:

(a) to perform the distance or off-premises contract; or

(b) to conclude the distance or off-premises contract, in cases where an offer was made by the consumer.

Article 13

Obligations of the trader in the event of withdrawal

1. The trader shall reimburse all payments received from the consumer, including, if applicable, the costs of delivery without undue delay and in any event not later than 14 days from the day on which he is informed of the consumer's decision to withdraw from the contract in accordance with Article 11.

   The trader shall carry out the reimbursement referred to in the first subparagraph using the same means of payment as the consumer used for the initial transaction, unless the consumer has expressly agreed otherwise and provided that the consumer does not incur any fees as a result of such reimbursement.

2. Notwithstanding paragraph 1, the trader shall not be required to reimburse the supplementary costs, if the consumer has expressly opted for a type of delivery other than the least expensive type of standard delivery offered by the trader.

3. Unless the trader has offered to collect the goods himself, with regard to sales contracts, the trader may withhold the reimbursement until he has received the goods back, or until the consumer has supplied evidence of having sent back the goods, whichever is the earliest.

Article 14

Obligations of the consumer in the event of withdrawal

1. Unless the trader has offered to collect the goods himself, the consumer shall send back the goods or hand them over to the trader or to a person authorised by the trader to receive the goods, without undue delay and in any event not later than 14 days from the day on which he has communicated his decision to withdraw from the contract to the trader in accordance with Article 11. The deadline shall be met if the consumer sends back the goods before the period of 14 days has expired.

   The consumer shall only bear the direct cost of returning the goods unless the trader has agreed to bear them or the trader failed to inform the consumer that the consumer has to bear them.

   In the case of off-premises contracts where the goods have been delivered to the consumer's home at the time of the conclusion of the contract, the trader shall at his own expense collect the goods if, by their nature, those goods cannot normally be returned by post.

2. The consumer shall only be liable for any diminished value of the goods resulting from the handling of the goods other than what is necessary to establish the nature, characteristics and functioning of the goods. The consumer shall in any event not be liable for diminished value of the goods where the trader has failed to provide notice of the right of withdrawal in accordance with point (h) of Article 6(1).

3. Where a consumer exercises the right of withdrawal after having made a request in accordance with Article 7(3) or Article 8(8), the consumer shall pay to the trader an amount which is in proportion to what has been provided until the time the consumer has informed the trader of the exercise of the right of withdrawal, in comparison with the full coverage of the contract. The proportionate amount to be paid by the consumer to the trader shall be calculated on the basis of the total price agreed in the contract. If the total price is excessive, the proportionate amount shall be calculated on the basis of the market value of what has been provided.

4. The consumer shall bear no cost for:

   (a) the performance of services or the supply of water, gas or electricity, where they are not put up for sale in a limited volume or set quantity, or of district heating, in full or in part, during the withdrawal period, where:

      (i)   the trader has failed to provide information in accordance with points (h) or (j) of Article 6(1); or

      (ii) the consumer has not expressly requested performance to begin during the withdrawal period in accordance with Article 7(3) and Article 8(8); or

   (b) the supply, in full or in part, of digital content which is not supplied on a tangible medium where:

      (i)   the consumer has not given his prior express consent to the beginning of the performance before the end of the 14-day period referred to in Article 9;

      (ii) the consumer has not acknowledged that he loses his right of withdrawal when giving his consent; or

      (iii) the trader has failed to provide confirmation in accordance with Article 7(2) or Article 8(7).

5. Except as provided for in Article 13(2) and in this Article, the consumer shall not incur any liability as a consequence of the exercise of the right of withdrawal.

Article 15

Effects of the exercise of the right of withdrawal on ancillary contracts

1. Without prejudice to Article 15 of Directive 2008/48/EC of the European Parliament and of the Council of 23 April 2008 on credit agreements for consumers, if the consumer exercises his right of withdrawal from a distance or an off-premises contract in accordance with Articles 9 to 14 of this Directive, any ancillary contracts shall be automatically terminated, without any costs for the consumer, except as provided for in Article 13(2) and in Article 14 of this Directive.

2. The Member States shall lay down detailed rules on the termination of such contracts.

Article 16

Exceptions from the right of withdrawal

Member States shall not provide for the right of withdrawal set out in Articles 9 to 15 in respect of distance and off-premises contracts as regards the following:

   (a) service contracts after the service has been fully performed if the performance has begun with the consumer's prior express consent, and with the acknowledgement that he will lose his right of withdrawal once the contract has been fully performed by the trader;

26

(b) the supply of goods or services for which the price is dependent on fluctuations in the financial market which cannot be controlled by the trader and which may occur within the withdrawal period;

(c) the supply of goods made to the consumer's specifications or clearly personalised;

(d) the supply of goods which are liable to deteriorate or expire rapidly;

(e) the supply of sealed goods which are not suitable for return due to health protection or hygiene reasons and were unsealed after delivery;

(f) the supply of goods which are, after delivery, according to their nature, inseparably mixed with other items;

(g) the supply of alcoholic beverages, the price of which has been agreed upon at the time of the conclusion of the sales contract, the delivery of which can only take place after 30 days and the actual value of which is dependent on fluctuations in the market which cannot be controlled by the trader;

(h) contracts where the consumer has specifically requested a visit from the trader for the purpose of carrying out urgent repairs or maintenance. If, on the occasion of such visit, the trader provides services in addition to those specifically requested by the consumer or goods other than replacement parts necessarily used in carrying out the maintenance or in making the repairs, the right of withdrawal shall apply to those additional services or goods;

(i) the supply of sealed audio or sealed video recordings or sealed computer software which were unsealed after delivery;

(j) the supply of a newspaper, periodical or magazine with the exception of subscription contracts for the supply of such publications;

(k) contracts concluded at a public auction;

(l) the provision of accommodation other than for residential purpose[s], transport of goods, car rental services, catering or services related to leisure activities if the contract provides for a specific date or period of performance;

(m) the supply of digital content which is not supplied on a tangible medium if the performance has begun with the consumer's prior express consent and his acknowledgment that he thereby loses his right of withdrawal.

Chapter IV Other Consumer Rights

Article 17
Scope

1. Articles 18 and 20 shall apply to sales contracts. Those Articles shall not apply to contracts for the supply of water, gas or electricity, where they are not put up for sale in a limited volume or set quantity, of district heating or the supply of digital content which is not supplied on a tangible medium.

2. Articles 19, 21 and 22 shall apply to sales and service contracts and to contracts for the supply of water, gas, electricity, district heating or digital content.

Article 18
Delivery

1. Unless the parties have agreed otherwise on the time of delivery, the trader shall deliver the goods by transferring the physical possession or control of the goods to the consumer without undue delay, but not later than 30 days from the conclusion of the contract.

2. Where the trader has failed to fulfil his obligation to deliver the goods at the time agreed upon with the consumer or within the time limit set out in paragraph 1, the consumer shall call upon him to make the delivery within an additional period of time appropriate to the circumstances. If the trader fails to deliver the goods within that additional period of time, the consumer shall be entitled to terminate the contract.

The first subparagraph shall not be applicable to sales contracts where the trader has refused to deliver the goods or where delivery within the agreed delivery period is essential taking into account all the circumstances attending the conclusion of the contract or where the consumer informs the trader, prior to the conclusion of the contract, that delivery by or on a specified date is essential. In those cases, if the trader fails to deliver the goods at the time agreed upon with the consumer or within the time limit set out in paragraph 1, the consumer shall be entitled to terminate the contract immediately.

3. Upon termination of the contract, the trader shall, without undue delay, reimburse all sums paid under the contract.

4. In addition to the termination of the contract in accordance with paragraph 2, the consumer may have recourse to other remedies provided for by national law.

Article 19

Fees for the use of means of payment

Member States shall prohibit traders from charging consumers, in respect of the use of a given means of payment, fees that exceed the cost borne by the trader for the use of such means.

Article 20

Passing of risk

In contracts where the trader dispatches the goods to the consumer, the risk of loss of or damage to the goods shall pass to the consumer when he or a third party indicated by the consumer and other than the carrier has acquired the physical possession of the goods. However, the risk shall pass to the consumer upon delivery to the carrier if the carrier was commissioned by the consumer to carry the goods and that choice was not offered by the trader, without prejudice to the rights of the consumer against the carrier.

Article 21

Communication by telephone

Member States shall ensure that where the trader operates a telephone line for the purpose of contacting him by telephone in relation to the contract concluded, the consumer, when contacting the trader is not bound to pay more than the basic rate.

The first subparagraph shall be without prejudice to the right of telecommunication services providers to charge for such calls.

Article 22

Additional payments

Before the consumer is bound by the contract or offer, the trader shall seek the express consent of the consumer to any extra payment in addition to the remuneration agreed upon for the trader's main contractual obligation. If the trader has not obtained the consumer's express consent but has inferred it by using default options which the consumer is required to reject in order to avoid the additional payment, the consumer shall be entitled to reimbursement of this payment.

26

Chapter V General Provisions

Article 23
Enforcement
1. Member States shall ensure that adequate and effective means exist to ensure compliance with this Directive.
2. The means referred to in paragraph 1 shall include provisions whereby one or more of the following bodies, as determined by national law, may take action under national law before the courts or before the competent administrative bodies to ensure that the national provisions transposing this Directive are applied:
   (a) public bodies or their representatives;
   (b) consumer organisations having a legitimate interest in protecting consumers;
   (c) professional organisations having a legitimate interest in acting.

Article 24
Penalties
1. Member States shall lay down the rules on penalties applicable to infringements of the national provisions adopted pursuant to this Directive and shall take all measures necessary to ensure that they are implemented. The penalties provided for must be effective, proportionate and dissuasive.
2. Member States shall notify those provisions to the Commission by 13 December 2013 and shall notify it without delay of any subsequent amendment affecting them.

Article 25
Imperative nature of the Directive
If the law applicable to the contract is the law of a Member State, consumers may not waive the rights conferred on them by the national measures transposing this Directive.

Any contractual terms which directly or indirectly waive or restrict the rights resulting from this Directive shall not be binding on the consumer.

Article 26
Information
Member States shall take appropriate measures to inform consumers and traders of the national provisions transposing this Directive and shall, where appropriate, encourage traders and code owners as defined in point (g) of Article 2 of Directive 2005/29/EC, to inform consumers of their codes of conduct.

Article 27
Inertia selling
The consumer shall be exempted from the obligation to provide any consideration in cases of unsolicited supply of goods, water, gas, electricity, district heating or digital content or unsolicited provision of services, prohibited by Article 5(5) and point 29 of Annex I to Directive 2005/29/EC. In such cases, the absence of a response from the consumer following such an unsolicited supply or provision shall not constitute consent.

Article 28

Transposition

1. Member States shall adopt and publish, by 13 December 2013, the laws, regulations and administrative provisions necessary to comply with this Directive. They shall forthwith communicate to the Commission the text of these measures in the form of documents. The Commission shall make use of these documents for the purposes of the report referred to in Article 30.

   They shall apply those measures from 13 June 2014. When Member States adopt those measures, they shall contain a reference to this Directive or be accompanied by such a reference on the occasion of their official publication. Member States shall determine how such reference is to be made.

2. The provisions of this Directive shall apply to contracts concluded after13 June 2014.

Article 29

Reporting requirements

1. Where a Member State makes use of any of the regulatory choices referred to in Article 3(4), Article 6(7), Article 6(8), Article 7(4), Article 8(6) and Article 9(3), it shall inform the Commission thereof by 13 December 2013, as well as of any subsequent changes.

2. The Commission shall ensure that the information referred to in paragraph 1 is easily accessible to consumers and traders, inter alia, on a dedicated website.

3. The Commission shall forward the information referred to in paragraph 1 to the other Member States and the European Parliament. The Commission shall consult stake-holders on that information.

Article 30

Reporting by the Commission and review

By 13 December 2016, the Commission shall submit a report on the application of this Directive to the European Parliament and the Council. That report shall include in particular an evaluation of the provisions of this Directive regarding digital content including the right of withdrawal. The report shall be accompanied, where necessary, by legislative proposals to adapt this Directive to developments in the field of consumer rights.

Chapter VI Final Provisions

Article 31

Repeals

Directive 85/577/EEC and Directive 97/7/EC, as amended by Directive 2002/65/EC of the European Parliament and of the Council of 23 September 2002 concerning the distance marketing of consumer financial services and by Directives 2005/29/EC and 2007/64/EC, are repealed as of 13 June 2014.

References to the repealed Directives shall be construed as references to this Directive and shall be read in accordance with the correlation table set out in Annex II.

26

Article 32

Amendment to Directive 93/13/EEC

In Directive 93/13/EEC, the following Article is inserted:

'Article 8a

1. Where a Member State adopts provisions in accordance with Article 8, it shall inform the Commission thereof, as well as of any subsequent changes, in particular where those provisions:
   — extend the unfairness assessment to individually negotiated contractual terms or to the adequacy of the price or remuneration; or,
   — contain lists of contractual terms which shall be considered as unfair,
2. The Commission shall ensure that the information referred to in paragraph 1 is easily accessible to consumers and traders, inter alia, on a dedicated website.
3. The Commission shall forward the information referred to in paragraph 1 to the other Member States and the European Parliament. The Commission shall consult stakeholders on that information.'

Article 33

Amendment to Directive 1999/44/EC

In Directive 1999/44/EC, the following Article is inserted:

'Article 8a

Reporting requirements

1. Where, in accordance with Article 8(2), a Member State adopts more stringent consumer protection provisions than those provided for in Article 5(1) to (3) and in Article 7(1), it shall inform the Commission thereof, as well as of any subsequent changes.
2. The Commission shall ensure that the information referred to in paragraph 1 is easily accessible to consumers and traders, inter alia, on a dedicated website.
3. The Commission shall forward the information referred to in paragraph 1 to the other Member States and the European Parliament. The Commission shall consult stakeholders on that information.'

Article 34

Entry into force

This Directive shall enter into force on the 20th day following its publication in the *Official Journal of the European Union*.

Article 35

Addressees

This Directive is addressed to the Member States.

(*Signatures omitted*)

27

Directive 1999/44 on Certain Aspects of the Sale of Consumer Goods and Associated Guarantees

THE EUROPEAN PARLIAMENT AND THE COUNCIL OF THE EUROPEAN UNION,

Having regard to the Treaty [on the Functioning of the European Union], and in particular Article [114] thereof,

Having regard to the proposal from the Commission,

Having regard to the opinion of the Economic and Social Committee,

Acting in accordance with the procedure laid down in Article [294] of the Treaty in the light of the joint text approved by the Conciliation Committee on 18 May 1999 ...

HAVE ADOPTED THIS DIRECTIVE:

Article 1

Scope and definitions

1. The purpose of this Directive is the approximation of the laws, regulations and administrative provisions of the Member States on certain aspects of the sale of consumer goods and associated guarantees in order to ensure a uniform minimum level of consumer protection in the context of the internal market.

2. For the purposes of this Directive:

(a) consumer: shall mean any natural person who, in the contracts covered by this Directive, is acting for purposes which are not related to his trade, business or profession;

(b) consumer goods: shall mean any tangible movable item, with the exception of:
   — goods sold by way of execution or otherwise by authority of law,
   — water and gas where they are not put up for sale in a limited volume or set quantity,
   — electricity;

(c) seller: shall mean any natural or legal person who, under a contract, sells consumer goods in the course of his trade, business or profession;

(d) producer: shall mean the manufacturer of consumer goods, the importer of consumer goods into the territory of the [Union] or any person purporting to be a producer by placing his name, trade mark or other distinctive sign on the consumer goods;

(e) guarantee: shall mean any undertaking by a seller or producer to the consumer, given without extra charge, to reimburse the price paid or to replace, repair or handle consumer goods in any way if they do not meet the specifications set out in the guarantee statement or in the relevant advertising;

(f) repair: shall mean, in the event of lack of conformity, bringing consumer goods into conformity with the contract of sale.

3. Member States may provide that the expression 'consumer goods' does not cover second-hand goods sold at public auction where consumers have the opportunity of attending the sale in person.

4. Contracts for the supply of consumer goods to be manufactured or produced shall also be deemed contracts of sale for the purpose of this Directive.

Article 2
Conformity with the contract

1. The seller must deliver goods to the consumer which are in conformity with the contract of sale.

2. Consumer goods are presumed to be in conformity with the contract if they:
   (a) comply with the description given by the seller and possess the qualities of the goods which the seller has held out to the consumer as a sample or model;
   (b) are fit for any particular purpose for which the consumer requires them and which he made known to the seller at the time of conclusion of the contract and which the seller has accepted;
   (c) are fit for the purposes for which goods of the same type are normally used;
   (d) show the quality and performance which are normal in goods of the same type and which the consumer can reasonably expect, given the nature of the goods and taking into account any public statements on the specific characteristics of the goods made about them by the seller, the producer or his representative, particularly in advertising or on labelling.

3. There shall be deemed not to be a lack of conformity for the purposes of this Article if, at the time the contract was concluded, the consumer was aware, or could not reasonably be unaware of, the lack of conformity, or if the lack of conformity has its origin in materials supplied by the consumer.

4. The seller shall not be bound by public statements, as referred to in paragraph 2(d) if he:
   — shows that he was not, and could not reasonably have been, aware of the statement in question,
   — shows that by the time of conclusion of the contract the statement had been corrected, or
   — shows that the decision to buy the consumer goods could not have been influenced by the statement.

5. Any lack of conformity resulting from incorrect installation of the consumer goods shall be deemed to be equivalent to lack of conformity of the goods if installation forms part of the contract of sale of the goods and the goods were installed by the seller or under his responsibility. This shall apply equally if the product, intended to be installed by the consumer, is installed by the consumer and the incorrect installation is due to a shortcoming in the installation instructions.

Article 3
Rights of the consumer

1. The seller shall be liable to the consumer for any lack of conformity which exists at the time the goods were delivered.

2. In the case of a lack of conformity, the consumer shall be entitled to have the goods brought into conformity free of charge by repair or replacement, in accordance with

paragraph 3, or to have an appropriate reduction made in the price or the contract rescinded with regard to those goods, in accordance with paragraphs 5 and 6.

3. In the first place, the consumer may require the seller to repair the goods or he may require the seller to replace them, in either case free of charge, unless this is impossible or disproportionate.

   A remedy shall be deemed to be disproportionate if it imposes costs on the seller which, in comparison with the alternative remedy, are unreasonable, taking into account:
   — the value the goods would have if there were no lack of conformity,
   — the significance of the lack of conformity, and
   — whether the alternative remedy could be completed without significant inconvenience to the consumer.

   Any repair or replacement shall be completed within a reasonable time and without any significant inconvenience to the consumer, taking account of the nature of the goods and the purpose for which the consumer required the goods.

4. The terms 'free of charge' in paragraphs 2 and 3 refer to the necessary costs incurred to bring the goods into conformity, particularly the cost of postage, labour and materials.

5. The consumer may require an appropriate reduction of the price or have the contract rescinded:
   — if the consumer is entitled to neither repair nor replacement, or
   — if the seller has not completed the remedy within a reasonable time, or
   — if the seller has not completed the remedy without significant inconvenience to the consumer.

6. The consumer is not entitled to have the contract rescinded if the lack of conformity is minor.

Article 4

Right of redress

Where the final seller is liable to the consumer because of a lack of conformity resulting from an act or omission by the producer, a previous seller in the same chain of contracts or any other intermediary, the final seller shall be entitled to pursue remedies against the person or persons liable in the contractual chain. The person or persons liable against whom the final seller may pursue remedies, together with the relevant actions and conditions of exercise, shall be determined by national law.

Article 5

Time limits

1. The seller shall be held liable under Article 3 where the lack of conformity becomes apparent within two years as from delivery of the goods. If, under national legislation, the rights laid down in Article 3(2) are subject to a limitation period, that period shall not expire within a period of two years from the time of delivery.

2. Member States may provide that, in order to benefit from his rights, the consumer must inform the seller of the lack of conformity within a period of two months from the date on which he detected such lack of conformity.

   Member States shall inform the Commission of their use of this paragraph. The Commission shall monitor the effect of the existence of this option for the Member States on consumers and on the internal market.

27

Not later than 7 January 2003, the Commission shall prepare a report on the use made by Member States of this paragraph. This report shall be published in the Official Journal of the European [Union].

3. Unless proved otherwise, any lack of conformity which becomes apparent within six months of delivery of the goods shall be presumed to have existed at the time of delivery unless this presumption is incompatible with the nature of the goods or the nature of the lack of conformity.

Article 6
Guarantees

1. A guarantee shall be legally binding on the offerer under the conditions laid down in the guarantee statement and the associated advertising.
2. The guarantee shall:
   — state that the consumer has legal rights under applicable national legislation governing the sale of consumer goods and make clear that those rights are not affected by the guarantee,
   — set out in plain intelligible language the contents of the guarantee and the essential particulars necessary for making claims under the guarantee, notably the duration and territorial scope of the guarantee as well as the name and address of the guarantor.
3. On request by the consumer, the guarantee shall be made available in writing or feature in another durable medium available and accessible to him.
4. Within its own territory, the Member State in which the consumer goods are marketed may, in accordance with the rules of the Treaty, provide that the guarantee be drafted in one or more languages which it shall determine from among the official languages of the [Union].
5. Should a guarantee infringe the requirements of paragraphs 2, 3 or 4, the validity of this guarantee shall in no way be affected, and the consumer can still rely on the guarantee and require that it be honoured.

Article 7
Binding nature

1. Any contractual terms or agreements concluded with the seller before the lack of conformity is brought to the seller's attention which directly or indirectly waive or restrict the rights resulting from this Directive shall, as provided for by national law, not be binding on the consumer.

   Member States may provide that, in the case of second-hand goods, the seller and consumer may agree contractual terms or agreements which have a shorter time period for the liability of the seller than that set down in Article 5(1). Such period may not be less than one year.
2. Member States shall take the necessary measures to ensure that consumers are not deprived of the protection afforded by this Directive as a result of opting for the law of a non-member State as the law applicable to the contract where the contract has a close connection with the territory of the Member States.

Article 8

National law and minimum protection

1. The rights resulting from this Directive shall be exercised without prejudice to other rights which the consumer may invoke under the national rules governing contractual or non-contractual liability.

2. Member States may adopt or maintain in force more stringent provisions, compatible with the Treaty in the field covered by this Directive, to ensure a higher level of consumer protection.

Article 8a

Reporting requirements

1. Where, in accordance with Article 8(2), a Member State adopts more stringent consumer protection provisions than those provided for in Article 5(1) to (3) and in Article 7(1), it shall inform the Commission thereof, as well as of any subsequent changes.

2. The Commission shall ensure that the information referred to in paragraph 1 is easily accessible to consumers and traders, inter alia, on a dedicated website.

3. The Commission shall forward the information referred to in paragraph 1 to the other Member States and the European Parliament. The Commission shall consult stake-holders on that information.

Article 9

Member States shall take appropriate measures to inform the consumer of the national law transposing this Directive and shall encourage, where appropriate, professional organisations to inform consumers of their rights.

Article 10

The Annex to Directive 98/27/EC shall be completed as follows:

'10. Directive 1999/44/EC of the European Parliament and of the Council of 25 May 1999 on certain aspects of the sale of consumer goods and associated guarantees (OJ L 171, 7.7.1999, p. 12).'

Article 11

Transposition

1. Member States shall bring into force the laws, regulations and administrative provisions necessary to comply with this Directive not later than 1 January 2002. They shall forthwith inform the Commission thereof.

   When Member States adopt these measures, they shall contain a reference to this Directive, or shall be accompanied by such reference at the time of their official publication. The procedure for such reference shall be adopted by Member States.

2. Member States shall communicate to the Commission the provisions of national law which they adopt in the field covered by this Directive.

27

Article 12
Review

The Commission shall, not later than 7 July 2006, review the application of this Directive and submit to the European Parliament and the Council a report. The report shall examine, inter alia, the case for introducing the producer's direct liability and, if appropriate, shall be accompanied by proposals.

Article 13
Entry into force

This Directive shall enter into force on the day of its publication in the Official Journal of the European [Union].

Article 14

This Directive is addressed to the Member States.

28

Council Directive 93/13/EEC on Unfair Terms in Consumer Contracts

THE COUNCIL OF THE EUROPEAN [UNION],

Having regard to the Treaty [on the Functioning of the European Union], and in particular Article [114] thereof,

Having regard to the proposal from the Commission,

In cooperation with the European Parliament,

Having regard to the opinion of the Economic and Social Committee …

HAS ADOPTED THIS DIRECTIVE:

Article 1

1. The purpose of this Directive is to approximate the laws, regulations and administrative provisions of the Member States relating to unfair terms in contracts concluded between a seller or supplier and a consumer.
2. The contractual terms which reflect mandatory statutory or regulatory provisions and the provisions or principles of international conventions to which the Member States or the [Union] are party, particularly in the transport area, shall not be subject to the provisions of this Directive.

Article 2

For the purposes of this Directive:
   (a) 'unfair terms' means the contractual terms defined in Article 3;
   (b) 'consumer' means any natural person who, in contracts covered by this Directive, is acting for purposes which are outside his trade, business or profession;
   (c) 'seller or supplier' means any natural or legal person who, in contracts covered by this Directive, is acting for purposes relating to his trade, business or profession, whether publicly owned or privately owned.

Article 3

1. A contractual term which has not been individually negotiated shall be regarded as unfair if, contrary to the requirement of good faith, it causes a significant imbalance in the parties' rights and obligations arising under the contract, to the detriment of the consumer.
2. A term shall always be regarded as not individually negotiated where it has been drafted in advance and the consumer has therefore not been able to influence the substance of the term, particularly in the context of a pre-formulated standard contract.

   The fact that certain aspects of a term or one specific term have been individually negotiated shall not exclude the application of this Article to the rest of a contract if an overall assessment of the contract indicates that it is nevertheless a pre-formulated standard contract.

Where any seller or supplier claims that a standard term has been individually negotiated, the burden of proof in this respect shall be incumbent on him.

3. The Annex shall contain an indicative and non-exhaustive list of the terms which may be regarded as unfair.

Article 4

1. Without prejudice to Article 7, the unfairness of a contractual term shall be assessed, taking into account the nature of the goods or services for which the contract was concluded and by referring, at the time of conclusion of the contract, to all the circumstances attending the conclusion of the contract and to all the other terms of the contract or of another contract on which it is dependent.

2. Assessment of the unfair nature of the terms shall relate neither to the definition of the main subject matter of the contract nor to the adequacy of the price and remuneration, on the one hand, as against the services or goods supplie[d] in exchange, on the other, in so far as these terms are in plain intelligible language.

Article 5

In the case of contracts where all or certain terms offered to the consumer are in writing, these terms must always be drafted in plain, intelligible language. Where there is doubt about the meaning of a term, the interpretation most favourable to the consumer shall prevail. This rule on interpretation shall not apply in the context of the procedures laid down in Article 7(2).

Article 6

1. Member States shall lay down that unfair terms used in a contract concluded with a consumer by a seller or supplier shall, as provided for under their national law, not be binding on the consumer and that the contract shall continue to bind the parties upon those terms if it is capable of continuing in existence without the unfair terms.

2. Member States shall take the necessary measures to ensure that the consumer does not lose the protection granted by this Directive by virtue of the choice of the law of a non-Member country as the law applicable to the contract if the latter has a close connection with the territory of the Member States.

Article 7

1. Member States shall ensure that, in the interests of consumers and of competitors, adequate and effective means exist to prevent the continued use of unfair terms in contracts concluded with consumers by sellers or suppliers.

2. The means referred to in paragraph 1 shall include provisions whereby persons or organizations, having a legitimate interest under national law in protecting consumers, may take action according to the national law concerned before the courts or before competent administrative bodies for a decision as to whether contractual terms drawn up for general use are unfair, so that they can apply appropriate and effective means to prevent the continued use of such terms.

3. With due regard for national laws, the legal remedies referred to in paragraph 2 may be directed separately or jointly against a number of sellers or suppliers from the same economic sector or their associations which use or recommend the use of the same general contractual terms or similar terms.

Article 8

Member States may adopt or retain the most stringent provisions compatible with the Treaty in the area covered by this Directive, to ensure a maximum degree of protection for the consumer.

Article 8a

1. Where a Member State adopts provisions in accordance with Article 8, it shall inform the Commission thereof, as well as of any subsequent changes, in particular where those provisions:
   — extend the unfairness assessment to individually negotiated contractual terms or to the adequacy of the price or remuneration; or
   — contain lists of contractual terms which shall be considered as unfair.
2. The Commission shall ensure that the information referred to in paragraph 1 is easily accessible to consumers and traders, inter alia, on a dedicated website.
3. The Commission shall forward the information referred to in paragraph 1 to the other Member States and the European Parliament. The Commission shall consult stake-holders on that information.

Article 9

The Commission shall present a report to the European Parliament and to the Council concerning the application of this Directive five years at the latest after the date in Article 10(1).

Article 10

1. Member States shall bring into force the laws, regulations and administrative provisions necessary to comply with this Directive no later than 31 December 1994. They shall forthwith inform the Commission thereof.
   These provisions shall be applicable to all contracts concluded after 31 December 1994.
2. When Member States adopt these measures, they shall contain a reference to this Directive or shall be accompanied by such reference on the occasion of their official publication. The methods of making such a reference shall be laid down by the Member States.
3. Member States shall communicate the main provisions of national law which they adopt in the field covered by this Directive to the Commission.

Article 11

This Directive is addressed to the Member States.

ANNEX TERMS REFERRED TO IN ARTICLE 3(3)

1. Terms which have the object or effect of:
   (a) excluding or limiting the legal liability of a seller or supplier in the event of the death of a consumer or personal injury to the latter resulting from an act or omission of that seller or supplier;
   (b) inappropriately excluding or limiting the legal rights of the consumer vis-à-vis the seller or supplier or another party in the event of total or partial non-performance or in adequate performance by the seller or supplier of any of the contractual

obligations, including the option of offsetting a debt owed to the seller or supplier against any claim which the consumer may have against him;

(c) making an agreement binding on the consumer whereas provision of services by the seller or supplier is subject to a condition whose realization depends on his own will alone;

(d) permitting the seller or supplier to retain sums paid by the consumer where the latter decides not to conclude or perform the contract, without providing for the consumer to receive compensation of an equivalent amount from the seller or supplier where the latter is the party cancelling the contract;

(e) requiring any consumer who fails to fulfil his obligation to pay a disproportionately high sum in compensation;

(f) authorizing the seller or supplier to dissolve the contract on a discretionary basis where the same facility is not granted to the consumer, or permitting the seller or supplier to retain the sums paid for services not yet supplied by him where it is the seller or supplier himself who dissolves the contract;

(g) enabling the seller or supplier to terminate a contract of indeterminate duration without reasonable notice except where there are serious grounds for doing so;

(h) automatically extending a contract of fixed duration where the consumer does not indicate otherwise, when the deadline fixed for the consumer to express this desire not to extend the contract is unreasonably early;

(i) irrevocably binding the consumer to terms with which he had no real opportunity of becoming acquainted before the conclusion of the contract;

(j) enabling the seller or supplier to alter the terms of the contract unilaterally without a valid reason which is specified in the contract;

(k) enabling the seller or supplier to alter unilaterally without a valid reason any characteristics of the product or service to be provided;

(l) providing for the price of goods to be determined at the time of delivery or allowing a seller of goods or supplier of services to increase their price without in both cases giving the consumer the corresponding right to cancel the contract if the final price is too high in relation to the price agreed when the contract was concluded;

(m) giving the seller or supplier the right to determine whether the goods or services supplied are in conformity with the contract, or giving him the exclusive right to interpret any term of the contract;

(n) limiting the seller's or supplier's obligation to respect commitments undertaken by his agents or making his commitments subject to compliance with a particular formality;

(o) obliging the consumer to fulfil all his obligations where the seller or supplier does not perform his;

(p) giving the seller or supplier the possibility of transferring his rights and obligations under the contract, where this may serve to reduce the guarantees for the consumer, without the latter's agreement;

(q) excluding or hindering the consumer's right to take legal action or exercise any other legal remedy, particularly by requiring the consumer to take disputes exclusively to arbitration not covered by legal provisions, unduly restricting the evidence available to him or imposing on him a burden of proof which, according to the applicable law, should lie with another party to the contract.

2. Scope of subparagraphs (g), (j) and (l)[:]

(a) Subparagraph (g) is without hindrance to terms by which a supplier of financial services reserves the right to terminate unilaterally a contract of indeterminate duration without notice where there is a valid reason, provided that the supplier is required to inform the other contracting party or parties thereof immediately.

(b) Subparagraph (j) is without hindrance to terms under which a supplier of financial services reserves the right to alter the rate of interest payable by the consumer or due to the latter, or the amount of other charges for financial services without notice where there is a valid reason, provided that the supplier is required to inform the other contracting party or parties thereof at the earliest opportunity and that the latter are free to dissolve the contract immediately.

Subparagraph (j) is also without hindrance to terms under which a seller or supplier reserves the right to alter unilaterally the conditions of a contract of indeterminate duration, provided that he is required to inform the consumer with reasonable notice and that the consumer is free to dissolve the contract.

(c) Subparagraphs (g), (j) and (l) do not apply to:
— transactions in transferable securities, financial instruments and other products or services where the price is linked to fluctuations in a stock exchange quotation or index or a financial market rate that the seller or supplier does not control;
— contracts for the purchase or sale of foreign currency, traveller's cheques or international money orders denominated in foreign currency;

(d) Subparagraph (l) is without hindrance to price-indexation clauses, where lawful, provided that the method by which prices vary is explicitly described.

29

Directive 2005/29 Concerning Unfair Business-to-Consumer Commercial Practices in the Internal Market ('Unfair Commercial Practices Directive')

Contents

THE EUROPEAN PARLIAMENT AND THE COUNCIL OF THE EUROPEAN UNION,
Having regard to the Treaty [on the Functioning of the European Union], and in particular Article [114] thereof,
Having regard to the proposal from the Commission,
Having regard to the opinion of the European Economic and Social Committee,
Acting in accordance with the procedure laid down in Article [294] of the Treaty ...
HAVE ADOPTED THIS DIRECTIVE:

Chapter 1 General Provisions

Article 1
Purpose
The purpose of this Directive is to contribute to the proper functioning of the internal market and achieve a high level of consumer protection by approximating the laws, regulations and administrative provisions of the Member States on unfair commercial practices harming consumers' economic interests.

Article 2
Definitions
For the purposes of this Directive:

(a) 'consumer' means any natural person who, in commercial practices covered by this Directive, is acting for purposes which are outside his trade, business, craft or profession;

(b) 'trader' means any natural or legal person who, in commercial practices covered by this Directive, is acting for purposes relating to his trade, business, craft or profession and anyone acting in the name of or on behalf of a trader;

(c) 'product' means any goods or service including immovable property, rights and obligations;

(d) 'business-to-consumer commercial practices' (hereinafter also referred to as commercial practices) means any act, omission, course of conduct or representation, commercial communication including advertising and marketing, by a trader, directly connected with the promotion, sale or supply of a product to consumers;

(e) 'to materially distort the economic behaviour of consumers' means using a commercial practice to appreciably impair the consumer's ability to make an informed decision, thereby causing the consumer to take a transactional decision that he would not have taken otherwise;

(f) 'code of conduct' means an agreement or set of rules not imposed by law, regulation or administrative provision of a Member State which defines the behaviour of traders who undertake to be bound by the code in relation to one or more particular commercial practices or business sectors;

(g) 'code owner' means any entity, including a trader or group of traders, which is responsible for the formulation and revision of a code of conduct and/or for monitoring compliance with the code by those who have undertaken to be bound by it;

(h) 'professional diligence' means the standard of special skill and care which a trader may reasonably be expected to exercise towards consumers, commensurate with honest market practice and/or the general principle of good faith in the trader's field of activity;

(i) 'invitation to purchase' means a commercial communication which indicates characteristics of the product and the price in a way appropriate to the means of the commercial communication used and thereby enables the consumer to make a purchase;

(j) 'undue influence' means exploiting a position of power in relation to the consumer so as to apply pressure, even without using or threatening to use physical force, in a way which significantly limits the consumer's ability to make an informed decision;

(k) 'transactional decision' means any decision taken by a consumer concerning whether, how and on what terms to purchase, make payment in whole or in part for, retain or dispose of a product or to exercise a contractual right in relation to the product, whether the consumer decides to act or to refrain from acting;

(l) 'regulated profession' means a professional activity or a group of professional activities, access to which or the pursuit of which, or one of the modes of pursuing which, is conditional, directly or indirectly, upon possession of specific professional qualifications, pursuant to laws, regulations or administrative provisions.

Article 3
Scope

1. This Directive shall apply to unfair business-to-consumer commercial practices, as laid down in Article 5, before, during and after a commercial transaction in relation to a product.

29

2. This Directive is without prejudice to contract law and, in particular, to the rules on the validity, formation or effect of a contract.

3. This Directive is without prejudice to [Union] or national rules relating to the health and safety aspects of products.

4. In the case of conflict between the provisions of this Directive and other [Union] rules regulating specific aspects of unfair commercial practices, the latter shall prevail and apply to those specific aspects.

5. For a period of six years from 12 June 2007, Member States shall be able to continue to apply national provisions within the field approximated by this Directive which are more restrictive or prescriptive than this Directive and which implement directives containing minimum harmonisation clauses. These measures must be essential to ensure that consumers are adequately protected against unfair commercial practices and must be proportionate to the attainment of this objective. The review referred to in Article 18 may, if considered appropriate, include a proposal to prolong this derogation for a further limited period.

6. Member States shall notify the Commission without delay of any national provisions applied on the basis of paragraph 5.

7. This Directive is without prejudice to the rules determining the jurisdiction of the courts.

8. This Directive is without prejudice to any conditions of establishment or of authorisation regimes, or to the deontological codes of conduct or other specific rules governing regulated professions in order to uphold high standards of integrity on the part of the professional, which Member States may, in conformity with [Union] law, impose on professionals.

9. In relation to 'financial services', as defined in Directive 2002/65/EC, and immovable property, Member States may impose requirements which are more restrictive or prescriptive than this Directive in the field which it approximates.

10. This Directive shall not apply to the application of the laws, regulations and administrative provisions of Member States relating to the certification and indication of the standard of fineness of articles of precious metal.

Article 4
Internal market

Member States shall neither restrict the freedom to provide services nor restrict the free movement of goods for reasons falling within the field approximated by this Directive.

Chapter 2 Unfair Commercial Practices

Article 5
Prohibition of unfair commercial practices

1. Unfair commercial practices shall be prohibited.

2. A commercial practice shall be unfair if:

   (a) it is contrary to the requirements of professional diligence, and

   (b) it materially distorts or is likely to materially distort the economic behaviour with regard to the product of the average consumer whom it reaches or to whom it is addressed, or of the average member of the group when a commercial practice is directed to a particular group of consumers.

3. Commercial practices which are likely to materially distort the economic behaviour only of a clearly identifiable group of consumers who are particularly vulnerable to the practice or the underlying product because of their mental or physical infirmity, age or credulity in a way which the trader could reasonably be expected to foresee, shall be assessed from the perspective of the average member of that group. This is without prejudice to the common and legitimate advertising practice of making exaggerated statements or statements which are not meant to be taken literally.

4. In particular, commercial practices shall be unfair which:
   (a) are misleading as set out in Articles 6 and 7, or
   (b) are aggressive as set out in Articles 8 and 9.

5. Annex I contains the list of those commercial practices which shall in all circumstances be regarded as unfair. The same single list shall apply in all Member States and may only be modified by revision of this Directive.

SECTION 1 MISLEADING COMMERCIAL PRACTICES

Article 6
Misleading actions

1. A commercial practice shall be regarded as misleading if it contains false information and is therefore untruthful or in any way, including overall presentation, deceives or is likely to deceive the average consumer, even if the information is factually correct, in relation to one or more of the following elements, and in either case causes or is likely to cause him to take a transactional decision that he would not have taken otherwise:
   (a) the existence or nature of the product;
   (b) the main characteristics of the product, such as its availability, benefits, risks, execution, composition, accessories, after-sale customer assistance and complaint handling, method and date of manufacture or provision, delivery, fitness for purpose, usage, quantity, specification, geographical or commercial origin or the results to be expected from its use, or the results and material features of tests or checks carried out on the product;
   (c) the extent of the trader's commitments, the motives for the commercial practice and the nature of the sales process, any statement or symbol in relation to direct or indirect sponsorship or approval of the trader or the product;
   (d) the price or the manner in which the price is calculated, or the existence of a specific price advantage;
   (e) the need for a service, part, replacement or repair;
   (f) the nature, attributes and rights of the trader or his agent, such as his identity and assets, his qualifications, status, approval, affiliation or connection and ownership of industrial, commercial or intellectual property rights or his awards and distinctions;
   (g) the consumer's rights, including the right to replacement or reimbursement under Directive 1999/44/EC of the European Parliament and of the Council of 25 May 1999 on certain aspects of the sale of consumer goods and associated guarantees, or the risks he may face.

29

2. A commercial practice shall also be regarded as misleading if, in its factual context, taking account of all its features and circumstances, it causes or is likely to cause the average consumer to take a transactional decision that he would not have taken otherwise, and it involves:

    (a) any marketing of a product, including comparative advertising, which creates confusion with any products, trade marks, trade names or other distinguishing marks of a competitor;

    (b) non-compliance by the trader with commitments contained in codes of conduct by which the trader has undertaken to be bound, where:

        (i) the commitment is not aspirational but is firm and is capable of being verified, and

        (ii) the trader indicates in a commercial practice that he is bound by the code.

Article 7
Misleading omissions

1. A commercial practice shall be regarded as misleading if, in its factual context, taking account of all its features and circumstances and the limitations of the communication medium, it omits material information that the average consumer needs, according to the context, to take an informed transactional decision and thereby causes or is likely to cause the average consumer to take a transactional decision that he would not have taken otherwise.

2. It shall also be regarded as a misleading omission when, taking account of the matters described in paragraph 1, a trader hides or provides in an unclear, unintelligible, ambiguous or untimely manner such material information as referred to in that paragraph or fails to identify the commercial intent of the commercial practice if not already apparent from the context, and where, in either case, this causes or is likely to cause the average consumer to take a transactional decision that he would not have taken otherwise.

3. Where the medium used to communicate the commercial practice imposes limitations of space or time, these limitations and any measures taken by the trader to make the information available to consumers by other means shall be taken into account in deciding whether information has been omitted.

4. In the case of an invitation to purchase, the following information shall be regarded as material, if not already apparent from the context:

    (a) the main characteristics of the product, to an extent appropriate to the medium and the product;

    (b) the geographical address and the identity of the trader, such as his trading name and, where applicable, the geographical address and the identity of the trader on whose behalf he is acting;

    (c) the price inclusive of taxes, or where the nature of the product means that the price cannot reasonably be calculated in advance, the manner in which the price is calculated, as well as, where appropriate, all additional freight, delivery or postal charges or, where these charges cannot reasonably be calculated in advance, the fact that such additional charges may be payable;

(d) the arrangements for payment, delivery, performance and the complaint handling policy, if they depart from the requirements of professional diligence;

(e) for products and transactions involving a right of withdrawal or cancellation, the existence of such a right.

5. Information requirements established by [Union] law in relation to commercial communication including advertising or marketing, a non-exhaustive list of which is contained in Annex II, shall be regarded as material.

SECTION 2 AGGRESSIVE COMMERCIAL PRACTICES

Article 8

Aggressive commercial practices

A commercial practice shall be regarded as aggressive if, in its factual context, taking account of all its features and circumstances, by harassment, coercion, including the use of physical force, or undue influence, it significantly impairs or is likely to significantly impair the average consumer's freedom of choice or conduct with regard to the product and thereby causes him or is likely to cause him to take a transactional decision that he would not have taken otherwise.

Article 9

Use of harassment, coercion and undue influence

In determining whether a commercial practice uses harassment, coercion, including the use of physical force, or undue influence, account shall be taken of:

(a) its timing, location, nature or persistence;

(b) the use of threatening or abusive language or behaviour;

(c) the exploitation by the trader of any specific misfortune or circumstance of such gravity as to impair the consumer's judgement, of which the trader is aware, to influence the consumer's decision with regard to the product;

(d) any onerous or disproportionate non-contractual barriers imposed by the trader where a consumer wishes to exercise rights under the contract, including rights to terminate a contract or to switch to another product or another trader;

(e) any threat to take any action that cannot legally be taken.

Chapter 3 Codes of Conduct

Article 10

Codes of conduct

This Directive does not exclude the control, which Member States may encourage, of unfair commercial practices by code owners and recourse to such bodies by the persons or organisations referred to in Article 11 if proceedings before such bodies are in addition to the court or administrative proceedings referred to in that Article.

Recourse to such control bodies shall never be deemed the equivalent of foregoing a means of judicial or administrative recourse as provided for in Article 11.

Chapter 4 Final Provisions

Article 11
Enforcement
1. Member States shall ensure that adequate and effective means exist to combat unfair commercial practices in order to enforce compliance with the provisions of this Directive in the interest of consumers.

   Such means shall include legal provisions under which persons or organisations regarded under national law as having a legitimate interest in combating unfair commercial practices, including competitors, may:
   (a) take legal action against such unfair commercial practices; and/or
   (b) bring such unfair commercial practices before an administrative authority competent either to decide on complaints or to initiate appropriate legal proceedings.
   It shall be for each Member State to decide which of these facilities shall be available and whether to enable the courts or administrative authorities to require prior recourse to other established means of dealing with complaints, including those referred to in Article 10. These facilities shall be available regardless of whether the consumers affected are in the territory of the Member State where the trader is located or in another Member State.

   It shall be for each Member State to decide:
   (a) whether these legal facilities may be directed separately or jointly against a number of traders from the same economic sector; and
   (b) whether these legal facilities may be directed against a code owner where the relevant code promotes non-compliance with legal requirements.
2. Under the legal provisions referred to in paragraph 1, Member States shall confer upon the courts or administrative authorities powers enabling them, in cases where they deem such measures to be necessary taking into account all the interests involved and in particular the public interest:
   (a) to order the cessation of, or to institute appropriate legal proceedings for an order for the cessation of, unfair commercial practices; or
   (b) if the unfair commercial practice has not yet been carried out but is imminent, to order the prohibition of the practice, or to institute appropriate legal proceedings for an order for the prohibition of the practice,
   even without proof of actual loss or damage or of intention or negligence on the part of the trader.

   Member States shall also make provision for the measures referred to in the first subparagraph to be taken under an accelerated procedure:
   — either with interim effect,
   or
   — with definitive effect,
   on the understanding that it is for each Member State to decide which of the two options to select.

   Furthermore, Member States may confer upon the courts or administrative authorities powers enabling them, with a view to eliminating the continuing effects of unfair commercial practices the cessation of which has been ordered by a final decision:

(a) to require publication of that decision in full or in part and in such form as they deem adequate;

(b) to require in addition the publication of a corrective statement.

3. The administrative authorities referred to in paragraph 1 must:

(a) be composed so as not to cast doubt on their impartiality;

(b) have adequate powers, where they decide on complaints, to monitor and enforce the observance of their decisions effectively;

(c) normally give reasons for their decisions.

Where the powers referred to in paragraph 2 are exercised exclusively by an administrative authority, reasons for its decisions shall always be given. Furthermore, in this case, provision must be made for procedures whereby improper or unreasonable exercise of its powers by the administrative authority or improper or unreasonable failure to exercise the said powers can be the subject of judicial review.

Article 12

Courts and administrative authorities: substantiation of claims

Member States shall confer upon the courts or administrative authorities powers enabling them in the civil or administrative proceedings provided for in Article 11:

(a) to require the trader to furnish evidence as to the accuracy of factual claims in relation to a commercial practice if, taking into account the legitimate interest of the trader and any other party to the proceedings, such a requirement appears appropriate on the basis of the circumstances of the particular case; and

(b) to consider factual claims as inaccurate if the evidence demanded in accordance with (a) is not furnished or is deemed insufficient by the court or administrative authority.

Article 13

Penalties

Member States shall lay down penalties for infringements of national provisions adopted in application of this Directive and shall take all necessary measures to ensure that these are enforced. These penalties must be effective, proportionate and dissuasive.

Article 14

Amendments to Directive 84/450/EEC

Directive 84/450/EEC is hereby amended as follows:

1. Article 1 shall be replaced by the following:

'Article 1

The purpose of this Directive is to protect traders against misleading advertising and the unfair consequences thereof and to lay down the conditions under which comparative advertising is permitted.';

2. in Article 2:

— point 3 shall be replaced by the following:

'3. "trader" means any natural or legal person who is acting for purposes relating to his trade, craft, business or profession and any one acting in the name of or on behalf of a trader.',

29

— the following point shall be added:

'4. "code owner" means any entity, including a trader or group of traders, which is responsible for the formulation and revision of a code of conduct and/or for monitoring compliance with the code by those who have undertaken to be bound by it.';

3. Article 3a shall be replaced by the following:

'Article 3a

1. Comparative advertising shall, as far as the comparison is concerned, be permitted when the following conditions are met:

(a) it is not misleading within the meaning of Articles 2(2), 3 and 7(1) of this Directive or Articles 6 and 7 of Directive 2005/29/EC of the European Parliament and of the Council of 11 May 2005 concerning unfair business-to-consumer commercial practices in the internal market;

(b) it compares goods or services meeting the same needs or intended for the same purpose;

(c) it objectively compares one or more material, relevant, verifiable and representative features of those goods and services, which may include price;

(d) it does not discredit or denigrate the trade marks, trade names, other distinguishing marks, goods, services, activities, or circumstances of a competitor;

(e) for products with designation of origin, it relates in each case to products with the same designation;

(f) it does not take unfair advantage of the reputation of a trade mark, trade name or other distinguishing marks of a competitor or of the designation of origin of competing products;

(g) it does not present goods or services as imitations or replicas of goods or services bearing a protected trade mark or trade name;

(h) it does not create confusion among traders, between the advertiser and a competitor or between the advertiser's trade marks, trade names, other distinguishing marks, goods or services and those of a competitor.'

4. Article 4(1) shall be replaced by the following:

'1. Member States shall ensure that adequate and effective means exist to combat misleading advertising in order to enforce compliance with the provisions on comparative advertising in the interest of traders and competitors. Such means shall include legal provisions under which persons or organisations regarded under national law as having a legitimate interest in combating misleading advertising or regulating comparative advertising may:

(a) take legal action against such advertising; or

(b) bring such advertising before an administrative authority competent either to decide on complaints or to initiate appropriate legal proceedings.

It shall be for each Member State to decide which of these facilities shall be available and whether to enable the courts or administrative authorities to require prior recourse to other established means of dealing with complaints, including those referred to in Article 5.

29

It shall be for each Member State to decide:

(a) whether these legal facilities may be directed separately or jointly against a number of traders from the same economic sector; and

(b) whether these legal facilities may be directed against a code owner where the relevant code promotes non-compliance with legal requirements.';

5. Article 7(1) shall be replaced by the following:

'1. This Directive shall not preclude Member States from retaining or adopting provisions with a view to ensuring more extensive protection, with regard to misleading advertising, for traders and competitors.'

Article 15

Amendments to Directives 97/7/EC and 2002/65/EC

1. Article 9 of Directive 97/7/EC shall be replaced by the following:

'Article 9

Inertia selling

Given the prohibition of inertia selling practices laid down in Directive 2005/29/EC of 11 May 2005 of the European Parliament and of the Council concerning unfair business-to-consumer commercial practices in the internal market, Member States shall take the measures necessary to exempt the consumer from the provision of any consideration in cases of unsolicited supply, the absence of a response not constituting consent.'

2. Article 9 of Directive 2002/65/EC shall be replaced by the following:

'Article 9

Given the prohibition of inertia selling practices laid down in Directive 2005/29/EC of 11 May 2005 of the European Parliament and of the Council concerning unfair business-to-consumer commercial practices in the internal market and without prejudice to the provisions of Member States' legislation on the tacit renewal of distance contracts, when such rules permit tacit renewal, Member States shall take measures to exempt the consumer from any obligation in the event of unsolicited supplies, the absence of a reply not constituting consent.'

Article 16

Amendments to Directive 98/27/EC and Regulation (EC) No. 2006/2004

1. In the Annex to Directive 98/27/EC, point 1 shall be replaced by the following:

'1. Directive 2005/29/EC of the European Parliament and of the Council of 11 May 2005 concerning unfair business-to-consumer commercial practices in the internal market (OJ L 149, 11.6.2005, p. 22).'

2. In the Annex to Regulation (EC) No. 2006/2004 of the European Parliament and of the Council of 27 October 2004 on cooperation between national authorities responsible for the enforcement of the consumer protection law (the Regulation on consumer protection cooperation) the following point shall be added:

'16. Directive 2005/29/EC of the European Parliament and of the Council of 11 May 2005 concerning unfair business-to-consumer commercial practices in the internal market (OJ L 149, 11.6.2005, p. 22).'

Article 17

Information

Member States shall take appropriate measures to inform consumers of the national law transposing this Directive and shall, where appropriate, encourage traders and code owners to inform consumers of their codes of conduct.

Article 18

Review

1. By 12 June 2011 the Commission shall submit to the European Parliament and the Council a comprehensive report on the application of this Directive, in particular of Articles 3(9) and 4 and Annex I, on the scope for further harmonisation and simplification of [Union] law relating to consumer protection, and, having regard to Article 3(5), on any measures that need to be taken at [Union] level to ensure that appropriate levels of consumer protection are maintained. The report shall be accompanied, if necessary, by a proposal to revise this Directive or other relevant parts of [Union] law.

2. The European Parliament and the Council shall endeavour to act, in accordance with the Treaty, within two years of the presentation by the Commission of any proposal submitted under paragraph 1.

Article 19

Transposition

Member States shall adopt and publish the laws, regulations and administrative provisions necessary to comply with this Directive by 12 June 2007. They shall forthwith inform the Commission thereof and inform the Commission of any subsequent amendments without delay.

They shall apply those measures by 12 December 2007. When Member States adopt those measures, they shall contain a reference to this Directive or be accompanied by such a reference on the occasion of their official publication. Member States shall determine how such reference is to be made.

Article 20

Entry into force

This Directive shall enter into force on the day following its publication in the *Official Journal of the European Union*.

Article 21

Addressees

This Directive is addressed to the Member States.

    (*Signatures omitted*)

ANNEX I COMMERCIAL PRACTICES WHICH ARE IN ALL CIRCUMSTANCES CONSIDERED UNFAIR

Misleading commercial practices

1. Claiming to be a signatory to a code of conduct when the trader is not.
2. Displaying a trust mark, quality mark or equivalent without having obtained the necessary authorisation.
3. Claiming that a code of conduct has an endorsement from a public or other body which it does not have.
4. Claiming that a trader (including his commercial practices) or a product has been approved, endorsed or authorised by a public or private body when he/it has not or making such a claim without complying with the terms of the approval, endorsement or authorisation.
5. Making an invitation to purchase products at a specified price without disclosing the existence of any reasonable grounds the trader may have for believing that he will not be able to offer for supply or to procure another trader to supply, those products or equivalent products at that price for a period that is, and in quantities that are, reasonable having regard to the product, the scale of advertising of the product and the price offered (bait advertising).
6. Making an invitation to purchase products at a specified price and then:
   (a) refusing to show the advertised item to consumers; or
   (b) refusing to take orders for it or deliver it within a reasonable time; or
   (c) demonstrating a defective sample of it,
   with the intention of promoting a different product (bait and switch).
7. Falsely stating that a product will only be available for a very limited time, or that it will only be available on particular terms for a very limited time, in order to elicit an immediate decision and deprive consumers of sufficient opportunity or time to make an informed choice.
8. Undertaking to provide after-sales service to consumers with whom the trader has communicated prior to a transaction in a language which is not an official language of the Member State where the trader is located and then making such service available only in another language without clearly disclosing this to the consumer before the consumer is committed to the transaction.
9. Stating or otherwise creating the impression that a product can legally be sold when it cannot.
10. Presenting rights given to consumers in law as a distinctive feature of the trader's offer.
11. Using editorial content in the media to promote a product where a trader has paid for the promotion without making that clear in the content or by images or sounds clearly identifiable by the consumer (advertorial). This is without prejudice to Council Directive 89/552/EEC.
12. Making a materially inaccurate claim concerning the nature and extent of the risk to the personal security of the consumer or his family if the consumer does not purchase the product.
13. Promoting a product similar to a product made by a particular manufacturer in such a manner as deliberately to mislead the consumer into believing that the product is made by that same manufacturer when it is not.

29

14. Establishing, operating or promoting a pyramid promotional scheme where a consumer gives consideration for the opportunity to receive compensation that is derived primarily from the introduction of other consumers into the scheme rather than from the sale or consumption of products.

15. Claiming that the trader is about to cease trading or move premises when he is not.

16. Claiming that products are able to facilitate winning in games of chance.

17. Falsely claiming that a product is able to cure illnesses, dysfunction or malformations.

18. Passing on materially inaccurate information on market conditions or on the possibility of finding the product with the intention of inducing the consumer to acquire the product at conditions less favourable than normal market conditions.

19 Claiming in a commercial practice to offer a competition or prize promotion without awarding the prizes described or a reasonable equivalent.

20. Describing a product as 'gratis', 'free', 'without charge' or similar if the consumer has to pay anything other than the unavoidable cost of responding to the commercial practice and collecting or paying for delivery of the item.

21. Including in marketing material an invoice or similar document seeking payment which gives the consumer the impression that he has already ordered the marketed product when he has not.

22. Falsely claiming or creating the impression that the trader is not acting for purposes relating to his trade, business, craft or profession, or falsely representing oneself as a consumer.

23. Creating the false impression that after-sales service in relation to a product is available in a Member State other than the one in which the product is sold.

Aggressive commercial practices

24. Creating the impression that the consumer cannot leave the premises until a contract is formed.

25. Conducting personal visits to the consumer's home ignoring the consumer's request to leave or not to return except in circumstances and to the extent justified, under national law, to enforce a contractual obligation.

26. Making persistent and unwanted solicitations by telephone, fax, e-mail or other remote media except in circumstances and to the extent justified under national law to enforce a contractual obligation. This is without prejudice to Article 10 of Directive 97/7/EC and Directives 95/46/EC and 2002/58/EC.

27. Requiring a consumer who wishes to claim on an insurance policy to produce documents which could not reasonably be considered relevant as to whether the claim was valid, or failing systematically to respond to pertinent correspondence, in order to dissuade a consumer from exercising his contractual rights.

28. Including in an advertisement a direct exhortation to children to buy advertised products or persuade their parents or other adults to buy advertised products for them. This provision is without prejudice to Article 16 of Directive 89/552/EEC on television broadcasting.

29. Demanding immediate or deferred payment for or the return or safekeeping of products supplied by the trader, but not solicited by the consumer except where the product is a substitute supplied in conformity with Article 7(3) of Directive 97/7/ EC (inertia selling).

29

30. Explicitly informing a consumer that if he does not buy the product or service, the trader's job or livelihood will be in jeopardy.

31. Creating the false impression that the consumer has already won, will win, or will on doing a particular act win, a prize or other equivalent benefit, when in fact either:
   — there is no prize or other equivalent benefit, or
   — taking any action in relation to claiming the prize or other equivalent benefit is subject to the consumer paying money or incurring a cost.

ANNEX II [UNION] LAW PROVISIONS SETTING OUT RULES FOR ADVERTISING AND COMMERCIAL COMMUNICATION

Articles 4 and 5 of Directive 97/7/EC

Article 3 of Council Directive 90/314/EEC of 13 June 1990 on package travel, package holidays and package tours

Article 3(3) of Directive 94/47/EC of the European Parliament and of the Council of 26 October 1994 on the protection of purchasers in respect of certain aspects of contracts relating to the purchase of a right to use immovable properties on a timeshare basis

Article 3(4) of Directive 98/6/EC of the European Parliament and of the Council of 16 February 1998 on consumer protection in the indication of the prices of products offered to consumers

Articles 86 to 100 of Directive 2001/83/EC of the European Parliament and of the Council of 6 November 2001 on the [Union] code relating to medicinal products for human use

Articles 5 and 6 of Directive 2000/31/EC of the European Parliament and of the Council of 8 June 2000 on certain legal aspects of information society services, in particular electronic commerce, in the Internal Market (Directive on electronic commerce)

Article 1(d) of Directive 98/7/EC of the European Parliament and of the Council of 16 February 1998 amending Council Directive 87/102/EEC for the approximation of the laws, regulations and administrative provisions of the Member States concerning consumer credit

Articles 3 and 4 of Directive 2002/65/EC Article 1(9) of Directive 2001/107/EC of the European Parliament and of the Council of 21 January 2002 amending Council Directive 85/611/EEC on the coordination of laws, regulations and administrative provisions relating to undertakings for collective investment in transferable securities (UCITS) with a view to regulating management companies and simplified prospectuses

Articles 12 and 13 of Directive 2002/92/EC of the European Parliament and of the Council of 9 December 2002 on insurance mediation

Article 36 of Directive 2002/83/EC of the European Parliament and of the Council of 5 November 2002 concerning life assurance

Article 19 of Directive 2004/39/EC of the European Parliament and of the Council of 21 April 2004 on markets in financial instruments

29

Articles 31 and 43 of Council Directive 92/49/EEC of 18 June 1992 on the coordination of laws, regulations and administrative provisions relating to direct insurance other than life assurance (third non-life insurance Directive)

Articles 5, 7 and 8 of Directive 2003/71/EC of the European Parliament and of the Council of 4 November 2003 on the prospectus to be published when securities are offered to the public or admitted to trading

30

Directive 85/374 on the Approximation of the Laws, Regulations and Administrative Provisions of the Member States Concerning Liability for Defective Products

THE COUNCIL OF THE EUROPEAN [UNION],

Having regard to the Treaty [on the Functioning of the European Union], and in particular Article [115] thereof,

Having regard to the proposal from the Commission,

Having regard to the opinion of the European Parliament,

Having regard to the opinion of the Economic and Social Committee ...

HAS ADOPTED THIS DIRECTIVE:

Article 1

The producer shall be liable for damage caused by a defect in his product.

Article 2

For the purpose of this Directive, 'product' means all movables even if incorporated into another movable or into an immovable. 'Product' includes electricity.

Article 3

1. 'Producer' means the manufacturer of a finished product, the producer of any raw material or the manufacturer of a component part and any person who, by putting his name, trade mark or other distinguishing feature on the product presents himself as its producer.
2. Without prejudice to the liability of the producer, any person who imports into the [Union] a product for sale, hire, leasing or any form of distribution in the course of his business shall be deemed to be a producer within the meaning of this Directive and shall be responsible as a producer.
3. Where the producer of the product cannot be identified, each supplier of the product shall be treated as its producer unless he informs the injured person, within a reasonable time, of the identity of the producer or of the person who supplied him with the product. The same shall apply, in the case of an imported product, if this product does not indicate the identity of the importer referred to in paragraph 2, even if the name of the producer is indicated.

Article 4

The injured person shall be required to prove the damage, the defect and the causal relationship between defect and damage.

30

Article 5

Where, as a result of the provisions of this Directive, two or more persons are liable for the same damage, they shall be liable jointly and severally, without prejudice to the provisions of national law concerning the rights of contribution or recourse.

Article 6

1. A product is defective when it does not provide the safety which a person is entitled to expect, taking all circumstances into account, including:
   (a) the presentation of the product;
   (b) the use to which it could reasonably be expected that the product would be put;
   (c) the time when the product was put into circulation.
2. A product shall not be considered defective for the sole reason that a better product is subsequently put into circulation.

Article 7

The producer shall not be liable as a result of this Directive if he proves:
   (a) that he did not put the product into circulation; or
   (b) that, having regard to the circumstances, it is probable that the defect which caused the damage did not exist at the time when the product was put into circulation by him or that this defect came into being afterwards; or
   (c) that the product was neither manufactured by him for sale or any form of distribution for economic purpose nor manufactured or distributed by him in the course of his business; or
   (d) that the defect is due to compliance of the product with mandatory regulations issued by the public authorities; or
   (e) that the state of scientific and technical knowledge at the time when he put the product into circulation was not such as to enable the existence of the defect to be discovered; or
   (f) in the case of a manufacturer of a component, that the defect is attributable to the design of the product in which the component has been fitted or to the instructions given by the manufacturer of the product.

Article 8

1. Without prejudice to the provisions of national law concerning the right of contribution or recourse, the liability of the producer shall not be reduced when the damage is caused both by a defect in product and by the act or omission of a third party.
2. The liability of the producer may be reduced or disallowed when, having regard to all the circumstances, the damage is caused both by a defect in the product and by the fault of the injured person or any person for whom the injured person is responsible.

Article 9

For the purpose of Article 1, 'damage' means:
   (a) damage caused by death or by personal injuries;
   (b) damage to, or destruction of, any item of property other than the defective product itself, with a lower threshold of 500 ECU, provided that the item of property:

(i) is of a type ordinarily intended for private use or consumption, and

(ii) was used by the injured person mainly for his own private use or consumption. This Article shall be without prejudice to national provisions relating to non-material damage.

Article 10

1. Member States shall provide in their legislation that a limitation period of three years shall apply to proceedings for the recovery of damages as provided for in this Directive. The limitation period shall begin to run from the day on which the plaintiff became aware, or should reasonably have become aware, of the damage, the defect and the identity of the producer.

2. The laws of Member States regulating suspension or interruption of the limitation period shall not be affected by this Directive.

Article 11

Member States shall provide in their legislation that the rights conferred upon the injured person pursuant to this Directive shall be extinguished upon the expiry of a period of 10 years from the date on which the producer put into circulation the actual product which caused the damage, unless the injured person has in the meantime instituted proceedings against the producer.

Article 12

The liability of the producer arising from this Directive may not, in relation to the injured person, be limited or excluded by a provision limiting his liability or exempting him from liability.

Article 13

This Directive shall not affect any rights which an injured person may have according to the rules of the law of contractual or non-contractual liability or a special liability system existing at the moment when this Directive is notified.

Article 14

This Directive shall not apply to injury or damage arising from nuclear accidents and covered by international conventions ratified by the Member States.

Article 15

1. Each Member State may:

   ——————

   (b) by way of derogation from Article 7(e), maintain or, subject to the procedure set out in paragraph 2 of this Article, provide in this legislation that the producer shall be liable even if he proves that the state of scientific and technical knowledge at the time when he put the product into circulation was not such as to enable the existence of a defect to be discovered.

2. A Member State wishing to introduce the measure specified in paragraph 1(b) shall communicate the text of the proposed measure to the Commission. The Commission shall inform the other Member States thereof.

30

The Member State concerned shall hold the proposed measure in abeyance for nine months after the Commission is informed and provided that in the meantime the Commission has not submitted to the Council a proposal amending this Directive on the relevant matter. However, if within three months of receiving the said information, the Commission does not advise the Member State concerned that it intends submitting such a proposal to the Council, the Member State may take the proposed measure immediately.

If the Commission does submit to the Council such a proposal amending this Directive within the aforementioned nine months, the Member State concerned shall hold the proposed measure in abeyance for a further period of 18 months from the date on which the proposal is submitted.

3. Ten years after the date of notification of this Directive, the Commission shall submit to the Council a report on the effect that rulings by the courts as to the application of Article 7(e) and of paragraph 1(b) of this Article have on consumer protection and the functioning of the common market. In the light of this report the Council, acting on a proposal from the Commission and pursuant to the terms of Article [115] of the Treaty, shall decide whether to repeal Article 7(e).

Article 16

1. Any Member State may provide that a producer's total liability for damage resulting from a death or personal injury and caused by identical items with the same defect shall be limited to an amount which may not be less than 70 million ECU.

2. Ten years after the date of notification of this Directive, the Commission shall submit to the Council a report on the effect on consumer protection and the functioning of the common market of the implementation of the financial limit on liability by those Member States which have used the option provided for in paragraph 1. In the light of this report the Council, acting on a proposal from the Commission and pursuant to the terms of Article [115] of the Treaty, shall decide whether to repeal paragraph 1.

Article 17

This Directive shall not apply to products put into circulation before the date on which the provisions referred to in Article 19 enter into force.

Article 18

1. For the purposes of this Directive, the ECU shall be that defined by Regulation (EEC) No. 3180/78, as amended by Regulation (EEC) No. 2626/84. The equivalent in national currency shall initially be calculated at the rate obtaining on the date of adoption of this Directive.

2. Every five years the Council, acting on a proposal from the Commission, shall examine and, if need be, revise the amounts in this Directive, in the light of economic and monetary trends in the [Union].

Article 19

1. Member States shall bring into force, not later than three years from the date of notification of this Directive, the laws, regulations and administrative provisions necessary to comply with this Directive. They shall forthwith inform the Commission thereof.
2. The procedure set out in Article 15(2) shall apply from the date of notification of this Directive.

Article 20

Member States shall communicate to the Commission the texts of the main provisions of national law which they subsequently adopt in the field governed by this Directive.

Article 21

Every five years the Commission shall present a report to the Council on the application of this Directive and, if necessary, shall submit appropriate proposals to it.

Article 22

This Directive is addressed to the Member States.

APPENDIX
United Kingdom Statutes on the European Union

A. EUROPEAN COMMUNITIES ACT 1972 (EXTRACTS)

2 General Implementation of Treaties

(1) All such rights, powers, liabilities, obligations and restrictions from time to time created or arising by or under the Treaties, and all such remedies and procedures from time to time provided for by or under the Treaties, as in accordance with the Treaties are without further enactment to be given legal effect or used in the United Kingdom shall be recognised and available in law, and be enforced, allowed and followed accordingly; and the expression enforceable EU right and similar expressions shall be read as referring to one to which this subsection applies.

(2) Subject to Schedule 2 to this Act, at any time after its passing Her Majesty may by Order in Council, and any designated Minister or department may by order, rules, regulations or scheme, make provision —

    (a) for the purpose of implementing any EU obligation of the United Kingdom, or enabling any such obligation to be implemented, or of enabling any rights enjoyed or to be enjoyed by the United Kingdom under or by virtue of the Treaties to be exercised; or

    (b) for the purpose of dealing with matters arising out of or related to any such obligation or rights or the coming into force, or the operation from time to time, of subsection (1) above;

and in the exercise of any statutory power or duty, including any power to give directions or to legislate by means of orders, rules, regulations or other subordinate instrument, the person entrusted with the power or duty may have regard to the objects of the EU and to any such obligation or rights as aforesaid.

In this subsection "designated Minister or department" means such Minister of the Crown or government department as may from time to time be designated by Order in Council in relation to any matter or for any purpose, but subject to such restrictions or conditions (if any) as may be specified by the Order in Council.

(3) There shall be charged on and issued out of the Consolidated Fund or, if so determined by the Treasury, the National Loans Fund the amounts required to meet any EU obligation to make payments to the EU or a member State, or any EU obligation in respect of contributions to the capital or reserves of the European Investment Bank or in respect of loans to the Bank, or to redeem any notes or obligations issued or created in respect of any such EU obligation and, except as otherwise provided by or under any enactment —

    (a) any other expenses incurred under or by virtue of the Treaties or this Act by any Minister of the Crown or government department may be paid out of moneys provided by Parliament; and

    (b) any sums received under or by virtue of the Treaties or this Act by any Minister of the Crown or government department, save for such sums as may be required for disbursements permitted by any other enactment, shall be paid into the Consolidated Fund or, if so determined by the Treasury, the National Loans Fund.

(4) The provision that may be made under subsection (2) above includes, subject to Schedule 2 to this Act, any such provision (of any such extent) as might be made by Act of Parliament, and any enactment passed or to be passed, other than one contained in this part of this Act, shall be construed and have effect subject to the foregoing provisions of this section; but, except as may be provided by any Act passed after this Act, Schedule 2 shall have effect in connection with the powers conferred by this and the following sections of this Act to make Orders in Council or orders, rules, regulations or schemes.

(5) … and the references in that subsection to a Minister of the Crown or government department and to a statutory power or duty shall include a Minister or department of the Government of Northern Ireland and a power or duty arising under or by virtue of an Act of the Parliament of Northern Ireland.

(6) A law passed by the legislature of any of the Channel Islands or of the Isle of Man, or a colonial Law (within the meaning of the Colonial Laws Validity Act 1865) passed or made for Gibraltar, if expressed to be passed or made in the implementation of the Treaties and of the obligations of the United Kingdom thereunder, shall not be void or inoperative by reason of any inconsistency with or repugnancy to an Act of Parliament, passed or to be passed, that extends to the Island or Gibraltar or any provision having the force and effect of an Act there (but not including this section), nor by reason of its having some operation outside the Island or Gibraltar; and any such Act or provision that extends to the Island or Gibraltar shall be construed and have effect subject to the provisions of any such law.

B. EUROPEAN UNION ACT 2011 (EXTRACTS)

2 Treaties Amending or Replacing TEU or TFEU

(1) A treaty which amends or replaces TEU or TFEU is not to be ratified unless —
   (a) a statement relating to the treaty was laid before Parliament in accordance with section 5,
   (b) the treaty is approved by Act of Parliament, and
   (c) the referendum condition or the exemption condition is met.

(2) The referendum condition is that —
   (a) the Act providing for the approval of the treaty provides that the provision approving the treaty is not to come into force until a referendum about whether the treaty should be ratified has been held throughout the United Kingdom or, where the treaty also affects Gibraltar, throughout the United Kingdom and Gibraltar,
   (b) the referendum has been held, and
   (c) the majority of those voting in the referendum are in favour of the ratification of the treaty.

(3) The exemption condition is that the Act providing for the approval of the treaty states that the treaty does not fall within section 4.

3 Amendment of TFEU under Simplified Revision Procedure

(1) Where the European Council has adopted an Article 48(6) decision subject to its approval by the member States, a Minister of the Crown may not confirm the approval of the decision by the United Kingdom unless —

    (a) a statement relating to the decision was laid before Parliament in accordance with section 5,

    (b) the decision is approved by Act of Parliament, and

    (c) the referendum condition, the exemption condition or the significance condition is met.

(2) The referendum condition is that —

    (a) the Act providing for the approval of the decision provides that the provision approving the decision is not to come into force until a referendum about whether the decision should be approved has been held throughout the United Kingdom or, where the decision also affects Gibraltar, throughout the United Kingdom and Gibraltar,

    (b) the referendum has been held, and

    (c) the majority of those voting in the referendum are in favour of the approval of the decision.

(3) The exemption condition is that the Act providing for the approval of the decision states that the decision does not fall within section 4.

(4) The significance condition is that the Act providing for the approval of the decision states that –

    (a) the decision falls within section 4 only because of provision of the kind mentioned in subsection (1)(i) or (j) of that section, and

    (b) the effect of that provision in relation to the United Kingdom is not significant.

4 Cases where Treaty or Article 48(6) Decision Attracts a Referendum

(1) Subject to subsection (4), a treaty or an Article 48(6) decision falls within this section if it involves one or more of the following —

    (a) the extension of the objectives of the EU as set out in Article 3 of TEU;

    (b) the conferring on the EU of a new exclusive competence;

    (c) the extension of an exclusive competence of the EU;

    (d) the conferring on the EU of a new competence shared with the member States;

    (e) the extension of any competence of the EU that is shared with the member States;

    (f) the extension of the competence of the EU in relation to —

       (i) the co-ordination of economic and employment policies, or

       (ii) common foreign and security policy;

    (g) the conferring on the EU of a new competence to carry out actions to support, co-ordinate or supplement the actions of member States;

    (h) the extension of a supporting, co-ordinating or supplementing competence of the EU;

    (i) the conferring on an EU institution or body of power to impose a requirement or obligation on the United Kingdom, or the removal of any limitation on any such power of an EU institution or body;

(j) the conferring on an EU institution or body of new or extended power to impose sanctions on the United Kingdom;

(k) any amendment of a provision listed in Schedule 1 that removes a requirement that anything should be done unanimously, by consensus or by common accord;

(l) any amendment of Article 31 (2) of TEU (decisions relating to common foreign and security policy to which qualified majority voting applies) that removes or amends the provision enabling a member of the Council to oppose the adoption of a decision to be taken by qualified majority voting;

(m) any amendment of any of the provisions specified in subsection (3) that removes or amends the provision enabling a member of the Council, in relation to a draft legislative act, to ensure the suspension of the ordinary legislative procedure.

(2) Any reference in subsection (1) to the extension of a competence includes a reference to the removal of a limitation on a competence.

(3) The provisions referred to in subsection (1)(m) are —

(a) Article 48 of TFEU (social security),

(b) Article 82(3) of TFEU (judicial co-operation in criminal matters), and

(c) Article 83(3) of TFEU (particularly serious crime with a cross-border dimension).

(4) A treaty or Article 48(6) decision does not fall within this section merely because it involves one or more of the following —

(a) the codification of practice under TEU or TFEU in relation to the previous exercise of an existing competence;

(b) the making of any provision that applies only to member States other than the United Kingdom;

(c) in the case of a treaty, the accession of a new member State.

5 Statement to be Laid Before Parliament

(1) If a treaty amending TEU or TFEU is agreed in an inter-governmental conference, a Minister of the Crown must lay the required statement before Parliament before the end of the 2 months beginning with the date on which the treaty is agreed.

(2) If an Article 48(6) decision is adopted by the European Council subject to its approval by the member States, a Minister of the Crown must lay the required statement before Parliament before the end of the 2 months beginning with the date on which the decision is adopted.

(3) The required statement is a statement as to whether, in the Minister's opinion, the treaty or Article 48(6) decision falls within section 4.

(4) If the Minister is of the opinion that an Article 48(6) decision falls within section 4 only because of provision of the kind mentioned in subsection (1)(i) or (j) of that section, the statement must indicate whether in the Minister's opinion the effect of that provision in relation to the United Kingdom is significant.

(5) The statement must give reasons for the Minister's opinion under subsection (3) and, if relevant, subsection (4).

(6) In relation to an Article 48(6) decision adopted by the European Council before the day on which this section comes into force ("the commencement date"), the condition in section 3(1)(a) is to be taken to be complied with if a statement under this section is laid before Parliament before the end of the 2 months beginning with the commencement date.

6 Decisions Requiring Approval by Act and by Referendum

(1) A Minister of the Crown may not vote in favour of or otherwise support a decision to which this subsection applies unless —
   (a) the draft decision is approved by Act of Parliament, and
   (b) the referendum condition is met.

(2) Where the European Council has recommended to the member States the adoption of a decision under Article 42(2) of TEU in relation to a common EU defence, a Minister of the Crown may not notify the European Council that the decision is adopted by the United Kingdom unless —
   (a) the decision is approved by Act of Parliament, and
   (b) the referendum condition is met.

(3) A Minister of the Crown may not give a notification under Article 4 of Protocol (No.21) on the position of the United Kingdom and Ireland in respect of the area of freedom, security and justice annexed to TEU and TFEU which relates to participation by the United Kingdom in a European Public Prosecutor's Office or an extension of the powers of that Office unless —
   (a) the notification has been approved by Act of Parliament, and
   (b) the referendum condition is met.

(4) The referendum condition is that set out in section 3(2), with references to a decision being read for the purposes of subsection (1) as references to a draft decision and for the purposes of subsection (3) as references to a notification.

(5) The decisions to which subsection (1) applies are —
   (a) a decision under the provision of Article 31(3) of TEU that permits the adoption of qualified majority voting;
   (b) a decision under Article 48(7) of TEU which in relation to any provision listed in Schedule 1 —
      (i) adopts qualified majority voting, or
      (ii) applies the ordinary legislative procedure in place of a special legislative procedure requiring the Council to act unanimously;
   (c) a decision under Article 86(1) of TFEU involving participation by the United Kingdom in a European Public Prosecutor's Office;
   (d) where the United Kingdom has become a participant in a European Public Prosecutor's Office, a decision under Article 86(4) of TFEU to extend the powers of that Office;
   (e) a decision under Article 140(3) of TFEU which would make the euro the currency of the United Kingdom;
   (f) a decision under the provision of Article 153(2) of TFEU (social policy) that permits the application of the ordinary legislative procedure in place of a special legislative procedure;

(g) a decision under the provision of Article 192(2) of TFEU (environment) that permits the application of the ordinary legislative procedure in place of a special legislative procedure;

(h) a decision under the provision of Article 312(2) of TFEU (EU finance) that permits the adoption of qualified majority voting;

(i) a decision under the provision of Article 333(1) of TFEU (enhanced co-operation) that permits the adoption of qualified majority voting, where the decision relates to a provision listed in Schedule 1 and the United Kingdom is a participant in the enhanced co-operation to which the decision relates;

(j) a decision under the provision of Article 333(2) of TFEU (enhanced cooperation) that permits the adoption of the ordinary legislative procedure in place of a special legislative procedure, where —

  (i) the decision relates to a provision listed in Schedule 1,

  (ii) the special legislative procedure requires the Council to act unanimously, and

  (iii) the United Kingdom is a participant in the enhanced co-operation to which the decision relates;

(k) a decision under Article 4 of the Schengen Protocol that removes any border control of the United Kingdom.

(6) In subsection (5)(k) "the Schengen Protocol" means the Protocol (No. 19) on the Schengen *acquis* integrated into the framework of the European Union, annexed to TEU and TFEU.

7 Decisions Requiring Approval by Act

(1) A Minister of the Crown may not confirm the approval by the United Kingdom of a decision to which this subsection applies unless the decision is approved by Act of Parliament.

(2) The decisions to which subsection (1) applies are —

(a) a decision under the provision of Article 25 of TFEU that permits the adoption of provisions to strengthen or add to the rights listed in Article 20(2) of that Treaty (rights of citizens of the European Union);

(b) a decision under the provision of Article 223(1) of TFEU that permits the laying down of the provisions necessary for the election of the members of the European Parliament in accordance with that Article;

(c) a decision under the provision of Article 262 of TFEU that permits the conferring of jurisdiction on the Court of Justice of the European Union in disputes relating to the application of acts adopted on the basis of the EU Treaties which create European intellectual property rights;

(d) a decision under the third paragraph of Article 311 of TFEU to adopt a decision laying down provisions relating to the system of own resources of the European Union.

(3) A Minister of the Crown may not vote in favour of or otherwise support a decision to which this subsection applies unless the draft decision is approved by Act of Parliament.

(4) The decisions to which subsection (3) applies are —

(a) a decision under the provision of Article 17(5) of TEU that permits the alteration of the number of members of the European Commission;

(b) a decision under Article 48(7) of TEU which in relation to any provision not listed in Schedule 1 —

   (i) adopts qualified majority voting, or

   (ii) applies the ordinary legislative procedure in place of a special legislative procedure requiring the Council to act unanimously;

(c) a decision under the provision of Article 64(3) of TFEU that permits the adoption of measures which constitute a step backwards in European Union law as regards the liberalisation of the movement of capital to or from third countries;

(d) a decision under the provision of Article 126(14) of TFEU that permits the adoption of provisions to replace the Protocol (No. 12) on the excessive deficit procedure annexed to TEU and TFEU;

(e) a decision under the provision of Article 333(1) of TFEU (enhanced cooperation) that permits the adoption of qualified majority voting, where the decision relates to a provision not listed in Schedule 1 and the United Kingdom is a participant in the enhanced co-operation to which the decision relates;

(f) a decision under the provision of Article 333(2) of TFEU (enhanced cooperation) that permits the adoption of the ordinary legislative procedure in place of a special legislative procedure, where —

   (i) the decision relates to a provision not listed in Schedule 1,

   (ii) the special legislative procedure requires the Council to act unanimously, and

   (iii) the United Kingdom is a participant in the enhanced co-operation to which the decision relates.

8 Decisions under Article 352 of TFEU

(1) A Minister of the Crown may not vote in favour of or otherwise support an Article 352 decision unless one of subsections (3) to (5) is complied with in relation to the draft decision.

(2) An Article 352 decision is a decision under the provision of Article 352 of TFEU that permits the adoption of measures to attain one of the objectives set out in the EU Treaties (but for which those Treaties have not provided the necessary powers).

(3) This subsection is complied with if a draft decision is approved by Act of Parliament.

(4) This subsection is complied with if —

(a) in each House of Parliament a Minister of the Crown moves a motion that the House approves Her Majesty's Government's intention to support a specified draft decision and is of the opinion that the measure to which it relates is required as a matter of urgency, and

(b) each House agrees to the motion without amendment.

(5) This subsection is complied with if a Minister of the Crown has laid before Parliament a statement specifying a draft decision and stating that in the opinion of the Minister the decision relates only to one or more exempt purposes.

(6) The exempt purposes are —

(a) to make provision equivalent to that made by a measure previously adopted under Article 352 of TFEU, other than an excepted measure;

(b) to prolong or renew a measure previously adopted under that Article, other than an excepted measure;

(c) to extend a measure previously adopted under that Article to another member State or other country;

(d) to repeal existing measures adopted under that Article;

(e) to consolidate existing measures adopted under that Article without any change of substance.

(7) In subsection (6)(a) and (b), "excepted measure" means a measure adopted after the commencement of this section and resulting from a decision in relation to which a Minister of the Crown had relied on compliance with subsection (4).

9 Approval Required in Connection with Title V of Part 3 of TFEU

(1) A Minister of the Crown may not give a notification to which this subsection applies unless Parliamentary approval has been given in accordance with subsection (3).

(2) Subsection (1) applies in relation to a notification under Article 3 of Protocol (No. 21) on the position of the United Kingdom and Ireland in respect of the area of freedom, security and justice annexed to TEU and TFEU (the "AFSJ Protocol") that the United Kingdom wishes to take part in the adoption and application of a measure proposed under any of the following —

(a) the provision of Article 81(3) of TFEU (family law) that permits the application of the ordinary legislative procedure in place of a special legislative procedure;

(b) the provision of Article 82(2)(d) of TFEU (criminal procedure) that permits the identification of further specific aspects of criminal procedure to which directives adopted under the ordinary legislative procedure may relate;

(c) the provision of Article 83(1) of TFEU (particularly serious crime with a cross-border dimension) that permits the identification of further areas of crime to which directives adopted under the ordinary legislative procedure may relate.

(3) Parliamentary approval is given if —

(a) in each House of Parliament a Minister of the Crown moves a motion that the House approves Her Majesty's Government's intention to give a notification in respect of a specified measure, and

(b) each House agrees to the motion without amendment.

(4) Despite any Parliamentary approval given for the purposes of subsection (1), a Minister may not vote in favour of or otherwise support a decision under a provision falling within any of paragraphs (a) to (c) of subsection (2) unless the draft decision is approved by Act of Parliament.

(5) A Minister of the Crown may not give a notification under Article 4 of the AFSJ Protocol that the United Kingdom wishes to accept a measure to which this subsection applies unless the notification in respect of the measure has been approved by Act of Parliament.

(6) The measures to which subsection (5) applies are —

    (a) a measure adopted under a provision described in any of paragraphs (a) to (c) of subsection (2), or

    (b) a measure established under Article 81(3), 82(2)(d) or 83(1) of TFEU by virtue of a previous decision adopted, without the participation of the United Kingdom, under a provision falling within any of those paragraphs.

10 Parliamentary Control of Certain Decisions Not Requiring Approval by Act

(1) A Minister of the Crown may not vote in favour of or otherwise support a decision under any of the following unless Parliamentary approval has been given in accordance with this section —

    (a) the provision of Article 56 of TFEU that permits the extension of the provisions of Chapter 3 of Title IV of Part 3 of that Treaty (free movement of services) to nationals of a third country;

    (b) Article 129(3) of TFEU (amendment of provisions of the Statute of the European System of Central Banks or of the European Central Bank);

    (c) the provision of Article 252 of TFEU that permits an increase in the number of Advocates-General;

    (d) the provision of Article 257 of TFEU that permits the establishment of specialised courts attached to the General Court;

    (e) the provision of Article 281 of TFEU that permits the amendment of the Statute of the Court of Justice of the European Union;

    (f) the provision of Article 308 of TFEU that permits the amendment of the Statute of the European Investment Bank.

(2) A Minister of the Crown may not vote in favour of or otherwise support a decision to which this subsection applies unless Parliamentary approval has been given in accordance with this section.

(3) Subsection (2) applies to a decision under Article 48(7) of TEU which in relation to a provision of TFEU applies the ordinary legislative procedure in place of a special legislative procedure not requiring the Council to act unanimously.

(4) A Minister of the Crown may not confirm the approval by the United Kingdom of a decision under Article 218(8) of TFEU for the accession of the European Union to the European Convention for the Protection of Human Rights and Fundamental Freedoms in accordance with Article 6(2) of TEU unless Parliamentary approval has been given in accordance with this section.

(5) Parliamentary approval is given if —

    (a) in each House of Parliament a Minister of the Crown moves a motion that the House approves Her Majesty's Government's intention to support the adoption of a specified draft decision, and

    (b) each House agrees to the motion without amendment....

18 Status of EU Law Dependent on Continuing Statutory Basis

Directly applicable or directly effective EU law (that is, the rights, powers, liabilities, obligations, restrictions, remedies and procedures referred to in section 2(1) of the European

Communities Act 1972) falls to be recognised and available in law in the United Kingdom only by virtue of that Act or where it is required to be recognised and available in law by virtue of any other Act.

C. EUROPEAN UNION (NOTIFICATION OF WITHDRAWAL) ACT 2017 (EXTRACTS)

1 Power to Notify Withdrawal from the EU

(1) The Prime Minister may notify, under Article 50(2) of the Treaty on European Union, the United Kingdom's intention to withdraw from the EU.

(2) This section has effect despite any provision made by or under the European Communities Act 1972 or any other enactment.

D. CONSTITUTIONAL REFORM AND GOVERNANCE ACT 2010 (EXTRACTS)

20 Treaties to be Laid Before Parliament Before Ratification

(1) Subject to what follows, a treaty is not to be ratified unless —
  (a) a Minister of the Crown has laid before Parliament a copy of the treaty,
  (b) the treaty has been published in a way that a Minister of the Crown thinks appropriate, and
  (c) period A has expired without either House having resolved, within period A, that the treaty should not be ratified.

(2) Period A is the period of 21 sitting days beginning with the first sitting day after the date on which the requirement in subsection (1)(a) is met.

(3) Subsections (4) to (6) apply if the House of Commons resolved as mentioned in subsection (1)(c) (whether or not the House of Lords also did so).

(4) The treaty may be ratified if —
  (a) a Minister of the Crown has laid before Parliament a statement indicating that the Minister is of the opinion that the treaty should nevertheless be ratified and explaining why, and
  (b) period B has expired without the House of Commons having resolved, within period B, that the treaty should not be ratified.

(5) Period B is the period of 21 sitting days beginning with the first sitting day after the date on which the requirement in subsection (4)(a) is met.

(6) A statement may be laid under subsection (4)(a) in relation to the treaty on more than one occasion.

(7) Subsection (8) applies if —
  (a) the House of Lords resolved as mentioned in subsection (1)(c), but
  (b) the House of Commons did not.

(8) The treaty may be ratified if a Minister of the Crown has laid before Parliament a statement indicating that the Minister is of the opinion that the treaty should nevertheless be ratified and explaining why.

(9) "Sitting day" means a day on which both Houses of Parliament sit.

21 Extension of 21 Sitting Day Period

(1) A Minister of the Crown may, in relation to a treaty, extend the period mentioned in section 20(1)(c) by 21 sitting days or less.

(2) The Minister does that by laying before Parliament a statement —
   (a) indicating that the period is to be extended, and
   (b) setting out the length of the extension.

(3) The statement must be laid before the period would have expired without the extension.

(4) The Minister must publish the statement in a way the Minister thinks appropriate.

(5) The period may be extended more than once.

22 Section 20 Not to Apply in Exceptional Cases

(1) Section 20 does not apply to a treaty if a Minister of the Crown is of the opinion that, exceptionally, the treaty should be ratified without the requirements of that section having been met.

(2) But a treaty may not be ratified by virtue of subsection (1) after either House has resolved, as mentioned in section 20(1)(c), that the treaty should not be ratified.

(3) If a Minister determines that a treaty is to be ratified by virtue of subsection (1), the Minister must, either before or as soon as practicable after the treaty is ratified —
   (a) lay before Parliament a copy of the treaty,
   (b) arrange for the treaty to be published in a way that the Minister thinks appropriate, and
   (c) lay before Parliament a statement indicating that the Minister is of the opinion mentioned in subsection (1) and explaining why.

23 Section 20 Not to Apply to Certain Descriptions of Treaties

(1) Section 20 does not apply to —
   (a) ……………………………..
   (b) a treaty covered by section 5 of the European Union (Amendment) Act 2008 (treaty amending Treaty establishing European Atomic Energy Community not to be ratified unless approved by Act of Parliament)[;]
   (c) a treaty that is subject to a requirement imposed by Part 1 of the European Union Act 2011 (restrictions on treaties and decisions relating to EU).

(2) Section 20 does not apply to a treaty in relation to which an Order in Council may be made under one or more of the following —
   (a) section 158 of the Inheritance Tax Act 1984 (double taxation conventions);
   (b) section 2 of the Taxation (International and Other Provisions) Act 2010 (double taxation arrangements);
   (c) section 173 of the Finance Act 2006 (international tax enforcement arrangements).

(2A) Section 20 does not apply to a treaty in relation to which an order may be made under paragraph 66 of Schedule 19 to the Finance Act 2011 (bank levy: arrangements affording double taxation relief).

(2B) Section 20 does not apply to any treaty referred to in section 218(1) of the Finance Act 2012.

(3) Section 20 does not apply to a treaty concluded (under authority given by the government of the United Kingdom) by the government of a British overseas territory, of any of the Channel Islands or of the Isle of Man.

(4) Section 20 does not apply to a treaty a copy of which is presented to Parliament by command of Her Majesty before that section comes into force.

24 Explanatory Memoranda

In laying a treaty before Parliament under this Part, a Minister shall accompany the treaty with an explanatory memorandum explaining the provisions of the treaty, the reasons for Her Majesty's Government seeking ratification of the treaty, and such other matters as the Minister considers appropriate.

25 Meaning of "Treaty" and "Ratification"

(1) In this Part "treaty" means a written agreement —
    (a) between States or between States and international organisations, and
    (b) binding under international law.

(2) But "treaty" does not include a regulation, rule, measure, decision or similar instrument made under a treaty (other than one that amends or replaces the treaty (in whole or in part)).

(3) In this Part a reference to ratification of a treaty is a reference to an act of a kind specified in subsection (4) which establishes as a matter of international law the United Kingdom's consent to be bound by the treaty.

(4) The acts are —
    (a) deposit or delivery of an instrument of ratification, accession, approval or acceptance;
    (b) deposit or delivery of a notification of completion of domestic procedures.

E. EUROPEAN UNION (WITHDRAWAL) BILL 2017 (EXTRACTS)

1 Repeal of the European Communities Act 1972

The European Communities Act 1972 is repealed on exit day.

2 Saving for EU-Derived Domestic Legislation

(1) EU-derived domestic legislation, as it has effect in domestic law immediately before exit day, continues to have effect in domestic law on and after exit day.

(2) In this section "EU-derived domestic legislation" means any enactment so far as —
    (a) made under section 2(2) of, or paragraph 1A of Schedule 2 to, the European Communities Act 1972,
    (b) passed or made, or operating, for a purpose mentioned in section 2(2)(a) or (b) of that Act,
    (c) relating to anything —
        (i) which falls within paragraph (a) or (b), or
        (ii) to which section 3(1) or 4(1) applies, or

(d) relating otherwise to the EU or the EEA,

but does not include any enactment contained in the European Communities Act 1972.

(3) This section is subject to section 5 and Schedule 1 (exceptions to savings and incorporation).

3 Incorporation of Direct EU Legislation

(1) Direct EU legislation, so far as operative immediately before exit day, forms part of domestic law on and after exit day.

(2) In this Act "direct EU legislation" means —

(a) any EU regulation, EU decision or EU tertiary legislation, as it has effect in EU law immediately before exit day and so far as —

(i) it is not an exempt EU instrument (for which see section 14(1) and Schedule 6),

(ii) it is not an EU decision addressed only to a member State other than the United Kingdom, and

(iii) its effect is not reproduced in an enactment to which section 2(1) applies,

(b) any Annex to the EEA agreement, as it has effect in EU law immediately before exit day and so far as —

(i) it refers to, or contains adaptations of, anything falling within paragraph (a), and

(ii) its effect is not reproduced in an enactment to which section 2(1) applies, or

(c) Protocol 1 to the EEA agreement (which contains horizontal adaptations that apply in relation to EU instruments referred to in the Annexes to that agreement), as it has effect in EU law immediately before exit day.

(3) For the purposes of this Act, any direct EU legislation is operative immediately before exit day if —

(a) in the case of anything which comes into force at a particular time and is stated to apply from a later time, it is in force and applies immediately before exit day,

(b) in the case of a decision which specifies to whom it is addressed, it has been notified to that person before exit day, and

(c) in any other case, it is in force immediately before exit day.

(4) This section —

(a) brings into domestic law any direct EU legislation only in the form of the English language version of that legislation, and

(b) does not apply to any such legislation for which there is no such version,

but paragraph (a) does not affect the use of the other language versions of that legislation for the purposes of interpreting it.

(5) This section is subject to section 5 and Schedule 1 (exceptions to savings and incorporation).

4 Saving for Rights etc. under Section 2(1) of the ECA

(1) Any rights, powers, liabilities, obligations, restrictions, remedies and procedures which, immediately before exit day —

(a) are recognised and available in domestic law by virtue of section 2(1) of the European Communities Act 1972, and

(b) are enforced, allowed and followed accordingly,

continue on and after exit day to be recognised and available in domestic law (and to be enforced, allowed and followed accordingly).

(2) Subsection (1) does not apply to any rights, powers, liabilities, obligations, restrictions, remedies or procedures so far as they —

    (a) form part of domestic law by virtue of section 3, or

    (b) arise under an EU directive (including as applied by the EEA agreement) and are not of a kind recognised by the European Court or any court or tribunal in the United Kingdom in a case decided before exit day (whether or not as an essential part of the decision in the case).

(3) This section is subject to section 5 and Schedule 1 (exceptions to savings and incorporation).

5 Exceptions to Savings and Incorporation

(1) The principle of the supremacy of EU law does not apply to any enactment or rule of law passed or made on or after exit day.

(2) Accordingly, the principle of the supremacy of EU law continues to apply on or after exit day so far as relevant to the interpretation, disapplication or quashing of any enactment or rule of law passed or made before exit day.

(3) Subsection (1) does not prevent the principle of the supremacy of EU law from applying to a modification made on or after exit day of any enactment or rule of law passed or made before exit day if the application of the principle is consistent with the intention of the modification.

(4) The Charter of Fundamental Rights is not part of domestic law on or after exit day.

(5) Subsection (4) does not affect the retention in domestic law on or after exit day in accordance with this Act of any fundamental rights or principles which exist irrespective of the Charter (and references to the Charter in any case law are, so far as necessary for this purpose, to be read as if they were references to any corresponding retained fundamental rights or principles).

(6) Schedule 1 (which makes further provision about exceptions to savings and incorporation) has effect.

6 Interpretation of Retained EU Law

(1) A court or tribunal —

    (a) is not bound by any principles laid down, or any decisions made, on or after exit day by the European Court, and

    (b) cannot refer any matter to the European Court on or after exit day.

(2) A court or tribunal need not have regard to anything done on or after exit day by the European Court, another EU entity or the EU but may do so if it considers it appropriate to do so.

(3) Any question as to the validity, meaning or effect of any retained EU law is to be decided, so far as that law is unmodified on or after exit day and so far as they are relevant to it —

    (a) in accordance with any retained case law and any retained general principles of EU law, and

    (b) having regard (among other things) to the limits, immediately before exit day, of EU competences.

(4) But —

(a) the Supreme Court is not bound by any retained EU case law,

(b) the High Court of Justiciary is not bound by any retained EU case law when —

    (i) sitting as a court of appeal otherwise than in relation to a compatibility issue (within the meaning given by section 288ZA(2) of the Criminal Procedure (Scotland) Act 1995) or a devolution issue (within the meaning given by paragraph 1 of Schedule 6 to the Scotland Act 1998), or

    (ii) sitting on a reference under section 123(1) of the Criminal Procedure (Scotland) Act 1995, and

(c) no court or tribunal is bound by any retained domestic case law that it would not otherwise be bound by.

(5) In deciding whether to depart from any retained EU case law, the Supreme Court or the High Court of Justiciary must apply the same test as it would apply in deciding whether to depart from its own case law.

(6) Subsection (3) does not prevent the validity, meaning or effect of any retained EU law which has been modified on or after exit day from being decided as provided for in that subsection if doing so is consistent with the intention of the modifications.

(7) In this Act —

"retained case law" means —

(a) retained domestic case law, and

(b) retained EU case law;

"retained domestic case law" means any principles laid down by, and any decisions of, a court or tribunal in the United Kingdom, as they have effect immediately before exit day and so far as they —

(a) relate to anything to which section 2, 3 or 4 applies, and

(b) are not excluded by section 5 or Schedule 1,

    (as those principles and decisions are modified by or under this Act or by other domestic law from time to time);

"retained EU case law" means any principles laid down by, and any decisions of, the European Court, as they have effect in EU law immediately before exit day and so far as they —

(a) relate to anything to which section 2, 3 or 4 applies, and

(b) are not excluded by section 5 or Schedule 1,

    (as those principles and decisions are modified by or under this Act or by other domestic law from time to time);

"retained EU law" means anything which, on or after exit day, continues to be, or forms part of, domestic law by virtue of section 2, 3 or 4 or subsection (3) or (6) above (as that body of law is added to or otherwise modified by or under this Act or by other domestic law from time to time);

"retained general principles of EU law" means the general principles of EU law, as they have effect in EU law immediately before exit day and so far as they —

(a) relate to anything to which section 2, 3 or 4 applies, and

(b) are not excluded by section 5 or Schedule 1,

(as those principles are modified by or under this Act or by other domestic law from time to time).

7 Dealing with Deficiencies Arising from Withdrawal

(1) A Minister of the Crown may by regulations make such provision as the Minister considers appropriate to prevent, remedy or mitigate —

    (a) any failure of retained EU law to operate effectively, or

    (b) any other deficiency in retained EU law,arising from the withdrawal of the United Kingdom from the EU.

(2) Deficiencies in retained EU law include (but are not limited to) where the Minister considers that retained EU law —

    (a) contains anything which has no practical application in relation to the United Kingdom or any part of it or is otherwise redundant or substantially redundant,

    (b) confers functions on, or in relation to, EU entities which no longer have functions in that respect under EU law in relation to the United Kingdom or any part of it,

    (c) makes provision for, or in connection with, reciprocal arrangements between —

        (i) the United Kingdom or any part of it or a public authority in the United Kingdom, and

        (ii) the EU, an EU entity, a member State or a public authority in a member State,

    which no longer exist or are no longer appropriate,

    (d) makes provision for, or in connection with, other arrangements which —

        (i) involve the EU, an EU entity, a member State or a public authority in a member State, or

        (ii) are otherwise dependent upon the United Kingdom's membership of the EU, and which no longer exist or are no longer appropriate,

    (e) makes provision for, or in connection with, any reciprocal or other arrangements not falling within paragraph (c) or (d) which no longer exist, or are no longer appropriate, as a result of the United Kingdom ceasing to be a party to any of the EU Treaties,

    (f) does not contain any functions or restrictions which —

        (i) were in an EU directive and in force immediately before exit day (including any power to make EU tertiary legislation), and

        (ii) it is appropriate to retain, or

    (g) contains EU references which are no longer appropriate.

(3) But retained EU law is not deficient merely because it does not contain any modification of EU law which is adopted or notified, comes into force or only applies on or after exit day.

(4) Regulations under this section may make any provision that could be made by an Act of Parliament.

(5) Regulations under this section may (among other things)—

(a) provide for functions of EU entities or public authorities in member States (including making an instrument of a legislative character or providing funding) to be —
  (i) exercisable instead by a public authority (whether or not newly established or established for the purpose) in the United Kingdom, or
  (ii) replaced, abolished or otherwise modified, or
(b) provide for the establishment of public authorities in the United Kingdom to carry out functions provided for by regulations under this section.

(6) But regulations under this section may not —
  (a) impose or increase taxation,
  (b) make retrospective provision,
  (c) create a relevant criminal offence,
  (d) be made to implement the withdrawal agreement,
  (e) amend, repeal or revoke the Human Rights Act 1998 or any subordinate legislation made under it, or
  (f) amend or repeal the Northern Ireland Act 1998 (unless the regulations are made by virtue of paragraph 13(b) of Schedule 7 to this Act or are amending or repealing paragraph 38 of Schedule 3 to the Northern Ireland Act 1998 or any provision of that Act which modifies another enactment).

(7) No regulations may be made under this section after the end of the period of two years beginning with exit day.

(8) The reference in subsection (1) to a failure or other deficiency arising from the withdrawal of the United Kingdom from the EU includes a reference to any failure or other deficiency arising from that withdrawal taken together with the operation of any provision, or the interaction between any provisions, made by or under this Act.

8 Complying with International Obligations

(1) A Minister of the Crown may by regulations make such provision as the Minister considers appropriate to prevent or remedy any breach, arising from the withdrawal of the United Kingdom from the EU, of the international obligations of the United Kingdom.

(2) Regulations under this section may make any provision that could be made by an Act of Parliament.

(3) But regulations under this section may not —
  (a) make retrospective provision,
  (b) create a relevant criminal offence,
  (c) be made to implement the withdrawal agreement, or
  (d) amend, repeal or revoke the Human Rights Act 1998 or any subordinate legislation made under it.

(4) No regulations may be made under this section after the end of the period of two years beginning with exit day.

9 Implementing the Withdrawal Agreement

(1) Minister of the Crown may by regulations make such provision as the Minister considers appropriate for the purposes of implementing the withdrawal agreement

if the Minister considers that such provision should be in force on or before exit day.

(2) Regulations under this section may make any provision that could be made by an Act of Parliament (including modifying this Act).

(3) But regulations under this section may not —

    (a) impose or increase taxation,

    (b) make retrospective provision,

    (c) create a relevant criminal offence, or

    (d) amend, repeal or revoke the Human Rights Act 1998 or any subordinate legislation made under it.

(4) No regulations may be made under this section after exit day.

Index